Teaching Reading to Every Child

SECOND EDITION

Teaching Reading to Every Child

Diane Lapp
SAN DIEGO STATE UNIVERSITY

James Flood
BOSTON UNIVERSITY

Macmillan Publishing Co., Inc.
New York

Collier Macmillan Publishers
London

Dedicated to our favorite readers

Eric, Shannon, Johanna, and Bartholomew

Macmillan Publishing Co., Inc.
866 Third Avenue, New York, New York 10022

Collier Macmillan Canada, Inc.

Library of Congress Cataloging in Publication Data

Lapp, Diane.
Teaching reading to every child.

Includes bibliographies and index.
1. Reading. I. Flood, James. II. Title.
LB1050.L365 1983 372.4′1 82-10097
ISBN 0-02-367640-X

Printing: 3 4 5 6 7 8 Year: 5 6 7 8 9 0

ISBN 0-02-367640-X

Preface

Regardless of the grade level or the content area, all teachers help students to learn from their texts. The ability of students to comprehend information from texts is related to their language, reading, and thinking abilities.

These processes have been examined in the second edition of *Teaching Reading to Every Child.* Since the objective of this new edition is essentially the same as the first—to assist the prospective teacher of reading in understanding the integral processes of learning to read—the original text has been revised, updated, and expanded to provide the most current theoretical information, research, and classroom applications of the entire reading process.

We have divided the book into four major sections: (I) your role as a teacher, (II) your students, (III) the reading process, (IV) your reading program.

Since the teaching profession requires an enormous commitment, we have introduced and discussed the professional responsibilities of teachers in general and teachers of reading in particular in Section I, Your Role as a Teacher. This section provides assistance to the teacher who is asked to make many decisions about the role of a teacher, the students' needs, and the curriculum.

The second section of the book provides information that will enable you to explore your students in light of current biological, psychological, and linguistic factors that affect and influence student development. This section includes detailed information about the development of children from infancy to preschool and on to the school years. Current trends in preschool reading programs, the importance of parental involvement in the education of the child, and the effects of television are discussed. Various activities for the preschool reading program as well as language arts activities for primary-, intermediate-, and middle-school-aged children are provided as well.

The third section of the text focuses on two distinct aspects of the reading process: decoding and comprehending. An understanding of "decoding" will help the teacher in instructing children in the beginning steps of reading: visual and auditory discrimination and recognition of letters, sounds, and words. Activities that will reinforce these early activities for beginning readers are included throughout this section of the text.

As the focus shifts to "comprehending," we introduce the topics of implicit and explicit understanding of texts, reading study skills strategies, and content area learning. Many activities that will help to develop an effective reading program are included in this section of the book.

Your Reading Program, the fourth and final section of this book, provides information and methods to assist you, the teacher, in understanding and designing a diagnostic-prescriptive reading program. This section includes a chapter on special-needs students, entitled Reading Instruction as Special Education, to help you understand and meet the needs of special children who may be in your classroom. There is a thorough discussion of Public Law (P.L.) 94-142 and mainstreaming, along with important theoretical and practical applications for the classroom teacher.

The entire fourth section of the text focuses on the integration of theory and practice. In addition to the needs of mainstreamed children, this section includes chapters on the bilingual student, students' interests and attitudes, assessment, and ways in which to manage an effective reading program.

The teacher's tasks are difficult, complex, and exciting. As a teacher, one of your most significant tasks will be to provide instruction that will enable all your students to be good readers of *all* their texts. The accomplishment of this task is imperative since reading is essential to a child's success in school and in life. You, the teacher, are the key to each child's success. Remember, your students *will* learn to read, with your help.

ACKNOWLEDGMENTS

We gratefully acknowledge the assistance of Jacqueline Collins, Jean Sheckler Beebe, Sharon Ryan Flood, Lynne Thrope, Shannon Dundon, Dr. Roselmina Indrisano of Boston University, and Dr. Robert Aaron of the University of Georgia for their valuable contributions toward the publication of this book. We especially want to thank our photographer, Dr. Linda Lungren, for her extensive work on this manuscript.

Diane Lapp
James Flood

Contents

SECTION I

Your Role as a Teacher

This book is designed to assist you in understanding the processes involved in learning to read. It introduces you to a variety of methods of teaching reading and provides theoretical considerations and practical applications.

The purpose of this section is to help you consider the personal commitment you must be willing to make if you have chosen teaching as your profession. Many factors contribute to the complexity of your task. You will be constantly involved in making decisions about *your role as a teacher, your students,* and *your curriculum.*

We examine your role as a teacher first, in this text, because a thorough understanding of this aspect of your professional commitment is essential to your success as a teacher. *All* teachers must try to enable students to learn from texts, regardless of grade level or content specialization, because the mastery of any and all information involves the integrated processes of language, reading, and thinking.

CHAPTER 1

Teaching Reading to All Your Students

All that people have ever thought, done or dreamed lies waiting to be discovered in a book.

Charlotte S. Huck, 1976

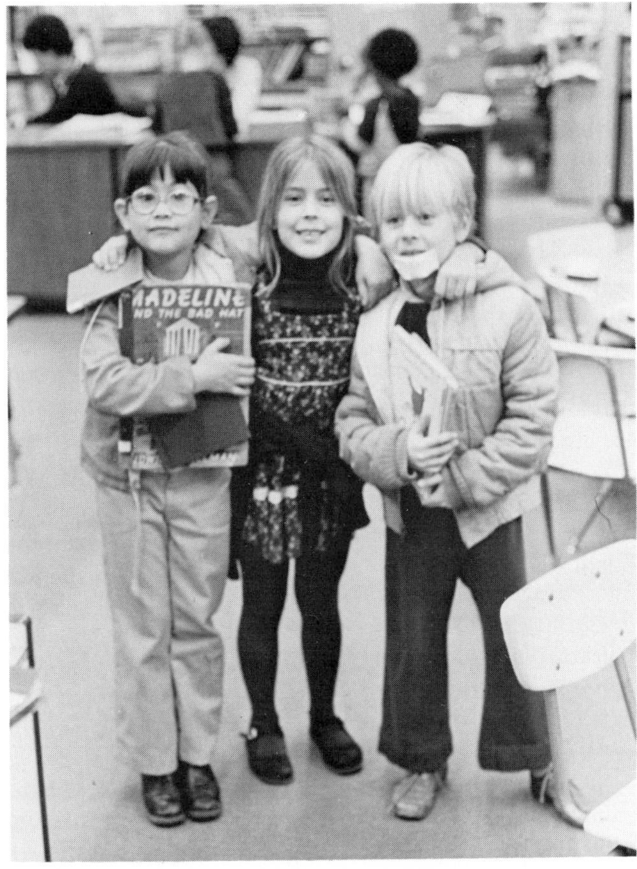

Your decisions about your classroom programs must be based on the needs, interests, and abilities of your students. (Photo by Linda Lungren.)

GOALS: To help the reader to

1. Understand the necessity of generating a personal definition of reading.
2. Examine the multifaceted role of the reading teacher.
3. Perceive the student of reading as an individual.
4. Understand the existence of a variety of possible reading curricula.

As teachers you know that teaching requires education, patience, long hours, sharing, enthusiasm, creativity, and a host of other personal attributes. You may already have encountered those who feel that teaching kindergarten, third grade, or sixth grade requires little more than a seventh-grade education and a bag full of tricks. Eventually, you will be harassed by well-meaning parents who believe that they know more about teaching than you do. After all, everyone has been to school, and many people believe that their own experience is all that is required in order to teach. Isn't it peculiar that this "experience by going" philosophy does not apply to all professionals: doctors, dentists, clergy?

You will have to accept these social realities with a smile, knowing that your job is the most important one society has to offer: the education of its young. Take pride in knowing that tomorrow's citizens will be sitting before you each morning as you enter your classroom door. Yes, yours is a very important task. You are a *teacher*, and you will experience life in a way that no other professional person can. You will meet all kinds of people, some of whom you will cherish and always remember. You will touch the lives of hundreds of people, but be prepared to meet all kinds, all sizes, all shapes.

> I have taught school for ten years. During that time I have given assignments, among others, to a murderer, an evangelist, a pugilist, a thief, and an imbecile.
>
> The murderer was a quiet little boy who sat on the front seat and regarded me with pale blue eyes; the evangelist, easily the most popular boy in school, had the lead in the junior play; the pugilist lounged by the window and let loose at intervals a raucous laugh that startled even the geraniums; the thief was a gay-hearted Lothario with a song on his lips; and the imbecile, a soft-eyed little animal seeking the shadows.
>
> The murderer awaits death in the state penitentiary; the evangelist has lain a year now in the village churchyard; the pugilist lost an eye in a brawl in Hong Kong; the thief, by standing on tiptoe, can see the windows of my room from the county jail; and the once gentle-eyed little moron beats his head against a padded wall in the state asylum.
>
> All of these pupils once sat in my room, sat and looked at me gravely across worn brown desks. I must have been a great help to these pupils—I taught them the rhyming scheme of the Elizabethan sonnet and how to diagram a complex sentence.
>
> (White, 1937, pp. 151, 192)

The message is clear. We must attempt to make our reading curriculum relevant to the lives and needs of our students. We must focus on their interests rather than rely on the familiar components of a "classical" education. During the course of your career, they will, indeed, *all be seated before you.*

Many children claim to dislike reading. Do they dislike reading because they perceive it as a perennial bore equated with unrealistic stories? The same children who do not want to read the basal reader are often found reading comic books, sports or movie magazines, and baseball cards during their free time. What they may dislike is not reading but rather the materials and methods that are often used to teach reading.

At the end of each summer, as September approaches, we hear children making unfortunate comments about the beginning of school. Why does this happen? Why do children think of schools as such disheartening places? It is irrelevant curricula? Are the rules too strict, or are they even unnecessary? Do teachers lack a sense of humor? Do our activities encourage boredom?

What can *you* do about it? How do you plan to make school learning relevant to the life experiences of your students? How do you plan to engage them in a reading program that will make a difference?

Your decisions about your classroom programs must be based on the needs, interests, and abilities of your students. Durr (1967) cautioned us about teaching methods when he said,

> The best methods and wisest methods lose their effectiveness when we know too little about our pupils. (p. 104)

This text is designed to help you accomplish the development of an effective reading program. The central focus of the text is on helping you to teach reading effectively to all students.

PURPOSE OF THIS BOOK

This book is designed to help you, the teacher of reading, plan learning experiences that will make a difference in the lives of your students. If you are concerned about being called a "teacher of reading," take pride and remember that you must teach reading regardless of your content specialization. All content areas

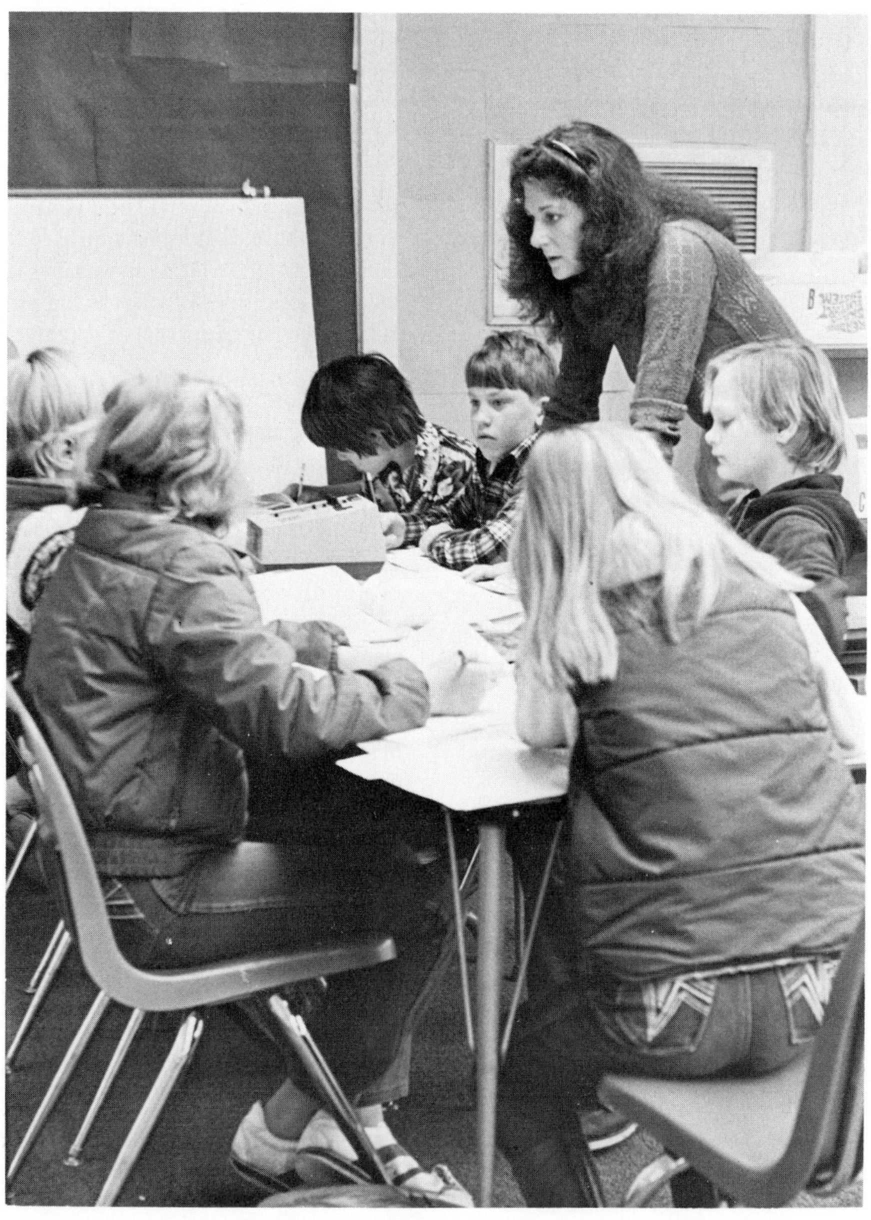

Your role is to provide children with the skills that will enable them to read for information and for enjoyment. All teachers at all grade levels in all content areas are teachers of reading. (Photo by Linda Lungren.)

present students with facts to be learned and texts to be read. Students are required to read, and read, and reread. Your role is to provide children with the skills that will enable them to read for *information* and for *enjoyment. All* teachers at *all* grade levels in *all* content areas are teachers of reading.

To prepare you for this task, each chapter of this text deals with important issues in the field of reading and presents current theoretical concerns and effective instructional applications. Our belief is that both teacher and students need to be prepared for reading. In a sense, then, this book is intended to help you for the task of teaching children to read.

WHAT IS READING?

Everyone knows what reading is—or do they? Educators, linguists, psychologists, and information scientists who are interested in the reading process have filled volumes with their definitions of reading. These definitions are frequently contradictory, each emphasizing a different aspect of the reading process. It would be unproductive to present a long list of definitions here because each of you will have to develop your own definition of the process after you understand its components. It is this development that should be your goal in reading this text. Your definition will continue to change and grow with new evidence from research. However, it is extremely important for you to formulate a definition of reading because you will be forced to develop an instructional program as soon as you enter the classroom.

Some research studies suggest that classroom teachers are influenced by theoretical orientations toward reading. According to Mitchell (1980), "If teachers' reading instruction is being influenced by their knowledge base and/or belief system, then they need to become aware of what these influences are." If you have not given any thought to the question, "What is reading?", your program will probably suffer from a fragmented and incomplete notion of the reading process.

In general, all definitions of reading fall into two categories: reading as a *decoding process*, that is, as a breaking of a visual/auditory code, and reading for *meaning*, that is, as a comprehension process.

Although there are differences of opinion about a precise definition of reading, most educators agree that the reading process includes

1. Letter and word perception and recognition.
2. Comprehension of the concepts conveyed by the printed word(s).
3. Reaction to and assimilation of the new knowledge with the reader's prior knowledge and experiences.

All instructors of reading must decide for themselves what reading is. Several authors have devised definitions and have established approaches on the basis of their definitions. These approaches, along with subsequent definitions of reading, are presented in detail in Chapter 10, "Approaches and Methods of Teaching Reading."

We believe that reading is an interaction between the author and the reader. To receive the printed message, the reader must perceive, interpret, hypothesize, and evaluate. These processes occur in varying degrees depending on the reader's familiarity with the text.

This type of processing happens quickly in the mind of a proficient reader; however, the amount of time that is required for text processing may not be the critical element. The critical element in proficient reading may be the *active participation* of the reader. However, there is a period of development that occurs prior to the *proficient reading* period that we shall call the *learning to read period*. It is during this learning to read period that the learner acquires and practices the strategies needed to be a proficient reader.

A reader may be aided to participate actively in the learning encounter during either the *learning to read* or the *proficient reading* period if the appropriate curricular considerations are a prerequisite to the encounter.

The quality of the reader-text interaction will be dependent on whether the reader is at the *learning to read* or the *proficient reading* period of development. While these periods *are not age dependent*, the proficient reader will be able to apply the necessary strategies to ensure comprehension. Reading strategies are applied by the proficient reader to ensure a successful experience, whereas during the learning to read period the student is acquiring and practicing these strategies until they become automatic.

Active participation during either the learning to read or the proficient reading period may be encouraged if

1. Strategies that aid readers in comprehending stories and texts are taught prior to reading.
2. Activities that foster and encourage concentration and observation by the reader are explained as part of the reading process.
3. Goals that are comprehensible are made apparent to the reader.
4. Materials that provoke reader interest are available in the environment.

After exploring the various definitions of reading presented in this text, you will need to develop your own personal definition of reading. Once you have done so, you will be able to *evaluate* your classroom reading program to see if it meets your desired goals. (We provide you with more detailed information about an evaluation procedure in Chapter 15, "Developing and Managing Your Reading Program.")

Given this general framework of what reading is and what the reading process entails, we turn now to the most important elements in the reading process: the teacher and the learner. The act of teaching reading is a play with two main characters, teacher and learner, who are dependent upon each other to produce a masterpiece. Each character is important; each receives his or her cues from the other before progress is made.

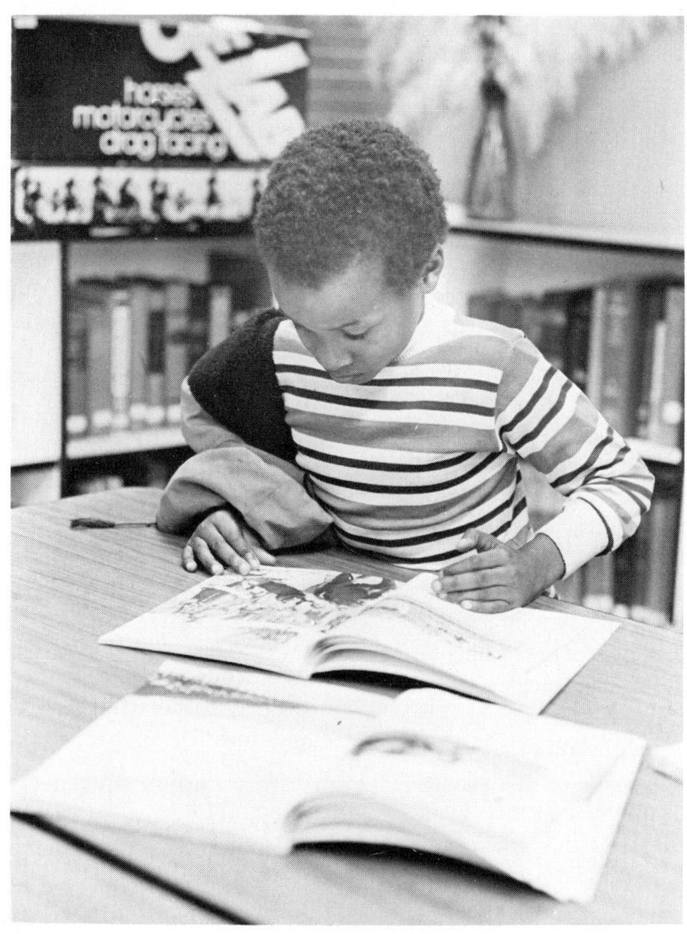

Materials which provoke reader interest should be available in the student's environment. (Photo by Linda Lungren.)

THE TEACHER

The teacher is extremely important in the process of acquiring reading competence. In fact, after reviewing the massive federally funded study, "The Cooperative Research Program in First-Grade Reading Instruction," Malmquist (1973) stated that "studies indicate that the teacher is a more important variable in reading instruction than are the teaching methods and instructional materials" (p. 142).

G. Spache (1973) also commented on the importance of the teacher after analyzing the results of these first-grade studies, comparing several methods of reading instruction:

> Our reading research into the effectiveness of various instructional methods in classroom or remedial situations is often pointless. Such comparative research tends to ignore the fact that the dynamic practices of the teacher and the kinds of teacher-pupil interaction she promotes are the most important determinants of pupils' achievements. The collected results of the large-scale First Grade Reading Studies . . . strongly reaffirm this fact. Hardly any real differences in pupil achievement were found in comparisons among a half-dozen different approaches in carefully equated populations. Rather, in almost every study, achievement varied more from one teacher's classroom to the next than it varied according to the methods or materials employed. (pp. 43–44)

After analyzing experimental/control group comparative studies, Tinker and McCullough (1975) concluded that greater achievement in reading scores by the experimental classes is a reflection of the teacher's drive and enthusiasm during the experimental stage. They also stated that the teacher is a greater factor in this achievement than specific methods or materials. Similarly, King (1973) stated that the differences in teaching styles and professional competencies among teachers have a definite effect on children's reading achievement. Likewise, Goldbecker (1975) stressed the importance of the teacher in a reading program by stating: "The salient point remains that no reading program operates by itself. The teacher is still the single catalyst who can determine success or failure of a reading program no matter where its emphasis lies" (p. 4).

With the teacher as the primary factor in the learning encounter, it becomes incumbent upon you to examine many of your values, to assess your philosophy of teaching, and to learn a great deal about the children who have been assigned to you. You need to consider theories of learning as well as the physical, mental, psychological, and sociological developmental patterns of children. You also need to process this information and integrate it into a cohesive approach to teaching.

This book will provide you, the teacher, with a great deal of the background information essential to teaching reading. However, it cannot provide you with your philosophy of teaching; only you can do that.

THE TEACHER'S ROLE

Every individual has several roles in life, roles that overlap and are interrelated to varying degrees. Your role as a *teacher* is a reflection of your role in society, in the school, and in the classroom.

As a teacher, you need to be certain that children who spend one year of their lives with you are helped in the development of knowledge that will assist them in becoming successful in life. You will encounter students who are experiencing great difficulty with a particular book, assignment, or project even though they really want to succeed and are making serious efforts to do so. Recognizing these students and/or situations is not the difficult task; dealing with them effectively is the job of a good teacher. The sources of difficulty are very complex.

As a teacher, your task is to identify your most effective style of relating to students to encourage comfortable teacher-student interaction and to promote maximum learning. To determine your most effective teaching style, you first have to understand yourself, your values, your approach to people, your place in society, your school, and your classroom. Insights into self may be gained by exploring some of the following questions:

1. What purpose does education play in my view of the world?
2. What are my personal definitions of "teaching," "learning," and "education"?
3. Recognizing that students learn in many ways, how do I think they learn best?
4. How do my overall priorities fit with my educational priorities?

5. What are the values that I may be transmitting to my students, consciously or unconsciously?

These are personal questions, and the answers can only be generated by you. Your answers will emerge and evolve bit by bit over a period of time. Teaching is a personal experience; teachers' answers will reflect their educational individuality. In answering these questions, you will gain insight into that identity. "The teacher's understanding and acceptance of herself [are] the most important requirement(s) in any effort she makes to help students to know themselves and to gain healthy attitudes of self-acceptance" (Jersild, 1955, p. 3).

Once you have thought about your values and your social position in the world, you need to determine your feelings about your position in the school and in your classroom. You have to begin to develop a philosophy of teaching and begin to deal with the important question, "What is my personal role as a teacher?"

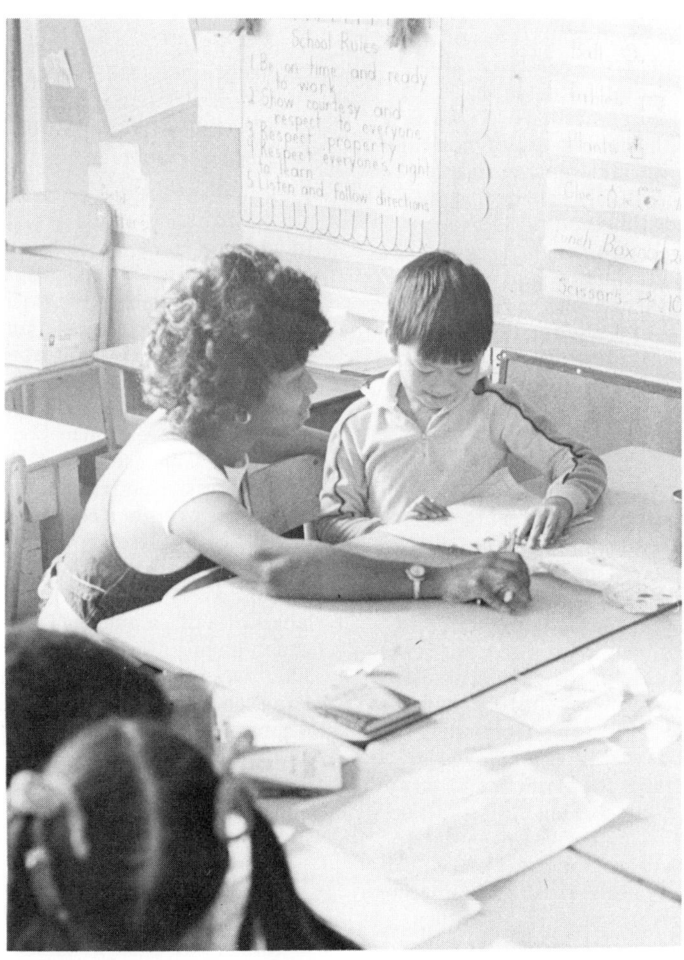

As a teacher you must begin with the attitude that you are educating the whole child and must consider language factors, cognitive factors, sensory and perceptual factors, and socioeconomic factors. (Photo by Linda Lungren.)

THE LEARNER

Now that you have explored some questions about yourself, you must come to appreciate many facts about your students. Essentially, you must begin with the attitude that you are educating the whole child. Educators (Rousseau, 1964; Drucker, 1967; Dewey, 1938) for decades have been espousing the development of the total child. As Dewey (1938) states:

> In this period [ages four to eight] the connection of the school life with that of the home and neighborhood is, of course, especially intimate. The children are largely occupied with direct social and outgoing modes of action, with doing and telling. There is relatively little attempt made at intellectual formulation, conscious reflection, or command of technical methods. As, however, there is continual growth in the complexity of work and in the responsibilities which the children are capable of assuming, distinct problems gradually emerge in such a way that the mastery of special methods is necessary.
>
> Hence, in the second period [from eight to ten], emphasis is put upon securing ability to read, write, handle numbers, etc., not in themselves, but as necessary helps and adjuncts in relation to the more direct modes of experience. Also, in the various forms of handwork and of science, more and more conscious attention is paid to the proper ways of doing things, methods of reaching results, as distinct from the simple doing itself. This is the special period for securing knowledge of the rules and technique of work.
>
> In the third period, lasting until the thirteenth year, the skill thus acquired is utilized in application to definite problems of investigation and reflection, leading to recognition of the significance and necessity of generalizations. When this latter point is reached, the period of distinctly secondary education may be said to have begun. This third period is also that of the distinctive differentiation of the various lines of work, history, and science, the various forms of science, etc., from one another. So far as the methods and tools employed in each have been mastered, so far is the child able to take up the pursuit [of] each by itself, making it, in some sense, really a study. If the first period has given the child a common and varied background, if the second has introduced him to control of reading, writing, numbering, manipulating materials, etc., as instruments of inquiry, he is now ready in the third for a certain amount of specialization without danger of isolation or artificiality. (pp. 53-54)

Cleland (1980) stated succinctly, "Reading is a personal process deeply rooted within the reader, and . . . any complete understanding of reading must necessarily concern itself with the totality of the person engaged in the reading act" (p. 11).

To achieve the goal of educating the whole child, the teacher of reading must understand at least four different factors that affect the reading ability of a child:

1. Language factors.
2. Cognitive factors.
3. Sensory and perceptual factors.
4. Socioeconomic factors.

Language Factors

Reading is a language process that involves the ability to interpret printed symbols. As Bonney (1962) points out,

> In addition to being a more or less efficient instrument of semantic transfer, language is the individual's personal equipment by means of which he organizes the world around him into principles and concepts; it is his means of coping with external reality. He must be able to use this equipment with confidence, to use it freely so he can live and act freely. If you hedge in his language, you hedge in his development, because as the psychologists point out, language behavior is not one among many, but an all-pervasive activity. The world—everything outside us—comes to us in a confusion of limitless numbers of impressions provoking endless associations. One of the ways man tries to achieve order out of the chaos is through his language. It is with words that the infant labels his environment. They serve him as handles with which he begins quickly to manipulate his environment. This gives him a hold . . . . This verbalizing becomes internal and silent . . . but continues to be the process whereby the individual reduces reality to chunks he can manage. (p. 59)

How language or linguistic skills are developed is a subject of constant research and debate. Such theories as Lenneberg's (1970) stress the innate aspects of language acquisition, whereas others, such as Skinner's (1972), emphasize behavioral *reinforcement* as a prime factor in language development. Still others, such as Piaget's (1962), focus on the child's *interactions* within his or her environment as an essential factor in establishing concepts that will be communicated later through language. After reviewing, grouping, and labeling existing theories as nativistic, behavioristic, and cognitive, Wanat (1971) states:

> Group differences have generally been ignored in research on language development. Thus, dialect differences, possible ethnic differences in capacities and strategies for processing information, differences in thinking style, and emotionally related factors are not adequately taken under consideration. None of the theories reviewed (Nativistic, Behavioristic, Cognitive) gives an adequate explanation of the way a child acquires his language. Each of the theories is wrong in that each unjustifiably claims to provide a complete explanation. Yet, each of these theories is valuable in that each provides part of the information we need to understand language. (p. 147)

Klein (1981), in a discussion of generalizations about children's language, suggests that language is acquired in orderly stages:

> Children do not learn language by simply imitating adults, nor do they acquire language accidentally. Instead, they develop language systematically with the system becoming more complex and language use more elegant throughout the years. Each of the various stages of development from beginning of speech through the beginning school years reflects attributes common to all children in the stage. (p. 445)

Although there is a need for continued research on language development, existing theories do offer much of what is needed in understanding the language base of the reading process. A child may enter school with a "private" language (dialect) as well as a "formal" (public) language. If the private language is better developed than the formal or public language, the child may find reading to be a difficult task, since most reading materials are written in formal or public language. Children from cultural backgrounds other than the teacher's may have difficulty with school experiences becuase their private language is often misunderstood or misinterpreted. *All* children must be encouraged to accept both their *private* and *public* languages while becoming aware of the phonological and grammatical variations that exist between these two systems. Then, the student will learn, respect, and apply the appropriate language at the appropriate time.

We believe that language refinement and growth are highly dependent upon teacher acceptance. We encourage you, as reading teachers, to accept the language presented by the student and then provide further learning through your examples. For example, if your first-grader says, "I *busted* it!" you reply, "I see that you *broke* it. Delicate things *break* easily. *Broken* things are hard to repair, but let's try." In this way, you help the child to acquire public language skills, while still accepting his or her private language. If you can offer children such nonthreatening verbal interactions, they will continually learn language by using it.

Cognitive Factors

Cognitive factors relating to reading achievement represent an array of mental processes as well as general intelligence.

Mental Processes. Cognitive processes can be described in different ways, and experts have developed sophisticated notational systems for sharing complex ideas about cognition. These thinking processes may be categorized under two broad headings. The first of these, *logical thinking*, deals with the formal, well-structured thought processes that are used in the ordered solving of problems. The second category, *creative thinking*, is more divergent. If the school is to nurture the individual, it must concern itself with both these thinking processes.

Gordon (1961), Piaget (1962), and many other psychologists and educators deal with the developmental stages of the mental processes. They assert that a large portion of cognitive growth takes place in the early years and is a biological function. Cannella (1980) however, cautions that "results concerning cognition and reading have been tentative and nonconclusive." Realizing this caution, a more detailed discussion on cognition is presented in Chapter 2, "The Reader Develops."

Intelligence. Although many factors have been correlated with reading and language achievement, intelligence and reading have been thought to be very closely related. Two examples illustrate this point:

> And he who shall be said to be a sot and idiot from his birth, is such a person who cannot account of number twenty pence, nor can tell who his father or mother, or how old he is, etc., so as it may appear that he hath no

understanding of reason what shall be for his profit, nor what for his loss. But if he hath such understanding, that he know and understand his letters, and do read by teaching or information of another man, then it seemeth that he is not a sot nor a natural "idiot."

(Fitzherbert, 1534, p. 18)

After an Old Home Week in the school system, when those we flunked return in Rolls-Royces to patronize us, we are positive of one thing:

Either it takes no intelligence to make money, and education is of comparatively little value, or teachers don't know a smart child when they see one.

(Preston, 1938, p. 176)

Many researchers and educators have conducted studies to examine the relationship between intelligence and reading. In 1972, Lohnes and Gray, after reanalyzing the data from the "The Cooperative Research Program in First-Grade Reading Instruction," concluded that "the best single explanatory principle for observed variance in reading skills was variance in general intelligence" (p. 59). Tremans-Ziremba et al. (1980) found that "the relationship between intelligence and reading achievement found in previous studies was verified" (p. 264).

There are many definitions of intelligence in operation; we define intelligence as a combination of biological factors and environmental experiences. Unfortunately, the most common computation of the IQ score, while considering MA (mental age) and CA (chronological age), gives little attention to the experiential background of the child. Generally, it focuses on a child's present level of intellectual functioning. Often, an IQ score is computed, the child is labeled "bright," "average," or "dull," and the case is closed. In so doing, the following questions remain unanswered:

1. Was the child ready to be tested?
2. Was the child motivated?
3. Were the child's life experiences similar to those of the "average" child?
4. If these experiences were different from the norm, which set of experiences should be tested?
5. Does the child need exposure to a specific set of experiences before being given a particular test?

Many children who score poorly on intelligence tests in the first grade are erroneously labeled "dull" or "retarded." They are then assigned to the lowest reading group, where they deteriorate mentally for the remainder of their school lives. Frequently, we misinterpret low IQ scores as a lack of potential and, thus, excuse ourselves from planning personalized programs for these children. The findings of Cohen and Glass (1968) are frightening; they state that there is no significant relationship between first-grade reading ability and IQ scores but that there are significant relationships by grade four. Bond and Wagner (1966) suggest that:

The correlation between mental age, as measured by individual Stanford-Binet tests, and reading comprehension at the end of the fifth grade it is approximately .60; during the high school years it approaches .80. (p. 119)

The exact nature of the relationship between reading and intelligence is still unknown. Much of the research is contradictory and sheds little light on this topic because the larger question of the precision of IQ testing is still unanswered. Durkin's study (1966) tells us an interesting bit of information related to this controversial question. Children with a range of IQ scores who began to read before first grade in New York and Oakland, California, scored consistently higher on standardized reading tests than did their IQ counterparts who did not begin reading until formal instruction in first grade. From this data we can infer that intelligence is not particularly related to early reading; we can also infer that children who begin to read early stay ahead of children with comparable IQs.

Sensory and Perceptual Development

One of the greatest initial concerns for the teacher of reading is a child's visual and auditory readiness for printed material. Silbiger and Woolf (1965) and other educators have suggested that there is no one best age at which a child should begin a visual or auditory readiness program.

Neuman (1981) conducted a study that showed that first-grade children can be taught auditory perceptual skills; this training, however, did not have a significant effect on their reading skills. It should be noted that perceptual development as well as sensory development often is dependent on physical, emotional, linguistic, and environmental factors. The specifics of assessment of readiness factors are discussed in detail in Chapter 4.

Socioeconomic Factors

Many reading studies have shown significant correlations between reading failure and low socioeconomic status. Rogers (1969) may have offered a possible explanation for this phenomenon when he pointed out that, until quite recently, educators

> frequently fail[ed] to recognize that much of the material presented to students in the classroom has, for the student, the perplexing, meaningless quality that learning a list of nonsense syllables has for us. This is especially true for the child whose background provides no context for the material with which he is confronted. Thus, education becomes the futile attempt to learn materials which have no personal meaning.
>
> Such learning involves the mind only. It is learning which takes place "from the neck up." It does not involve feelings or personal meanings: it has no relevance for the whole person. (pp. 3–4)

Tremans-Ziremba et al. (1980) suggest that "it is necessary to obtain a better description of the ongoing family environmental processes that influence reading before a full understanding of the relationship between reading and socioeconomic status can be obtained" (p. 264). Many questions remain unanswered and must be studied before we can fully understand the impact of socioeconomic factors and reading. In Chapter 2, we discuss several issues that concern the home and the preschool experiences of children who are beginning to learn to read.

CURRICULUM

What do I do to be an effective reading teacher? The role of the classroom teacher is extremely complex and demands extensive treatment throughout the book. The "What do I do?" part of this question is discussed in depth in Chapter 15, "Developing and Managing Your Reading Program."

Both your philosophical and methodological beliefs will determine the structures of your classroom. You must consider such questions as: How will information be transmitted? What type of student-teacher interactions will I try to develop? Such questions will help you, an educational facilitator, to reassess existing curricula, methods, and materials continuously as the strengths and needs of your students change. As a teacher of reading, you will be called upon to make many similar curricular decisions.

Classroom Simulation

When the close of summer signals the start of the school year, teachers begin to think about their curriculum and begin to plan their teaching strategies.

As you begin to do this, ask yourself the following questions:

TEACHER

1. What is my world view? What part does education play in this view?
2. What is my role as a teacher? Who am I to my students? Which word best describes my role: *facilitator, expert, resource person, equal, confronter*?
3. What societal values am I conveying to my students?
4. What is my view of humanity? What am I specifically doing through day-to-day interactions to produce the ideal, mature, human being?
5. What are my basic values? Do I encourage children to accept my value structure, or do I teach them a process for developing and selecting their own value system?
6. With what type of student-teacher interactions am I most comfortable? Is the flow of communication one-way or two-way, open-ended or planned and determined?
7. To what types of motivational sources do I ascribe? Does the motivational source come from within the student, or does the class have a materialistic reward system, or both? Does the motivational source distort the learning process or insert noneducational values into the educational process?
8. What types of discipline will I employ? How do I handle individual problems? Group problems? Total class problems? What are the emotional and educational results of my discipline?

STUDENTS

1. What will be the role of the student? What expectations do I have for my students?
2. Who are these children? What do I know of their experiential readiness for learning?

3. Which word or phrase best describes the relationship of the students to me and to the learning process: *receivers of the word, creators, individualists, technicians, obedient children*?
4. How do children learn? How will they view my role in teaching them?
5. How are students evaluated? Do students have a clear understanding of the evaluative process? How are these children affected emotionally, socially, and cognitively by the evaluative processes of the classroom?

CURRICULUM

1. What will be the learning climate? Will it be quiet, active, friendly, individually oriented, teacher dominated, task oriented, almost unstructured, enthusiastic, altering in tempo, or even paced? Will the atmosphere be friendly, fearful, respectful, "hard-at-work," or personal growth oriented? What will be my role in determining the learning environment?
2. What will be the major purpose, or goal, of education in this classroom? What specific social, psychological, emotional, and cognitive learning will occur within the classroom?

Although answering these questions may seem burdensome, we encourage you to attempt to formulate answers that will help you to integrate your philosophical, psychological, and curricular beliefs. This attempt at integration may best begin by describing the principles of your philosophy, the effects of these principles on the psychological development of your students, and the practical curricular implementation.

Once you have formulated or refined your educational beliefs, you can begin to plan a curriculum that will provide your students with the experiences and information needed to become a successful reader. Our role in this process is to provide you with a comprehensive view of reading literature and methods for implementing this theory. You will then be a *practitioner* as well as a *theoretician.*

QUESTIONS AND RELATED READINGS

If you feel that you have not acquired adequate knowledge to answer the following questions successfully, we suggest additional related readings.

1. What is your personal definition of reading?
2. What is the relationship between the teacher and the learning process?
3. Why is it important for the teacher of reading to view the student as an individual?
4. What are some possible curricula available to the reading teacher?

Goal 1: To help the reader to understand the necessity of having an individual definition of reading.

Question 1: What is your personal definition of reading?

DeStefano, J. S. *Language, the Learner, and the School.* New York: John Wiley & Sons, Inc., 1978.

LaBerge, D., and S. J. Samuels. "Toward a Theory of Automatic Information Processing in Reading." In *Theoretical Models and Processes of Reading*, ed. by H. Singer and R. Ruddell. Newark, Del.: International Reading Association, 1976, pp. 548–79.

Wolf, T. "Reading Reconsidered." In *Thought and Language/Language and Reading*, ed. by M. Wolf, M. McQuillan, and E. Radwin. Cambridge, Mass.: President and Fellows of Harvard College, 1980, pp. 109–27.

Goal 2: To help the reader to examine the multifaceted role of the reading teacher.

Question 2: What is the relationship between the teacher and the learning process?

Dennard, K. "Commentary: A Black Educator Speaks About 'Black English'." *The Reading Teacher* 35:2 (November 1981), 133.

Feeley, J. T. "Teaching Non-English Speaking First-Graders to Read." *Elementary English* 47 (February 1970), 199–208.

Santa, C. M., and B. L. Hayes. *Children's Prose Comprehension: Research and Practice.* Newark, Del.: International Reading Association, 1981.

Goal 3: To help the reader to perceive the student of reading as an individual.

Question 3: Why is it important for the teacher of reading to view the student as an individual?

DuBois, D., and G. Stice. "Comprehension Instruction: Let's Call It for Repair." *Reading World* 20 (March 1981), 173–84.

Dunn, R., and M. Garbo. "The Reading Game: How to Improve the Odds for Every Youngster." *Learning* 8 (August–September 1979), 34–36ff.

Harris, L. A., and C. B. Smith, eds. *Individualizing Reading Instruction: A Reader.* New York: Holt, Rinehart and Winston, 1977.

Goal 4: To help the reader to understand the existence of a variety of possible reading curricula.

Question 4: What are some possible curricula available to the reading teacher?

Glatthorn, A. A. *A Guide for Developing an English Curriculum for the Eighties.* Urbana, Ill.: National Council of Teachers of English, 1980.

Noyce, R. M. "Try the Enrichment Triad in Reading Class." *Journal of Reading* 24:4 (January 1981), 326–30.

Stewig, J. W. "Planning Environments to Promote Language Growth." In *Discovering Language with Children*, ed. by G. S. Pinnell. Urbana, Ill.: National Council of Teachers of English, 1980, pp. 52–56.

BIBLIOGRAPHY

Bond, G. L., and F. B. Wagner. *Teaching the Child to Read.* New York: Macmillan Publishing Co., Inc., 1966.

Bonney, M. "An English Teacher Answers Mario Pei." *Saturday Review*, 15 September 1962, pp. 58–60, 75.

Cannella, G. S. "Beginning Reading: Cognitive Developmental Research." *Journal of Instructional Psychology* 7 (Fall 1980), 139.

Cleland, C. J. "Piagetian Implications for Reading Models." *Reading World* 20 (October 1980), 10–15.

Cohen, A., and G. G. Glass. "Lateral Dominance and Reading Ability." *The Reading Teacher* 21 (November 1968), 343–48.

Dawson, M. *Developing Comprehension Including Critical Reading.* Newark, Del.: International Reading Association, 1968.

Dewey, J. *Experience and Education.* New York: Macmillan Publishing Co., Inc., 1938.

Drucker, P. "The New Philosophy Comes to Life." *Harper's Magazine*, August 1957, pp. 37–40.

Durkin, D. *Children Who Read Early: Two Longitudinal Studies.* New York: Bureau of Publications, Teachers College, Columbia University, 1966.

Durr, W. K. *Reading Instruction: Dimensions and Issues.* Boston: Houghton Mifflin Company, 1967.

Fitzherbert, A. S. *The New Natura Breuium.* England, 1534, p. 18.

Flood, J., and Lapp, D. "In Search of the 'Perfect Question': Questioning Strategies for Developing Story Comprehension in Young Children." *Principal* LVI:3 (October 1980), 20–23.

Goldbecker, S. S. *Reading: Instructional Approaches.* Washington, D.C.: National Education Association, 1975.

Gordon, W. J. J. *Synectics: The Development of Creative Capacity.* New York: Harper & Row, Publishers, 1961.

Guthrie, J. T. *Comprehension and Teaching: Research Reviews.* Newark, Del.: International Reading Association, 1981.

Harris, T. L., and R. E. Hodges. *A Dictionary of Reading.* Newark, Del.: International Reading Association, 1981.

Huck, Charlotte S. *Children's Literature in the Elementary School.* 3rd. ed. New York: Holt, Rinehart, and Winston, 1976.

Hunt, R. L. "Why Teachers Fail." *The Clearing House*, 12 (April 1938), 176.

Jersild, A. T. *When Teachers Face Themselves.* New York: Bureau of Publications, Teachers College Press, Columbia University, 1955.

King, E. M. "The Influence of Teaching on Reading Achievement." In *Reading for All,* ed. by R. Karlin, Proceedings of the Fourth IRA World Congress on Reading. Newark, Del.: International Reading Association, 1973, pp. 110–15.

Klein, M. L. "Key Generalizations About Language and Children." *Educational Leadership* 38 (March 1981), 446.

Lapp, D. "Individualizing Reading Instruction Made Easy for Teacher." *Early Years* (February 1977), 34–37.

____ "Beyond the Redbirds, Bluebirds, and Yellowbirds." *Reporting on Reading* 5:2 (March 1979), 1–9.

Lenneberg, E. H. "On Explaining Language." In *Language and Reading–An Interdisciplinary Approach*, ed. by D. V. Gunderson. Washington, D.C.: Center for Applied Linguistics, 1970, pp. 3–25.

Lohnes, P. R., and M. M. Gray. "Intelligence and the Cooperative Reading Studies." *Reading Research Quarterly* 7 (Spring 1972), pp. 466–476.

Malmquist, E. "Perspectives on Reading Research." In *Reading for All*, ed. by R. Karlin. Proceedings of the Fourth IRA World Congress on Reading. Newark, Del.: International Reading Association, 1973, pp. 142–55.

Mitchell, K. A. "Patterns of Teacher-Student Responses to Oral Reading Errors as Related to Teachers' Theoretical Frameworks." *Research in the Teaching of English* 14 (October 1980), 259.

Neuman, S. B. "Effect of Teaching Auditory Perceptual Skills on Reading Achievement in First Grade." *Reading Teacher* 34 (January 1981), 422–26.

Patin, H. "Class and Caste in Urban Education." *Chicago School Journal* 45 (1964), 305–10.

Piaget, J. *Plays, Dreams, and Imitation in Childhood.* New York: W. W. Norton & Company, Inc., 1962.

Preston, E. F. "Those We Flunked." *The Clearing House* 12 (April 1938), 176.

Rogers, C. *Freedom to Learn.* Columbus, Ohio: Charles E. Merrill Publishing Company, 1969.

Rousseau, J. J. *Emile, Julie, and Other Writings.* New York: Barron's Educational Series, Inc., 1964.

Silbiger, F., and D. Woolf. "Perceptual Difficulties Associated with Reading Disability." *College Reading Association Proceedings* 6 (Fall, 1965), 98–102.

Skinner, B. F. *Beyond Freedom and Dignity.* New York: Alfred A. Knopf, Inc., 1972.

Spache, G. D. "Psychological and Cultural Factors in Learning to Read." In *Reading for All*, ed. by R. Karlin. Proceedings of the Fourth IRA World Congress on Reading. Newark, Del.: International Reading Association, 1973, pp. 43–50.

Spivak, G. C. "Reading the World: Literacy Studies in the 80's." *College English* 43:7 (November 1981), 671–79.

Tinker, M., and C. M. McCullough. *Teaching Elementary Reading.* 4th ed. Englewood Cliffs, N.J.: Prentice-Hall, Inc., 1975.

Tremans-Ziremba, M., J. Michayluk, and L. Taylor. "Examination of Some Predictors of Reading Achievement in Grade 4 Children." *Reading Improvement* 17 (Winter 1980), 264.

Wanat, S. F. "Language Acquisitions: Basic Issues." *The Reading Teacher* 25 (November 1971), 142–47.

White, N. J. "I've Taught Them All." *The Clearing House* 12 (November 1937), 151, 192.

Your Students

This section concerns the development of the young child and the potential effects of preschool programs that seek to prepare young children for reading. As a teacher, it is important to have this background information to understand better how a child becomes a reader.

The development of the child from birth throughout his or her school career is both an internal and external process. Given minimal input from their external learning environment, all children will acquire the language used in that environment. The most important internal process is the development of the brain. Linguists and biologists studying cognition have now come to some agreement that the pattern of brain development is essentially the same for all children. Jean Piaget, one of the most celebrated of the developmental psychologists, specifies chronological age correlates of cognition.

This section also deals with parental involvement in the prereading preparation of young children and includes the specifics for helping the young child prepare for reading. The merits of preschool and kindergarten programs are discussed in detail, and the historical and philosophical correlates of reading preparation are presented.

CHAPTER 2

The Reader Develops

The reason the young child learns [to talk] so well and so fast is that *his* way of learning is his own best way. When he is allowed this freedom to explore the world of language, he pursues his own interest and curiosity. . . . He comes at things from many directions and is therefore more likely to see the way they fit together and relate to one another. . . . He learns not to please others, but to please himself.

Eda LeShan

The reason the young child learns to talk so well and so fast is that his way of learning is his own best way. (Photo by Linda Lungren.)

GOALS: To help the reader to

1. Understand the stages of cognitive development.
2. Examine language acquisition and development.
3. Recognize the home environment and family involvement as an influence on the developing reader.
4. Examine television as an influence on the developing reader.

Cognitive and linguistic development of the child, as well as home and family factors, contribute to a child's success in school. Background information about these aspects of child development is consequently very important to the prospective teacher of reading. We have designed this chapter as an information resource system for you. It is filled with important background information that is absolutely essential for you to think about before you begin to teach reading.

There are internal and external stimulants that shape the growth of the human organism. In this chapter, we discuss two general aspects of internal growth: *cognition* and *language development*. Obviously, each of these is determined in part by outside factors, but in the growth pattern of "normal" children, cognition and language development occur roughly at the same time, suggesting that there is something innate in the biological composition of all children that causes the organism to grow at a determined rate. The external stimulants to human growth that we discuss in this chapter are family influences and environmental factors, including the effects of television and educational materials on the prereading skills of young children.

HUMAN DEVELOPMENT: INTERNAL STIMULANTS

Although there are innumerable internal factors that affect human development, we have selected the following four areas for discussion in this chapter because they are thought to be the factors most closely related to later reading success:

1. Cognitive development.
2. Perceptual development.
3. Language development.
4. Human performance and information processing.

Developing Cognition

When discussing the cognitive development of the child, it is important to begin with a detailed explanation of the mental processes operating in human beings. As explained in Chapter 1, the mental processes, or thinking processes, can be categorized under two broad headings that indicate two somewhat different mental processes. The first of these is *logical thinking*, which deals with the formal, well-structured thought processes used in the ordered solving of problems. The second category, *creative thinking*, is an informal, divergent kind of thinking. In any curriculum designed to nurture the individual, the teacher must be concerned with both kinds of thought processes.

Logical Thinking. Under this broad heading, a number of processes are examined, namely, *concept formation and attainment*, the *generalizing process*, and *hypothesizing* and *predicting*.

Concept Formulation. A concept is a word or phrase that identifies or classifies a group of objects, events, or ideas. We tend to observe similarities and differences in any group of objects; we then classify the similarities under a concept label. A concept may be concrete: *dog* or *car*; or it may be abstract: *democracy* or *love*. The concept may be more or less inclusive, as well. *Animal* is more inclusive than is *mammal; mammal* is more inclusive than is *dog*; and *dog* is more inclusive than is *English Shepherd*. Authors sometimes focus on one of these elements rather than on another; thus, inclusiveness may be stressed by one author, whereas abstractness may form the basis for another author's definition of a specific concept.

Concept formation is a mental state or process whereby we construct an understanding of objects and experiences, particularly in relation to other objects and experiences. Conception or concept formation denotes process, whereas concept denotes product. The designation of a concept in words is called a *term*.

The transition from perception, or mere awareness, to conception is complex, and much remains to be learned about it. As a child moves from perception to conception, Piaget (1963) observed that (1) the amount of redundant material decreases, (2) the amount of irrelevant information that can be tolerated without affecting the responses increases, and (3) the integration of the spatial and temporal separation over the total information contained in the stimulus field increases. As a concept is formed, repetition becomes less essential, irrelevant information distracts less, and time and space separation can be greater without disturbing the learner.

Vygotsky (1962) studied the complex process of concept formation in some detail and concluded that a child, in his or her early years, birth to two years of age, associates a number of objects with a word. Sometimes the association is based only on a chance impression, for example, *doggie* may equal *horse, cow, cat, donkey, oddly shaped chair*, and *teddy bear.* From this somewhat random collection of objects, the child improves the unorganized *congerie*, or "heap" (Vygotsky's term), in three ways: trial and error methods, organization of the visual field, and reorganization of the heaps by associating elements from different heaps with a new word. This tendency continues as the child matures, however, and the child begins to think about objects on the basis of more concrete or factual bonds. The child does not yet distinguish between the essential and the nonessential (relevant and irrelevant) attributes of objects. The child may associate objects on the basis of similarities, contrasts, or proximity in space or time or on the basis of his or her own practical experiences. In this phase of concept formation, which Vygotsky refers to as thinking in complexes, the subjective associations are supplemented by more objective bonds, but the child still groups objects *in toto* with all of their attributes, regardless of their importance.

In the final stage of concept formation, the child isolates elements and is able to consider these elements apart from the concrete experience in which they were encountered. The application of a concept to new situations presents an even greater difficulty for the child. "When the process of concept formation is seen in all its complexity, it appears as a movement of thought within the pyramid of concepts, constantly alternating between two directions from the particular to the general and from the general to the particular" (Vygotsky, 1962, pp. 80–1).

Concept formation in its simplest form consists of three basic steps:

1. Differentiation of properties and/or elements of objects and/or events. This involves the breaking down of global wholes into specific criteria or parts.
2. Grouping or collecting these specific elements. This necessitates a careful analysis of common characteristics. These commonalities aid the process of pattern detection.
3. Elements are named, labeled, or categorized by the individual. Pattern recognition is involved; as decisions about exclusion or inclusion of a new element in the category are based on common characteristics.

The following example may serve to present these ideas in a practical way: (1) A very young child perceives that the object he or she knows to be a lawn mower has wheels and makes a loud noise. Other objects in the child's environment also have wheels and make noise, such as cars, motorcycles, and vacuum cleaners, so the child calls them all lawn mowers. (2) Eventually the child learns that the large ones that people ride inside are called cars and that lawn mowers are pushed by hand; consequently, now all large things that have wheels, that make a loud noise, and that people ride in are called cars, be they trucks, buses, tractors, and so on. Lawn mowers the child now knows are smaller than cars, but the concept of lawn mower becomes finalized when the child can distinguish those characteristics particular to a lawn mower that make it distinct from other small, noisy, wheeled, hand-pushed objects. (3) Lawn mowers cut grass; none of those other things do.

Because young children are growing both mentally and physically, they need to be given many opportunities to subject the concepts they have already developed to careful scrutiny, and they need to be provided with experiences that will expose them to new objects, events, and ideas.

Concept Realization. Several factors affect the realization of a concept. The *kind* of concept (abstract or concrete) and the *developmental age* of the child are factors in concept attainment. The *number* and *degree* of intensity of *experiences* that the individual has also affect the attainment of concepts. This suggests that there is a time and a kind of experience that is appropriate for a child. Several of Piaget's concepts, which deal specifically with this idea, follow:

1. *Accommodation.* When encountering something new that does not fit an existing mental structure, the individual accommodates the new by modifying or reorganizing his or her present structure of thought.

2. *Assimilation.* When internalizing the change so as to handle the new experience with ease, as a part of his or her own life space, the individual has assimilated the new information.

In dealing with children, some time must be allowed for this process. Ginsburg and Opper (1969) give a prime example of infant accommodation:

> Suppose an infant of four months is presented with a rattle. He has never before had the opportunity to play with rattles or similar toys. The rattle, then, is a feature of the environment to which he needs to adapt. His subsequent behavior reveals the tendencies of assimilation and accommodation. The infant tries to grasp the rattle. In order to do this successfully he must accommodate in more ways than are immediately apparent. First, he must accommodate his visual activities to perceive the rattle correctly; then he must reach out and accommodate his movements to the distance between himself and the rattle; in grasping the rattle he must adjust his fingers to its shape; and in lifting the rattle he must accommodate his muscular exertion to its weight. In sum, the grasping of the rattle involves a series of acts of accommodation, or modifications of the infant's behavioral structures to suit the demands of the environment. (p. 19)

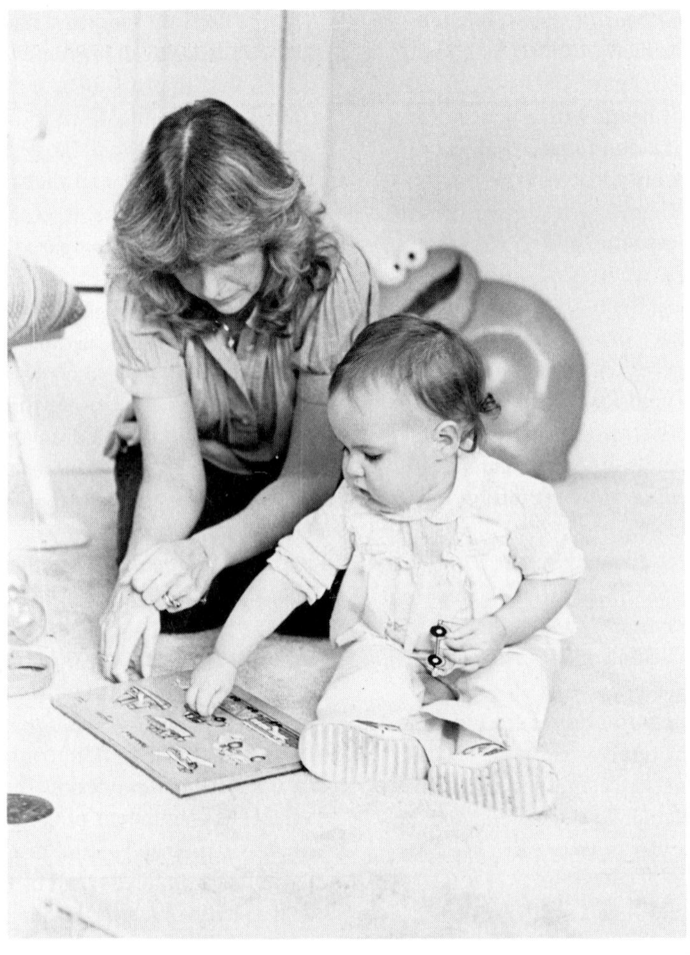

The grasping of a rattle or small puzzle piece involves a series of acts of accommodation—viewing the object, reaching out, judging distance, adjusting fingers, and accommodating muscular exertion. (Photo by Linda Lungren.)

One can consider the accommodation/assimilation process by a single term: *adaptation*. The child adapts to the environment when the concepts of accommodation and assimilation are integrated.

Piaget suggests that the evolution of thought takes place in the following stages that coincide roughly with age-developmental stages:

1. *Sensorimotor* stage, or preverbal intelligence, roughly from birth to eighteen months or two years, wherein the child responds to a stimulus in a noncognitive way.
2. *Preoperational*, the stage in which children group and categorize on a functional basis, for example, combining pencil with paper. One child grouped a knife with a carrot and a potato because "you peel them with it." This is common in young children of two to seven years of age.
3. *Concrete operational* stage, in which the child can reason logically about concrete things but not necessarily about abstract thoughts; this generally occurs between the ages of seven to eleven years.
4. *Formal operations*, the stage of conceptual or formal thought, beginning at about eleven years of age. At this stage, the child likes to think in abstract terms and enjoys hypothesizing—producing thoughts about thought.

Piaget asserts that cognitive developmental changes are related to biological developmental processes. Thus, each stage of cognitive growth, with its concomitant changes, emerges logically, and inevitable connections stem from each of the preceding stages. The stages are not reversible, and no stage is avoidable. "As Piaget suggests, every child must pass through the stages of cognitive development in the same order" (Wadsworth, 1971, p. 28). The child cannot go through the concrete operations stage and then the preoperational stage in reverse order. Piaget is a true developmental-stage theorist and postulates that one stage builds on another, that the child accomplishes certain learning tasks before proceeding to more complex tasks.

Although these stages are identified within certain age ranges, the ranges are not precise or binding; they are only approximations. The rate at which children pass through these processes is not fixed; it may be affected by intelligence, general health, social conditions, and other variables.

Generalization. The formation of a generalization is the end result of differentiation and synthesis of ideas. The innumerable facts in a life experience must be ordered and connected, that is, generalized, if they are to have any meaning for the learner. The learner must be the primary agent in generalizing meaning in his or her own collection of facts.

Prediction and Hypothesis. Isolated facts alone are useless unless we can group them to generalize and, based on these generalizations, make predictions. A fact observed will almost never be repeated. All that can be affirmed is that under analogous circumstances an analogous fact will be produced. To predict we must, therefore, invoke the aid of analogy. While we base our prediction on as large a number of facts as possible, we can never be sure that further investigation will support our hypothesis (Poincaré, 1952). Even so, it is far better to predict without complete certainty than not to hypothesize at all. It is important that students learn to hypothesize and then carry out experimentation that will verify or negate their hypotheses.

According to Piaget, there are several indications of when a child is in transition between the concrete operations level of thinking and the formal thinking stage. One indicator is the child's ability to transcend time and space via symbolic representation (sometimes this is called *symbolism*), that is, to see the hypothetical consequences of a proposed solution and to suggest alternate solutions. Here, the child goes beyond the time and space barriers and solves problems intellectually. Usually this occurs during adolescence, and the youth delights in considering "that which is not." The child is engaging in what is called antecedent/consequent thinking, in predicting what will happen. On the basis of this, the child selects the consequence that will be least hazardous and/or expensive to him.

Creative Thinking. Kagen (1971) expressed the notion that "the mission of education is to persuade each child that he is a richer source of ideas than he suspects and to enable him to experience the exhilaration that is inherent in the creative use of mind" (p. 4). We hope to stress in this book the importance of this "creative use of the mind" and the teacher's responsibility to provide ample opportunities for creative thinking.

The teacher might best encourage creativity by serving as a model, demonstrating interest in novel situations and curiosity about different and unique ideas. Having shown this interest and delight in learning to a child, the teacher must provide the child with opportunities to develop and pursue such interests in learning. Some educators call this approach discovery learning. There are several advantages to *discovery learning*:

1. It enables the child to identify problems and possible solutions.
2. It develops the learner's self-confidence and attitudes toward trying alternative solutions.
3. It encourages the student to discover broad principles and larger connections between different bodies of knowledge.

As a cautionary note about the process of discovery learning, it must be said that there can be an arbitrary nature about the ideas of knowledge gained this way. A sense of ownership emerges about the conclusions; that is, "Because I discovered it, it must be right." Continuous self-evaluation of one's ideas may be difficult, and consequently there is a need for highly skilled teacher guidance in the discovery process.

While discovery is sometimes considered as a completely creative process, it should be noted that some researchers believe that the function of discovery is specialized and limited and that there are certain kinds of discovery possible in certain content areas:

1. Discovery involves skill or knowledge about the subject. Pribram (1964) notes that "novelty rises out of variations of the familiar" (p. 10). This means that a person does not create on a completely "knowledgeless" basis but that he or she has probably already done considerable work in the field in question.
2. A second requirement for creative thinking is a combination of talent and background unique to the individual. Some skills and information are necessary to be able to produce,but they will not guarantee significant discovery in a field. People who are truly creative seem to be able to detect a delicate balance between too much information and freedom and too little of each and combine this with elements from their unique experiences to produce a new product—a refining of their world views.
3. A third element necessary for discovery is the appropriate mind set of the person involved. Some persons are highly motivated, whereas others are determined, and still others believe that the job they set out to do requires a great deal of persistence. These qualities are mind set. It is obvious that the execution of the task involved in the discovery process usually requires determination; for example, an idea for the development of a new piece of jewelry or for a new curricular design may come to a person's mind rather quickly, but the transformation of this idea into a product that others can share may be time consuming and necessitate perseverance to task completion.
4. There is evidence of emotional involvement in the creative act. Persons indicate an unusual degree of satisfaction with a creative accomplishment because they have been emotionally involved in the production of the idea and/or product.

One psychologist, Gordon (1961), discusses mental states that help a person to become better able to discover new relationships. Gordon is interested in the area of scientific discovery and uses the term "synectics," which means "the joining together of different and apparently irrelevant elements" (p. 18). Gordon delineates the mental states that are beneficial to the synectic process as follows:

1. Detachment-involvement: removing a problem from its familiar settings, seeing it differently; then becoming involved in order to produce a new insight.
2. Deferment: resisting the first solution that comes along.
3. Speculation: permitting the mind to run free to search for solutions.
4. Autonomy of the object: crystallizing ideas into some kind of solution. (pp. 18–19)

Gordon further explains ways in which persons may achieve these mental states. For example, he states that the use of *personal analogy* is one way in which a teacher can help a student to be more productive in solving a problem. In role-playing sessions in which we ask a child to assume the role of another and ask, "How did you feel when you were Brian?", we are using personal analogy.

A second way in which a person achieves problem-solving mental states is through direct analogy. We use *direct analogy* when we compare and contrast or use parallel facts, knowledge, or technology. We say, for instance, "You need to know how the people in the Fiji Islands solve their housing problem. How can thinking about how the people in the Arctic solved their housing problems help us?" or "You have studied how baboons behave in groups. Can we find similar areas of behavior in human group behavior?"

The third way is through the use of *symbolic analogy.* We might use impersonal and objective objects to solve a problem. When using this thinking style, we are trying to discover the relationships between past knowledge and new information.

A fourth means of achieving these mental states is that of *fantasy analogy*. "Wild ideas" should be scrutinized to determine if there are situations in which they do, in fact, make sense, before they are discarded as irrelevancies (Gordon, 1961).

Gallagher (1964) has investigated the phenomenon of original thought and has suggested that the following procedures are useful in original, productive thinking:

1. *Preparation:* During this stage the problem is investigated from all directions. This is primarily a period of identification and fact gathering.
2. *Incubation:* The person does not consciously think about the problem. Perhaps some kind of internal process of association of new information with past information and some internal reorganization of the information may occur during this period.
3. *Illumination:* "Aha phenomenon"—it is this stage in which the creator finds the solution to the problem.
4. *Verification:* During this stage the ideas is tested to determine its validity. (p. 359)

The implication of much of this research on cognition is that by carefully assessing cognitive abilities and by structuring learning activities where discovery can take place teachers can accelerate and expand a child's mental growth. Familiarity with the major issues and theories in the area of cognitive development is undoubtedly important for your consideration as a teacher of children. The degree to which you are able to integrate your awareness of the types and processes of thinking that can be expected of children will be reflected in your success in the classroom.

Developing Perception

As we have emphasized throughout this chapter, many factors influence a child's ability to cope with a learning situation. Chief among them is the internal stimulant of perception that is predicated on sensory development. External factors such as emotional and physical condition, linguistic ability, and motivation developed at home interrelate to influence perceptual development.

Perception and its relationship to the reading process has been a topic of research for decades. A child's perceptual ability involves the factors of *seeing* (visual), *hearing* (auditory), *smelling, tasting,* and *touching* (kinesthetic). Primary emphasis has been placed on visual and auditory perception in the studies investigating perception and reading. The question of when the child's perceptual abilities (especially visual) are mature enough to cope with the reading process is central to "reading readiness" research. The topic of when to begin reading instruction is discussed in greater detail in Chapter 4, "Readiness for Reading: Preparation, Program, and Activities."

Although perception of a stimulus may differ from individual to individual, Vernon (1959) suggests that the perceptual process as it pertains to the reading act consists of the following four points: (1) *discriminating* visual stimulus from its background characteristics, or recognizing that sound patterns within words are separate entities; (2) *recognizing* essential similarities necessary for the general classification of sound patterns into a succession of word patterns; (3) *classifying* visual symbols within their broader class, which are reflected as sounds; and (4) *identifying* words, usually through naming.

Therefore, perception involves the process of associating meaning with a concept that previously has been isolated through experience. After successful identification and recognition, the perceptual process involves one's ability to modify and relate the previous association with the present situation. Here we see how children refine the factors of *identification* and *recognition, categorization, generalization, analysis,* and *synthesis* to arrive at an understanding of the world around them.

Until the child enters school, he or she has been involved primarily with the sounds of whole words and their symbolic representations. For example, the child has been exposed to concretes: the word *cookie* refers to the good-tasting treat offered by his or her mother, and the word *shoe* refers to something one wears on one's feet. Through exposure, the child learns that there are many categories of cookies and shoes.

Because perceptual development is affected by emotional, physical, and socioeconomic factors, children entering first grade may have substantially different perceptual backgrounds and abilities. In view of potential

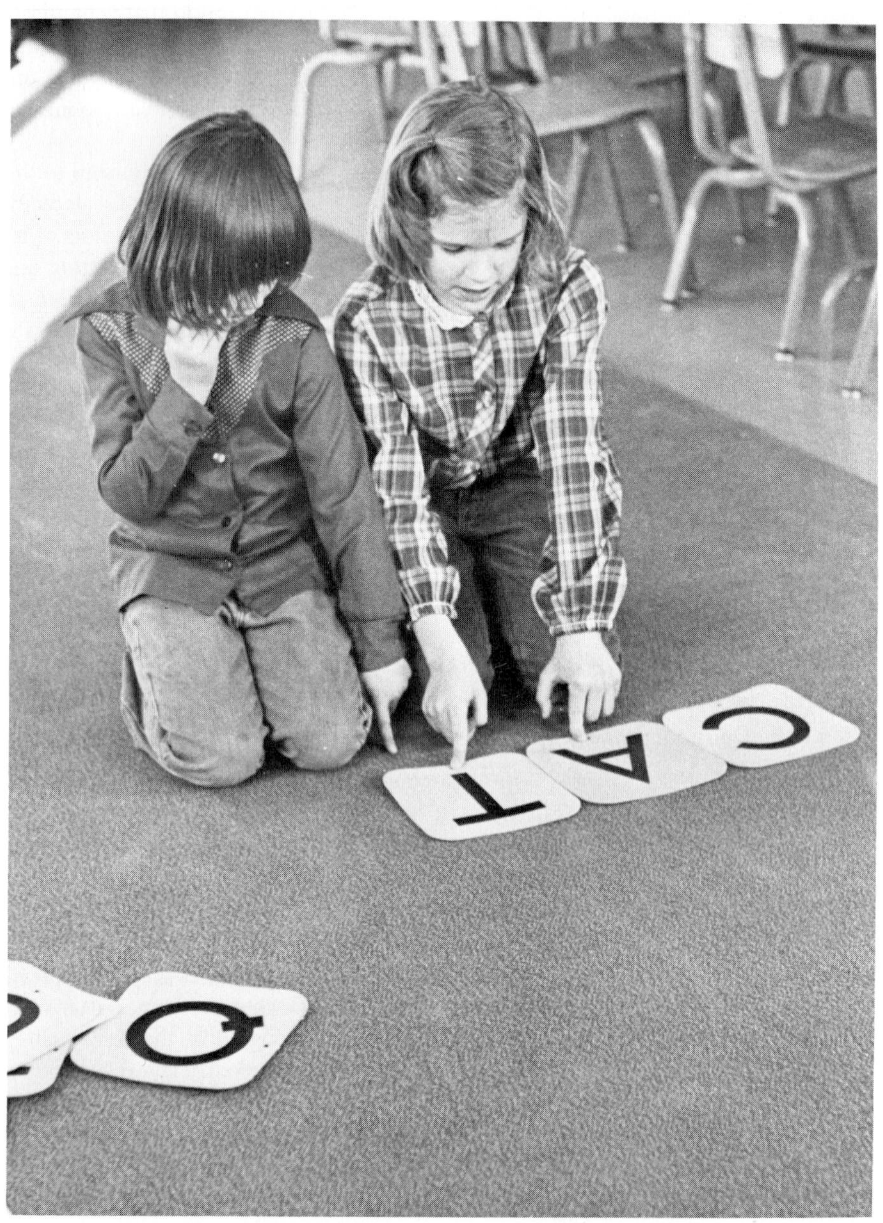

It is not sufficient for a beginning reader to see letters and to hear words. He must be perceptually able to discriminate differences in the letter shapes in order to form words. (Photo by Linda Lungren.)

differences, a wide variety of exposures to similar experiences must be offered to the beginning reader. It is not sufficient for a beginning reader to *see* letters and to *hear* words. The child must be able perceptually to discriminate differences in the letter shapes in order to form words. Most young children will need similar practice in perceiving word parts and whole words.

Developing Language

It is almost axiomatic to say that teachers who are preparing to instruct children in reading need to know a great deal about the language development of the child. The relation between the language development of young children and the reading process has become a major focus in linguistic and educational research in recent years. Psycholinguistics also has contributed considerably to our understanding of language acquistion and development of language in young children. Efforts have been made to incorporate the findings of this research into a viable instructional approach to reading. For this reason, a brief overview of the current research on language acquisition is presented in the following section.

Language Acquisition

Although human infants are born with immature nervous systems, they are still very capable of communicating, in a primitive linguistic manner, their basic needs. The central nervous system—the brain and the spinal cord—is more mature than is the peripheral nervous system. Infants learn to control their muscles, and with this maturation of the system, they become more capable of discriminating between sets of sounds, shapes, and colors. Researchers have reported a chronology for certain types of linguistic performance. For almost all children the schedule looks something like this:

Age	Vocalization
At birth	Crying
1-2 mo.	Cooing and crying
3-6 mo.	Babbling, cooing, and crying
9–14 mo.	First words
18–24 mo.	First sentences
3–4 yr.	Almost all basic syntactic structures
4–8 yr.	Almost all speech sounds correctly articulated
9-11 yr.	Semantic distinctions established

Although there is a range in which the stages in this table occur, Lenneberg (1967) has stated that they occur in the same sequential order for every child. When a child is born, he is incompletely equipped either to perceive or produce speech. He does not produce sounds directly related to those that will later be part of his language.

Based on what is known about language acquisition, Chomsky (1962) and others have advanced the idea that humans possess an innate, specific language-acquisition device. They tell us that all infants acquire this language tool without overt teaching: every physiologically "normal" child learns to talk, given a minimal amount of language input. Even mentally retarded children with IQs of 60 learn to talk, though often not as rapidly as the normal child, and often with a smaller vocabulary than the "normal" child.

Components of Language

Let us look now at the various components of language and the specifics of their acquisition in the child. In discussing language, the basic components usually are

1. *Phonology*—the sound system.
2. *Morphology*—inflections, tense markers.
3. *Syntax*—the order of words in an utterance.
4. *Semantics*—the meaning of words.

Phonology. One of the major concerns of linguists is to examine the specific speech sounds that make up language. The study of these speech sounds is called *phonology*. Because many researchers believe that the reading process includes the decoding of sounds in print, it is important that teachers of reading understand how the child acquires and uses the phonology of his or her language.

An interesting point about emerging sound systems in very young children is that, during their first year, the direction of the development of consonant like sounds is from back to front in the mouth, and for vowel-like sounds it is from front to back (McCarthy, 1954); however, during the last part of the first year of life, the direction is switched.

Roman Jakobson, a linguist, asserts that the development of the phonemic system is the result of the child's attempts to establish a system of oppositions within a sound continuum (1968). The first oppositions are maximal ones between a consonant and a vowel; usually they are the opposition between the most open central, farthest back vowel, /a/, and the farthest front, stopped consonant, /p/. Thus, /a/ is the "optimal" vowel, and /p/ is the "optimal" consonant. There is great frequency of /papa/ as a first syllable sequence in young children. Sometimes there is less than optimal control over the larynx and over the velum, which is the flap of skin at the back of the roof of mouth. In this case, the first syllable sequences are /baba/ or /mama/. Jakobson points out that this is why "papa," "baba," and "mama" are often the child's first-remembered or quoted sequences; it also explains why they are used as parental names or substitutes in many cultures.

As the child continues to develop, so does his or her ability to use a wider variety of consonant sounds. Some linguists suggest rough age correlates for production of English consonants:

Age	Proficient Consonant Articulation
3½ yr.	b p m w h
4½ yr.	d t h g k y ŋ
5½ yr.	f
6½ yr.	v ǰ ž š l
7½ yr.	s z θ f

For a detailed discussion of developmental distinctions between speech sounds and how and where they are formed in the mouth, see Alyeshmerni and Tauber (1975).

Morphology. Morphology is the term used by linguists to refer to the study of morphemes. The smallest units of meaning in language are called *morphemes*. Inflectional endings and tense markers, as well as the root words to which they are attached, all represent types of morphemes. In the study of morphology, the teacher is interested in looking briefly at how the child demonstrates growth in understanding about the effect that inflectional endings and tense markers have on meaning in language.

In an important study on the acquisition of morphology, Jean Berko-Gleason (1958) showed children a picture of a cartoon figure, telling the children in the study, "This is a *wug*." She then told the children that there were two animals, showed them a picture and said: "These are two ______," expecting the children to supply the plural "wugs" / wugz/. She used nonsense words that elicited all three of the English plural morphemes into consideration (/-s/ as in *hats*; /-z/ as in *rugs*; and /-iz) as in roses). Berko-Gleason found that children in the age range of 4 years made 6 percent errors with the /-iz/ forms but only 25 percent errors with /-z/ forms. She also found that the children have /-iz/ forms in their lexicons, for 91 percent had the correct plural for *glass*. She concluded that at a relatively early age children are able to account for morphological changes in language.

Syntax. Linguists use the term *syntax* to refer to the arrangement of words in a meaningful order. The expansion of the child's language from single to multiple utterances suggests the need for consistency in ordering such utterances so that they will be sensible to others. Since clarity of meaning in written language also depends on this consistent ordering, the child's ability to use proper syntax in speaking may facilitate understanding written sentences.

Telegraphic Speech and Pivots. The child produces his or her first word between nine and fourteen months of age; within six months of that age range, the child has a lexicon or vocabulary of at least fifty items. At this point, the child begins to put these words together. Most of these early combinations are *telegraphic*. According to Brown and Fraser (1963), articles, prepositions, and auxiliaries are not used at this stage. Here are some samples of telegraphic speech:

Daddy car
Baby cookie

Shortly after this period, children begin to use some of their words as *pivots*—that is, the pivot words are fixed and other words, often known as "open-class" words, are attached to them. The following illustrations exemplify this phenomenon:

Position Pivot 1	Position Pivot 2
allgone truck	shoe on
allgone cracker	hat on
allgone milk	pants on

Brown and Fraser indicate further that the child divides his or her lexicon into "function" words and "object" words. These divisions may be the basis of functional divisions that later become formal word classes, for example, nouns, verbs, and adjectives. As such, this process may lay the groundwork for contextual word analysis when the child begins the task of reading.

Slobin (1979) presents examples of some of these pivot structures:

Function	English	Function	English
Modify, qualify	pretty ___	Describe act	___ away
	my ___		___ on
	allgone ___		___ off
	all ___		___ it
Locate, name	there ___	Demand	more ___
	here ___		give ___
	see ___	Negate	no ___
	it ___		don't ___

Complex Syntactic Forms. *Forming questions* follows a path from simple to complex just as statement formation does. In the early stages, children begin simply by incorporating the rising intonation typical of English sentences into the same sentences they used for statements and demands, for example, "Daddy home?" More complex questions using either a verb or the auxiliary (*do, did*) in the initial position, called "yes/no" questions ("Does Mike go to school?)" and the "wh-" questions (*who, what, where, when, why, how*) form as the child progresses with language comprehension. *Relative clauses* are one of the last syntactic concepts to be understood by children. Carol Chomsky (1969) has found that many eight-year-olds do not fully understand a sentence such as "Tell Hugo what to buy at the store." She suggests further that most children between the ages of five and ten regard the first noun phrase in a sentence as the subject and the second noun phrase as the object. In a sentence such as "The cupcake was baked by Bill Deacon," the cupcake is thought of as the subject perpetrating a horrible fate on the object, Bill Deacon.

The ability to formulate and ask questions about words and ideas encountered in the text is essential to reading comprehension, as is minimizing miscues provoked by such syntactic complications as relative clauses. As the child acquires competence with these language forms, the ability to proceed smoothly through a written text increases.

Semantics. In its simplest form, *semantics* is the study of word meaning. Single words can have multiple meanings for the child, and even "fixed" multiple meanings can be altered by syntactic and contextual constraints. A four-year-old child knows that a figurative meaning is being attached to the word *puppy* when his mother says, "Kevin, you're acting like a puppy." Furthermore, the child knows whether or not "puppy" is being used in a good or bad sense by the mother's tone and by contextual considerations (for example, is the child chewing on the sofa?).

If we take this consideration one step farther and the utterance is changed to "Kevin, you're acting like a zumtoadbat," the child can use his or her knowledge of syntax, intonation, and context to arrive at an acceptable synonym for "zumtoadbat." Semantics, then, is the study of word meaning, including phonology, syntax, and pragmatics (i.e., contextual usage).

While the importance of semantics in the acquisition of syntax has been both minimized (Chomsky, 1972) and emphasized (Clark, 1976; Ferguson, 1971), there can be little argument that knowledge of word meaning, including phonology, syntax, and pragmatics (contextual usage), is essential to reading comprehension. Simply breaking the code phonetically does the reader little good without the semantic information necessary to give it meaning.

Human Performance and Information Processing

In recent years, psychologists, educators, mathematicians, and linguists have begun to study the phenomenon of human information processing. They have examined such complex areas of human performance as the role of perception and memory in processing information, the speed and quantity of information processing and storage, and the type of information that is processed and stored most easily by the human brain.

As mentioned earlier, the field of human information processing crosses many disciplines and involves a great deal of technical and experimental research that is beyond the scope of this text. It is important for you to be aware of this area of endeavor because an understanding of how we process perceptual and linguistic information will enhance our comprehension of the reading process. Advances in this field may one day revolutionize the theories and models of reading that are currently considered valid (see Chapter 7). Many reaction-time experiments involving letter discrimination and target words have offered insight into the functions of attention, recognition, and memory in processing visual information. For example, Neisser (1967) found that literate adults could scan a list of stimulants for ten targets as quickly as they could for one. He found that subjects could scan a list of words for members from a particular class (e.g., fruits) almost as fast as they could for a single item (e.g., store). Scanning for items from other large, open classes such as animals or names was slower. Chase (1973) found that rate increases linearly with memory size, although it does *not* depend on the form of the task, preview, or the probability of a target.

Results of studies such as these may indicate direction for reading instruction in structural analysis, configuration clues, classification systems, and techniques for scanning.

In more recent studies on cognition, psychologists and educators have examined interactions among sensori-perceptual and attentional processes, short-term retention, and associative factors in memory. Most research related to the reading process studies the coding transformations that occur within a matter of seconds in most literate adults. There is presently evidence that supports the following: (1) these information-processing operations may entail both sensory and associative storage; (2) when subjects are given a few seconds to study a list of familiar items, memory rates are comparable for letters or numbers, words, or word categories (Smith, 1967); and (3) both memory and visual search rates depend heavily on the familiarity of the materials, the relative emphasis given to speed and accuracy, and the practice time. Indications for reading instruction based on research findings in this area may include work on improving visual and auditory memory, previewing material to be taught, and implications for re-evaluation of testing instruments.

Although this body of information may not seem particularly relevant or necessary to you as a teacher, it is important that you be aware of current research in the field as well as new, and often varied, directions that researchers are investigating to find more efficient ways in which to help children learn to read. For a detailed discussion of work in the field of human information processing, see Fitts and Posner (1979).

HUMAN DEVELOPMENT: EXTERNAL STIMULANTS

The child who sits before you in the classroom is not only developing in time with a complex multiplicity of internal factors, but is also being shaped physically, emotionally, and psychologically by external stimulants, or factors within the environment. In the past, the significance of the environment as an influence on learning has often been underestimated, and many educators now feel that external stimulants are as important if not more important than inherent qualities in developing full learning and achievement potential. In the area of reading instruction, it appears that the external stimulants associated with the home environment are directly related to success in learning to read.

We examine external stimulants in two categories: family and parental influences and home environment. There are no simple answers to questions about how or why a child does or does not learn to read. All we can present here are the findings of current research that has examined some of these relations and the reading achievement of the child.

Family and Parental Influence

As soon as a child is able to respond to language, the family may begin to influence attitudes toward reading. Oral language provides the foundation for success in reading. To encourage language development, parents need to talk to their child as soon as he or she is born to provide the child with a model. Through the physical act of holding a baby snugly and securely while showing him or her the pictures in a book, parents and other family members begin to reinforce the association that reading is a pleasurable experience.

As the child matures, parents can begin reading to him or her, holding the book so that the child can view the illustrations as well as the printed page. The intent here is not to initiate reading but to establish and to reinforce an understanding of the relationship between the printed pages and spoken words. Parents should discuss the ideas in the material they read to their children. Such interaction may introduce new words that the parents can help the child incorporate into his or her vocabulary. Parents can gain insight into their child's growth and maturity in this way.

Anecdotes and reminiscences abound when parents and teachers try to remember how they began to read. As adults, the most successful readers vividly remember parts of the process of their introduction to reading. For example, one teacher recalls the arrival of the daily newspaper and the fact that her father, an energetic and hardworking policeman, always read it before going to bed. She recalled her daily anticipation of crawling up into his lap to hear her favorite comic strips read and her motivation to learn to read so she could "read the paper" before he did. She also recalled a book of stories from which her mother read after tucking her into bed at night. Although she could not recall specific comic strips or stories, the pleasure of these situations remained with her and continued to influence her attitude toward reading. As children observe their parents in the act of reading, they become involved with imitative and identification behavior. Such children are aware of a complicated task (reading) that they wish to accomplish as they observe a master craftsman at work.

Reading-Related Models. Many studies have shown that children who view their parents reading, who are read to, and who have books and educational toys succeed at prereading tasks. Hess and Shipman (1965) and Klaus and Gray (1968) have found that modeling in all cases causes higher performance than when parental noninvolvement exists. However, most modeling research is not related specifically to readiness for reading. Durkin's studies (1966, 1972) are exceptions because she discovered that, in cases of early readers, modeling was an important predictor of reading success.

Verbal Interaction Between Parent and Child. McCarthy (1954) postulated that the degree of verbal and reading efficiency was dependent on the frequency and quality of the parent's contact with the child. Also, Hess and Shipman suggested that a child's performance on cognitive tasks is associated with the "teaching style" of the mother. This maternal teaching style is particularly evident in reading episodes between parent and child.

Oral Reading Episodes. Be it classic children's stories read chapter by chapter or a favorite comic book read until the reader and the child know every word, being read to is not only a joy to both parties, but it is also beneficial to the young reader. There is an extensive body of normative literature suggesting that reading to young children enhances language development (Templin, 1957; MacKinnon, 1959; Durkin, 1974; Bullock, 1975) and is related to reading success (Almy, 1958; Durkin, 1974, 1980). Educators have urged frequent oral reading to young children (Durkin, 1974). Several methodological texts on the teaching of reading urge parents to read to young children because books and stories provide children with important models of book language (Durkin, 1974) and with models of life-lifting language.

There is also an historical body of normative literature suggesting that children should be read to during the school day. Chapparo (1975) maintains that "storytime reading to children should be an integral part of every reading program—children need models." Durkin (1974) argues in favor of reading to young children on the grounds that an oral reading episode "can be a vehicle for learning about children's readiness for reading" (p. 125).

Few educators will dispute the need for reading to young children, but even fewer educational researchers have investigated the most efficacious ways in which this reading should be done. Bullock's report, "A Language for Life" (1975), addresses the "how" of reading to young children by stressing the importance of the socio-emotional implications of the child's first contacts with books. The report advised that "the best way to prepare the very young child for reading is to hold him on your lap and read aloud to him stories he likes—over and over again" (p. 28).

There has been limited empirical research on the effects of style of reading to young children and cognitive growth. One of the few studies in this area was reported by Swift (1970), who explained the success of a parent training program called *Get Set*, which first presented the value of reading to young children. The purpose of the program was to enable mothers to lengthen thoughts, elaborate on ideas, and improve observational skills. Parents were taught to retell certain parts of stories to extend their children's verbalization and communication skills; parents were also taught to develop their children's thoughts by asking experiential questions during the readings.

Another study by Flood (1977) found that parents can enhance their children's experiences by following these four steps during a reading episode:

1. Prepare children for the story by asking warm-up questions.
2. Interact with the child during the story by asking and answering many questions.
3. Reinforce the child during the episode in a positive manner.
4. Finish the episode by asking evaluative questions.

Reading episodes provide parents and teachers with unique opportunities for verbal interaction with young children. Some researchers believe that this interaction is directly related to language and reading success. It has been frequently reported that the interaction of adults and children creates an environment that fosters language growth in the child (Durkin, 1966, 1974). Durkin found that it was important for parents to talk with

Whether it be classic children's stories read chapter by chapter, or a favorite comic book, being read to is not only a joy to all parties, but beneficial to the reader. (Photo by Paul Hill.)

their children and to answer their questions, thereby providing them with experiences that result in new vocabulary.

Reading-Rich Environment. While parental contact in a reading context is perhaps the most important factor in establishing a rich atmosphere for developing interest and skill in reading for the young child, other factors in the home environment are also significant to the reading readiness task. Chief among these factors are educational materials and television.

Books and Materials

An extensive body of literature suggests that children need to have books and other educational materials available to them in the home to prepare more successfully for reading (Bernstein, 1967; Beck, 1973; Durkin, 1974). Materials may include such items as chalkboards, magnetic letter sets, toys that utilize the alphabet, children's magazines, paper, pencils, and a desk or table where the child can "work," "study," or play "school." In her analysis of environmental variables related to the development of verbal abilities and reading, Jones (1972) found that the availability of materials and organizational opportunities were important influences in developing reading readiness. Success in reading is often related to the importance placed on it in the home. By incorporating reading-related activities in the recreational pursuits of the child, parents and other family members can create an environment that is rich in reading.

Television Viewing

Perhaps the greatest single nonhuman environmental influence on the child's later cognitive abilities, including reading ability, is the effect of television viewing. There is no longer a question of whether educational shows are effective, but rather to what degree they are effective. As early as the mid-1950s, Templin (1957) argued in favor of periodic studies about children's language because of the influence of television on changing norms of language ability. In the introduction to *Certain Language Skills in Children* (1957), she states that

> The present study was begun after the introduction of television into many homes. Thus, it is likely that more adult language was present in the environment than would have been true earlier. . . . It may be that the effect of such language stimulation in the child's environment would be even greater today than when the first data for this study was gathered just a few years ago. (p. vii)

SLOW
SCHOOL
ZONE
"How come we were born with the ability to watch TV, but we have to learn how to read?"

TV Guide, 23 August 1981.

Templin's warning for updated norms to account for the influence of television certainly has been heard, and there has been a great deal of television research. However, seventeen years later, Leifer (1974) reported: "To date we understand little about the combined roles of television, the home, and the school in influencing child development" (p. 74). A great deal of research has been conducted on the social and cognitive effects of television, but few have studied the interrelations between television and language learning and reading.

Similarly, there have been few studies investigating the role of parents in the cognitive development of children *via* television. That parents are important in shaping attitudes toward television has been demonstrated by several researchers. Lyle and Hoffman (1972) report: "Mothers who watch television at least three hours per day are likely to have children who watch a great deal of television" (p. 70). Leifer (1974) states: "Parents need to be especially active in limiting and guiding their young children's exposure to television" (p. 191). Unfortun-

The effect of TV on childrens' performance.

"The Family Circus" by Bill Keane reprinted courtesy The Register and Tribune Syndicate, Inc.

ately, researchers have found that only one third of parents have definite viewing rules (Lyle and Hoffman, 1972). Leifer reports that parental interaction with children during and after television viewing may influence the ways in which children integrate what they have seen.

Sesame Street. *Sesame Street*, the result of a joint venture of the Carnegie and Ford Foundations and the U.S. Office of Education, turned public attention to the positive educational aspects of television. The show was fine-tuned by extensive pretesting and observation of the viewers' responses. As a result, the proposed format of the show underwent some changes. Vocabulary, letter names, and beginning sounds were taught through rhyme, puppetry, songs, stories, and direct instruction.

Although general television may or may not have a beneficial effect on children's language growth, there is a significant body of literature suggesting that educational television, in general, and the Children's Television Workshop, in particular, are beneficial for children. The Educational Testing Service's evaluation of *Sesame Street* conducted by Ball and Bogatz (1972) stated that "the facts are that the show was seen to have a marked effect, not only in the areas of rote learning of basic skills, such as counting, and in simple contiguity association learning, as in learning the names of letters and numbers, but also in higher areas of cognitive activity, such as sorting and classifying pictorial representations" (p. 7). Frequent viewing of *Sesame Street* seemed to be a better predictor of performance at posttest than was age. In this study, posttest frequency of viewing matched the pretest data. Ball and Bogatz maintain that the implication of this finding is that "we should think of beginning with younger than four-year-old children and perhaps raise our expectations of what these young children can learn" (p. 18).

According to them,

> The children who watched the most learned the most, and skills that received the most attention in the program were the best learned by the children. The goals of the program directly related to reading included recognizing, naming, and matching capital and lowercase letters, recognizing and matching letters in words, recognizing initial sounds and reading words. . . . The results from *Sesame Street* point up the importance of being specific about educational goals and directing the educational program toward these goals. (p. 18)

Blanton (1972) proposed the following list of objectives as comprehensive and appropriate for an early education program.

Blanton's Educational Television Prereading Objectives*

Letters

1. *Matching:* Given a printed letter, the child can select the identical letter from a set of printed letters.
2. *Recognition:* Given the verbal label for a letter, the child can select the appropriate letter from a set of printed letters.
3. *Labeling:* Given a printed letter, the child can provide the verbal sound.
4. *Letter sounds:*
   a. For sustaining consonants (f, l, m, n, r, s, v), given the printed letter, the child can produce the letter's corresponding sound.
   b. Given a set of words presented orally, all beginning with the same letter sound, the child can select from a set of words another word with the same initial letter sound.
5. *Recitation of the alphabet:* The child can recite the alphabet.

Words

1. *Matching:* Given a printed word, the child can select an identical word from a set of printed words.
2. *Boundaries of a word:* Given a printed sentence, the child can correctly point to each word in the sentence.
3. *Temporal-sequence/spatial-sequence correspondence:* (Words and sentences are read from left to right.)
   a. Given a printed word, the child can point to the first and last letter.
   b. Given a printed sentence, the child can point to the first and last word.
4. *Decoding:* Given the first five words on the reading vocabulary list (ran, set, big, mop, fun), the child can decode other related words generated by substitutions of a new initial consonant. (Example: given the word ran, the child can decode man and can.)

*From "How Effective Is *Sesame Street?*" by William Blanton in the ERIC/CRIER column in the May 1972 issue of *The Reading Teacher*, p. 807. Reprinted by permission.

5. *Word recognition:* For any of the words on the *Sesame Street* word list, the child can recognize the given word when it is presented in a variety of contexts.
6. *Reading:* The child can read each of the 20 words on the *Sesame Street* word list.

While some may advocate "widening" the street to include other theories of learning (Beck, 1979), most everyone would hate to see a "road closed" sign on *Sesame Street.*

The Electric Company. The Electric Company was designed to pick up where *Sesame Street* left off, that is, to supplement the reading of seven- to ten-year-olds.

Roser (1972) noted that the show was designed to emphasize these curricular items:

1. The left-to-right sequence of print corresponds to the temporal sequence of speech.
2. Written symbols stand for speech sounds. They "track" the stream of speech.
3. The relation between written symbols and speech sounds is sufficiently reliable to produce successful decoding most of the time.
4. Reading is facilitated by learning a set of strategies for figuring out sound-symbol relationships. (p. 684)

In summary, television cannot and should not be ignored as a vehicle of potential for children's learning. Even though there are those who are concerned only with reading via print, the world of television (and indeed it is here to stay) should be used, making it possible for children to respond more easily to print with greater understanding.

QUESTIONS AND RELATED READINGS

The following questions are based on the goals stated at the beginning of the chapter. If you feel that you have not attained adequate knowledge to answer the questions successfully, we suggest additional related readings.

1. Explain the various stages of human cognitive development.
2. Explain the process of language acquisition and development in the child.
3. How does the family, especially the parents and home surroundings affect prereading development and attitudes toward reading?
4. In what way can television be useful for developing prereading skills?

Goal 1: To help the reader to understand the stages of cognitive development.

Question 1: Explain the various stages of human cognitive development.

Flavell, J. H. *Cognitive Development.* Englewood Cliffs, N.J.: Prentice-Hall, Inc., 1977.

Peill, E. J. *Invention and Discovery of Reality.* London: Wiley, 1975.

Piatelli-Palmarini, M. *Language and Learning: The Debate Between Jean Piaget and Noam Chomsky.* Cambridge, Mass.: Harvard University Press, 1980.

Goal 2: To help the reader to examine language acquisition and development.

Question 2: Explain the process of language acquisition and development in the child.

Clark, E. "Non-linguistic Strategies in the Acquisition of Word Meanings." *Cognition* 2 (1973), 161–82.

Lenneberg, E., ed. *Foundations of Language Development: A Multidisciplinary Approach.* New York: Academic Press, Inc., 1975.

Slobin, D. I., ed. *The Ontogenesis of Grammar.* New York: Academic Press, Inc., 1971.

Goal 3: To help the reader to recognize home environment and family involvement as an influence on the developing reader.

Question 3: How do the family, especially the parents, and home surroundings affect prereading development and attitudes toward reading?

Bradley, R. H. "Home Environment and Cognitive Development in the First 2 Years: A Cross-Lagged Panel Analysis." *Developmental Psychology* 15:3 (May 1979), 246–50.

Gotts, E. E. "Long-Term Effects of a Home-Oriented Preschool Program." *Childhood Education* 56:4, (February–March 1980), 228–34.

Horan, M. "A Prekindergarten Program: Policy Implications of the Research." *Education and Urban Society* 12:2 (February 1980), 193–210.

Goal 4: To help the reader to examine television as an influence on the developing reader.

Question 4: In what way can television be useful for developing prereading skills?

Becker, G. J. *Television and the Classroom Reading Program.* Reading Aids Series. Newark, Del.: International Reading Association, 1973.

Brown, R., ed. *Children and Television.* 1st Amer. ed. Beverly Hills, Calif.: Sage Publications, 1976.

Dorr, A. "Television Literacy for Young Children." *Journal of Communication* 30:3 (Summer 1980), 71–83.

BIBLIOGRAPHY

Almy, M. "The Importance of Children's Experience to Success in Beginning Reading." In *Research in the Three R's*, ed. by Hunnicutt and W. Iverson. New York: Harper & Row, Publishers, 1958, pp. 48–52.

Alyeshmerni, M., and P. Tauber. *Working with Aspects of Language.* New York: Harcourt Brace Jovanovich, 1975.

Ball, S., and G. A. Bogatz. "Research on *Sesame Street*: Some Implications for Compensatory Education." Paper presented at the Second Annual Blumberry Symposium in Early Childhood Education. Baltimore, Md.: Johns Hopkins University Press, 1972.

Beck, I. L. *A Longitudinal Study of the Reading Achievement Effects of Formal Reading Instruction in the Kindergarten: A Summative and Formative Evaluation.* Unpublished doctoral dissertation, University of Pittsburgh, 1973.

Beck, T. K. "Widening *Sesame Street.*" *Journal of Educational Television and Other Media* 5:2 (Summer 1979), 39–42.

Berko-Gleason, J. "The Child's Learning of English Morphology." *Word* 14 (1958), 150–77.

Blanton, W. "How Effective Is Sesame Street?" in the ERIC/CRIER column, *The Reading Teacher* 25 (May 1972), 807.

Brown, R., and C. Fraser. "The Acquisition of Syntax." In *Verbal Behavior and Learning*, ed. by C. N. Cofer and B. Musgrave. New York: McGraw-Hill Book Company, 1963, 158–97.

Bullock, Sir A. "A Language for Life." Report for the British Government, 1975.

Chapparo, J. "A New Look at Language Experience." Paper presented at *A Successful Foundation for a Reading in a Second Language Conference*, San Diego, Calif: February 1975.

Chase, W. G., ed. *Visual Information Processing.* New York: Academic Press, Inc., 1973.

Chomsky, C. S. *The Acquisition of Syntax in Children from 5 to 10.* Cambridge, Mass.: The MIT Press, 1969.

Chomsky, N. *Syntactic Structures.* The Hague: Mouton, 1957.

____. *Language and Mind.* New York: Harcourt Brace Jovanovich, 1972.

Clark, H. H. *Semantics and Comprehension.* The Hague: Mouton, 1976.

Durkin, D. *Children Who Read Early: Two Longitudinal Studies.* New York: Bureau of Publications, Teachers College Press, Columbia University, 1966.

____. "Listen to Your Children." *Instructor* 8:6 (February 1972), 87–88.

____. *Teaching Them to Read.* Boston: Allyn & Bacon, Inc., 1974.

____. *Teaching Young Children to Read.* 3rd ed. Boston: Allyn & Bacon, Inc., 1980.

Fitts, P. M., and M. I. Posner. *Human Performance.* Westport, Conn.: Greenwood Press, Publishers, 1979.

Flood, J. "Parental Styles in Reading Episodes with Young Children." *The Reading Teacher* 30 (May 1977), 864–67.

Gallagher, J. J. "Productive Thinking." In *Review of Child Development Research*, ed. by M. L. Hoffman and L. W. Hoffman. Vol. 1. New York: Russell Sage Foundation, 1964.

Ginsberg, H., and S. Opper. *Piaget's Theory of Intellectual Development.* Englewood Cliffs, N.J.: Prentice-Hall, Inc., 1969.

Gordon, W. J. *Syntectics–The Development of Creative Capacity.* New York: Harper & Row, Publishers, 1961.

Hess, R. D., and V. C. Shipman. "Early Experience and the Socialization of Cognitive Modes in Children." *Child Development* 36 (1965), 869–86.

Jakobson, R. *Kindersprache, Aphasie, und Allegmeine Lautgesetze.* Uppsala: Almquist and Wiksell, 1941. (English translation: *Child Language, Aphasia, and Phonological Universals.* The Hague: Mouton, 1968.

Jones, J. P. *Intersensory Transfer, Perceptual Shifting, Modal Preference, and Reading.* Newark, Del.: International Reading Association, 1972.

Kagen, J. *Change and Continuity in Infancy.* New York: John Wiley & Sons, Inc., 1971.

Klaus, R. A., and S. W. Gray. *The Early Training Project for Disadvantaged Children: A Report After Five Years.* Society for Research in Child Development Monographs, Serial no. 120, 1968, pp. 33–4.

Leifer, G. "Children's Theater Workshop." Cambridge, Mass.: Harvard Educational Workshop, 1974.

Lennenberg, E. H. *Biological Foundations of Language.* New York: John Wiley & Sons, Inc., 1967.

LeShan, Eda. *The Conspiracy Against Childhood.* N.Y.: Atheneum, 1967, p. 61.

Lyle, R., and J. Hoffman. "Children's Use of Television and Other Media." In *Television and Social Be-*

havior, ed. by E. A. Rubinstein, G. A. Comstock, and J. P. Murray. Vol. 4. Washington, D.C.: U.S. Government Printing Office, 1972.

MacKinnon, P. *How Do Children Learn to Read?* Montreal: The Copp Clark Co., 1959.

McCarthy, D. "Language Development in Children." In *Manual of Child Psychology*, ed. by L. Carmichael. 2d ed., New York: John Wiley & Sons, Inc., 1954, pp. 492–630.

Martin, J. G. *Mediated Transfer in Two Verbal Learning Paradigms.* Unpublished doctoral dissertation, University of Minnesota, Minneapolis, 1960.

Neisser, U. *Cognitive Psychology.* New York: Appleton-Century-Crofts, 1967.

Piaget, J. *The Origins of Intelligence in Children.* New York: W. W. Norton & Company, Inc., 1963.

Poincaré, H. *Science and Hypothesis.* New York: Dover Publications, Inc., 1952.

Pribram, K. A. "Neurological Notes in the Art of Educating." In *Theories of Learning and Instruction.* National Society for the Study of Education. Chicago: University of Chicago Press, 1964.

Roser, N. L. "*Electric Company* Critique: Can Great Be Good Enough?" *The Reading Teacher* 17:7 (April 1972), 680–4.

Slobin, D. I. *Psycholinguistics.* Glenview, Ill.: Scott, Foresman and Company, 1979.

Smith, H. K. "The Responses of Good and Poor Readers When Asked to Read for Different Purposes." *Reading Research Quarterly* 3 (1967), 53–83.

Spache, G. D., and E. B. Spache. *Reading in the Elementary School.* 3rd ed. Boston: Allyn & Bacon, Inc., 1973.

Swift, M. "Training Poverty Mothers in Communication Skills. *The Reading Teacher* 23 (January 1970), 360–7.

Templin, M. *Certain Lcnguage Skills in Children.* Minneapolis: University of Minnesota Press, 1957.

Vernon, M. D. "The Perceptual Process in Reading." *The Reading Teacher* 13 (October 1959), 2–8.

Vygotsky, L. S. *Thought and Language.* Cambridge, Mass.: The MIT Press, 1962.

Wadsworth, B. J. *Piaget's Theory of Cognitive Development.* New York: David McKay Co., Inc. 1971.

CHAPTER 3

The Integrated Language Arts

There is an art of reading, as well as an art of thinking, and an art of writing.
Isaac D'Israeli

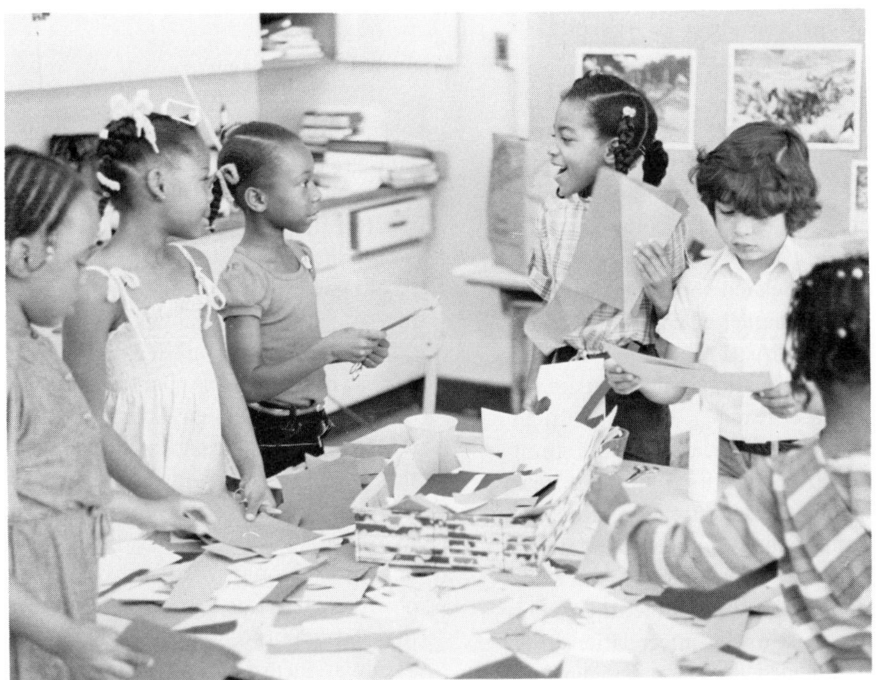

Language is the foremost means of communicating the majority of one's ideas and feelings. (Photo by Linda Lungren.)

GOALS: To help the reader to

1. Develop an understanding of listening skills.
2. Understand how speaking skills are acquired.
3. Enhance students' reading skills.
4. Improve students' writing skills.
5. Comprehend the interrelatedness of all the language arts.

Language is the foremost means of communicating the majority of one's ideas and feelings. Language is one of the systems we use to express ourselves. For example, *encoding* occurs when we use speech and writing as codes to convey our thoughts. As our thoughts are conveyed or received, they are decoded. Therefore, *decoding* involves extracting meaning, as in listening and reading.

The ability to convey our ideas occurs *via* the language arts. The term *language arts* describes our communication processes as well as a major portion of the school curriculum. Language arts include the communication processes of *listening, speaking, reading,* and *writing.* The development of these interrelated communication processes is important for the learner when gaining information as well as giving information.

Consider for a moment situations when you are listening, speaking, writing, or reading. More often than not, you use more than one of the language arts simultaneously. From this perspective, it is natural to view the act of communication as an interrelated process. Loban's (1976) research findings support this view; he states that students who have low abilities in oral language also have difficulty in reading and writing. He suggests further that the inverse of this interrelationship is true. He found that students with adequate language abilities show little, if any, difficulty in acquiring other communication skills.

One of your many tasks as a classroom teacher will be to integrate the language arts among themselves and to integrate them throughout the entire curriculum. When a student is engaged in a math, science, or social studies activity, he or she can be using all the language arts. A student *listens* to instructions or ideas, shares ideas by *speaking, reads* content materials, and *writes* detailed reports to express his or her thoughts. Students use the language arts throughout the curriculum. You can see how unrealistic it is to believe that language arts can be taught in a single, separate, forty-minute-a-day period.

If your task as a reading/language arts teacher seems overwhelming, let us stop and ponder the following questions:

1. What specific information will I need to know about each of the language arts?
2. Which communication skills are appropriate for the students at a given stage of development?
3. How can I teach all the language arts in conjunction with all the content area skills?
4. Are there activities I can use to facilitate learning these skills?
5. Where do I begin?

Each time a teaching task seems overwhelming to you, you must stop, pose the questions to which the answers will solve your dilemma, and then set out through reading, thinking, student observation, or talking with your colleagues to answer your queries.

No one ever knows all there is to know about teaching. As you teach, you will continuously pose new questions and confront new problems and then will seek to answer them. This chapter is designed to serve as a model to aid you in answering your questions about the teaching of the language arts. We plan to accomplish this task in the following ways.

First, you will be introduced to information related to extending listening, speaking, and writing skills within your classroom. A discussion of the language art of *reading* will not be a prime focus of this chapter since it is the central purpose of this text. Second, you will explore a simulated curriculum that illustrates the integration of the language arts within content areas of study.

PART I THE LANGUAGE ARTS

LISTENING

Some say that owls are wise
Because they keep so quiet.
Could most of us fare better
On an expert listening diet?
(Quoted in Lundsteen, 1979, p. 128)

Listening occupies a major portion of time spent in school. One study of elementary schoolchildren by Wilt (1950) estimates this listening time to be 57.5 percent of a student's day. In today's complex world, a child also watches television and listens to the radio, record players, telephones, tape recorders, and other teaching machines. Too often, parents and teachers have assumed that quiet children are *listening* children. But are they? Children need to develop listening skills that will enable them to function well in a complex society. Teachers can facilitate this process by teaching listening skills and by fostering an environment in which of these skills can be acquired easily.

The Beginning Years

Children are exposed to sounds from the very earliest moments of life. By the age of four, the young child is silent for only nineteen minutes of a waking day (Brandenburg, 1915). The earliest listening patterns are developed in the home and the degree of listening activity reinforcement supplied by the home affects the development of beginning listening skills (Feldman, 1967).

Listening should not be confused with *hearing*; hearing is part of the listening process. An active listener does a great deal more than simply hear and obey. Listening involves *hearing* information, *processing* the information, *reflecting* on the information, and *responding* to it. Although hearing involves the intake of information, the listening process encourages one to *process* and *reflect* on the information and, through language, respond to what has been heard.

Brown (1954) refers to this listening/language process as auding.

> "Auding is to the ears what reading is to the eyes." If reading is the gross process of looking, recognizing, and interpreting written symbols, auding may be defined as the gross process of listening to, recognizing, and interpreting spoken symbols. (p. 86)

Brown further explains this point of view further through the following formula (p. 3).

Seeing is to Hearing
as
Observing is to Listening
as
Reading is to Auding

Parents and caregivers are most important in the early development of listening skills.

The School Years

Children enter school with a wide range of auding abilities. Part of your job as a classroom teacher will be to identify children with hearing disabilities, rather than poor listening/auding skills. Detecting these problems is not always an easy task; through observation, however, you may notice that a student

1. Is abnormally inattentive or abnormally attentive.
2. Relies on gestures when speech would be more effective.
3. Is behind in speech development.
4. Strains to hear what is being said around him or her.
5. Gives inappropriate answers to your questions.
6. Ignores a speaker with whom he or she does not have direct eye contact.
7. Has difficulty relating sequences to that which he or she has listened.
8. May be unable to reproduce consonant phonemes.
9. Has difficulty repeating long, detailed sentences.
10. Evidences voice production (pitch, stress, rhythm) difficulties.

In addition, be particularly alert to any student who may exhibit one or more of these signs when you have knowledge of the child having any of these medical complaints:

1. Frequent colds or ear infections.
2. Allergies.
3. Measles, mumps, or rubella.

If you detect possible hearing difficulties, refer the child to a speech and hearing specialist or school doctor or nurse. If, after a checkup, the child is diagnosed as having no hearing loss, you will have to plan curricula to facilitate the progress of these underdeveloped listening skills. Duker (1968) encourages the development of such curricula because he believes that listening skills can be effectively taught.

THE FAMILY CIRCUS® By Bil Keane
HUMMMMMM...
UMMMMMM...
Copyright 1981
The Register and Tribune
Syndicate, Inc.
BIL KEANE

"I'm trying to practice my reading but Dolly won't listen."

Be careful in your diagnostic efforts not to confuse linguistic variations in speech patterns with hearing impairment. You may observe omissions, additions, distortions, and substitutions in the speech patterns of your children that are an outgrowth of dialect rather than a function of hearing difficulty. If you are working with children who have dialects other than your own, be careful not to diagnose their listening/language needs incorrectly.

In addition to language variations, attitudes toward listening may vary depending on a child's culture. For example, some cultures prohibit the male from listening to female commands; others restrict the singling out of an individual for the purpose of a compliment; and still others may limit the frequency of child-adult conversations.

As you begin to select from commercially prepared programs or develop your own curricula, be careful to remember the following developmental and environmental constraints:

> It is not uncommon, however, for children to have to listen far beyond their reasonable attention spans. This they must do while lawn mowers clatter, other children shout outside the window, people walk on noisy flooring, and they sit in sweltering temperatures—in short, they encounter every imaginable kind of inhibition to attention.
>
> (Lundsteen, 1979, p. 32)

Classroom Programs

As you attempt to integrate listening activities throughout your curriculum, it is important to be aware of the following dimensions of the student and environment.

Planning your Classroom Environment. Increasing your students' receptiveness to what they hear may be possible by manipulating the following factors in your classroom:

1. Develop a classroom environment (seating arrangements or bulletin boards) that can help to focus attention on the speaker.

2. Speak clearly and loudly enough to be heard. Don't "talk to the chalkboard." Whenever possible, be animated.
3. Emphasize concrete, not abstract, ideas (for example, say "Hancock Elementary School" not "school").
4. Use contrast when you are speaking to keep shifting the students' attention so they continue listening to you.

As well as planning an environment that ensures productive listening, be sure to plan situations that encourage positive listening attitudes and habits.

Developing Positive Listening Attitudes. The development of a positive attitude toward listening is accomplished by

1. Discussing with your children the importance of listening.
2. Beginning each lesson by establishing a specific purpose.
3. Encouraging children to listen and share ideas.
4. Reinforcing good listening habits.
5. Being a good listener yourself.

Listening and Sharing the Sounds of One's World. You can learn a great deal about your students by having them share the sounds of their personal world. Ask your students to share such things as

1. Sounds they hear on the way to school.
2. Sounds of emotions (happiness, sadness, amazement, etc.).
3. Sounds of things they enjoy the most.
4. Sounds of seasons.
5. Sounds of home and family.
6. Sounds of a quiet, relaxed time.
7. Sounds that remind them of school.
8. Sounds of someone they love.

Creating Sounds. Children of all ages enjoy producing sounds from such objects as metal lids, water taps, paper, and other materials that are easy to collect. Provide a large cardboard box where "sound makers" may be stored. Each time a child devises a new sound, encourage the child to share it with others. Keep your curriculum flexible enough to accommodate new developments.

Listening for a Definite Purpose. Listening involves not only hearing, but inferring meaning from what is heard. You may encourage the development of comprehensive listening by planning lessons that

1. Illustrate sequencing (numbers, letters, directions).
2. Encourage the students to listen and anticipate what may follow. For example, read the children a story or poem and omit some obvious words. Encourage the children to listen for context clues that will help them to supply missing information.

   Mary was going to the_______ to get a book. She _______Harold on Palm Street. _______ decided to _______ with her.

3. Encourage the children to infer meaning from what they have heard. This may be done by reading short paragraphs or stories followed by questions such as

   Why do you think . . .?
   How would you feel . . . ?
   What would you do . . . ?
   How do you know . . . ?

4. Encourage children to answer questions. This may be accomplished by reading a passage similar to

   Sharon and Hanna were spending the summer with Grandmother. Sharon awakened early one morning and tiptoed into Grandmother's kitchen. As she crept around the corner of the pantry feeling for the cookie jar, she jumped with fright! A shadow! Someone else was in the kitchen. She momentarily forgot about the cookie jar and groped for the light. There was Hanna also inching her way toward the cookie jar.

   After reading the passage, ask

   At what time do you think the story occurred?
   How did Sharon know Hanna was in the kitchen?
   How many girls stayed at Grandmother's?
   What were the girls doing in the kitchen?

It is important to ask a wide range of questions because answering them encourages the student in various thinking activities.

Evaluating Listening Competencies. Encourage your students to evaluate their strengths as listeners. They may do this by observing if they

1. Direct their attention toward the speaker.
2. Listen until the speaker has completed the statement.
3. Think carefully about the message being sent.
4. Listen for the organizational style of the speaker.
5. Determine the validity of the statement.
6. Think of appropriate responses.
7. Weigh the value of their response.

Stammer (1981) has suggested the following four-step method (MAPP) that may aid you in developing curricula to ensure that your students will develop more effective listening behaviors:

1. *Modeling*—Consciously or unconsciously, students will see you as a role model. Consider these questions:
   a. Do I look at the speaker?
   b. Are my responses prompt and thoughtful?
   c. Do I listen to what the students mean as well as what they say?
2. *Assessment*—Listening is a complex process. You can assess your own awareness of what is involved when students listen to you (or try to) by answering these questions:
   a. Do I understand what makes up the listening process?
   b. Do I let my students know what to listen to?
   c. Am I aware of individual student limitations?
3. *Preparation*—Take children's listening habits into consideration when planning your lessons. Ask yourself the following questions:
   a. Is my classroom conducive to careful listening?
   b. Do I plan directions carefully?
   c. Are my listening directions specific?
   d. Do I paraphrase accurately when I must repeat instructions?
   e. Do I complement spoken directions with visual clues?
4. *Practice*—Encourage your students to be as active and alert when they listen as when they speak. See if you can answer "yes" to these questions:
   a. Is there a positive listening atmosphere in the classroom?
   b. Is listening an active rather than a passive activity?
   c. Do my activities help shape and improve listening skills?

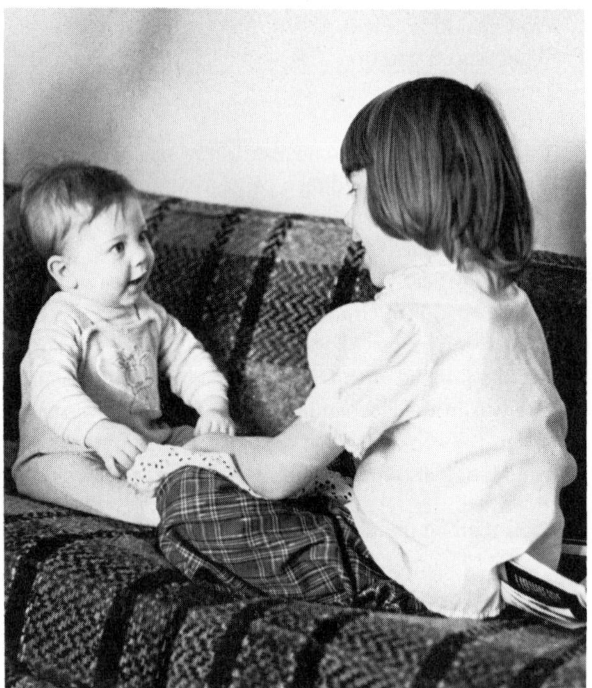

Regardless of the age of acquisition, each child progresses through stages of cooing, babbling, single words, word commands, phrases, sentences, and the mastery of grammatical rules. (Photo by Linda Lungren.)

Additional classroom activities have been provided at the end of this chapter. These activities will enable you to develop adequate listening practices for your classroom.

SPEAKING

Talking and eloquence are not the same: to speak, and to speak well, are two things.

(Ben Jonson, 1573–1637)

A primary purpose of language is communication. Communication is an ongoing problem area because parents and teachers tend to emphasize "correct" communication rather than to determine the extent to which correct communication encourages effective communication.

In some curricula, too much emphasis has been placed on the memorization of "correct" syntactic rules and applications of these rules. Such rule knowledge may provide a general understanding of the syntax of written communication, but it cannot serve as a total program.

Before an intended message can be received, some cultural contact must be experienced. For the receiver to receive the intended message, there must be as little semantic interference as possible. It should be noted that increased cultural exposure decreases the potential for interference.

Sender	Message	Receiver

Writings by Smith and others (1970) suggest that, within a cultural setting, one can observe the language development of children approximating adult language. As this occurs, more effective communication between sender and receiver occurs. In this way, language serves as a means of transmitting what is understood about culture.

The basic structures of language are learned by the age of five or six. By the time children begin elementary school, they have developed extensive speaking vocabularies, consisting of approximately 2,500 words. In addition, children develop language "habits," which are determined by age, socioeconomic group, and geographic region. These language habits are difficult to alter once they are acquired. The concept of "correct" language is impossible because of pronunciation, word collection, phrasing, and construction variations.

Most children come to school with language and the desire to communicate. So inherent is the desire to communicate that, throughout history, language has been developed wherever people have congregated. Given this potential, why is there so often a communication breakdown in the classroom? Perhaps it is because a teacher insists on "correct" language and fails to take into account discrepancies in the child's pronunciation, phrasing, lexicon, and construction. Studies by Loban (1976) suggest that the dichotomy between correct language (the language of the school or teacher) and effective language (the language of the child) can lead to student failure.

The Early Years

A child is exposed to sound and encouraged to speak from the very earliest days of life. During this early stage, the child listens to sounds, attempts sounds, and combines and experiments with the production of speech sounds. The child eventually strings these unintelligible sounds together, continually receiving ample positive reinforcement from the doting adults and siblings of his or her extended family. Eventually, the words and word strings acquire comprehensibility. These early language patterns soon begin to include sentences so that:

> After the age of six there is relatively little in the grammar or syntax of language that the average child needs to learn, except to achieve a school imposed standard of speech or writing to which he may not be accustomed in his home environment.
>
> (Carroll, 1971, pp. 200–11)

Speech, one of the most commonly used communication processes, is believed by some to begin as early as five months after conception (Wilkinson, 1971), whereas others believe that it begins with the child's first cry at birth. Most children utter their first intelligible word sometime in the second six months of life (Bellugi and Brown, 1964). Regardless of the age of acquisition, each child progresses through stages of cooing, babbling, single words, word commands, phrases, sentences, and the mastery of grammatical rules. The basics of language are learned long before a child enters your classroom, but you, the teacher, can continue to encourage language experience and language expressions within the classroom setting.

The School Years

The elementary school curriculum is designed in such a way that you can build on the early language structures of children. As you attempt to implement such curricula within your classroom, it is important for you to understand the comprehensiveness of any individual's language usage.

Language is a means of *expressing the self.* Our earliest attempts at self-expression may be simple sounds, such as a grunt or cry. Eventually, more sophisticated forms of language are used to convey our needs, desires, and emotions.

The language of self-expression is seldom neutral because it conveys our ideas, love, humor, hate, anger, excuses, and other human sensations. As classroom teachers, you must encourage the use of language as self-expression through a climate of acceptance. A student will interpret rejection of his or her language or ideas as personal rejection, rejection of himself or herself. One of the functions of life is the continual identification of self in a constantly changing environment of social interaction. Encouraging and accepting a child's self-expression will help him or her during these formative years as well as in later life.

One's ability to use language as a process through which extended thinking is shared is heavily dependent on an ever-increasing vocabulary. Your classroom, therefore, must be rich with exposure to language. See the activities sections of Chapters 5 and 6 for examples of ways in which to accomplish vocabulary development.

An important factor in the development of self-expressive speech is *time.* One must *try* sharing a small amount of information, *weigh* the results and consequences of giving oneself through language, and perhaps, if the consequences are not too harsh, *try again*. If these early attempts at self-expression are rejected, the student will be very wary of taking such a risk again. A student may even alter his or her own ideas to express those that will receive the teacher's positive acceptance.

The language of young children is often *egocentric*. As the child is engaged in group situations or when the child must listen to others to complete a task, this egocentric language will lessen. As students become involved in more sender-receiver exchanges, their language becomes more *expository*, which ultimately enables them to receive a wider variety of messages. Language is a means of acquiring information as well as a means of self-expression. Alone, a person is unable to understand totally the world around him or her; however, through language interchanges, a person continually experiences larger segments of the universe. Many of these interchanges are verbal. How do I get to city hall? What are your views regarding . . . ? Have you read . . .? Such interchanges supply us with topics of discussion as well as bits of valuable information.

Information may also be acquired through *gestures, graphics,* and *mechanical codes.* There is a wide range of sources and activities that can be utilized to help children become familiar with these symbols. Role-playing and pantomime activities can assist children with the interpretation of *gestures.* Graphic messages are received by interpreting traffic signs, advertisements, books, and other printed materials. The interpretation of mechanical messages can come to the receiver through traffic lights, flashing lights on a police car or ambulance, and train crossings. These unspoken expositions of language offer a wide range of facts and ideas.

Other tasks and activities that can give your students an opportunity to expand their oral language skills might include interviewing, reader's theater, storytelling, presentation of formal and informal speeches, role playing, choral speaking, puppetry, and creative dramatics. These activities are not only valuable tools for building oral language skills, they are fun for the teacher and students. Some sample activities are included at the end of this chapter.

Language Styles

Experiences with language continually enable the student to accommodate each encounter with the appropriate language style. As Joos (1967) suggests, *informal* situations shared with intimate friends allow us to exhibit our private language styles. This style is often comprised of one-word or one-phrase utterances. The receiver is so well aware of our thinking patterns that he or she can anticipate what we will say almost before it is said. *Casual* situations shared with friends who are not quite as intimate may still allow us to use our private language; however, our utterances may need to be more explanatory. The *consultative* style of language is one that is used to convey factual information. Speakers may use this style when expressing their ideas to an audience comprised of people who are not members of their private communities. The need arises for an alternate style of language, a more public language that will be shared and understood by most of the audience. Certain contexts require *frozen* styles of language, such as written messages or speeches to colleagues, which are often heavily dependent on the use of an extremely formal language. It will become obvious that the development of various dialects must receive some attention in your classrooms if you are to prepare students to accommodate the multilanguage interactions that they will experience throughout their lives. Additional activities are provided at the end of this chapter to help you accomplish this task.

WRITING

The purpose of fostering . . . writing in the classroom is to make a contribution to each child's academic and personal growth.

(Cramer, 1975, p. 507)

Writing, like speaking, provides the student with an outlet for the expression of ideas. Murray (1968) maintains that writing is a process of using language to bring meaning to our experiences. Written expression may be conveyed through many different forms, e.g., compositions, letters, poems, reports, and short stories. At the outset, writing involves inventing, devising, selecting, eliminating, and arranging one's ideas. Proofreading, editing, and correcting one's ideas are laborious but critical tasks in the writing process.

Many educators distinguish between "creative" and "practical" writing experience by referring to stories and poems as acts of creativity. Although we understand their rationale, we believe that any time a person conveys his or her thoughts through written language, regardless of the form, that person has engaged in an act of creativity. Throughout this chapter, we avoid a distinction between creative and practical writing.

The Writing Process

Far too often, "teaching writing" has been a matter of (1) the teacher assigning a topic, (2) the student agonizing over the assignment, (3) the student turning in the completed assignment, and (4) the teacher making comments and corrections, assigning a grade, and returning it to the student. Foley (1981) suggests that classroom writing problems may be traced to risk taking:

> One reason that students do not learn to write easily is because they are not taught to take risks. Similarly, some teachers do not teach writing easily because they feel uncomfortable or uncertain about the process. Instead of risking failure, they reduce writing instruction to thoughtless drill in grammar and mechanics (p. 4).

Let us examine the writing process and some ways for you, the teacher, to become comfortable with writing instruction in the classroom.

Theory. Many educators have examined the components of the writing process and have generated models to describe it (Petrosky and Brozick, 1979; Hayes and Flower, 1980; Foley 1981). Foley (1981) offers this model as an illustration of the traditional teacher-dominated approach to writing instruction:

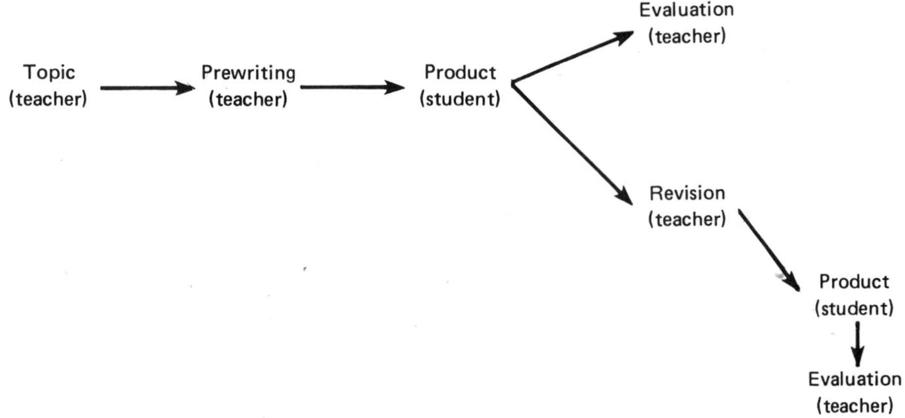

Source: D. Foley. *Teaching Writing on the Elementary Curriculum.* Indianapolis, Indiana: Indiana Public Schools/Lilly Endowment, Inc., 1981.

Foley suggests that, in this traditional model approach, the teacher is constantly in control of the writing process. "The result is that the teacher evaluates his own work, in effect, because he is evaluating how closely the writer followed what he was asked to do on the corrections the teacher included" (p. 74).

Current theories of writing instruction tend to emphasize writing as process rather than writing as product. Within this framework, writers are not only concerned with correctness of form, but also with learning, generating, and discovering through writing (Flood and Salus, 1983). A successful writing program will probably take on a form similar to the following:

1. Developing the assignment
   a. Establish the purpose of the writing
   b. Identify the intended audience
   c. Allow the students to develop their topics while the teacher guides and supports them. Children "write best about what they know." (Foley, 1981, p. 4).
2. Discussing and planning for writing
3. Prewriting
4. Discussing
5. Writing
6. Sharing
7. Editing and rewriting

Any particular writing assignment may extend over several days. Additionally, many educators suggest that children should have a particular time each day set aside for writing. This writing can be in a journal or can be any other form of writing the student chooses.

The content and form of writing may be different between the elementary school student and the intermediate-level student, but the *process* remains the same.

The following sections provide more specific suggestions and activities for your student writers at each grade level.

The Primary Years

During the early school years, writing is often the result of listening and speaking experiences. You will find that children love to listen and to create stories. When encouraged, young children will engage freely in storytelling. If you capitalize on these situations by recording their stories, your students can listen to their own stories and tales while creating illustrations for them. An activity such as this may serve as the basis for an entire writing curriculum.

Writing must give the child some degree of satisfaction—it should attract attention. Children's writing should be displayed and have a readily understood purpose (Sealey et al., 1979). Some examples might be stories to be read, charts, and interesting information.

What you do as an early primary teacher may definitely influence your students' attitudes toward writing. Be flexible with your assignments, remembering that there are many ways in which to complete any task. Through early language discussions, you will be able to encourage students to believe that they have many things to write about. Correct style, form, and spelling may need to receive secondary attention during these early writing attempts. Any device that encourages children to *talk*, and eventually to turn that talk to *writing*, can be viewed as a positive motivational device.

The following story is an example of turning one's talk and experiences to writing.

This story (p. 49) was written by Shannon, a second-grade student. At this early age, narratives are frequently a reflection of the student's experiences rather than an exercise in creativity.

It is not necessary to correct every error in these early writing attempts; this may discourage the child. Note that Shannon's spelling errors are all phonetic representations of the words she chose to use. After she checks the proper spelling of these words, she will realize that not all words are spelled phonetically. This can be a valuable part of the writing experience for a young child.

During the early primary grades, your language and writing programs will be closely intertwined. The following activities may be used or adapted to foster successful writing experiences in your classroom:

1. Provide various sensory experiences, such as
   a. smelling (orange, perfume, onion).
   b. touching (sandpaper, velvet, clay).
   c. seeing (pictures, cartoons, books).
2. After the sensory exposure, encourage the children to share their reactions verbally.

My Dog Had a Cold

Once upon a time there was a dog named Muffen. he was so cute. one day we went Outside. he began to sneeze then. I ran down to the docter's. he said that Muffen had the flu. Muffen was very scared so I said Muffen you're your lucky. I broke my finger. you better hurry and get better so you can come to my Birthday Monday. I'll all have the doctor give you a shot. arrrr said Muffen. you have to have a shot it's the only way to get better for my Birthday Monday. The next morning was a desaster. I took Muffen to the docter and then the stuff began. Muffen bit the docter's leg bit my hand and he didn't get a shot he got a spanken instead.

The End

by Shannon (age: 8)

TEACHER COMMENT

This sentence is a little too long.

TEACHER COMMENT

Shannon,

Don't forget to start a new sentence with a capital letter. Also, each sentence should end with a period. Please check the spelling of the words I have circled. I hope Muffin was able to come to your birthday party!

3. Make recordings of their shared reactions.
4. Encourage the children to listen to the recordings and then illustrate their thoughts.
5. Have children add descriptive words or phrases with your help.
6. Encourage the children to edit their work. Editing may be an arduous task, but point out to your students that it is a necessary task in which all writers engage. Too often the editing process is not explained to students. The student thus incorrectly assumes that a successful writer/author produces a finished piece of prose after only one attempt. When students/writers are not able to do the same, they view themselves as being punished when they engage in the editing process. Because they feel that they have failed when they are asked to edit, many students view themselves as poor writers and consequently never explore themselves as writers.
7. Have the children share the written product aloud with other students. The students may share their work with their families by writing a note or a letter to accompany it.

Activities such as these integrate the language arts (listening, speaking, reading, and writing) through stories, poems, letters, and notes.

As you listen to the text your students create, you will observe that the best stories are often shared accounts of in-depth perceptions. It is very important to plan activities that will heighten the sensory awareness of your students. The following activities can serve to encourage students' awareness of their world while extending language development:

1. Ask children to describe the face of someone they love.
2. Have the children close their eyes and listen to a variety of sounds. Then have them describe the sounds.
3. Let the students try to identify objects by touch. A variety of objects can be placed in paper bags.
4. Ask the students to describe pleasant or frightening odors.

The Intermediate Years

During the intermediate school years, opportunities abound for engaging students in the writing process. It is important to emphasize writing in your curriculum because writing activities (1) provide students with an opportunity for self-expression, (2) provide an additional channel for extending language development, and (3) arouse students' interest in literary materials.

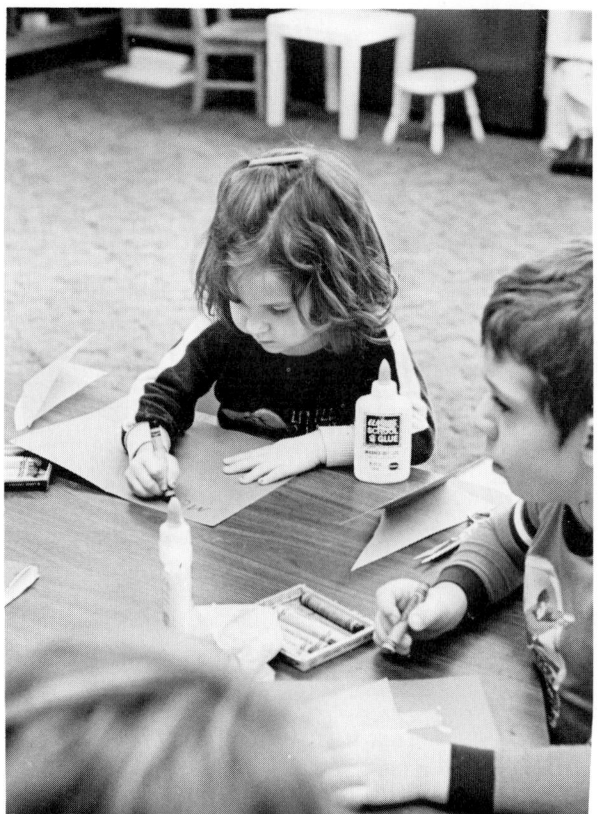

It is important to emphasize writing in your curriculum because writing activities provide self-expression, language development, and arouse students' interest in literary materials. (Photo by Linda Lungren.)

The story on pages 51–52 was written by Eric, a fifth-grade student. Note the wry humor and the imagination displayed in the story.

The contents of this story exemplify how children are influenced by their experiences. Eric very willingly shared his fascination of *Star Wars, Raiders of the Lost Ark*, and other science space ventures. Because his teacher encouraged conversation, writing, and editing, he gladly shared his ideas through a fictional piece.

You may enounter students who are not anxiously awaiting an opportunity to participate in a writing ac-

Missy Martian's Mission

One day a very, very small spaceship came out of the sky. It looked like a beer can. It even opened like one. I know that because I saw it.

A little person came out and said, "La ba." I said, "Ha ha". She said, "Oh, that's the launguge you speak." "Yes, it is," I said. "I have been taught to speak all langues on the planet Earth.

**T.C. Please check the proper spelling!

"What planet do you come from?" "Ram Bam," she said. "Will you say T.V. in your language," I said. "Boob tube, by the way, what is T.V.?" "It's a picture that flashes on a box." "Oh, then what does picture, flash, and box mean?" "Never mind."

**T.C. Is this a question?

"What is your name?" "Missy! What is yours?" "Charles." "My mission is to bring back a human being. Will you come?" "How long will it be?" "Only about a nagratriairn." "How long will that be in my time?" "Oh, only

**T.C. I like the way you created new words.

about ten minuts. "Ok, I'll go." Caboom and we were there. "What was that, double light speed?" We came down out of the sky and landed on a landing pad. I was taken for test.

**T.C.

One test or more than one?

"Hey, that's a needle!" "We are going to test your blood." "Ouch!" "Hey, your blood is red, ours is green! We're ready to take you back." Caboom and we were home. We said goodbye to each other and then of to Ram Bam she flew again.

by Eric (age: 11)

**T.C. Eric,
your story is very good and very creative. Each time a new character (person) speaks you should begin a new paragraph. Please check the spelling of the circled words before you turn in your final copy.

**T.C.

Eric, your pictures add a lot to your story!

**T.C. = TEACHER COMMENTS

tivity. For the reluctant writer or the student who has difficulty with writing, you may need to provide

1. "Starter" packets (possible topics, locales, characters, themes, etc.)
2. Basic language activities
3. Word lists
4. Alternate assignments
5. Areas of interest that can be integrated into writing activities

One excellent activity that you may want to use in your writing curriculum is sentence combining.

Teaching Sentence Combining

Several researchers in the field of written composition have reported successful attempts at having students manipulate sentences to expand their ability to organize. This device of manipulating sentences organizationally is called *combining.*

Mellon (1969) and O'Hare (1973) were among the first to create sentence-combining activities for children. Combs (1976) found that practice in sentence combining has a significant positive effect on children's syntactic fluency. McAfee (1980) conducted a study of fifth-grade children who had received sentence-combining instruction and reported these findings.

1. Students who received sentence-combining instruction had significantly improved reading comprehension scores compared with students who did not receive this instruction.
2. Students who received sentence-combining instruction had significantly improved written language scores when compared with the control group.
3. Students who received sentence-combining instruction had scores that showed significant improvement in free writing compared with students who did not receive this instruction.

The following examples illustrate sentence combining:

A. One day a dog came into our yard.
B. The dog was little and brown.
Combined: One day a little brown dog came into our yard.

A. Elaine is tall.
B. Elaine is slender.
C. Elaine is pretty.
Combined: Elaine is tall, slender, and pretty.

Depending on the age and abilities of your students, the sentences may be more complex.

A. The old woman stood silently on the street corner.
B. She was watching a burning apartment building.
C. She was wearing a tattered coat.
D. A solitary tear trickled down her cheek.
Combined: An old woman in a tattered coat stood silently on the street corner watching a burning apartment building while a solitary tear trickled down her cheek.

Explain to your students that they may change the words or the order of the words as long as they do not change the meaning.

Sentence combining will help students with most types of writing and can be especially valuable in editing compositions. It is important, however, that students be aware that sentence combining may not be appropriate for all forms of writing. Poetry, tall tales, or musical creations are some examples of writing activities that may not lend themselves well to sentence combining.

Haiku is a form of Japanese poetry that children find enjoyable to write. Like all poetry, haiku writing uses a language base different from prose. Since it does not use the sentence as its basic element, you can see how inappropriate it would be to attempt sentence combining with haiku writing.

Haiku writing is an excellent and enjoyable activity for students. The poems have three lines containing a total of seventeen syllables. The first and third lines contain five syllables and the second line has seven syllables. These poems are usually written about nature. All your students can write haiku. An example of haiku is

The sun is peeking (5 syllables)
Into my bedroom window. (7 syllables)
The rain is slowing. (5 syllables)

Other activities that foster student interest in writing can be found at the end of this chapter.

PART II THE LANGUAGE ARTS CURRICULUM

Although the language arts (listening, speaking, reading, and writing) may be separated for discussion, it is very difficult to separate them when teaching. This part of the chapter includes a simulated curriculum that illustrates the integration of all of the language arts within content areas of study.

THE THEME

As you begin to consider the development of your language arts curriculum, you must select a central focus through which all the communication skills can be explored. Select topics such as

1. Literature
2. Poetry
3. Music

For the purpose of this simulated unit, we will select the *literature* strand of the curriculum for use as our central point. *Do not stop reading if you are a primary-grade teacher.* Through the study of literature, children of all ages can explore

1. Their cultural heritage
2. People of all ages
3. The vicarious experiences of others

Literature can also provide exposure to

1. Various writing styles
2. Language
3. Listening skills
4. A variety of reading materials

The exploration of literature encourages students to learn the wonders of self through the vicarious explorations of others. The following literary texts show you that literature exists for all ages.

AGES 2 TO 6

1. Milgram, Mary. *Brothers Are All the Same.* New York: E. P. Dutton, 1978.
2. Wildsmith, Brian. *The Lazy Bear.* New York: Franklin Watts, Inc., 1974.

AGES 6 TO 9

1. Baylor, Byrd. *The Way to Start a Day.* New York: Charles Scribner's Sons, 1977.
2. Lobel, Arnold A. *A Treeful of Pigs.* New York: Greenwillow Books, 1979.

AGES 10 TO 14

1. Lampman, Evelyn Sibley. *Squaw Man's Son.* New York: Atheneum, 1978.
2. Pevsner, Stella. *Keep Stompin' Till the Music Stops.* New York: The Seabury Press, 1977.

THE SCOPE AND SEQUENCE

Once you have decided on a central focus, or *thematic* area, it is necessary to determine the (1) general unit goals as well as (2) the specific skills you want to develop.

Because our topic is the exploration of literature, our goals might include

1. Developing an understanding of the organization of a given literary work:
   a. Form (story, poem, drama).
   b. Main theme.
   c. Plot.
   d. Characters.
   e. Author's writing style.
2. Developing an understanding of the possibility of self-exploration through literature.
3. Introducing students to a variety of reading and writing styles.
4. Increasing listening skills through reading and sharing ideas about a given literary work.
5. Increasing students' awareness of the variety of social values evidenced by literary characters.
6. Acquainting students with the scientific progress made through history.

These are only a few of the goals that might be explored through the study of literature. The six goals listed have incorporated all the language arts and several areas of content study. Once you are satisfied with your overall goals, you need to list the specific skills that you want to cover in each of the language arts and content areas that have been incorporated in your thematic unit.

Reading

1. Vocabulary extension
2. Comprehension of a wide variety of writing styles

Writing

1. Practice with cursive writing
2. Self-expression through writing

Listening

1. Following directions through listening
2. Developing listening skills as the basis for good conversational practices

Speaking

1. Exhibiting organizational skills in language
2. Increasing language fluency

Social Studies

1. Understanding others through their writings
2. Understanding self through story characters

Science

1. Exploring new environments described through literature
2. Exploring social awareness regarding the environment through statements made by literary characters

Math

1. Developing basic skills: addition, subtraction, and division
2. Developing logical thinking skills

After deciding which skills you plan to develop, you must decide which skills can be incorporated appropriately within the given unit of study. Realistically, any one unit cannot serve as the means for covering all of the skills and objectives you have for *all* the content and language arts areas of the curriculum. This unit can be given a separate time slot in the curriculum or it can become part of your already existing English and reading program.

OBJECTIVES AND ASSESSMENT

The next steps in the development of your language arts curriculum are (1) to develop *specific behavioral objectives* and (2) to *assess* your students to determine their existing competencies within the area of study. Once you have determined your students' competencies, as related to the stated behavioral objectives, you can begin to determine the composition of your study groups. Consider these typical behavioral objectives for this literary unit:

1. After listening to a dramatic selection, the children will write a detailed description of the reasons they are like or unlike the main character.
2. After reading or listening to *Across Five Aprils*, the student will be able to state at least one of the reasons that led the families to war.
3. After the children have read *Henny-Penny*, they will be able to state the reasons why Henny-Penny and her friends never come out of Foxy-Loxy's den.

When you compare these objectives with the general unit goals and the general skills to be taught, you can see that they have been designed in an attempt to integrate all of these areas. For example, behavioral objective 2 includes the development of reading, listening, and social studies skills. Remember when planning your unit to always refer to your general goals and skills to formulate your specific behavioral objectives. For further assistance in the development of behavioral objectives, refer to Chapter 15.

Once you have determined your specific behavioral objectives, you can adapt the program to meet the needs of your students. This can be accomplished through formal and informal assessments of your students. Informal assessment might include an analysis of

1. The reading levels of the texts to be read.
2. Which children can easily read the texts: who will require minimal help; and who needs a great deal of help.
3. The writing, listening, and speaking skills required to complete each task.
4. The types of abilities each child has as they relate to each area.
5. The content area concepts being explored.
6. What children know about the content areas that are being explored.

Procedures for informal assessment might include (1) general class discussion, (2) knowledge from previous assignments, or (3) a game, worksheet, or reading assignment. After determining the relationship between the goals to be accomplished and the skills and information possessed by each child, you can begin to determine *basic grouping patterns.*

LESSON PLANNING

Unit lessons should reflect (1) a theme, (2) skills to be mastered, and (3) content areas to be explored. More than one lesson may need to be operating simultaneously because of varying degrees of student competency within your classroom. Plan your lessons in such a way that *you are not* the central focus of each one. Include games, media, and student-directed activities in the lessons. In this way, each lesson will be able to function even when you are not there. Classroom management is an arduous task and one that will need your constant attention.

EVALUATION

Evaluation is an ongoing process. Assessing the competencies of your students to plan your groups is an evaluative process. A further evaluation is necessary after the lesson is implemented to determine who has completed it successfully. For those children, you will plan a lesson related to the next unit objective, remembering again to engage in the diagnostic assessment pro-

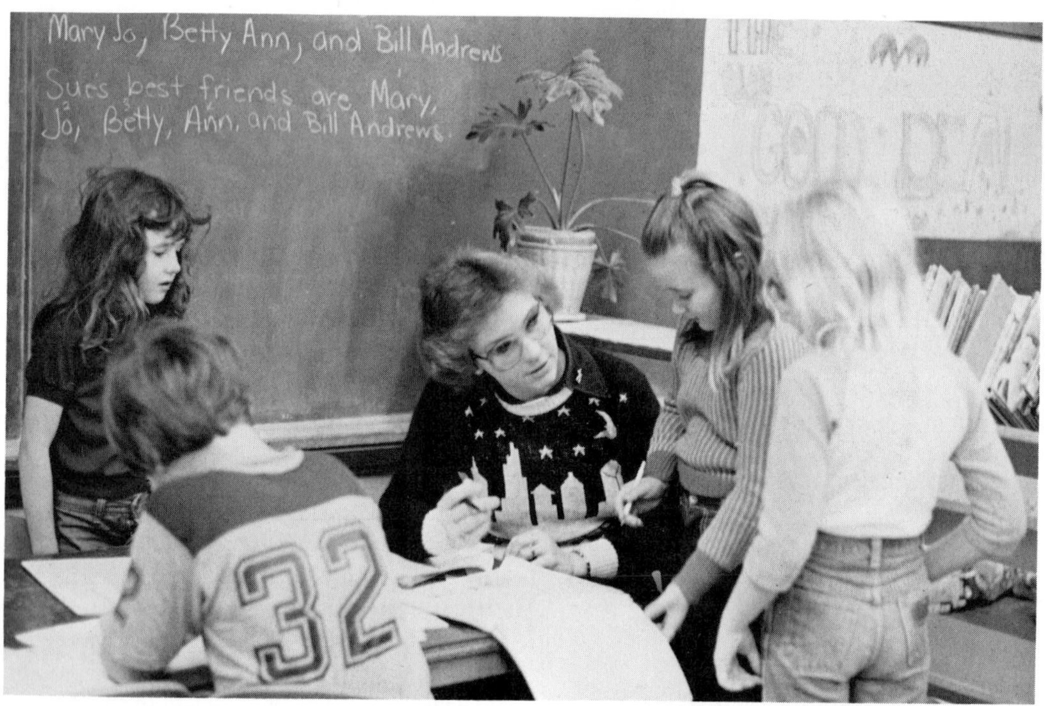

Evaluation is an ongoing process. Assessing the competencies of your students in order to plan your groups is an evaluative process. (Photo by Linda Lungren.)

cess you used during the planning of the initial lesson. For the children who have not mastered the lesson, you will need to ask "Why?"

You may ask yourself

1. Was the lesson implemented successfully?
2. Did the children possess the skills necessary to master the lesson?
3. Was the lesson too involved? Did it convey too much information?

Once you have determined why the lesson was not mastered, you will be better able to continue instruction with each group.

ARE YOU READY?

In this chapter, you have been introduced to the various components of a language arts program and the classroom management procedures involved in implementing integrated units. The task may seem complicated, but once you begin, the process becomes clear. Children do not *learn* language arts in isolation, nor do they *use* them in isolation; therefore it is more realistic to learn them in an integrated curriculum. Although this type of classroom management is probably unlike the one under which you learned your language art skills, we encourage you to try to implement this model, to attempt to *individualize* as well as to *integrate* the language arts curriculum. The following activities are included to help you develop a language arts curriculum.

LANGUAGE ARTS ACTIVITIES

1. What Was That?

Goal: Developing listening skills

Grade Level: 2–8

Construction: Make a tape recording of various sounds from the student's environment, such as a ringing doorbell, a whistling teapot, a telephone ringing, running water, and paper crumbling. For younger students, you may want to collect pictures that match these sounds.

Utilization: Students try to identify the sounds or match the pictures with the sounds.

2. Musical Moves

Goal: Developing skills in body movement

Grade Level: 1-4

Construction: Have a class discussion on the role of body movement in the communication process. Ask the students to describe the different feelings that music can evoke: happiness, sadness, fear, and so on.

Utilization: Play various kinds of music capable of involving the children in a variety of feelings. Encourage them to sway, shake, twist, hop, jump, or move in whatevery way the music makes them feel.

3. And Then . . .

Goal: Developing skills in listening and writing

Grade Level: 4–9

Construction: Find a record that tells a story or tape record yourself reading a story. Explain to the students that they will have to listen very carefully to complete the exercise.

Utilization: Stop the record or tape recorder at an exciting part of the story. Ask the students to write the ending for the story, including an appropriate title.

4. Silence Is Golden

Goal: Developing skills in attentive listening

Grade Level: 3–8

Construction and Utilization: Have the students be absolutely quiet for three minutes. Then have the students discuss what sounds they heard during the silent time. Some possibilities are a clock ticking, traffic sounds, lawn mower, siren, and breathing.

5. Add-on

Goal: Developing skills in listening and speaking

Grade Level: 3–9

Construction: Prepare a file of index cards with unusual story ideas. Some examples might be (a) If dinosaurs still roamed the earth . . . ; (b) If we were students in 1997 . . . ; (c) If my pet could talk . . . ; (d) The day the sun stopped shining . . . ; (e) My wonderful new invention is . . . .

Utilization: Have a student draw one of the index cards. The student starts telling the story. After three or four sentences, stop the student and select another student to continue with the story. Continue with several students; then choose a student to supply an ending to the story.

6. Painting to Music

Goal: Developing skills in listening appreciatively

Grade Level: 1-4

Construction and Utilization: Provide each child with finger paints and finger-painting paper. Select music capable of evoking emotion. Selections should differ in volume and tempo throughout the recording. Before the finger painting begins, have the children explore moving their bodies according to how the music makes them feel. Play the music a second time, encouraging the children to express their feelings using the finger paint.

7. Using the Telephone

Goal: Developing telephone skills

Grade Level: 1-4

Construction: Set up a classroom telephone system. You can use toy telephones or a string and tin cans, or you may be able to borrow a Teletrainer from your local phone company. With this set, someone can press buttons that will cause the phone to ring or give a busy signal. Make up index cards giving such situations as, "You just saw a building on fire; what is the proper way to phone for help?" Before enacting the situations, review with the class how to make collect, person-to-person, and direct long-distance calls; how to take messages; how to interpret the different signals; and how to call for information.

Utilization: Each student draws a card and demonstrates the proper way in which to use the telephone. Two people may be needed for some situations.

8. Homophones, Homophones

Goal: Developing skills in listening, speaking, and writing

Grade Level: 4-9

Construction: Review the meaning of homophones with the class. Divide the class into two teams. Have each student write five sentences, each containing two homophones. For example, "Wearing two hats is one too many."

Utilization: The students take turns reading a sentence to a player on the other team. The other player must then state the two words that are homophones; if correct, the player scores one point for the team. The team scoring the most points at the conclusion of the contest is the winner. This activity can also be done with antonyms or compound words.

9. Complete the Family Tree

Goal: Tracing word histories

Grade Level: 4-9

Construction: Prepare a ditto or laminated sheet making a large tree with many branches. On the trunk write the original Latin or Greek derivative.

Utilization: Have the child complete the family tree by writing on the branches words that developed from Latin or Greek. If phono were written on the trunk, the child would label the branches with phonograph, telephone, and so on.

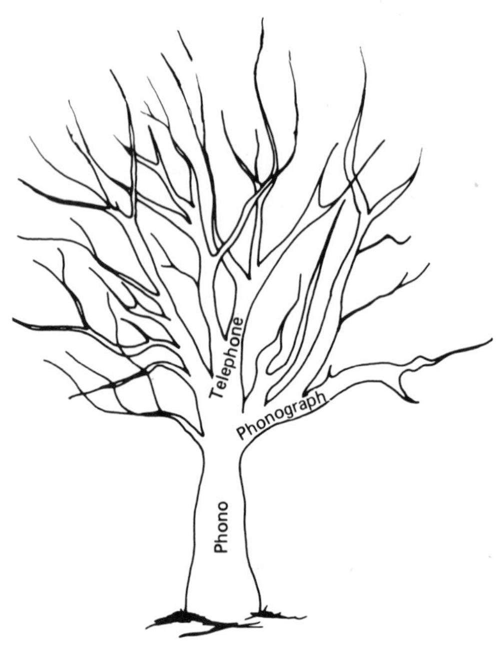

10. Fill In the Blank

Goal: Developing skills in listening appreciatively

Grade Level: 4–8

Construction: Make up four- to six-line poems or limericks, preferably ones that rhyme. Leave out one word at the end that the student must fill in. The student should be able to guess the word using context clues or rhyming words.

Utilization: The student fills in the correct word. Examples of rhymes and limericks can be found in Arbuthnot et al. (1971)

11. Budding Playwrights

Goal: Developing skills in listening, speaking, reading, and writing

Grade Level: 4–8

Construction: Read aloud a favorite story.

Utilization: Have students redesign the story, changing it to a play using a narrator and dialogue. Students could also specify the scenery and costumes to be used. After practicing, they can perform the play for the rest of the class.

12. The Best News in Town

Goal: Developing skills in writing

Grade Level: 6–9

Construction and Utilization: Have several copies of newspapers in the classroom for the students to use as samples. Have each student write three headlines that he or she would like to see in the newspaper. Some possibilities are "Principal Announces Four-Day School Week"; "Bill Thompson Wins Lottery"; "No School on Sunny Days." The students then write a newspaper story about one of the headlines.

13. Speaking at the O-K "Chor-al"

Goal: Developing skills in listening, speaking, reading, and writing

Grade Level: 3–8

Construction: Assist the class in writing a poem for choral speaking. Either the refrain or the lines of the poem whould be repetitive. Perhaps the teacher could read other poems used for choral speaking to give the children some idea of what choral speaking is.

Utilization: Six to ten students read the main lines of the poem, and the remainder of the class listens in order to know when to join in with the refrain.

14. Like It or Not

Goal: Developing skills in listening appreciatively

Grade Level: 1–7

Construction: Prepare a tape of various sounds from the environment: a barking dog, music, a baby crying, laughter, a siren, for example.

Utilization: Have the students divide a piece of paper into two columns labeled "Sounds I Like" and "Sounds I Don't Like." After listening to the tape, have them supply sounds of their own. For young children, the teacher can write the students' suggestions on a large chart to reinforce the language experience.

15. How to Find Timbuktu

Goal: Developing skills in listening, speaking, reading and writing

Grade Level: 4–8

Construction: Display a large map of the world in front of the room. Divide the group into two teams and have each member locate a specific place on the map. Each member should then write five steps of directions, using cardinal directions, latitude, and longitude.

Utilization: In turn, a player from team A reads his directions to player B. If player B finds the location using the five steps, player B gets the point for the team. The team with the most points, after everyone has had a turn finding a location, wins.

16. Acting Out Your Feelings

Goal: Interpreting and using nonverbal communication

Grade Level: 1–8

Construction: Discuss with your class the different ways people show their true feelings without using words. Describe differences between how a person might act and what he or she really thinks. Design situations for the students to act out, utilizing nonverbal communication. Situations may be written on 3" X 5" index cards.

Utilization: Two or more students select a card and act out the situation. The remainder of the group must guess what the person using nonverbal communication is really thinking and name the techniques that he or she is using.

17. Dear Aunt Sue

Goal: Developing skills in writing

Grade Level: 5–9

Construction: Provide several copies of sample advice columns (Dear Abby, Ann Landers, or a local advice columnist). Prepare a file of questions or problems students might ask for advice (for example, "My friends don't have to go to bed until 9:30 P.M., but my parents make me go to bed at 9:00 P.M.. What should I do?"

Utilization: Have students write replies to the situation they have selected in the style of the advice columnists. If desired, several students can write responses to the same question. The class can vote on the "best" reply.

18. One-Two-Three

Goal: Developing skills for giving directions

Grade Level: 1–8

Construction: Have students choose a how-to-do-it topic for which they will give the class directions. The topic can be one with which the children are either familiar or unfamiliar. Suggested topics are dialing a phone, tying a shoe, and brushing teeth.

Utilization: After each student has given instructions, have the class discuss the strengths and weaknesses of each attempt at direction giving.

19. Make Your Own Movie

Goal: Developing words from a standard Latin or Greek base

Grade Level: 4–8

Construction: Secure a large cardboard box and make a slit in two sides. Also secure a roll of white shelf paper and several colored magic markers.

Utilization: Have children select Latin or Greek word bases from the dictionary and list several words containing the bases. Example:

port	mono
import	monotone
transport	monologue
portable	monopoly
export	monorail

Have the children write a story, play, or script incorporating several of the derived words. The meanings of the words should be understood through the events in the story. Have the children illustrate their script on the shelf paper. Pull one end of the paper through the slits of the cardboard box and then roll it around a paper towel tube.

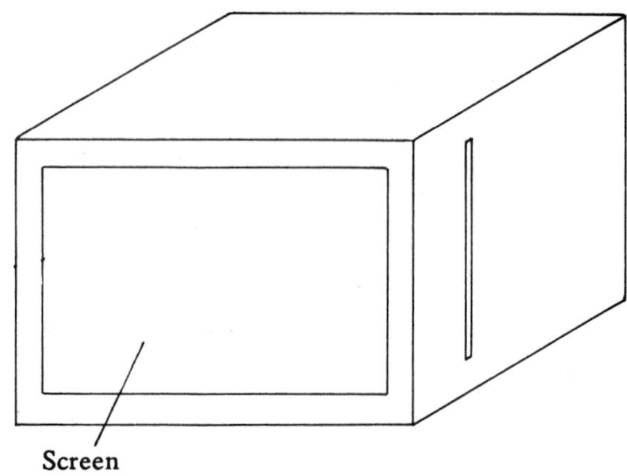

20. Improvisational Theater

Goal: Developing skills in listening and speaking

Grade Level: 4–8

Construction and Utilization: Have an improvisational type of theater performance in which the audience makes suggestions as to what the actors must improvise. The actors can ask for the names of a song, place, or a short plot from the viewers; the actors then develop a skit based on the audience's suggestions.

21. The Great Debate

Goal: Developing skills in listening and speaking

Grade Level: 4–9

Construction: Review with students the techniques and procedures of debating. Assist them in selecting topics. Choose four volunteers, two for each team. The topic that will be debated is called the proposition, which is stated in the affirmative. For example, "Resolved: Students should be allowed to set up a student lounge in the school." The affirmative team is in favor of the proposition, and the negative team is against it. Traditionally, constructive speeches prepared in advance are given first, followed by rebuttal speeches, in which the students disagree with the content of the other team's speeches and defend their own stances. The order in which the team members give their speeches is usually

Constructive speeches	Rebuttal speeches
1. First affirmative	5. First negative
2. First negative	6. First affirmative
3. Second affirmative	7. Second negative
4. Second negative	8. Second affirmative

Utilization: A chairperson reads the topic and introduces the team members. A timekeeper makes sure they do not go over the established time limit (fifteen minutes). The remaining members of the class serve as judges. They should decide which team performed better with regard to supporting statements, speaking clearly, and holding interest.

22. Both Sides

Goal: Developing skills in critical listening

Grade Level: 4-9

Construction: Prepare, with a helper, a tape cassette imitating two historical people having an argument, for example, Aaron Burr and Alexander Hamilton, Stephen Douglas and Abraham Lincoln, two people currently running for president, or a rock musician and a conductor of classical music.

Utilization: Have the students listen to the tape offered by each speaker as many times as necessary and write down the supporting statements. They should determine the person with whom they agree most and state the reasons.

23. Guessword

Goal: Developing skills in listening, speaking, reading, and writing

Grade Level: 4-9

Construction: Provide students with a list of twenty to twenty-five vocabulary words. Divide the class into two teams and have them make up clues for a part of one or two words on the list. For example, if one of the words is *belittle*, the student could make up a clue for "bee" or "little."

Utilization: In turn, a player from one team reads a clue for one of the words to a player on the other team. That person must try to guess the complete word after he has guessed the clue. Score five points for each word guessed correctly. The first team to reach seventy-five points wins.

24. Be Careful with This Code!

Goal: Developing skills in interpretive listening

Grade Level: 4-8

Construction: Prepare a code formula substituting letters for numbers. For example, A = 1, B = 2, C = 3. Translate a secret message from letters to the code numbers. Prepare dittos consisting of ten to fifteen lines of numbers in random order.

3	5	8	10	15	4	6
9	11	12	18	4	2	1

Prepare directions for the student to circle one of the numbers in each line. For example: "Mark the number that is fourth from this end," or "Mark the second number after 18." When all of the numbers are circled, tell the students the secret formula.

Utilization: The student changes the numbers to letters and figures out the coded message.

25. Mystery Word

Goal: Developing skills in attentive listening

Grade Level: 3-9

Construction and Utilization: Advise the class that they are to listen for the mystery word, which you will use at least once every thirty minutes. The first student to identify the mystery word correctly gets a prize (popcorn, star, bonus points, etc.).

QUESTIONS AND RELATED READINGS

If you feel that you have not attained adequate knowledge to answer the following questions successfully, we suggest additional related readings.

1. What specific information will I need to know about each of the language arts?
2. Which communication skills are appropriate for the students at a given stage of development?
3. How can I teach all the language arts in conjunction with all the content area skills?
4. Are there activities I can use to facilitate learning these skills?
5. Where do I begin?

Goal 1: To help the reader to develop an understanding of listening skills.

Question 1: As a classroom teacher, how would you set about the task of developing students' listening skills?

Devine, T. G. "Listening: What Do We Know After Fifty Years of Research and Theorizing?" *Journal of Reading* 21(January 1978), 296–304.

Friedman, P. G. *Listening Processes: Attention, Understanding, Evaluation. What Research Says to the Teacher.* Washington, D.C.: National Education Association, 1978.

Wilt, M. "A Study of Teacher Awareness of Listening as a Factor in Elementary Education." *Journal of Educational Research* 43 (April 1950), 626–36.

Goal 2: To help the reader understand how speaking skills are acquired.

Question 2: As a classroom teacher, how would you set about the task of developing students' speaking skills?

Fletcher, D. B. "Oral Language and the Language Arts Teacher." *Language Arts* 58 (February 1981), 219–24.

Shane, H. G., and J. Walden, eds. *Classroom-Relevant Research in the Language Arts.* Washington, D.C.: Association for Supervision and Curriculum Development, 1978.

Stewig, J. "Instructional Strategies: The Owl, the Pussy-Cat and Oral Language." *Elementary English* 50 (1973), 325–30.

Goal 3: To help the reader enhance students' reading skills.

Question 3: As a classroom teacher, how would you set about the task of developing students' reading skills?

Anderson, P. S., and D. Lapp. *Language Skills in Elementary Education.* New York: Macmillan Publishing Co., Inc., 1979.

Chall, J. S. *Learning to Read: The Great Debate.* New York: McGraw-Hill Book Company, 1967.

Powell, W. R., and E. L. Wenzel. *Indicators for Learning and Teacher Compentencies in the Basic Skills: Reading and Listening.* Gainesville: Florida Educational Research and Development Council, 1979.

Goal 4: To help the reader improve students' writing skills.

Question 4: As a classroom teacher, how would you set about the task of developing students' writing skills?

Graves, D. H. "Writing Research for the Eighties: What Is Needed." *Language Arts* 58 (February 1981), 197–206.

Kantor, K. J. "Appreciating Children's Writing." *Language Arts* 56 (October 1979), 742–6.

Sealey, L., et al. *Children's Writing (An Approach for the Primary Grades).* Newark, Del.: International Reading Association, 1979.

Goal 5: To help the reader comprehend the interrelatedness of all the language arts.

Question 5: What is meant by the "interrelatedness" of the language arts?

Donoghue, M. R. *The Child and the English Language Arts.* Dubuque, Iowa: William C. Brown Company, Publishers, 1979.

Glatthorn, A. A. "Using Separate Objectives in Integrated Units." In *A Guide for Developing an English Curriculum for the Eighties.* Urbana, Ill.: National Council of Teachers of English, 1980.

Lee, D. M., and J. B. Rubin. *Children and Language: Reading and Writing, Talking and Listening.* Belmont, Calif.: Wadsworth Publishing Co., 1979.

BIBLIOGRAPHY

Anderson, P. S., and D. Lapp. *Language Skills in Elementary Education.* New York: Macmillan Publishing Co., Inc., 1979.

Arbuthnot, M. H., et al. *The Arbuthnot Anthology of Children's Literature,* 3rd ed. New York: Lothrop, Lee & Shephard Books, 1971.

Bellugi, U., and R. Brown, eds. *The Acquisition of Language.* Monographs of the Society for Research in Child Development, No. 29. Chicago: University of Chicago Press, 1964.

Brandenburg, R. "The Language of a Three-Year-Old Child." *Pedagogical Review* 21 (March 1915), 89.

Brown, D. "Auding as the Primary Language Ability." Unpublished doctoral dissertation, Stanford University, Palo Alto, Calif., 1954.

Burrows, A. T., et al. *They All Want to Write.* New York: Holt, Rinehart and Winston, 1964, p. 88.

Carroll, J. B. "Language Development." In *Child Language*, ed. by A.Bar-Adon and F. L. Weiner, Englewood Cliffs, N. J.: Prentice-Hall, Inc., 1971, pp. 200–11.

Colum, P. *Roofs of Gold.* New York: Macmillan Publishing Co., Inc., 1964.

Combs, W. E. "Further Effects of Sentence Combining Practice on Writing Ability." *Research in the Teaching of English* 10 (Fall 1976), 147.

Cramer, R. L. "The Nature and Nurture of Creative Writing." *Elementary School Journal* 75 (May 1975), 507-12.

Devine, T. G. "Listening: What Do We Know After Fifty Years of Research and Theorizing?" *Journal of Reading* 21 (January 1978), 296-304.

D'Israeli, Isaac. *Literary Character.* New York: W. J. Middleton, Publisher, 1891, p. 177.

Duker, S. *Listening Bibliography.* 2nd ed. Metuchen, N. J.: The Scarecrow Press, Inc., 1968.

Feldman, A. K. "The Effect of Reinforcement of Listening Skills of the Culturally Deprived." Unpublished master's thesis, The Ohio State University, Columbus, 1967.

Flood, J., and D. Lapp. *Language/Reading Instruction for the Young Child.* New York: Macmillan Publishing Co., Inc., 1981.

Flood, J., and P. H. Salus. *Language and the Language Arts.* Englewood Cliffs, N.J.: Prentice-Hall, Inc., 1983.

Foley, D. *Teaching Writing in the Elementary Curriculum.* Indianapolis, Ind.: Indianapolis Public Schools/Lilly Endowment, Inc., 1981.

Friedman, P. G. *Listening Processes: Attention, Understanding, Evaluation. What Research Says to the Teacher.* Washington, D.C.: National Education Association, 1978.

Glatthorn, A. A. *A Guide for Developing an English Curriculum for the Eighties.* Urbana, Ill.: National Council of Teachers of English, 1980.

Hayes, J. R., and L. Flower. "The Process of Writing." In *Cognitive Processes in Writing* by L. Gregg and E. Steinberg, Potomac, Md.: Lawrence Erlbaum Associates, Publishers, 1980. pp. 3-30.

Hunt, I. *Across Five Aprils.* Chicago: Follett Publishing Company, 1964.

Jacobs, J. *Time for Fairy Tales Old and New.* New York: G. P. Putnam's Sons, 1972.

Joos, M. *The Five Clocks.* New York: Harcourt Brace Jovanovich, 1967.

Kantor, K. J. "Appreciating Children's Writing." *Language Arts* 56 (October 1979), 742-6.

Larrick, N. *On City Streets.* New York: Evans, M. & Co., Inc. 1968.

Loban, W. *The Language of Elementary School Children.* Urbana, Ill.: National Council of Teachers of English, 1976.

Lundsteen, S. W. *Listening: Its Impact on Reading and the Other Language Arts.* NCTE/ERIC Clearinghouse on Reading and Communication Skills. Urbana, Ill.: National Council of Teachers of English, 1979.

McAfee, D. C. "Effect of Sentence-Combining Instruction on the Reading and Writing Achievement of Fifth-Grade Children in a Suburban School District." Unpublished doctoral dissertation, Texas Woman's University, Denton, Texas, 1980.

Mellon, J. C. *Transformational Sentence-Combining: A Method for Enhancing the Development of Syntactic Fluency in English Compositions.* Urbana, Ill.: National Council of Teachers of English, 1969.

Mollick, L. B., and K. S. Etra. "Poor Learning Ability . . . or Poor Hearing?" *Teacher* 98 (March 1981), 42-43.

Murray, D. M. *A Writer Teaches Writing: A Practical Method of Teaching Composition.* Boston: Houghton Mifflin Company, 1968.

O'Hare, F. *Sentence Combining: Improving Student Writing Without Formal Grammar Instruction.* Urbana, Ill.: National Council of Teachers of English, 1973.

Petrosky, A., and J. Brozick. "A Model for Teaching Writing Based Upon Current Knowledge of the Composing Process." *English Journal* 68 (January 1979), 96-101.

Russell, D. H., and E. J. Russell. *Listening Aids Through the Grades.* New York: Bureau of Publications, Teachers College Press, Columbia University, 1959.

Sager, C. "Improving the Quality of Written Composition Through Pupil Use of Rating Scale." Unpublished Ed.D. dissertation, Boston University School of Education, Boston, Mass., 1972.

Sealey, L., N. Sealey, and M. Millmore. *Children's Writing (An Approach for the Primary Grades).* Newark, Del.: International Reading Association, 1979.

Shane, H. G., and M. Walden, eds. *Classroom-Relevant Research in the Language Arts.* Washington, D.C.: Association for Supervision and Curriculum Development, 1978.

Smith, E. B., et al. *Language and Thinking in the Language Arts in the Elementary School.* New York: Holt, Rinehart and Winston, 1970.

Stammer, J. D. "MAPPing Out a Plan for Better Listening." *Teacher* 98 (March 1981), 37-38.

Wilkinson, A. *The Foundations of Language.* London: Oxford University Press, 1971.

Wilt, M. "A Study of Teacher Awareness of Listening as a Factor in Elementary Education." *Journal of Educational Research* 43 (April 1950), 626-36.

CHAPTER 4

Readiness for Reading: Preparation, Programs, and Activities

Readiness is a continuously developing process: It begins at conception and continues at ever higher cognitive levels until death, as each experience and strengthening of skill makes the individual ready for the next step.

Robert Hillerich, 1977

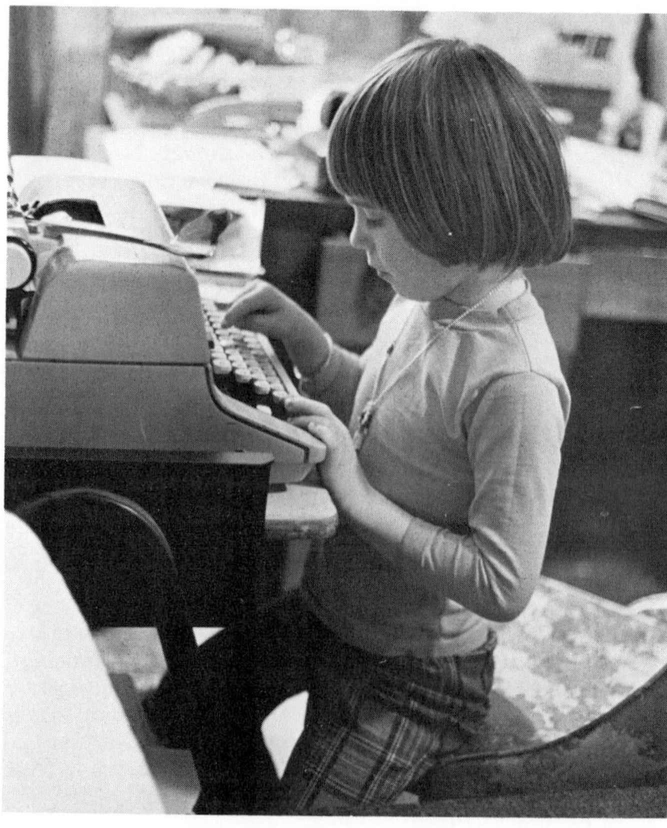

Readiness is a continuously developing process. It begins at conception and continues at ever higher cognitive levels as each experience and strengthening of skill makes the individual ready for the next step. (Photo by Linda Lungren.)

GOALS: To help the reader to

1. Acquire an understanding of the historical development of readiness practices in the United States.
2. Understand the nature of readiness as it applies to each individual student.
3. Examine the components of model prereading programs in preschool and kindergarten.
4. Learn about assessment instruments that measure aspects of readiness.

WHEN IS THE CHILD READY TO READ?

The question of when a child is ready to read is not only extremely controversial but its answer is complex. A brief historical overview demonstrates how the answer to this question has changed and been revised over the years.

Beginning Reading Instruction at a Mental Age of 6.5 Years: History

In the United States, learning to read and beginning school were almost simultaneous events until 1931. Thus, most students began reading instruction at about six years of age, and few educators questioned the acceptability of this practice. Huey (1908) spoke specifically against this practice and seemed to favor a more spontaneous approach: "[the child] is concerned about the printed notices, signs that come his way, and should be told what these things say when he makes inquiry" (p. 28).

In two separate studies (Holmes, 1927; Reed, 1927) it was reported that many children failed first grade because they were not ready "to read." Researchers attempted to explain this failure and many, including Holmes, concluded that children entering first grade were not ready to learn to read. Frequently, relevant variables such as teacher preparation, instructional method, materials, and class size were not examined in these investigations; however, readiness programs began to emerge throughout the country.

Gesell, a physician, believed that children were not ready to learn to read at six years of age and that instruction should be postponed until they were "readied." Since his position stemmed from his interest in neural maturation, he looked for an explanation of biologically determined developmental stages from the point of view of intrinsic growth, neural ripening, and unfolding behaviors. He was convinced that the ability to read occurred at one of these stages. His suggestions may have been so widely accepted because the prevailing psychological trends of the time placed great importance on the "natural" development of the child.

Mental Age Formula to Determine Reading Readiness Age

Exactness of measurement was in vogue, and the public was not interested in vague notions of stages of development. Educators and psychologists set out to determine the exact age at which reading instruction should begin. In the 1920s, group intelligence tests became available to the educational community. The numerical equivalent of a child's mental age provided by these tests became the catalyst for pinpointing the moment at which a child would be able to begin reading instruction. The commonly accepted formula for determining mental age was

$$\text{Mental age} = \frac{\text{intelligence quotient} \times \text{chronological age}}{100}$$

Many studies in the 1920s reported a high correlation between reading achievement and intelligence. One study (Arthur, 1925) concluded that a mental age of 6.0 to 6.5 was "necessary for standard first-grade achievement." The study that was the most famous and that had the most profound effect on beginning reading instruction was conducted by Morphett and Washburne and was reported in 1931. They stated unequivocally that 6.5 was the proper mental age to begin reading instruction, although their study was conducted on children using only *one* method of instruction in *one* school system (Winnetka, Illinois). The conclusion of their report read: "Mental age alone showed a larger degree of correlation with reading progress than did intelligence quotient or the average of mental and chronological age" (p. 502). This report became the foundation for reading readiness programs for the next thirty years.

Beginning Reading Instruction at 6.5 Years: Objections

It was only a few years before educators began to question the merits of the mental age concept of reading readiness. In a research report on reading readiness, Gates and Bond (1936) stressed the importance of individual strengths and weaknesses on beginning reading instruction:

> This study emphasizes the importance of recognizing and adjusting to individual limitations and needs . . . rather than merely changing the time for beginning reading. It appears that readiness for reading is something to develop rather than merely to wait for . . . . (p. 681)

Several theories of the times may help to explain why a mental age of 6.5 years continued to be *the* age at which reading instruction should begin. Gesell's (1946) views supported the popular notions that readiness for reading resulted from maturation—that is, the passing of time. Olson's (1949) concept of organismic age and Havighurst's (1953) "teachable moment" further supported the proponents of the mental age theory. Durkin (1972) suggested that psychologists were to blame: "They were the reason for too little change over too many years . . . psychological conceptions of human growth and development changed very little from the 20s to the 50s" (p. 73).

Gradually, the concept of reading readiness focused on aspects other than a precise mental age for beginning reading instruction. MacGinitie (1969) summarized Durkin's theory that readiness and beginning reading instruction should not be viewed as two separate entities in his concise statement: "When a child is taught a little, he is then ready for a little more" (p. 399). Along with Gates (1937), Durkin (1972) suggests that, rather than inquire about the correct age for beginning instruction, the researcher should ask, "Is the child ready to succeed with this particular kind and quality of instruction?"

Calfee and Hoover (1973) suggested that programs and teaching methods that are not individualized to meet the needs of beginning readers will not be effective:

> Early admission of mentally advanced children seems to yield desirable outcomes, whereas early admission of children on a non-selective basis to programs without provision for individual difference is less effective. (p. 10)

Later in this chapter we discuss a definition of readiness that includes many factors: the particular task at hand, the child's ability at the moment, the child's response to a specific teaching method, and other essential components that, in combination, can be termed "readiness."

Reading Readiness Tests and Alternatives. From the 1930s through the 1950s, many reading readiness tests were developed and they attained some measure of popularity. However, criticisms of such tests ultimately led educators to search for other methods of predicting reading success. Criticisms included:

1. They do not adequately assess potential reading ability.
2. The competencies measured by the tests are not directly related to reading.
3. Visual discrimination tasks are often too difficult.
4. Total readiness programs are built on the results of diagnostic tests, the components of which may not have measured later reading success.

As an alternative to reading readiness tests, teachers and researchers began to look for tests that could predict the *potential* of a child to be able to learn to read. An assessment of four prereading skills (alphabet recognition, vocabulary, whole-word recognition, and visual discrimination) can help you to identify students who will probably succeed in reading and those who may experience some difficulty. These predictors may help you to plan appropriately individualized programs for young children who appear to have a high risk of failure or for those children who exhibit potentially serious reading problems.

Alphabet Recognition. Many research reports have indicated a close relationship between reading and letter recognition. One of the four major conclusions of a study by Carswell (1978) was that "knowledge of letter names is present among all children who learn to read words, whether the letter names are learned in school or before school entry" (p. 216). Monroe (1935), Durrell (1958), Silvaroli (1965), and Silberberg et al. (1968) all found that the ability to name letters at the beginning of first grade was highly predictive of reading achievement at the end of the school year. Weiner and Feldman (1963) reported that letter recognition was related more closely to reading achievement than to matching printed words. Studies by Bond and Dykstra (1967) and Jansky and De-

Hirsch (1972) indicated that the single greatest predictor of later reading success was letter naming.

In related studies, Olson (1958) found that the knowledge of letter names was not causally related to high reading achievement but that lack of this knowledge was frequently associated with low achievement. Muehl and Kremenack (1966) reported that letter knowledge was advantageous for reading but that a lack of letter-name knowledge was not causally related to reading problems.

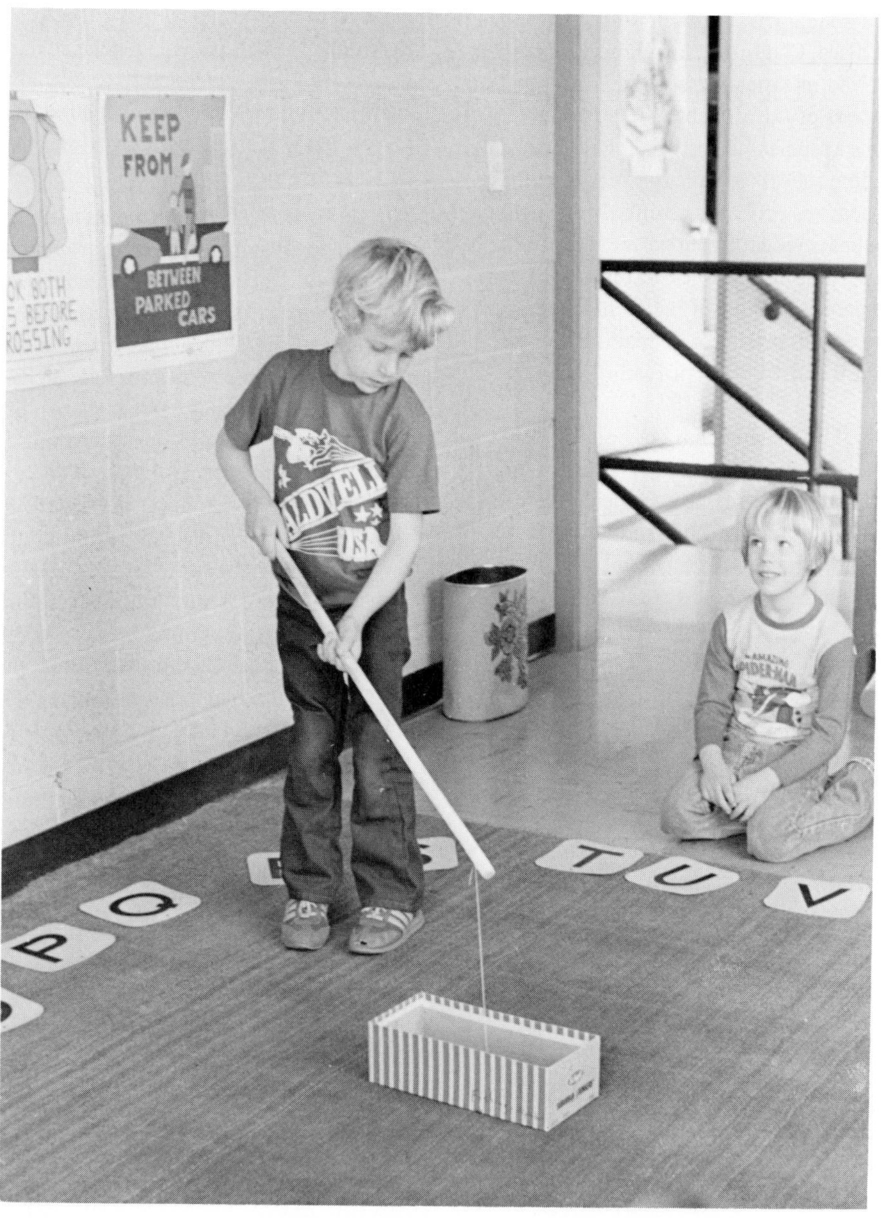

Studies suggest that the quickest way to predict reading success is alphabet recognition and that this knowledge is probably essential for learning to read English. (Photo by Linda Lungren.)

Samuels (1972) has reported that two separate experimental studies failed to support the assumption that letter-name knowledge facilitates reading. In partial replication of Samuels' study, Chisholm and Knafle (1975) found opposite results; they discovered that letter-name knowledge was highly predictive of reading achievement. They concluded that their study "supported the statement by Calfee, Chapman, and Venezky (1972): 'to read English a child must learn to isolate, differentiate, and identify the letters of the alphabet' " (p. 145).

Cumulatively these studies suggest that the quickest way to predict reading success is alphabet recognition and that this knowledge is probably essential to learning to read English. It bears repeating, however, that there is no cause-effect relationship between letter-name knowledge and reading success. Alphabet recognition can be used as an efficient, useful predictor of reading success, but not as a method for instruction of reading.

Vocabulary. General intelligence has been shown to be closely related to reading achievement. Lohnes and Gray (1972) concluded that "the best single explanatory principle for observed variance in reading skills was variance in general intelligence" (p. 60). In turn, the most common component of IQ tests is the vocabulary subtest.

Almenoff (1979) conducted a study to assess the predictive efficiency of certain standardized readiness tests to determine how well they forecasted second-grade reading achievement. This was a retrospective study, using second-grade students on whom complete kindergarten testing data was available. One of the three best kindergarten predictors of second-grade reading achievement was found to be the Vocabulary subtest of the Vane Kindergarten Test. Almenoff also found that two of the three "most efficient predictors of second grade reading achievement" were the Vocabulary subtest of the Vane Kindergarten Test and the Word Meaning subtest of the Metropolitan Readiness Test.

Picture-recognition tasks can be used as a vocabulary measure. Morgan (1960) and DeHirsch et al. (1966) concluded that achievement on picture-recognition vocabulary tests was highly correlated to reading achievement.

Commenting on student performance on an oral vocabulary task, Artley (1948) pointed out that "any limitation in word meaning . . . would have a bearing on reading ability" (p. 351). Robinson (1963) found that vocabulary was related to predicting reading success. Loban (1963) also reported that kindergarten children who possessed extensive vocabularies continued to exceed the performance of other children through grade six.

A third type of vocabulary task is categorization, in which children provide a generic name for a group of words. In 1966 DeHirsch et al. found that this test significantly correlated with second-grade reading achievement. A 1972 study by Jansky and DeHirsch also found categorization to be related to later reading achievement.

Whole-Word Recognition. Research has shown that word recognition and reading are highly related. Gavel (1958) and DeHirsch et al. (1966) found that recognition of words that the child had been taught was highly predictive of reading achievement at the first-grade level. Examples of these words include a child's full name (for example, Mary Agnes Cunningham), or a date (July 4, 1776), or words with special meaning for the child (Big Bird, candy, monster).

In a study reported in the *Reading Research Quarterly* (1977-1978), Richek tested kindergarten children on seven reading readiness tasks and two word-learning tasks. The word-learning tasks were similar to a sight-word and a sound-symbol method of initial reading instruction. Richek found that a large proportion of the students scored higher on the sight-word than on the sound-symbol word-learning task.

Visual Discrimination. Although it is frequently cited as a necessary skill for reading readiness, visual discrimination is a very controversial predictor of reading achievement. It is generally accepted that visual discrimination of nonalphabetic forms and shapes is probably not an effective method of prereading instruction. The question of the predictive value of visual discrimination ability, however, remains unanswered.

Goins (1958) and DeHirsch et al. (1966) found that matching two- and three-letter sequences is highly predictive of reading achievement. For example,

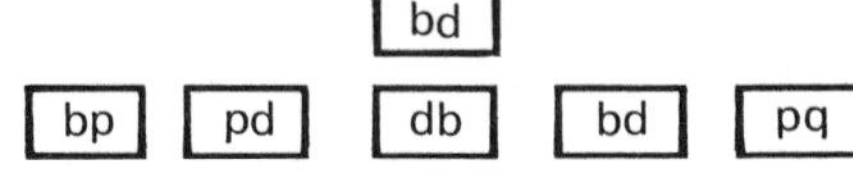

Directions for this test might state: "Color the box in the second line that contains the same letters as the box on the first line."

Kak (1980) used computer-generated alphanumeric characters with kindergarten children to test their ability to process the features of patterns. Kak's data suggest that children with reading problems may process elements (e.g., line lengths, angles) less efficiently or less accurately.

Many researchers (Wilson and Fleming, 1940; Bryan, 1964; Barrett, 1965) have reported that visual discrimination ability in young children correlates highly with later reading achievement. Barrett (1965) found that scores on word-matching tests correlated very closely with reading achievement, but he also suggested that visual perception was unable to "bear the entire burden of prediction." In a study by Buktenica (1969), visual discrimination ability was found to be a far more reliable predictor of reading achievement than was intelligence.

However, Calfee et al. (1972) were unable to demonstrate that visual discrimination was an adequate predictor of reading achievement. Olson and Johnson (1970) also found that visual discrimination, as measured by the Frostig Developmental Test of Visual Perception, was the least effective predictor of the five readiness predictors (spatial relations, position in space, form constancy, figure-ground, eye-motor coordination) that they investigated.

In short, alphabet recognition, vocabulary knowledge, word recognition, and visual discrimination *may* be useful as predictors of later reading success. They *may* help

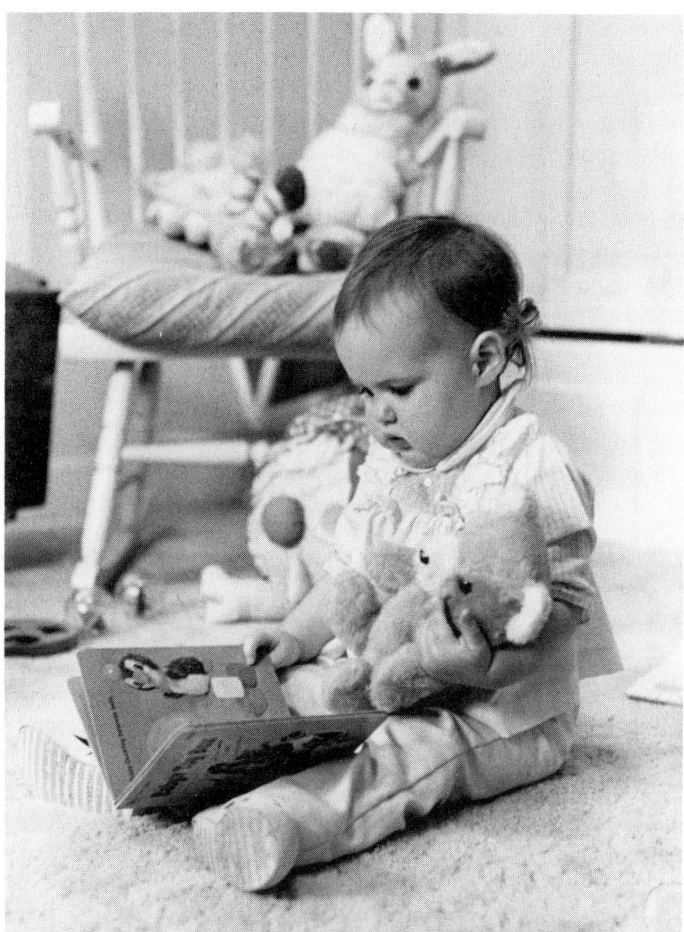

When a child exhibits an interest in printed material, that child is demonstrating an interest in learning to read. (Photo by Linda Lungren.)

you to identify children who would be appropriate candidates for early reading programs.

EARLY PROGRAMS

Within the historical and theoretical framework presented here, we now attempt to answer the question, "When should a child be taught to read?"

When cannot be pinpointed to an age or a time; it will vary with each child. When a child exhibits an interest in printed material, that child is demonstrating an interest in learning to read. Some may see this as a simplistic answer to a complex question, but it makes sense in many ways.

Farr and Roser (1979) remind us that a child's literacy development begins very early. If the child grows up in a literate society, the basic structure of literacy is developing before the beginning of school instruction. Today's children are constantly exposed to print in the form of books, magazines, television, advertisements, billboards, and household products (cereal boxes, toothpaste, etc.). When a young child asks a parent, "What does that say?" he or she is asking for reading instruction. When he or she can say, "That says Wheaties," he or she is indeed reading.

To answer the important question, "When should a child be taught to read?" with the relatively simple answer, "When he or she indicates an interest in printed material," avoids the question to a degree. If we are talking about formal instruction and educational strategies, a more sophisticated answer seems necessary. We need to investigate the meaning of "readiness."

Readiness Reconsidered

Initially, scores from readiness tests were used to determine when a child would be mentally capable of benefiting from reading instruction. However, the climate of the times persuaded educators to focus too strongly on the test scores and too little on the child as an individual with a unique history and individual needs.

Ausubel (1959) suggested that readiness is "the adequacy of existing capacity in relation to the demands of a given learning task" (p. 246). In other words, he suggested that the "when" of reading instruction depends on the child, the instruction, and the specific components of what is being taught. Children with the same chronological age may range from those who are "ready" to learn that their name begins with "J" to those who are able to "read" a short sentence. The children in the latter group have already learned to decode some words and have committed them to their sight-word vocabulary.

As classroom teachers, you must be cautious not to infer or assume that these differences in "readiness" are caused by intelligence differences among the children. Rather, you should recognize that their readiness preparation is merely at a different stage of development.

Readiness varies from child to child; there is no single "proper" age at which to begin reading instruction. This is recognized in some other countries where reading instruction begins much earlier than in the United States. At about five years of age, children begin reading in the United Kingdom; children in Israel often begin instruction at four years of age.

An area of interest related to initial instruction of reading is the phenomenon of early reading. Many researchers have investigated the effects of early reading programs. We review some here to determine whether early reading is a help or a hindrance to the young child.

Early Reading

One of the best known studies on early reading was conducted for six years by Durkin in New York City and in Oakland, California, in 1966. Some of the children read before their entry into first grade and before receiving any formal reading instruction. Durkin concluded that early reading was not necessarily a function of socioeconomic status, ethnicity, or intelligence. She further reported that the early readers achieved higher reading scores during their entire elementary school careers.

In a similar but later study conducted in Illinois with four-year-old children, Durkin did not reach the same conclusions. In this study, early readers who had been trained in a special two-year preschool language arts/reading program scored significantly higher than did their nonearly reading classmates on standardized reading tests in grades one and two, but the differences between the two groups were not statistically significant in grades three and four.

Durkin hypothesized that a family that fostered preschool reading ability would probably continue to foster achievement, with or without school instruction. Another possible explanation may lie in the analysis of test data. Durkin's original data analysis did not take into account the phenomenon of increased variance in the scores of the upper-grade students. A reanalysis of the data might indeed show that the early readers did outperform nonearly readers even in the later grades.

Although some studies have provided insight into the *effects* of early reading, many questions remain unanswered as to its causes. For example: What type of environment (if any) is conducive to early reading? Which home factors contribute to the success of early reading? How much influence does a parent have on early reading?

One final note on early reading is necessary. Despite stories and anecdotes to the contrary, young children *do not* learn to read by themselves (Durkin, 1966, 1972). Interviews with parents of early readers uncovered these characteristics:

1. These parents converse a great deal with their children.
2. Early readers tend to ask many questions.
3. Parents of early readers take the time to answer their questions.
4. A very common question is, "What's that word?"

Effects of Early Reading Programs. Generally, research findings support the idea that early reading usually produces successful readers. Although some of the research reports are flawed by design problems and/or data analysis, the evidence does suggest that early reading programs have a positive influence on successful reading.

McKee, Brzeinski and Harrison (1966) reported that kindergarteners who were taught to read were able to sustain their early achievement if the reading program in subsequent years was coordinated with the early program. In another study on kindergarten children, King and Friesen (1972) found that early readers who were selected for the study outperformed nonearly readers at the end of first grade. However, intelligence was not taken into consideration in reporting these findings, and the mean intelligence score of early readers was 115 versus the 104 mean intelligence score of nonearly readers.

Gray and Klaus (1970) reported that high-risk children who had participated in intervention programs achieved well at the end of first grade, but they found no continued growth after first grade. Unfortunately, this study did not take into account the instruction received by each child after first grade.

Beck (1973) found that early readers had significantly higher intelligence scores than did nonearly readers. Adjusting for intelligence, she found that children who started to read in kindergarten outperformed their nonearly reading classmates in grades one through five. The selection process for early readers in this study was unique—*teachers* selected them as being "ready" to read. She suggests that her results should be interpreted very cautiously because of her unusually small sample, which dwindled to only eight early readers by fifth grade.

Although there are some flaws in the design and analysis of these studies, it can be concluded that early readers score higher than nonearly readers in many cases. If this is true, why isn't more emphasis placed on early reading? Let us examine some of the traditional objections.

Objections to Early Reading

There are four criticisms of early reading that are sometimes cited, but we believe that the objections can all be countered easily. A brief discussion of each appears in the following table.

Objections	
1. Early reading will hurt the child's vision	There is little evidence to support this position. On the contrary, children's own activities seem to indicate that a child's vision is ready for reading by four or five years of age. Many children are writing by four or five years of age, an activity that requires similar visual acuity.
2. Parents are not qualified to teach reading.	Parents may not have taken formal reading and/or education courses, but there are many activities that they can do with their children. Some of these activities are included at the end of this chapter.

3. Early readers will be bored in school.	Children will only be bored with reading if they have to start over again. If classroom programs are tailored to the individual needs of each child, there seems to be no logical or inherent need for boredom.
4. Childhood is a time for play, not academics.	Reading can be a playful and enjoyable activity for children. If children spend as much time on reading activities as they seem to want, then the concern about introducing too much academics seems unwarranted.

The Case for Early Intervention

Despite the lack of evidence to support their position, some educators still feel that prereading or early reading programs are unnecessary, or even counterproductive. Many researchers, however, argue that there is a great need for early programs. Their belief is that high-risk, potentially handicapped children need to be identified when they are very young so that remediation of their problems can be begun before they are overwhelming. As in the field of medicine, we have now entered an age of prevention in education. Educators are examining preventive measures to avoid later serious educational problems.

Money (1966) stressed the importance of early identification of high-risk children in efforts to alleviate childhood learning disabilities. Similarly, the report of the National Task Force on Dyslexia and Related Reading Disorders (1969) also stated that the early identification of children who may have potential reading problems is urgently needed to protect children from the psychological trauma of reading failure and to ensure appropriate intervention to prevent this failure.

Research positions that support early intervention frequently stem from the belief that the causes of reading failure can be found in a child's earliest stages of development (Hallgren, 1950; DeHirsch et al., 1966; Ingram, 1970; Owens et al., 1968; Silver, 1971; Satz and van Nostrand, 1973).

Educators who supported the concept of timely intervention argue that very young children are frequently more receptive to remediation than are older children. For example, according to Caldwell (1969), "There is some evidence to suggest that the child may be more sensitive to environmental stimulation (for example, remedial intervention) during that period in which maturation of the brain is evolving and when behavior is less differentiated" (p. 220). Research also indicates that basic language ability in children develops between birth and the age of five or six (Menyuk, 1963). This evidence, too, suggests that the amelioration of reading difficulties in elementary school children might be accomplished best through intervention during the preschool years.

In 1961, Hunt utilized his theories of cognitive development in young children as a rationale for early intervention programs. Programs such as Head Start were based largely on Hunt's theories. These programs have been monitored closely, evaluated, and updated to strengthen their effectiveness. Program modifications have included (1) starting intervention earlier and incorporating parent involvement as an integral part of the intervention (parent and child centers; Home Start), (2) extending the intervention support into the primary grades (Follow Through), (3) coordinating services to children and their families over an extended period of time (child and family resource centers), and (4) supporting the development of innovative educational programs (Planned Variation).

Although it seems obvious that the development of early intervention programs is important, one significant issue remains to be discussed. Some detractors of early intervention programs base their objections on this belief, namely, that there is a developmental, biologically determined *critical period* for the acquisition of reading. They further believe that to tamper with this biological clock is unnatural and is bound to have an adverse effect on the child. This notion bears further examination.

Critical Period for Language Acquisition. There are linguistic theroies that support the notion of a critical period in the language acquisition of human beings. Some educators have extended this concept and applied it to the reading process as well. We first examine the linquistic theory; then we look at its possible appropriateness for reading.

Critical period can be defined as a nonchronological period or stage in which the human organism is especially sensitive to the specifics of language development (phonology, syntax, morphology, semantics, and pragmatics). It is possible that there are certain periods that foster the development of each of these components. These periods of heightened sensitivity might parallel psychophysiological theories of the rate of growth in the human brain, which closely parallel Piaget's (1963a) stages of cognitive development. The perception of a critical period as a sensitive stage, however, merely means that there are periods of sensitivity to language development—*not* that there are terminal points after which language development will not occur.

Several factors affect sensitivity to language development, three of which we examine briefly: *neurophysiology, psychology,* and *environment.*

Neurophysiology. The theory of critical periods states that a particular behavior is acquired at a specific time. Although formulated originally as a biological concept, it has been applied by some to the acquisition and development of language.

Lennenberg (1967) and others have claimed that language cannot be learned after the lateralization of the brain is complete, a phenomenon that Lennenberg though occurred at puberty. Others, however, have theorized that lateralization may be complete by age five, or may even be a neonatal phenomenon.

These concepts and theories are important to educators because they seem to parallel Piaget's sensorimotor stage, and future investigations may examine the relationship between the critical period of language acquisition and the sensorimotor period.

Psychology. In examining the components of language development, the psychological makeup of the individual must be considered. Factors such as experience, cognition, attitude, intellectual functioning, culture, and motivation must be taken into account when proposing a theory to explain a sensitive stage of development.

Environment. The case of Genie, a fictitious name, demonstrates the profound effect of environment of language. In 1970, Genie was a thirteen-year-old girl who was brought to Children's Hospital in Los Angeles; she had been virtually "locked in a closet" for most of her life. Many of the actual details of the case are unknown, but at the time of her entry into Children's Hospital, she had no speech and limited signs of nonverbal language and was barely able to control her vocal muscles. After several years of life in a normal foster home and work with educators, psychologists, and speech pathologists, Genie exhibited an amazing amount of growth.

Genie's progress far exceeded the expectations of those who would hold to a strict theory of critical period development. She comprehends speech, uses expressive speech, and demonstrates some understanding of cognitive relationships. Since Genie's language acquisition began with the onset of puberty, her case certainly contradicts Lennenberg's theory, in which he suggested that the critical period for language acquisition occurs between birth and puberty.

Although we recognize that neurophysiology, psychology, and environment are determinants affecting an individual's sensitivity to language development, the exact nature of the interrelationships among these factors is unknown. It is also unclear as to which determinant occurs first or is most significant for the acquisition of language.

IS THERE A CRITICAL PERIOD FOR THE ACQUISITION OF READING?

Few educators support the theory of a critical period for the spontaneous acquisition of reading, largely because it is not generally agreed that there is a critical period for the acquisition of language. However, related research on cognitive development suggests that there may be a critical period in which to *begin* reading instruction. This theory suggests that initial reading instruction should take place between four and six years of age, a time when the child is rather sophisticated, having acquired most of the rules of English syntax.

Reading has traditionally been taught when a child is six to eight years old. Piaget (1963a) describes this as a time when the child is involved in "concrete operations." For the child who is experiencing difficulty in learning to read, it may be that the repetitive drills involved in beginning reading are interruptive. Another partial explanation of the problem may be a mismatch between the child's cognitive development and beginning reading instruction.

Many researchers already have reported a major change in cognitive behavior at five or six—the age at which American children enter school. White (1975) states that "four contemporary points of view concerning cognitive development have held the five-seven period to be important, each on its own evidence and in its own terms" (p. 210). These four positions are (1) Piaget, (2) the Russian researchers, typified by Luria, (3) the stimulus-response behaviorists, and (4) Freud.

It is important to recognize that there is a major change in skill performance between the ages of five and seven. This change may be due to:

1. General level of intellectual functioning and/or language
2. Improved organizational abilities
3. Changes in attention (i.e., duration and fixation)

The best answer to the question of when to begin reading instruction seems to come from Gates (1937) and Calfee and Hoover (1973), who have suggested that instruction should match the needs of the child.

Components of a Prereading or Early Reading Program

The single greatest factor in assessing any prereading or early reading program is the extent to which it meets the needs of the individual child. Additionally, a model program guides children, but it allows them to progress at their own rate; it also provides a rich language environment. While there is probably no causal relationship between environmental factors and success in reading, Teale (1978) suggests that the following factors be considered:

1. There should be an availability and range of printed material in the environment.
2. Children *read* in the environment to promote the idea that print is meaningful.
3. The environment should facilitate contact with paper and pencil.
4. Those in the environment should respond to what the child is trying to do.

At this time, it is important to stress some factors about the ways in which children learn, because they must be part of the foundation of any model prereading program. Piaget (1963a) suggests that children learn by abstracting features from a stimulus and integrating these features into an existing framework. He and other cognitively oriented psychologists and educators believe that children learn by generating hypotheses and testing them against the input they recieve. This theory is consistent with the views of such linguists as Menyuk (1971), who maintains that children acquire language by generating rules, testing them, and reformulating them.

If you adhere to Piaget's views of learning, then reading must be an accessible adventure for children. A rich variety of materials must be made available to children for them to be able to extract letter-sound relationships. Children must see books and other printed materials; they must hear the words read over and over. Only in this way will they be able to generate and test hypotheses about letter-sound correspondences.

Reading as a Prop for Play. Whenever possible, you should try to incorporate reading into children's play. When children interact with reading in this manner, they begin to perceive reading as an important "real-life" process. This can be done by creating environments in which children need to "read" to play. By using a variety of simple props with appropriate words, signs, and descriptions, the children begin to utilize and recognize words that have meaning for them. The following examples may be helpful:

1 Housekeeping Corner
   a. Include empty boxes, cartons, and cans. You can intervene in children's play by asking, "I wonder what the baby wants to eat?" Go to the empty containers and start to read, "I wonder if she wants *peaches, pears,* or *apple sauce*?" Children will begin to model this behavior.
   b. Include menus that have been made by the children for their restaurant play.
   c. Create little homemade books for the children to read to their dolls.
2. Block Area
   a. Include many different kinds of signs in this area. If your children are building a city or town, intervene in their play by asking them, "Is this the drugstore?" If they say, "Yes," ask them, "Do you want to make a sign?" You can attach signs to the blocks by using paper and toothpicks. In this way the signs can be saved.

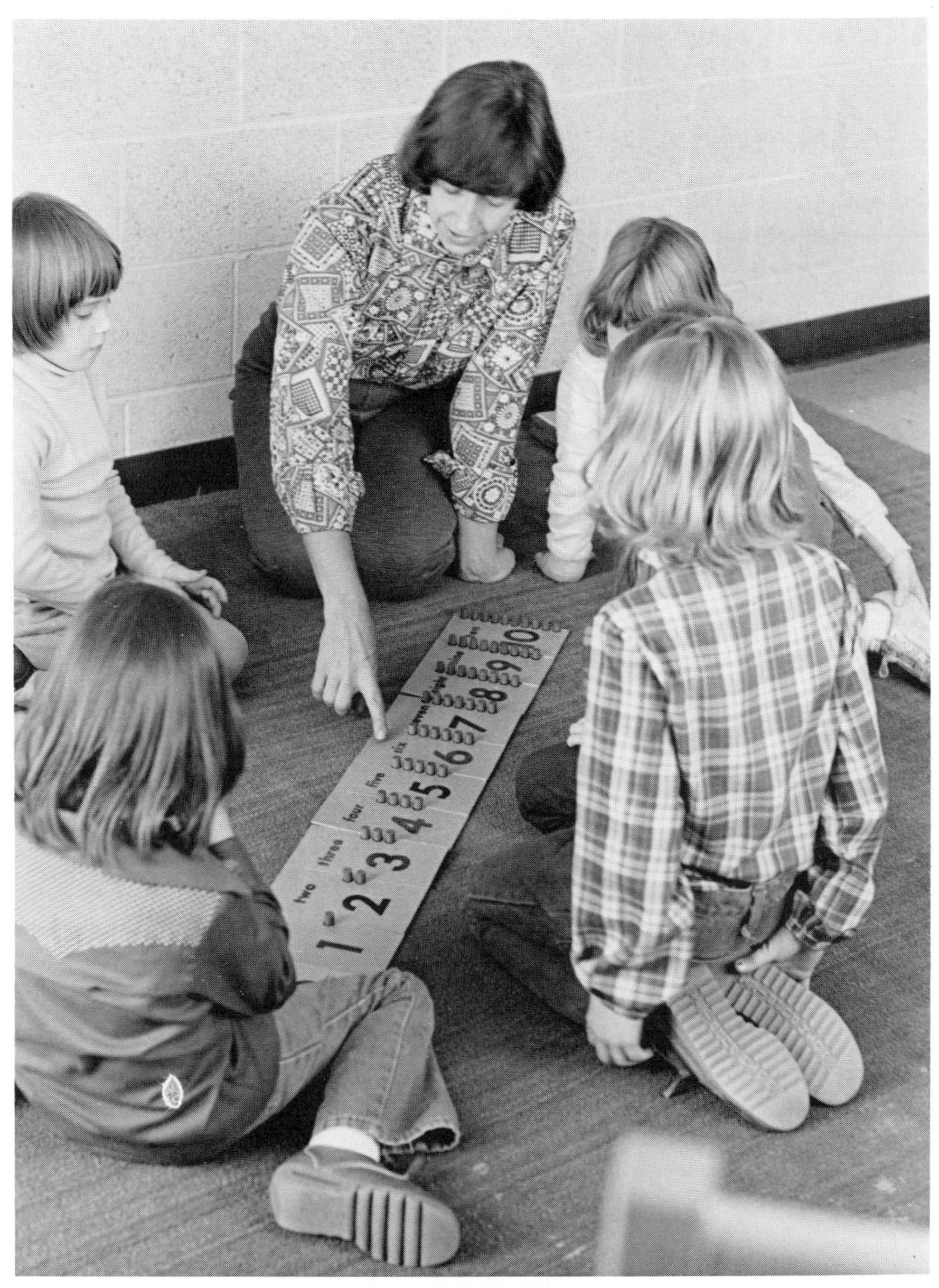

Whenever possible, you should try to incorporate number recognition and reading letters into children's play. (Photo by Linda Lungren.)

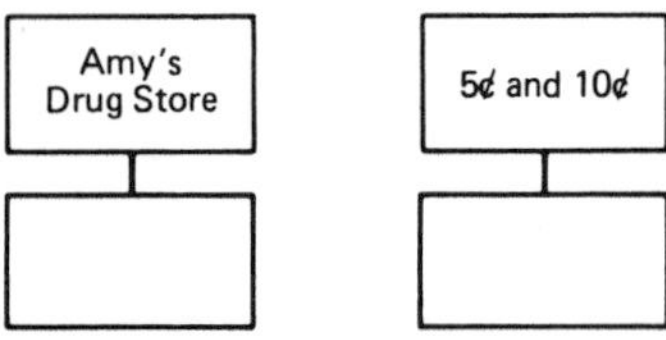

b. Sometimes children enjoy building "cars" and "airplanes" out of blocks. This seems like a perfect opportunity for including signs (reading props) in the play situation. Signs can be made that are interchangeable; they can be saved and used in many different situations.

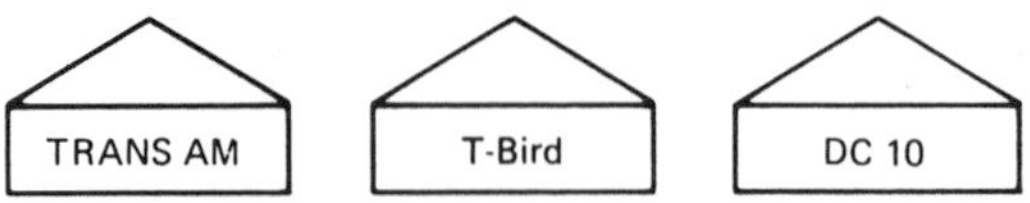

3. Dramatic Play Corner
   a. "Doctor/hospital" is a perfect situation in which reading can be incorporated into children's play. Signs can be made to enhance the play; for example,

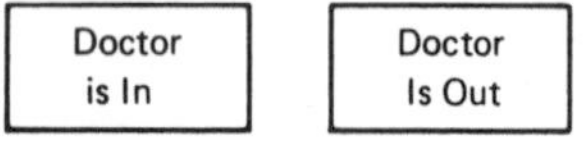

   b. Playing "store" is also an excellent opportunity to incorporate reading into play. Children can "make" money and use it to buy groceries. Children can also prepare a shopping list before they embark on this adventure.

Guidelines for a Prereading or Early Reading Program

There are many important elements to a successful early reading program. As with any goal, it is necessary to identify your objectives and to plan your classroom strategies to meet these objectives. The following chart lists fourteen objectives that we consider essential in a good prereading program, and strategies that can be implemented to meet these objectives.

GENERAL OBJECTIVES AND STRATEGIES FOR A PREREADING PROGRAM

Objectives	Strategies
1. Improvement of general language ability: phonology, morphology, syntax, semantics, and pragmatics. For bilingual children and non-English-speaking children, support language development in child's native language and provide opportunities for the acquisition of English as a second language.	Language-experience approaches. Children who show interest in beginning reading instruction will be afforded the opportunity to begin a personalized language-experience reading program. These children can make word cards and will be taught to "read" single words.
2. Enjoyment of books and an understanding of books as resources. Books represent a wide variety of backgrounds. Children whose first language is not English should have the opportunity to be read stories in their own languages.	Reading to children individually and in small groups, in other languages (where appropriate) and in English. Asking questions relating to the story and encouraging children to retell it in their own words. Picture books readily available to children in a reading corner. Films of familiar stories. Trips to libraries and museums and other neighborhood places of interest.
3. Comprehension of material related orally such as in understanding simple directions or a story that has been read.	Listening experiences via records and tapes of stories, songs, and nursery rhymes. Listening experiences that result in following simple directions. Musical listening, singing, and movement experiences.
4. Appreciation of the relationship between oral and written language.	Language-experience approaches. Children who show interest in beginning reading instruction will be afforded the opportunity to begin a personalized language-experience reading program. These children can make word cards and can be taught to "read" single words.
5. Confidence in their ability to create written materials; for example, stories dictated to a teacher.	Taking down children's dictated stories and helping children make their own books. Opportunities for dramatic play.
6. Recognition of the alphabet.	Games and other manipulative materials (felt letters and

	felt board; magnetic letters and magnetic board; alphabet bingo) that develop alphabet recognition and letter-sound associations.
7. Sight vocabulary that is familiar and important to the child, such as the child's name and the names of frequently used classroom materials (for example, door, a window).	Use of labels in the classroom to indicate names of things and places for their storage. Use of children's names on lockers, tote boxes, and artwork.
8. Letter-sound associations, particularly initial phonemes, consonants, and recognition of familiar sounds.	Phonics training for those children who show interest and who, it appears, will profit from such a program.
9. Recognition of rhyming words.	Phonics training for some children who show interest and who, it appears, can profit from such a program.
10. Introduction to and/or development of effective viewing of educational television.	Use of educational television in selected classrooms.
11. Ability to communicate about concrete objects.	Use of referential communication games.
12. Recognition of sequence.	Use of recipe charts for cooking activities. Use of sequencing materials; for example, puzzles, stories (some without endings), and picture cards.
13. Simple categorization.	Work with children on visual discrimination skills; for example, matching letters, shapes, and designs.
14. Acquisition of directionality.	Exercises and games on directionality (left-right, up-down, etc.).

Sample Lesson Plan

The following lesson plan is presented as an example of how you might use the suggested strategies to implement one of your objectives. This lesson could be used to teach sequencing (objective 12).

Objective/goal

Recognition of sequence

Behavioral objective

Given three different pictorial sequences, the child will be able to choose the one that accurately represents the events from the story.

Materials

Book or story, cardboard, pictures or illustrations.

Strategy and Implementation

1. The teacher reads a story to the children. (Alternative: the child can listen to a story the teacher has recorded, and "follow along" in the book.)
2. The children and teacher discuss the events in the story.
3. Using pictures, illustrations, or even appropriate cartoons, the teacher arranges the characters or pictorial events in three different sequential arrangements.
4. The child is asked to select the pictorial arrangement that depicts the story correctly.

Instructional Program. Any effective instructional program must be based on clearly defined goals and objectives. The instructional techniques and activities that complement the objectives itemized in the previous section fall into four major categories: letter recognition, whole-word techniques, phonics techniques, and language experiences.

Letter Recognition. Once a child has exhibited an interest in print, the teacher should capitalize on this interest by beginning letter-recognition activities. Most three-year-old children, having been exposed to such shows as *Sesame Street*, are capable of recognizing the letters of the alphabet. The needs of the child must determine the type of letter-recognition task that is employed, and these activities fall into three categories:

1. Matching the same letter shapes from two groups of letters
2. Using an auditory modality
3. Teaching children the letters of their names

Reinforcement activities might include tracing letters from stencils, drawing letters in sand or clay, or writing letters on the chalkboard with water and watching them "mysteriously" disappear.

Whole-Word Techniques. It is likely that the first words that children will memorize will be their own names. You can encourage this whole-word recognition by allowing children to put name labels on such items as desks, lockers, lunch boxes, or cubicles.

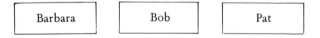

Barbara	Bob	Pat

You might teach lessons on *the days of the week, the weather,* or *dates* to encourage whole-word recognition. For example, you may have a chart where the child is asked to choose the correct day and put the name in a slot:

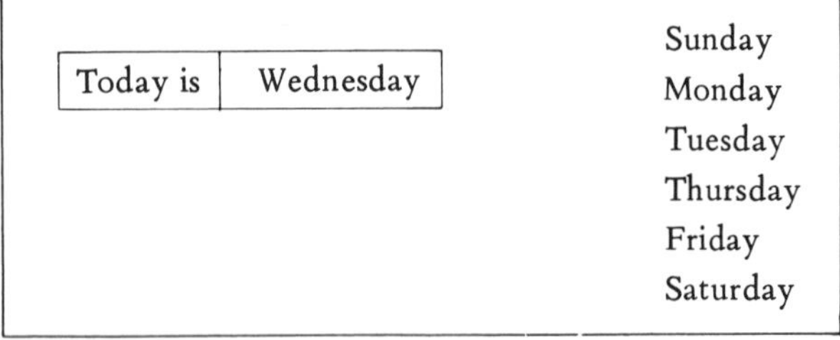

or you may have a sign describing the daily weather with a spinwheel:

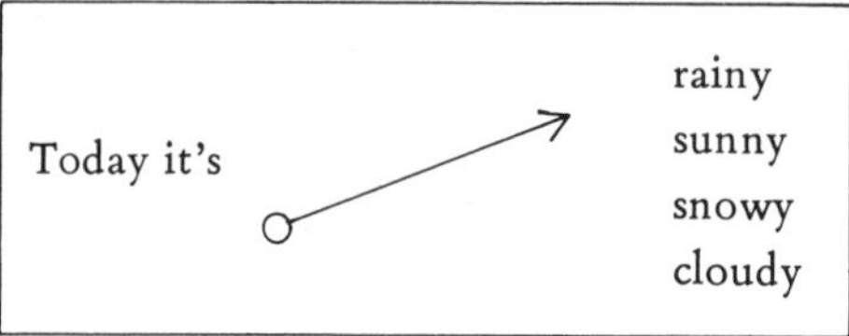

Each child may take a turn pointing the arrow to the weather for each day.

Birthdays are always useful for helping children with sight words. You may make a display like this one:

April Birthdays

Another excellent idea is to label objects or areas in the classroom. Not only will this help children with whole-word recognition, but it can also acquaint children with categorization, a useful technique for beginning readers. You may label parts of the classroom: reading area, play corner, coats and hats, library, and tapes and records. Shelves or materials may also be labeled: puzzles, games, toys, books, paints, crayons, newspapers, and paste. In addition, signs can be useful for teaching sight words:

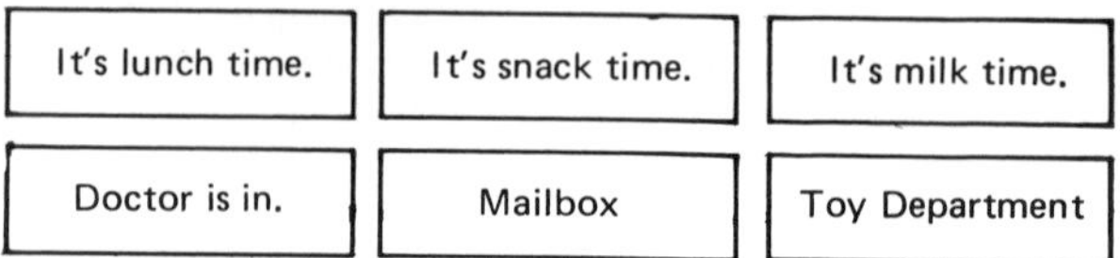

Phonics Techniques. A fun way to introduce children to working with sounds is through rhyme. Ask children to rhyme as many words as they can with the following words: pane, tin, brother. "Name of the Day" is another activity that children enjoy. The teacher says, "The name for today is Paul. Who has a name that begins with the same sound as Paul?" Activities such as these also afford the teacher the opportunity to determine which children seem ready for more phonics activities. Additional phonics activities are included at the end of this chapter.

Language-Experience Techniques. The language-experience approach to reading instruction uses the actual language of the child as its foundation. The key to this activity is participation. You might begin by asking, "Nancy, what is your favorite color?" On a large piece of construction paper (or on the chalkboard) write

Nancy's favorite color is yellow.

Next you should elicit related statements from the other children by asking, "John, can you think of something yellow?"

The sun is yellow.

Lynne's house is yellow.

Anita has a yellow banana.

A lemon is yellow.

Labeling objects or areas in the classroom helps with whole-word recognition and with categorization. (Photo by Linda Lungren.)

You can then end, for example, with

Many things are yellow.

These charts can be illustrated with the children's own art or by using pictures clipped from magazines. Sometimes the illustrations alone create great interest for the children.

Language-experience charts like the one shown here can be constructed for special occasions:

We are going to have a Halloween party.
We will wear costumes.
Jimmy is going to be a ghost.
Robin is going to be a clown.
Frank is going to be a pirate.
Margaret is going to be a farmer.
Hanna is going to be a bunny.
Lena is going to be a rabbit.
Michael is going to be an owl.
Debby is going to be a cowboy.
Sharon is going to be a swan.
Anthony is going to be a monster.
We will have candy and cookies.

At first, the teacher reads the entire chart to the children. Later, children are asked to read their own entries. Eventually, the children will read the entire story.

ASSESSMENT

Growth is a very important measurement for educators. Inevitably, the question will arise as to how to assess the child and the program to determine growth. You may also want to assess some children's readiness with a diagnostic measure. Throughout the next few pages we present some example of assessment instruments that may be useful in the preschool.

Assessing Reading Readiness

These are two basic methods of assessing reading readiness: (1) observation of children using a checklist of characteristics known to be important to success in reading and (2) reading readiness tests. The best measure of a child's readiness involves a combination of both.

Observations and Checklists

Teachers' observations can be potent tools when they are used to foster reading success in the classroom. After making observations, the teacher should record some brief notes about each child's progress. Three checklists are included here that may prove useful to you: (1) Russell's Checklist, (2) the Prereading Rating Scale, and (3) an informal teacher checklist. The Santa Clara County Inventory of Developmental Tasks, an observation instrument, is also included.

Russell's Checklist. Russell's Checklist (1967) can be used to help teachers better organize the knowledge they have acquired about a child or a group of children:

Checklist for Reading Readiness*

Physical Readiness

	Yes	No
1. Eyes		
a. Does the child seem comfortable in the use of his eyes (does not squint, rub eyes, hold materials too close or too far from eyes)?	1. ☐	☐
b. Are the results of clinical tests or an oculist's examination favorable?	2. ☐	☐
2. Ears		
a. Is it apparent through his response to questions or directions that he is able to hear what is said to the class?	3. ☐	☐
3. Speech		
a. Does he articulate clearly?	4. ☐	☐
b. Does he speak in a group with some confidence?	5. ☐	☐
c. Does he speak without gross errors in pronunciation?	6. ☐	☐
d. Does he respond to suggestions for speech improvement?	7. ☐	☐
4. Hand-eye coordination		
Is he able to make his hands work together in cutting, using tools, or bouncing a ball?	8. ☐	☐
5. General health		
a. Does he give an impression of good health?	9. ☐	☐
b. Does he seem well nourished?	10. ☐	☐
c. Does the school physical examination reveal good health?	11. ☐	☐

Social Readiness

	Yes	No
1. Cooperation		
a. Does he work well with a group, taking his share of the responsibility?	12. ☐	☐
b. Does he cooperate in playing games with other children?	13. ☐	☐
c. Can he direct his attention to a specific learning situation?	14. ☐	☐
d. Does he listen rather than interrupt?	15. ☐	☐
2. Sharing		
a. Does he share materials, without monopolizing their use?	16. ☐	☐
b. Does he offer help when another child needs it?	17. ☐	☐
c. Does he await his turn in playing or in games?	18. ☐	☐
d. Does he await his turn for help from the teacher?	19. ☐	☐
3. Self-reliance		
a. Does he work things through for himself without asking the teacher about the next step?	20. ☐	☐
b. Does he take care of his clothing and materials?	21. ☐	☐
c. Does he find something to do when he finishes an assigned task?	22. ☐	☐
d. Does he take good care of materials assigned to him?	23. ☐	☐

Emotional Readiness

	Yes	No
1. Adjustment to tasks		
a. Does the child seek a task, such as drawing, preparing?	24. ☐	☐
b. Does he accept changes in school routine calmly?	25. ☐	☐
c. Does he appear to be happy and well adjusted in schoolwork, as evidenced by relaxed attitude,	26. ☐	☐

*Reprinted from pages 55–7 of the *Manual for Teaching the Readiness Program* by David H. Russell, Odille Ousky, and Grace B. Haynes, rev. ed. Boston: Ginn & Company, 1967.

		Yes	No
	pride in work, and eagerness for a new task?		
d.	Does he follow adult leadership without showing resentment?	27. ☐	☐

2. Poise

a.	Does he accept a certain amount of opposition or defeat without crying or sulking?	28. ☐	☐
b.	Does he meet strangers without displaying unusual shyness?	29. ☐	☐

Psychological Readiness

1. Mind set for reading — 30. ☐ ☐

a.	Does the child appear interested in books and reading?		
b.	Does he ask the meanings of words or signs?	31. ☐	☐
c.	Is he interested in the shapes of unusual words?	32. ☐	☐

2. Mental maturity

a.	Do the results of the child's mental test predict probable success in learning to read?	33. ☐	☐
b.	Can he give reasons for his opinions about his own work or the work of others?	34. ☐	☐
c.	Can he make or draw something to illustrate an idea as well as most children his age?	35. ☐	☐
d.	Is his memory span sufficient to allow memorization of a short poem or song?	36. ☐	☐
e.	Can he tell a story without confusing the order of events?	37. ☐	☐
f.	Can he listen to work for five minutes without restlessness?	38. ☐	☐

3. Mental habits

a.	Has the child established the habit of looking at a succession of items from left to right?	39. ☐	☐
b.	Does his interpretation of pictures extend beyond mere enumeration of details?	40. ☐	☐
c.	Does he grasp the fact that symbols may be associated with spoken language?	41. ☐	☐
d.	Can he predict possible outcomes for a story?	42. ☐	☐
e.	Can he remember the central thought of a story as well as the important details?	43. ☐	☐
f.	Does he alter his own method to profit by another child's example?	44. ☐	☐

4. Language Patterns

a.	Does he take part in class discussions and conversations?	45. ☐	☐
b.	Is he effective in expressing his needs in classroom situations?	46. ☐	☐
c.	Are the words used in the preprimers and the primer part of his listening and speaking vocabulary?	47. ☐	☐
d.	Does he understand the relationship inherent in such words as up and down, top and bottom, big and little?	48. ☐	☐
e.	Does he listen to a story with evidence of enjoyment and the ability to recall parts of it?	49. ☐	☐
f.	Is he able to interpret an experience through dramatic play?	50. ☐	☐

Not all of the items in Russell's checklist will pertain to any one child. However, the primary teacher will help children make a good start if he or she watches the behavior of the children related to the overlapping categories of their physical, social, emotional, and psychological readiness.

Prereading Rating Scale. To use the prereading rating scale, place a check in the appropriate box in front of the following questions. The test manual describes the use and interpretation of this scale in detail.

I. Facility in Oral Language

Yes	No	
☐	☐	1. Does the child take part in class discussions and conversations?
☐	☐	2. Is he effective in expressing his needs in classroom situations?
☐	☐	3. Can he tell a story or relate an experience effectively?

II. Concept and Vocabulary Development

☐ ☐ 4. Is he familiar with the words and concepts related to his environment: for example, people, places, things, and activities?

☐ ☐ 5. Does he have a knowledge of nursery rhymes and traditional children's stories and can he talk about them?

☐ ☐ 6. Has he travel experiences within the community and to other places and can he describe them?

III. Listening Abilities

☐ ☐ 7. Is the child able to understand directions read or told to him?

☐ ☐ 8. Does he possess the ability to recall stories heard by providing the essential information and a sequence of events?

☐ ☐ 9. Is he able to memorize a short poem or story?

☐ ☐ 10. Is he a retentive and responsive listener?

IV. Skills in Critical and Creative Thinking

☐ ☐ 11. Does the child's interpretation of pictures extend beyond mere enumeration of details?

☐ ☐ 12. Can he predict possible outcomes for a story?

☐ ☐ 13. Does he express unique ideas about personal experiences, classroom happenings, and stories he has heard?

☐ ☐ 14. Does he demonstrate flexibility in his thinking patterns or does he have a "one-track mind"?

V. Social Skills

☐ ☐ 15. Is the child accepted by other children?

☐ ☐ 16. Can he play competitively with others?

☐ ☐ 17. Does he listen rather than interrupt?

☐ ☐ 18. Does he await his turn for help from the teacher?

VI. Emotional Development

☐ ☐ 19. Can the child accept some opposition or defeat?

☐ ☐ 20. Is he eager for new tasks and activities?

☐ ☐ 21. Can he accept changes in routine?

☐ ☐ 22. Does he appear to be happy and well adjusted in school work?

VII. Attitude Toward and Interest in Reading

☐ ☐ 23. Does the child ask questions about letters, words, and numbers?

☐ ☐ 24. Has he grasped the fact that "writing is talk written down"?

☐ ☐ 25. Is he enthusiastic about beginning to learn to read?

VIII. Work Habits

☐ ☐ 26. Can the child work by himself?

☐ ☐ 27. Can he see a task through to completion?

☐ ☐ 28. Can he find something to do when he finishes an assigned task?

Before assessing specific cognitive competencies, teachers should be certain that a child is not experiencing visual or auditory difficulties. Auditory and visual acuity may often be assessed initially through observation.

Vision. Vision is obviously a very important factor in reading because reading is basically a visual act. Seeing is central to reading because the printed stimulus enters the mind through the eye.

Spache (1973) describes the visual aspect of the reading process:

> his eyes hop or glide from one stop to the next, from left to right. He does not read in a smooth sweep along the line but only when the eyes are at rest in each fixation. During the sweeps or swings from one fixation to the next, the reader sees nothing clearly, for his eyes are temporarily out of focus. Each fixation, during which reading actually occurs, lasts from about a third of a second in young children to about a quarter of a second at the college level. In all probability most of the thinking that occurs during reading is done during this fractional part of a second, for a number of studies show that the duration of the fixation often lengthens if the reading material is very difficult. The fixations are the heart of the visual reading act, for they occupy about 90 per cent of the time for reading, while interfixation and return sweeps account for the rest.
>
> If the reader fails to recognize what he sees in a fixation, or to understand the idea offered, he tends to

INFORMAL TEACHER CHECKLIST

Student's name: ____________________

Date: ____________________

Skill	Definitely Yes	To a Degree	No	Comment
a. Can recognize letters				
b. Can rhyme				
c. Has memorized alphabet				
d. Can describe actions and pictures				
e. Can sound out words				
f. Can tell story about picture				
g. Can hold a pencil				
h. Can match objects that are the same kind or different				
i. Knows that written words mean spoken words				
j. Can put pictures in order				
k. Can write letters of alphabet				
l. Knows numbers				
m. Can write numbers				
n. Can name the colors				
o. Knows words about time (before, after, until)				
p. Can "read" simple stories				
q. Knows abstract words (happy, brave)				
r. Knows words about space (front, back, above)				
s. Knows common nouns (dog, lake)				

make regression. That is, he makes another fixation at approximately the same place or he swings backward to the left to read again. He may regress several times until the word is recognized or the idea comprehended before resuming the normal left-to-right series of fixations. Then near the end of each line he makes one big return sweep to a fixation close to the beginning of the next line. (p. 9)

The alert classroom teacher is in an excellent position to detect students' vision problems. Any of the following behaviors observed while a child is reading may be a clue that the reader is experiencing visual difficulty: tilting of the head, facial contortions, thrusting the head forward, books held too closely to the face, body tension while observing distant objects, tension during visual work, excessive hand movements, avoidance of close visual work, poor sitting positions, frequent rubbing of eyes, or loss of place while reading.

Hearing. The development of hearing acuity is important enough to be viewed as a reading readiness base.

Both language development and reading *may* be adversely affected by even the smallest hearing impairment. To what degree the lack of auditory ability may impede the reading process is unknown. We do know however, that a child's ability to hear small sound units and add meaning to the units is a word-analysis skill that is essential to reading. Readiness programs should provide tasks that help children perceive partial- as well as whole-word utterances.

Through classroom observation, you may be able to detect children who are experiencing hearing difficulties. Some common symptoms to be alert to are inability to discriminate like or unlike sounds, slurred or inaudible language, cupping one's ear when listening, turning one's ear toward the speaker, requesting that sentences be repeated, interchanging words with similar sounds, frequent colds, earaches, and unnatural tonal quality of the voice.

SANTA CLARA UNIFIED SCHOOL DISTRICT INVENTORY OF DEVELOPMENTAL TASKS

This checklist was developed by the Santa Clara Unified School District in Santa Clara, California to assess vision and hearing and language/thought development. It can also be used to assess certain aspects of readiness.

This instrument is extremely comprehensive and should be examined in terms of the authors' approach and objectives. It has been described in terms of sequential and hierarchical skills; a taxonomic approach was used in its creation. If you look at the scoring sheet first, the ordering will be quite clear.

Each of the skills from coordination to conceptualization is ordered by ascending difficulty. Each of the tasks on the horizontal axis (2.2, creep, to 1.12, jump rope alone) are also ordered by ascending difficulty. The complete list of tasks is presented with a model page from the *Santa Clara Guide.* This example page demonstrates the scoring procedure for each task; tasks 5.8, 5.9, and 5.10 are presented as examples.

Instructional Activities

Level

1. Attending Behavior
2. Coordination

I. 2.2 Can creep—crawling in homolateral, then cross-pattern
2.3 Can walk—timed: Rooster Walk, Elephant Walk, Bear Ostrich
2.4 Can run—3-legged race, Bird Run, Crab Run, Dog Run, Horse Gallop
2.5 Can jump—chairs, blocks, hopscotch
2.6 Can hop—height, time
2.7 Can balance on one foot

II. 2.8 Can use hands and arms—right/left: Follow the Leader, Simon Says, Twister, teach body parts
2.9 Can skip and play skip-ball tag, lean while skipping

III. 2.10 Can balance on walking beam—hands behind back
2.11 Can jump rope, assisted

IV. 2.12 Can jump rope, unassisted

I. 3. Visual motor

3.3.1 Walking—a sitting student watching is able to follow a teacher walking around the room
2 Skipping—a sitting student watching is able to follow another child skipping around the room
3 Object focus—look at ________ until I count to 5
4 Ball roll count aloud until ball stops
5 Gliders
6 Thumb focus
7 Pencil tracking—practice directional objects
3.4 String beads, thread needles, sorting tasks (timed) make chains of colored strips (own patterns)
3.5 Can copy circle—simple forms, complex forms, mazes

II. 3.7 Can copy cross—follow numbers (dot-to-dot)
3.8 Can copy square—the Clock Game

III. 3.6 Can use scissors—zigzag strips, geometric forms
3.10 Can copy letters—copy-speed tests
3.11 Can copy simple words, then cut up and rearrange
3.12 Form patterns—Tinker Toy construction projects (Play Tiles), ball and jacks, drawing people, catching the ball (see Hackett and Jenson, 1966), copying diamond

Santa Clara Unified School District

Name *Jim N.* Date ______

Birthdate ______ School ______

Teacher ______ Grade/Type of Class ______

Area (0 1 2)	1	2	3	4	5	6	7	8	9	10	11	12
Conceptual									9.9 assign number value	9.10 identify position	9.11 tell how 2 items are alike	9.12 sort objects 2 ways
Language								8.8 give personal information	8.9 describe simple objects	8.10 relate words and pictures	8.11 define words	8.12 use correct grammar
Auditory Memory							7.7 perform 3 commands	7.8 repeat a sentence	7.9 repeat a tapping sequence	7.10 repeat 4 numbers	7.11 recall story facts	7.12 repeat 5 numbers
Auditory Perception						6.6 discriminate between com. sound	6.7 identify common sounds	6.8 Locate source of sound	6.9 match beginning sounds	6.10 hear diff. between words	6.11 match rhyming sounds	6.12 screen sounds
Visual Memory					5.5 recall animal pictures	5.6 name objects from memory	5.7 recall 3 color sequence	5.8 recall 2 picture sequence	5.9 reproduce design from memory	5.10 recall picture sequence	5.11 recall 3 part design	5.12 recall word forms
Visual Perception				4.4 match color objects	4.5 match form objects	4.6 match size objects	4.7 match size and form on paper	4.8 match numbers	4.9 match letter forms	4.10 match direction on design	4.11 isolate visual images	4.12 match words
Visual Motor			3.3 follow target with eyes	3.4 string beads	3.5 copy a circle	3.6 cut with scissors	3.7 copy a cross	3.8 copy a square	3.9 tie shoes	3.10 copy letters	3.11 copy sentence	3.12 form patterns
Coordination		2.2 creep	2.3 walk	2.4 run	2.5 jump	2.6 hop	2.7 balance on one foot	2.8 skip	2.9 balance on walking beam	2.10 show left and right	2.11 jump rope assisted	2.12 jump rope alone
	1.1	1.2	1.3	1.4	1.5	1.6	1.7	1.8	1.9	1.10	1.11	1.12
			Level I	Pre-School				Level II 5–5½ yrs		Level III 6–6½ yrs		Level IV 7– yrs

Santa Clara School District inventory of development tasks: an observation guide.

Level

I. 4. Visual perception

4.4 Can match color objects—color-code typing

4.5 Can match form objects—use shape to make pictures; child has to match shapes to build the picture:

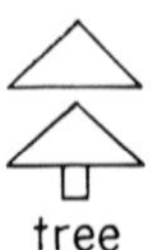

4.6 Can match size objects—parquetry blocks to have child work a design on top of a marked paper

4.7 Can match size and form on paper—have child match a shape on paper

II. 4.8 Can match numbers

4.9 Can match letters

III. 4.10 Can match direction of design—toy card (same direction?), mirror patterns, play camera, obstacle course

IV. 4.11 Can isolate visual images—cloud pictures

4.12 Can match words

I. 4. Visual memory

5.5 Recall animal pictures

5.6 Can name objects from memory—chalk, button

5.7 Reproduce a visual sequence of three colors from memory, five color chips, three color flashcards—tell child to reproduce the order you just gave him or her

5.8 Can recall a picture sequence
One tachistoscope for building visual memory in one frame:

5.9 Can reproduce design from memory, draw from memory:

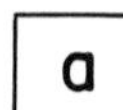

Have children put one letter in a square.

III. 5.10 Can reproduce a sequence of three pictures from memory

5.11 Can recall impart design

IV. 5.12 Can recall word forms:

Arzo | Arpo Arno Arzo

Expose target word for five seconds
Internal design

Match words in a list

Level

6. Auditory perception

6.6 Can discriminate between common sounds; have children close eyes and listen for familiar sounds.

6.7 Can identify common sounds—Cross the Road game

6.8 Can locate source of sounds

6.9 Can match beginning sounds
I'm going to the _______ and I'm taking _______
Rissen-Act game (aural version of Simon Says)
Come Letter game
Shopping at the Supermarket game
Lost Squirrel game

III. 6.10 Can hear fine differences between similar words: badder-lantern/sheep-sleep/cub-cup

IV. 6.11 Can match ending sounds

7. Auditory memory

7.7 Can perform three commands

II. 7.8 Can repeat a sentence—play Echo, rote poem

7.9 Can repeat a tapping sequence
Worksheet . . . .

III. 7.10 Child repeats a series of four numbers:
6 2 9 7 forward, backward

7.11 Can recall story facts—simple comprehension

7.12 Can repeat five numbers:
2 - 4 - 2 - 7 - 8 or A - R - C - K - L

II. 8. Language

8.8 Can give personal information—Who am I?

8.9 Can describe simple objects

The gift box
Who was it?
Come and find it
What do I have in my hand?
Feel box
The Mystery box

III. 8.10 Can relate words and pictures—giraffe/tall, rabbit/hop

8.11 Can define words

IV. 8.12 Can use correct grammar
Improve usage of see/saw
(see *And to Think I Saw It on Mulberry Street*, Dr. Seuss)
Improve usage of was/were

II. 9. Conceptual

9.9 Can assign number value; which is bigger? 5 or 8

III. 9.10 Can identify first, last, or middle

9.11 Can tell how two things are alike
Riddles
Grouping/card-sorting tasks
Find identical objects in a room
Subclasses—for example, animals, dogs, collies
Complete functional sentences—for example, knives are to cut

9.12 Can sort objects two ways:
Place things in categories
Learning-to-think series

Sample Sheet from Guide

Visual Memory Level II Task 5.8

5.8 Reproduce a sequence of two pictures from memory.

Material: Five picture cards, three flashcards

Procedure: Show child a flashcard for five seconds. Say: "First this, then this." Remove card from view. Say: "Make one just like mine." Child reproduces the sequence seen on the flashcard by arranging two pictures in the proper order.

Scoring Procedure

Scoring:

0	1	2
Child has two or more errors.	Child has one error.	Child has all correct.

Visual Memory Level II Task 5.9

5.9 Reproduce designs from memory

Material: Three picture flashcards

Procedure: Say: "I'm going to show you a card with a drawing on it. After I turn the card over, you draw one just like the one on the card." Show child the card for five seconds.

Scoring:

0	1	2
Child cannot reproduce two or more designs.	Child fails to reproduce one design.	Child can reproduce the three forms accurately.

Visual Memory Level III Task 5.10

5.10 Reproduce a sequence of three pictures from memory.

Material: Five picture cards and three picture flashcards.

Procedure: Show child a flashcard for five seconds. Say: "First this, then this," (point left to right). Remove card from view. Say: "Make one just like mine." Child reproduces the sequence seen on the flashcard by arranging three pictures in the proper order.

Scoring:

0	1	2
Child has two or more errors.	Child has one error.	Child has them all correct.

READING READINESS TESTS

In addition to informal checklists and subjective observations, you may also wish to use standardized readiness tests for assessment purposes.

Some readiness tests that may be utilized are the Clymer-Barrett Prereading Battery, Gates-MacGinitie Readiness Skills Test, Harrison-Stroud Reading Readiness Profiles, Macmillan Reading Readiness Test, and the Metropolitan Readiness Test. Most of these include subtests that check vocabulary, knowledge of the letters of the alphabet, visual and auditory discrimination, and hand-eye coordination. By evaluating the child's performance on these tests, the teacher can also gain insight into the child's attention span and ability to listen to and follow directions.

In some school districts, first-grade intelligence tests may also be used. These are similar in some ways to readiness tests; however, readiness tests are believed to provide a better prediction of beginning reading success.

Most formal reading readiness tests include some or all of these tasks: sentence comprehension, associating words and pictures, copying, counting and writing numbers, visual discrimination, auditory discrimination, word recognition, and drawing a human figure.

In special cases, you may desire a comprehensive evaluation of a child's language development. The Illinois Test of Psycholinguistic Abilities (ITPA) will meet this need; however, you should be aware of the following factors;

1. The ITPA is administered individually.
2. It has many subtests and requires a considerable amount of time to administer in total.
3. Considerable practice is required for effective administration and scoring.

For these reasons, it is usually given by a speech or language specialist.

ACTIVITIES FOR PRESCHOOL

The following section lists many activities and games that can be used by teachers who are preparing young children for reading. They have been categorized according to directionality, auditory memory and discrimination, visual memory and discrimination, oral expression and concept building, listening, and activities for parents.

Directionality

Directionality is the ability to know left from right, up and down, backward and forward, and directional orientation. A child's inability to deal accurately with directionality causes frustration and embarrassment.

According to Spache (1972), discriminations of forms and shapes are based fundamentally on the bodily hand-eye experience of each child. These discriminations (left-right, up-down) are first learned in the muscles. During the early years, a child gradually learns to transfer these muscular cues into visual cues. Then the child is ready to apply these visual cues to reading.

Not every child needs training in this area. Bienlien (1981) points out, however, that "because many learning and problem-solving situations require directional orientation, it is important that these skills be specifically taught, if necessary" (p. 43). Following are some practical games and exercises that a classroom teacher might find helpful to aid children in developing skills in directionality.

1. Will You Help?

Goal: Working from left to right

Grade Level: Preschool

Construction and Utilization: Give the children a worksheet divided into different sections. Each section is a separate story, with each story consisting of the same direction from left to right. Ask the children to trace the dashed arrow leading from left to right. See examples on page 89.

2. Simon Says

Goal: Directional orientation

Grade Level: Preschool +

Construction and Utilization: Using the popular Simon

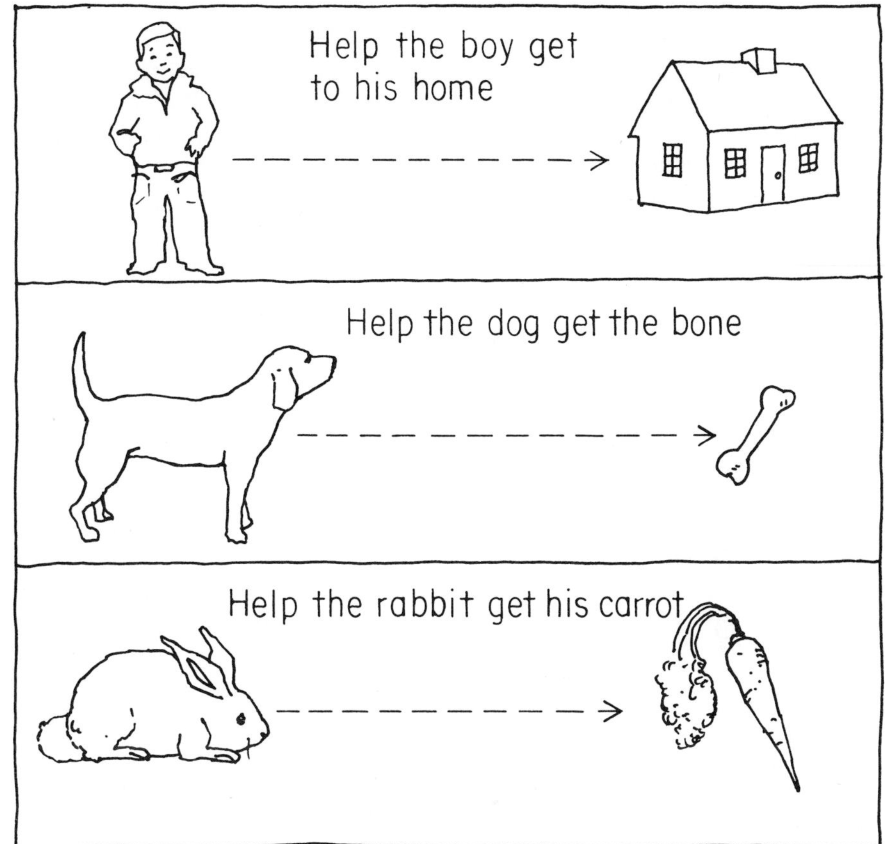

Help the boy get
to his home
Help the dog get the bone
Help the rabbit get his carrot

Says format, incorporate several commands dealing with left and right, up and down, forward and backward. Some examples might be put your left hand on your head, jump forward two steps, turn to the right, point your fingers up.

3. Copy Cats

Goal: Left to right

Grade Level: Preschool +

Construction: The teacher should cut long strips of paper. The paper should be divided in the center. Using a stamp pad and stamps of various shapes or pictures, the teacher stamps several designs in a row on the left of the paper.

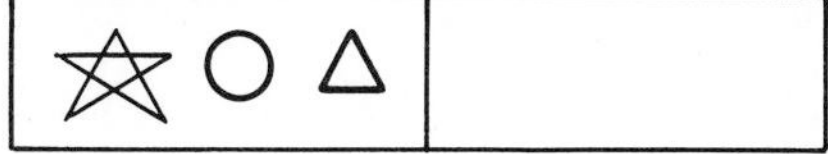

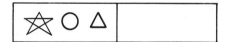

Utilization: The child follows the pattern and duplicates the design.

4. Labeling

Goal: Left and right discrimination

Grade Level: K+

Construction and Utilization: If the child has an individual desk, label the upper-left hand corner with an "L" and the upper-right-hand corner with an "R." At various times during the day, instruct the children to "put your papers on the left side of your desk." Refer to left and right frequently during the day, using the children's labeled desks as reference points.

5. Sewing ABCs

Goal: Left-to-right alphabet recognition

Grade Level: Preschool

Construction: Make large cards out of oak tag. On the left, make capital letters going from top to bottom. Punch a hole to the right of each capital letter. On the right side of the card, make corresponding lowercase alphabet letters with holes punched to the left of the letters.

Utilization: The child then takes colored yarn and "sews" the capital letters to the corresponding small letter, by threading left to right. A variation of this activity would be to use pictures instead of letters.

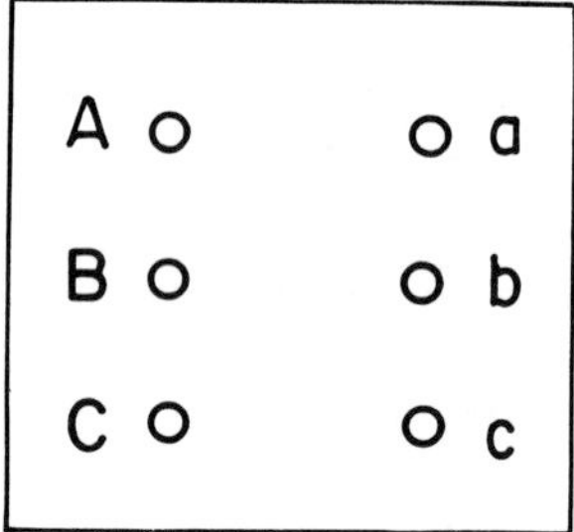

Auditory Memory and Discrimination

The relation between auditory memory and discrimination ability and success in beginning reading is an area of importance to reading educators who continue to debate which sounds a child should be able to discriminate auditorially to succeed in reading. Durkin (1972) feels that discrimination tasks should focus on real words because the children will be working with these words in reading. Spache (1976), on the other hand, feels that this ultimate goal of having children discriminate letter sounds in different words is founded on *many* types of listening exercises. She claims that the child must first be able to discriminate loudness, rhythmic patterns, and pitch, for example. These skills, in her view, are directly related to phonics and structural analysis, for it is here that the child is asked to discriminate the pitches of letter sounds, the loudness that determines accent, and the comparative duration of the sounds of vowels and consonants.

Auditory discrimination is an important skill, and the following section will prove helpful in teaching it.

6. Rhyme Time

Goal: Auditory discrimination

Grade Level: K-1

Construction: Prepare lists of word pairs in which most of the words rhyme. Decide in advance how many sounds you wish to use with your particular group at one time.

rake	band	bed	bend
take	hand	head	send
cot	tall	father	seat
lot	fall	brother	meet
some	fox	man	mint
come	locks	Pam	sent
bet	pen	can	fine
set	pin	ran	pine

Utilization: This activity can be used with individuals or with groups. If the game is to be played with one student, the words should be pronounced distinctly and correctly (but without exaggeration). The student is asked whether or not the pair of words sound alike (rhyme).

To use the game with a group, give each player several red and white tokens or pieces of construction paper. Have each player select a red token if the words rhyme and a white token if they do not. The tokens should be arranged in a straight row across the player's desk. After reading the list, the teacher may check each child's arrangement of tokens quickly to determine is he or she is succeeding or is having difficulty. The teacher may need to remind children of color coding as the game is being played: "If these words rhyme, place a red token in the line; if they do not, place a white token in the line." If some children have difficulty with some of the pairs or if additional reinforcement would be helpful, the teacher can repeat the list and let children respond orally while they check their own arrangements of the tokens.

A circular seating arrangement is not recommended for this game. Children should be seated so that the activities of the other players are not distracting.

7. Musical Medials

Goal: Auditory discrimination—medial sounds

Grade Level: K-1

Construction and Utilization: This activity can be an excellent lead-in to music class. Distribute several instruments such as triangles, bells, shakers, sticks, and tambourines. The teacher reads word pairs, some of which will have the same medial sounds. Whenever the children hear two words with the same medial sound they "make music" with the instruments.

8. What's in a Name?

Goal: Auditory discrimination—beginning sounds

Grade Level: K-1

Construction: This game requires no specially prepared materials. It should be played in a setting having many objects that children can identify.

Utilization: Have children name pairs of objects found in the playing area that begin with the same sound. Examples: cabinet, corner; window, wall; chalk, chair; blocks, blanket; picture, pencil.

Variation: One player may name an object or simply give a word that the player on his or her right must match. Occasional exchanging of positions in a circle is helpful if the game continues very long.

9. Middle Sound Matches

Goal: Auditory discrimination—medial sounds

Grade Level: K-1

Construction: Develop clusters of words similar to those listed here:

	sit		leaf		pet
bat		seen		his	
	man		boat		bill

Utilization: Pronounce the words in each cluster. Ask the child to listen for the word that has the same middle sound as the first word that was read.

Variation: This same technique can be applied to beginning and ending sounds.

10. Sounds Alive!

Goal: Auditory discrimination—heightened awareness and perception of sound.

Grade Level: K-1

Construction: Secure a piano or a xylophone (or you may want to use your own voice for this).

Utilization: Play (or sing) two series of notes and have the children tell you (a) which note was higher or lower and (b) which note was louder or softer.

Variations: Play (or sing) two series of notes and have the children tell you (a) whether the two were the same or different and (b) whether one series was faster or slower. Choose a familiar song and play it (or hum the melody) with varying tempos to suggest different moods. Have children decide how the changes made them feel. For example, "Mary Had a Little Lamb" played with a fast, rollicking rhythm might make them feel like dancing. A slow, heavy rhythm might make them feel tired. To extend the use of this, the children might express their interpretations through facial expressions or body movements.

11. Matched Pairs

Goal: Auditory discrimination—initial sounds

Grade Level: K-1

Construction: Prepare a file of picture cards. On each card have pictures of two common objects, most of which have names beginning with the same sound. Examples might include car, can; dog, door; rug, radio.

Utilization: Children may play this game individually, placing cards with pictures of objects beginning with the same sound in one stack and those that do not in another.

Variation: Prepare picture cards having only one object on each card. Seat a group of children around a table or in a circle on the floor. Deal three cards to each child in the group. Place additional cards in a stack in the center of the group. Each player checks to see if he or she has any matching sound cards. If the child does, he or she places them on the table. Beginning with a designated student, one player draws a card from the hand of the player on his or her left and makes any matches possible. The person from whose hand a card was drawn may pick up a new card from the stack but cannot place any cards on the table until it is his or her turn to play. Proceed around the circle until the stack of cards has been used. Then players having cards left may check around the circle as their turn to play comes, to see who has a matching card. They may then claim it. When the cards have all been matched, each player in turn must call the names of his or her pairs while others listen to determine if the caller is correct.

Note: In this exercise, players must listen to and follow directions, they must cooperate, and they must articulate the names of the pictured objects.

Visual Memory and Discrimination

Research related to the development of visual skills is controversial. Durkin (1974) strongly recommends dealing with visual skills through letters and words. Spache (1976) argues the opposite, suggesting that the first developmental stage of form discrimination is followed by discrimination of three-dimensional materials and, finally, by the use of paper and pencil in two-dimensional materials and, finally, by the use of paper and pencil in two-dimensional reproduction and matching. She feels that shapes and forms *are* closely related to the hand-eye movements of writing and the visual movements of reading.

A 1978 research review states, "We do not recommend perceptual training using nonalphabetic shapes as a means of facilitating reading acquisition, but we do recommend that children learn to discriminate, recognize, and produce letters of the alphabet" (Weaver and Shonkoff, 1978, p. 40).

Whatever view you adopt, it is clear that some children entering school have not reached the stage of development where certain visual cues can be applied to reading. In the following section, the classroom teacher is provided with some useful games to help the child who needs visual skills development.

12. Good Connections

Goal: Visual discrimination—word forms

Grade Level: K-1

Construction: Prepare word cards or worksheets having three-word clusters. If word cards or worksheets are used, they should be similar to the following:

tall	tall bell	time	time tune
same	some same	apple	about apple
bun	bee bun	ram	run ram

Utilization: Players should be asked to draw a line to connect the words that look the same. Or, if word cards are used, they can put the matching words together.

13. Watch Me

Goal: Visual memory

Grade Level: K-1

Construction and Utilization: The teacher walks around the room and touches three objects. In turn, each child touches the same three objects but adds another to the series. Play continues until someone forgets to touch an object.

14. Match the Word

Goal: Visual discrimination—word forms

Grade Level: K-1

Construction: Mark off a piece of heavy chart paper in word-sized squares. Using a magic marker, fill the blocks with word forms. Make a set of word cards.

ball	bee	Ann
town	music	house
mother	goat	school

Utilization: Ask players to match word pairs by placing cards on the square having the same word. This can be an individual game, or, if larger charts are made, it can become a group activity with children taking turns matching word cards that have been distributed to them.

Variation: Children may select a card from the face-up (or face-down) cards to match with a chart word.

15. All Shapes, Sizes, and Colors

Goals: Visual discrimination—shapes, colors, and sizes

Grade Level: K-1

Construction: Prepare a collection of geometric shapes of graduated sizes in the basic colors. (Or prepare wooden shapes that can be painted.) This collection might include circles, squares, rectangles, triangles, hexagons, and octagons.

Utilization: Numerous uses can be made of these:

a. All objects of the same color can be grouped.
b. All objects of the same shape can be grouped.
c. All objects of the same shape and color can be grouped. These also can be arranged in order of size.

Note: It is not necessary for children to be able to name the different geometric forms to play or to benefit from this game. However, the names can be taught as directions are given and games are played.

16. Picture Possibilities

Goal: Visual discrimination—matching pictures that are the same or have some common element

Grade Level: K–1

Construction: Collect and mount individually on cards:

a. Several pairs of identical pictures
b. Several pictures having different content but some similar element
c. Series of pictures that tell a story

Utilization: Suggested uses for each of the collections:

a. Identical picture pairs:
   (1) An individual is given the set and asked to match all pairs.
   (2) Individuals in a group are given a card. Then each player matches his or her card to the identical card of another player.
b. Having several pictures to examine, the player is asked to choose those having (1) something green, (2) a house, (3) people, (4) animals, (5) a country setting, (6) a city setting. The possibilities are limitless.
c. The player is given a set of cards portraying a story and is asked to arrange them in the correct order.

Variation: The player is given one picture that does not belong or is asked to tell the story shown by the cards.

17. Same or Different?

Goal: Visual discrimination—letters

Grade Level: K–1

Construction: This can be played with plastic or styrofoam letters, construction paper letters, or letters on worksheets. Directions here are for using plastic letters.

Utilization:

a. Arrange groups of letters, all of which are identical except for one which is strikingly different. Ask players to find and remove the different letters. Example:

   G G X G G G

   e e e e r e

b. Arrange groups of letters that are more similar. Again, have the students find the different letter. Example:

   B R B B B B

   A A O A A A

c. Give each player several letters and have him or her group the ones that are the same.
d. Make a pattern with letters and let players copy with their letters. Your design may or may not spell a word.

18. Mind Readers

Goal: Color, size, and shape discrimination

Grade Level: K–1

Construction: Use attribute blocks of variously colored and sized triangles, circles, and squares.

Utilization: The teacher tells the class, "I am thinking of an object. You must guess which object I am thinking about by asking me questions that can only be answered with yes or no. For example, you may ask if it is blue, or if it is small, or if it is a triangle." Put out simple objects first, such as circles. When the children get the idea of identifying the selected object, progress to more varied blocks, such as triangles and squares.

Oral Expression and Concept Building

Most educators would agree that what cannot be understood when spoken cannot be understood when written. Quite simply, all the different aspects of language are interrelated and interdependent. The teacher who cares about reading generally plans a program that extends her children's language learning through their everyday experiences. The need for this continuous language learning is stressed by Brown (1958):

> The usefulness of being able to sound a new word depends on the state of the reader's speaking vocabulary. If the word that is unfamiliar in printed form is also unfamiliar in spoken form the reader who can sound it out will not understand the word any better than the reader who cannot sound it. . . . The real advantage in being able to sound a word that is unfamiliar in print only appears when the word is familiar in speech. (p. 69)

The following games and activities may be useful in your language development curriculum.

19. Do You See What I See?

Goal: Listening and using concept-loaded words

Grade Level: Preschool +

Construction and Utilization: The teacher or a child looks around and finds an object in the room. The child then gives other children clues such as "I see something that is big and green. Do you see it?" The other children must keep guessing from these clues.

20. Tell the Story

Goal: Oral interpretation

Grade Level: K-1

Construction: Collect, mount, and laminate pictures of scenes or situations to which prereaders can relate readily.

Utilization: Choose a picture. Allow children in a small group to study the picture for a minute while they decide what story the picture tells. Then let them take turns telling their stories to the class. Encourage reticent children to tell all they can about the picture.

21. That Reminds Me of . . .

Goal: Increase oral vocabulary

Grade Level: Preschool +

Construction and Utilization: Place the name of each new month on chart paper. Then have the class think of as many words as they can that have to do with that month. Children can use these words later to create their own stories. Examples:

November

fall	colorful
birthdays (of students)	pumpkins
chilly	leaves
Thanksgiving	

22. Eat a Letter

Goal: Letter formation

Grade Level: K-1

Construction and Utilization: For reinforcement of letter formation use a cookie or bread recipe to make a dough. Have children form the dough into letter shapes and then bake the shapes. If children need practice in forming particular letters, they may be handed cards that say which letters they are to form.

23. Color Collage

Goal: Color identification

Grade Level: K-1

Construction and Utilization: Each child draws the name of a color from a hat. The teacher can read the name for the child if necessary. The students then look through magazines to find pictures using the color. Pictures should be cut and made into a collage. The teacher should display the collages in the room for the entire class to see.

24. Sharing: Things and Feelings

Goal: Social readiness—sharing

Grade Level: K-1

Construction: Select two children. Secretly plan with them a role-playing situation in which they are to share crayons for work they are doing. (This can be incorporated into regular class activities.) One of the two children uses more than his part of the crayons and refuses to share them. The other student snatches the crayons and runs away with them. Then she refuses to share.

Utilization: Have the situation played as naturally as possible. Then reveal to the rest of the class that this was "make believe." Lead them to discuss how they felt about the situation. Ask them to consider whether they have ever behaved in a similar manner and how such behavior might be changed. Work for suggestions of self-discipline.

25. Troublesome Tongue Twisters

Goal: Taking turns

Grade Level: K-1

Construction and utilization: The teacher recites a tongue twister and selects a student to repeat it. Each speaker selects another student to repeat the tongue twister.

Listening

It has been estimated that elementary school children spend as much as 57.5 percent of their school time listening (Wilt, 1950), yet students do not always know what to listen for or how to listen. For this reason, there has been an increasing emphasis on the teaching of listening as a necessary skill to be developed in the classroom.

Listening is an important skill for group living. The young child needs to listen to and be able to follow directions, enjoy stories, and share the experiences of others. Studies by Pratt (1963) and Duker (1968) indicate that listening skills can be taught in the classroom. Smith (1973) suggests that children who listen well seem to stand a much better chance of developing an extensive oral vocabulary.

Because young children are usually very active and talkative, they are regarded as poor listeners and, therefore, need listening activities that are simple and short. In the following section, some listening games are included that you may find helpful for classroom utilization.

26. Did You Hear?

Goal: Attentive listening

Grade Level: K–1

Construction and Utilization: The teacher (or a child) picks a special word. The teacher sets a time limit and then instructs the children to clap their hands once each time they hear that word.

27. Silence (Montessori technique)

Goal: Attentive listening

Grade Level: Preschool

Construction and Utilization: Have the children close their eyes and listen while the teacher whispers a child's name. When that child hears his name, he may then whisper the name of another child. This can continue until all the children have had a chance to whisper a name.

28. What Was That?

Goal: Attentive listening and discrimination

Grade Level: Preschool–2

Construction and Utilization: The teacher makes a tape recording with a variety of sounds on it. Examples might include dripping water, whistle, bird chirping, whistling teapot, and animal sounds. The students are asked to identify the various sounds they hear.

Parent Activities

Parents often ask what activities they can do with their children to help prepare them for reading. This list of activities may be useful in responding to such a request.

29. Read to Your Child

Goal: Getting the child interested in reading

Grade Level: Preschool

Construction and Utilization: One of the most important things that parents can do for their children is to read to them. This can foster a love of and an interest in reading; it also motivates the children to learn to read so that they can read independently. A child learns many things by imitating adult behavior, and reading is no exception.

30. Day in and Day out Reading

Goal: Recognition of words in everyday experiences

Grade Level: Preschool–1

Construction and Utilization: Your everyday experiences with your child are filled with opportunities to point out and identify words. When preparing a meal, for example, you can point out labels on boxes, cans, and packages. When you and your child go somewhere together, you can discuss street signs, store names, advertisements, vehicle logos, and even numbers (addresses, telephone numbers).

31. Where Does It Go?

Goal: Simple classification

Grade Level: Preschool

Construction and Utilization: You will need an assortment of buttons in different sizes, shapes, and colors and an empty egg carton. The child can sort the buttons by any criterion (for example, by color) and put them into the sections of the egg carton. A simillar activity can also be done with playing cards, which the child can sort by suit, color, number, or picture categories.

32. Identifying Colors

Goal: Association of color name with colors

Grade Level: Preschool

Construction and Utilization: Talk about objects in terms of color. Color surrounds the child. "Let's put on your *blue* shirt today." "Would you like some *orange* sherbet?" Take a walk with your child and have him or her notice the *green* trees and the *red* and *yellow* flowers. Children love to be helpers. Encourage the child to do such things as "Take Daddy his *brown* shoes." Opportunities for using color words are plentiful, and even if using them sounds silly to an adult, the child is learning from them.

QUESTIONS AND RELATED READINGS

If you feel that you have not acquired sufficient knowledge to answer the following questions successfully, we suggest additional related readings.

1. How did readiness become a part of the curriculum in American education?
2. How can readiness be defined as it applies to the child as an individual?
3. What are some of the strategies that can be employed in preschool and kindergarten?
4. In what ways can readiness be assessed?

Goal 1: To help the reader to acquire an understanding of the historical background for readiness practices in the United States.

Question 1: How did readiness become a part of the curriculum in American education?

Durkin, D. "When Should Children Begin to Read?" *Innovation and Change in Reading Instruction.* Sixty-seventh Yearbook of the National Society for the Study of Education, Part II. Chicago: University of Chicago Press, 1968, Chap. 20.

Gates, A. I., and G. L. Bond, "Reading Readiness: A Study of Factors Determining Success and Failure in Beginning Reading." *Teachers College Record* 37 (May 1936), 679–85.

Hillerich, R. *Reading Fundamentals for Preschool and Primary Children.* Columbus, Ohio: Charles E. Merrill Publishing Company, 1977.

Goal 2: To help the reader to understand the nature of readiness as it applies to each student individually.

Question 2: How can readiness be defined as it applies to the child as an individual?

Aukerman, R. C., ed. *Some Persistent Questions on Beginning Reading.* Newark, Del.: International Reading Association, 1972.

Cleland, C. J. "Learning to Read: Piagetian Perspectives for Instruction." *Reading World* 20 (March 1981), 223–4.

Durkin, D. "Pre-test Grade Starts in Reading: Where Do We Stand?" *Educational Leadership* 36 (December 1978), 174–7.

Goal 3: To help the reader to examine components of model prereading programs in preschool and kindergarten.

Question 3: What are some of the strategies that can be employed in preschool and kindergarten?

Hillerich, R. *Reading Fundamentals for Preschool and Primary Children.* Columbus, Ohio: Charles E. Merrill Publishing Company, 1977.

Hoffman, S., and H. T. Fillmer. "Thought, Language, and Reading Readiness." *The Reading Teacher* 33 (December 1979), 290–4.

Weaver, P., and F. Shonkoff. *Research Within Reach: A Research-Guided Response to Concerns of Reading Educators.* Research and Development Interpretation Service/National Institute of Education, Washington, D.C.: U.S. Department of Health, Education and Welfare, 1978.

Goal 4: To help the reader to learn about assessment instruments that measure aspects of readiness.

Question 4: In what ways can readiness be assessed?

Lewkowica, N. J. "Phonemic Awareness Training: What to Teach and How to Teach it." *Journal of Educational Psychology* 72 (October 1980), 686–700.

Mancy, P. T. *Complete Book of Illustrated K–3 Alphabet Games and Activities.* New York: The Center for Applied Research in Education, Inc., 1980.

Weller, T. G., and G. E. MacKinnon, eds. *Reading Research: Advances in Theory and Practice.* Vol. I. New York: Academic Press, Inc., 1979.

BIBLIOGRAPHY

Almenoff, P. "A Comparison of Kindergarten Predictors for Forecasting Second Grade Reading Achievement." Unpublished doctoral dissertation, Hofstra University, Hempstead, N.Y., 1979.

Almy, M. "The Importance of Children's Experiences to Success in Beginning Reading." In *Research in the Three R's*, ed. by R. Hunnicutt and W. Iverson. New York: Harper & Row, Publishers, 1958, pp. 168–93.

Arthur, G. "A Quantitative Study of the Results of Grouping First Grade Children According to Mental Age." *Journal of Educational Research* 12 (October 1925), 173-85.

Artley, A. S. "A Study of Certain Factors Presumed to be Associated with Reading and Speech Difficulties." *Journal of Speech and Hearing Disorders* 13 (1948), 351-60.

Ausubel, D. P. "Viewpoints from Related Disciplines: Human Growth and Development." *Teachers College Record* 60 (February 1959), 245-54.

Ball, S., and G. A. Bogatz. "Research on *Sesame Street*: Some Implications for Compensatory Education." Paper presented at the Second Annual Blumberg Symposium in Early Childhood Education. Baltimore: John Hopkins University Press, 1981.

Barrett, T. C. "Visual Discrimination Tasks as Predictors of First Grade Reading Achievement." *The Reading Teacher* 18 (January 1965), 276-82.

Beck, I. L. "A Longitudinal Study of the Reading Achievement Effects of Formal Reading Instruction in the Kindergarten: A Summative and Formative Evaluation." Unpublished dissertation, University of Pittsburgh, 1973.

Bellugi, U., and R. Brown, eds. *The Acquisition of Language.* Chicago: University of Chicago Press, 1971.

Bienlien, L. R. "Directionality."*Delta Kappa Gamma Bulletin* 47 (Spring 1981), 42-44.

Bond, G. L., and R. Dykstra. "The Cooperative Research Program in First Grade Reading Instruction." *Reading Research Quarterly* 2 (Summer 1967), 5-142.

Brown, R. *Words and Things.* New York: The Free Press, 1958, p. 69.

Bruno-Golden, B., and B. Cutler. "The Development of Perception, Memory, and Counting Skills: At Home or School." *Exceptional Parent* 9 (April 1979), 58-59.

Bryan, B. "Relative Importance of Intelligence and Visual Perception in Predicting Reading Achievement." *California Journal of Educational Research* 15 (February 1964), 2-6.

Buktenica, N. "Group Screening of Auditory and Visual Perception Abilities: An Approach to Perceptual Aspects of Beginning Reading." Paper presented at the American Education Research Association Convention, Washington, D.C., April 1969.

Burns, P., and B. Broman. *The Language Arts in Childhood Education.* Skokie, Ill.: Rand McNally & Company, 1975.

Caldwell, B. M. "The Usefulness of the Critical Period Hypothesis in the Study of Filiative Behavior." In *Contemporary Issues in Developmental Psychology*, ed. by N. D. Endler, L. R. Boulter, and H. Osser. New York: Holt, Rinehart and Winston, 1969, pp. 213-23.

Calfee, R., R. Chapman, and R. Venezky. "How a Child Needs to Think to Learn to Read." In *Cognition in Learning and Memory*, ed. by L. Gregg. New York: John Wiley & Sons, Inc., 1972, pp. 139-82.

Calfee, R., and K. Hoover. "Policy and Practice in Early Education Research." Paper presented at the California Council for Educational Research, Los Angeles, Calif., November 1973.

Carswell, M. D. "Attainment of Selected Concepts Related to Reading by Kindergarten and First Grade Children." Unpublished dissertation, University of Georgia, Athens, 1978.

Central New York Study Council. *Some Helps for Building Guides for Skill Development in the Language Arts: Listening.* Report no. 7. Syracuse, N.Y.: Syracuse University Press, 1957.

Chisholm, D., and J. Knafle. "Letter-Name Knowledge as a Prerequisite to Learning to Read." Paper presented at the American Education Research Association Convention, Washington, D.C., April 1975.

Croft, D. R. *An Activities Handbook for Teachers of Young Children.* 2nd ed. Boston: Houghton Mifflin Company, 1975.

DeHirsch, K., J. J. Jansky, and W. S. Langford. *Predicting Reading Failure.* New York: Harper & Row, Publishers, 1966.

Duker, S. "Listening." In *Encyclopedia of Educational Research,* ed. by R. L. Ebel. 4th ed. New York: Macmillan Publishing Co., Inc., 1969, pp. 747-53.

Durkin, D. *Children Who Read Early: Two Longitudinal Studies.* New York: Bureau of Publications, Teachers College Press, Columbia University, 1966.

____. "A Language Arts Program for Pre-First Grade Children: Two-Year Achievement Report." *Reading Research Quarterly* 5 (Summer 1970), 534-65.

____. *Teaching Them to Read.* Boston: Allyn & Bacon, Inc., 1974.

____. *Teaching Young Children to Read.* Boston: Allyn & Bacon, Inc., 1972.

Durrell, D. D. "First-Grade Reading Success Story: A Summary." *Journal of Education* 140 (February 1958), 2-6.

Farr, R., and N. Roser. *Teaching a Child to Read.* New York: Harcourt Brace Jovanovich, 1979.

Fromkin, V., and R. Rodman. *An Introduction to Language.* New York: Holt, Rinehart and Winston, 1974.

Gates, A. I. "The Necessary Mental Age for Beginning Reading." *Elementary School Journal* 37 (March, 1937), 497-508.

____. "The Role of Personality Maladjustment in Reading Disability." In *Children with Reading Problems,* ed. by G. Matchez. New York: Basic Books, Inc., Publishers, 1968, pp. 80-6.

Gates, A. I., and G. L. Bond. "Reading Readiness: A Study of Factors Determining Success and Failure in Beginning Reading." *Teachers College Record* 37 (May 1936), 679-85.

Gavel, S. R. "June Reading Achievements of First-Grade Children." *Journal of Education* 140 (February 1958), 37–43.
Gesell, A. *The First Five Years of Life.* New York: Harper & Row, Publishers, 1940.
Gesell, A., and F. Ilg. *"The Child From Five to Ten."* New York: Harper & Row, Publishers, 1946.
Gibson, E., and H. Levin, *Psychology of Reading.* Cambridge, Mass.: The MIT Press, 1975.
Gibson, E. J., J. J. Gibson, A. D. Pick, and H. A. Osser. "A Developmental Study of the Discrimination of Letter-Like Forms." *Journal of Comparative and Physiological Psychology* 55 (December 1962), 897–906.
Goins, J. T. "Visual Perception Abilities and Early Reading Progress." *Supplementary Educational Monograph* 87 (1958), 116–28.
Gray, W. S., and R. Klaus. "The Early Training Project: A Seventh-Year Report." *Child Development* 41 (December 1970), 900–24.
Hacket, B., and R. Jenson. *A Guide to Movement Exploration.* Palo Alto, Calif.: Peck Publications, 1966.
Hallgren, B., "Specific Dyslexia: A Clinical and Genetic Study." *Acta Psychiatrica et Neurologia* 65 (1950), 1–287.
Havighurst, R. *Human Development and Education.* New York: Longman, Inc., 1953.
Hiebert, E. H. "Developmental Patterns and Interrelationships of Preschool Children's Print Awareness." *Reading Research Quarterly* 16 (1981) 238–59.
Hillerich, R. *Reading Fundamentals for Preschool and Primary Children.* Columbus, Ohio: Charles E. Merrill Publishing Company, 1977. Chapter opening quotation appears on page 19.
Holmes, M. C. "Investigation of Reading Readiness of First Grade Entrants." *Childhood Education* 3 (January 1927), 215–21.
Huey, E. B. *The Psychology and Pedagogy of Reading.* New York: Macmillan Publishing Co., Inc., 1908.
Hunt, J. M. *Intelligence and Experience.* New York: The Ronald Press Company, 1961.
Ingram, T. T. S. "The Nature of Dyslexia." In *Early Experience and Visual Information Processing in Perceptual and Reading Disorders,* ed. by F. A. Young and D. B. Lindsley. Washington, D.C.: National Academy of Sciences, 1970, pp. 405–44.
Jansky, J., and K. DeHirsch. *Preventing Reading Failure.* New York: Harper & Row, Publishers, 1972.
Kak, A. K. "Schemata: Its Role in the Early Reading Process of Children." *Reading World* 19 (March 1980), 295–301.
King, E. M., and D. T. Friesen. "Children Who Read in Kindergarten." *Alberta Journal of Educational Research* 18 (September 1972), 147–61.
Kohlberg, L. "Early Education: A Cognitive Developmental View." *Child Development* 39 (December 1968), 1013–62.
Lenneberg, E. H. *Biological Foundations of Language,* New York: John Wiley & Sons, Inc., 1967.
"Let's Look at First Graders—A Guide to Understanding and Fostering Intellectual Development in Young Children." New York: New York City Board of Education, 1965.
Loban, W. D. *The Language of Elementary School Children.* Urbana, Ill.: National Council of Teachers of English, 1963.
Lohnes, P. R., and M. M. Gray. "Intellectual Development and the Cooperative Reading Studies." *Reading Research Quarterly* VIII:I (Fall 1972), 53–61.
Lundsteen, S. W. *Listening: Its Impact on Reading and the Other Language Arts.* NCTE/ERIC Clearinghouse on Reading and Communication Skills. Urbana, Ill.: National Council of Teachers of English, 1979.
MacGinitie, W. N., Evaluating Readiness for Learning to Read: A Critical Review and Evaluation of Research." *Reading Research Quarterly* 4 (Spring 1969), 396–410.
McKee, D., Brzeinski, J., and L. Harrison. "The Effectiveness of Teaching Reading in Kindergarten." Cooperative Research Project No. 5-1371. Denver Public Schools and Colorado State Department of Education, 1966.
McNeill, D. "Developmental Psycholinguistics." In *The Genesis of Language,* ed. by F. Smith and G. A. Miller. Cambridge, Mass.: The MIT Press, 1966.
Menyuk, P. "Syntactic Structures in the Language of Children." The *Journal of Child Development* 34 (1963), 407–22.
_____. *The Acquisition and Development of Language.* Englewood Cliffs, N.J.: Prentice-Hall, Inc., 1971.
Money, J. "On Learning and Not Learning to Read." In *The Disabled Reader: Education of the Dyslexic Child,* ed. by J. Money. Baltimore: Johns Hopkins University Press, 1966, pp. 21–40.
Monroe, M. "Reading Aptitude Tests for the Prediction of Success and Failure in Beginning Reading." *Education* 56 (September 1935), 7–14.
Morgan, E. "Efficacy of Two Tests in Differentiating Potentially Low from Average and High First Grade Readers." *Journal of Educational Research* 53 (April 1960), 300–4.
Morphett, M., and C. Washburne. "When Should Children Begin to Read?" *Elementary School Journal* 31 (March 1931), 496–503.

Muehl, S., and S. Kremenack. "Ability to Match Information Within and Between Auditory and Visual Sense Modalities and Subsequent Reading Achievement," *Journal of Educational Psychology* 57 (August 1966), 230–9.

National Task Force. *Dyslexia and Related Reading Disorders.* Washington, D.C.: U.S. Department of Health, Education, and Welfare, 1969.

Neuman, S. B. "Effect of Teaching Auditory Perceptual Skills on Reading Achievement in First Grade." *The Reading Teacher* 34 (January 1981), 422–6.

"New York City Guide to Understanding and Fostering Intellectual Development." In *Young Child,* New York City Schools, 1965.

Olson, A. V. "Growth in Word Perception Ability as It Relates to Success in Beginning Reading." *Journal of Education* 140 (February 1958), 25–36.

Olson, A. V., and C. Johnson. "Structure and Predictive Validity of the Frostig Developmental Test of Visual Perception in Grades One and Three." *Journal of Special Education* 4 (1970), 49–52.

Olson, W. C. *Child Development.* Lexington, Mass.: D. C. Heath & Company, 1949.

Owens, F., P. Adams, and T. Forrest. "Learning Disabilities in Children: Sibling Studies." *Bulletin of the Orton Society* 18 (1968), 33-62.

Piaget, J. *The Origins of Intelligence in Children.* New York: W. W. Norton & Company, Inc., 1963. (a)

____. *Plays, Dreams, and Imitation in Childhood.* New York: W. W. Norton & Company, Inc., 1963 (b)

Pratt, L. E. "The Experimental Evaluation of a Program for the Improvement of Listening in the Elementary School." Unpublished doctoral dissertation, State University of Iowa, Ames, 1963.

Reed, M. M. *An Investigation of Practices in First Grade Admission and Promotion.* New York: Bureau of Publications, Teachers College Press, Columbia University, 1927.

Richek, M. A. "Readiness Skills That Predict Initial Word Learning Using Two Different Methods of Instruction." *Reading Research Quarterly* 13 (1977–1978), 200–21.

Robinson, H. M. "Vocabulary: Speaking, Listening, Reading and Writing." In *Reading and the Language Arts,* ed. by H. A. Robinson. Chicago: Universtiy of Chicago Press, 1963.

Russell, D. *Manual for Teaching the Reading Readiness Program.* Lexington, Mass.: Ginn and Company, 1967.

Russell, D., and E. Karp. *Reading Aids Through the Grades.* New York: Bureau of Publications, Teachers College, Columbia University, 1956.

Samuels, S. J. "The Effect of Letter-Name Knowledge on Learning to Read." *American Educational Research Journal* 9 (Winter 1972), 65–74.

Satz, P., and G. K. van Nostrand. "Developmental Dyslexia: An Evaluation of a Theory." In *The Disabled Learner: Early Detection and Intervention,* ed. by P. Satz and J. J. Ross. The Netherlands: University of Rotterdam Press, 1973.

Schickedanz, J., M. York, I. Stewart, and D. White. *Strategies for Teaching Young Children.* Englewood Cliffs, N.J.: Prentice-Hall, Inc., 1977.

Schickedanz, J., and J. Flood. U.S. Office of Education Proposal for Reading Improvement Act Pre-elementary Grant, January 1976.

Shapiro, B., and R. Willford. "ITA. Kindergarten or First Grade?" *The Reading Teacher,* (January 1969), 307–11.

Silberberg, N., et al. "The Effects of Kindergarten Instruction in Alphabet and Numbers on First Grade Reading." Final Report. Minneapolis: Kenny Rehabilitation Institute, 1968.

Silvaroli, N. J. "Factors in Predicting Children's Success in First Grade Reading." In *Reading and Inquiry International,* Vol. 10. Reading Association Conference Readings, ed. by J. A. Figure. Newark, Del.: IRA Publications, 1965, pp. 296–8.

Silver, L. B. "Familial Patterns in Children with Neurologically Based Learning Disabilities." *Journal of Learning Disabilities* 4 (August–September 1971), 349–58.

Smith, J. *Creative Teaching of the Language Arts in the Elementary School.* Boston: Allyn & Bacon, Inc., 1973.

Spache, E. *Reading Activities for Child Involvement.* 2nd ed. Boston: Allyn & Bacon, Inc., 1976.

Spache, G. D., and E. B. Spache, *Reading in the Elementary School.* 3rd ed. Boston: Allyn & Bacon, Inc., 1973.

Suppes, P. "Mathematical Concept Formation in Children." *American Psychologist* 21 (February 1966), 139–50.

Teale, W. H. "Positive Environments for Learning to Read: What Studies of Early Readers Tell Us." *Language Arts* 55 (November–December 1978), 922–32.

Weaver, P., and F. Shonkoff. *Research Within Reach: A Research-Guided Response to Concerns of Reading Educators.* Research and Development Interpretation Service/National Institute of Education. Washington, D.C.: U.S. Department of Health, Education, and Welfare, 1978.

Weiner, M., and S. Feldman. "Validation Studies of a Reading Prognosis Test for Children of Lower and Middle Socio-Economic Status." *Educational and Psychological Measurement* 23 (Winter 1963), 807–14.

White, B. *First Three Years.* Englewood Cliffs, N.J.: Prentice-Hall, Inc., 1975.

Wilson, F. T., and C. W. Fleming. "Grade Trends in Reading Progress in Kindergarten and Primary Grades." *Journal of Educational Psychology* 31 (January 1940), 1–13.

Wilt, M. "A Study of Teacher Awareness of Listening as a Factor in Elementary Education." *Journal of Educational Research* 43 (April 1950), 626–36.

SECTION III

The Reading Process

In this section, we identify, isolate, and discuss each component of reading to explore the complex processes that are involved in understanding texts.

Reading and comprehension are synonymous. Reading comprehension is the acquisition of information from printed materials. For students to construct meaning from written language, they must have an understanding of *graphophonemic* cues, to help them to decode words; *syntactic* cues, to assist them to understand words in texts; and *semantic* cues, to enable them to understand the meaning of the words as they are written in a particular text.

The chapters of this section are concerned with reading comprehension as an active process that requires the reader to integrate new information include the development of schema, organizing aids for the topics of the text, the language of the text, and the rhetorical style of the text.

Also included is a discussion of reading study skills and reading skills and strategies needed by students to master the complexities of content area materials. Too often, these areas do not receive appropriate instructional attention; therefore, the theory and activities in this section have been designed specifically to help *all* teachers plan and implement content area reading teaching strategies.

CHAPTER 5

Breaking the Code: Understanding and Using *Phonics* as a Word Analysis Strategy

Poor readers have a specific difficulty in accessing a phonetic representation derived from script.

M. Leonard et al., 1977

The teaching of reading involves the specialized task of helping children to decode the written symbolic representation of a language they already know. (Photo by Linda Lungren.)

GOALS: To help the reader to

1. Understand the relation between the visual mode and reading.
2. Comprehend the relation between the auditory mode and reading.
3. Determine what constitutes phonics.
4. Establish a phonics instruction program.

The teaching of reading involves the specialized task of helping children to decode the written, symbolic representation of a language they already know. They can say and hear, with understanding, words that they have never seen written down. When faced with their own language in this written "code," many children fail to understand that they really already know what is on that page.

Educators have argued that children have a *spoken* as well as a *listening, writing,* and *reading* vocabulary. It should be noted that a knowledge of the language of one of these vocabularies does not necessarily ensure transfer to knowledge of any other vocabularies. The first vocabulary that a child acquires is a listening vocabulary, followed closely by the development of a spoken vocabulary. The individual's expressive capabilities generally exceed his or her expressive vocabulary. Most individuals auditorially comprehend a far greater range of language patterns than they use in their spoken text. Listening vocabulary also exceeds one's early writing and reading vocabularies.

As we discussed in Chapter 2, most children have acquired a basic understanding of the syntax of the English language by the age of four. By the time children begin formal instruction in reading, they have also acquired a substantial listening and speaking vocabulary, and they can discriminate between most of the sounds of the English language. By using these natural abilities, the transition from the listening and speaking vocabulary to the reading vocabulary can be made.

In this chapter we describe the process of beginning reading by explaining the phenomenon of decoding. Considerable background information and implementation strategies are presented here in order to help you teach children to read.

PERCEPTION: THE VISUAL MODE

Visual perception is the ability to visually "take in" objects in the environment. By four years of age the

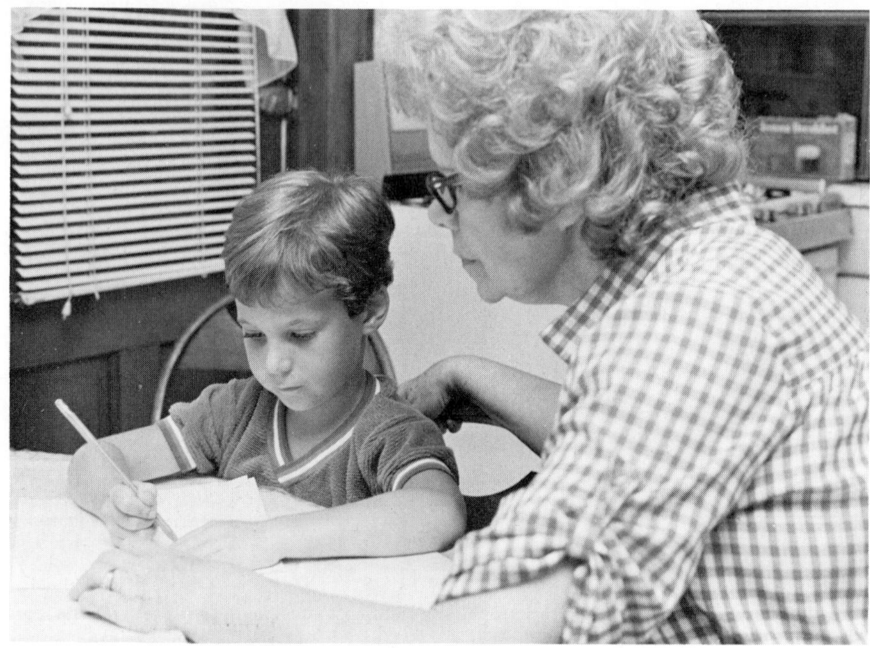

The child who begins first grade knowing the letter names is more likely to succeed in learning to read than the child who has not acquired this knowledge. (Photo by Paul Hill.)

normal child not only is able to perceive objects but, more important to the task of reading, he or she is able to discriminate among fine details.

Letter Discrimination

mn bd oc qg and OO JT EF RP

Even competent readers will admit that the differences between the letters in these pairs are very subtle. It is therefore easy to understand why children may not always see the differences between them. Difficulty with visual discrimination of letters becomes even more obvious when one reads the following sentences quickly:

Sam sat in the sand in front of the band.

The band man said to Sam, "Sit on the land, not the sand."

Sam's son ran on the land and landed in the sand by the band.

Did Sam and his son land by the band man on the sand?

Did you have any difficulty in discriminating between letters as you read sentences? Gibson and Levin (1975) have researched the ways in which children identify abstract visual symbols, and they suggest that they use a set of distinctive features to discriminate between these symbols. The four distinctive features that children attend to are the following:

1. *Straight-Line Segments.* In the roman alphabet there are several letters that are made up of this type of visual symbol:

   E F H I L T

2. *Curved Segments.* In the roman alphabet the following letters are examples of curved segmental visual symbols:

   C O

3. *Symmetries.* The following alphabetic letters constitute examples of symmetries:

   M W X

4. *Discontinuities.* Several alphabetic letters are examples of discontinuities:

   K B G J

Children process these features to arrive at a solution. For example, one child might look at the letter *J* and see straight-line segments and curved segments. A second child may see only the top part of the letter *J*, which looks like *T*, and may fail to perceive the curved line segments and to attend to both stimuli. To avoid initial difficulties, teachers can instruct children in letter discrimination using a developmental plan similar to the one described here:

Step 1: Ask children to look at single letters.

1. a d
2. d b
3. b a
4. b b

Step 2: Ask children if the letters are the same or different.

Step 3: Ask children to look at sets of letters and to determine if the sets are the same or different.

ad ba db ad

Step 4: Ask children to examine sets of words and determine if they are the same or different.

| pat | mat | | sat | rat | | cat | bat |

After children have completed this assignment, it is important to explain to them that one word can be written in at least four different forms. Then you may want to progress to

Step 5: Ask children to examine the following set of words and to determine if they are the same or different.

MAT mat *mat* *Mat*

Knowledge of Letter Names

The importance of letter-name knowledge in the acquisition of reading skills has long been a subject of interest and study for teachers and researchers. Durkin (1974) argues convincingly that knowledge of letter names is helpful in carrying out initial reading instruction. Murphy and Durrell (1972) use a letter-naming system for initial phonics instruction.

D:	Initial	Medial	Final
	dean	audience	lad
	decent	comedian	speed
	decide	radio	plaid

With the creation of *Sesame Street*, most middle-class children arrive in kindergarten knowing the names of the letters of the English alphabet. The child who begins first grade knowing the letter names is more likely to succeed in learning to read than is the child who has not acquired this knowledge. This is correlation, not causality. Several studies have shown that teaching the letter names in isolation does not have much effect on later success in reading (Jenkins et al., 1972; Silberberg et al., 1972). However, knowledge of letter names is an indicator of the student's readiness for reading. The student who has learned the alphabet before coming to school most likely comes from a reading-rich environment and is eager to learn to read. Letter names are relatively easy to learn, and the experience may, through general transfer, facilitate in the more difficult task of making letter-sound associations.

PERCEPTION: THE AUDITORY MODE

Although children may not be able to produce all the sounds of English until they are eight or nine years old, they are capable of perceiving almost all the sounds of their environment by the age of four. However, an inability to produce sounds does not necessarily interfere with the ability to begin reading.

Auditory Discrimination

As well as being able to perceive, or "take in," the sounds in their environment, young children are capable of discriminating between the sounds of English; they can distinguish between minimal pairs of sounds (e.g., *mit* and *pit* and *man* and *pan*) and match sounds (e.g., *box* begins with a /b/ sound). Which of the following words begin with the same sound?

tail pail bail snail

As a teacher, your task is to assist the child in "breaking the code" by helping him or her to recognize the correspondence between letters and sounds. The child has language—*phonology, syntax*, and *vocabulary*—and can discriminate visually between many different symbols. The child often knows the names of the letters of the alphabet and can discriminate between them. All that the child needs now is the knowledge of the code, the link between letters and sounds.

Letter-Sound Correspondence (Grapheme-Phoneme Correspondence)

The following charts containing consonant and vowel correspondences in various positions within a word can be extremely useful to you in teaching students how to analyze words. The lists represent most of the sounds of the English language. If a child is able to read all these correspondences within meaningful contexts, he or she can probably be considered a competent decoder. The phonemes in these lists, written between slash marks (e.g., /t/), are symbols for the sounds of English. Each single symbol stands for only one sound. (See pp. 107–110.)

Discriminating Between Words

A Chinese woman studying in the United States for the first time quipped, "All words in English look alike." Most first-graders who are beginning to read might quickly agree with her. As competent adult readers of English, we might argue with her that all words in Chinese look the same to us. If you were beginning to learn to read in Chinese, you would probably see sentences like these:

日日有明月

秋季末森林内村人採木材

CONSONANT CORRESPONDENCE IN VARIOUS POSITIONS

Letter-Sound (Grapheme-Phoneme) Relationships

Phoneme	Grapheme	Phoneme in Initial Position	Phoneme in Medial Position	Phoneme in Final Position
/b/	b	bake	cabin	tub
		baby		
/k/	c	cat	become	zinc
	k	kite	making	work
	ck		tracking	back
	x		complexion	
	ch	charisma	anchor	monarch
			echo	
	qu	queen	racquet	bisque
	cc		account	
/s/	s	suit	insert	porous
	ss		massive	miss
			possessive	possess
	c	cite	pencil	face
			glacier	
	st		gristle	
			listen	
			fasten	
	ps	pseudonym		
	sc	scissors	Pisces	
			visceral	
/č/	ch	cherry	lecher	such
	t		picture	
			nature	
			virtue	
/d/	d	dish	body	hard
	dd		middle	odd
/f/	f	fish	safer	roof
	ff		raffle	muff
	ph	phonograph	telephone	graph
		phrase	cephalic	
	gh		roughness	tough
/g/	g	good	rigor	bag
	gh	ghetto		ugh
		ghost		
	gg		trigger	egg
	gu	guest	beguile	rogue
/ǰ/	g	gin	wager	
	du		schedule	
	j	jug	prejudice	raj
	dg		dredger	hedge
	dj	djinn	adjoin	
/h/	h	horse	behead	
	wh	who		
/l/	l	long	bailer	boil
	ll		falling	doll
/m/	m	moon	hamper	dream
	mb		tombstone	dumb
	mm		drummer	

Phoneme	Grapheme	Phoneme in Initial Position	Phoneme in Medial Position	Phoneme in Final Position
/n/	n	nest	diner	pin
	nn		thinner	
	gn	gnat	signing	assign
	kn	knight		
	pn	pneumonia		
	mn	mnemonic		
/ŋ/	ng		stinger	song
	n		think	
/p/	p	point	viper	hip
	pp		hopping	
/r/	r	rat	boring	tear
	rr		merry	purr
	wr	write		
	rh	rhyme	hemorrhage	myrrh
/š/	sh	shadow	crashing	dish
	s	sure	nauseous	
	ci		precious	
	ce		ocean	
	ss		obsession	
			pressure	
			assure	
	ch	chic	machine	
		chevron		
	ti		motion	
/t/	t	test	water	cat
	tt		letter	putt
	pt	ptomaine		receipt
	bt		debtor	debt
/θ/	th	thin	ether	wreath
/ð/	th	then	either	bathe
/v/	v	violet	hover	dove
/w/	w	will	throwing	how
	ui		sanguine	
/ks/	x		toxic	box
	cc		accent	
/y/	y	yarn	lawyer	day
/z/	z	zipper	razor	blaze
	s		visit	logs
			amuser	
	zz		drizzle	fizz
			nozzle	
	x	xanadu		
		xylophone		
/ž/	z	Xanadu	azure	
	su		treasure	
	si		allusion	
	ss		fissure	
	g	genre	regime	decoupage
/gz/	x	xeroxes	exhibit	
			exert	
			exact	
	gs			digs
/θ/	th	think, thin	mythology	bath, lath
/ð/	th	thy, this	bother	bathe, lathe

VOWEL CORRESPONDENCES

Sound Label	Vowel	Letter Label	Example
Unglided or short	/æ/	a	an
		au	laugh
Glided or long	/ey/	a.e*	pane, bake
		ai	rain
		ea	steak
		ei	feign
		ay	tray
		ey	obey
		ua	guard
Unglided or short	/e/	e	pen
		ea	lead
		eo	jeopardy
		ei	heifer
		ai	stair
		ie	friendly
Glided or long	/iy/	e.e*	mete
		e	he
		ea	heat
		ee	tree
		ei	conceive
		ie	believe
Unglided or short	/i/	i	hit
		ui	guild
		y	gym
		u	business
Glided or long	/ay/	i.e	write
		uy	buyers
		ie	tries
		ai	aisle
		ia	trial
		y	spy
		i	find
		ei	height
		igh	night
Unglided or short	/a/	oo	not
Glided or long	/ow/	o.e	shone
		oa	goat
		ow	snow
		o	no
		ew	sewing
		ough	dough, through
		oo	floor
		eau	beau, bureau
		oe	hoe, doe
Unglided or short	/ə/	u	nut
		oo	flood
		ou	enough, curious, pretentious
		ough	rough
		o	hover, cover, come
Glided or long	/yuw/	u.e	yule
		eau	beauty
		ew	dew

*The dot stands for omitted letter.

Sound Label	Vowel	Letter Label	Example
Unglided or short	/u/	oo	good
		u	put
Unglided or short	/ɔ/	a	walk
		au	maul
		o	frog
		aw	saw
Unglided or dipthong	/aw/	ow	down
		ou	cloud
Glided or dipthong	/ y/	oy	boy
		oi	loin

Do the words in each of these sentences look alike to you? This is what happens to the young child when he or she first sees written words in English. We have to be extremely patient to make sure that the child can distinguish each separate word.

In English the two Chinese sentences mean

Every day the moon is bright.

At the end of autumn, the villager gathers wood in the forest.

We have no difficulty in distinguishing each word in the English translation. This proficiency is the result of a great deal of exercise, practice, and experience. Most children in the first grade are able to distinguish the letters of the English alphabet in a relatively short period of time and with little practice, but it is not uncommon to hear a young child say, "I have trouble reading the little words." This might mean that young children have difficulty in quickly identifying little words such as *in, and, on, an, or, for, from, form, foam.* Test yourself again by quickly reading these "little" words aloud.

inn on and
ache ate ace atom
to too toe tow
it in if
of off oft often
for from form foam
each eat ear earn
here her hear heart

Now read this brief passage as quickly as possible.

He often saw Susie swimming in the sea just short of the shore and today he saw her sink several times. With his ear Hank tried to hear her heart beat as he dragged her drowning from the foam. As he towed her up to the beach she reached over and tickled his toes twice. "Just a joke!" she cried as she crawled across the street.

After learning to identify letters by processing visual and/or auditory stimuli the child acquires the ability to discriminate between words. The next step in the process is the *decoding* of written words for meaning—children attach these written symbols to concepts. One of the first decoding strategies that children use is a phonics strategy. An explanation of the content of phonics and its application to reading is presented throughout the remainder of this chapter.

TEACHING PHONICS

The Sound System of English

The study of speech sounds is called *phonetics.* The phonetician studies the physiological and acoustical aspects of speech sounds. The study of the sound system of a language is *phonology*. The phonologist seeks information about the relevant sounds of a language. Educators have taken the analysis of the relevant sounds of English and used them to set up letter-sound correspondences to aid in the teaching of reading. The educator has taken the most useful parts of this knowledge for the teaching of reading and has attempted to develop a body of knowledge called *phonics.* This subset, phonics, includes the most common sounds of English and the most frequently used letter or strings of letters that record these sounds.

The Origin of Phonics Instruction

Phonics instruction originated in the 1890s, before which time most children learned to read by memorizing and reciting the alphabet. Emphasis began to shift from exercises in naming letters to exercises in naming the sounds of the letters. Phonics exercises were unrelated to meaning. Children would recite "phonics"; for example, they would practice the following drill:

da	ra	pa	sa	la	na	ma
di	re	pi	si	li	ne	me

Rebecca Pollard's *Synthetic Method* was introduced to schools in 1890. In this method she advocated the following practices:

1. Articulation drills in single letters before reading instruction began.
2. Drills for each consonant; each consonant had the sound of a syllable: /bə/, /kə/, /də/, /fə/, /gə/, /lə/, /mə/, /nə/, /pə/, /rə/, /sə/, /tə/.
3. Drills on phonograms (word families): *bill, pill, mill, drill, trill; back, pack, track.*
4. Drills on diacritical markings in sentences: The lamb̸ ate the grass̸ at nīg̸h̸t.
5. Drills on phrases in sentences: The dog/sat/on his tail,/and/he yelped.

Syllable Strategies

The teaching of syllabication as a tool for decoding written words is one of the many controversial areas in reading instruction. (For a discussion of this controversy, see Groff, 1981.) The research does, however, seem to indicate that teaching vowels out of the context of the syllable has little meaning for the beginning reader. You may, therefore, wish to begin phonics instruction with the introduction of the syllable. But what is a syllable?

As Groff (1971) points out in his discussion of the syllable, English is "stress-timed language"; therefore, it is easy to identify the number of syllables in a given word, but it is very difficult to determine syllable boundaries. The syllable presents a problem similar to that of a cartographer deciding exactly how much of the valley between the two hills belongs to each hill.

Syllables are usually determined by the existence of a vowel, and the phonological features that exist within a syllable are a vowel and often consonants; together they result in emphasis on one part of the syllable. Gibson and Levin (1975) found that some children use such units quite automatically when they are decoding; instruction in the visual recognition of larger letter units facilitates many children's word-recognition abilities. It should also be noted that the visual identification of letter sequences for pronunciation can facilitate the decoding process.

Knowledge of syllables and stress in English will also be helpful for you when you are structuring an application of phonics strategies. It is therefore important to remember that the following generalizations are subject to scrutiny and exception.

1. All syllables have a vowel sound: pen - cil, why.
2. When a final *e* appears as a vowel in a word, it usually does not add another sound: tale.
3. When two consonants exist between two vowels, a syllable division usually exists between the consonants: spar - tan.
4. When a consonant exists between two vowels, a division occurs between the first vowel and the consonant: o - dor.
5. If the single consonant preceded and followed by vowels is *x*, the *x* and the preceding vowel are in the same syllable: ex - it.
6. When a word ends in *le*, and it is preceded by a consonant, the consonant and *le* make up a new syllable: bun - dle, can - dle.

Stress Point Rules

English is a time-sequence language; it contains stress points that are essential to pronunciation and meaning. Knowledge of the stress rules of English will provide children with one more tool to help them to decode unknown words. The following brief set of rules may help you in teaching stress points as part of your phonics program:

1. If a root has two syllables, the first is *usually* stressed: mother, battle, summer.
2. If a root has two syllables and the second syllable con-

tains a long vowel, the syllable with the long vowel is stressed: precede, canteen.

3. If the first vowel in a multisyllabic root is a short vowel and it precedes two consonants, the first syllable is stressed: permanent, sacrosanct.
4. If the first vowel in a multisyllabic root is a long vowel and it precedes two consonants, the syllable that contains the long vowel is stressed: alliance.
5. If a final syllable contains *le*, it is not stressed: table, preamble.

Although stress is an important component in learning to read, it is extremely difficult to write an exhaustive list of rules that do not have a long list of exceptions. Most children, however, who have heard a word spoken will be able to find the stress pattern while they are decoding the constituent parts of the word. When decoding con. sti. tu. tion, the child will be able to match the stress with his or her knowledge of the spoken word.

Before beginning our discussion of consonant and vowel sounds, it seems important to present the total array of English phonemes with a transcription key, using the symbols of a modified International Phonetic Alphabet. This key will help you to aid children in deciphering words that they are unable to pronounce. For example, if a child did not know how to pronounce *treasure*, he might say /*tri . sur*/ instead of /trezr/. The phoneme list follows.

ENGLISH PHONEMES WITH KEY FOR PRONUNCIATION

Consonants

Phoneme Symbol	Key Word (target underlined)	Transcription of Key Word
/p/	pin	/pIn/
/b/	bin	/bIn/
/t/	tile	/taIl/
/d/	dime	/daIm/
/k/	cope	/kop/
/g/	goat	/got/
/č/ modified	church	/čərč/
/ǰ/ modified	judge	/ǰəǰ/
/f/	find	/faInd/
/v/	vine	/vaIn/
/θ/	thin	/θIn/
/ð/	that	/ðæt/
/s/	sin	/sIn/
/z/	zip	/zIp/
/š/ modified	shoot	/šut/
/ž/ modified	treasure	/trɛžar/
/l/	lid	/lId/
/r/	rid	/rId/
/m/	mean	/min/
/n/	neat	/niyt/
n	sing	/sIŋ/
/w/	wit	/wIt/
/y/	yelp	/yɛlp/

Vowels

Phoneme Symbol	Key Word (target underlined)	Transcription of Key Word
iy	seat	/sit/
I	sit	/sIt/
ei	gait	/get/
ɛ	get	/gɛt/
æ	rat	/ræt/
a	top	/tap/
ɔ	bought	/bɔt/
oʊ	coat	/koʊt/
ʊ	put	/pʊt/
	root	/rut/
ə or ^	but	/bət/
oI oi	toy	/toI/
aʊ	cow	/kaʊ/
ai	kite	/kait/

Consonants

Before beginning our discussion of the phonetic elements, it may be useful to add a cautionary note about teaching children the actual technical language used to describe sounds in English (cluster, digraph, dipthong, etc.). Research indicates that, while many children use correspondences accurately, they may have difficulty understanding the terms used to explain these sounds. Examples often are easier to cope with than are definitions (Tovey, 1980).

It is important to understand the difference between sounds and letters and the correspondences (or lack of correspondence) among them. Several consonant letters have only one sound in English; others have a variety of sounds. In the next few pages we introduce you to a series of rules that governs the pronunciation of consonant graphemes.

The beginning sounds in the following words are representative of the most common consonant sounds. Each of these sixteen graphemes (letters) usually has only one sound in initial position in English words (especially in common ones).

b	baby	n	not
d	doll	p	pipe
f	fan	r	ran
h	home	s	saw
j	juice	t	took
k	kit	v	very
l	lady	w	was
m	me	z	zoo

As you have noticed, words beginning with the consonants *c, g, q,* and *x* were not included in the list. *C* and *g* were not included because they have two sounds: *hard* and *soft* sounds. *Q* and *x* do not represent sounds of their own.

C

For example, the *hard* sound of *c* is heard in words such as cat, candy, cape, coat, cuff, cough, calf, fabric, and picnic. The *hard* sound of *c* is heard as /k/.

The *soft* sound of *c* is heard in words such as city, cell, cent, cigar, and cyst. The *soft* sound of *c* is heard as /s/.

Hard *c* sound	Soft *c* sound
cat	city
candy	cell
coat	cent
cuff	cigar

When the consonant *c* is followed by *a, o,* or *u*, the sound of /k/ is often heard. When *c* is followed by *e, i,* or *y*, the sound of /s/ is often heard.

G

The *hard* sound of *g* is heard in words such as game, give, get, gate, goat, good, gulp, and guest and in the final position in words such as bag and gag. The *hard* sound of *g* is heard as /g/.

The *soft* sound of *g* is heard in words such as gym, gentle, gender, and gent and in the final position in badge and rage. The *soft* sound of *g* is heard as /ǰ/.

Hard *g* sound	Soft *g* sound
game	gender
good	gentle
guest	gym

In many words when the consonant *g* is followed by *e, i,* or *y*, the sound of /ǰ/ is heard; and when *g* is followed by *a, o,* or *u*, the hard or /g/ sound is heard. This principle is not as reliable in its application to *g* as it is in application to *c*.

Q

The consonant *q* always appears with the vowel *u*. Together they represent the following sounds:

qu as the /k/ sound: antique, queue

qu as the /kw/ sound: quack, quail, quarrel, queen, quiz, quote.

X

The letter *x*, like the letter *q*, represents no sound of its own and is used to represent the following sounds:

x as the /z/ sound: xylem, xylophone, Xavier, Xenia

x as the /ks/ sound: sox, taxi

x as the /gz/ sound: exist, exotic

W and Y

The letters *w* and *y* are unique because they can function as both consonants and vowels.

The letters *w* and *y* function as consonants only when they appear as the initial letter in a syllable.

yard canyon war wallow

yawn	you	walnut	went
young	yelp	wilt	wonder
yellow			

Consonant Clusters (sometimes called blends). When two or more consonants appear in succession in a word and are both pronounced or are blended when pronouncing the word, they are referred to as consonant blends. The following examples constitute a sample of consonant blends in the initial position:

bloom	flee	prize	screw
bright	free	scout	straight
clown	glad	skate	stop
cradle	grape	sled	sweep
draw	kraut	smile	train
dwarf	plum	snap	twinkle

The following words are examples of consonant blends in the final position:

-st	-sk	-sp	-nt	-nd
must	ask	crisp	went	bend
fast	desk	grasp	spent	send
rest	brisk	clasp	want	sand
coast	task	wisp	ant	hand
most	dusk	rasp	bent	wind
last	risk		elephant	hind
best	mask			blind
toast	tusk			
chest	flask			

-mp	-ft	-lm	-nk	-lt
limp	left	calm	bunk	felt
skimp	lift	balm	sunk	melt
lamp	loft		brink	belt
clamp	graft		sink	malt
lump	raft		honk	salt
dump			spunk	bolt
bump				silt
				hilt
				pelt

-lp	-ld
help	held
gulp	hold
kelp	old
scalp	mold
	told
	cold

Consonant Digraphs. When two consonants appear together in a word and form one sound, they are referred to as a *consonant digraph.* The following words contain examples of consonant digraphs:

chair them ring

In the case of the /th/ sound, it is necessary to distinguish between the voiced sound and voiceless sound.

Voiced sound /ð/	Voiceless sound /θ/
they	thigh
them	thimble
bathe	bath
breathe	breath

The following list contains examples of consonant digraphs in the initial position:

ch	sh	ð th (voiced)
chin	ship	this
chip	shall	those
chop	shop	that
chuck	shell	there
chill	shut	them
chest	shot	they
chair	shout	these
chick	shed	the
chain	shoe	than
cherries	shine	their

θ th (voiceless)	wh
thin	whip
thank	whistle
thick	whale
thump	whisper
thorn	whack
thumb	wheel
thing	white
thunder	when
thud	where
thermometer	why

The following lists contain consonant digraphs in the final position:

ch	sh	th (θ)	ng
much	wish	tooth	bang
rich	mash	both	sang
lunch	dash	health	sing
such	dish	math	ring
crunch	crush	with	song
march	flash	breath	strong
branch	fresh	wealth	rung
ranch	fish	myth	hung
bunch	wash	bath	gang
pinch	rash	path	wing

Some additional terminology may be useful for you when you are implementing your reading program.

Voiced Consonants. The consonants /b/, /d/, /g/, /j/, /l/, /m/, /n/, /r/, /v/, /w/, /th/ (this), and /z/ are referred to as *voiced consonants*. When these consonants are articulated, they cause the vocal chords to vibrate.

Voiceless Consonants. The consonants /p/, /f/, /h/, /k/, /s/ (sand), /t/, /th/ (thin), /sh/, /ch/, and /wh/ are referred to as *voiceless consonants*. When these consonants are articulated the vocal chords do not vibrate.

Stops. The consonants /b/, /p/, /d/, /t/, /k/, and /g/ are referred to as *oral stops*. They must be pronounced instantaneously; they cannot be held as the phoneme /m/ is.

Vowels

The vowel sounds of English are often complex for children learning to read because each vowel letter may represent several sounds. In the next few pages, we introduce you to English vowels and their orthographic representations and the rules governing them. It is extremely important for you to familiarize yourself with these rules to adapt these principles to your reading instruction program.

The following letters represent vowel sounds in English:

a e i o u (y, w, and h)

	Long vowel sound	Short vowel sound
a	able	apple
e	evil	elephant
i	ice	igloo
o	ocean	octopus
u	universe	umbrella

The long vowel sounds can be marked with a macron (–):

ā	ē	ī	ō	ū
āim	ēat	īce	ōld	ūse
gāme	bēlow	bīke	hōme	fūse
bāit		tīe	bōat	mūse

If you are assisting children who need work on vowel sounds, the following systematic list of long and short vowels in the initial and medial position may be of some help to you. You could make flashcards or charts of these lists to help your children who are having trouble with these sounds.

Long Vowel Sounds in the Initial Position

ā	ē	ī	ō	ū
able	evil	ice	ocean	universe
ache	even	ivy	okay	unicorn
ace	evening	ivory	Oklahoma	unite

acre	equal	item	over	use
age	equation	icing	obey	useless
acorn	Egypt	identify	oh	usual
ape	ecology	idea	old	ukelele
alien	ego	I	open	Utah
Asia	eve	Irish	oval	uniform
April	Edith	iodine	oboe	unicycle

Long Vowel Sounds in the Medial Position

ā	ē	ī	ō	ū
cake	Pete	like	cone	cube
race	Steve	nine	stove	mule
game	beet	white	note	cute
place	tree	ride	home	fume
cage	feet	bike	nose	mute
gate	seed	kite	smoke	fuse
face	meet	mile	hope	fuel
save	sweet	wipe	stone	hue
snake	green	line	vote	mule
lake	wheel			

The short vowel sounds can be marked with a breve (˘):

ă	ĕ	ĭ	ŏ	ŭ
at	egg	if	odd	us
bat	set	kit	flop	run

Short Vowel Sounds in the Initial Position

ă	ĕ	ĭ	ŏ	ŭ
apple	elephant	igloo	octopus	umbrella
as	Eskimo	it	ox	uncle
astronaut	enter	is	on	us
after	exit	if	ostrich	under
ant	edge	invade	olive	umpire
alligator	eggs	ill	October	ugly
actor	enemy	itch	object	up
am	engine	improve	odd	unlucky
afternoon	escape	ignore	otter	until
anniversary	energy	insect	opera	usher

Short Vowel Sounds in the Medial Position

ă	ĕ	ĭ	ŏ	ŭ
bad	pet	big	pot	bus
bat	ten	ship	fox	tub
black	fell	tin	block	puppy
cap	bed	hill	box	jump
cat	help	sit	top	much
can	step	stick	doll	sum
clap	red	pig	sock	cup
dad	sled	kit	mop	duck
fan	spell	win	hot	cut
map	yes	pin	shop	rug
rag	west	dig	rock	drum
tan	tent	hid	lock	club
sad	hen	bit	drop	fun
man	well	will	spot	but

When you are introducing vowel usage, the following rules may be extremely useful.

SHORT VOWELS

1. A vowel grapheme represents a short vowel when it is followed by a consonant unit (closed syllable); for example, fat, crab, pet, pit, skin, put, rat.
2. A vowel grapheme represents a short vowel when it is followed by a compound consonant unit; for example, dg/ǰ/ or -x/ks/: badge, tax.
3. A vowel grapheme represents a short vowel when it is followed by a *cluster* of consonants; *tt* or *st* as in fast.
4. A vowel grapheme represents a short vowel when it is followed by a double consonant; for example, little, ball, bottle.

LONG VOWELS

1. A vowel grapheme represents a long vowel sound when it is followed by a consonant, which in turn is followed by *l* or *r* and another vowel, usually a final *e*; for example, cradle, table, ogre.
2. The vowel graphemes *oi* and *oy* represent the gliding sound /ɔy/ in boil and boy. The vowel graphemes *ou* and *ow* represent the gliding sound /aw/ in bout and how.

3. When the vowel grapheme occurs as the last unit of a syllable and when it is preceded by a consonant unit, the grapheme will represent the long vowel (open syllable sound; for example, Jimmy, tree, knee.

Schwa Sound. The schwa sound /ə/ appears often in unaccented syllables of polysyllabic words, and in many recent dictionaries the symbol appears in some accented syllables. The schwa /ə/ is illustrated in the following words:

about	/əbaut´/
April	/e´prəl/
arrogant	/ær´əgənt/
taken	/tei´kən/
lemon	/lɛ´mən/
circus	/sər´kəs/
upon	/əpon´/

As you can see, the schwa sound may be represented by any vowel letter if the vowel is found in an unaccented syllable. It may also represent the short *u* sound and the vowel sound in *er, ir,* and *ur.*

Y as a Vowel. The letter *y* generally represents the short *i* sound when it appears within a syllable not containing another vowel letter.

myth system lymph

The letter *y* generally represents the long $\bar{i}$ sound when it appears as the final sound in a one-syllable word.

by cry my

The letter *y* generally represents the long $\bar{e}$ sound when it appears as the final letter in a multisyllabic word.

fairy dairy berry briskly

The letter *y* generally represents the long $\bar{i}$ sound when it appears as the final letter of a syllable that is not the last syllable in a multisyllabic word.

cycle dynamo asylum

Vowel Digraphs. A vowel digraph is written as two vowel letters that represent the equivalent of *one* vowel sound.

treat	bait	touch	cough
through	caught	wood	cool
shook	loan	weigh	soup
receive	bread	read	

Burmeister (1968) examined the frequency of adjacent vowel pairs that act as vowel digraphs and found that certain vowel pairs consistently acted as digraphs and certain vowel pairs rarely acted as digraphs:

Grapheme	Example	Pronunciation	Frequency (number of cases)	Percentage
ay	gray	/ā/	132/137	96.4
oa	road	/ō/	129/138	93.5
ai	villain	/ə/	9/309	2.9
ea	sergeant	/ə/	3/545	0.5

Based on information reported in L. E. Burmeister, "Vowel Pairs," *The Reading Teacher* (February 1968), 447--8. Reprinted by permission of the International Reading Association and the author.

Burmeister's work suggests that teachers should be extremely cautious when they use phonics as their principal mode of instruction. Many of the rules of phonics are consistent and extremely useful, but some phonics principles need constant re-examination.

Vowel Diphthong. A vowel diphthong consists of two vowel letters in one syllable, *both* of which are sounded. The first vowel is strongly sounded, whereas the second becomes a glided or semivowel sound.

Example of vowel diphthongs in English are:

Diphthong	Example
oi	soil
oy	toy
ou	pout
ow	howl

Burmeister (1968) also researched the frequency of adjacent vowel pairs that act as diphthongs and found similar patterns of consistency and inconsistency (see below).

When reviewing this information, it becomes obvious that phonics rules may need re-examination.

Generalized Vowel Rules. The following rules may be of help to you when you introduce your students to the concept of vowel sounds:

1. When a single vowel in a syllable is followed by the letter *r*, the vowel is affected or influenced by it.

chart	dollar	fir	for	work
cart	her	first	fort	curl

2. When the letter *a* is followed by *ll* or *lk* in a syllable, the *a* represents the sound of *ou* or *au*. (as in <u>aw</u>ful)

all	wall	enthrall	walk
ball	call	chalk	talk

3. When the letter combinations *gn, gh, ght, ld,* or *nd* follow the single letter *i* in a syllable, the *i* represents a long vowel sound.

sign	tight	mild
sigh	light	mind

4. When the letter combination *ld* follows the single letter *o* in a syllable, the letter *o* generally represents a long vowel sound.

cold	fold	mold
told	old	behold

5. When the letter combination *re* follows a single vowel in a syllable, one generally hears an *r* sound.

core	tire	bore	lure
here	tore	cure	

6. *E*'s at the end of a monosyllabic word usually make the first vowel a long sound. This is sometimes called the Magic *E* Rule.

cape	time	dote	vane	note
hate	wine	cube	Pete	code
made	bite	cute	dime	hope
pane	ripe	dude	hide	rode
rate	pine	tube	kite	robe

Grapheme	Example	Pronunciation	Frequency (number of cases)	Percentage
oi	moist	oi	100/102	98.0
au	auction	ɔ aw	167/178	93.8
oy	coyote	oi ay	1/50	2.0
oo	blood	ə or Λ	7/315	2.2

Phonics Generalizations

Clymer (1963), Bailey (1967), and Emans (1967) published comprehensive views of the overall usefulness of traditional phonics rules, which were generally substantiated by a more recent study (Caldwell et al., 1978). Perhaps you recognize these rules because, as children, many of you had to memorize them in isolation. The rules may or may not have been valuable in teaching you to read. Some were probably useful, and some may have confused you. The confusion may have resulted from rules that were too complex to be useful while decoding or were not consistent. The figures that are presented in the following chart explain the usefulness of most of the rules of phonics and the frequency with which these rules apply in English. Rules with high frequency (consistent about 75 per cent of the time) are especially helpful when you are teaching children how to decode. Rules with low frequency (inconsistent) should not be taught because they are not useful in learning decoding skills; no phonics rules should ever be taught in isolation. These rules are only useful in applied contexts.

It is one thing to understand the theoretical principles behind phonics instruction and quite another thing to know how to actually use phonics strategies to help children develop meaningful decoding skills. Answers to questions such as these may help you to design your phonics program: "How do I begin phonics instruction?" "Is there a proper sequence for instruction?" "How should I incorporate syllabication into a phonics program?" and "Do I teach a formal program of phonics to children who already understand and use most of the phonics strategy rules?"

Of course every teaching situation is unique, based totally on the teacher and the students involved. You, as the instructor, must be knowledgeable and comfortable with phonics strategies to generate enthusiasm and comprehension in your students. We hope to answer some instructional questions that teachers of reading often ask, re-emphasizing the fact that *every situation is different*. The instructional answers that are provided here are only guidelines for you as a teacher. You will have to implement the teaching of phonics in your own particular manner to meet the specific needs of your students.

Phonics is one of the most difficult and important strategies for the student to learn. While the controversy over how much phonics to teach still continues, with professional opinion now perhaps swinging back in favor of more intensive phonics programs (Fulwiler and Groff, 1980), not every child necessarily can or should learn phonics.

The question that is asked most frequently when one is teaching phonics strategies is "What should I teach first?" This question implies an effective introductory sequence for teaching consonant and vowel correspondences. The answer to this involved question is complex, but recent research has offered us a number of reasonable suggestions:

Suggestion #1: Offer vowel instruction early in the program.

Many teachers and publishers of packaged programs have delayed in teaching the vowels because they believed that all the consonants needed to be taught first. They argued that the regularity of the letter-sound correspondence of the consonants helped the child to learn to read. This view failed to consider the high correlation between the letter-sound correspondences of many vowels and the importance of the ability to decode vowels to read independently without adult guidance. Most children can clearly articulate vowels by the ages of four or five, and most children have had some experience in decoding vowels, such as when they memorize certain sign words like *Mary* or *Happy Birthday*. The early introduction of vowels will help children to become involved independently in the reading process from the beginning of instruction.

Suggestion #2: Structure vowel sequence on decibel rating.

A logical question follows: Which vowel sounds should be introduced in early stages of instruction? Fairbanks's (1966) work may provide us with some meaningful answers. He found that the vowels in the following words have different decibel levels:

Vowel		Decibel
cap	/æ/	4.5
talk	/ə/	3.8

FORTY-FIVE PHONIC GENERALIZATIONS

	Percentage of Utility		
	Clymer	Bailey	Emans
	Grades 1–3	Grades 1–6	Grades 4+
1. When there are two vowels side by side, the long sound of the first vowel is heard and the second vowel is usually silent: leader.	45	34	18
2. When a vowel is in the middle of a one-syllable word, the vowel is short: bed.	62	71	73
3. If the only vowel letter is at the end of a word, the letter usually stands for a long sound: go.	74	76	33
4. When there are two vowels, one of which is a final *e*, the first vowel is long and the *e* is silent: cradle.	63	57	63
5. The *r* gives the preceding vowel a sound that is neither long nor short: part.	78	86	82
6. The first vowel is usually long and the second silent in the digraphs *ai, ea, oa,* and *ui*: claim, beam, roam, suit.	66	60	58
ai		71	
ea		56	
oa		95	
ee		87	
ui		10	
7. In the phonogram *ie*, the *i* is silent and the *e* is long: grieve.	17	31	23
8. Words having double *e* usually have the long *e* sound: meet.	98	87	100
9. When words end with silent *e*, the preceding *a* or *i* is long: amaze.	60	50	48
10. In *ay*, the *y* is silent and gives *a* its long sound: spray.	78	88	100
11. When the letter *i* is followed by the letters *gh*, the *i* usually stands for its long sound and the *gh* is silent: light.	71	71	100
12. When *a* follows *w* in a word, it usually has the sound of *a* as in *was*: wand.	32	22	28
13. When *e* is followed by *w*, the vowel sound is the same as that represented by *oo*: shrewd.	35	40	14
14. The two letters *ow* make the long *o* sound: row.	59	55	50
15. *W* is sometimes a vowel and follows the vowel digraph rule: arrow.	40	33	31
16. When *y* is the final letter in a word, it usually has a vowel sound: lady.	84	89	98
17. When *y* is used as a vowel in words, it sometimes has the sound of long *i*: ally.	15	11	4
18. The letter *a* has the same sound (o) when followed by *l, w,* and *u*: raw.	48	34	24
19. When *a* is followed by *r* and final *e*, we expect to hear the sound: charge.	90	96	100
20. When *c* and *h* are next to each other, they make only one sound: charge.	100	100	100
21. *Ch* is usually pronounced as it is in *kitchen, catch,* and *chair*, not like *ah*: pitch.	95	87	67

	Grades 1–3	Grades 1–6	Grades 4+
22. When *c* if followed by *e* or *i*, the sound of *s* is likely to be heard: glance.	96	92	90
23. When the letter *c* is followed by *o* or *a*, the sound of *k* is likely to be heard: canal.	100	100	100
24. The letter *g* is often sounded as the *j* in *jump* when it precedes the letters *i* or *e*: gem.	64	78	80
25. When *ght* is seen in a word, *gh* is silent: tight.	100	100	100
26. When a word begins with *kn*, the *k* is silent: knife.	100	100	100
27. When a word begins with *wr*, the *w* is silent: wrap.	100	100	100
28. When two of the same consonants are side by side, only one is heard: dollar.	91	100	100
29. When a word ends in *ck*, it has the same last sound as in *lock*: neck.	100	100	100
30. In most two-syllable words, the first syllable is accented: bottom.	85	81	75
31. If *a, in, re, ex, de,* or *be* is the first syllable in a word, it is usually unaccented: reply.	87	84	83
32. In most two-syllable words that end in a consonant followed by *y*, the first syllable is accented and the last is unaccented: paltry.	96	97	100
33. One vowel letter in an accented syllable has its short sound: banish.	61	65	64
34. When *y* or *ey* is seen in the last syllable that is not accented, the long sound of *e* is heard: paltry.	0	0	1
35. When *ture* is the final syllable in a word, it is unaccented: future.	100	100	100
36. When *tion* is the final syllable in a word, it is unaccented: notion.	100	100	100
37. In many two- and three-syllable words, the final *e* lengthens the vowel in the last syllable: costume.	46	46	42
38. If the first vowel sound in a word is followed by two consonants, the first syllable usually ends with the first of the two consonants: dinner.	72	78	80
39. If the first vowel sound in a word is followed by a single consonant, the consonant usually begins the second syllable: china.	44	50	47
40. If the last syllable of a word ends in *le*, the consonant preceding the *le* usually begins the last syllable: gable.	97	93	97
41. When the first vowel element in a word is followed by *th, ch,* or *sh*, these symbols are not broken when the word is divided into syllables and may go with either the first or second syllable: fashion.	100	100	100
42. In a word of more than one syllable, the letter *v* usually goes with the preceding vowel to form a syllable: covet.	73	65	40
43. When a word has only one vowel letter, the vowel sound is likely to be short: crib.	57	69	70
44. When there is one *e* in a word that ends in a consonant, the *e* usually has a short sound: held.	76	92	83
45. When the last syllable is the sound *r*, it is unaccented: ever.	95	79	96

shop	/a/	3.7
choke	/ow/	3.0
check	/e/	2.2
coop	/yu/	1.9
cup	/ə/	1.1
cheek	/iy/	1.0
cook	/u/	0.3
pit	/i/	0.0

These findings suggest that children can discriminate vowel sounds with the highest decibel ratings. This natural phenomenon should dictate the sequence of instruction.

Suggestion #3: Present visually contrastive pairs (*d* and *b*) very early in the program.

In the past teachers have been encouraged not to introduce simultaneously two letters that are easily confused with one another, such as *d* and *b*. However, the current opinion is that the introduction of contrastive pairs *d* and *b, q* and *p, m* and *n* has instructional value because the child has to focus on the distinctive features of each of the letters within a specific context (*d*og, *b*og). Researchers argue that this initial struggle will reduce later confusion for the child.

Suggestion #4: Teach the first consonants by using the /f/, /s/, /v/, /m/ sound in words.

Coleman (1967) maintains that children find continuants, *consonants* that are produced by the constant release of air, for example, /s/, easier to blend with other sounds than consonants that are formed by stopping the air flow, for example, /t/. He suggests that the continuants are easily learned and should be among the first consonants that are taught to the beginning reader. Continuants include

/s/	sat
/f/	fat
/v/	vat

Suggestion #5: Introduce children to variations in letter-sound correspondences.

One criticism of the linguistic method of reading instruction, which is described in detail in Chapter 10, is that children begin to expect one-to-one letter-sound correspondence (pan, man, can), and they find it difficult to transfer their phonics strategies to new words that do not fit the pattern. These findings suggest that children should be introduced to variations in letter-sound correspondence from the very beginning, such as *tap* and *tape*, to prepare them for later reading.

Suggestion #6: Make good use of natural order strategies.

Marchbanks and Levin (1965) maintain that it is also important to note that children use definite *order* strategies when they are decoding. First they look at the initial letter(s), then they look at the final letter(s), then the middle letter(s), then the configuration of the word. This phenomenon underlines the need for children to learn independent phonics strategies so that they will be able to cope with new and unfamiliar words.

Suggestion #7: Introduce children to word families through phonograms.

Teachers often use word families to teach phonics. These word families are sometimes called phonogram lists. Teachers can use these lists to create games or activities for children. (See activity 11 at the end of this chapter.)

Brainstorming as a group is another way of establishing the concept of phonograms. Write *an* on the board and have them tell you as many words as they can that have this sound. Then change *an* to *ane* and ask them again to give you words that have the same ending sound as *ane.*

"Vocabulary of Rhymes," *Webster's Collegiate Dictionary*, is a very useful list of phonograms that may help you in developing students' early reading vocabularies. Examples from that list are ace brace, face, grace, lace, place, race, space

eal deal, heal, meal, real, seal, veal

ig big, dig, fig, jig, pig, rig, wig

oat boat, coat, float, goat, throat

Suggestion #8: Practice new words by verbalizing.

Kibby (1979) found that words learned by the phonics method were retained best when practiced in the production mode or by verbalization. Using the concept of phonograms in oral games or using the tape recorder may facilitate retention of words learned phonetically.

Based on these suggestions, the following questions and answers will help you to develop a sequential, effective phonics teaching program.

1. Q. Should consonants or vowels be introduced first?

   A. They should be introduced simultaneously, taking into consideration the information we have acquired about continuants /f/, /s/, /v/, and /m/; visually similar graphemes *b* and *d*; and decibel loading for certain vowel sounds.

2. Q. Should short vowels or long vowels be introduced first?

   A. Short vowels should be introduced in the order

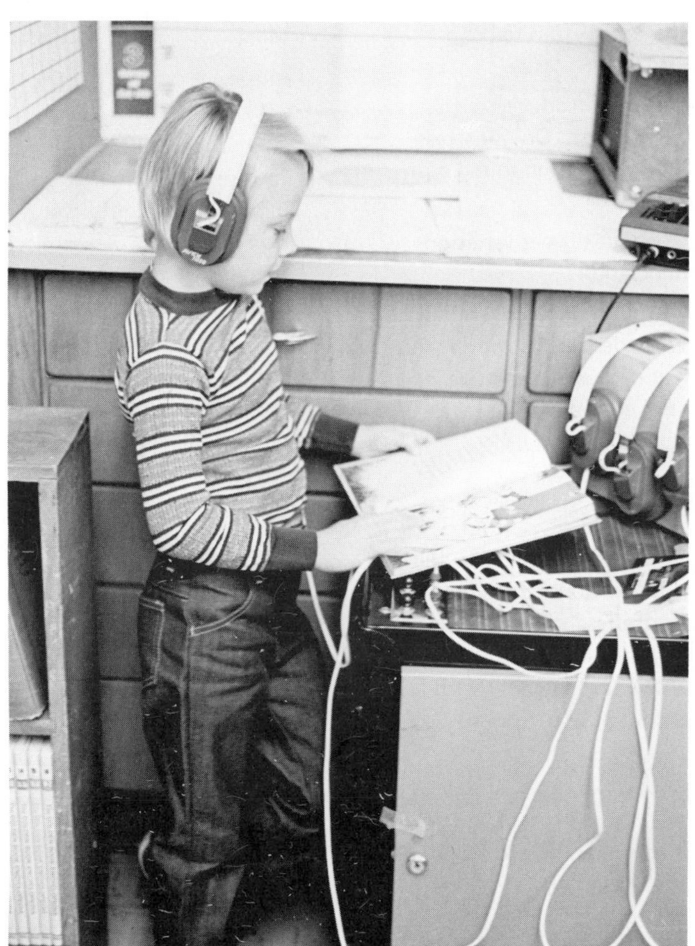

Using the concept of phonograms in oral games or employing the tape recorder may facilitate retention of words learned phonetically. (Photo by Linda Lungren.)

presented in the decibel-loading chart. Long vowel sounds should be introduced as contrasts to short vowel sounds, using words that have become part of the child's sight vocabulary, such as *cap* and *cape.* When you are introducing graphemes and graphemic patterns, you should tell the children that graphemes represent sounds, not that graphemes make phonemes.

3. Q. Should I reinforce vowel correspondence by teaching vowels within words, such as *cat, bat, rat*?

   A. Definitely. Children should be introduced to the concept of syllable and word meaning from the beginning of their reading programs.

4. Q. Should I emphasize the sound of initial consonants within the word?

   A. Yes. Consonants should be introduced within CVC words (e.g., *pan, bat, sun*). Do not stress the sounds; instead, emphasize each sound within the context of the word.

5. Q. Should I be concerned about dialect variations in my children's pronunciation?

   A. Dialect variation will result in different sounds for letter-sound correspondences. However, this should not concern you because your students will develop letter-sound equivalents which reflect their own dialect.

Sample Lessons for Teaching Phonics Strategies

Keeping in mind the suggestions and answers to the questions offered in the previous section, the following lesson plan illustrates *one* way of presenting an introductory lesson on the topic of letter-sound correspondence of the grapheme *m* that may provide you with a framework on which to build your phonics lessons.

Lesson Plan

Goal: To introduce the grapheme *m* and its corresponding phoneme /m/.

Grade/Grade Level: Primary

Construction and Utilization:

1. Write *m* on the board. Ask children if they can name words that begin with /m/.
2. Assess the degree to which children need this exercise. If some children have difficulty naming words, continue using this lesson. The other children who have already mastered this information or who are not yet ready to pursue this lesson should be provided with activities to meet their needs.

Procedure:

1. List on the board the words that children have named:

   mother

   mouse

   moose

   monkey

   Mike

   music

2. To reinforce this skill, divide an oak-tag board into four sections. In section 1, draw a picture of a man; in section 2, a mit; in section 3, a mouse; and in section 4, a mask. Ask children to name the picture, then write the words *man, mitt, mouse,* and *mask* under each of the pictures. Have the children copy the same pictures and words on their own papers. When the children seem to have grasped the idea, have them present their pictures and help them write their own words under each picture.

Evaluation: Put another *m* on the board and ask children to draw pictures and write words under each one.

man

mitt

mouse

mask

This lesson can be followed by a lesson on *n*. Point out the similarities of these two letters to children and ask them to explain the differences. The board may look like the following:

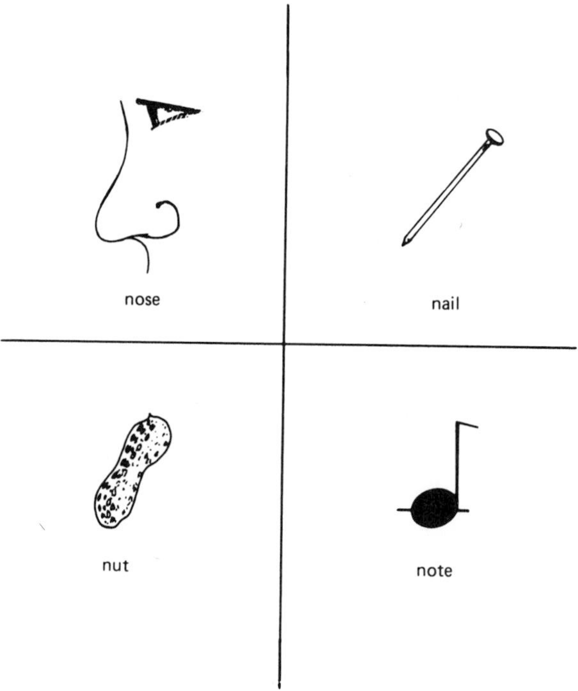

Another lesson for introducing initial consonants is substitution practices. Children can be introduced to patterned substitution drills in which they can infer that there are relationships between words. For example, in the following exercise the child must fill in the appropriate word by changing the first letter of each word.

fan	The __man__ sat on the chair.
tan	He __ran__ to the store.
sit	He ________ the ball.
kit	I want a little ______ of the cake.
tone	Feed the dog the ______ .
lone	I want an ice cream ______ .

Using the same CVC words, you may want to introduce short vowel sounds within the context of a word. Using the same or similar CVC words, you may introduce the final consonant sounds. Once the consonants and vowels have been introduced in the context of words, you may wish to develop word family charts to be on display in your classroom. In this manner, the words are continually reinforced through sight-word strategies. A sample word family chart is the following.

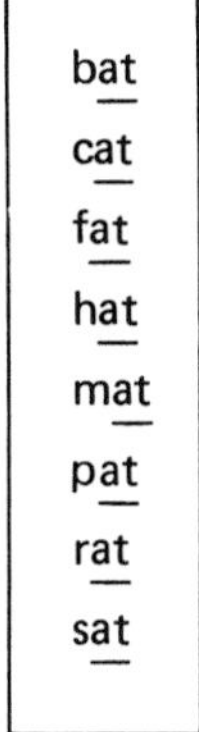

bat
cat
fat
hat
mat
pat
rat
sat

Short vowels may also be introduced through patterned exercises in which children substitute both initial and final consonants as well as the medial vowel within a word. For example, children have these three options:

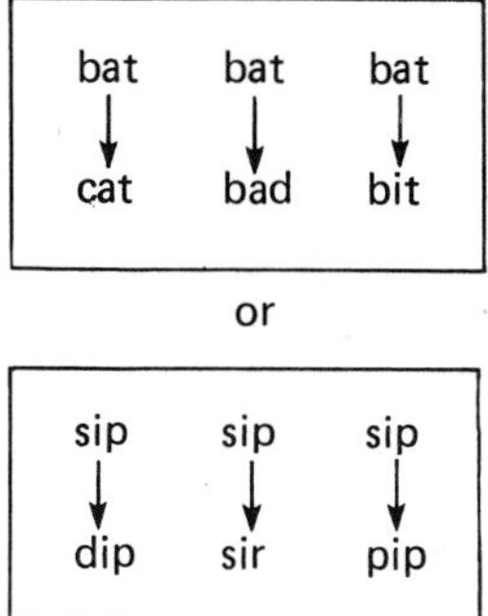

Consonant blends (clusters) may come before or after your lessons on short vowels. Blends should be taught in the same way that the initial and final consonants were taught; they should be taught within the context of a word family:

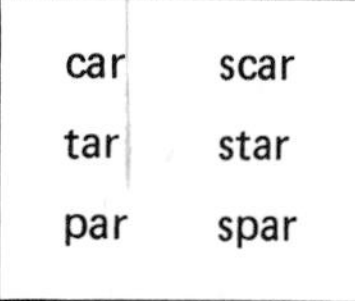

Long vowels may be introduced by contrasting CVC words and CVC-*e* words. For example,

mat	māte
kit	kīte
not	nōte

Incorporating Syllable Strategies

The argument for presenting vowel sounds within the context of the syllable was presented earlier in this chapter, and if you agree with this theory, you need no further encouragement to teach syllabication as part of your phonics program. For those who are skeptical of the syllable's usefulness in phonics instruction, there can be little argument that some rules for "breaking" words apart are extremely important to the decoding process. In some ways, this is an easy task because children already understand the principles of syllabication. An inductive method of teaching can be used by asking children to pull apart words that they have in their sight vocabulary, such as *hap • py* and *birth • day*. Then ask them to read, for example,

mis • chief	Tues • day	to • day
ap • ple	sun • shine	re • port

The following rules may be helpful to you when you are teaching your children the principles of syllabication:

1. Look at the word. Ask yourself if it is a compound word. If it is, name the parts that make up the word, such as base • ball.
2. Look for affixes in the words and look for tense markers like *-ed*. Look for word parts within the word with which you are familiar, such as *-ness*. If there are word parts that you know, separate them from the word and read the rest of the word—this will be the root word, for example, good/ness. Now put the stress on the root, *good*, and read the whole word: goodness.
3. Look in the midst of the word for a cluster of consonants or for a consonant digraph. If there is a cluster of two consonants, try to separate the word into two parts between the two letters of the cluster: ras • cal. If the cluster has three consecutive consonants, separate after the second of the three consonants: frank • ly. If there is a consonant digraph, divide the word after the digraph. Put the stress on the first syllable; thatch • er.
4. If no cluster of consonants exists within the middle of the word, you might want to try the following: separate the word after the consonant that comes after the first vowel in the word and read the word by making the vowel in the first syllable a short vowel and putting the stress on the first syllable: Pan • a • ma. Vowel sounds in the second syllable will usually be a schwa sound /ə/. If you still do not know the word, separate the first vowel after the first vowel digraph, such as *ai* in raisin, and read the first syllable as a CV word. Give the vowel a long sound and put the stress on this syllable.

Reteaching Phonics

It is often difficult to know how much formal phonics instruction is necessary before you are re- or overteaching this strategy. Some students may have a working understanding of phonics without being able to use the rules accurately all the time. For example, if a child looks at this sentence

Ellen Lewis hit the tennis ball out into Dorcester Park.

and reads

Ellen Lewis hit the

and stops, you might say, "Let's break the word apart; you know the parts of the word: ten-nis." Then you might tell the child to read the next word, "ball," and ask him or her to guess the preceding word. After having succeeded in decoding the word, the child may continue the sentence

ball out into

and stop again. You may continue with the same technique:

Dor/ces/ter (Dorcester)

One final suggestion may be crucial in establishing an effective reading program: If a child reads the sentence *"Senator Lawrence Darrell of California* voted in favor of the bill" as *"Senator Lawrence Dar of Connecticut* voted for the law," and answers the comprehension question *"Did Senator Darrell oppose the legislation?"* with a *"no,"* then understanding may have taken place and further phonics instruction may not be necessary for this sentence. In fact further phonics instruction may be counterproductive; it may interfere with the student's progress. However, the child must be encouraged to read carefully, since word substitution *may* result in comprehension errors.

In conclusion, you may want to remember the following general guidelines when you are establishing your reading program:

1. Phonics is a means of decoding. If it is too confusing for the child, try another strategy.
2. Try to break the words into parts for the child, using the syllabication rules that were presented in the preceding section.
3. If the child cannot decode the word and you sense that frustration is overwhelming, tell the child the word.
4. Phonics is a means to an end: comprehension. When phonics decoding hinders comprehension, it is no longer useful. Decide just how many words the child can struggle through in each sentence before there is serious comprehension loss and structure your teaching accordingly.

This chapter intended to introduce you to visual and auditory perception and to the content of phonics strategies.

QUESTIONS AND RELATED READINGS

If you feel that you have not attained adequate knowledge to answer the following questions successfully, we suggest additional related readings.

1. Explain the developmental processes of visual perception and letter and word discrimination.
2. Explain the relationship between auditory processing and reading.
3. List and explain the basic components of phonics.
4. Explain some effective ways of teaching children how to decode by using phonics principles.

Goal 1: To help the reader to understand the relations between the visual mode and reading.

Question 1: Explain the developmental processes of visual perception and letter and word discrimination.

Chase, W., ed. *Visual Information Processing.* New York: Academic Press, Inc., 1973.

Ehri, L. C., and K. T. Roberts. "Do Beginners Learn Printed Words in Context or in Isolation?" *Child Development* 50 (September 1979), 675–85.

Gibson, E., and H. Levin. *The Psychology of Reading.* Cambridge, Mass.: The MIT Press, 1975.

Goal 2: To help the reader to comprehend the relations between the auditory mode and reading.

Question 2: Explain the relationship between auditory processing and reading.

Kiraly, J., and A. Furlong. "Teaching Words to Kindergarten Children with Picture Configuration and Initial Sound Cues in a Prompting Procedure." *Journal of Educational Research* 67 (March 1974), 295–8.

Smith, F. *Understanding Reading.* 2nd ed. New York: Holt, Rinehart and Winston, 1978.

Wittrock, M. C., and J. Carter. "Generative Processing of Hierarchically Organized Words." *American Journal of Psychology* 88 (January 1975), 489–501.

Goal 3: To help the reader to determine what constitutes phonics.

Question 3: List and explain the basic components of phonics.

Anderson, P., and D. Lapp. *Language Skills in Elementary Education.* 3rd ed. New York: Macmillan Publishing Co., Inc., 1979, pp. 384–7.

Durkin, D. *Phonics and the Teaching of Reading.* New York: Teachers College Press, Columbia University, 1965.

Heilman, A. *Phonics in Proper Perspective.* Columbus, Ohio: Charles E. Merrill Publishing Company, 1976.

Goal 4: To help the reader to establish a phonics instruction program.

Question 4: Explain some effective ways of teaching children how to decode by using phonics principles.

Durkin, D. *Teaching Them to Read.* 2nd ed. Boston: Allyn & Bacon, Inc., 1974.

Heilman, A. *Phonics in Proper Perspective.* Columbus, Ohio: Charles E. Merrill Publishing Co., 1976.

Ruddell, R. *Reading-Language Instruction.* Englewood Cliffs, N.J.: Prentice-Hall, Inc., 1974.

In the next few pages, we present several activities that you might find useful for your reading program.

1. Xylo-phonics

Goal: Letter discrimination

Grade Level: K-3

Construction: Use an old xylophone or a toy one. Choose a different letter for each key and tape it to the key. Make small index cards with a series of four to five letters on each—preferably those that are usually confused by children: b, d, p, and q.

Utilization: The child draws a card from the stack and has to hit the letters on the xylophone in the same order as those on the card. Score one point for each series performed correctly.

2. Space Shuttle Voyage

Goal: Letter recognition

Grade Level: K-3

Construction: Make large flashcards showing frequently confused letters such as b, d, g, p, q (one letter per card).

Utilization: Have the children sit in a circle on the floor. One child begins by standing behind the person on his right. Hold up a flashcard (in the shape of a star) while both children attempt to name the correct letter. Whoever is first (or correct) gets to continue around the circle. The child who beats everyone wins by going into orbit and back to earth.

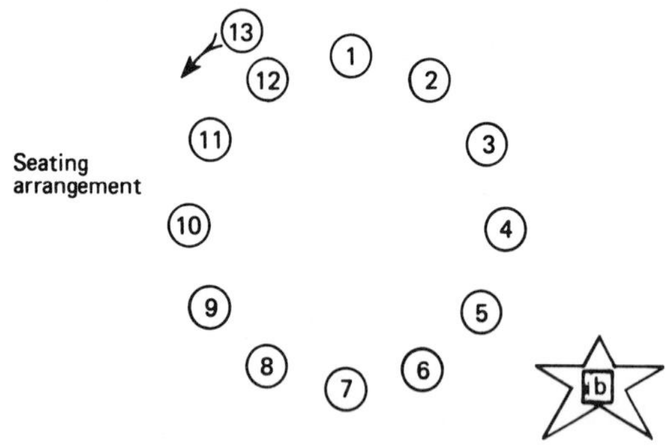

3. Bug-Eyed Monster

Goal: Visual discrimination of beginning or ending letters

Grade Level: K-3

Construction: Make a deck of twenty-five cards containing twelve pairs of various words that begin or end with the same letter. Write one of the twelve words on each card. Also design one card for the Bug-Eyed Monster, which is a word that cannot be paired with any of the other cards.

Utilization: Have all the cards dealt out and have each take turns drawing a card from the person on his left. If he gets a pair, he puts it down on the table, saying the two words and whether they end or begin with the same letter. The game ends when all the cards are paired and someone is left with the Bug-Eyed Monster.

4. Letter Bingo

Goal: Recognition of frequently confused letters

Grade Level: K-1

Construction: Make a Bingo board with the following letters:

B	Q	C	O	F
b	q	c	o	f
D	G	J	T	E
d	g	j	t	e
R	r	N	n	m

Utilization: Play this game with the regular Bingo rules. The caller names a letter (e.g., "capital B," "small b"), and the players have to cover the correct letter.

5. Roll Your Word

Goal: Discriminating between letters and their use in spelling words

Grade Level: K-3

Construction: Construct two piles of index cards representing each letter of the alphabet. One pile contains the vowels; the second pile, the consonants. Make at least five cards for each vowel.

Utilization: Each child rolls the dice and is allowed to pick up the number of cards he has rolled on the dice. He is allowed to select from either the consonant or vowel pile. The child receives one point for each letter of the word he has created. The object of the game is to collect points.

PHONICS ACTIVITIES

6. "Phonics-Made-Easy"

Goal: Phonics review

Grade Level: 3–7

Construction: Design a board (similar to a Parcheesi board) on oil cloth using felt markers or on cardboard hinged in the center. On each square write game instructions (lose a turn, roll again, go back two spaces, etc.) and, most important, phonics concepts that require the players to name a word that has a long *o*, short *e*, begins with the blend *bl*, and so on. You will also need dice and markers to play this game.

Utilization: Players roll dice to move their markers. If the player responds successfully, he or she stays put, but if the response is incorrect (as determined by the other players), the marker is moved back one square. The player to get back home first wins.

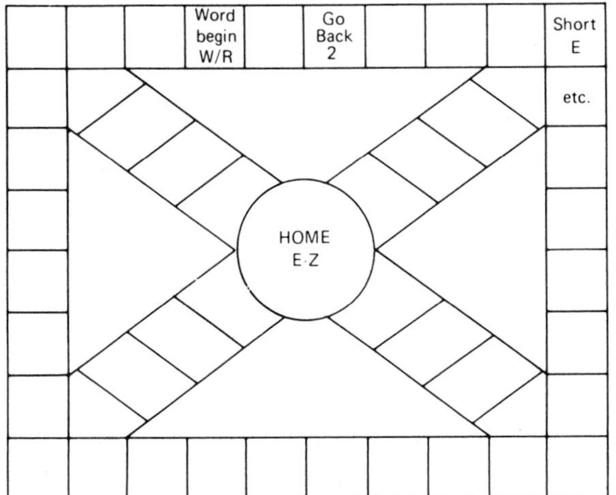

7. Clip the Clothespins

Goal: Discriminating long vowel sounds

Grade Level: K–3

Construction: Construct a large cardboard circle. The circle should be subdivided into five sections. Collect pictures that represent the long vowel sounds of *a, e, i, o, u*. Pictures can be taken from discarded workbooks. Paste pictures containing the same vowel sounds in each section. On the reverse side of each section, write the letter sound being represented by the pictures. Secure six clothespins with clips. With paint or nail polish write one letter on each clothespin leg. The same letter should be written on both legs of one clothespin.

Utilization: Have the child name the pictures in the first section by selecting the clothespin bearing the letter heard in the words he or she has just pronounced. The child then checks the answer by looking at the back side of the cardboard circle.

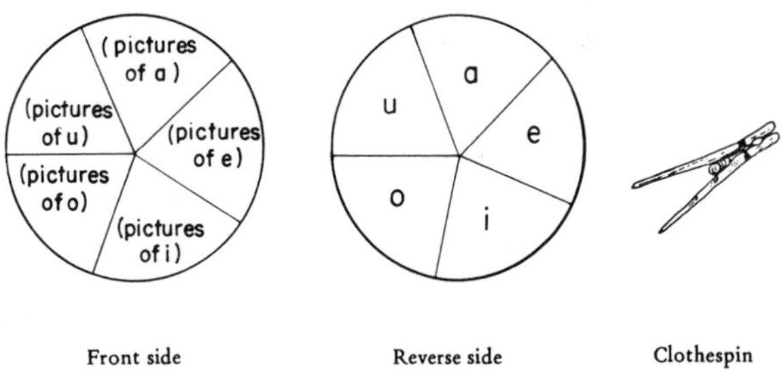

Front side Reverse side Clothespin

8. Phonics Concentration

Goal: Short and long vowel sounds

Grade Level: 3–8

Construction: Similar to activity 7, choose or draw pictures that represent long (and short) vowel sounds and paste (or draw) them on one side of a card, one to each card. You must make or find pairs of pictures, at least two pairs for each vowel sound (more for older students). On the other side of the card, write the vowel sound it represents.

Utilization: Mix up the cards and place them picture side down. Each in turn, players flip over two cards with the same vowel sound hoping to find a pair or match. If they don't match, the cards are turned back over and the next player has a turn. When the cards are matched, they are removed from the game. The player with the most pairs at the end wins. (Players must be able to say the word indicated by the pictures in order to take the pair.)

Variations: Any sound you wish to teach may be represented. The more sounds and more pairs, the more complex the game.

9. Welcome to the Short Vowel Hotel

Goal: Discriminating short vowel sounds

Grade Level: 1-3

Construction: Construct a large chart. The chart should be large enough to be subdivided into five columns. At the top of the first column write an *a*. On the tops of columns 2 through 5, write the letters *e, i, o, u*. Write one letter on the top of each column. Draw several rectangles in each column. Design forty to fifty rectangular cards. On each card write one word containing a short vowel sound.

Utilization: Word cards are placed on a deck. The first child selects a card and pronounces the word without exposing it to the other players. The child beside him identifies the column containing the correct vowel sound heard in the word. If the child is correct, he places the card in the correct column (the proper "hotel") and scores one point. The game continues until all the cards have been placed in the proper hotel.

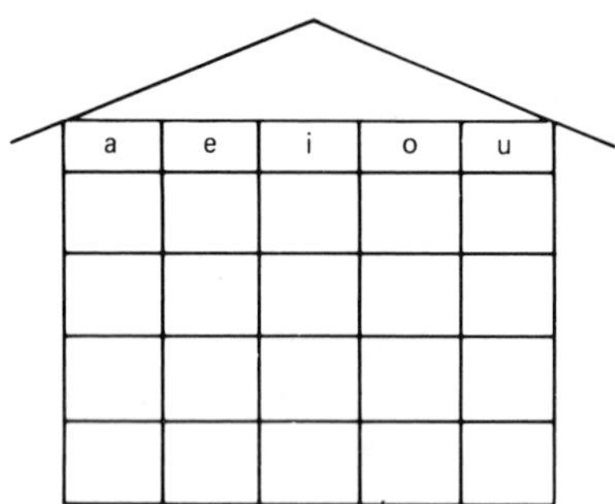

10. The Vowel Express

Goal: Distinguishing long and short vowel sounds

Grade Level: 1-3

Construction: Design cards as in activity 9 but include words with the long vowel sound as well. On a ditto master, draw two train engines pulling cars with lines on them. Label one "long vowel express" and the other "short vowel express."

Utilization: The game is played in the same way as "Welcome to the Short Vowel Hotel" (activity 9), except that in this game, the child must write the word behind the correct engine.

11. Spin the Word Family

Goal: Instruction in phonograms (initial consonants)

Grade Level: 2-5

Construction: Make a wheel out of cardboard and write various phonograms at different points on the wheel. Attach the wheel to another piece of cardboard and write four initial consonants that form words with the phonograms at four sides of the cardboard. (Examples of phonograms are *ack, ag, ay, ug, at, ell, an, ent, ank.* Initial consonants to go with these are *s, b, t, r.*)

Utilization: Have the child spin the wheel and try to form a word from the phonogram and initial consonant. Award a point for each one formed correctly. The child with the most points wins.

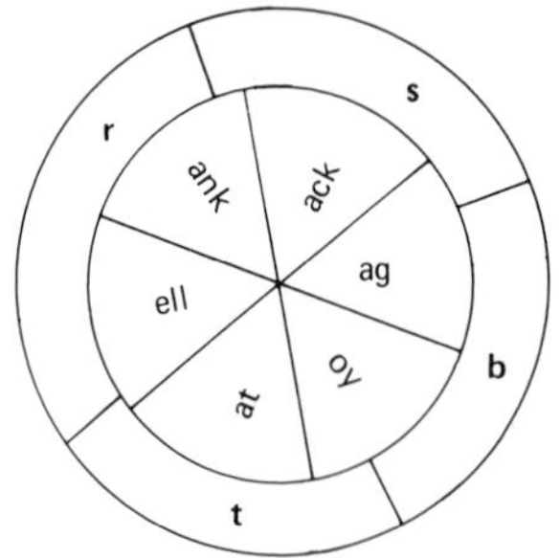

12. Hang a Word

Goal: Using consonant clusters (blends) to make words

Grade Level: 1-3

Construction: Make a "blend board" from a piece of

wood you have painted or decorated. Pound six columns of nails into the board. Cut several cards from thick paper. Punch holes into the tops of all the cards. Write various blends on half the number of cards and word endings on the other half. Hang blends on the first two columns. Leave columns 3 and 5 blank. Hang word endings on columns 4 and 6.

Utilization: Have the child hang blends in front of the endings, making as many different words as possible. Then the child writes down the word and uses it in a sentence.

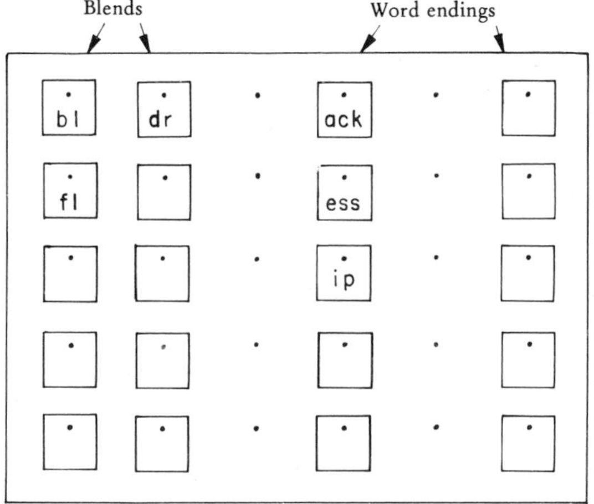

13. Listen and Write

Goal: Practice in identifying consonant digraphs.

Grade Level: 1-3

Construction: Prepare a cassette tape of sentences that contain words spelled with consonant digraphs. Make up an accompanying ditto master or laminated sheet containing pictures of the words and the part of the word without the digraph.

Utilization: The child listens to the tape and follows along on the paper, filling in the consonant digraphs. If desired, children can then make their own cassette tape, using the words in a story.

14. Picture Story

Goal: Recognizing consonant digraphs

Grade Level: 1-3

Construction: Write a short story on a ditto master or laminated paper. Replace some of the words containing consonant digraphs with a picture. At the bottom of the page show the pictures again, along with part of the word, omitting the consonant digraph.

Utilization: The student must insert the correct consonant digraph. This activity also gives good practice in using contextual clues.

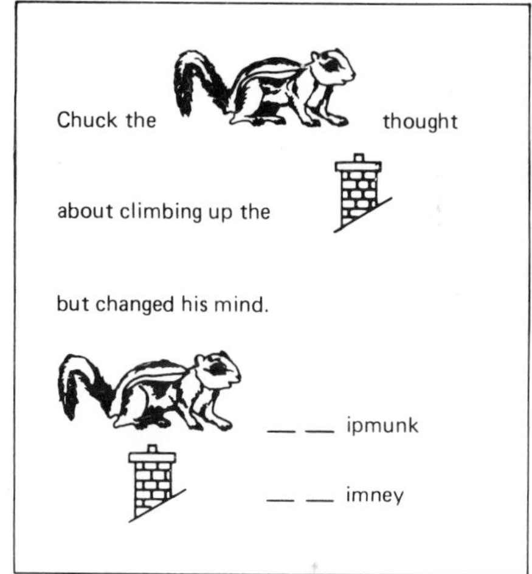

15. Color the Clown's Hat

Goal: Distinguishing vowel digraphs

Grade Level: 1-3

Construction: On a sheet of paper, list several rows of words containing the same vowel digraphs. Each row should contain three words. Although each row should contain words having the same vowel digraph, it is not necessary that all words within a row have the same digraph sound (touch). At the end of each row, draw the outline of a clown's hat.

Utilization: Instruct the child to pronounce the words in each row. If all the words have the same vowel digraph sound, the clown's hat should be colored yellow. If all of the words do *not* have the same vowel digraph sound, the clown's hat should be colored blue. Example:

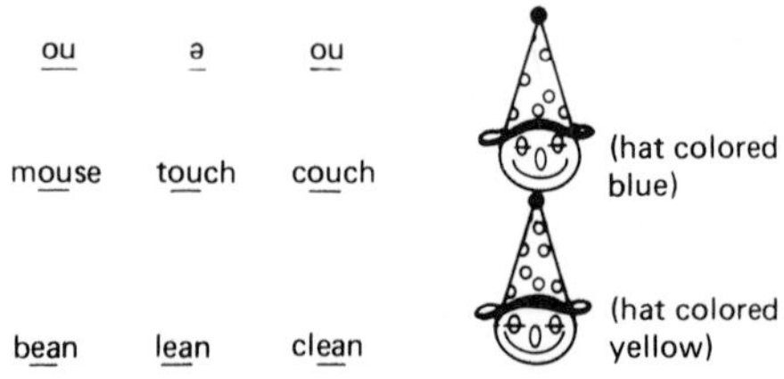

Traffic lights could be substituted for the clown's hat. The child would then be instructed to color the traffic light green if all of the words *do* have the same vowel digraph sound, and to color the traffic light red if all of the words *do not* have the same vowel digraph sound.

16. The Diphthong Journal/Book

Goal: Recognition of vowel diphthongs (or other phonic elements)

Grade Level: 1-6

Construction: A loose-leaf book may be made by cutting out two 8" X 10" cardboard covers. Place two holes along the end of each cover. Place several pieces of 7" X 9" colored construction paper between the cardboard covers. The paper should contain the same holes as the cover. Tie yarn or put rings through the holes to secure the book and decorate the cover with wallpaper, children's art designs, or graphics appropriate to the students' ages and interests.

Utilization: Children should be asked to cut pictures from magazines or draw pictures that represent words containing vowel diphthongs. The children paste the pictures into the book, label each picture, and draw a line under each vowel diphthong. For older students, the pictures can be used to inspire stories, thoughts, or sentences for a daily or weekly journal.

17. Crazy Eights

Goal: Practice in matching final endings

Grade Level: 1-3

Construction: Make a deck of forty cards with words containing five different word endings (eight cards for each ending, for example, *ite, ood, eigh*. Make five extra cards with the number 8 on them.

Utilization: This game is played like the card game Crazy Eights. Five cards are dealt to each player. One card is turned face up in the center. Players in turn try to get rid of their cards by putting down a card with the same ending as the word card turned up (saying the word orally as it is placed down). If the player doesn't have a card, he can play an 8, or he can draw a card from the deck. If he does have an 8 he can also place it in the center and begin another ending. If the player does not read the word card correctly, he must keep the card and lose his turn.

18. Syllable Scrabble

Goal: Syllabication of given words

Grade Level: 4-6

Construction: Cut in half several 3" X 10" word cards. Print the individual syllables of multisyllabic words on each card. A word list of all possible words can be provided if desired. Construction paper and glue will also be needed.

Utilization: Have the child find the correct syllables to make up the word and paste them on construction paper in any design he chooses. Accent marks should also be added. If desired, the child can then illustrate the word on the piece of construction paper.

19. "Break" the Word

Goal: Practicing syllabication

Grade Level: 4-6

Construction: Prepare a list of words, identifying the proper syllables. Examples:

turkey	tur / key
ball	ball
alphabet	al / pha / bet

Utilization: Divide the class into teams of five players each. An "MC" (master of ceremonies) calls out a word from the list, and each player writes its syllabicated form. Teams may score ten points for each player who divides the word correctly. A bonus of five points is given if two players on a team are correct, and two additional points are given for other team members with correct answers. The team earning the most points wins.

BIBLIOGRAPHY

Bailey, M. "The Utility of Phonic Generalizations in Grades One Through Six." *The Reading Teacher* 20 (February 1967), 412–8.

Burmeister, L. "Vowel Pairs." *The Reading Teacher* 21 (February 1968), 447–98.

Caldwell, E. C., S. R. Roth, and R. R. Turner. "A Reconsideration of Phonic Generalizations." *Journal of Reading Behavior* 10 (Spring 1978), 91–6.

Clymer, T. "The Utility of Phonics Generalization in the Primary Grades." *The Reading Teacher* 16 (January 1963), 252–8.

Coleman, E. *Collecting a Data Base for an Educational Technology*, Parts I and III. El Paso: University of Texas Press, 1967.

Dolch, E. "A Basic Sight Vocabulary." *Elementary School Journal* 36 (February 1936), 456–60.

Durkin, D. *Teaching Them to Read.* 2nd ed. Boston, Mass.: Allyn & Bacon, Inc., 1974.

Emans, R. "The Usefulness of Phonics Generalizations Above the Primary Grades." *The Reading Teacher* 20 (February 1967), 419–25.

Ernst, M. *Words.* 3rd ed. New York: Alfred A. Knopf, Inc., 1955.

Fairbanks, G. *Experimental Phonetics: Selected Articles.* Urbana: University of Illinois Press, 1966.

Fries, C. *Linguistics and Reading.* New York: Holt, Rinehart and Winston, 1963.

Fulwiler, G., and P. Groff. "The Effectiveness of Intensive Phonics." *Reading Horizons* 21 (Fall 1980), 50–4.

Gibson, E., and H. Levin. *The Psychology of Reading.* Cambridge, Mass.: MIT Press, 1975.

Gleason, J. "Language Development in Early Childhood." In *Oral Language and Reading*, ed. by J. Walden. Urbana, Ill.: National Council of Teachers of English, 1969.

Groff, P. *The Syllable: Its Nature and Pedagogical Usefulness.* Portland, Ore.: Northwest Regional Educational Laboratory, 1971.

____. "Teaching Reading by Syllables." *The Reading Teacher* 34 (March 1981), 659–64.

Guszak, F. *Diagnostic Reading Instruction in the Elementary School.* New York: Harper & Row, Publishers, 1972.

Heilman, A. *Principles and Practices of Teaching Reading.* Columbus, Ohio: Charles E. Merrill Publishing Company, 1972.

Hoover, K. "The Effect of Sequence of Training in Kindergarten Children." Unpublished doctoral dissertation, Stanford University, Palo Alto, Calif., 1975.

Jenkins, J., R. Bausel, and L. Jenkins. "Comparison of Letter Name and Letter Sound Training as Transfer Variables." *American Educational Research Journal* 9 (February 1972), 75–86.

Kibby, M. W. "The Effects of Certain Instructional Conditions and Response Modes on Initial Word Learning." *Reading Research Quarterly* 15 (No. 1) 1979, 145–71.

Leonard, M., D. Shankweiller, I. Leberman, and K. Fowler. "Phonetic Recoding and Reading Difficulty in the Beginning Reader." *Memory and Cognitions* (1977), pp. 623–9.

Marchbanks, B., and H. Levin. "Cues by Which Children Recognize Words." *Journal of Educational Psychology* 56 (September 1965), 57–61.

Murphy, H., and D. Durrell. *Speech to Print Phonics.* New York: Harcourt Brace Jovanovich, 1972.

Pollard, R. S. *Pollard's Synthetic Method.* Chicago: Western Publishing House, 1889.

Ruddell, R. *Reading-Language Instruction.* Englewood Cliffs, N.J.: Prentice-Hall, Inc., 1974.

Silberberg, N., M. Silberberg, and I. Iverson. "The Effects of Kindergarten Instruction in Alphabet and Numbers on First Grade Reading." *Journal of Learning Disabilities* 5 (March 1972), 254–61.

Spache, G., and E. Spache. *Reading in the Elementary School.* 3rd ed. Boston: Allyn & Bacon, Inc., 1973.

Thorndike, E. *The Teaching of English Suffixes.* New York: Bureau of Publications, Teachers College, Columbia University, 1932.

Tovey, D. R. "Children's Grasp of Phonics Terms Vs. Sound-Symbol Relationships." *The Reading Teacher* 33 (January 1980), 431–7.

CHAPTER 6

Breaking the Code: Understanding and Using Sight Words and Structural and Contextual Clues as Word Analysis Strategies

Oh, this learning, what a thing it is!

Shakespeare, *The Taming of the Shrew*, I, ii 1594

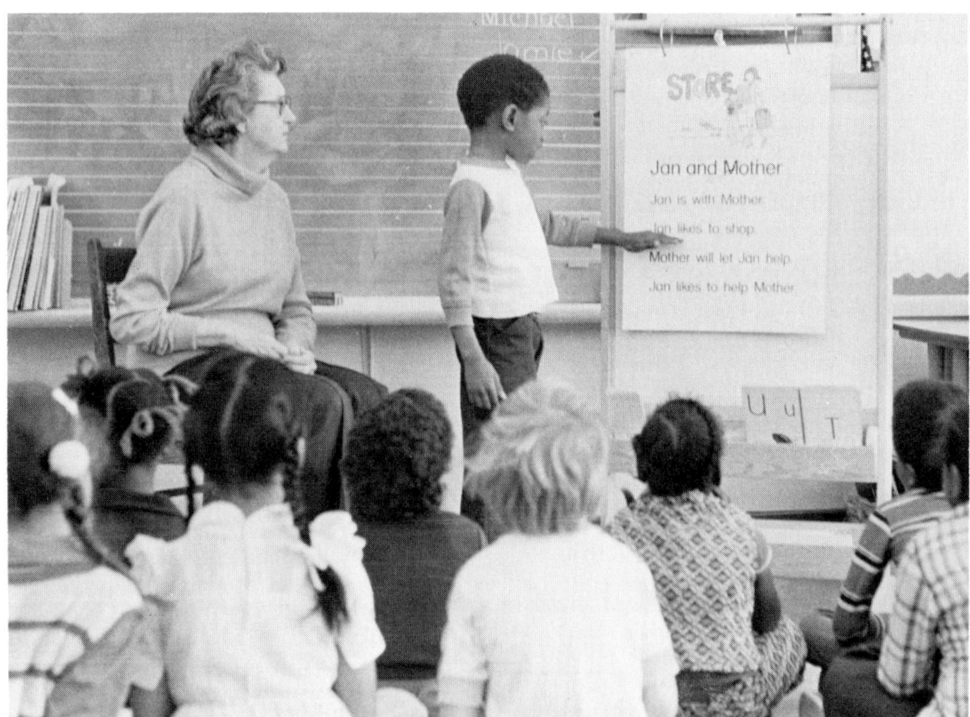

The sight-word approach to beginning reading is often used with high-frequency words to begin a basal reading program. Children are then able to participate immediately in the reading process. (Photo by Linda Lungren.)

sight words
structur·al clue·s
and contextual ____________
help us ____________ what
we ________ .

GOALS: To help the reader to

1. Understand the use of sight-word strategies as a word-recognition skill.
2. Understand the use of structural analysis as a word-recognition skill.
3. Understand the use of contextual analysis as a word-recognition skill.

In addition to phonics skills and strategies, you will want to instruct your children in three other word analysis strategies that will help them to decode unknown words. In this chapter, we present additional word analysis strategies in these areas—*sight-word skills, structural analysis skills,* and *contextual analysis skills*—and some instructional principles that may help you to implement your word analysis knowledge.

STRATEGIES FOR SIGHT-WORD ANALYSIS

The *sight-word approach* to beginning reading, also known as the "whole-word" or "look-say" method, is often used with high-frequency words to begin a basal reading program. The rationale for this method is that children are able to participate immediately in the reading process.

Children are able to recognize many words prior to beginning reading instruction. These words are usually highly meaningful for the child. Sometimes they can (1) read words affecting their daily activities (Happy Birthday, Merry Christmas, Chanukah); (2) read words naming frequent interactions (Jack-in-the-box, bike, candy); (3) read certain signs (stop, go); and (4) read their own names.

One way in which to increase this list of sight words is to use "organic" words (Ashton-Warner, 1963) or "key" words (Veatch et al., 1979), both terms referring to personal, secret words that have special meaning to the individual child. Ask the children to tell you a secret word; then write it on an index card and let the children keep the cards in their special files.

Review these words periodically with the children and use them as catalysts for storytelling, language-experience charts, or play productions. A language-experience method of teaching reading, which will be explained in detail in Chapter 10, begins instruction with the child's experiences, which are expressed by the words the child already knows and uses. By studying these private words themselves and sharing them with classmates, children develop sight-word recognition of words that are important to them, and the interaction among the children in activities using these words develops a classroom atmosphere that is very congenial and conducive to learning (Brown, 1981).

Basal programs that begin with the introduction of sight words introduce new words in such ways that they can be compared with and contrasted to the words that have already been presented. For example, initial stories might introduce a phonogram (a word family such as *at*) and then introduce the following words: *mat, cat, rat, bat, pat.*

As competent adult readers, we tend to identify and utilize many clues when we are reading. Among these clues are configuration clues; for example, if the following array is presented to us and we are told that the answer is a familiar holiday song, we examine the word configurations to arrive at an answer:

a	—	—	—
—	—	n	g
s	—	n	—

In the following pattern we are told that the answer is the name of a college:

U	—					
—	a	—	a	l		
a	—	a	—	—	m	y

We use configuration clues to arrive at our two answers, *Auld Lang Syne* and U.S. Naval Academy.

Shapes of words also offer configuration clues; for example, [p e t] is different in shape from [b a b y]. Readers often attend to and depend upon configuration when they are decoding. While there is a controversy among researchers as to how important these word shapes are in the overall reading process, recent research seems to indicate that word shape information is indeed quite useful as an aid to word recognition (Haber and Haber, 1981; Rayner, 1976, 1978; Haber and Schindler, 1981). One concern that has been voiced about the introduction of the phonogram is the child's dependence upon the configuration and a phenomenon called "first letter guessing." The child realizes that [ran] means *ran*; the child is introduced to [man] and is told that this says *man*. What sometimes happens is the following: the child internalizes this information: ran = *ran*. When the child sees the word "run" in a sentence, he or she recognizes the "r" and *guesses* that the word says "ran." In other cases, the child who has learned ran = *ran* might even say "ran" when encountering such words as *rooster, rabbit, rye,* or *rough*.

The selection of appropriate words to be taught as sight words needs to be examined carefully by teachers so that children's memories do not become overtaxed; for example, children may not be able to learn long words like *nightingale* or *superintendent* as sight words. An appropriate starting point is the child's own name. Color names and numeral names are also useful because of their convenient visual referents, such as *black, gray, 4 (four).*

The next step is to determine appropriate criteria for introducing sight words. The best single criterion seems to be to select high-frequency functional words, such as *the*; for example,

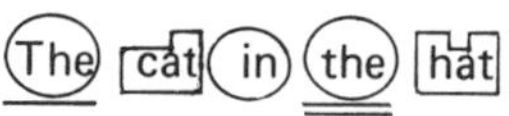

The following is an extended list for use as a sight-word vocabulary.

THE DALE LIST OF 769 EASY WORDS

A	anything	begin	bow	can	cloth	D	E
a	apple	behind	box	cap	clothes	dance	each
about	are	being	boy	captain	cloud	dark	ear
above	arm	believe	branch	car	coal	day	early
across	around	bell	brave	care	coat	dead	earth
act	as	belong	bread	careful	cold	dear	east
afraid	ask	beside	break	carry	color	deep	easy
after	at	best	breakfast	case	come	did	eat
afternoon	away	better	bridge	catch	coming	die	edge
again	B	between	bright	cause	company	different	egg
against	baby	big	bring	cent	cook	dinner	eight
ago	back	bill	broken	center	cool	do	either
air	bad	bird	brother	chair	corn	doctor	else
all	bag	bit	brought	chance	corner	does	end
almost	ball	black	brown	change	cost	dog	England
alone	band	bless	build	chief	could	done	English
along	bank	blind	building	child	count	don't	enough
already	basket	blood	built	children	country	door	evening
also	be	blow	burn	choose	course	double	ever
always	bear	blue	busy	Christmas	cover	down	every
am	beat	board	but	church	cow	draw	everything
American	beautiful	boat	butter	circle	cried	dream	except
an	because	body	buy	city	cross	dress	expect
and	bed	bone	by	class	crowd	drink	eye
animal	bee	book	C	clean	crown	drive	F
another	been	born	cake	clear	cry	drop	face
answer	before	both	call	clock	cup	dry	fair
any	began	bottom	came	close	cut	dust	fall

family
fancy
far
farm
farmer
fast
fat
father
feed
feel
feet
fell
fellow
felt
fence
few
field
fight
fill
find
fine
finger
finish
fire
first
fish
fit
five
fix
floor
flower
fly
follow
food
foot
for
forget
fourth
found
four
fresh
friend
from
front
fruit
full
G
game
garden
gate
gave
get
gift
girl
give
glad
glass
go
God
going
gold
golden
gone
good
got
grain
grass
gray
great
green
grew
ground
grow
guess
H
had
hair
half
hall
hand
hang
happy
hard
has
hat
have
he
head
hear
heard
heart
heavy
help
here
herself
hid
high
hill
him
himself
his
hold
hole
home
hope
horse
hot
house
how
hundred
hunt
hurry
hurt
I
I
ice
if
in
Indian
instead
into
iron
is
it
its
J
jump
just
K
keep
kept
kill
kind
king
kiss
knee
knew
know
L
lady
laid
lake
land
large
last
laugh
lay
lead
learn
leave
left
leg
lesson
let
letter
lie
lift
light
like
line
lion
lips
listen
little
live
load
long
look
lost
lot
loud
love
low
M
made
mail
make
man
many
march
mark
market
matter
may
me
mean
measure
meat
meet
mean
met
middle
might
mile
milk
mill
mind
minute
miss
money
month
moon
more
morning
most
mother
mountain
mouth
move
Mr.
Mrs.
much
music
must
my
myself
N
name
near
neck
need
neighbor
neither
nest
never
New York
next
nice
night
nine
no
noise
none
noon
nor
north
nose
not
note
nothing
now
number
O
oak
ocean
of
off
office
often
old
on
once
one
only
open
or
other
our
out
outside
over
own
P
page
paint
pair
paper
part
party
pass
path
pay
pen
people
pick
picture
piece
place
plain
plant
play
please
point
poor
post
pound
present
press
pretty
pull
put
Q
quarter
queen
quick
quiet
quite
R
race
rain
ran
rather
reach
read
ready
real
reason
red
remember
rest
rich
ride
right
ring
river
road
rock
roll
roof
room
rose
round
row
run
S
said
sail
salt
same
sand
sat
save
saw
say
school
sea
season
seat
second
see
seed
seem
seen
self
sell
send
sent
serve
set
seven
several
shake
shall
shape
she
sheep
shine
ship
shoe
shop
short
should
shoulder
show
shut
sick
side
sign
silk
silver
sing
sir
sister
sit
six
size
skin
sky
sleep
slow
small
smile
smoke
snow
so
soft
sold
soldier
some
something
sometime
song
soon
sound
south
space
speak
spot
spread
spring
square
stand
star
start
station
stay
step
stick
still
stone
stood
stop
store
storm
story
straight
street
strike
strong
such
sugar
suit
summer
sun
suppose
surprise
sweet
T
table
tail
take
talk
tall
taste
teach
teacher
tear
tell
ten
than
thank
that
the
their
them
then
there
these
they
thick
thin
thing
think
this
those
though
thought
thousand
three
through
throw
tie
till
time
tire
to
today
together
told
tomorrow
tongue
too
took
top
touch
town
trade
train
tree
true

try
turn
twelve
twenty
two
U
uncle
under
until
up
upon

us
use
V
valley
very
visit
W
wait
walk
wall
want

war
warm
was
wash
waste
watch
water
wave
way
we
wear

weather
week
well
went
were
west
what
wheat
wheel
when
where

whether
which
while
white
who
whole
whom
whose
why
wide
wild

will
win
wind
window
wing
winter
wish
with
without
woman
wonder

wood
word
work
world
would
write
wrong
XYZ
yard
year
yellow

yes
yesterday
yet
you
young
your

THE DOLCH BASIC SIGHT VOCABULARY OF 220 WORDS

a
about
after
again
all
always
am
an
and
any
are
around
as
ask
at
ate
away

be
because
been
before
best
better
big
black
blue
both
bring
brown
but
buy
by

call
came
can
carry
clean
cold
come
could
cut

did
do
does
done
don't
down
draw
drink

eat
eight
every

fall
far
fast
find
first
five
fly
for
found
four

from
full
funny

gave
get
give
go
goes
going
good
got
green
grow

had
has
have
he
help
her
here
him
his
hold
hot
how
hurt

I
if
in
into
is
it
its

jump
just

keep
kind
know

laugh
let
like
light
little
live
long
look

made
make
many
may
me
much
must
my
myself

never
new
no
not
now

of
off
old

on
once
one
only
open
or
our
out
over
own

pick
play
please
pretty
pull
put

ran
read
red
ride
right
round
run

said
saw
say
see
seven
shall
she
show

sing
sit
six
sleep
small
so
some
soon
start
stop

take
tell
ten
thank
that
the
their
them
then
there
these
they
think
this
those
three
to
today
together
too
try
two

under
upon
us
use

very

walk
want
warm
was
wash
we
well
went
were
what
when
where
which
white
who
why
will
wish
with
work
would
write

yellow
yes
you
your

In teaching sight words to beginning readers, repetition is essential. This is especially true of high-frequency words that defy phonetic generalization.

TEACHING CONTRACTIONS AS SIGHT WORDS

Teaching contractions as sight words helps to alleviate problems encountered with the inconsistency of their formation patterns. An easy rule for children to remember as an aid for recognizing contractions is the following: when two or more words combine to form a new, shorter word, an apostrophe (') is substituted for one or more letters in the new word. The following is a list of contractions:

I have	I've	cannot	can't
I am	I'm	do not	don't
I will	I'll	had not	hadn't
he will	he'll	must not	mustn't
she is	she's	they have	they've
she will	she'll	have not	haven't
was not	wasn't	will not	won't
did not	didn't	of the clock	o'clock
does not	doesn't	would not	wouldn't
will not	won't	there is	there's
they are	they're	is not	isn't
she is	she's	should not	shouldn't
has not	hasn't	could not	couldn't
are not	aren't	you are	you're
it is	it's		
he is	he's		
he will	he'll		

Lack of correspondence between spelling and pronunciation in words that the student encounters throughout his or her school years makes it important to continue teaching both whole words and contractions as sight words past the initial reading instruction level. More difficult and less frequently used words that may be taught effectively as sight words include *pneumonia, phlegm, mnemonic.*

Certain borrowings from other languages that have entered English have unusual spellings that children may find difficult. Some of these words may be taught effectively as sight words. Ruddell (1974) provides us with the following list:

Language Source	Plants and Animals	Food	Culture	Miscellaneous
American Indian	sequoia catawba cayuse	supawn pemmican	manitou kayak	Chautauqua
French	caribou	brioche à la mode parfait sazarac	bureau bateau pirogue	Cajun charivari rotisserie
Spanish	mesquite marijuana mosquito palomino	frijol tequila enchilada	sombrero serape lariat pueblo	coquina hombre savvy
German		blutwurst schnitzel zwieback	pinochle rathskeller turnverein	katzenjammer phooey spiel
Italian		spaghetti ravioli	duet opera piano virtuoso	granite balcony
Persian	lilac lemon	sherbet	caravan khaki borax	paradise check
Greek			acrobat barometer catastrophe	tactics tantalize elastic
Russian		vodka	ruble droshky	steppe

Regardless of the grade level or the content that you are teaching, you will be introducing and reinforcing sight-word skills. As you observed in the Dolch or Dale word lists and the list of contractions, many of the words you will be teaching as sight words do not lend themselves to visual representations, such as *the* and *I'm*. Therefore, they must be taught in context. The following rules may aid you to help your children to develop their sight-word vocabularies.

GUIDELINES FOR SIGHT-WORD INSTRUCTION

1. Use pictures to illustrate the word being taught when it is appropriate to do so. Encourage your students to study the picture and the number of words on the page and try to guess what is being said in the passage.
2. Ask the students to look at the words as you read them. This helps the children to decide if their guesses are correct.
3. Point to the picture and reread the passage while the children follow the story visually.
4. Encourage the children to read the passage with you.
5. Ask individual children to read the sentences while the other children follow the story visually.
6. After reading the sentence, point out the individual words you are introducing.
7. Discuss the meaning of each word. Explain that some words serve as helpers to complete sentences, such as *the, is,* and *am.*
8. "Tell" children certain words that have extremely irregular patterns: *sight, of, who, laugh, though, the, should.*
9. While framing each word, assist students in recognizing the length and configuration, initial letter(s), and ascending letter features.
10. Finally, encourage students to reread the sentence with you.

Exercises for Reinforcing Sight Words

In addition to the activities section at the end of the chapter, the following vocabulary exercises are provided as aids.

1. Un-Scramble

Write each word of a sentence on an individual index card and place the cards in an envelope. Do this for several sentences making some more complex by allowing several possibilities. The children then try to form a sentence (or sentences) by unscrambling the words. For example,

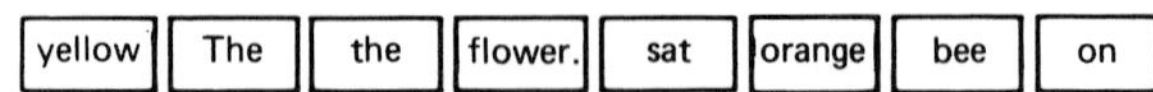

(Include uppercase letters and punctuation to make it easier; exclude them for more difficult work.)

may unscramble to

Suddenly the car stopped.

The car stopped suddenly.

The car suddenly stopped.

Such exercises tend to encourage students to focus on meaning. They are reinforcing these words as part of their sight repertoire. This same activity can be conducted with words printed on dice. The dice can be thrown and students will have to assemble a sentence. To prepare the dice, print items of a particular class, either grammatical or semantic, on each die.

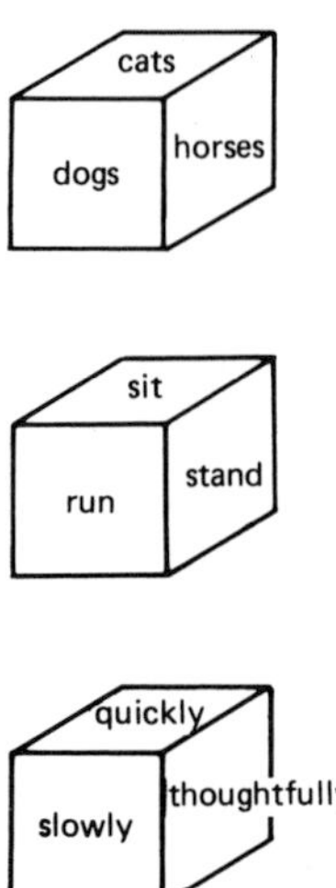

On the other three sides appear

bears	jump	joyfully
cows	fly	sadly
rabbits	kneel	pensively

Students can roll as many dice as you decide to keep in the cup at one time. When the dice have been rolled, the children would have to make sentences from the words that appear on each die.

Cats jump quickly.

Horses kneel sadly.

Cows fly thoughtfully.

2. Sentence Completion

The same principle is used in this exercise. When you encourage students to focus on comprehension, they will be reinforcing their sight vocabulary.

Ask students to complete the following sentences:

The bird in the tree was frightened by ________.

The ________ sounded like ________.

3. Classification

For beginning readers, it is sometimes useful to give them the opportunity to organize their ideas by classifying them into appropriate categories. Ask students to name a category and then ask them to name examples of the category:

Fruit	States	Flowers
apple	California	daisy
orange	Texas	rose
banana	Massachusetts	petunia

4. Word Building

Write the words that are part of your students' sight vocabulary on the board and ask the children to read the cognates:

back ward	house fly
pop corn	side walk
honey moon	lip stick
blue berry	base ball
under wear	up stairs

Building compound words from known sight words is helpful for beginning readers and is lots of fun.

5. Configurations

Teachers of reading need to provide children with a great deal of practice in visual discrimination of word configurations as a basis for developing sight-word skills. Durrell (1966) suggests that young children need a great deal of practice and training to be able to recognize and quickly distinguish between words with very similar configurations. Here are some examples:

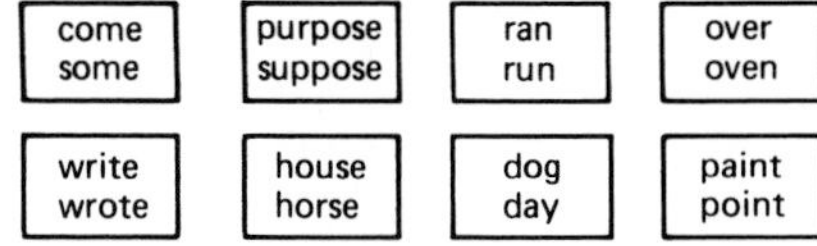

When teachers say to the children, "What do you think the word looks like?" they are actually helping children to use configuration analysis as a strategy for decoding a word by sight; for example, the configurations of the following words are quite different.

kettle jog quick

However, relying too heavily on configurations has obvious limitations, as is demonstrated by the following list of words that have similar configurations:

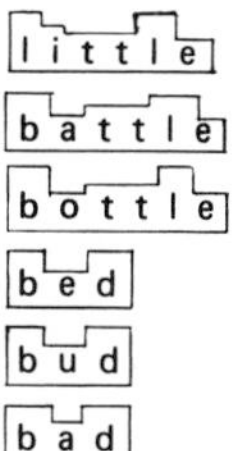

6. Initial Skills

Some children rely on the first letter as a clue to meaning; for example, they see *d* and read *don't* for *doesn't*. They may need continued instruction in analyzing all of the letters before they try to read the word. A useful example may be to cover the first letter and have the children guess the word:

_____ oy _____ unt _____ alk

After you have taught several sight words, you may wish to evaluate your students' competence in reading sight words. One effective way of doing this is to select certain words from the Dolch list or the contraction list and write them on a piece of paper. Put a dash in front of each word. If you are working with an individual, you can ask the child to read each word. You may want to check the words that the child reads correctly. If you are using this format with a group of students, ask the children to number the words as you call them out. An example of this format is

_____ the _____ this
_____ of _____ had
_____ and _____ not
_____ to _____ are
_____ a _____ but

This becomes a useful record-keeping system as well as a diagnostic base for effective teacher decision making.

STRATEGIES FOR STRUCTURAL ANALYSIS

Structural analysis entails the breaking of words into their smallest parts, which is a useful decoding skill when the word is not in the child's sight vocabulary. Finding meaning in parts of a word may help not only in decoding it but in understanding its meaning. Children who can unravel the parts of a word like *un • sports • man • like* by knowing that the prefix *un* = *not* and the suffix *like* = *as* will be able to say the word and know that it means "not as a sportsman." Knowledge of the rules of morphology will be helpful in establishing the structural analysis segment of your word analysis program.

Morphology. The morpheme is the smallest unit of meaning in any language. A morpheme is not necessarily a word, as a word may be composed of a single morpheme (e.g., *venture*) or several morphemes (e.g., *ad • venture • some*) There are two types of morphemes, one generally referred to as "free," meaning that it is uninflected and can stand alone as a word (e.g., *box*), and "bound," meaning that it cannot stand alone (e.g., *-ing* as in *boxing*). Free morphemes are often found as *root words*; bound morphemes are usually *affixes*. The following chart provides examples of bound and free morphemes.

Bound Morpheme	Free Morpheme	Bound Morpheme
pre	view	
re	view	
	view	er
	view	ing
pre	view	er
re	view	ing
pre	test	
re	test	
	test	er
	test	ing
pre	test	ing
re	test	ing

Root words (free morphemes) are also sometimes called stem or base words. Examples of root words are

walk	pay	sleep	agree	fear
boy	box	cover	part	stand

Affixes. Helping children to understand how words are constructed is an important step in assisting them in unlocking word meanings. To do so, children must be introduced to the affixes of English. Affixes are called bound morphemes, and they include prefixes and suffixes. The following chart illustrates the affixes of the English language.

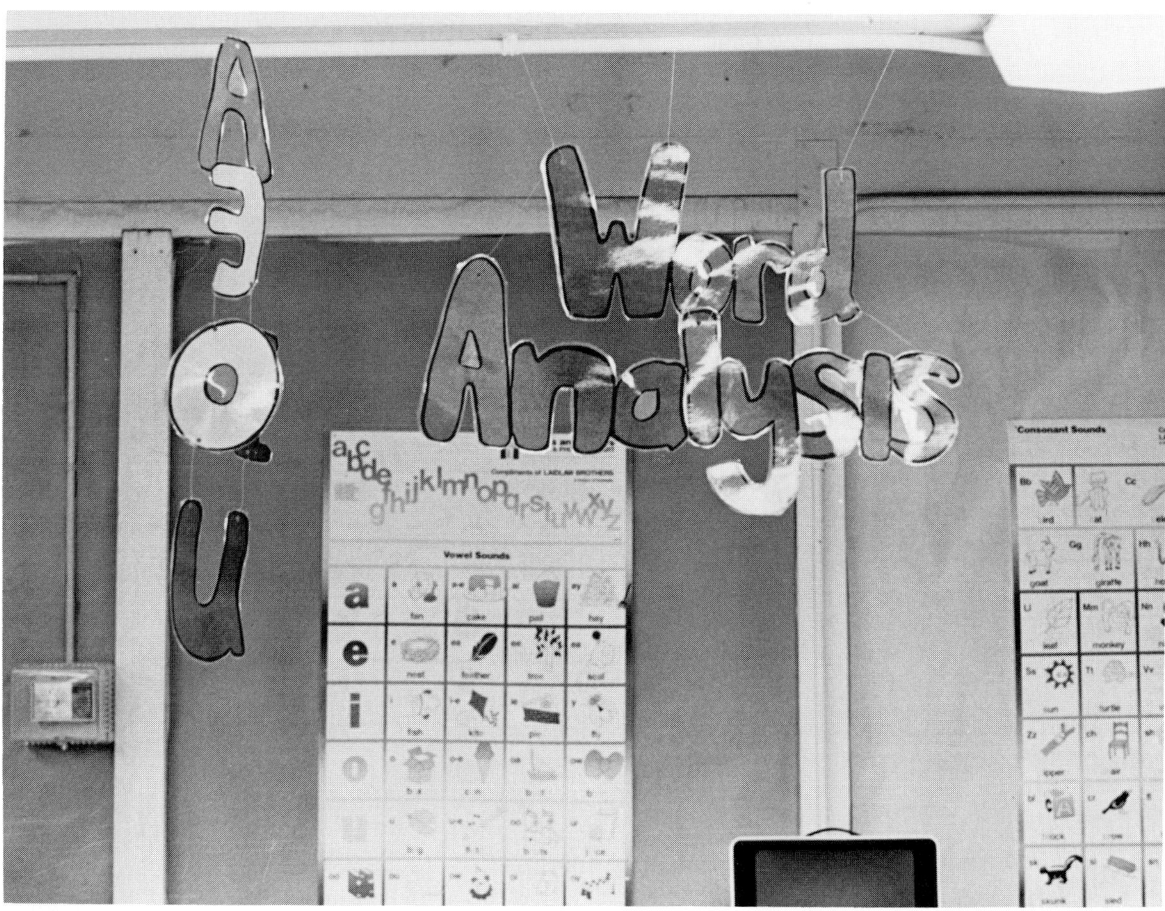

Helping children understand how words are constructed is an important step in assisting them in unlocking word meanings. (Photo by Linda Lungren.)

Word Class	Affix	When Affix Is Added to	Example
ADVERB	-ly	ADJ	hardly, slowly
		derived ADJ	carelessly stereotypically advantageously relatively
	-wise	N	otherwise
	-ward	N	frontward
	a-	N	aside, ahead
		V	afloat
		ADJ	alive, afresh, aloud
		STEM	aghast
	al-	ADV	almost already
	-fore	ADV	therefore
	-most	N	foremost
ADJECTIVE	-y	N	lengthy
		STEM	pretty
	-al	N	functional
		STEM	terminal integral
	-ible	V	reversible
		STEM	fallible visible
	-able	V	adorable
		STEM	viable durable
	-ful	N	careful
	-less	N	guileless

	Suffix	Base	Examples
	-en	N	wooden
	-ive	V	possessive
		N	defective
		STEM	native
	-ar	N	particular
		STEM	regular, linear
	-ary	N	honorary
		STEM	ordinary
	-ic	N	aromatic
		STEM	arctic analytic
	-ish	N	foolish
		STEM	squeamish
	-ous	N	mischievous
		STEM	fabulous
	-ent	V	abhorrent
		STEM	resident expedient
	-ose	ADJ	grandiose
		STEM	morose
	-ed	N	spotted
		V	determined
	-id	STEM	morbid, lurid
	-ing	N	conflicting
		V	hanging
	-ate	N	proportionate
		STEM	literate
	-ile	STEM	mercantile juvenile
	-ory	V	contradictory
		STEM	illusory
	-ant	N	concordant
		STEM	rampant verdant
	-some	V	meddlesome
VERB	-ate	N	fabricate
		STEM	separate
	-ize	N	idolize
		ADJ	vitalize
		STEM	emphasize mesmerize
	-ify	N	citify
		ADJ	simplify clarify
		STEM	liquify modify
	-ish	STEM	finish, polish
	-en	N	hasten
		ADJ	moisten
		STEM	glisten
	en-	N	engulf, enjoy
		V	enliven, enjoin
		ADJ	embitter, enrich
		STEM	endure, endow
	-le	N	handle
		STEM	amble
	-er	V	loiter, saunter
NOUN	-age	V	spoilage
	-ance	V	preponderance hindrance perserverance
	-cy	N	leniency agency
		ADJ	obstinacy consistency
	-ee	V	employee refugee
	-er	N	boxer biographer
		V	skier
		STEM	matter
	-ian	N	historian
	-ile	N	projectile
	-ism	N	despotism
		STEM	paroxism
	-ist	V	typist
		N	pianist
		ADJ	socialist
	-ive	N	objective
		V	relative
		STEM	missive
	-ity	STEM	animosity
		ADJ	generosity
	-ment	V	payment amusement
	-ness	ADJ	goodness liveliness
	-old	N	cuckold
	-ship	N	citizenship
		ADJ	hardship
	-ster	N	gangster roadster
		ADJ	oldster
		STEM	monster
	-um	V	continuum
		ADJ	ultimatum
		STEM	curriculum
	-us	N	modulus
		STEM	stimulus animus
	-tion	derived V	solution
		V	eruption vibration
	-hood	N	statehood motherhood

New affixes are constantly being added to English. Many of these pass quickly from the English language, but some of them remain in the general language usage: for example, from *hamburger*, we derive *burger* and *cheeseburger*.

sandwich	wich	fishwich
panorama	orama	cinerama
marathon	thon	telethon

Prefixes. A prefix is added to the beginning of a word, changing its meaning. There may be one or several prefixes added to a given word. Some of the most frequently recurring prefixes and their meanings in English are

dis (not, apart)	em (in)
in (not)	de (from)
mis (wrong)	inter (between)
anti (against)	ex (out, from)
non (not)	en (in)
com (with)	op, ob (against)
con (with)	pro (in front of)
pre (before)	per (fully)
super (over)	im (not, in)
tri (three)	un (not, opposite of)

Suffixes. When the meaning of a word is modified by the addition of a *new* ending, a suffix has been added to the root word. Thorndike's text *The Teaching of English Suffixes* (1932) allows us some insight into the frequency with which some suffixes appear. For example, the five most common suffixes in English are

ion	decoration
er	harder
ness	awareness
ity	purity
y	rainy

Other suffixes that appear frequently are

able	objectionable
ant	pleasant

A list of recurring English suffixes with their meanings is presented below:

ness (being)	ling (little)
ment (result of)	ty (state)
ward (in direction of)	ity (state)
our (full of)	ure (denoting action)
ious (like, full of)	ion (condition or quality)
eous (like, full of)	ian, or, ist, er (one who does)
et (little)	en (made of, to become)
able, ible, ble, (capable of being)	ly (similiar in appearance or manner)
ic (like, made of)	ful (full of)
ish (like)	ness (quality or state of being)
and (being)	less (without)
ent (one who)	y (like a, full of)
age (collection of)	al (pertaining to)
ance (state of being)	man (one who)
ence (state or quality)	
wise (ways)	

Inflectional Endings. Because English has evolved into a word order language, there are few remaining inflections. Those that still exist are used for forming plurals, possessives, marking tenses, and comparatives. All commonly used tenses are included in the following listing.

Plural, Possessive, and Third Singular Verb Markers

1. If the word ends in any of these phonemes (/s, z, c, j/), the inflectional ending is /z/.

mass /mæs/	masses /mæs z/
barage /bəraǰ/	barages /bərajəz/

2. If the word ends in a voiceless consonant, the appropriate ending is /s/.

bit /bɪt/	bits bɪts/
sip /sɪp/	sips /sɪps/

3. If the word ends in either a voiced consonant or a vowel, the appropriate ending is /z/.

crib /krɪb/	cribs /Krɪbz/
rid /rɪd/	rids /rɪdz/

Tense Markers

1. *Past tense and past participle.* Both of these forms use the same rules to produce their appropriate endings
   a. If the verb ends in /t/ or /d/, the ending is /əd/.

      rate /ret/ rated /retəd/

   b. If the verb ends in a voiceless consonant, the ending is /t/.

      dip /dɪp/ dipped /dɪpt/

   c. If the verb ends in a voiced consonant or a vowel, the ending is /d/.

      rib /rɪb/ ribbed /rɪbd/

2. *The progressive.* When the progressive is used, for example, *ing*, as in "He is going," /ɪŋ/ is added to the verb form, following the *be*, to form the present participle.

he will sell	/hi wɪl sel/
he will be selling	/hi wɪl bi selɪŋ/

Comparatives

When forming the comparative or the superlative of many adjectives and adverbs, *-er* and *-est* are added, respectively.

tall	taller	tallest
narrow	narrower	narrowest

Compound Words. Due to their natural familiarity with the words that combine to form compound words, children are generally able to use this word analysis skill quickly and easily. Gleason (1969) conducted a study of children's definitions of compound words and offers the following definitions for the words *airplane, breakfast*, and *Friday.*

> They knew what the words referred to and how to use them, but their ideas about the words were rather amusing. One little boy said that an airplane is called an airplane because it is a plain thing that goes in the air. Another child said that breakfast is called breakfast because you have to eat it fast to get to school on time. Several subjects thought that Friday is called Friday because it is the day you eat fried fish. (p. 19).

During beginning reading programs children may be taught to identify many compound words as sight words.

policeman	mailman
grandmother	football
grandfather	doghouse
thanksgiving	toothpick
breakfast	seaweed
outcome	filmstrip

Because many of these words are part of the spoken vocabularies of your children, they can be used as a base for drawing generalizations about other compound words. The following is a list of compound words that are frequently used in basal programs:

township	anthill	anyway	toothache
wheelbarrow	countryside	something	marksman
policeman	peppermint	whenever	spellbound
soapstone	grasshopper	himself	sharpshooter
teenage	flagpole	snowman	beeswax
nighttime	peacetime	windshield	rowboat
Marblehead	lifejacket	toothbrush	drawbridge
needlepoint	Northwest	toothpaste	raincoat
understatement	downpour	motorcycle	hatbox
gentlemen	fingertip	broadcast	bathtub
wristwatch	shortstop	aircraft	chessboard
overpower	houseboat	anyone	doormat
airplane	floodlight	afternoon	sailboat
baseball	eyeball	evergreen	bellhop
basketball	otherwise	airport	cowboy
football	pigtail	sandbox	eyeglass
skydive	classmate	railroad	clothesline
underground	slowpoke	bookcase	wishbone
fireman	blacksmith	horseshoe	doghouse
sweatshirt	notebook	lighthouse	sidewalk
Eiderdown	pushpin	upset	pocketbook
uptown	taxpayer	salesman	cookbook
downtown	riverbank	lifetime	faraway
classroom	undersize	without	bedroom
homework	birthday	clubhouse	nowhere
lunchbox	weatherman	typewriter	barefoot

By providing your students with the skills of structural analysis, you are giving them yet one more approach to recognizing words and understanding their meanings. With a knowledge of the rules of morphology, children are easily able to analyze complex words that might otherwise have been daunting. When you are implementing your structural analysis program, you may want to follow some of these rules.

1. Encourage children to analyze the ending of each word, such as *s, ed,* as tense markers, *'s* as possession, and *s* as a plural marker.
2. Encourage children to split words into parts with which they are already familiar, for example, re/*view*/ing.
3. Encourage children to guess the pronunciation of a new word by looking at the parts of the word that are familiar to them.
4. Encourage children to make their own "new" compound words. This will help them to understand better how compound words are formed.

An understanding of structural analysis will help your children deal with many new words. Structural analysis, like phonics and sight-word strategies, is only one way of helping children learn to decode words. Each strategy is useful only as an aid to learning—no strategy can substitute for learning.

STRATEGIES FOR CONTEXTUAL ANALYSIS

Because word meaning is often dependent on the context in which it is used, skill in recognizing and understanding unknown words by utilizing clues in the surrounding context is essential to readers of all levels of maturity.

All language . . . concerns itself with meanings. Or, perhaps, we should say rather that human beings are basically concerned with meanings and use language as their tool to grasp, to comprehend, and to share meanings. It is the linguist's business to turn the spotlight on the tool—language itself—in order to examine the physical material

Because word meaning is often dependent on the context in which it is used, skill in recognizing and understanding unknown words by utilizing clues in the surrounding context is essential to readers of all levels of maturity. (Photo by Paul Hill.)

of which it is composed and to determine the ways this material has been selected and shaped to accomplish its function of mediating meaning.

(Fries, 1963, p. 97)

These literary devices provide much needed information about the words they seek to explain, and it is therefore important for readers to be able to recognize these *contextual clues* when they are provided. By instructing beginning readers to examine not only the unknown word itself but also what the author has provided surrounding the word, we can expose students to all the available clues for understanding the unknown word.

While the actual role of the use of contextual analysis in the decoding process is still under investigation and is causing controversy among researchers (see Biemiller, 1979; Juel, 1980), there is little question that the ability to use context clues is an integral part of the reading process.

Each of the devices mentioned is important, and before we suggest instructional activities for each of these clues, we need to understand them thoroughly.

Definition. As children's materials are being written, authors closely monitor the introduction of new words. One common way of providing children with an understanding of the new word is to *introduce* and *define* it within the same context.

The cornea is the transparent outer coating of the eyeball.

Synonym. By using a word that means the same thing as the new word, the author provides a useful clue to word meaning.

a. I hanker to visit California. This restless longing never ends.

b. It was an accident, since it occurred as happenstance.

Summary. A brief listing of the qualities or characteristics evoked by a word can provide a summary that will clarify the new word for the reader.

a. They all said Toby was uncouth. His loud, harsh voice, crude language, and disgusting manners seemed to bear them out.

b. Mary is a student who is interested in intellectual inquiry as well as research.

Simile. A simile uses the words *like* or *as* to make a comparison or provide information about a word or idea.

a. Her hair was as blond as harvested wheat.

b. Her lips were as taut as a steel pipe.

c. The boy's eyes glistened like bright stars in the sky.

Examples. Illustration through examples is a clear and useful method for providing information about a new word.

a. Linda is an ambitious girl. For example, she spends every evening doing extra work for her assignments.

b. The words running, going, doing, and crying are examples of the incorporation of the suffix -ing to root words.

Apposition. A statement, in a word or a phrase, that is equivalent to the subject is a statement of *apposition*. Statements of apposition are usually adjacent to each other and may or may not be set off by commas.

a. The dictionary, a book that contains an alphabetic arrangement of the words of one language, was of help to the child.

b. *A Christmas Carol* is a classic by the English novelist Dickens.

Antonym. An *antonym*, a word opposite in meaning from another, is often provided in printed material as a contextual clue.

a. Lynne is often calm. Anxiety is a characteristic that cannot be ascribed to her.

b. We stood silently watching the raucous waves.

Groupings. When an unfamiliar word is classified in context with other words to depict similarities, the meaning of the word is often more readily recognized by the reader.

a. His tie was a combination of many colors: yellow, red, and chartreuse.

b. I bought a chamois, sponges, wax, and detergent on my way home from school.

Spache and Spache (1973) clearly delineate the importance of teaching children contextual analysis strategies when they explain the relationship between contextual analysis and inferential thinking skills:

> Apparently most context clues demand some degree of inferential thinking. As a result, some teachers assume that contextual analysis is not much more than guesswork and therefore should not be promoted. The truth is that such inferential thinking is an essential part of the reading process at all maturity levels and should be strongly encouraged. Pupils should not be burdened with learning the technical terms which might be employed to describe the types of context clues. Rather the emphasis should be placed upon helping the reader use the sense of the sentence or the surrounding sentences as an aid in identifying the probable meaning of a difficult word. The goal of contextual analysis is not always an exact recognition of a word or its pronunciation. These may be approached by other means such as phonic or structural analysis. But when these techniques are successful, they do not necessarily result in the derivation of the meaning of the word, for it may not be encompassed in the reader's auditory vocabulary. Thus contextual analysis takes the reader beyond pronunciation to meaning, which in many situations is more significant for his ultimate comprehension. (p. 497)

It should be noted that other contextual clues may also benefit the reader: *italics, footnotes, capitalization, boldface type, quotation marks,* and *parenthetical statements.* Teachers can encourage children to use contextual clues to extract meaning from the printed word.

Teaching children contextual analysis strategies will not ensure the effective reading of every word but may provide the child with an added possibility for decoding the unknown word. You can instruct children in contextual analysis strategies by calling their attention to the following: picture clues, lexical clues (word and sentence meaning of clues), relational clues (word order clues in sentence), and interpretation clues. You can do this by instructing children through the use of cloze exercises like the following:

1. Deleting words from sentences

    Lena Valentino, elected senator from Massachusetts, ______ for the Equal Rights Amendment.

2. Deleting words from language experience stories

    We went to the zoo.
    Anita Deasy liked the gorillas.
    Jim Hill liked the ______.

Additionally, contextual clues can be taught using some of the following strategies:

PICTURE CLUES

a. Justin pushed the ______ across the grass.

b. Surprisingly, ______ enjoy eating carrots, apples, and lettuce as well as peanuts.

LEXICAL CLUES

a. Ripe, red, round, and juicy, the ______ crunched as she took a bite.

b. ______, the rich and creamy brown substance, is made of peanuts and oil.

RELATIONAL CLUES

a. The tiny spotted ______ barked with anticipation as his owner walked up the path.

b. The woman held her ______ up over her head as the rain poured down on top of it.

INTERPRETIVE CLUES

a. The dazzling light was like a ______ in the darkened sky.

b. The spider spun its ensnaring ______ in the corner of the room.

Contextual analysis may be viewed as another aid in developing reading comprehension. When children use contextual analysis strategies as a process to further their understanding of the printed page, they are using another set of clues which will help them to decode and acquire meaning. The mature, competent reader greatly depends upon context clues to help accelerate his or her reading and increase comprehension of difficult and unfamiliar texts. It is important to encourage your children to pay attention to the context of a passage. When your students are unable to continue in a passage because they are stumped by an unfamiliar word, tell them to ask themselves the following questions:

1. Are there clues to the meaning of this word in the surrounding words?
2. Will I understand this word if I continue to the end of the sentence?
3. Have I examined the pictures for clues to the meaning?

In the next few pages, we present several activities that may be useful reinforcements for your word analysis program.

SIGHT-WORD ACTIVITIES

1. Word Stacks

Goal: Discrimination of sight words with similar configurations

Grade Level: K–3

Construction: On heavy cardboard write words that have similar configurations; then cut them out following the edges of the letters. Make several words for each configuration.

saw	pig	bell	bill
was	jog	dell	hill

Utilization: Mix up the cards; then have the students sort them into stacks according to configuration, pronouncing each word as they stack it.

2. Dip in the Well

Goal: Discrimination of function sight words

Grade Level: K–3

Construction: Write a list of function sight words on separate index cards. Write sentences leaving out one word space. Ask the children to supply the correct sight words.

Function words:	Sentences:
of, the, off, if	Keep ____ the grass.
then, over, above	The sky is ________ the earth.

Utilization: The game can be played like Go Fish. Deal each player seven cards and put the rest of the deck in the middle of the table. The object of the game is to match two cards, Keep ______ the grass and off.

If a player cannot make a match, he asks the player to his right, "Do you have an off card?" If he does not have it, he tells the original player to "Dip in the Well."

3. Words-O

Goal: Recognizing sight words

Grade Level: K–3

Construction: Draw a Bingo card using the WORDS-O. Write sight words in each of the boxes.

W	O	R	D	S	O
of	every	off	sight	how	would
the	is	FREE	might	should	where
each	as	from	what	who	when

Utilization: The caller draws the sight words from a pile of prepared index cards. He names the card as each student examines his board to see if he has the word. If he has, he covers it with a chip. The first to have all the spaces covered wins the game.

4. Word Grams

Goal: Developing word-recognition skills by reinforcing the visual structure of words

Grade Level: Pre K–3

Construction: Select a series of words that have a distinctive visual structure. Words should be those that can be combined into meaningful sentences. Write each word on a piece of oak tag. Cut the oak tag to emphasize the visual structure.

Utilization: Each child selects a series of words and from these forms a sentence.

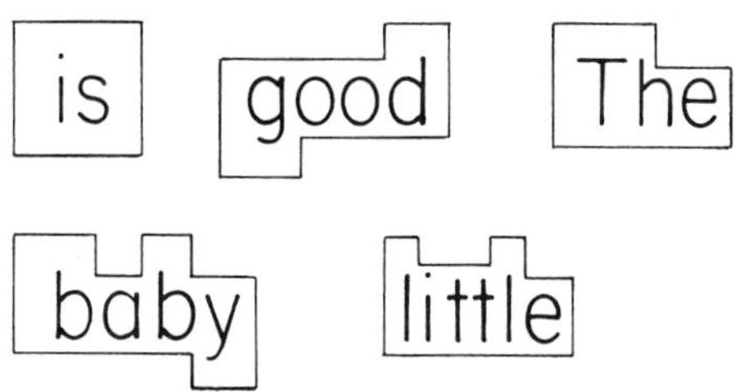

5. Sight-Word Basketball

Goal: Recognizing sight words

Grade Level: 1–4

Construction: On the chalkboard, draw a scoreboard such as the one illustrated here. Make up cards in the shape of basketballs and print sight words on them.

	HOME	VISITORS
1		
2		
3		
4		

Utilization: Divide the class into two teams—Home and Visitors (or have them invent names). Appoint a scorekeeper and a timekeeper. Hold up one word for the "tip off," and whichever team answers first gets to start (or flip a coin). Show each team a card, alternating between teams. When one team misses a word, the other one gets a "free throw," or a chance to name it, plus a new word. The game is divided into four quarters; each "quarter" is timed (two minutes or more depending on time available). The team with the most points at the end of four quarters wins.

6. Calendar Words

Goal: Practice in word recognition

Grade Level: K–3

Construction: Design or acquire a calendar with large daily squares. Construct cardboard number squares for each day of the month. On each page of the calendar write the name of the month; on each cardboard square write the number of the day and a sight word.

November						
Sun.	Mon.	Tues.	Wed.	Thurs.	Fri.	Sat.
1	2	3	4	5	6	7
8	9	10	11	12	13	14
15	16	17	18	19	20	21
22	23	24	25	26	27	28
29	30					

15 saw

26 the

Utilization: In turn, each child draws a cardboard number card. He or she must then pronounce the corresponding word appearing on the calendar for that day. If correct, the child receives the number of points appearing as the number of the day on the cardboard card. Whoever has the most points when all of the cards are drawn wins.

7. Checker Words

Goal: Recognition of sight words

Grade Level: K–3

Construction: Draw a checker board on oak tag. In each square write a sight word twice, having it face both directions. You will need checkers or chips (or dried lima beans).

to to		am am		were were
	it it		saw saw	
have have		the the		stop stop
	go go		book book	
you you		day day		this this

Utilization: To jump a piece or land on a square, the child must pronounce the word on the space to which he or she is moving. The rules for checkers are followed.

8. Pick-a-Plural

Goal: Forming plurals

Grade Level: 3–6

Construction: Attach three envelopes to a bulletin board. Label one envelope for 6 points, one 10 points, and one 15 points. On 3" X 5" cards, write the singular form of the words. Place the words in the envelopes. Five-point words should be less difficult than 10- or 15-point words.

5	10	15
train	fox	leaf
grape	latch	man
toy	candy	wolf

Utilization: Divide the class into two teams. In turn, players from each team select an envelope. A word is then drawn. The team has fifteen seconds in which to spell the plural form of the word. If the team can supply the correct word form, it is given the number of points appearing on the envelope. If the team cannot supply the plural form, it must subtract the number from its existing score. The team first earning 75 points wins.

9. Attractions

Goal: Forming compound words

Grade Level: 4–6

Construction: Write parts of compound words on two pieces of masking tape and affix each to a paper clip. A horseshoe magnet is also needed.

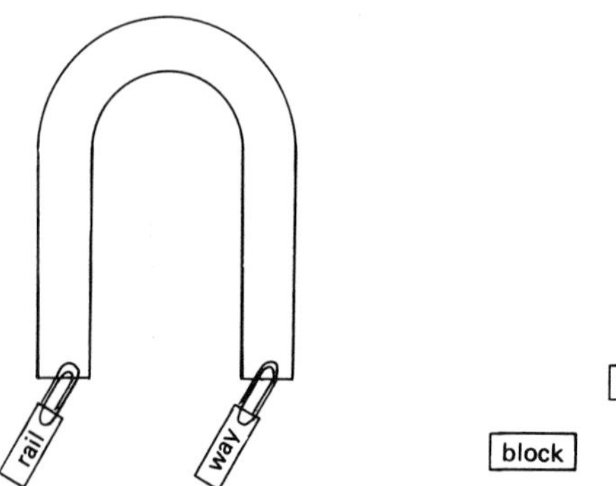

Utilization: Children pick up two words with a horseshoe magnet that, when they are joined together, form a compound word. The child writes the word and tries to form as many different words as possible.

10. Concentration

Goal: Forming compound words

Grade Level: 4–6

Construction: Make 3" X 5" word cards so that, when two are combined, they form a compound word.

Utilization: Sixteen cards are placed down and children take turns turning over two cards. If a compound word is formed from the two that are turned up, the child gets to keep it as a "match." If the two cards do not make a match, the cards are returned to their face-down positions, and another child tries to find the match. Whoever has the most pairs when all the cards are used wins.

11. Contraction Galaxy

Goal: Matching contractions with the original two words

Grade Level: 3–6

Construction: On an oak-tag board, draw an arrangement of circles to represent a galaxy of stars. Make up cards in the shape of starships and write the two words that form the contractions on each wing of the ship.

Utilization: The child must "claim" the planet by matching the two words on the ship with the contraction on the planet. A point is given each time a ship properly claims a planet.

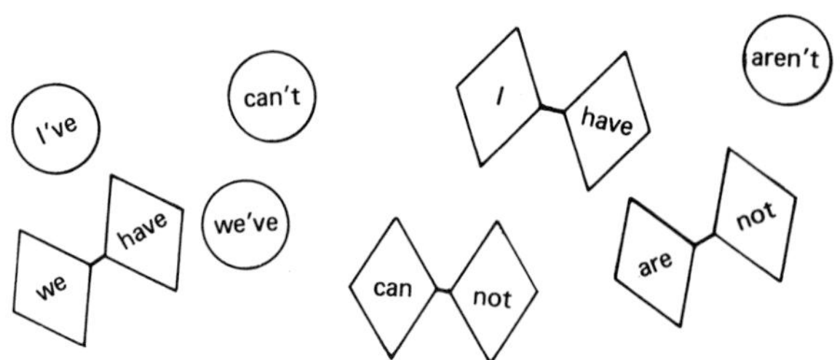

12. 3-2-1 Contract

Goal: Making a contraction out of two spoken words

Grade Level: 3–6

Construction: Record on cassette tape sentences containing words that could be made into contractions.

Utilization: The student writes on paper the proper words in contraction form.

13. Finding the Ending

Goal: Completing stories by selecting appropriate root words and prefixes

Grade Level: 3-6

Construction: Write a short story, leaving out several words that contain prefixes. The story could be written on a piece of oak tag, with slits cut into the blanks. Two decks of small cards should be designed, one set containing all the root words and one set containing all the prefixes. To facilitate a large group of children, the root words and prefixes could also be listed in two separate columns at the bottom of the printed story.

Utilization: A child selects the missing root word and prefix and inserts them into the proper blank.

14. Connection Puzzles

Goal: Matching appropriate suffixes with a root word

Grade Level: K-3

Construction: Design pairs of puzzle pieces out of heavy cardboard. On some pieces write root words, and on connecting pieces write appropriate suffixes (there may be more than one suffix for each root word).

Utilization: The child connects word pieces to appropriate suffix pieces to make new words. If the suffix is incorrect, the child will not be able to connect them.

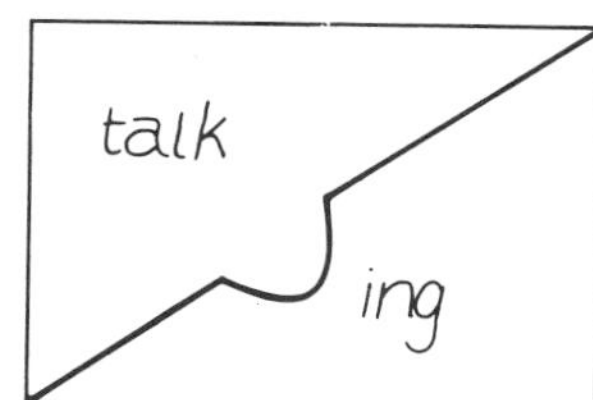

15. Simply Suffixes

Goal: Adding suffixes to given root words

Grade Level: K-3

Construction: You will need an overhead projector, blank transparencies, and a felt-tipped pen.

Utilization: Divide the group into two teams. The first member of team A writes a word on the transparency, to which a suffix could be added. The first member of team B must attach an appropriate suffix, making all the necessary changes in the root word. If team B's player is correct he writes a root word, and the second member of team A attempts to add a suffix. A point is scored for each correct suffix. If a player is unable to add the correct suffix, the next team member on the opposing team makes an attempt. The team having the most points after a twenty-minute time period is the winner.

16. Affix Relay

Goal: Making new words by adding a suffix

Grade Level: All grades

Construction: All that is needed is a chalkboard and chalk.

Utilization: Divide the class into two teams. Write two words on the board to which endings could be added to make new words. The difficulty of the word will depend on the age and abilities of the students. The first member of each team goes up to the board and writes a new word, using the derivative. They run back and give the chalk to the next team members, who must then add a new ending. Whichever team writes the most words in one minute wins. Examples:

adventure	tire	note
adventures	tires	notes
adventured	tired	noted
adventuring	tiring	noting
adventuresome	tiresome	notation

This game can be modified to stress prefixes or both prefixes and suffixes.

17. Wordy Spider

Goal: Adding prefixes and suffixes to root words

Grade Level: 3-5

Construction: Draw a spider on a bulletin board, chalkboard, or ditto master. The body of the spider should contain a root word. On the arms of the spider write various prefixes and suffixes.

Utilization: Each child writes as many different word combinations as possible. Whoever makes the most words wins.

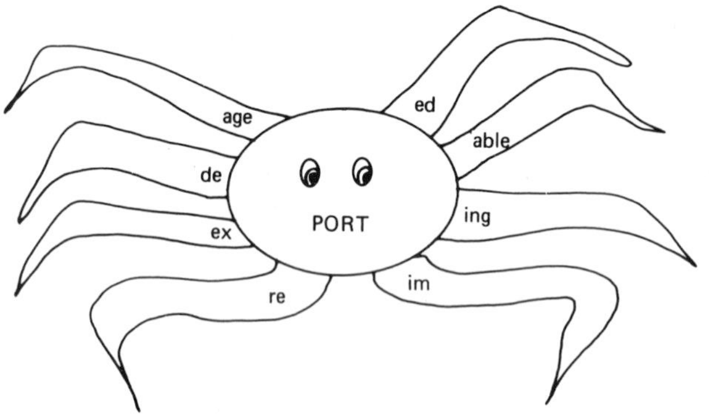

18. Can of Words

Goal: Adding prefixes and suffixes to root words

Grade Level: 3-6

Construction: Secure three coffee cans and label them prefixes, root words, and suffixes. Construct several 3" X 5" cardboard-backed cards. On each card write a prefix, suffix, or root word.

Utilization: The child draws a card from each can and attempts to make a word using all three pieces. Examples:

pre	tend	ing

If the prefix or suffix does not apply, only one need be used. The child tries to make as many different words as possible.

19. Clay Comparisons

Goal: Understanding and identifying inflectional changes within adjectives as they relate to tangible objects

Grade Level: 4-6

Construction: Supply several children with equal amounts of clay. Design word cards with each card containing a series of adjectives with inflectional endings. Examples:

big, bigger, biggest

tall, taller, tallest

long, longer, longest

Give each child a word card.

Utilization: Each child reads a card and designs clay objects to illustrate the concept shown on the card. For example, the child could design three stars:

big star

bigger star

biggest star

20. Speedway Words

Goal: Modification of word forms through inflectional endings

Grade Level: 4-6

Construction: Design a gameboard by drawing a race-track either on the board or on a piece of paper that is then pasted to the board. Write a base word in each of the first few squares; then several squares farther on write a word partner to each of the base words, mixing them up. Continue to fill in the squares with more base words and derivatives of all the base words. Also include pictures (free squares) and directions to miss a turn, take another turn, go back to START, and so on.

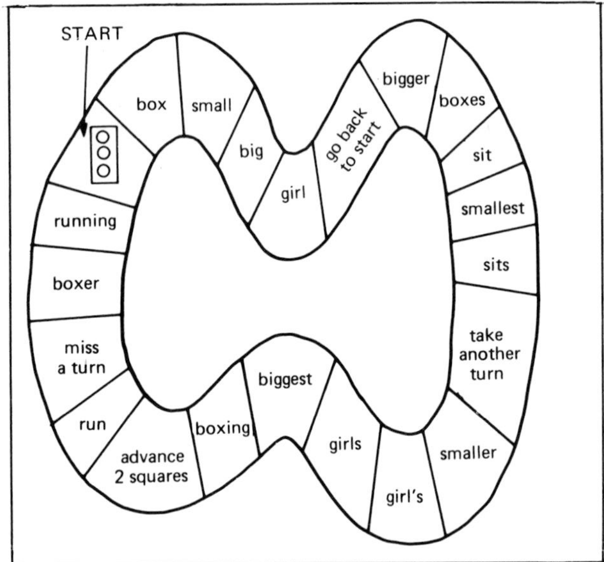

Utilization: In turn, players roll the dice and move the appropriate number of spaces When a player lands on the appropriate square, he or she is to identify the word and also the very next word partner appearing on the board. If the child makes the correct identification, he may move his playing piece to the word partner. For example, if the child lands on big, he should move to bigger, or biggest depending on which appears first. The first player to move around the board is the winner.

21. Fish Families

Goal: Altering word structures with inflectional endings

Grade Level: 4-6

Construction: Make up 4" X 5" word cards from oak-tag board. Four cards from the same family comprise a "book." For example,

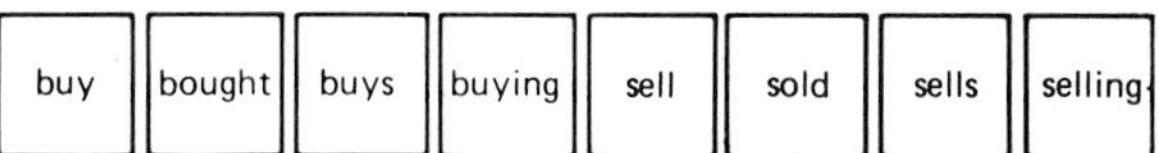

Utilization: Players are dealt four cards and the rest are scattered face down on the table. In turn, each player asks any other player for a card that could help to make a "book." If he receives it he can ask again; if the person does not have the card, he says "Fish," and the asker must draw a card. If he draws the card he was asking for, he gets another turn. Whoever has the most books when there are no more cards wins. Each player then must say the words in his books.

22. John and He

Goal: Changing nouns to pronouns, and vice versa

Grade Level: 4-6

Construction: Write a short story on a chart or ditto. Underline all nouns and pronouns.

Utilization: Have children replace all the nouns in the story with pronouns and all the pronouns with nouns. Children should recopy the story on another sheet of paper and tell which story sounds better to them and whether the original meaning of the story is still the same.

23. Pronoun Slaps

Goal: Distinguishing between nouns and pronouns

Grade Level: 4-6

Construction: Design a deck of cards that contains a variety of nouns and pronouns.

Utilization: Deal out all the cards and keep them face down. Instruct the children to slap only the words that are pronouns. Players in turn place a card in the center of the table. If it is a pronoun, the first to slap it gets to keep the card. When all a player's cards are used up, he is out of the game. Whoever has the most cards at the end wins.

24. Possessive Jeopardy

Goal: Forming possessives of nouns and pronouns

Grade Level: 4-6

Construction: Design a question board by securing a large square piece of oak tag. The board should be divided into four columns: nouns, pronouns, possessive nouns, and possessive pronouns. Cut several squares from cardboard or material. Staple five squares to each cardboard column, leaving enough slack for the cardboard squares to be used as pockets. Squares within each column should be labeled 5, 10, 15, 20, and 25, respectively. Question cards, of increasing difficulty, dealing with the title of the column should be placed in the pockets. For example, use the question, "How do you spell the possessive form of children?"

Utilization: In turn, players choose a category (noun, pronoun, possessive noun, possessive pronoun) and the pocket number from which they want to draw their question. If the player answers correctly, he gains the score listed in the pocket from which his card was drawn (5, 10, 15, 20, 25). If the player cannot answer the question, he forfeits his turn. The player accumulating the most points is the winner.

Nouns	Pronouns	Possessive nouns	Possessive pronouns
5	5	5	5
10	10	10	10
15	15	15	15
20	20	20	20
25	25	25	25

CONTEXTUAL ANALYSIS ACTIVITIES

25. Crosswords

Goal: Utilizing contextual definitions

Grade Level: 3-6

Construction: Design a crossword puzzle in which students have to choose a word from a list to complete a sentence. The selected word is to be defined within the context of the sentence.

Utilization: The child completes each sentence and then writes the correct letters in the appropriate puzzle boxes. Examples:

censor candy car

a. A ________ is an official who examines a book.
b. A piece of ________ is a sweet treat made with sugar.
c. An automobile is often defined as a ________.

26. Guess What?

Goal: Utilizing contextual groupings

Grade Level: 4-6

Construction: Design a series of groupings that describes the uses of one instrument or the tasks of an occupation. The end of the sentence that tells the name of the instrument or occupation is omitted. Clickers or some sort of noisemaker will also be necessary.

Utilization: Divide the class into teams each consisting of five players. Each team is given a noisemaker to be used for signaling. The master of ceremonies reads the description and calls on the team who signals first with the noisemaker. The player must supply the missing word. If the player is correct, the team scores five points. If he is incorrect, the other team is allowed to answer. The team with the most points at the end of the game wins. Examples:

I answer the alarm, ride on the truck, and put out the fire.

I am a firefighter.

I love old bones, hate cats and bark at strangers.

I am a (dog).

I am used to plow fields, pull wagons, plant seeds, and mow large fields. I am a (tractor).

27. Don't Do What I Do

Goal: Utilizing contextual antonyms

Grade Level: 1-3

Construction: Make up descriptive sentences that contain antonyms.

Utilization: Read a sentence containing antonyms and have members of the class act out the sentence at the same time showing opposite actions. For example; "She laughed so hard she cried." One child should pantomime laughter and another child should pantomime crying.

28. Scrambled Synonyms

Goal: Utilizing contextual synonyms

Grade Level: 3-6

Construction: Design sentences that utilize synonyms to introduce or define unfamiliar words. Do not include the new word in the sentence context. Instead, construct a chart consisting of missing words and deceptive letters mixed vertically, horizontally, diagonally, forward, and backward. Examples:

a. I ______ to visit California. This restless longing never ends.
b. The old ______ is a tired female horse.
c. My grandmother is my mother's ______.

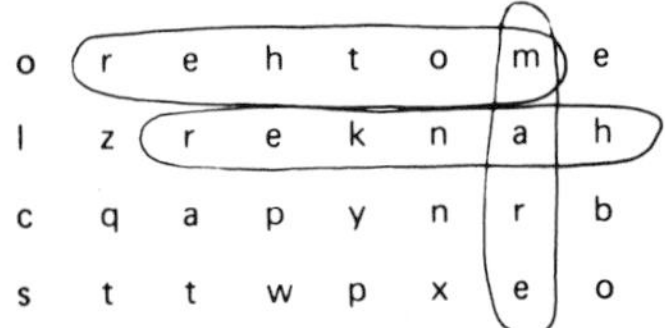

Utilization: Each child is given a dittoed copy of the sentences and word chart. The child reads the sentence and then looks to the chart and selects the missing synonym. The child circles the synonym and also writes it in the sentence.

29. Send the Dragon Home

Goal: Utilizing contextual summaries

Grade Level: 3-6

Construction: On a large piece of oak tag, draw a gameboard with small squares. At one end of the board draw a dragon, and at the opposite end draw a cave. Design a set of 3" X 5" cards that offer detailed, descriptive statements. A summary of each statement is written in various squares on the board. Secure buttons, beans, or other desired playing pieces.

Utilization: In turn, each player draws a descriptive card. After reading the descriptive statement, the student moves his playing piece to the square on the board that offers a summary statement. If the player cannot identify the summary statement, he returns his playing pieces to "dragon" and awaits his next turn. The first player to reach the "cave" wins the game. If a student selects a descriptive card, the summary of which would move him in reverse, he remains where he is if he can identify the summary square. If he cannot identify the summary square, he should be aided in doing so and returned to "dragon."

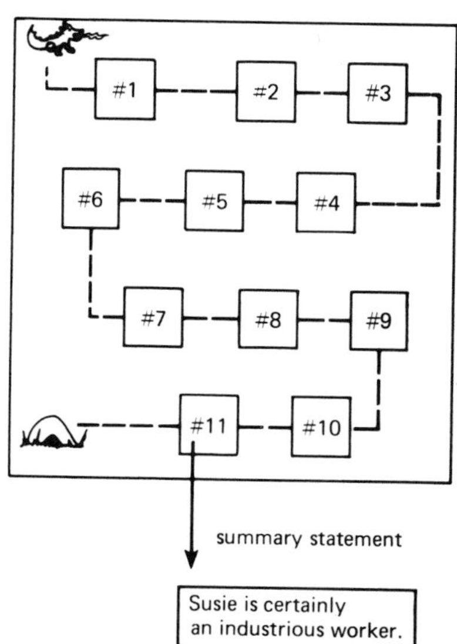

30. For Example

Goal: Utilizing contextual examples

Grade Level: 4-6

Construction: Prepare a list of introductory sentences. One sentence should appear at the top of a blank sheet of paper.

Utilization: One paper, with an introductory sentence, is given to the first person in each row or at a learning center. The paper is passed throughout the group or row and each child adds an example that clarifies the introductory statement. When all groups have finished, the statements are read and one point is given for each acceptable example. The team receiving the most points wins. Examples:

Linda is an ambitious girl.
Linda has red hair.
Linda does all her homework.
Linda has read two books today.

31. Drawing Similes

Goal: Utilizing contextual similes

Grade Level: 2-5

Construction: Divide large pieces of drawing paper into sections. Design a series of sentences using similes with one word omitted. Example:

His voice sounded like the roar of a ______ .

Utilization: A child selects a sentence and mentally fills in the blank. He then illustrates the sentence on a piece of drawing paper and labels the picture with the completed sentence.

32. Make a Monkey

Goal: Utilizing contextual appositions

Grade Level: 2-4

Construction: On the board, draw a monkey's face.

Utilization: Divide the class into two teams. In turn, a member from each team is given a sentence that contains a word in apposition. However, the main word has been replaced by a blank line. Each time a player is correct, he may add a new part to the monkey. Whichever team completes the monkey first wins by making a "monkey" of the other team. Examples:

The ______, an instrument used in a baseball game, was thrown by the pitcher. (ball)

The ______, a soft sweet mixture, began to drip from the cone. (ice cream)

QUESTIONS AND RELATED READINGS

If you feel that you have not attained adequate knowledge to answer the following questions successfully, we suggest additional related readings.

1. Describe the theory and practice of teaching sight-word strategies.
2. Describe the elements of structural analysis.
3. Explain the use of contextual analysis strategies in the word-recognition process.

Goal 1: To help the reader to understand the use of sight-word strategies as a word-recognition skill.

Question 1: Describe the theory and practice of teaching sight-word strategies.

Baker, G. "Learning to Read: Children's Responses to 'Look and Say' Method." *Educational Review* 32 (June 1980), 133–50.

Floriani, B. P. "Word Expansions for Multiplying Sight Vocabulary." *The Reading Teacher* 33 (November 1979), 155–7.

Harris, A. J., and E. R. Sipay. *How to Increase Reading Ability: A Guide to Developmental and Remedial Methods.* 6th ed. New York: Longman, Inc., 1978.

Goal 2: To help the reader to understand the use of structural analysis as a word-recognition skill.

Question 2: Describe the elements of structural analysis.

Huston, B. A. "Moving Language Around: Helping Students Become Aware of Language Structure." *Language Arts* 57 (September 1980), 614–20.

Smith, N. B., and H. A. Robinson. *Reading Instruction for Today's Children*, 2nd ed. Englewood Cliffs, N.J.: Prentice-Hall, Inc., 1980, pp. 162–72.

Thomas, E. L., and H. A. Robinson. *Improving Reading in Every Class: A Sourcebook for Teachers.* 2nd ed. Boston: Allyn & Bacon, Inc., 1977.

Goal 3: To help the reader to understand the use of contextual analysis as a word recognition skill.

Question 3: Explain the use of contextual analysis strategies in the word-recognition process.

Durkin, D. *Teaching Them to Read.* 2nd ed. Boston: Allyn & Bacon, Inc., 1974.

Spache, G., and E. Spache. *Reading in the Elementary School.* 3rd ed. Boston: Allyn & Bacon, Inc., 1973.

West, R. F., and K. E. Stanovich. "Automatic Contextual Facilitation in Readers." *Child Development* 49 (September 1978), 717–27.

BIBLIOGRAPHY

Ashton-Warner, S. *Teacher.* New York: Bantam Books, Inc., 1963.

Biemiller, A. "Changes in the Use of Graphic and Contextual Information as Functions of Passage Difficulty and Reading Achievement Level." *Journal of Reading Behavior* 11 (Winter 1979), 307–18.

Brown, B. "Enrich Your Reading Program with Personal Words." *The Reading Teacher* 35 (October 1981), 40–3.

Coleman, E. *Collecting a Data Base for an Educational Technology,* Parts I and III. El Paso: University of Texas Press, 1967.

Dolch, E. "A Basic Sight Vocabulary." *Elementary School Journal* 36 (February 1936), 456–60.

Durrell, D. D. *Improving Reading Instruction.* New York: Harcourt Brace Jovanovich, 1966.

Fries, C. C. *Linguistics and Reading.* New York: Holt, Rinehart and Winston, 1963.

Gleason, J. B. "Language Development in Early Childhood." In *Oral Language and Reading*, ed. by J. Walden. Urbana, Ill.: National Council of Teachers of English, 1969.

Guszak, F. *Diagnostic Reading Instruction in the Elementary School.* New York: Harper & Row, Publishers, 1972.

Haber, R. N., and L. R. Haber. "The Shape of a Word Can Specify Its Meaning." *Reading Research Quarterly* 16 (No. 3, 1981), 334–45.

Haber, R. N., and R. Schindler. "Errors in Proofreading: Evidence of Syntactic Control of Letter Processing?" *Journal of Experimental Psychology: Human Perception and Performance* 7 (1981), 573–9.

Juel, C. "Comparison of Word Identification Strategies with Varying Context, Word Type, and Reader Skill." *Reading Research Quarterly* 15 (No. 3, 1980), 358–76.

Kucera, H., and W. Francis. *Computational Analysis of Present-Day American English.* Providence, R. I.: Brown University Press, 1967.

Marchbanks, B., and H. Levin. "Cues by Which Children Recognize Words." *Journal of Educational Psychology* 56 (September 1965), 57–61.

McHugh, J. "Words Most Useful in Reading." Compiled at California State University, Hayward, 1969.

Murphy, H., and D. Durrell. *Letters in Words.* Wellesley, Mass.: Curriculum Associates, Inc., 1970.

Rayner, K. "Developmental Changes in Word Recognition Strategies." *Journal of Educational Psychology* 68 (June 1976), 323-9.

____. "Eye Movements in Reading and Information Processing." *Psychological Bulletin* 85 (May 1978), 618–60.

Ruddell, R. *Reading-Language Instruction.* Englewood Cliffs, N.J.: Prentice-Hall, Inc., 1974.

Shuy, R. "Some Relationships of Linguistics to the Reading Process." In *Teachers' Edition of How It Is Nowadays*, ed. by T. Clymer and R. Ruddell. Reading 360 Series. Lexington, Mass.: Ginn and Company, 1973.

Spache, G. D., and E. Spache. *Reading in the Elementary School.* 3rd ed. Boston: Allyn & Bacon, Inc., 1973.

Thorndike, E. *The Teaching of English Suffixes.* New York: Bureau of Publications, Teachers College, Columbia University, 1932.

Veatch, J., et al. *Key Words to Reading: The Language Experience Approach Begins.* 2nd ed. Columbus, Ohio: Charles E. Merrill Publishing Company, 1979.

CHAPTER 7

Understanding Reading Comprehension

To read is to translate, for no two persons' experiences are the same. A bad reader is like a bad translator: he interprets literally when he ought to paraphrase and paraphrases when he ought to interpret literally. In learning to read well, scholarship, valuable as it is, is less important than instinct; some great scholars have been poor translators.

W. H. Auden, 1962

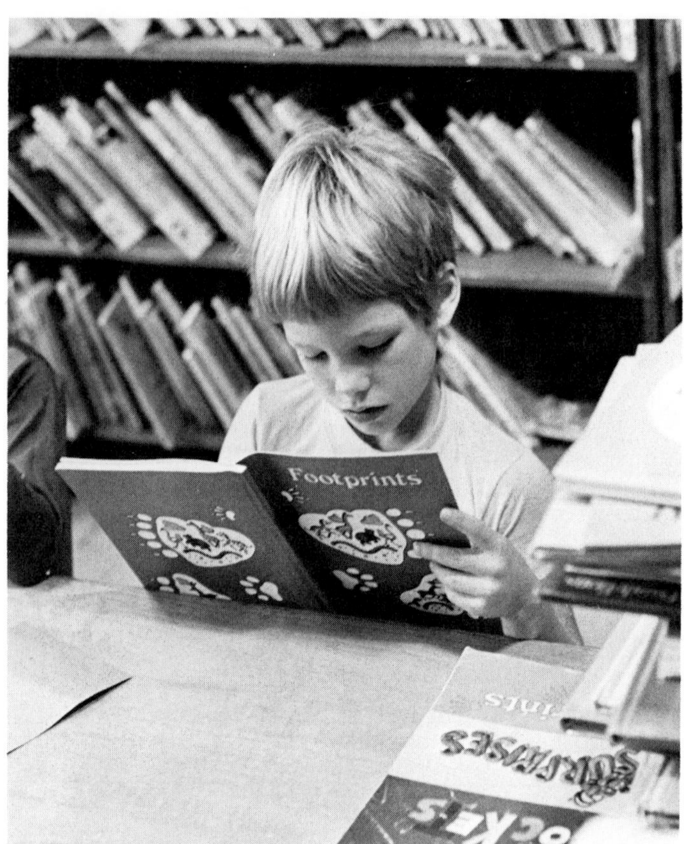

If information is not processed, if comprehension has not taken place, then reading has not occurred. (Photo by Linda Lungren.)

GOALS: To help the reader to

1. Understand the processes involved in reading comprehension.
2. Comprehend schema theory development.
3. Explain text structures and textual cohesion.
4. Develop various instructional practices that aid students in acquiring comprehension strategies.

OVERVIEW OF READING COMPREHENSION

Most broadly, reading comprehension is the acquisition of information from printed materials. If information is not processed, if comprehension has not taken place, then reading has not occurred. Reading *is* comprehension.

Lapp et al. (1982) have pointed out that there are many viewpoints regarding the exact nature of the comprehension of written discourse. One group of theorists holds a "bottom-up" view of reading; they claim that reading takes place in two stages: (1) decoding of words and (2) reading for meaning. This viewpoint implies that reading takes place in the following way: letter identification, letter-sound correspondence, the putting together of sounds, and lexical search for word meaning. The meaning of each word in a group is used to comprehend the meaning of the group. The inverse point of view, held by a second group of theorists, is a "top-down" view of reading. These theorists hold that higher-order cognitive structures are used to comprehend lower-order morphemic (word) and phonological (sound) information. A third viewpoint, and one held by many theorists (Menyuk and Flood, 1981; Rumelhart, in press), is a parallel processing or interactive viewpoint. These theorists claim that letter-sound correspondences, letter-sequence correspondences, and syntactic structures are used in parallel to arrive at the meaning of a string of words. This third view is the most reasonable position; it is based on the premise that readers must be aware of what they are doing, that is, readers must bring their knowledge of language to conscious awareness to be able to derive meaning from texts.

When students become experienced readers and when the reading material is familiar to them lexically and structurally, the process of reading becomes automatic. However, when the material is unfamiliar to them lexically or structurally, readers have to consciously bring all their knowledge of the world to a greater level of awareness to make sense of the text.

Different levels of language are required for different reading tasks. Menyuk (in press) illustrates these levels of language in the following diagram:

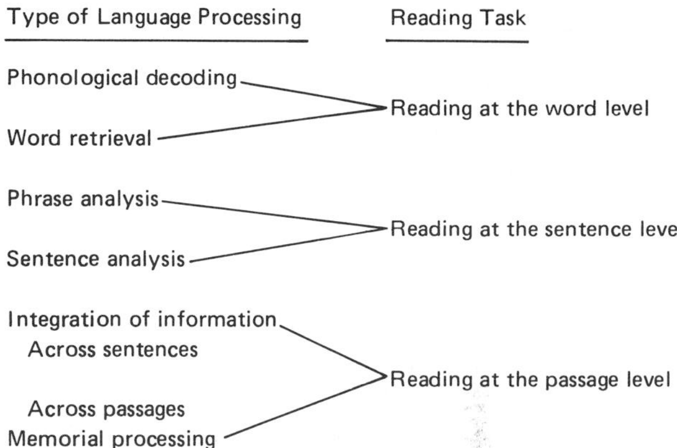

The steps in reading include the following: (1) all linguistic categorizations are brought to conscious awareness in the initial acquisition of reading in the translation process; (2) materials that are structurally well within the grasp of the reader are read automatically (i.e., from page to mind); and (3) material that contains structures that are in the process of being mastered require conscious processing. Each written word is categorized phonologically and lexically; the words in a phrase or sentence are initially made comprehensible to the reader in an explicitly conscious way. Once this has been done, they are related automatically. The processing of written language, like spoken language, takes place in a parallel fashion; that is, all levels of language are referred to, *when needed*, to determine meaning.

WHAT IS READING COMPREHENSION?

Although researchers are not positive about every aspect of reading comprehension, they are certain that the child who comprehends a story or text is the child who is actively involved in the written material. Reading is not a passive process; it demands active participation. The reader has to decode, search his memory, and think, think, think while processing a text.

Stauffer (1969) has stated that reading is a thinking process in which the reader has to be an active participant. Passivity and successful reading comprehension are mutually exclusive. Jenkins (1974) maintains that reading comprehension is closely linked with memory. He suggests that what is best remembered is that which has been experienced:

I think we will eventually conclude that the mind remembers what the mind *does*, not what the word does. That is, experience is the mind at work, not the active world impinging on a passive organism—and experience is what will be remembered. (p. 11)

The proficient reader processes written material by performing many operations while reading. This processing, an interaction between the reader's mind and the text, is an indivisible whole. Let us look at the following example:

Suppose that the text says

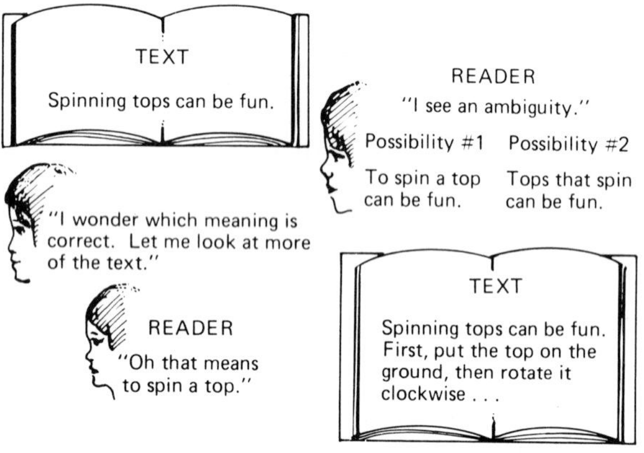

All this happens in the reader's mind in a moment. The time that it takes may not be the critical element in the reading process; the critical element may be the *active participation* of the reader. You can influence the active participation of your young readers in three essential ways:

1. *Motivation*—by providing interesting materials and provoking interest by setting clear, worthwhile goals.
2. *Strategies development*—by providing readers with the strategies that are necessary for comprehending stories and texts. These strategies must exist within the reader before he or she can become a full participant in reading.
3. *Concentration*—by providing teacher-generated activities that foster concentration and observation by the young reader. The activities can help your children to "zero in" on the materials that they are reading. Thorndike (1917) discussed the importance of recognizing reading as an active, participatory process when he wrote

Understanding a paragraph is like solving a problem in mathematics. It consists in selecting the right elements of the situation and putting them together in the right relations, and also with the right amount of weight or influence or force for each. The mind is assailed as it were by every word in the paragraph. It must select, repress, soften, emphasize, correlate and organize, all under the influence of the right mental set of purposes or demands. (p. 329)

THEORIES OF READING COMPREHENSION

Although we know that reading comprehension has to be an active process—the reader must work—we still do not have a totally adequate explanation of how reading comprehension works. In recent years, many researchers have attempted to explain the processes involved in comprehending written discourse.

As explained previously, there are three positions that are held on the nature of the reading process. Each is a point on a continuum, stressing one particular facet of the process. The continuum stretches from one end where it is believed that reading is essentially text-based (that is, the text defines the act of the reading), to the other end where it is believed that reading is essentially knowledge-based (in the mind of the reader); this view has been called the schema view of reading, based on Bartlett's (1932) notion that we have cognitive schema operating during the reading process. The text-based position is frequently referred to as a bottom-up process view of reading; that is, the text is the starting point of the reading act. The schema or knowledge-based position is frequently referred to as a top-down process view of reading.

In the middle of the continuum there is a third view of reading, one that suggests that reading is both text-based (bottom-up) and knowledge-based (top-down).

This position is called the interactive process view of reading.

In the next few pages, we present several views of reading. Each of the designers of these theories espouses an interactive view of reading. However, each can be placed on the continuum in approximately the following places:

Gough, LaBerge and Samuels	Rumelhart and Frederiksen	Smith
text-based bottom-up view of reading	interactive view of reading	knowledge-based top-down view of reading

In studying current theories, it is extremely important for us to attempt to understand as much as we can about the nature of reading comprehension to plan appropriate reading curricula.

Gough's Model (1972)

By describing the proceedings during "one second of reading," Gough has devised a model of reading that is serial in nature. In his proposal, reading is a chain reaction that is touched off by the initial visual fixation when the eye first focuses on a body of print. This purely physiological function produces an icon in the brain, or, stated differently, transmits a direct visual representation of the print. The icon consists of the contents of the fixation, usually 15-20 letters and spaces, which endures for a short time (about 250 milliseconds) until it is replaced with a second fixation, or naturally fades based on normal neural functioning. The letters in the icon are identified and read out at a speed of 10-20 milliseconds per letter. According to Gough, the time lapse from the initial fixation to the vocal production of the word is due to a mechanism of grapheme-phoneme mapping that is not mapped onto speech directly, but rather onto a somewhat abstract element of the language sound system called systematic phonemes. Gough does not elaborate on exactly what systematic phonemes are except to suggest that they are related to phonetic segments (the sounds of the language) "only by a complex system of phonological rules" (Gough, 1972, p. 337). He further refers to them as "abstract phonemic representations" and it is in this form that the original letter is introduced into the lexicon where a meaning search is initiated.

Once a word has been identified it is, in essence, put on "hold" in the primary memory which serves as a repository for successive words until it can be ascertained whether, according to the structure and content of the sentence it is in, the first meaning found for the word is correct.

It is at this point that Gough's "wondrous mechanism" (aptly named *Merlin*) works its magic on the words in the primary memory. By sorting out the deep structure or grammatical relationships of the fragments on "hold," *Merlin* provides a semantic interpretation of the words and comprehension is achieved. At that juncture the whole, now understandable contents of the fixation are relegated to the final memory register, the charming TPWSGWTAU (The Place Where Sentences Go When They Are Understood).

After all this has transpired and phonological rules provide the necessary instructions for pronunciation, speech is achieved and reading has been accomplished.

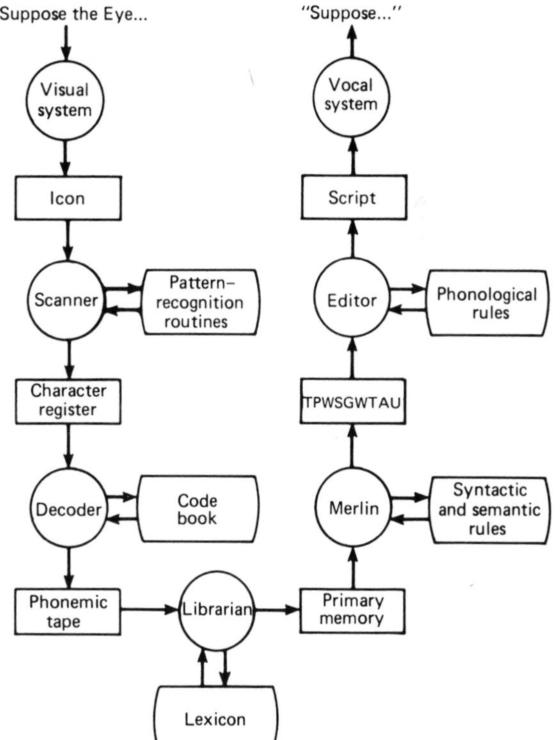

Gough might suggest that reading instruction should begin with letter-by-letter teaching and then progress to words. He might argue that lexical meanings are grouped into meaningful units and interpreted by the reader in conjunction with the syntactic and semantic knowledge that he possesses. According to Gough, the reader does not "guess" at words (as will be suggested in other models), rather the reader "plods" along, step by step. Higher levels of comprehension (such as inferences) are not included in his model.

LaBerge and Samuels' Model (1974)

The concept and role of attention provide the basis for LaBerge and Samuels' theory of automaticity. Since attention capabilities are limited, they feel that a person can attend to multiple tasks simultaneously if only one of them requires full attention. The function of automaticity in the information-processing task of reading is to free the reader's attention from decoding to allow for total concentration on comprehension. Decoding must, then, become automatic.

The operation of automaticity can be easily observed when comparing a beginning reader with an accomplished reader. Because a new reader has not yet achieved automaticity in decoding, attention must be applied to recognizing the words as well as understanding their meanings and implications. This constant shifting of attention from one task to the other results in the hesitant and labored effort characteristic of beginning readers. Once the decoding, or visual input, aspect of reading is automatic, full attention can be placed on the interpretation of the meaning of the context and fluent reading with full comprehension is possible.

The process involved for achieving comprehension as seen by LaBerge and Samuels has four components, all of which are linked with a feedback loop which interconnects. This allows for complex strategies of information processing depending on the ability of the reader and the difficulty of the material. The four stages represented in this model are:

1. *Visual Memory* (VM): In this first stage of information processing, the eye transmits to the brain various pieces of orthographic information for use in letter and word recognition.

2. *Phonological Memory* (PM): The second stage involves the mapping of sounds to letters and words through both acoustic (how they sound) and articulatory (how they are formed for speech) cues. Information to accomplish this stage may be supplied from any of the other components, even as feedback from the semantic memory. This is especially true of difficult words recognized from the meaning of the context.

3. *Semantic Memory* (SM): The main function of this component is to derive meaning from the information provided by the previous two stages.

4. *Episodic Memory* (EM): This is the "optional" stage that goes to work when there is difficulty in any of the normally automatic word recognition processes. In essence, this phase provides "booster" attention to a code, momentarily diverting full attention from the comprehension or SM stage.

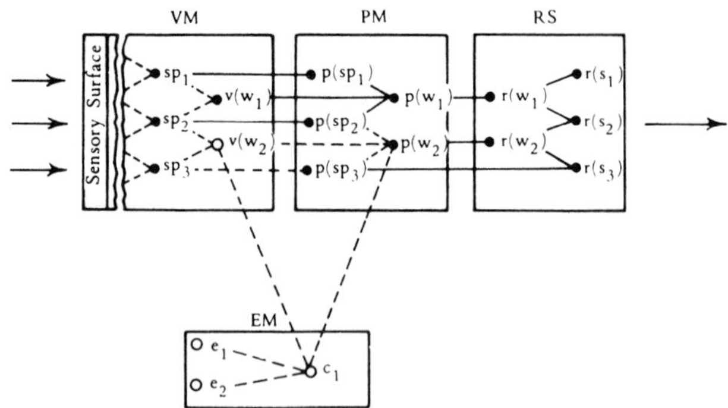

LaBerge and Samuels's Theory

LaBerge and Samuels view reading as a serial acquisition of skills which are testable, sequential, and teachable. The basic skills of reading are to be "overlearned" to the point that they become automatic. One of the main ways to achieve this automaticity through post-criterion learning is by repetition and reinforcement of the skill in question.

Rumelhart's Model (1976)

Using computerized language processing as a base, Rumelhart has devised a theory of reading comprehension that utilizes the principle of interactive stages. There are no fixed steps through which a reader must progress to arrive at comprehension; rather, Rumelhart conceives of a "message center" or "pattern synthesizer" which is bombarded with information from various independent "knowledge sources." These sources represent various components of the reading process and provide information simultaneously to the message center which generates hypotheses or expectations about what is being read. Thus information from any level of the reading process (i.e.: feature, letter, letter cluster, lexical, syntactic and semantic levels) can advance or nullify any hypothesis under consideration at a given moment. The following figure demonstrates the parallel and interactive function of what takes place in the message center for the phrase "the car."

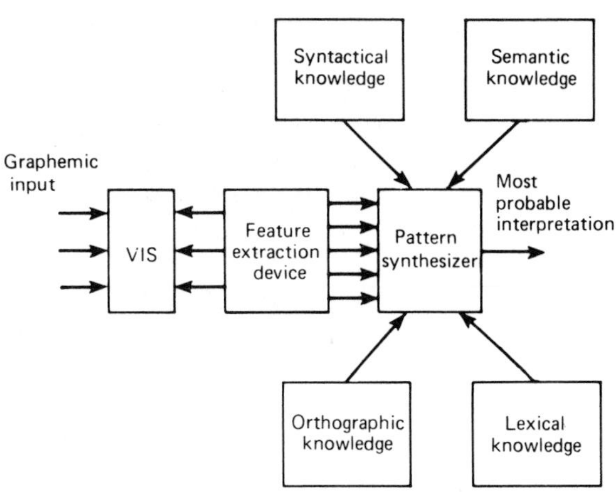

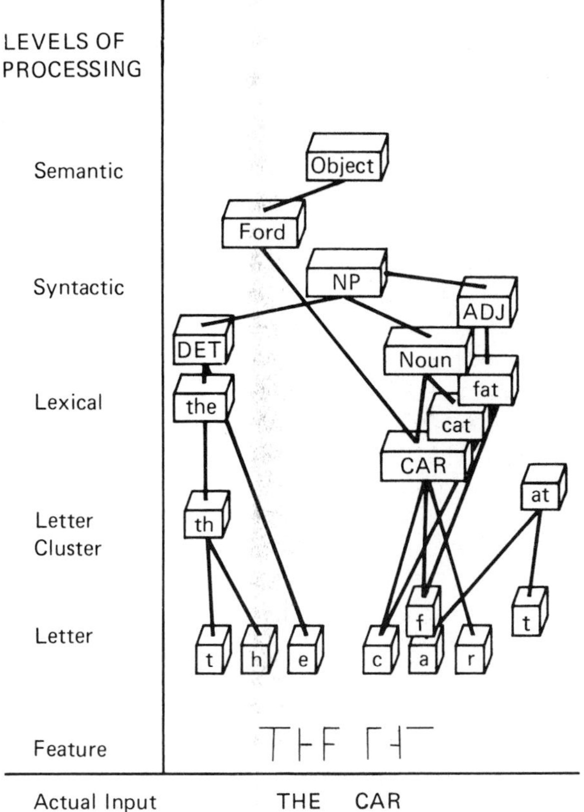

This constant input and evaluation of information from stage to stage produce the uniquely interactive nature of Rumelhart's theory. It is both a top-down and bottom-up process. The following representation of Rumelhart's theory depicts this dual process.

In bottom-up processing, the reader begins with graphemic input which is fed into the "VIS" (visual information store) which serves as a reservoir of orthographic features from which the "Feature Extraction Device" pulls the most critical features. These essential features then serve as input into the "Pattern Synthesizer" (the message center previously described) which extracts the "most probable interpretation" of the information received. The information from the other knowledge sources works on the pattern synthesizer furnishing further data for arriving at a conclusion about what has been read. While Rumelhart's theory is predicated on the belief that a reader will begin with graphemic input and advance through the other stages to comprehension, it does allow the reader to begin at any point and work in any direction. Thus, if a reader arrives at understanding by using semantic knowledge to formulate a correct hypothesis, the top-down process is at work.

Frederiksen's Model (1977)

Another theory of comprehension was presented by Frederiksen in 1977. This model is flexible because it operates from both the top-down (the reader begins with the high-level skills of comprehension and progresses to the low-level skills of decoding) and bottom-up model, thus agreeing with Rumelhart's interactive theory.

In addition, Frederiksen accounts for the higher-level comprehension skills by generating a taxonomy of text-based inference which describes classes of comprehension operations. These classes range from the most basic lexical operations through to the complex inferential task of determining the truth or value of a text. Using Frederiksen's theory it is possible to determine the relationship between the actual elements of a piece of discourse and its comprehensibility (Marshall and Glock, 1978–1979). The fact that text structure affects comprehension has important ramifications in such areas as school text selection and beginning reading instruction.

Frederiksen extends his theory to the act of writing by assuming that the thought process used in writing begins where the reading process ends—that is, with "knowledge structure" or area of comprehension. Starting with this broad network of what is known about the topic, a writer then decides what to put down on paper by selecting the most important information and the most effective words to convey that information. As suggested in the diagram, this process is achieved in levels, focusing, sequencing, and, finally, generating the actual text.

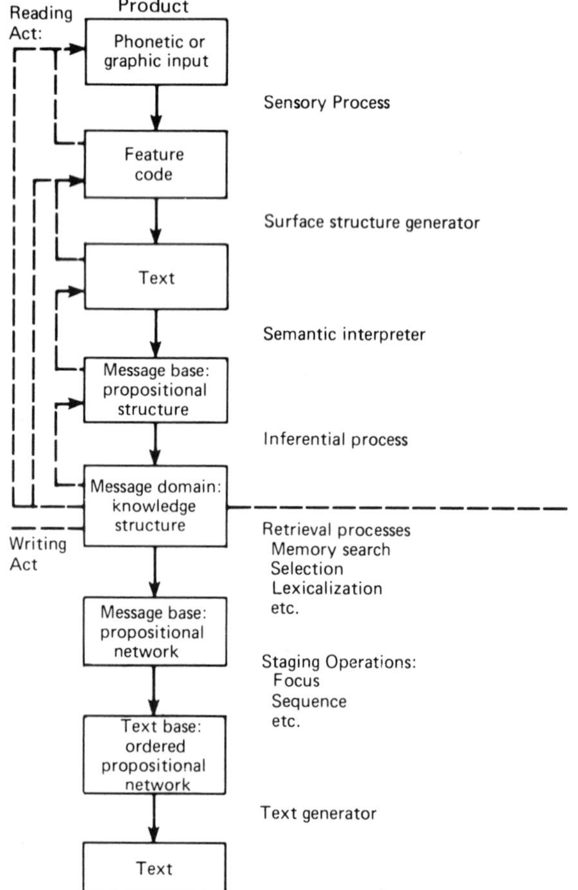

This model was developed based on the following assumptions:

1. A skilled reader's comprehension is based on the interaction between the high- and low-level skills in a top-down manner.
2. If a reader encounters difficulty in decoding or other low-level skills, he or she will revert to the bottom-up technique.

Based on these assumptions of the comprehension act, Frederiksen believes that early reading instruction should be oriented toward achieving two main goals:

1. Teaching children to process written material in the same manner as they process oral language.
2. Decoding skills should be taught so the reader is not bound by the bottom-up mode.

Smith's Theory (1971)

In Smith's theory of reading, he rejects the notion that reading is a decoding of printed words to spoken language; for example,

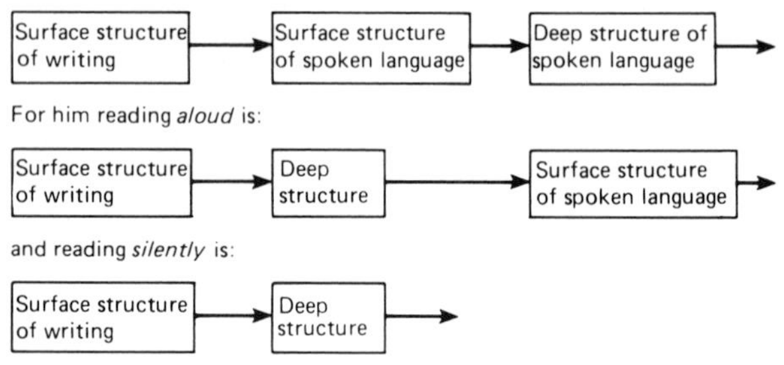

He believes comprehension must take place first and that the identification of individual words comes second. As an example of this phenomenon, he uses the following sentence: "We should *read* the *minute* print on the *permit*." None of the italicized words can be articulated until they have been understood in context. He believes that a reader sees four to five words ahead of and behind the actual word that he is reading. Research has shown that, when lights are turned out on an oral reader, the reader is able to recite the next four or five words of the passage that he is reading. Smith reasons that this occurs because the eye is ahead of the voice by four or five words.

Central to Smith's theory is the concept of "nonvisual information" or a previous familiarity with the manner in which words connect to form meaning. Smith expresses this notion that a reader's world knowledge enriches the printed word when he states; "The more that is known behind the eyeball, the less that is required to identify a letter, word, or meaning from the text." When the material is familiar to the reader, it is quickly comprehended. On the other hand, when the material is more unfamiliar and the vocabulary is more complex, the reader has difficulty comprehending the passage.

The actual process of reading for the competent adult reader can be illustrated in the following diagram:

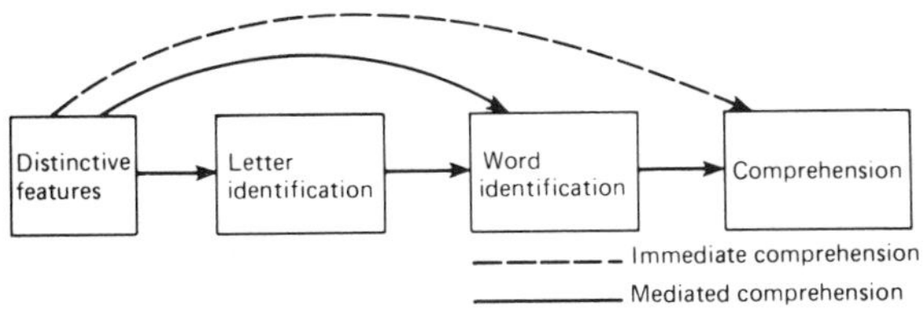

The main limitation of this view, however, is that it does not account for three well-known phenomena:

1. Children who have never seen most of the words that they have in their spoken vocabularies.
2. Fluent readers who encounter words that they have never seen before.
3. Second language learners whose aural/oral repertoire exceeds their visual repertoire.

Story Schemata

In an effort to further understand the comprehension process, researchers have been conducting extremely fruitful research on children's understanding of stories. These analyses have attempted to unravel the complex interrelations of story elements and children's understanding of stories. Stein (1979) reviewed the current state of the art; she reported that, in the past, researchers have maintained that there is a prototype grammatical structure for all stories. She suggests that listeners recognize the structures of stories they hear (or read). The ultimate questions in this research are: Does a particular structure exist in the listener (reader) or in the story itself? Does the structure exist in both the reader and text and does comprehension occur when the two match each other?

Bartlett (1932) argued that a story structure ("an active organization of past reactions and experiences which are always operating in any well-developed organism" would be affected by the listener's schema when the story structure was beyond the experience of the listener and that prototypical structures exist primarily in the mind of the listener.

According to Stein and Glenn (1977) the acquisition of schematic story structures is the result of having stories told or read to the young child. The child who is read to frequently is able to generate rules about story structures, and this child is able to change the actual story in such a way that it fits with his or her schema for stories.

SCHEMA THEORY

Several studies have demonstrated the facilitative effect of prior knowledge on comprehension (recall). The evidence supports the notion that schema or organized prior knowledge plays an active role in what we comprehend. Comprehension is seen as an active process that depends on a dynamic interactive memory structure or set of structures–schemata–used to organize and to interpret what is read or heard. Therefore, what we remember, and consequently infer from a passage, seems to be affected not only by linguistic cues and semantic content but also by the knowledge that we bring to a passage. This is because schema theory seems to account, in part at least, for some of the inferences we draw from our memory stores.

While the idea of schema theory has been traced to the philosopher Kant, it was reintroduced to the educational community in the works of Bartlett (1932), and its definition has undergone a number of transformations in later psychological works (Rumelhart and Ortony, 1977; Winograd, 1977).

Recently, Rumelhart (1981) has defined schema as representations of all one's knowledge, from situations to events, from actions to a sequence of actions, from objects to a sequence of events. If one accepts this definition, it must follow that readers have mental images for almost all their life experiences, ranging from the concrete to the abstract. Thus, when we read the word "ball," we actually have a schema for the concept of ball. This schema may include types of balls, our experiences with balls, and the properties of balls. In a similar manner, events may be encoded in our minds. So, when we read, we may be constantly referring to prototypic experiences that allow us to make sense of the text. For example, if we read about going to a play, proponents of schema theory would argue that our comprehension results from our relating the book experience to our own "going to a play" schema. Given the definition of schema, some theorists and researchers have attempted to identify types of schemata.

Housel and Acker (1979) have categorized schemata into two types: content schema and relational schema. *Content schema* is "receiver stored knowledge about objects and events" (p. 14). The schemata are not specifically related to other people. Examples of this type of schemata are knowledge of historical events and mathematical theorems. *Relational schema* is the "expectations for the different ways people relate to one another" (p. 14). Examples of relational schemata include one-upmanship, competition, love, and hate.

Calfee (1980) suggests that one may acquire schemata through experience and/or training. He argues that schemata are the result of abstracting "commonly occurring elements" from an event or "training in the use of such frameworks." Once these schemata are encoded in one's memory, they result in a set of expectations; once we discover that "X" follows "W," we begin to presume "X" will always follow "W."

Most of those who study the integration of ideas in memory assume that integration is a structural phenomenon occurring during storage. Integration combines isolated ideas into a coherent whole for the reader. Trabasso (1972, 1981) treats these isolated ideas as part of a "causal chain." This consists first of a conceptualization of the written sentence and then a link-up of these conceptualizations achieved by the generation of inferences which connect the ideas. Inferences, then, serve to fill in the blanks left by the explicit events of the text. These inferences are generated through a system of matching up the internal representation in the memory of what has been encoded with the reader's existing prior knowledge (schemata). When a match occurs and an inference is generated, the causal chain is complete and comprehension results. Thus, the product of comprehension is more than a simple aggregation of separate concepts, i.e., what is stored in memory is qualitatively different from its input. People do not treat surface and deep structures merely as components to be stored. They draw on a broad range of world knowledge, spontaneously integrating the information, making inferences, assumptions, and "best guesses." The surface form of the message is quickly transformed and often not remembered. Existing schemata provide the basis for the identification and organization of the critical semantic elements of a message.

Not all researchers accept the notions of schema theory. Schank and Abelson (1977) challenge schema theory with their concept of "scripts." Reder (1980) describes scripts as a series of causal scenes, each action helping the next action; they capture the essence of a stereotyped sequence of actions for a familiar situation. For example, based on one's expectations of going to a market, Schank and Abelson argue that people have scripts for going to the market. As such, when one reads about someone going to the market, readers use their scripts to make sense of the text and to make appropriate inferences.

Schema theory has also been challenged by a hybrid of the script model called the *script elaboration model.* The difference between the script and script elaboration model is the degree of emphasis placed on elaborative processing. For example, Reder claims that, based upon prior experience, readers employ not only past experience to understand a current situation but also add more information to the memory representation of the event. In the elaboration model, a "going to the market" script would also stimulate individual "idiosyncratic" embellishments of going to the market. The embellishments may include more elaborate descriptions of the script. Reder argues that this elaboration actually increases retention.

Many researchers have used the constructs of schemata, scripts, and script elaboration to explain the reader's use of prior knowledge in the reading process. For Rumelhart (in press), reading is really a reader's searching for a schemata that "offers a coherent account of the various aspects of the text." The readers are merely using their prior knowledge to make sense of the text. When comprehension fails on the part of the reader (as opposed to a lack of skill on the author's part), it may be due to a schemata deficiency wherein the reader has no experience at all with the subject, or it may be that through inattentive reading, the appropriate schemata, although existing in the reader's mind, is not summoned up to make sense of the text.

Mandler (1981) demonstrated quite effectively that

many young children have acquired schema for stories and that these schema govern their comprehension of stories. She argues that these children may or may not be able to articulate the structure of the story and that explicit knowledge of a story grammar is not necessary for comprehending a story; however, it may be useful for writing a story.

TEXTUAL ANALYSIS

Several researchers have examined texts in an attempt to extract the structures that underlie them, giving them cohesion and making them meaningful.

Most textual structure research begins with the assumption that there are two major structural categories for prose: *narration* and *exposition*. Although this is a controversial position, it is useful in understanding the research to date. In addition to prose structures per se researchers have also investigated the issue of text cohesion. Both issues, text structure and cohesion, are discussed in the pages that follow.

Narrative

Calfee (1980) described narrative text as episodic sequential prose. Elaborations of this definition have been discussed in the literature on story grammars. Tierney and Mosenthal (1980) define story grammars as "internalized story structures" and Guthrie (1977) has identified the elements of narrative that are common to particular sets of narratives: setting, theme, plot, and resolution; he also established a number of rules that govern these elements. Other researchers (Stein, 1979) have identified different types of stories. For example, Stein classified stories as simple and multiple episodic narratives. For Stein, simple stories consist of setting and episodic structure. The multiple episode stories consist of sequential, causal, or simultaneous happenings. In addition to conducting research on the elements and types of story grammars, researchers have attempted to identify the internal relationships of story grammars. Mandler and Johnson (1977) identified the relational terms that signal structural relations within stories; they maintain that such words as *and* and *then* signal the reader to elements in the story.

While these researchers have focused on the *what* of narrative structure, other researchers have examined the question of *how* structures are encoded. Stein and Glenn (1977) maintain that most people acquire "internalized story structures" through the telling and retelling of stories that contain such structures. As a result of familiarity with these structures, the reader or receiver uses information for hypothesis formation and testing. Flood and Lapp (1981) argue that "children and adults expect specified types of information to be explained in a fixed order within the framework of the story" (p. 36).

Story Grammars

Summers (1980) illustrated three different story grammars designed by Rumelhart, Thorndyke, and Stein and Glenn. The story *Bernie, the Bear* will serve to illustrate each grammar. Each grammar includes several categories of elements within a story; each of the grammars is slightly different.

The sentences in the *Bernie, the Bear* story are numbered. In each of the three diagrams that follow, the numbers that are included in the diagram refer to the sentences in the *Bernie, the Bear* story.

BERNIE, THE BEAR

1. Once upon a time there was a big brown bear named Bernie.
2. He lived in a dark hole deep in the forest.
3. One day, Bernie was wandering through the forest.
4. Then he spotted a big glob of honey on the stump of a tree.
5. Bernie knew how delicious honey tasted.
6. He wanted to taste it right away.
7. So he walked very close to the tree.
8. Then he licked the honey with his tongue.
9. Suddenly, Bernie was surrounded by swarming bees.
10. He had been stung by the bees.
11. He felt sad and hurt.
12. Bernie wished he had been more careful.

RUMELHART'S GRAMMAR

Rumelhart includes two major categories in his grammar: syntactic structures and semantic structures.

Syntactic Structure Categories

Action—activity by a being or by a natural force
Application—attempting to carry out a plan or desire
Attempt—formulation and application of the plan

Change of state—event of one object changing state
Consequence—outcome of the action
Desire—internal response in which one wants something and will probably try to get it
Emotion—an internal response; usually an expression of feeling
Episode—an event and reaction
Internal response—a mental response to an external event
Event—a change of state or action
Overt response—willful reaction to external event
Plan—creating a subgoal that will accomplish the desire
Preaction—activity done to allow planned action
Reaction—response to prior event
Setting—introduction of characters and conditions
State—condition of an object or stable relationship
Story—structural discourse that centers around the reactions of one or more protagonists to events
Subgoal—a goal developed in service to a higher goal

Semantic Structure

And—simultaneous relation
Allow—enabling relation
Initiate—relation between external event and reaction
Motivate—relation between internal response and action
Cause—causal relation
Then—temporal relation

His grammar is illustrated in the following diagram:

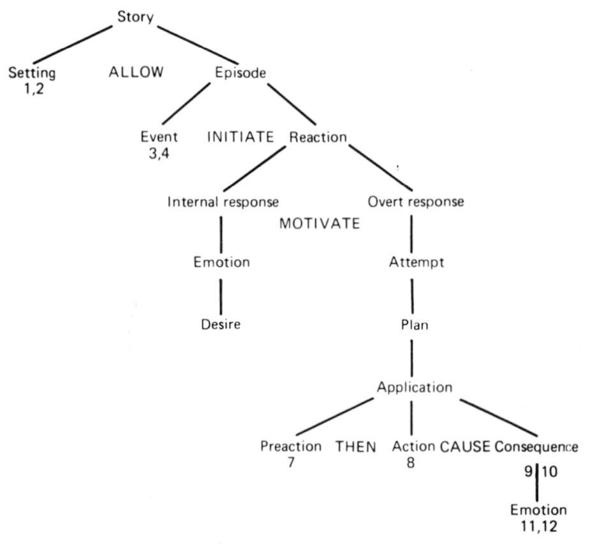

THORNDYKE'S GRAMMAR

Thorndyke includes nine categories in his grammar:

1. Story—setting + theme + plot + resolution
2. Setting—character + location + time
3. Theme—stated event and goal or implied goals introduced by events leading up to and justifying goal
4. Plot—*x* number of episodes (cluster of actions in attempts to achieve goal)
5. Episode—subgoal + attempt + outcome
6. Attempt—event or episode
7. Outcome—event or new state
8. Resolution—final result (event) or final state
9. Subgoal and goal—desired state

His grammar is illustrated below:

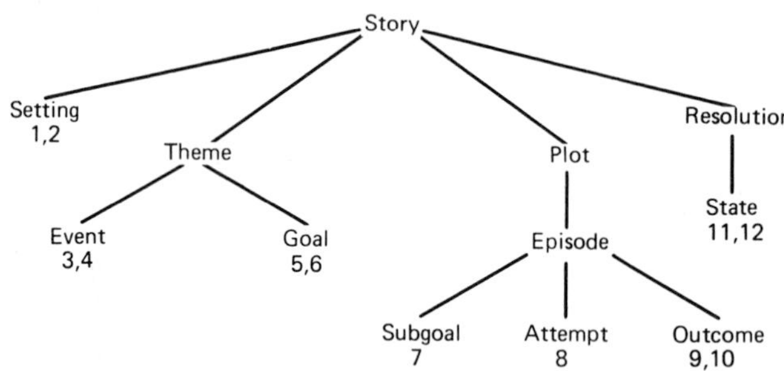

STEIN AND GLENN'S GRAMMAR

Stein and Glenn's grammar includes three major elements: story, setting, and episode.

Categories
Story—setting + episode
Setting—describes social and physical context
Episode

Episodic structures include five elements:

1. Initiating Event—change in environment which prompts character to respond
2. Internal Response—character's internal reaction including goals, effective states, and cognitions
3. Attempts—behavior motivated by internal response
4. Consequence—attainment or nonattainment of goal; results of behavior

5. Reaction—character's response to consequence; generally describing feelings and thoughts.

Their grammar is illustrated below:

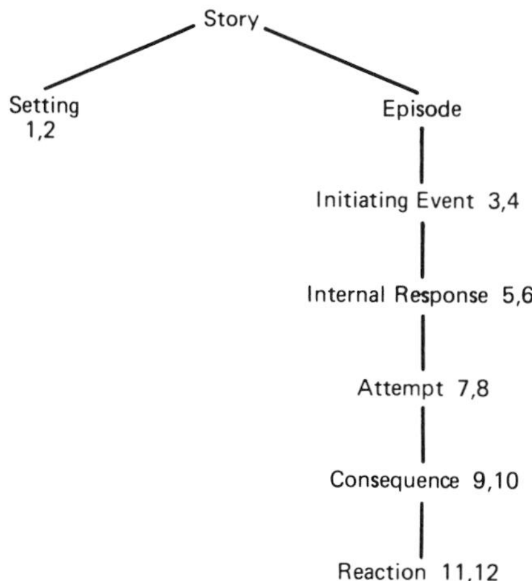

Exposition

Calfee (1980) described expository prose as an object/descriptive approach to writing. The importance of deciphering the structure of this approach has become quite important because educators realize that it is expository texts that are used to "educate" postprimary-grade students in most educational settings.

Research on the structure of expository prose has a history of working from the inside out. Rather than beginning with an overall story grammar examination of the elements and types of exposition, a review of the research shows that researchers first focused on the internal relations within the text.

Niles (1970), a pioneer in expository structural analysis research, identified four organizational patterns of internal relationships for expository writing:

Type	Example
1. Cause and effect	In history texts, causes and effects of revolutions
2. Comparison-contrast	In science texts, a comparison of planets in our solar system
3. Time-order relations	In history texts, chronological description of events
4. Simple listing	In mathematics texts, the steps in solving word problems

Vacca (1972) suggests that signal words within texts announce to the reader/listener the type of organizational pattern used by the writer or speaker. In his scheme, the word "because" is tied with the cause and effect pattern, "however" is tied to the comparison and contrast pattern, "when" with time-order, and "to begin with" with simple listing. This work is similar to the previously discussed story structure research of Mandler and Johnson (1977) and Rumelhart (1975).

In developing a grammar for exposition that is analogous to the narrative construct of story grammar, Meyer (1975) took these organizational patterns and placed them into broader categories called *content structures.* As described by Meyer and Rice (1980), "the content structure displays the way in which the author of the passage has organized the information in the text" (p. 5). The content structure of a passage can be pictured as a tree, with the overall shape of the tree determining the type of text. In Meyer's scheme, there are three different levels to a content structure:

Level 1	Main ideas (macropropositions)
2	Supporting details
3	Specific details

Meyer (in press) illustrates her view of the processes involved in reading an expository text on the following page.

Expository structure research has focused on the significance of the research as well as its definition and classification. In her recent work, Meyer (in press) has summarized much of the research that validates the content structure framework. The gist of her argument is that reading comprehension is enhanced when the reader is cognizant of the structure. Meyer cites the work of Taylor (1980), Elliot (1980), Meyer (1971, 1975, 1979), Meyer and Rice (1981), Bartlett (1978), and Armbruster and Anderson (1981), in asserting that there are

> five basic research findings [that] emerge from examining the relationship between the content structure of prose and what people remember after reading it: 1. Major ideas found in the upper levels of the content structure are better remembered than those found at the bottom. 2. The type of structure of expository relationships affect recall more when they occur at the upper levels of the content or tree structure than at the lower levels. 3. Different types of relationships have different effects on memory. 4. People skilled at identifying top level

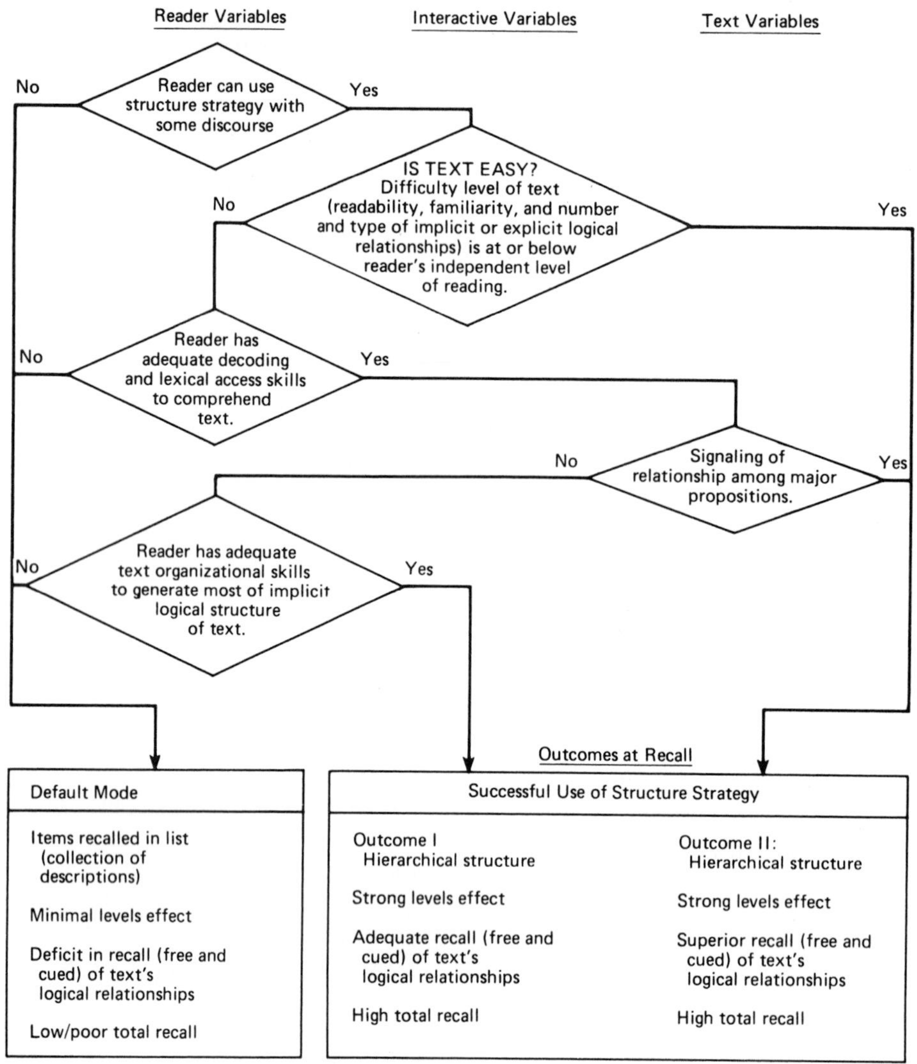

Model depicting the interaction of reader text variables that affect quality and quantity of recall from hierarchically organized text.

From Meyer, B. J. "Organizational Aspects of Text: Effects on Reading Comprehension and Applications for the Classroom," in *Understanding Reading Comprehension*, ed. by J. Flood. Newark, Delaware: International Reading Association, in press.

structures have better recall. 5. People can be taught to identify different top level structures.

In view of the research findings stating that comprehension is facilitated when readers understand the patterns of text organization, the following discussion will detail the four types of organizational patterns delineated by Niles (1970) and how they may be effectively used for reading instruction.

Cause and effect: This pattern of text organization answers the questions: "What is the cause of ______ ?" and "What are the effects of ______ ?" Cause and effect text organization is found in many content area materials.

The following selection illustrates a cause and effect pattern. The outline at the end of the passage depicts the cause and effect relationships operating within the discourse.

FROM "ME" TO "US"

The last half of the 1970's has been called the "Me" era, with people focusing a great deal of attention on themselves. Sociologists argue about the ultimate effect of this egocentric fascination. They are concerned with whether or not this lack of concern for greater social and political issues and disregard for traditional values including the importance of the family, planning for the future, and so on will have a deteriorating influence on our society. While the social scientists may disagree in many of these areas, one benefit of the "me" concentration on which they do agree is the increased awareness of the importance of physical fitness, often including fastidious attention to diet and exercise.

The general American public has now recognized that what they eat and what they do determine how they look. The number of calories taken into the body every day must equal the number of calories that the body burns up in a day in order to maintain a certain weight. If an excess of calories is consumed the body will turn these leftovers into fat, adding body weight. If the body burns up more calories than it is fed, it will use the extra fat for energy, thus reducing body weight. There are, of course, some sources of calories that are more beneficial to the body's functions than others. The calories in protein sources such as meat, eggs, and fish provide more nutrition than the same number of calories supplied by sugar.

For people to be healthy and maintain a desirable weight, they must balance the kind and number of calories they take in with the energy they put out. This is one reason so many Americans have begun regular exercise programs. Health clubs and spas which offer exercise classes and weight reduction machines have become very popular. Quite often people find that it is easier to exercise in groups than alone. In fact, health clubs have become a new place to meet people and develop friendships. Perhaps the sociologists should stop arguing and start exercising. They may find that the "Me" generation has inadvertantly become the"Us" generation.

A cause and effect outline:

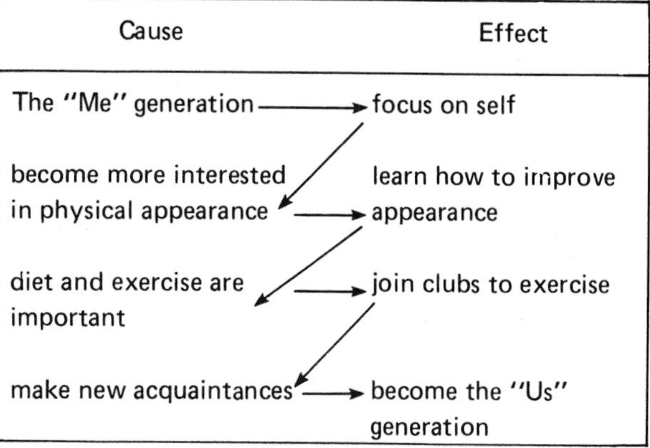

Student activities:

1. To provide practice for your students in recognizing this form of discourse, ask them to answer the test questions for cause and effect patterns mentioned earlier.
2. Present them with a partially completed outline for the passage and ask them to fill in the blanks.
3. After they are comfortable with this style of text organization, ask them to generate their own outlines or diagrams of the passage using the form described above or creating their own visual depiction of the text pattern.

Comparison-contrast: By determining how things are alike and how they are different, comparison-contrast discourse goes beyond simple descriptions to present relationships between and among topics. Text patterns of this sort provide answers to the questions of "How are _______ and _______ alike?" "How are _______ and _______ different?" and "How are these things related to each other or yet another factor?"

The following passage presents a comparison-contrast format for a discussion of certain aspects of life in England versus life in the United States. The chart presented after the illustration categorizes in a systematic way the details of the written discourse.

ENGLISH FEET VS. AMERICAN CARS

Just because we speak the same language and have common ancestors doesn't mean we live the same life.

Life in England is different from life in the United States. It is different in all the obvious ways—the money doesn't look like ours, and they use different words than we do to name various items found in daily life. Life in England is also different from life in the United States in lots of subtle ways. One of these ways is in the comparative methods of transporting oneself.

Although it is obvious that the English drive on the opposite side of the street than we do, it may not be quite so evident that there are fewer cars per capita over there and that there are fewer women drivers. While it is almost unheard of for an American over 18 to lack a driver's license, many English people, especially middle-aged women, have never learned to drive. How do they manage to get around, you ask? They use their feet! Both for walking and pedaling bicycles, feet are a much more useful body part in England than they are in the United States. English feet often walk or pedal the rest of the body to a bus stop, train station, or, if they are London feet, to a "tube" (subway) station. Public transportation in England is more efficient and convenient to use than most such systems in the USA. It must be remembered, however, that England is much smaller than America and consequently it is perhaps easier to have a more effective national train system.

Not only do the methods of transporting oneself differ from country to country, the means of taking children from place to place differ as well. In the United States, the safety conscious parent straps the child into a car seat (officially called an infant restraining device) to insure that the child does not go bouncing around inside the car either from youthful exuberance or from a sudden application on the brakes. The fancier and more complex the car seat, the more sophisticated and more expensive the car, the more the status enjoyed by the American parent. Those English women who are using their feet to get from place to place obviously do not strap an infant restraining device on their backs. No, they push their young loved ones in front of them, lying in or strapped into the English child's traditional mode of transport—the perambulator or "pram," as it is more commonly called. When these mothers walk down to the local shops pushing their babies in front of them, one somehow knows that there will indeed always be an England.

A comparison-contrast outline:

English	American
differences	
1. drive on the left	1. drive on the right
2. fewer cars	2. more cars
3. fewer women drivers	3. more women drivers
4. use feet more	4. use feet less
5. more efficient public transportation	5. less efficient public transportation
6. push children in prams	6. strap children into car seats
likenesses	
1. speak English	1. speak English
2. English ancestors	2. English ancestors
3. must travel to do daily business	3. must travel to do daily business

Student activities:

1. After reading a comparison-contrast ask the students to answer the questions about this format presented on page 173.
2. Make a list of the attributes discussed in the passage and ask the students to decide if they are shared by both/all subjects under discussion or not shared. For example:

	shared	unshared
drive on the right		X
speak English	X	
frequently walk		X
frequently use car seats		X

3. In preparation for writing an original comparison-contrast essay, have the students outline the differences and likenesses of the subjects of their paper.

Time-order relations (chronology): Very often found in history texts, this discourse pattern uses sequencing of events to organize information. The obvious questions answered by chronologies are: "What happened first? Second? Third?" and "What is the consequence of these events?" Time-order relation texts are among the easiest to recognize and comprehend because of their straightforward, time-line style of organization.

Student activities:

1. Have the students list, in order, the events detailed in a historical passage.
2. Provide a timeline which supplies only the appropriate dates. Have the students fill in information of various sorts relevant to the historical period. For example:

   Fill in the blanks with a description of a typical activity for each date given.

Before 1 A.D.	A.D. 79	1709	mid 1700s
________	________	________	________
________	________	________	________
________	________	________	________
________	________	________	________

3. For a variation of activity 2 students may be encouraged to provide a pictorial timeline; create a dialogue between two people of a town in each historical period; or write a newspaper headline or column that is representative of life in each period.
4. To further reinforce the time-order relation text pattern, students may wish to write a chronology or draw up a timeline of their own lives, the history of their town, school, state, etc.

Simple listing (taxonomy): Description and classification of characteristics is typical of the listing style of text organization. This format provides information about a subject in a taxonomic structure progressing from its most general aspects to the more detailed ones. Pertinent questions concerning a taxonomic pattern of discourse are: "What kind of thing is ______?" "What makes it so?" and "What varieties of it are there?"

The "tree" or "branching" style outline is useful for demonstrating the relationships among the attributes of subjects discussed in a listing style format.

THE MODERN PIANO

Of all the keyboard instruments, the piano is perhaps the most popular both for concert and home use. The reason for this may be in its unique versatility which allows the player to take charge of the entire musical score and interpret it with unlimited nuance and flexibility.

There are two main types of piano—the grand piano and the upright piano. The difference in their shapes controls the difference in their musical action and thus in the quality of the sound they produce.

The grand piano (which has two versions, the baby grand and the concert grand) houses the strings in a wing-shaped body which stands parallel to the floor. The hammers hit the strings in an upward movement, coming below the strings.

The upright piano, as the name suggests, is box-shaped and stands with its strings in a vertical position. The action of the hammers in an upright piano is a forward motion.

In addition to these two main types of pianos, the modern era's fascination with amplification and computers has produced the electronic piano. This instrument has permitted the versatile piano to keep pace with new developments in the ever-changing field of popular music.

A listing or taxonomic outline:

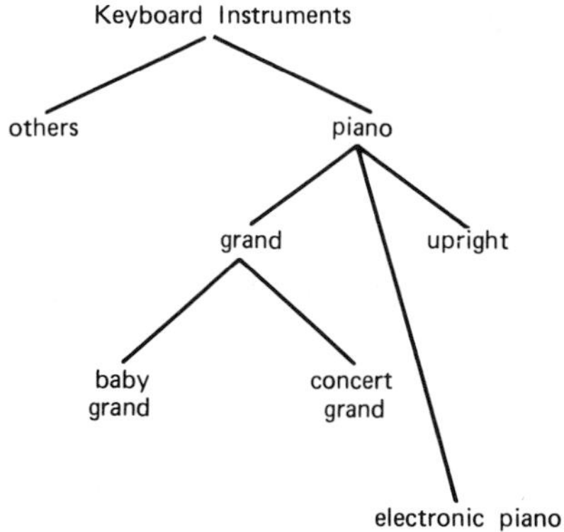

Student activities:

1. Provide students with an incomplete outline of a listing passage and ask them to fill in the blanks.
2. Ask the students to elaborate on the simple tree dia-

gram by providing the additional information in answer to the question "What makes it so?" In other words, they should provide the defining characteristics of the item being discussed. For example:

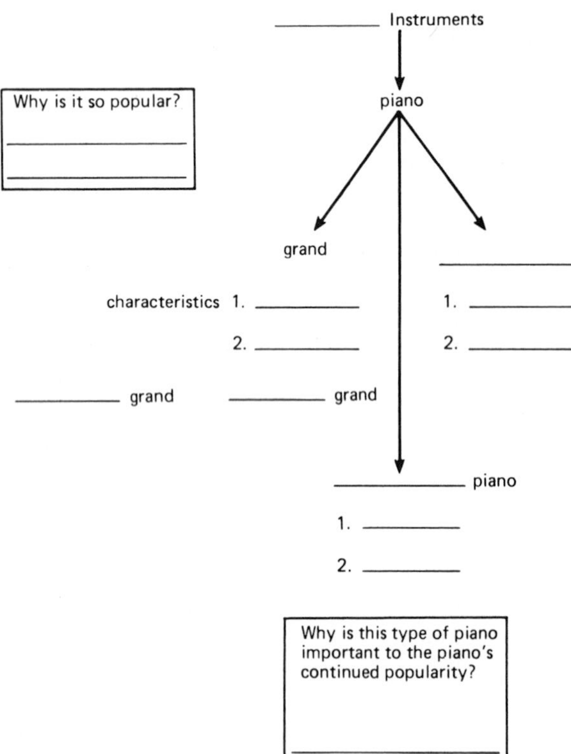

3. In preparation to writing an original essay in the listing format, ask students to organize their information in a taxonomic diagram before they begin writing.

By encouraging the students to become familiar with text structures, you will be providing them with valuable tools for attacking many types of content discourse which might otherwise be overwhelming due solely to the complexity of the information discussed. The ability to reduce the discourse to an elemental outline form may provide the key to unlocking its meaning.

Text Cohesion

While there is no single definition of cohesion, Halliday and Hasan (1976) maintain that cohesion is the relations of meaning that exist within a text. For Halliday and Hasan, cohesion occurs when the interpretation of any item in a text requires reference to other items in the text. Chapman (in press) has stated succinctly that cohesion is "the characteristic that makes a text a text rather than a haphazard collection of sentences."

We have made indirect references to cohesion throughout this chapter; Niles' organizational patterns, Vacca's signaling terms, and Meyer's rhetorical relations are direct and/or indirect examples of cohesion. Halliday and Hasan add more specific descriptions to these internal relations. In their scheme, the reference device is defined as referring the reader back to a prior definite thing. Substitution refers to the replacement of one thing by another. It must be noted, however, that cohesion is more of an interpretive aid than an addition to content. As Halliday and Hasan assert, "it is the continuity provided by cohesion that enables the reader or listener to supply all the missing pieces, all of the components of the picture which are not present in the text but are necessary for its interpretation" (p. 16).

LITERAL, INFERENTIAL, AND CRITICAL READING COMPREHENSION

Many practices in the teaching of comprehension are based on the idea that there are three levels of comprehension; these levels are usually called *literal* (on the line) comprehension, *inferential* (between the lines) comprehension, and *critical* (beyond the lines) comprehension. This distinction has been useful in the past because it divided the whole world of comprehension into three manageable categories. However, many problems arose from this design because educators began to think linearly about these three levels, assuming that they represented three levels of difficulty. It was assumed that these three levels were ordered hierarchically and that literal comprehension was easier than was inferential comprehension, which in turn was easier than critical comprehension.

This idea was probably the function of reading educators' attempts to model comprehension processes in a manner similar to the way that Bloom modeled levels of cognitive functioning. The following illustrates the way in which reading educators attempted to create a taxonomy of reading objectives based on Bloom's notions:

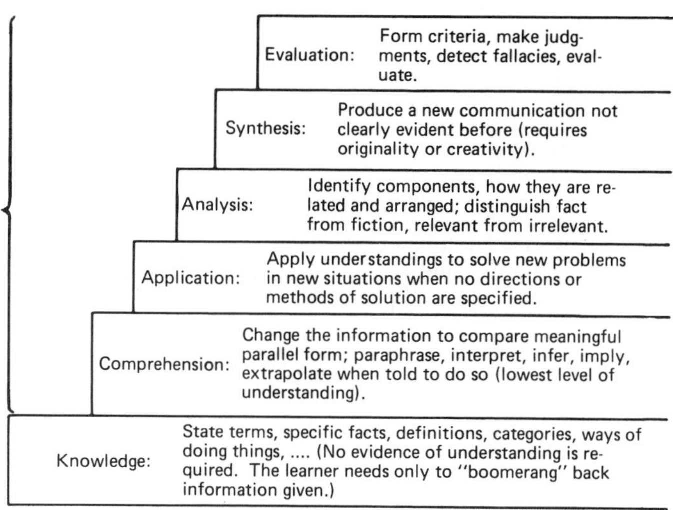

Bloom's taxonomy of educational objectives.

Bloom's taxonomy presents learning as a developmental process in which each category of the hierarchy became progressively more difficult. Mastery of one category may be dependent upon the preceding category.

Some reading educators have suggested that Bloom's taxonomy of educational objectives is closely related to the hierarchy of learning that encompasses the comprehension processes. In the past, researchers in reading have based reading comprehension taxonomies on Bloom's taxonomy. These schemata were similar to the following:

Levels of Cognitive Development	Reading Comprehension
	Text Explicit Information (literal comprehension)
Knowledge (recall)	Identifying sounds, letters, phrases, sentences, paragraphs Recognizing and recalling details, main ideas, sequence, comparison, cause and effect relationships, character traits, patterns
Comprehension (understanding)	Translating ideas or information explicitly stated: classifying, generalizing, outlining, summarizing, synthesizing
	Text Implicit Information (inferential comprehension)
Application (abstracting)	Realizing of one's experiences and textual exposures Inferring details, main ideas, sequence, comparisons, cause and effect relationships, character traits
Analysis (analyzing)	Predicting outcomes
Synthesis (production)	Interpreting figurative language, imagery, character, motives, and responses Synthesizing convergently and divergently
	World Knowledge Information (critical comprehension)
Evaluation (judging)	Making evaluative judgments of reality or fantasy, fact or opinion, adequacy and validity, appropriateness, worth, desirability, and acceptability Valuing Detecting propaganda euphemism, fallacy of reasoning, statistical fallacy (maps, charts), stereotyping, oversimplification
	Appreciation Emotional response to content Identification with characters or incidents Reactions to the author's use of language Reactions to the author's word pictures

Teachers at all grade levels in all content areas can use the idea of a reading comprehension taxonomy as a means to *develop* and *assess* the various levels of cognitive development in students. The first step in this process is to familiarize yourself with the various levels and to consciously make an effort to plan activities and questions that include portions of all (or at least most) of these categories.

Throughout a student's school day, he or she is asked to answer questions regarding stories, class activities, and printed materials. You can help foster reading *and* thinking skills by making an effort to include such questions as:

1. What are two things the story mentions . . . ? (Knowledge)
2. Write a short summary of . . . (Comprehension)
3. What was the effect of . . . ? (Application)
4. What might havelhappened if . . . ? (Analysis)
5. Why do you think this person acted this way? (Synthesis)
6. Is this a fact or opinion? (Evaluation)

You can determine which of your students needs additional practice to successfully answer questions at each cognitive level through informal (e.g., observation) or formal (e.g., questions tracking) methods. Observation in class discussions, for example, might demonstrate that some students have a reluctance to answer certain types of questions. Another student may not always be successful in answering a particular type of question. Observations such as these can help you plan curricula so that each student becomes more competent with all types of reading comprehension tasks. At times, you may want to track your students' needs and capabilities more formally.

When you assess student comprehension through a written text, you can write certain questions which are intended to measure a particular cognitive skill. By tracking these questions and recording each student's success rate, you can obtain a fairly accurate picture of each student's present level and thus plan instruction accordingly.

Of course, we recognize that not all questions can be neatly labeled in a category. However, recognizing and attempting to implement instruction based on a reading comprehension taxonomy is an important *first* step toward producing critical readers and thinkers.

Sources of Reading Comprehension

Because the three-part division of literal, inferential, and critical comprehension is still used by many publishers of reading comprehension tests and reading texts, it may be useful for you to think of this categorization scheme as an attempt to divide the sources of reading comprehension into three very important components:

1. Literal comprehension—*extracted from text explicit information.*
2. Inferential comprehension—*extracted from text implicit information.*
3. Critical comprehension—*extracted from world knowledge (experience).*

There are two major objections to a three-level (literal, inferential, and critical comprehension) classification scheme:

1. It is assumed that there is a linear progression of difficulty in these three levels of comprehension, and it is assumed that tasks that measure comprehension can be labeled correctly as literal, inferential, or critical.
2. The scheme only takes the source of comprehension into consideration. It does not take into account the dynamic active process of comprehension in which the reader participates. The operations of the learner during the reading process are ignored in this three-level scheme.

The first objection, the assumption that there is a linear progression of difficulty in these three levels of comprehension that can be labeled literal, inferential, or critical, stems from certain current discoveries. Let us try to determine the level that each of the following questions are measuring:

Text

(1) Zoe and Zeke, two talented masons, were building an internal fireplace for a cantankerous architect. (2) The architect was inflexible with his prints, insisting that the measurements had to be absolutely perfect despite his annoying habit of altering the plans every twenty min-

utes. (3) After three hours of utter frustration, Zoe and Zeke thought they understood the plans. (4) As they started to lay the foundation, the architect decided he wanted an external fireplace and announced, "I think your work is unprofessional. You're fired." (5) Zoe and Zeke, quite flabbergasted, said, "Sir, you are a poor excuse for an architect and the bane of all craftsmen. Your sense of professionalism is a sham."

L, I, C

________1. How many times did the architect alter the plans while Zoe and Zeke were working?

________2. Why did the architect tell the masons that they were unprofessional?

________3. What was the masons' reaction to being fired?

________4. When did the masons understand that the architect was troublesome?

The entire passage is straightforward and comprehensible. The details of the story are explicit, and the characterizations of the architect and the masons are direct and thorough (for interpreting the author's point of view). However, the four questions, while easily answered, are quite difficult to label as literal, inferential, or critical. The source for the answer to each question is in the text, thereby making the question appear to be a test of literal comprehension, but the exact answer is not in the text. For example,

Question:	How many times did the architect alter the plans while Zoe and Zeke were working?
Text source:	The architect was inflexible with his prints, insisting that the measurements had to be absolutely perfect despite his annoying habit of altering the plans every twenty minutes. After three hours of utter frustration, Zoe and Zeke thought they understood the plans.
Operation:	Convert 3 hours into 180 minutes. Divide 20 minutes into 180 minutes to arrive at the answer: 9 times.

The answer is not stated explicitly in the text; the reader is called upon to perform certain arithmetic operations beyond the text. Therefore, you may be tempted to label the question inferential. However, it is clear that the reader has to operationalize previous knowledge (arithmetic computation) to answer the question. Does this straying from the text qualify the question for the label critical comprehension?

The difficulty of assigning the correct label is at once apparent and unnecessary. We have carefully explained the entire process of answering the question without giving the question a label. This strongly suggests that we should be investigating the *processes* involved in answering the question (in comprehending) and that we may be wasting our time by fighting over inappropriate and misleading labels.

Operations During Reading Comprehension

A second objection to a three-level classification scheme proposed by some reading educators is that it only takes the source of comprehension into consideration. This is a reasonable objection because this scheme does not account for the multiplicity of operations in which the reader participates. Let us illustrate this point by analyzing several operations that are involved in answering these seemingly literal questions:

Question:	What did Zoe and Zeke do for a living?
Text source:	Two talented masons
Operations:	a. The reader has to understand apposition: Zoe and Zeke, two talented masons means that Zoe and Zeke are two talented masons. b. The reader has to process synonomy: step 1, "do for a living" = occupation/job; step 2, occupation/job = masons.

While the question is easily answered, the sophistication and complexity of the operations suggest that a facile label such as "literal comprehension" is an inadequate descriptor for the entire process of comprehension. Rather, it seems important to examine each of the steps involved in the processing of the original story, the processing of the question, and the formulation of a correct answer.

It is extremely important to begin to unravel some of the processes involved in proficient comprehension. An appropriate way to begin this unraveling is to examine the operations of the reader during reading episodes. We know the following facts about readers:

1. Readers process propositions, not sentences. A proposition is a relational structure established by a predicate term and one or more argument terms; for example, in the sentence "Sharon's daughter, Johanna, is an intelligent girl," there are at least six propositions.

   Sharon is a mother.

   Sharon has a daughter.

   The daughter is Johanna.

   Johanna has a mother.

   Johanna is a girl.

   Johanna is intelligent.

   These propositions are not articulated consciously by the reader. In this view of reading, it is suggested that the reader is ready to accept anything that follows logically from these propositions, such as Johanna can count backward, but the reader is also prepared to examine carefully new information that does not logically follow from these propositions, such as Johanna is a boy.

2. All readers process (infer) regardless of memory demands (Flood and Lapp, 1977).
3. Readers attend to certain semantic and/or syntactic elements in the initial propositions of texts (Flood, 1978; Trabasso, 1972). An example of this phenomenon was reported by Flood (1978) when he asked proficient readers to supply the second sentence for two passages that began in the following ways:

Passage A	Passage B
Christmas always meant going to Grandma's house.	One of the oldest drinks known to man is milk.

In passage A, all readers wrote in a personal narrative (reminiscent) style, supplying a second highly descriptive sentence about the event of Christmas. In passage B, all readers supplied a second data-filled sentence using a formal, nonnarrative style.

All proficient readers seem to participate in similar operations during comprehension. Most proficient readers, after being exposed to the following two sentences

Josie is laughing, smiling, and squealing.

She is hugging the master of ceremonies.

will probably infer something like "Josie is happy because she won the prize." The operations in which the reader participates can be described in the following way:

Type	Example
1. Clarification of anaphoric referent.	she = Josie.
2. Superordination of strings of lexical items.	laughing, smiling, squealing = happy.
3. Inferring causality.	Josie is laughing, smiling, and hugging the master of ceremonies <u>because</u> she won the prize.

Frederiksen (1977) suggests that there are at least twenty-six types of inferences that readers generate. These inferences are important for proficient reading, and there are certain conditions that elicit these operations. Some of the conditions that elicit these twenty-six inferences in reading are the following:

Type	Example
1. Ambiguity in sentences and clauses.	Flying planes can be dangerous. I like her cooking. She fed her dog biscuits.
2. Unclear anaphoric referents.	Zoe and Zeke were masons. They were paid by Vera and Velma. They were inflexible.
3. Unclear cataphoric referents	It was a beautiful day in spring when it happened.
4. Unclear deictic referents. (person, place, time).	Paula and Phyllis were meeting in the afternoon. She was so late that she left.

5. Unclear topical referents.	It was always this way. They had so much fun when they went there that they decided to go again.
6. Partial lexicalization.	The set disappeared.
7. Missing connective.	Tony drove too fast. The police didn't care about the emergency.
8. Unclear segmentation.	Mary went to the fire station. Bernard and Mary lived happily ever after. They got the firemen to help them put out the fire.
9. Need for reduction.	Danny was whining, coughing, vomiting, crying, tossing, bleeding, shouting, moaning.
10. Need for extensions.	Emma lost her tooth. Her father put her quarter in her piggy bank.
11. Pragmatic considerations.	The house was eighty years old and the crew arrived.

Although we are only at the threshold of our understanding of reading comprehension, we are coming to some agreement that we need to specify the operations that the readers must perform if they are reading with proficiency. Frederiksen (1977) has offered us a first step over the threshold by specifying twenty-six types of inferencing operations, listed on the following pages.

		Example	
Type of Operation	Definition	Actual Text	Recalled Text
Lexical Operation			
1. Lexical expansion	Expanding a concept into one or more propositions	The child is sick.	The child is vomiting, sore, feverish.
2. Lexicalization	Replacing a proposition with a lexical concept	The child is vomiting, sore, feverish.	The child is sick.
Identification Operation			
3. Attribute inference	Specifying an attribute	The boy has a bicycle.	The boy has a big bicycle.
4. Category inference	Classifying an object or action	Joan is buying an outfit.	Joan is buying a skirt and sweater outfit.
5. Time inference	Specifying a time	She is watering the roses.	She was watering the roses.
6. Locative inference	Specifying location	She is watering the roses.	Mary is watering the roses in the garden.
7. Part structure	Specifying part of an object	She is watering the roses.	She is watering the roots of the roses.
8. Degree inference	Specifying the degree of an attribute, e.g., very	We'll put them in a vase.	We'll put them in a nice vase.
Frame Operation			
9. Act inference	Filling in an action	Father will be sad.	Father will feel sad.
10. Case inference	Inferring agent or instrument	a. Agent—now the junk is all put away b. Instrument—Tom hit the boy.	a. Agent—Karen was putting away the party favors. b. Instrument—Scott hit the boy with the bat.
11. Instrumental inference	Generating a cause of an event	Paula got well.	Dr. Ryan made Keith well.
12. Result inference	Generating the result of an action	Take some of mine.	Sadie, you can have some of mine.
13. Source inference	Inferring a prior state	Jimmy, you don't have a soda.	Take some of mine.
14. Goal inference	Generating a goal for an action	Bobby cleaned his room.	Bobby cleaned his room so his father wouldn't get mad.

15. Theme inference	Generating a theme	Let's fix the mistake.	Mitchell rebuilds the structure.
16. Frame transformation	Transforming a frame of one type into a frame of another type	N_1VN_2—John bought shoes.	VN_2N_1—buy shoes, John.
17. Disembedding operation	Removing a proposition from an event frame.	He wants to take a vacation.	He . . . went to New England.
18. Embedding operation	Inserting a proposition into an event frame.	This is Pearl. She is buying a boat.	Pearl went to buy a boat.
Event Generation			
19. Event inference	New, more general proposition	He is sick.	He is vomiting, feverish, and cranky.
	More specific propositions	He is vomiting, feverish, and cranky.	He is sick.
Macrostructure Operation			
20. Superordinate inference			
21. Subordinate inference	Ten subtypes, corresponding to the different slots (processive and resultive event frames)	The parade was held on Tuesday.	The parade of the clowns was postponed until Tuesday because it rained on Monday.
Algebraic Operation			
22. Algebraic inference	Metric (degree) or nonmetric	A little boy was watering the flowers and then he ran down the lane.	A little boy watered the flowers and ran down the lane
Dependency Operations			
23. Causal inferences	Connect unconnected events with causal relations	Tony was washing the windows and crashed and broke the vase.	Because Tony was washing the window carelessly, he fell and broke the vase.
24. Conditional inferences	Specify antecedent conditions for an event	Now Sara thinks that Bootie will be sad. She wants to hug him.	She thought he might be sad.
25. Logical inferences	Specify the logic of the inferences	It's lightning outside.	It's lightning outside; it must be raining.
Truth Value Operation			
26. Truth value operation	Qualification or negation	Peter hurt Amy.	He thought she might be mad.

While Frederiksen's approach has been extremely helpful, there are certain limitations to his system. The following system, designed by Flood and Lapp (1977), is an attempt to create a scheme that is based directly on data collected from readers' processing of texts. These data were collected from readers of three age ranges. (twelve years old to adulthood; Flood and Lapp, 1977). The following chart illustrates this system with examples from such data:

Category	Text	Recall
1. Generating text identical information	soda	soda
2. Generating macro- and microstructures a. Synonomy—a narrowly defined category; traditionally acceptable synonyms. This category assumes a high degree of rater reliability. Synonyms can be conventionally acceptable such as couch/sofa (thesaurus) or text specific	couch	sofa
b. Colloquial (figurative) synonym—Acceptable synonym within a specific context	dollar	buck

Category	Text	Recall
c. Superordinate: recall of the larger unit to which text belongs	bear	animal
d. Subordinate: recall of smaller unit of which text element is a part	flower	daisy
e. Categorization: generation of larger concept that encompasses several text elements	uniforms, drums, batons, marching people	parade
3. Generating cause		
a. Text proactive: extracting previous information from text that explains events as effects of causes	Jason was a lawyer. He became a dentist.	Jason realized that he had made a mistake.
b. Text retroactive: extracting subsequent information from text that explains an event as a cause	Jason liked Chicago. Jason moved to Cheyenne where he enjoyed his business	Jason moved from Chicago to Cheyenne because he didn't like his job in Chicago.
c. Experience proactive: presumptions about events that preceded and caused the existing event	Jason's business was successful.	Jason's family gave him a great deal of money.
d. Experience retroactive: assumptions about events that succeeded the existing event	Jason's business was successful.	Jason was successful as a lawyer after he sold his business and converted his business assets into client contacts.
4. Generating dimension		
a. Space: placing an event in space (metric or nonmetric)	Jason practiced law.	Jason's business was transcontinental, stretching from urban to rural communities.
b. Time: placing an event in time (metric or nonmetric)	Jason studied law.	In the autumn, Jason studied law.
c. Motion: recalling movement	Jason's business was transcontinental.	Jason flew from coast to coast to help his business.
d. Manner: recalling specifiable characteristics	Jason studied.	Jason studied assiduously.
5. Accommodating referents		
a. Conjunctive: joining two elements	Jason was an architect. His fellow engineers praised him.	Jason was an architect and an engineer.
b. Syncretic: merging diverse elements into a single element	Jason was an architect. His fellow engineers praised him.	Jason was an architectural engineer.
c. Disjunctive: recall of one selected element	Jason was an architect. His fellow engineers praised him.	Jason was an engineer
d. Episodic: sequencing events in a temporally fixed, irreversible order	Jason was an architect. His fellow engineers praised him.	Jason was an architect but stopped being an architect. Then he became an engineer.
e. Additive: creating two sources to accommodate diverse information	Jason was an architect. His fellow engineers praised him.	One Jason was an architect. Another Jason was an engineer.
f. Anaphoric: establishing a referent.	They praised him.	The engineers praised him.
6. Generating case frames (traditional case grammar relations)	Jason learned law.	Jason was taught law by the faculty of Tulane Law School.
7. Generating attributes		
a. Actors	Jason studies law.	Mild-mannered Jason, the bookworm, studied law.
b. Events: attributing qualifications to events	Jason led the parade.	The parade was the grandest show in Dublin.
c. Place: adding specificity to places	Jason studied in Louisiana.	Jason studied in the humidity of the South.
d. Dimension: attributing characteristics to dimensions	He moved to Chicago.	He moved very far from Tulane.
8. Generating text erroneous information	Jason, once a lawyer, became an accountant.	Jason studied architecture, but practiced nothing.
9. Generating text external information	Jason was a lawyer.	I don't know why Jason was what he was.

INSTRUCTION IN DEVELOPING READING COMPREHENSION

At this point, you are probably asking, "What can I do to help children develop reading comprehension skills?" First, we suggest that you analyze the text for difficulties that your children may encounter. Ask yourself, "Is the passage written clearly, does it make sense?" If there are severe problems, you can (1) abandon the text and select an alternate text that is more clearly written or (2) rewrite the text, correcting it to clarify potentially troublesome areas. For example, if the text says "Dan and Dee are playing basketball, but Don is not. Don and Del are roller skating," you may want to

1. Change the names to avoid confusion.
2. Make the unclear reference to Don in the second sentence less ambiguous.

The reader could rightly wonder if the Don in the second sentence is the Don in the first sentence.

A corrected, more readable version of the text that adheres closely to original intent might be "Jay and Dee are playing basketball, but Jeffrey is not because he is roller skating with Marge."

Questioning Strategies

In addition to clarifying unclear texts, you can direct students' reading by developing comprehension tasks. The most frequently used task is *questioning.* There is an extensive body of research literature that demonstrates the importance of directing and focusing students' reading through teacher questions. It is absolutely critical for you to understand that a question is a useful tool, a stimulant for learning.

Too often in the past, teachers have fallen into the trap of thinking that a question automatically produces a certain type of thinking (a specific mental operation). The operation is done by the reader in his or her thinking processes, not by the question; the question is merely a device that may or may not stimulate the type of thinking that is desired by the teacher. We have spent a great deal of time and effort labeling questions as literal, inferential, and critical (evaluative). Much of this time and effort has been futile; we should turn our attention to examining the processes and operations that are involved during reading, remembering that questions can merely serve as stimulants to thinking, not as substitutes for it.

Because questions are sources for thinking, it seems obvious that we should ask our students many different types of questions to stimulate many different mental operations. It seems equally obvious that students interpret questions in many different ways; it is possible that a question that the test maker intended to elicit recall of explicitly stated information may not serve the purpose for some students. For example,

Ken Baxter, who was fifteen years old, wore a costume that was far too young for him. He came as a bunny rabbit.

Question:	What costume did the boy wear?
Intended answer:	A bunny rabbit costume.
Possible answers:	1. He wore a babyish animal costume. 2. His costume is appropriate only for young children to wear at parties. 3. He was the laughingstock of the party.

Each of the possible answers is relatively correct; each strays farther from the text and the actual question, but we must be ready for interpretive answers like number 3, "He was the laughingstock of the party," if we want to fully understand the way our students make sense of texts.

Questions as Stimulants for Thinking

A second way in which to look at questioning as a stimulant for thinking is to think of questions as a tool for ordering thinking, for putting the pieces of a puzzle together. When a student misinterprets or miscomprehends, as demonstrated by getting the single crucial question wrong, what do we know? We only know from the answer that something went awry; we need to go back to the passage and discover, with the child, the pieces of the puzzle that he or she does not understand. This retracing procedure can be done through systematic questioning that is based on the logical propositions within the text or story. The following example is based on the beginning of the children's book, *Where the Wild Things Are:*

1. The night Max wore his wolf suit and made mischief of one kind
2. and another
3. his mother called him "Wild Thing!"
4. and Max said "I'll eat you up!"
5. so he was sent to bed without eating anything.

Let us suppose that you asked your readers to answer this question: "Why did Max's mother send him to bed without eating?" The answer that you might expect from your students would be similar to the following: Max was sent to bed without eating

cause	action →	because he was fresh to his mother
↓ effect	↓ reaction →	↓ and therefore she got angry with him
↓ effect	↓ consequence →	↓ and sent him to bed

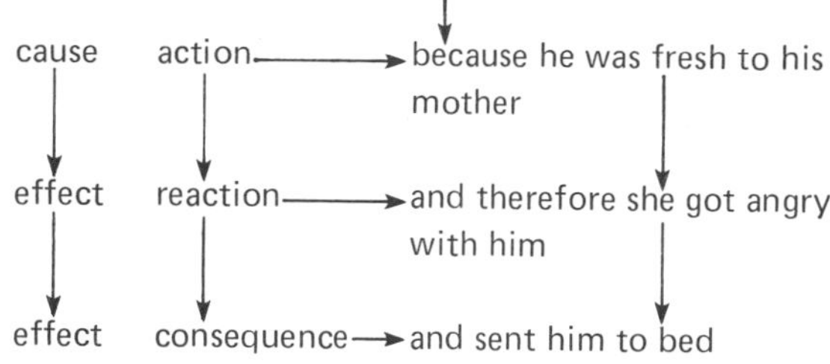

To arrive at the desired response, the reader has to (1) attend to the text and (2) perform numerous mental operations simultaneously.

The accompanying chart illustrates the complexity of the question by listing some of the operations (processes) that the child must perform and the text source for extracting the information needed to answer this question: if the child is unable to answer the question

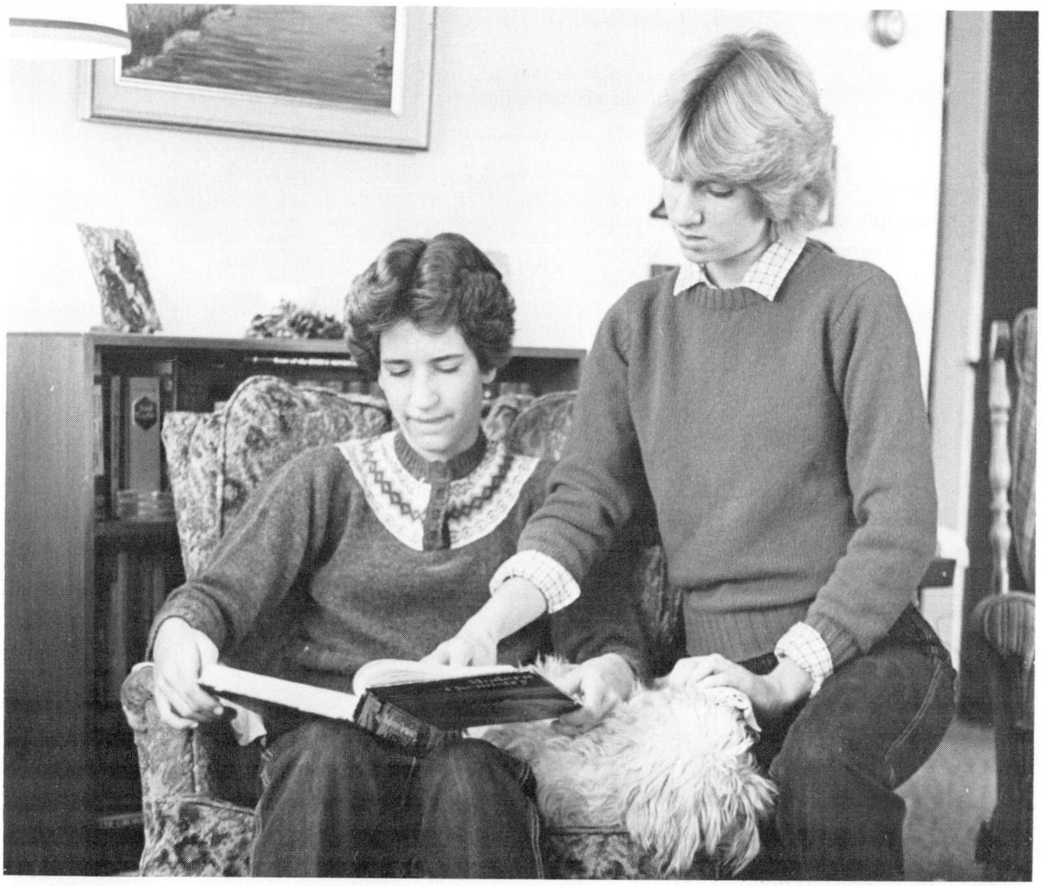

By encouraging the students to become familiar with text structures, you will be providing them with valuable tools for attacking many types of content discourse which might otherwise be overwhelming due solely to the complexity of the information discussed. (Photo by Linda Lungren.)

		Type of Information Processing		
Operation	Text Source	Explicit	Implicit	World Knowledge
1. Synonymy: "fresh" means the reader has extracted a. tone (Max's intent) b. dialogue rules c. mother's intention in her reply	and Max said "I'll eat you up!"			x
2. Conjoining: and = so, therefore (cause effect)	his mother called him Wild Thing and (so, therefore) Max said		x	
3. Transformational grammar deletion rule	"I'll eat you up"	x	x	
	(to her)		x	
4. Clarifying anaphoric referent	(his mother)		x	
5. Generating retroactive causality	(so his mother said "Go to your room without eating anything") so he was sent to bed without eating anything			x

correctly, you, as the teacher, can retrace the reader's steps by asking logically ordered questions that require fewer operations than the original text. This set of questions may aid you to assist the reader in reconstructing the text:

Question 1: What did Max's mother call him on the night he made mischief of one kind and another?

Text source: 1. The night Max wore his wolf suit and made mischief of one kind
2. and another
3. his mother called him "Wild Thing!"

Operation: syntactic transformation of question to subject-verb-object sentence (i.e., Max's mother called him "Wild Thing!")

Question 2: Why did Max's mother call him Wild Thing?

Text source: 1. The night Max wore his wolf suit and made mischief of one kind
2. and another
3. his mother called him "Wild Thing!"

Operations: syntactic deletion—Max . . . made mischief of one kind and another
inferred causality—[so] his mother called him "Wild Thing."

Question 3: What did Max say to his mother when she called him Wild Thing?

Text source: 4. and Max said "I'll eat you up!"

Operation: elongation—I'll eat you up [to her]

Question 4: What do you think Max's mother thought of that?

Text source: 5. so he was sent to bed without eating anything.

Operation: extracting Max's purpose/tone

application of world knowledge

Question 5: Then what did Max's mother say/do?
Text source: 5. so he was sent to bed without eating anything.
Operations: passive to active transformation—he was sent → _______ sent Max to bed; syntactic substitution (elongation—Mom sent Max to bed
world knowledge of (rule)—Mom's turn to talk—"*I* send *you* to bed without dinner"
deleted imperative—Go to bed)

There are additional tasks. The child must extract that dialogue is occurring and must know the rules of dialogue:

Mom: "Wild Thing!"

Max: "I'll eat you up!"

Mom's turn: "Go to bed without eating!"

Leading students through the text in this step-by-step manner may be a productive procedure for helping them to understand the interrelatedness of the entire text.

Narrow and Broad Questions

You can provide the opportunities for your students to engage in many and varied operations, to engage in different types of cognition through your questions. But you must acknowledge the fact that we cannot guarantee that your students will engage in a single, specific, logical operation as a result of the questions you ask. Rather, you must remember that it is important to constantly assess your students' responses to evaluate the effect of the questions that you are asking. Are your questions stimulating your students to think in a variety of ways? Do your questions elicit only one logical operation?

The task of stimulating your children's thinking is comprehensive, but you can begin by constructing appropriately challenging questions along a continuum similar to the continuum by Cunningham (1971). One continuum is

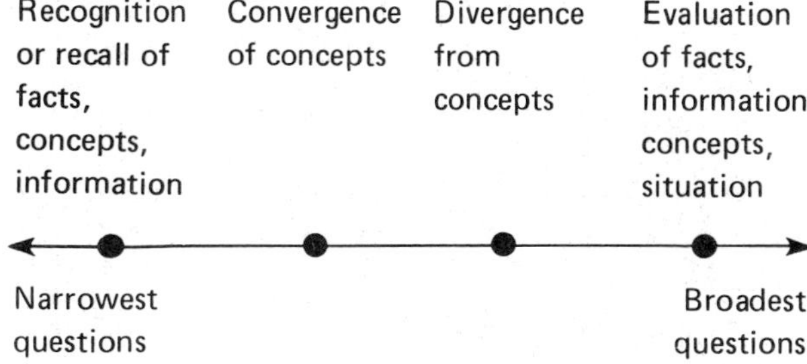

A second dimension of questioning strategies is the difficulty index of individual questions, which may shape a reader's response. There are easy narrow questions and difficult narrow questions; for example, after the student read "Jason rarely moved in springtime, but he moved to Minneapolis without warning one April morning," you asked "To which city did Jason move?" This would be an easy question, but the question "What is the eighth word in the original sentence?" is a difficult question. If a reader was unable to answer the second question, we could not conclude that student was unable to comprehend explicitly stated information. Rather, we would say that the question was extremely difficult (and absurd).

It should also be pointed out that readers need to be prepared to answer certain question types. If we always ask, "What was the eighth word . . .?", students can become attuned to this kind of question and can actually become quite capable of answering it. But they may be less successful in answering broader, more important questions if they have only had practice in answering a narrow memory type of question.

Therefore, it might be productive and useful to examine the types of questions we ask when we are encouraging comprehension in our classrooms. It may be informative to evaluate these questions along the dual dimensions we have established: ease/difficulty and narrowness/broadness. It may also be interesting to compare your in-class discussion questions with your test questions. You can do this by tape recording your classes and then by examining your end-of-unit test questions. You may want to plot your questions on a graph similar to the following one:

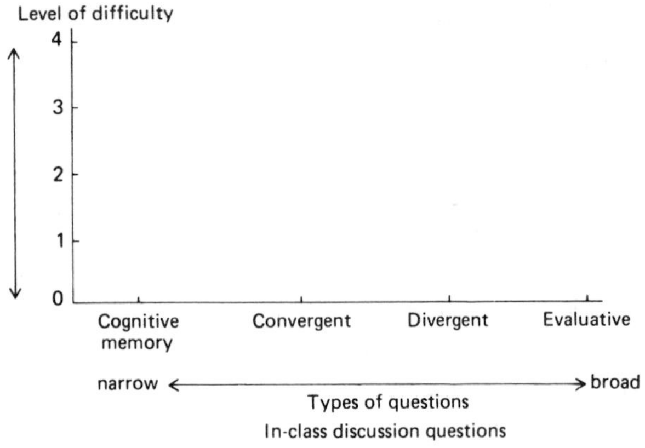

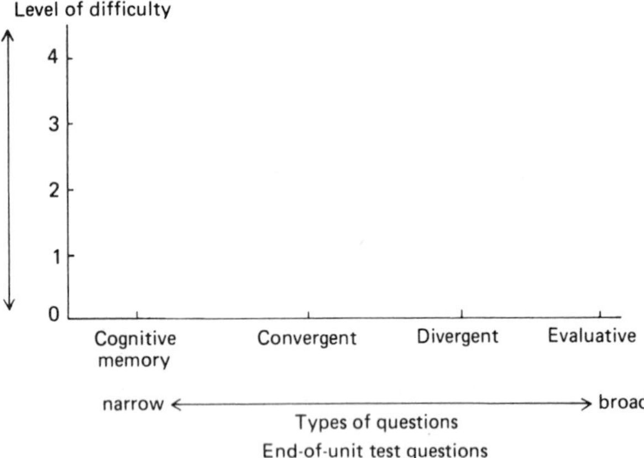

The Directed Reading Activity

In addition to establishing an effective questioning program, you may want to use a comprehensive teaching method, the *directed reading activity.* In a directed reading activity (DRA), you do the following:

1. During the first stage, encourage involvement with the subject matter by calling upon your students' prior knowledge of the subject. This use of prior knowledge is the calling up of one's schema.
2. During the second stage, introduce key vocabulary terms. This stage helps students to develop schema.
3. During the third stage, springboard questions are used by the teacher to provide the student with a guide for searching for the *key* content.

The following lesson on "Spiders" will illustrate the DRA. The topic of spiders is often included in middle-grade science texts (e.g., *Exploring Science*, by Blecha et al., 1980). Rather than merely telling the students to read the lesson and to answer some follow-up questions, a directed reading activity format includes the following.

1. Background

   The teacher involves the students in a discussion of spiders (e.g., Why do they like spiders?). The teacher may bring spiders to class to let children experience spiders with other children in a controlled educational setting.

2. Vocabulary

   The teacher needs to isolate and teach the words that will give the students problems with the reading material. For example, in the spider material, some potentially difficult words are spinnerets, lasso, and digest. By preteaching these words, the teacher helps children over the rough spots before they are frustrated unduly.

3. Springboard Questions

   The teacher needs to provide the students with reading guides to alert them to the important parts of each text. Some important prequestions might be (a) What are spiders like? (b) Where can spiders be found? The reader will note that sometimes authors use these questions as part of the text. With the directed reading activity format, the questions also precede the actual reading.

4. Silent or Oral Reading

   At this point, the text is read by the student.

5. Follow-up Questions

   The follow-up questions are used to check comprehension of text explicit learning while stimulating interpretive thought. To check text explicit learning, springboard questions can be repeated. To stimulate interpretive thought, activities requiring a greater number of schemata can be employed. For example, one could ask, "What would the world be like without spiders?"

ReQuest

Another useful technique for helping children to understand texts is called *ReQuest*. The ReQuest technique is related directly to the questioning technique and can be used as a replacement for the first two stages of the directed reading activity format. The technique involves teacher-student question and answer sessions. The technique begins with both the teacher and student silently reading the first sentence of a passage. The teacher reads the entire passage but the child does not; then the child asks as many questions as he or she desires. The teacher answers the questions as completely as possible. After the student has asked as many questions as desired, the teacher begins to ask questions and the student has to answer. Through this procedure, the student gains insight into the questioning process as both a participant and observer of the teacher who acts as a role model. The procedure continues until the student is capable of answering the question, for example, "What do you think is going to happen in the rest of the selection?" This procedure or technique results in the development and retrieval of one's schemata and concepts.

To illustrate the ReQuest technique, we turn again to the topic, "Spiders." The beginning of the fifth-level Laidlaw basal reader is "Many people think spiders are insects" (*Exploring Science*). To begin the ReQuest procedure, encourage the student to ask the teacher as many questions as possible about the first line. The student may ask, "What do most people think spiders are like?" or "Why do many people think that spiders are insects?" The teacher responds with appropriate answers. At this point it would also be useful to indicate to the student the type of mental processes involved in answering the questions. This could demonstrate the process of schema formation and information retrieval (i.e., the use of prior knowledge to answer questions). The teacher could follow the student's questions with a question such as "Do you think that spiders are insects?" This procedure could be repeated with each succeeding passage until the student feels comfortable.

It should be noted that this technique can be used as a partial substitute for some of the stages of the directed reading activity, for it naturally provides help with background information as well as vocabulary words. This process, in turn, serves as a springboard question exercise.

Concept Development

Many researchers have characterized schema as being synonymous with the idea of concepts; concept development can be considered as a form of schema development. Reading effectiveness can be enhanced through concept formation development.

Flood and Lapp (1981) have suggested two ways in which concept formation can be encouraged. One technique is to share with students a broad general experience. Once the students have shared a common experience, they are asked to group the components of the experience. This involves their becoming aware of the common properties of their groups. After the categories have been established, it is recommended that the students address the issue of labeling the categories. In this manner, the students are trained in organizing concepts and, as such, schema development.

A second technique is called question initiating. The technique begins, once again, with a shared experience. From this point, the student is asked to invent as many questions as possible that result from the experience and his or her reactions to that experience. The questions are listed and categorized. In both techniques, once the categories have been established, it is necessary to discuss why items belong in a category.

To exemplify the concept formation process, we will use a lesson from a third-grade social science text (*Communities and Social Needs*, King et al., 1977). The particular lesson that we have chosen deals with community government. To develop schema awareness through concept formation, we begin with a shared experience such as meeting with a member of city government, visiting city government, or seeing a film on city government. Then the teacher asks the students for a list or lists of what they have seen. The students may list the following: *councilmen, councilwomen, typists, visitors, security officers, discussions on police, money, fire, trash, big building, fancy offices, people working hard, people not working hard, people voting, people discussing, people arguing.*

From this list, the teacher asks the students to set up categories. They may categorize these words in three lists like the following:

Category A	Category B	Category C
big building	discussions	money
fancy offices	arguments	fire
security officers	votes	trash
councilmen	people working hard	police
councilwomen	people not working hard	
typists		

After the categories have been designed, the teacher can ask students to label the categories. For example, category A could become *Things and People We Met,* category B could become *What Government Workers Do,* and category C could become *What Government Workers Talk About.*

Once the categories and labels have been determined, a discussion regarding the similar characteristics of each item in each category can follow. This leads to a discussion on organization and the specific concepts (in this case) of the physical setting of government, the activities of government, and the functions of government.

You must remember that it is important to constantly assess your students' responses in order to evaluate the effect of the questions that you are asking. (Photo by Linda Lungren.)

Prediction Strategy

The prediction strategy, as discussed by Hansen (1981), is based on the notion that comprehension improves when readers can integrate the text into prior knowledge. To stimulate this integration, Hansen suggests activities that evoke prior knowledge and encourage its application to textual information. Based on studies with second-graders, she recommends the following procedure:

1. Prior to having the children read a story, select a few of the ideas that you, the teacher, find important.
2. Write two questions for each idea, one concentrating on previous experiences that relate to the idea and one that requires the students to make a text-related prediction.
3. Ask the students to write their answers and predictions.
4. Discuss the students' answers and predictions.
5. Ask students to read the passage.
6. Ask students to answer the follow-up questions (using both literal and interpretive questions).

To demonstrate this prediction strategy, we will use the topic of "Spiders" again. One idea that may be developed is "the functions of spider webs." To promote the comprehension of this concept, the teacher needs to ask two questions, one to stimulate prior knowledge awareness and one to encourage predictions. To stimulate prior knowledge awareness, you could ask for a list of characteristics of spider webs that children have seen. To promote predictions, you could ask children to speculate on why spiders make webs. Next, ask the children to write their lists, read the material, and answer follow-up questions.

Functional Literacy

After you have instructed your students in concept formation, you have begun to ready them for the task of reading. However, the demands of comprehension are so complex and varied in today's world that it is important for you to go beyond this preparatory process. Let us presume that you have effectively introduced your students to a new concept and that you have prepared appropriate questions for stimulating thinking. Now it is your task to help them through new, varied, lifelike materials that require the transfer of the reading strategies that they have acquired.

The 1981 National Assessment of Educational Progress* surveyed the reading strengths of American students. The findings may suggest that we as teachers need to expand our curriculum to include the teaching of comprehension strategies through materials that are relevant to older readers. The importance of such a curriculum expansion becomes obvious because we are surrounded daily by discussion of literacy. What is literacy? Who is literate? How is literacy related to reading comprehension?

Let's begin by defining *functional literacy*. Because of the many journal articles and national surveys that have described functional literacy as a dominant issue in American homes and schools, anyone who asks this question may appear to be somewhat naive. It is obvious to most of us, as teachers, that a person considered literate by the standard of one culture may be unable to meet the literary demands of another culture. Therefore, literacy tests must be suitable to assess the competencies of the general population with regard to life-coping tasks rather than only being applicable to a small part of the population. Once this issue has been addressed, it becomes necessary to ask, "Literacy for what purpose?"

The *advancement of literacy* is a basic goal of American education. The success of achieving this goal is often questioned as America continues to become an ever more *visual* nation, where films often replace rather than supplement books, and television supplants general newspapers and journal reading. At this time, when Americans appear to be spending less time with reading materials, we are witnessing an increase in both political propaganda and marketing advertisements. Every day consumers are required to make decisions regarding insurance, taxes, applications, credit loans, personal purchases, and government organizations. Can a person be considered literate if he or she can perform only academic tasks? If the answer is yes, one wonders why so many students have evidenced success in school subjects, yet seem to have difficulty with high-level comprehension tasks.

*The National Assessment of Educational Progress (NAEP) is an information-gathering project that surveys the educational attainments of nine-year-olds, thirteen-year-olds, seventeen-year-olds, and adults (twenty-six to thirty-five) in ten learning areas: art, career and occupational development, citizenship, literature, mathematics, music, reading, science, social studies, and writing. Information regarding any such surveys may be obtained by writing to NAEP, Suite 700, 1860 Lincoln Street, Denver, Colorado 80203.

A program designed to foster literacy may have dual complexity because it must include the development of language arts and computational skills as well as provide application strategies necessary in making decisions in life-coping situations. The following outline is presented in an attempt to explain this duality further:

I. Do you have the academic skills of literacy?
   A. Language arts
      1. Spoken language
         Are you able to communicate in the dominant language of the culture?
      2. Written language
         Can you express yourself through the written language of the dominant culture? (syntax, semantics, spelling)
      3. Reading
         Can you critically comprehend the printed materials of the dominant culture? (perceive, infer, evaluate, apply)
   B. Computation
      Can you add, subtract, multiply, divide, compute fractions and percentages, interpret graphs and thermometers?

II. Can you apply these skills to life-coping situations?
   A. Personal
      1. Restaurant functioning
      2. Driver's license application
      3. Transportation schedules
      4. Instructional manuals
      5. W2 forms
      6. Grocery slips
      7. Bank slips
      8. Insurance forms
      9. Savings accounts
      10. Home purchases
   B. Career
      1. Employment ads
      2. Pension plans
   C. Health
      1. Medications
      2. Health care
   D. Civic responsibilities
      1. Community resources
      2. Consumer economics
      3. Environmental issues

A curriculum designed to produce literate citizens must stress the *application* of basic academic skills to life-coping situations. To accomplish this task, students must be introduced to a common set of materials that is used by all people when they are involved in their daily functions.

Persuasion

Students need to be introduced to the art of persuasion to comprehend texts fully. They have to be able to ask themselves such questions as "What is the author's point of view? Is this a biased accounting of the facts?"

The theme of persuasion, the art of persuasion, and the art of persuading are certainly not new to any of us. Throughout history people have attempted to *influence*, or persuade, others. Persuasion, which can be accomplished through a variety of techniques, often uses forms of *propaganda* to promote products, ideas, and people. Propaganda involves one person or group's deliberate attempts to persuade another person or group of people to accept a differing point of view or action. The base of propaganda is heavily laden with syllogism.

Syllogistic Reasoning

A *syllogism* is an argument whose conclusion is supported by two premises. One of these premises, the major premise, contains the *major* term, which is the *predicate* of the conclusion. The other, the *minor* premise, contains the *minor* term, which is the subject of the conclusion. Common to both premises is the *middle* term, which is excluded from the conclusion.

A common example of syllogistic, or deductive, reasoning is the following:

A is B
B is C
therefore
A is C

In this instance,

A is B (major premise)
↓
(major term)
B is C (minor premise)
↓
(minor term)
B (middle term)
A is C

Now let us consider

A. All people are human.
B. Mildred Cunningham is a person.
C. Therefore, Mildred Cunningham is a human.

Is this conclusion true? Yes, when the *major* and *minor* premises are true, the conclusion is true.

Now let us consider

A. All people who live in the western United States are highly intelligent.
B. Lynne Thrope lives in the western United States.
C. Therefore, Lynne Thrope is highly intelligent.

Why is this considered syllogistic reasoning? Statement A contains the major premise, and statement B contains the minor premise. However, the major premise is false; therefore, the conclusion is false. It is important for a critical reader or listener to distinguish between *valid reasoning* and *truth.*

In trying to influence one's intended audience, it is a common device for the producer to present an argument in a manner that is *valid* but then to use *major* and *minor* premises that are false. If one is not a critical *thinker, reader,* and *listener*, it is quite easy to be fooled by what appears to be a logical argument or syllogistic reasoning.

Now let us consider

A. Anyone who opposes increased welfare payments for the poor is antidemocratic.
B. Harold Charles opposes increased welfare payments for the poor.
C. Therefore, Harold Charles is antidemocratic.

or

A. Anyone who is opposed to girls playing hockey is a sexist.
B. Gertrude Hill opposes girls playing hockey.
C. Therefore, Gertrude Hill is a sexist.

or

A. Reading a novel is an enjoyable hobby.
B. Linda Lungren is reading a book.
C. Therefore, Linda Lungren is engaged in an enjoyable hobby.

Are these conclusions true? The answer to this question can be determined only after you have decided if the major premise is true.

Remember, *all* persuasion is not *negative*; neither does it all contain *falsehoods.* Some persons or groups may be interested in persuading us to do good, happy, enjoyable, and morally sound things. Therefore, the reader or listener must be trained to detect the underlying *message within the message.* The critical reader or listener engages in an evaluative process that makes possible the determination of written or spoken propaganda. As readers and listeners, we are confronted daily with persuasion, or propaganda, from newspapers, magazines, textbooks, radio, movies, and television.

Let us consider

Things Go Better with Coke.
See the USA in Your Chevrolet.
You Can't Do Better than Sears.

Aren't the statements in these advertisements the major premises or syllogisms? For example,

A. See the USA in Your Chevrolet.
B. I want to see the USA.
C. I ought to buy a Chevrolet.

or

A. You Can't Do Better than Sears.
B. I want to do better.
C. I'll shop at Sears.

The basic line of each of these advertisements is a *major* premise within syllogistic reasoning. The reader/listener must be alerted to propaganda's appeal to his or her emotions, interests, needs, desires, fears, and prejudices. The questions posed by the critical reader are virtually the same as those needed for propaganda detection. Critical reading involves students posing and answering such questions as

A. *What* do you think happened next?
B. *Why* do you think this happened?
C. *What* other things might have happened?
D. *How* would you have acted differently?

The act of critical thinking demands that one address the many ways in which other persons or groups attempt to influence our thinking. Propaganda techniques are easily detected in advertisement. The following are common forms of propaganda that are used to influence consumers. We have selected one product—cereal—to illustrate how a noncritical thinker/reader/listener can be influenced to buy a particular product. Although these examples are designed to exert positive influence, the same techniques can be used to effect negative outcomes. You may wish to present these techniques to your students because they are the primary audience for whom cereal commercials are designed.

Propaganda Techniques

Bandwagon

MORE MOTHERS PREFER ZOOMIES CEREAL THAN ANY OTHER.

Although the bandwagon approach attempts to convince you that the vast majority of consumers prefer a particular product, it fails to alert you to the options.

Prestige

BOB GOMBAR, ACE GOALIE, EATS ODIES CEREAL.

The prestige approach implies that you might be more like this famous personality if you were to use this product.

Testimonial

TRACY BOSTON, TENNIS PRO, SAYS, "I EAT CIRCLES CEREAL EVERY MORNING AND YOU SHOULD, TOO."

The testimonial approach not only implies that you will be like the tennis pro, but it also tells you what this famous personality believes is good for you.

Repetition

POPPY CEREAL IS NOT ONLY GOOD FOR BREAKFAST, BUT ALSO YOU'LL WANT TO MUNCH, MUNCH, MUNCH POPPIES FOR YOUR LUNCH, LUNCH, LUNCH.

Repetition creates a catchy jingle that is easily repeated.

Plain Folks

THE PRESIDENT OF STARTERS CEREAL WAS ONCE A CABBIE. SHE STILL ENJOYS COFFEE CLUBS WITH NEIGHBORHOOD MOTHERS.

This type of propaganda implies that the president is just one of the family; therefore, she would never cheat or sponsor an unreliable product.

Snob Appeal

ALL THE FAMILIES IN HIGHTOWN VILLAGE EAT CHUNK-UMS. DO YOUR KIDS EAT CHUNK-UMS?

Snob appeal suggests that if you want to be considered a member of the upper class, your children must be Chunk-um eaters.

Emotional Word Appeal

GOOD MOTHERS BUY TARTIES CEREAL FOR THEIR CHILDREN.

This approach certainly implies the criterion necessary for successful motherhood.

Authority

MOST DOCTORS AGREE THAT FILLERS CEREAL IS BETTER FOR YOUR HEALTH.

Not only are you not informed as to what Fillers is better than, but you are also influenced by the fact that physicians have attested to its value.

Transfer

Although words may not be used to influence you, a picture is presented of a healthy child holding a box of

Fillers cereal. You are encouraged to draw the conclusion that your child can be just like this if she eats Fillers.

Labeling

A catchy label such as Wow cereal easily becomes part of your vocabulary. You look for it at the grocery store.

Ego Building

ARE YOU BRIGHT ENOUGH TO BUY SYSTEMS CEREALS?

Is there anyone of us who is not anxious to be labeled bright? We have the incentive to be readily persuaded.

Image Building

YOU'LL BE LIKE ATLAS IF YOU EAT MUSCLES CEREALS.

Again for the many, many people who wish to be a powerhouse of physical or emotional muscles, this becomes the perfect persuasive gimmick.

Oversimplification

GURGLES MAKES EVERY BREAKFAST EATER FEEL HEALTHIER.

How easy life is if only one follows the reasoning presented in this method of persuasion.

Buckshot

This persuasive method utilizes many approaches in a direct attempt to strike as many individuals as possible.

Smith (1963) suggests that, in an attempt to help children learn to analyze propaganda, they should be trained to ask and answer the following questions:

1. Who is the propagandist?
2. Whom is he serving?
3. What is his aim in writing on this subject?
4. To what human interests, desires, emotions does he appeal?
5. What technique does he use?
6. Are you or are you not going to permit yourself to be influenced through the tactics of this propagandist? (pp. 276–7)

One procedure that acquaints children with types of propagandists, as well as aids them in developing a questioning habit regarding propaganda, is to designate a specific wall, chart, scrapbook, or bulletin board as a propaganda center. Children then collect propaganda statements found in ballads, public speeches, posters, leaflets, journals, reports, newsletters, pamphlets, textbooks, newspapers, novels, radios, conversations, and button slogans. Categorizing statements by propaganda type will provide students with practice in answering the questions posed by Smith. Eventually this process of analysis will become automatic.

In addition to asking high-level questions and alerting children to propaganda techniques, you may need to offer demonstrations that will supply children with needed conceptual information. Experimenting with manipulating liquids, clay, and beads often encourages intellectual developmental processes. The selection of activities is dependent on the developmental stages of your students. Demonstrations may aid learning for some children who have reached a particular developmental stage, but it may be ineffective for those without sufficient "readiness." You must be *sensitive* to the developmental stages at which your students are operating.

Although many sociopsychological factors affect a child's learning, studies by Crossen (1948), McKillop (1952), Groff (1962), Johnson (1967), and Schnayer (1967) have emphasized that the child's *attitude* toward a particular topic affects his or her ability to draw inferences from the materials. Merritt (1967) suggests that it is the primary job of the classroom teacher to sequence instruction in reading to elicit desired comprehension behaviors. Merritt further cautions us that competency in reading comprehension can be developed *only* when materials are used in sequence according to the experiential readiness of the student.

As suggested by Merritt, one's ability to read is affected by many factors: cognitive, socioeconomic, sensory, perceptual, language, school, and teacher. The totality of such factors results in one's *background experience*, by which reading comprehension may be affected; thus, we are again faced with the complexity of the literacy issues.

As you attempt to implement any type of instruction designed to further the development of your students' reading and literacy and comprehension skills, keep in mind the following points:

1. Children must be able to decode and understand the words in context before they can critically evaluate the validity of their content.
2. Children must be able to gain needed information through interpretation of *all* graphic aids pertaining to the material which they are being asked to read.
3. Children cannot critically evaluate beyond their experiential and reasoning capacities.
4. Children must be encouraged to suspend judgments based on personal experience until they fully understand the presentation of the reading passage.
5. Children may need to be introduced to prereading activities that will expand their experiential backgrounds. Such expansions may be a must if you are asking children to draw conclusions which rely heavily on personal experiences.
6. Children are better able to accomplish a reading task if the objectives of the task have been clearly defined.
7. Children may be better able to react critically to a written passage if the author is somehow similar to the child, in age or ethnic background.

As classroom teachers, you must continuously supply activities and questions that help children in the developmental process of comprehension. (Photo by Linda Lungren.)

GUIDELINES FOR LESSONS ON COMPREHENSION

When you actually plan a lesson that is intended to encourage comprehension development, you should:

1. *Establish a purpose.* Ideally, the purpose of the lesson should be tied closely to the children's lives (planning the arrangement of the classroom, selecting a new game, discussing a classroom activity). Although your topic cannot always be totally related to the children's lives, it can be presented so that it establishes a new interest or capitalizes on an existing interest. Plan questions that will tap appropriate types of comprehension.

2. *Select materials.* The materials being selected should lend themselves to the teaching of a specified skill. Fiction, nonfiction, games, workbooks, high-interest-low-vocabulary materials are only a few examples of the extensive resources that are available. Remember that the selected materials should help you to accomplish the purpose of the lesson.

Any written document is a potential material source for teaching children how to comprehend texts. Any story, poem, essay, newspaper article, diary entry, or timetable can be used to help children to improve their comprehension.

Many publishers have designed extremely effective comprehension-development materials. *Comprehension Plus* was developed by Flood and Lapp (1983) in an effort to provide materials for teaching comprehension. Each lesson in the six grade-level series (A-F) is a self-contained instructional unit. The student is introduced to the focus skill before he or she is expected to use it in comprehending a text. Special emphasis is given to vocabulary development and using the newly learned strategy in context. A sample lesson is presented on pp. 198–200.

Other materials have been developed as kits filled with enjoyable additional reading material to supplement your program. An example of these materials is presented from *CLUES to Better Reading*, Kit 2 (see pp. 201–203).

3. *Plan experiences.* Through questions, materials, and follow-up activities, you will need to provide the child with opportunities to develop skill in finding main ideas, finding supporting details, detecting the organization plan of the material, detecting sequential arrangements, adjusting reading rate, and critically evaluating work.

The ability to comprehend printed material involves a myriad of skills that are not acquired as a once-and-for-all process. To learn and continue to comprehend requires continuous attention. As classroom teachers you must continuously supply activities and questions that help children in the developmental process of comprehension.

COMPREHENSION ACTIVITIES

1. Where and When?

Goal: Developing an understanding of time and place

Grade Level: 3-6

Construction: On a sheet of paper, type a series of short stories that involve various times and places. On another sheet, make up a crossword puzzle, asking questions involving time and place. For example, "The third story takes place in the season of ______ ." If desired, provide a separate answer sheet for self-correcting.

Utilization: The student completes the crossword puzzle after reading each story.

2. Post Office

Goal: Identifying declarative and interrogative sentences

Grade Level: 4-6

Construction: Get an empty carton with dividers that has been used to hold bottles. Divide the box into two parts by putting a long piece of colored tape down the middle of the side with dividers. Label one side with a card saying "declarative" and one side with "interrogative." Then, using masking tape, label each on the declarative side with "command," "statement," "narrative," and so on. Label the slots on the interrogative side with "asking information," "disbelief," and so on. On envelopes write sentences that could fit under one of the preceding categories, but do not use punctuation.

Utilization: A student inserts the envelopes into the appropriate slot, using the word clues in the sentence.

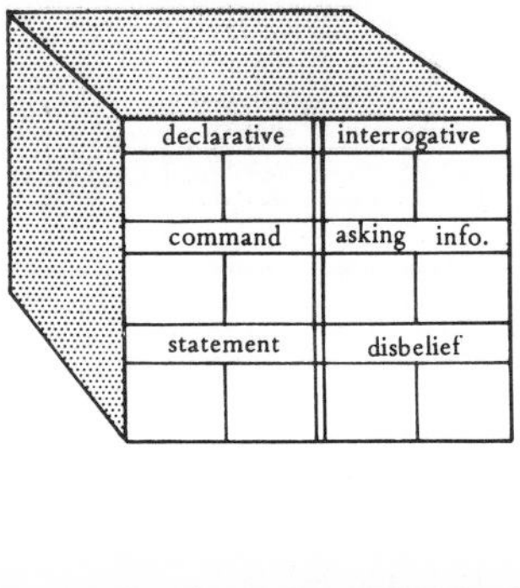

LESSON 18

Look at the picture of Tina. Is Tina really a queen? No. Tina is **imagining** that she is queen.

You can imagine many things that are not real. When you imagine something, it doesn't really happen. It happens only in your mind.

Read the story below. Draw a circle around each sentence in the story that tells something that could not be real.

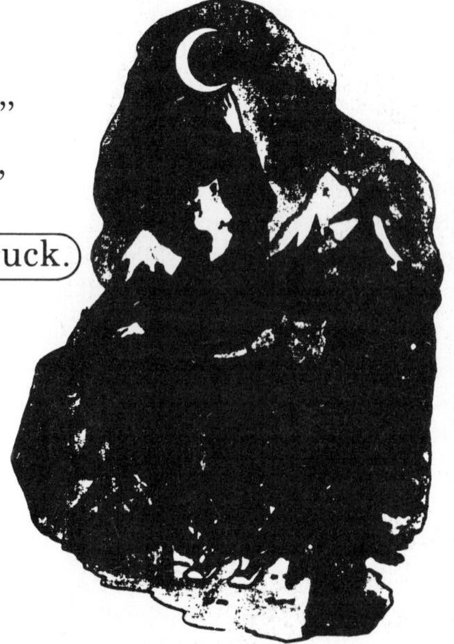

Harry did not like to drink milk. One day his mother said, "If you drink your milk, you will grow big and strong." Harry drank his milk. Then Harry said, "I am growing as tall as a mountain. I am so strong that I can pick up a big truck. I am going to drink some more milk. Then I will be able to touch the moon!"

Harry could see himself grow bigger and bigger. He imagined himself touching the moon.

Here is a **tip.** Sometimes the people in a story imagine things that are not real.

Read the story below. Can you tell what is real and what Tommy imagined?

Too Much TV?

Tommy Dale's mother was taking him to the dentist. Tommy wanted to stay home and watch TV.

"Now I won't know how the space show ended," Tommy said to his mother.

"That's all right," she said as they walked into the dentist's office. "They all end the same way. The good guys and the bad guys shoot at each other with their ray guns."

"And the good guys win," Tommy said.

"That's right," his mother said. "Now hurry. The dentist is waiting for you. I'll be right here in the waiting room."

Tommy went into the office. He sat in the chair and looked up at the dentist. The dentist told Tommy to open his mouth so he could shoot some X-rays.

As Tommy looked up, he saw a green spaceman holding a ray gun. "Oh, no, you don't!" Tommy shouted. He jumped out of the chair and ran out of the room. "Mother! Mother! He's trying to shoot me! He isn't a dentist. He's from space. He told me to open my mouth. And I did. Then he said he was going to shoot some X-rays. He was going to shoot me in the mouth with a ray gun!"

"Oh, Tommy! You have been watching too much TV," said his mother as she walked him back into the dentist's office.

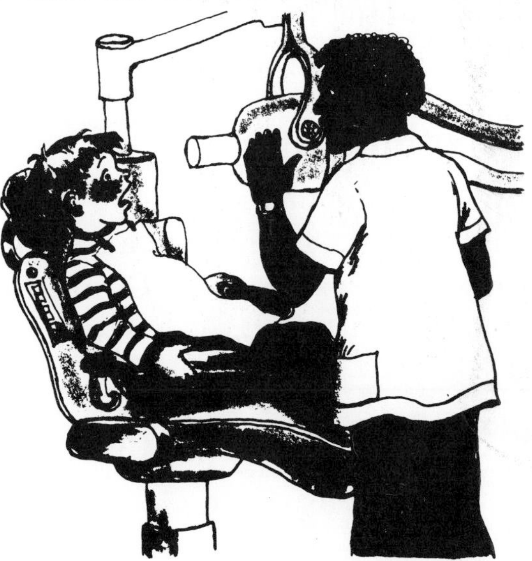

Word Hunt

Write the underlined word from the story to finish each sentence.

1. Tommy watched a TV show about places that are not on Earth. It was a space show.
2. Tommy went to the dentist to have his teeth checked.
3. X-rays are pictures of your teeth.

Something to Think About

Draw a line under the sentence in each pair that tells what Tommy imagined.

1. The dentist was from space.
   Tommy liked to watch space shows.
2. Tommy sat in the dentist's chair.
   The dentist was going to shoot Tommy.
3. The dentist was a green spaceman.
   The dentist was going to take pictures of Tommy's teeth.
4. The dentist had a ray gun.
   The dentist used an X-ray machine.

Something More

Look at the picture below. Write a sentence about it that could be real. Then write a sentence about it that could *not* be real.

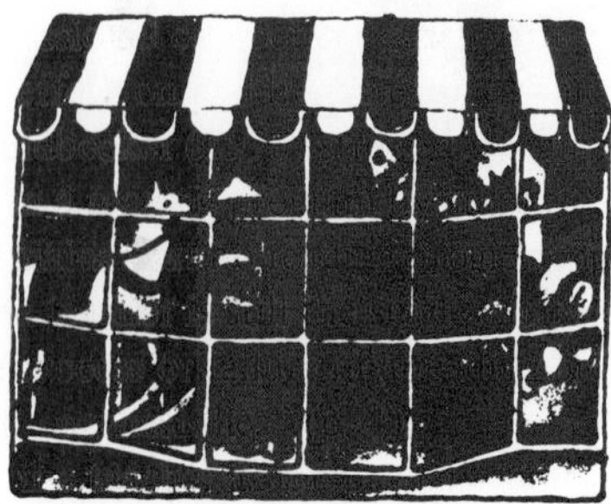

Could Be Real

Answers will vary.

Could *Not* Be Real

B8

SUPPORTING DETAILS

The Ghosts of Morgan Castle

I had heard that Morgan Castle had a ghost. That is why I went there during the storm. The best time to meet with a ghost is, of course, during a lightning storm.

The outside of Morgan Castle was in terrible shape. The face of the front wall had crumbled away. There wasn't an unbroken window to be seen anywhere. The lawn was wild with weeds. Someone had left an old bedspring leaning against the building, and the coils seemed to sing out a sad tune as the wind blew. There was no front door; only spider webs kept strangers away—spider webs and, perhaps, a ghost.

"Hello," I called softly. Hearing no answer, I tried it again—only louder. "Hel-lo-o-o-o!"

I pushed aside some of the webs and, still carrying my suitcase, stepped into Morgan Castle. "Is anyone here?" I shouted. "Anyone at all?"

Suddenly a bolt of lightning struck. In the blinding flash of light, I could see the inside of the castle. "A ghost would certainly feel comfortable in this ruin," I muttered to myself. Bats flew around the Great Hall! Dust covered everything as snow covers the ground. The furniture was broken and moldy. Water dripped in a number of places. In one place in particular, the water rushed down like a small waterfall. A rat ran across the room. Seconds later the rest of its family followed.

SUPPORTING DETAILS

There was a handbell sitting on the mantle over the fireplace. I picked it up and began to ring it loudly. Minutes passed. They seemed like hours. Finally, my signal was answered. I heard a noise; it sounded like feet dragging across a floor. As the noise came closer it grew louder. The suspense got to me. I rang the bell again, listening to its echoes ringing throughout the castle.

"You rang?" a voice asked.

I turned around quickly to see a thin white cloud coming down the stairs. It was a ghost! I hadn't been misled. Morgan Castle was indeed haunted.

I picked up my bag and floated over to the staircase.

"Boo to you," I said in that friendly manner we ghosts seem to have. "I hear that you're looking for a roommate."

Each of the numbered sentences below tells the main idea from a paragraph in the story. Number a sheet of paper from 1 to 3. Next to each number, write the letters of three sentences that give supporting details for the main idea.

Main Idea Sentences

1. The outside of Morgan Castle was in terrible shape.
2. The inside of Morgan Castle was in ruin.
3. I rang a bell and waited for my signal to be answered.

Supporting Detail Sentences

a. Minutes passed and seemed like hours.
b. The lawn was wild with weeds.
c. An old bedspring leaned against the building.
d. Bats flew around the Great Hall.
e. The suspense got to me.
f. Dust covered everything.
g. Water dripped in a number of places.
h. As the noise came closer it grew louder.
i. The face of the front wall had crumbled away.

Now float over to the answer card and check your answers.

3. The Hunting Game

Goal: Following instructions

Grade Level: 1-3

Construction: Choose one object the players are to find and hide it somewhere in the classroom. Make up a series of clues that the children have to follow *exactly* in order to find the object, such as "on the left side of the drawer you will find . . . , walk ten feet and turn right," and so on. Place the clues accordingly around the classroom.

Utilization: There should be only two players for each object hidden. Tell them they are to find a certain object without mentioning its name. Then just tell them where to find the first clue.

4. Organize These "Books"

Goal: Classifying ideas

Grade Level: 1-3

Construction: Put together shelves using cinder blocks and pieces of wood, or use red milk carton containers. Otherwise, shelves available in the classroom can be utilized. Books can be made from blocks of wood or small cardboard boxes. Write titles on the side. An alternative is to use a supply of books already in the classroom. Label each shelf for different ideas; for example, Places to Visit, Things to Make, Science Experiments, and so on. This can be an ongoing activity if the class has a revolving library.

Utilization: Children place the books on the proper shelf according to title or subject.

5. Spin the Meaning

Goal: Understanding how punctuation affects meaning

Grade Level: 3-4

Construction: Make up a folder of laminated sheets of paper that contain sentences with no punctuation. Construct a spinner with five sections: surprise, sadness, humor, disbelief, command, or whatever is desired.

Utilization: A student spins the dial and punctuates the sentence to show the emotion indicated by the spinner.

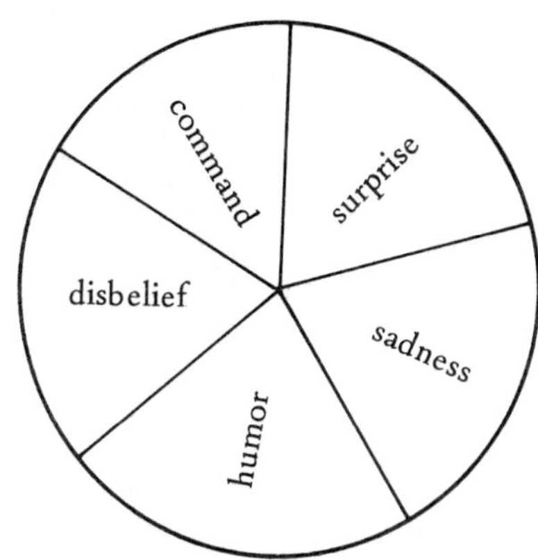

Alternative Game: Change the Meaning

Grade Level: 4-6

Construction: On sheets of paper, write sentences twice, using certain punctuation on one of them. Laminate the paper so that it can be reused.

Utilization: Using a felt-tipped pen, students must punctuate the second sentence so that the meaning is changed. For example,

"Joe," said Jim, "isn't here."

Joe said, "Jim isn't here."

6. Figure Out the Funnies

Goal: Understanding sequences

Grade Level: 5-8

Construction: Laminate and cut into sections several comic strips—the longer the better.

Utilization: Each child must arrange the comic strip sections in the proper order on a desk or table.

7. Tie Me Together

Goal: Inferring cause and effect

Grade Level: 2-6

Construction: Cut out a large piece of cardboard and label one side with phrases that could be "causes" and the other side with phrases to serve as "effects." Label each side with the appropriate heading. Punch holes along the side of each cause and each effect card and attach a shoestring or piece of yarn to each hole on the cause side.

Utilization: Student must thread the yarn into the effect side holes, matching cause with the appropriate effect.

8. Synthesize and Generalize

Goal: Inductive reasoning

Grade Level: 6–8

Construction: On a cassette tape, record paragraphs that give detailed information concerning any subject from which a generalization can be made.

Utilization: After listening to the paragraph, the child must state two generalizations that can be inferred.

9. Who's the Greatest?

Goal: Generalizing from given information

Grade Level: 4–6

Construction: Between two sheets of clear contact paper, place six to eight baseball cards. Place these in a folder, along with a laminated paper on which questions that require generalizations are written, such as "Who appears to be the best all-round pitcher? From these players' records, which team would you predict to win the World Series?"

Utilization: On another sheet of paper, the student writes the answers to these questions and then makes a short generalization concerning the ability of each player.

10. Make Your Own Comic Book

Goal: Forming stories

Grade Level: 4–6

Construction: Have students make a comic book using manila paper for the inside pages and shiny shelf or finger paint paper for the cover. Fold it over and staple it.

Utilization: Tell students to make up any story and characters they wish, and to illustrate their work accordingly. The only criterion is that the narrative parts must be written with red pen and the conversation in blue.

11. Don't Laugh Your Head Off

Goal: Making inferences about figurative language

Grade Level: 3–6

Construction: On large index cards, write stories using figurative expressions. Here are some suggestions of figurative expressions.

frog in my throat	keep your chin up
on pins and needles	take the floor
spill the beans	take the cake
money to burn	beat around the bush
drop me a line	eat his words
put your best foot forward	chip on your shoulder

Utilization: The student rewrites the story, replacing the figurative language with literal expressions. The student can then make up his or her own stories, using figurative expressions and exchanging them with a friend.

12. What Happens Next?

Goal: Predicting outcomes

Grade Level: 3-8

Construction: Make up short stories on large laminated index cards or record them on cassette tape. Leave out the endings, but give clues as to how they could end.

Utilization: The students read or listen to the story and write down an ending and illustrate it. (Accept any reasonable response.)

13. Help: Analogies in Jeopardy!

Goal: Evaluating analogies

Grade Level: 4-6

Construction: On a large piece of oak tag or cardboard attach twenty-five small envelopes in five rows each. On each envelope write \$5, \$10, \$15, \$20, or \$25 down the column. Then attach headings to each column, such as movies, sports, and food, for example. In each envelope, insert cards with an analogy involving the words that fit under each category. The correct answer is written on the back. Examples:

A dog is to a puppy as a cat is to a ______ . (kitten)

Bread is to a sandwich as ______ is to pie filling. (crust)

A conductor is to an orchestra as a ______ is to a football team. (coach)

Utilization: The student is the MC and there can be two or three players. Students take turns choosing which envelope they want to answer. The MC reads the analogy, and if the player can complete it cor-

Movies	Sports	Food	Animals	People
$5	$5	$5	$5	$5
$10	$10	$10	$10	$10
$15	$15	$15	$15	$15
$20	$20	$20	$20	$20
$25	$25	$25	$25	$25

rectly, he accumulates that amount of money and gets another turn. If he is wrong, another player gets to answer. Whoever has the most money when all the envelopes have been chosen wins.

14. Are You for Real?

Goal: Evaluating fact and fantasy

Grade Level: 4-6

Construction: Make thirty (or more) cards with "Fact" written on fifteen of them and "Fantasy" written on the other fifteen.

Utilization: Two players, in turn, draw a card and make up a sentence stating a fact or fantasy, according to the card he draws. The other players must guess which word was on the card; they score one point for each correct answer. Players should make sentences that are not easily distinguishable, thus eliminating the chance of accumulating many points.

15. Why Should I Buy This?

Goal: Evaluating the differences between fact and opinion

Grade Level: 4-6

Construction: Gather a collection of goods for sale from magazines or newspapers and mount it on cardboard.

Utilization: Instruct each student to choose a picture and make up a television or radio advertisement for it. The paragraph-length advertisement should contain information about what the product can be used for, what it's made of, and why a person should buy it. Of course the truth can be stretched, as in the real world of advertising. Then each student should go back and underline those sentences that are only opinion.

QUESTIONS AND RELATED READINGS

If you feel that you have not attained adequate knowledge to answer the following questions successfully, we suggest additional related readings.

1. What cognitive, linguistic, and affective factors are involved in the processes of reading?
2. How is schema theory developed in students?
3. What are the elements that provide cohesion to texts?
4. What teaching procedures enhance children's comprehension of texts?

Goal 1: To help the reader to understand the processes involved in reading comprehension.

Question 1: What are the cognitive, linguistic, and affective factors involved in the processes of reading?

Fisher, D., and C. Peter. *Comprehension and the Competent Reader.* New York: Prager Studies of Holt, Rinehart and Winston, 1981.

Menyuk, P., and J. Flood. "Linguistic Competence, Reading/Writing Problems and Remediation." *Orton Society Bulletin* 31 (1981), 13-28.

Rumelhart, D. "Understanding Understanding." In *Understanding Reading Comprehension,* ed. by J. Flood. Newark, Del.: International Reading Association, in press.

Goal 2: To help the reader to comprehend schema theory development.

Question 2: How is schema theory developed in students?

Bartlett, F. *Remembering: A Study in Experimental and Social Psychology.* Cambridge: Cambridge University Press, 1932.

Rumelhart, D. "Notes on a Schema for Stories." In *Representation and Understanding: Studies in Cognitive Science,* ed. by D. G. Bobrow and A. M. Collins. New York: Academic Press, Inc., 1975.

Stein, N. "How Children Understand Stories: A Developmental Analysis." In *Current Topics in Early Childhood Education,* ed. by L. G. Katz. Vol. 2. Norwood, N.J.: Ablex Publishing Corp., 1979.

Goal 3: To help the reader to explain text structures and textual cohesion.

Question 3: What are the elements that provide cohesion to texts?

Halliday, M., and R. Hasan. *Cohesion in English.* London: Longman Press, 1976.

Herber, H. *Teaching Reading in the Content Areas.* 2nd ed. Englewood Cliffs, N.J.: Prentice-Hall, Inc., 1978.

Meyer, B. *The Organization of Prose and Its Effects on Memory.* Amsterdam: North-Holland Publishing Company, 1975.

Goal 4: To help the reader to develop various instructional practices that aid students in developing comprehension strategies.

Question 4: What effective teaching procedures enhance children's comprehension of texts?

Hansen, J. "An Inferential Comprehension Strategy for Use with Primary Grade Children." *The Reading Teacher* 34 (March 1981), 665–9.

Strange, M. "Instructional Implications of a Conceptual Theory of Reading Comprehension." *The Reading Teacher* 33:4 (January 1980), 391–7.

Whaley, J. "Story Grammars and Reading Instruction." *The Reading Teacher* 34 (April 1981), 762–71.

BIBLIOGRAPHY

Anderson, R. C., R. J. Spiro, and W. E. Montague, eds. *Schooling and the Acquisition of Knowledge.* New York: Lawrence E. Erlbaum, 1977.

Armbruster, B. B., and Anderson, T. H. *The Effect of Mapping on the Free Recall of Expository Text.* ERIC ED 182 735. National Institute of Education (DHEW). Wash. D.C. Feb. 1980.

Auden, W. H. *The Dyer's Hand.* New York: Random House, Inc., 1962. The chapter opening quotation appears on pages 3–4.

Bartlett, B. *Top Level Structure as an Organizational Strategy for Recall of Classroom Text.* Unpublished doctoral dissertation, Arizona State University, 1978.

Bartlett, J. R. *Remembering: A Study in Experimental and Social Psychology.* Cambridge: Cambridge University Press, 1932.

Blecha, M. K., P. C. Gega, and M. Green. *Exploring Science.* River Forest, Ill.: Laidlaw Publishers, 1980, pp. 40–42.

Bloom, B. S., ed. *Taxonomy of Educational Objectives. Handbook I: Cognitive Domain.* New York: David McKay Co., Inc., 1956.

Calfee, R. "Acquisition and Development of Schema." Paper delivered at the National Reading Conference, San Diego, Calif., December 1980.

Chapman, J. "Comprehending and the Teacher of Reading." In *Understanding Reading Comprehension,* ed. by J. Flood. Newark, Del.: International Reading Association, in press.

Crossen, H. "Effect of the Attitudes of the Reader Upon Critical Reading Ability," *Journal of Educational Research* 42 (Dec. 1948), 289–98.

Cunningham, R. "Developing Question-Asking Skills." In *Developing Teacher Competencies*, ed. by J. Weigand. Englewood Cliffs, N.J.: Prentice-Hall, Inc., 1971.

Elliott, S. N. "Effect of Prose Organization on Recall: An Investigation of Memory and Metacognition." Unpublished doctoral dissertation, Arizona State University, Tucson, 1978. Cited by B. Meyer, "Organizational Aspects of Text: Effects on Reading Comprehension and Applications for the Classroom. In *Understanding Reading Comprehension,* ed. by J. Flood. Newark, Del.: International Reading Association, in press.

Fisher, D. F., and C. W. Peters, eds. *Comprehension and the Competent Reader.* New York: Praeger Publishers, Inc., 1981.

Flood, J. "The Effects of First Sentences on Reader Expectations in Prose Passages." *Reading World* 17 (May 1978), 306–15.

____. *Language/Reading Instruction for the Young Child.* New York: Macmillan Publishing Co., Inc. 1981, pp. 356, 361.

____. *Comprehension Plus, Levels A–F.* Englewood Cliffs, N.J.: Prentice-Hall, Inc., 1983.

Flood, J., and D. Lapp. "Inference: A Scoring System for Operations Performed by Readers in Text Recall." Paper presented at National Reading Conference, St. Petersburg, Florida, December 1977.

Flood, J., and D. Lapp. "In Search of the 'Perfect Question': Questioning Strategies for Developing Story Comprehension in Young Children." *Principal* (October 1980), 56, 20–3.

Flood, J., and D. Lapp. "Prose Analysis and the Effects of Staging on Prose Comprehension." Paper presented at the Second Annual Reading Association of Ireland Conference, Dublin, Ireland, 1977.

Frederiksen, C. H. "Inference and Structure of Children's Discourse." Paper for the Symposium on the Development of Processing Skills, Society for Research in Child Development Meeting, New Orleans, 1977.

Gibson, E., and H. Levin. *The Psychology of Reading.* Cambridge, Mass.: The MIT Press, 1975.

Gough, P. B. "One Second of Reading." In *Language by Eye and Ear,* ed. by J. F. Kavanaugh and I. G. Mattingly. Cambridge, Mass.: The MIT Press, 1972.

Groff, P. J. "Children's Attitudes Toward Reading and Their Critical Reading Abilities in Four Content Type Materials." *Journal of Educational Research,* 55 (1962), 313–7.

Guthrie, J. "Research Views: Story Comprehension." *The Reading Teacher* 30 (1977), 575–7.

____,ed. *Comprehension and Teaching: Research Reviews.* Newark, Del.: International Reading Associ-Association, 1981.

Halliday, M., and R. Hasan. *Cohesion in English.* London: Longman Press, 1976.

Hansen, J. "An Inferential Comprehension Strategy for Use with Primary Grade Children." *The Reading Teacher* 34 (March 1981), 665–9.

Housel, T. J., and S. J. Acker. *Schema Theory: Can It Connect Communication Discourse?* ERIC Document ED 177 614. Washington, D.C.: U.S. Educational Resources Information Center, May 1979.

Huey, E. B. *The Psychology and Pedagogy of Reading.* New York: Macmillan Publishing Co., Inc., 1908.

Jenkins, J. "Can We Have a Theory of Meaningful Memory?" In *Theories in Cognition Psychology: The Loyola Symposium*, ed. by R. L. Solso. New York: Harcourt Brace Jovanovich, 1974, 1–20.

Johnson, C. J., II. "A Study and Analysis of the Relationships at the Intermediate Grade Levels Between Attitude as Reflected in Certain Thematic Content and Recalled Comprehension." Unpublished doctoral dissertation, University of California, Berkeley, 1967.

King, F. M., D. K. Bracken, and M. A. Sloan. *Communities and Social Needs.* River Forest, Ill.: Laidlaw Publishers, 1977.

LaBerge, D., and S. J. Samuels. "Toward a Theory of Automatic Information Processing in Reading." *Cognitive Psychology* 6 (1974), 293–323.

Lapp, D., and J. Flood. *CLUES* For Better Reading. Wellesely, Mass.: Curriculum Associates, 1982. Kits for grades 1–8.

Lapp, D., J. Flood, and G. Gleckman. "Classroom Practices Can Make Use of What Researchers Learn." *The Reading Teacher* 35 (March 1982), 578–85.

Mandler, J. "What Is a Story Grammar Good For?" Paper presented at the Pre-IRA Conference of the Center for the Study of Reading, New Orleans, April 25, 1981.

Mandler, J. M., and N. S. Johnson. "Remembrance of Things Parsed: Story Structure and Recall." *Cognitive Psychology* 9 (1977), 111–51.

Marshall, N., and M. D. Glock. "Comprehension of Connected Discourse: A Study Into the Relationships Between the Structure of Text and Information Recalled." *Reading Research Quarterly* 14 (1978-1979), pp. 10–56.

McKillop, A. S. *The Relationship Between the Reader's Attitude and Certain Types of Reading Responses.* New York: Bureau of Publications, Teachers College Press, Columbia University, 1952.

Menyuk, P. "Syntactic Competence and Reading." In J. Stark and S. Wurzel (eds.), *Language Learning and Reading Disabilities: A New Decade.* Proceedings of Queens College CUNY Conference, 1981.

____. "Language Development and Reading." In *Understanding Reading Comprehension*, ed. by J. Flood. Newark, Del.: International Reading Association, in press.

Menyuk, P., and J. Flood. "Linguistic Competence, Reading, Writing Problems and Remediation." *Orton Society Bulletin* 31 (1981), 13–28.

Merritt, J. E. "Developing Competence in Reading Comprehension." In *Reading Instruction: An International Forum.* Proceedings of the First World Congress on Reading. Newark, Del.: International Reading Association, 1967, 91–8.

Meyer, B. J. *The Organization of Prose and Its Effects on Memory.* Amsterdam: North-Holland Publishing Company, 1975.

____. "Organizational Aspects of Text: Effects on Reading Comprehension and Applications for the Classroom." In *Understanding Reading Comprehension.* ed. by J. Flood. Newark, Del.: International Reading Association, in press

Meyer, B. J., and A. G. Rice. *The Amount, Type, and Organization of Information Recalled from Prose by Young, Middle, and Old Adult Readers.* ERIC Ed 191 003. Paper presented at the annual meeting of the American Psychological Association, Montreal, Canada. September 1980, p. 6.

National Assessment of Educational Progress. *Reading in America: A Perspective on Two Assessments.* Denver: NAEP, 1981.

Niles, O. *School Programs: The Necessary Conditions in Reading: Process and Program.* Urbana, Ill.: National Council of Teachers of English, 1970.

Pearson, P. D., and D. Johnson. *Teaching Reading Comprehension.* New York: Holt, Rinehart and Winston, 1978.

Reder, L. M. "The Role of Elaborations in the Comprehension and Retention of Prose: A Critical Review." *Review of Educational Research* 50 (Spring 1980), 5–53 (quotation taken from p. 38).

Rumelhart, D. "Toward an Interactive Model of Reading." Technical Report No. 56. Center for Human Information Processing, University of California, San Diego, 1976.

____. "Understanding Understanding." In *Understanding Reading Comprehension*, ed. by J. Flood. Newark, Del.: International Reading Association, in press.

Rumelhart, D., and A. Ontony. "The Representation of Knowledge in Memory." In *Schooling and the Acquisition of Knowledge,* ed. by R. C. Anderson, R. J. Spiro, and W. E. Montague. Hillsdale, N.J.: Erlbaum, 1977, 99–135.

Schank, R. C., and R. P. Abelson. *Scripts, Plans, Goals, and Understanding: An Inquiry into Human Knowledge Structures.* Hillsdale, N.J.: Erlbaum, 1977.

Sendak, M. *Where the Wild Things Are.* New York: Harper & Row, Publishers, 1969.

Senta, C., and B. Hayes. *Children's Prose Comprehension.* Newark, Del.: International Reading Association, 1981.

Smith, F. *Understanding Reading.* 2nd ed. New York: Holt, Rinehart and Winston, 1978.

Smith, N. B. *Reading Instruction for Today's Children.* Englewood Cliffs, N.J.: Prentice-Hall, Inc., 1963.

Stauffer, R. G. *Directing Reading Maturity as a Cognitive Process.* New York: Harper & Row, Publishers, 1969.

Stein, N. "How Children Understand Stories: A Developmental Analysis." In *Current Topics in Early Childhood Education*, ed. by L. Katz. Vol. 2. Hillsdale, N.J.: Ablex, Inc., 1979.

Stein, N. C., and C. Glenn. "The Role of Structural Variation in Children's Recall of Simple Stories." Paper presented at the Society for Research in Child Development, New Orleans, 1977.

Summers, P. "Story Grammars." Handout for Course RL 780, Reading and Language Department, Boston University, April 1980.

Taylor, B. M. "Children's Memory for Expository Text After Reading." *Reading Research Quarterly* 15 (1980), 399–411.

Thorndike, E. L. "Reading and Reasoning: A Study of Mistakes in Paragraph Reading." *Journal of Educational Psychology* 8 (1917), 323–32.

Tierney, R. and J. Mosenthal. *Discourse Comprehension and Production: Analyzing Text Structures and Cohesion.* ERIC ED 179 945 (January 1980), p. 31.

Trabasso, T. "Mental Operations in Language Comprehension." *Language Comprehension and the Acquisition of Knowledge.* Washington, D.C.: V. H. Winston, 1972.

Trabasso, T. "On the Making of Inferences During Reading and their Assessment." In J. Guthrie (ed.) *Comprehension and Teaching: Research Reviews.* Newark, Del.: International Reading Association, 1981.

Vacca, R. "An Investigation of a Functional Reading Strategy in Seventh Grade Social Studies." Unpublished doctoral dissertation, Syracuse University, Syracuse, N.Y., 1973.

Winograd, T., and P. Johnston. "Comprehension Monitoring and the Error Detection Paradigm." Technical Report No. 153. Center for the Study of Reading, University of Illinois, Champaign-Urbana, January 1980.

Woodworth, R. S. *Experimental Psychology.* New York: Holt, 1938.

CHAPTER 8

Reading Study Skills and Strategies

A major goal of teaching is that students become independent learners, able to apply knowledge when needed. In our constantly changing world the processes or methods for obtaining, integrating, and reviewing information are much more important than the mere memorization of specific data which may soon be obsolete.

M. Tonjes and M. Zintz, 1981

By helping students to acquire and use study skills, you are also helping them become independent learners. (Photo by Linda Lungren.)

GOALS: To help the reader to

1. Acquire an understanding of reading study skills.
2. Understand the importance of reading study skills.
3. Recognize and implement instructional strategies appropriate to students' grade levels and abilities.

Before we begin our discussion of specific reading study skills, it may be appropriate to examine our terminology. Lamberg and Lamb (1980) define *study skills* as "procedures, strategies, or techniques used by students to consciously direct their academic performances" (p. 407). Estes and Vaughan (1978) state that "skills are specific, overt, demonstrable capabilities that are required to perform a specific task" (p. 105). For students, this specific task is to acquire knowledge or information in a particular area, a field of *study.*

Reading study skills can be viewed as tools that help students accomplish this task. According to Shepherd (1978), "the goal of the study skills is the student's total independence to gain information for himself" (p. 112). By helping students to acquire and use study skills, you are also helping them become *independent learners.*

Many study skills are applicable to all content areas; some are related more specifically to a particular area of study. For this reason, the topic of study skills is analyzed twice in this text.

In this chapter, we define and discuss generally those study skills that are needed by elementary school children to experience success in learning. In Chapter 9, we explore the interpretation of these same study skills within specific content areas of study (math, science, social studies) and provide you with *methods* for classroom implementation. For example, the process of reading graphic data is discussed generally in this chapter as a generic study skill because it pertains to all content area reading in both the primary and intermediate grades. In Chapter 9 the processes involved in reading graphic data are discussed in relation to reading specific science, math, and social studies materials.

GENERIC STUDY SKILLS

Selection-Evaluation-Selection

One of the more intangible goals of education is the preparation of students to meet the challenges of everyday living. The process of selection-evaluation-selection is not only related to study situations, but it is basic to every choice in life. In an increasingly complex society, both students and adults must learn and understand the *process* of decision making. In making a decision one has to identify and select from many possible choices, evaluate the options according to predetermined standards and criteria, and then make a refined selection. Evaluation is a skill; its complexity depends on the complexity of selections to be made and the bases for those selections. If you find yourself in a situation where you must choose a reference, you may need to examine several possibilities, weigh or evaluate their content as it relates to your need, and make a final choice or selection based on your evaluations. An individual who is asked a direct question needs to sift through possible answers, evaluate their potential worth, and make a choice for a response. The child who is given an opportunity to choose a way to use a segment of time will need to consider all possibilities and make his or her choice accordingly. One might say that selection and evaluation are basic to the decision to get up and start each new day.

The process of selection-evaluation-selection does not lend itself to the primary-intermediate breakdown as readily as do several of the other common study skills. We have, therefore, discussed it first because it is common to the use of each of the others.

ORGANIZATION

Primary Years

Most children begin to develop a sense of order or organization at an early age in their homes (e.g., "put the ball back in the toy chest," "hang your sweater in the closet"). This early organizational training must be encouraged and promoted in school as the child matures. Success in using organizational skills depends on the child's ability to perceive relationships.

Young children can begin to develop organizational skills by grouping items of the same size, shape, or color. These skills can then be refined by grouping objects of varying shades of the same color or arranging objects of the same shape, but different sizes, in order from largest to smallest, or vice versa. This skill may also be developed by grouping objects or pictures that have some common elements. For example, in kindergarten, children might be asked to select and group a collection of pictures, for example, grouping the pictures that show children playing or all those that have something red in them.

Categorizing. From using these basic exercises, first-grade children are ready to advance to organizing words and sounds. Ask your children to classify words that have the same beginning, medial, or ending sounds.

banana	pen	had
bunny	fell	lid
boat	set	fed

They can categorize or group words that have related meanings, for example, all the words that name pieces of furniture or all the words that name actions.

Sequence, or the order of organization, is a significant part of writing, composing, or relating ideas. Young children particularly need guidance in organizing their thoughts and ideas. One activity that primary-school-aged children enjoy is arranging pictures or cartoons in a logical sequence so that they "tell a story." Another way for teachers to guide young students in developing a sense of sequence is to solicit ideas for a group story. The teacher works with the students, encouraging them to consider the appropriate sequence of events. The story, once composed and recorded on a chart, may be cut into sentence strips so that children can read the sentences and then reconstruct the original story.

For children to develop organizational skills, they must be able to see relationships among ideas. For example, after they have heard or read a story that took place in a specific country, they might be asked to identify the things in the story that indicate the setting of the story. Another approach is to have them write ideas about two characters (e.g., R2D2 and Luke Skywalker) from a story they know, then mix them up, and regroup the ideas that relate to each character.

The organization of the classroom itself can provide an excellent opportunity for primary children to develop organizational skills; therefore, your classroom should include a wide variety of books and other instructional materials. These materials need to be arranged and kept in some orderly fashion while the children are practicing their learning. Through classroom discussions, children can help to plan the organization and placement of these materials. Then individuals or small groups of students (on a rotating basis) can be responsible for returning items to their proper location.

Summarizing. "The ability to provide an adequate summary is a useful tool for understanding and studying texts" (Brown et al., 1981, p. 17). Both primary and intermediate children can be helped to develop this skill. Summarizing requires the ability to select the most significant points in a story, incident, or report and to relate them in a sequential order. Although the skills of sequencing and summarizing become refined during the intermediate grades, they can be initiated quite early by asking children to tell about some event or story in their own words. Even at these early levels, you can begin building organizational skills with children through examples and discussions. We suggest that you

1. Encourage children through questioning to observe the structure of the material being read.
   a. Am I reading an essay within a book or a total book?
   b. What clues do the pictures give me?
   c. Title clues
   d. Subtitle clues
   e. Summary
2. Survey lessons with children to determine the language clues that enable the student to better understand the author's organizational structure.
   a. Are there clue words that add to the total idea?

in addition	since	moreover
and	furthermore	too
another	otherwise	as well as
also	likewise	plus
again	besides	after all

   b. Are there clue words that emphasize the concluding idea?

finally	in conclusion
in sum	consequently
in brief	hence
this	then
in the end	at last

c. Are there clue words that emphasize reversing, qualifying, or modifying ideas?

but	on the other hand
nevertheless	either-or
still	conversely
in contrast	however
even if	opposed to

d. Are there clue words that indicate thought emphasis?

because	as
like	for instance

e. Are there clue words that indicate relationships in time, space, or degree?

last	here	many
now	there	more
later	close	little
after	for	some
previously	by	best
following	away	all
meanwhile	under	fewer
at the same time	above	greater
before	across	above all
immediately	beneath	worst

3. Encourage awareness of the headings and subheadings of the material being read.
   a. Position on page
   b. Type of print
4. Discuss the informational clues offered through headings, subheadings, and organizational pattern.
5. Read materials with students and ask questions that focus on organizational structure.
   a. What are the major headings? subheadings?
   b. Were time relationships evidenced through headings?
   c. Were irrelevant subheadings included?
   d. Were more subheadings needed?
   e. Was a summary provided?
6. Develop note taking skills.
   a. Begin reading a story.
   b. Stop when the emphasis of the story shifts.
   c. Write a sentence that summarizes what was read.
   d. Write a phrase containing the main points of the sentence.
   e. Continue reading, and repeat this process each time the emphasis of the story shifts.

Activities 1 and 2 at the end of this chapter are designed to help you to implement specific organization skills in your primary classroom.

Intermediate Years

As children enter the intermediate school years, they encounter materials that present more complex ideas, written in complex sentences and in longer paragraphs. At the intermediate level, the emphasis is on expanding the organizational skills developed in the early years to help students deal with more difficult materials. The development of organizational skills helps students to recognize relationships among facts. Once students have identified the organizational structure of the material, they have an operational base from which they can synthesize, compose, and evaluate newly learned facts.

It is important that students learn to recognize the way an author structures ideas and fits information together. As Vacca (1981) points out, "the perception of organizational patterns–relations–in single sentences, in paragraphs, and in long text passages has been considered basic to comprehension by many authorities in the field of reading" (p. 141). Through the development of this study skill, the reader follows the author's plan by recognizing organizational patterns, major ideas, and details. The organizational patterns commonly used by authors include time order, enumeration, comparisons, contrasts, and cause and effect relationships.

You can help your students to recognize common organizational patterns by pointing out that they are often suggested by the author's choice of *signal words.* Examples of signal words are

Time order:	before, after, when, on (date)
Enumeration:	first, next, finally, then
Comparison:	like, similarly, as well as
Cause and effect:	because, since, therefore, as a result

Outlining. Outlining is a useful tool for students to employ in organizing information. However, it can be a difficult skill to master if children are not taught to understand purpose and organization throughout the primary levels. The basis for success in outlining lies in being able to grasp the relationships among the ideas involved. The foundation for development of this skill is found in the primary skills: classifying (grouping ideas) and summarizing.

Friedland and Kessler (1980) reported that they were successful in teaching outlining to intermediate-level students through the use of a practical exercise. They introduced the concept of outlining (without naming it) by asking students how they could best arrange the contents (everything from clothing to pencils to gum wrappers) of a messy dresser. The next exercise was preparing and organizing a classroom inventory. Only then did the students advance from classifying items to classifying ideas; "from the simple and concrete to the complex and abstract."

The concept of outlining can be developed easily and naturally by children if the teacher makes a list of related ideas in a simple format. These lists may have the more important ideas set off by numerals and the supporting ideas indicated by letters. Move first into the use of major ideas, with supporting ideas indented, and then add letter and number designations. The use of such listings continually lends itself to the teaching of this skill.

As more formal outlining is practiced, a few basic principles of outlining should be taught. They are illustrated in the following outline form.

Topic

I. A major idea
    A.
        1.
            a.
                (1)
                    (a)
                    (b)
                (2)
            b.
        2.
    B.

This simple outline form goes as far, and perhaps farther, than the majority of elementary children will be able to go in understanding and outlining material. Ultimately, children need to understand that the purpose of outlining is to help them identify main ideas and supporting ideas in some body of information.

Children must be helped to understand that the author has already designed an outline for the material; the child has to interpret and use the outline as a clue for comprehension.

One of the easiest ways in which to help your students identify topics and subtopics is to provide them with an incomplete outline of a text excerpt. You provide the main topics and have the students supply the missing topics and subtopics. For example, give your students a text excerpt such as the following, which discusses some of the technological advances that affected the United States in the first half of the 1800s:*

Cotton Gin

One of the early problems with growing cotton was separating the seeds from the fibers. This was a slow, difficult, and expensive job. Hand-picking one pound of fibers from three pounds of seed had been a full day's work for one slave. Because of this, very little cotton was grown, and cotton cloth was rare. In 1793 Eli Whitney developed a machine for this job. Even in its first crude form, it could clean cotton fifty times faster than work by hands. Later, larger cotton gins (**gin** is short for engine) could clean hundreds of pounds each day.

Spinning Machine

English textile factories were more advanced than factories in America. Machines for spinning fibers into thread were developed in England, but the design of these machines was kept secret. Americans offered money to anyone who would bring the secret of the design to America. Samuel Slater, a young textile mechanic familiar with the machines, came to America and succeeded in building a spinning machine here in 1791. Many cotton-spinning mills were soon established.

Power Loom

Weaving thread into cloth was originally done slowly on hand looms. After several years of experiments, a successful power-driven loom was built around 1814. By 1840 one American town had nine mills with 4,000 power looms.

After the students have finished reading the passage, ask them to complete an outline similar to the following:

*M. Brady and H. Brady, *Idea and Action in American History* (Englewood Cliffs, N.J.: Prentice-Hall, Inc., 1977), p. 218.

TECHNOLOGICAL ADVANCES IN THE EARLY 1800s

Topic I. The cotton gin solved one of the problems of growing cotton.

Subtopic A.

Subtopic B.

Subtopic C.

Topic II. Spinning machines were available in England, but not in America.

Subtopic A.

Subtopic B.

Subtopic C.

Subtopic D.

Topic III. Power looms were used to weave thread into cloth.

Subtopic A.

Subtopic B.

Following are other activities that will help children to understand the significance of main headings and subheadings:

1. After children have read only chapter headings and subheadings, ask them to discuss the information that should be contained in each.
2. Encourage children to write a story summary using only the information provided in story headings and subheadings.
3. Ask children to read several paragraphs and develop a heading for each paragraph.
4. Select several newspaper articles Remove the titles. Ask children to read the articles and select the appropriate title.

In addition to main topics and subtopics, children need to understand (1) the format of an outline and (2) the different types of outlines.

Format. Some students experience difficulty with outlines because they do not understand the relationships presented in the organized text structure. A student must be taught that in an outline, one does not use a I unless one has information for II. The student may continue on through III, IV, V, and so on, but unless the information being dealt with can be broken into at least two parts of equal importance, one does not break the idea away from the preceding heading of greater importance. Therefore, if the student has I, he needs II; if he has A, he needs B; if he has 1, he needs 2, and so on.

Types. There are two basic types of outlines: the sentence outline and the word or phrase outline. The type of outline the student writes is determined by his or her own needs and the complexity of the material. If a great deal of time is going to elapse between development and use, the student may want to use the sentence form because it will be easier to remember the written selection of more information. The word or phrase outline is very useful for study purposes or when giving an oral review of printed materials.

Sentence Outline

Summer Vacation

I. Last summer my family visited California.
   A. It took four days to drive there.
   B. We stayed for two weeks.
II. We went to three major cities.
   A. In San Diego we spent a lot of time at the beach.
   B. In Los Angeles I saw a movie studio.
   C. I rode the cable cars in San Francisco.

Word or Phrase Outline

Summer Vacation

I. Visited California
   A. Four days' drive
   B. Stayed for two weeks
II. Things I saw
   A. San Diego beaches
   B. Los Angeles movie studio
   C. Cable cars in San Francisco

It is usually recommended that the different forms not be mixed. When outlining is first being learned, it is advisable to adhere to this principle. However, as the outliner becomes more skilled and prepares outlines for personal use, he or she may find a mixture more satisfactory.

When preparing outlines with your students, remember to emphasize these additional points:

1. Italicized or underlined words may indicate a foreign term.
2. Chapter introductions may provide them with an understanding of what can be anticipated within the text.
3. Chapter summaries may enable them to gain a complete understanding of the relationships that have been explored within the text.

Note Taking. Note taking is an important study skill that can help children's learning. Rickards (1980) discusses two possible functions of note taking:

1. Notetaking [sic] may facilitate comprehension and recall of facts through "encoding" of material.
2. Notetaking [sic] plus reviewing notes may be productive of recall.

The research data is as yet inconclusive; however, learning this skill requires careful and continuous teaching because it is such a useful skill for the students to acquire.

Children often resort to paragraph lifting in the name of note taking. It is important to help students make use of different clues and cues while taking notes. For instance, students need to focus attention on topics and subtopics. Subsequently, they need to read the material accompanying these topics and subtopics and make their notes in a form that they can understand and reuse. The notes should paraphrase the most significant information in the material. If students are taking notes from either an oral or written presentation, they must

1. Be able to pick out the important points and related ideas.
2. Realize the value of listening and reading before summarizing or paraphrasing.
3. Write notes in their own words.
4. List brief notes.
5. Develop notes that give structural clues: *first, most important, finally.*
6. Invent their own abbreviation code.
7. Be consistent.
8. Develop a topical note-filing system that includes a bibliographic reference to topic, date, and purpose of notes.

You can help students to develop good note taking skills by teaching them (1) to identify important facts and ideas, (2) to match the form of notes with the intended purpose, and (3) to determine what type of information to include. As a class activity, read a selection with your students and then discuss

1. The ideas that should be recorded as notes.
2. The best form of notes for the intended purpose.
   a. Outline
   b. List
   c. Chart
   d. Time line
   e. Parallel columns
3. The need for notes to include
   a. Who?
   b. What?
   c. When?
   d. Where?
   e. Why?
   f. How?

Note taking may be an arduous task for students who have not mastered the skill of summarizing. You can help your students to develop skill in preparing summaries by reading a newspaper or text selection with them and then

1. Stating the main theme.
2. Selecting the sentence that best summarizes each paragraph.
3. Combining these sentences to summarize several paragraphs.

If students appear to be having difficulty in selecting main ideas, present them with a passage and several sentences from the selection; discuss the main idea of the selection with them and look for clue words and phrases. Once the topic becomes clearer, difficulties in selecting main ideas will diminish.

Summarizing and Synthesizing. At the intermediate level, students begin to get involved in such projects as report writing, which requires synthesizing and restating information gathered from a variety of sources. This process is related to locational skills as well as to the ability to organize. Synthesizing requires the use of note taking, outlining, and summarizing skills.

Students must be able to

1. Identify available sources from which they can garner information.
2. Effectively use the sources they have identified.
3. Synthesize the information into a meaningful, logically ordered whole.

As a student becomes competent in the use of a few sources, the number can be increased gradually. Another requirement for effective use of this skill is knowledge of suitable sources from which information may be gathered. If students do not know direct sources, they must learn ways of identifying and locating such sources.

Summaries and synthesizations are both similar to outlines in that they all contain major facts and minor details in the students' own words. A summary presentation may take the form of a paragraph, a listing of events, or a record of procedural steps. In developing these skills, you might introduce students to a text excerpt that contains a summary. After reading the excerpt and summary, you may ask students to

1. List the main ideas and important details.
2. Discuss their rationale for listing these major ideas and details.
3. Determine if these bits of information are contained in the summary.
4. Analyze the different styles used to present major and minor points in the text and in the summary.

PREPARING GRAPHIC AIDS

Graphic aids, including pictures, charts, graphs, maps, and tables, can be valuable tools to enhance children's learning. Hawkins (1980) particularly encourages the use of graphs in the classroom because " graphs can make astronomical numbers understandable. Statistical data can be presented in simple and interesting forms through these devices. Comparisons can be made. Relationships which are not readily grasped from tables or statistics or narratives can be shown and clarified" (p. 1). Educational research also supports the use of graphic aids. In a study on the effect of pictorial aids, Truman (1981) reported the major finding to be that learning with pictures was significantly better than learning without pictures.

Children can learn to use and to develop tables or charts to convey information. To prepare an effective chart or graph that uses symbols to represent quantities, students need to be instructed in abstract reading skills. For example, if children were trying to prepare a graph portraying the population in their home area since 1900, they would have to decide which years to chart or graph, the type of symbol to use, and the number of people each symbol should represent. They would also have to select a general format for the chart, and they would need to prepare a legend explaining their use of symbols so that others could use the information. Examples of social studies and science graphs emphasizing these details are presented in Chapter 9. These examples will serve to emphasize the need to (1) read graphs with understanding and (2) allot ample time for developing graph-reading skills.

You can help children to recognize the value of graphic aids by preparing materials that have an obvious relevance to the students' lives. Some examples might be

1. A table showing the number of students in the school according to grade.
2. A map of the area around the school.
3. A chart illustrating the height of each student.
4. Diagrams showing how to use classroom audiovisual equipment.
5. A picture file depicting each child's hobby.

As students encounter graphic aids in texts, review the material with them and explain the illustrated concepts in detail. By continually using and emphasizing pictorial aids, you will encourage your students to use these aids as they attempt to understand printed materials.

Primary Years

Teachers can help children to develop skill in remembering by helping them set purposes for reading, listening, and viewing films to gain information. These purposes usually need to be stated in broad terms so that children do not focus their attention on small details and thereby fail to extract the larger meaning of the text.

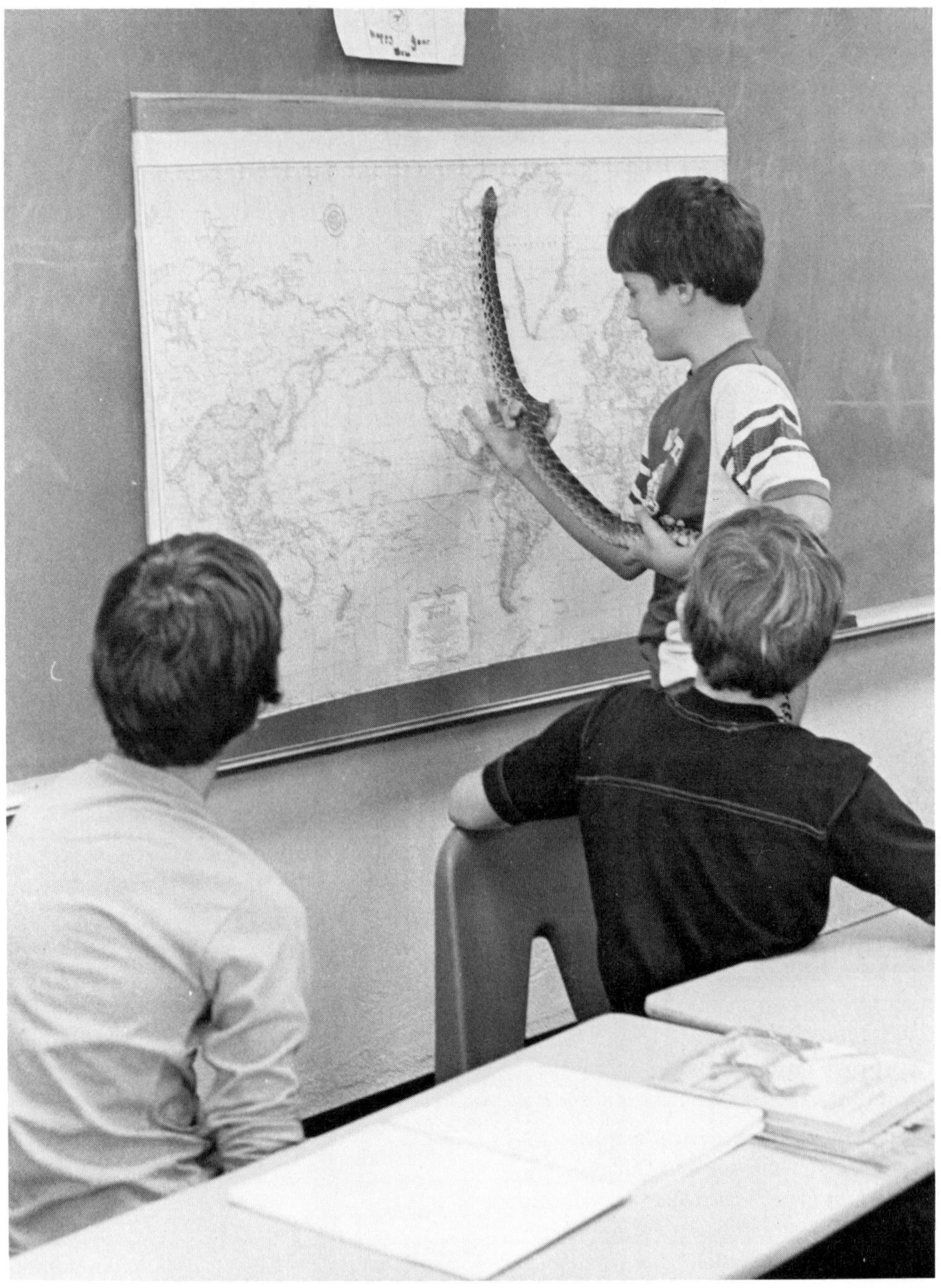

Graphic aids including pictures, charts, graphs, maps, and tables can be valuable tools to enhance children's learning. This student is giving a report on a snake he captured in his neighborhood. (Photo by Linda Lungren.)

Question asking is one of the oldest and most frequently used means of checking recall. Our purpose here is not to discuss techniques of question asking; rather, it is to point out the various ways in which children can provide answers to questions. Answers may be given orally or through demonstration, the carrying out of some direction, or role playing. Answers may also be shared through media, art, music, and dance.

Finally, we encourage you to allow children to verify information that they have recalled as an aid to accuracy as well as recall. This is particularly valuable if a difference of opinion exists as to the facts being recalled. Too often, the teacher simply supplies the correct answer and the issue is resolved. Although it may involve more time, let the children with differences of opinion reexamine their sources and discuss their differences. In the long run, this will be time well spent.

Intermediate Years

Throughout the intermediate years, the emphasis is on expanding and refining skills that were introduced at the primary level. As students encounter more factual and more complex materials, they sometimes experience difficulty recalling the amount of information that is required of them. One of the most useful strategies that students can learn is the *SQ3R technique.*

SQ3R. SQ3R is an acronym for *survey, question, read, recite, review.* This method helps students to understand and recall what they read through an organized, well-planned approach to reading. Let us examine each of the steps in this process.

Survey. Students survey the text or material to get a general idea of the content and organization. Surveying involves glancing over such items as chapter titles, main headings, subheadings, graphic aids, tables of contents, introductions, summaries (when provided), italicized words, introductory sentences, numbered points, and chapter exercises. This sets the stage, or provides a framework, for subsequent steps.

Question. Questioning relates to the major headings. The student can use the headings to pose questions that they believe the text will answer. This gives the student a purpose for reading—a question to answer. For example, if the heading is "Transportation in the Nineteenth Century," the student might pose the following questions:

1. What forms of transportation did people use in the nineteenth century?
2. How did these forms of transportation differ from modern methods of transportation?
3. What effects did these forms of transportation have on people's lives?

Read. The students are now ready to read the selection, keeping in mind the questions they have formulated. Encourage them to look for the main idea and supporting details.

Recite. The fourth step, the second R, is reciting the answers to the questions. This will aid comprehension and enhance recall of the material. Students must ask themselves if the answers make sense; if they do not, they may want to go to another source to check the same information.

Review. Finally, students review what they have read. Explain that reviewing is similar to surveying, but with the details filled in. Students can review the information in their minds, or they can write down notes or an outline.

You should encourage your students to learn and to utilize the SQ3R method of reading and studying. They will find it is a useful strategy to aid comprehension and to facilitate recall of the material they have read.

Psychological Aids. Psychological aids may be valuable tools to help our minds absorb and retain information. By examining the relationships or logical connection among a number of ideas, it is often possible to link them and recall them better than we can recall them separately.

Association. Association is a method that will enable students to relate and synthesize information. For example, if the students are reading about the branches of the U.S. government, you might want to develop questions that encourage them to integrate and associate the facts from the text; for example,

1. Political leaders felt that a stronger central government was necessary.
2. Legislative branch: a Congress to make laws.
3. Executive branch: a president to enforce the laws.
4. Judicial branch: a system of courts to see that justice was done.
5. The system of checks and balances was conceived to regulate and control each branch of the government.

To encourage students to associate these facts, you might ask a question such as "How does the system of checks and balances help keep the government strong?"

Another method of helping students to recall information is the delayed recall technique. Using this method, students periodically check their own recall and review of information until they have the facts at their fingertips. You can develop this technique by occasionally having students refer to material that they have already learned.

At times, it may be desirable or necessary for students to memorize particular information. In this case, the *whole and parts methods* of recall may be a useful tool. The length of the material to be memorized plays an important part in determining which of these techniques is most effective. In all cases, the initial focus should be on the "whole." Parts of the total material to be memorized should be studied until they are understood in total. Students should be introduced to all these methods of review and be encouraged to use them whenever appropriate.

LOCATING INFORMATION

Primary Years

The development of *locational skills* is absolutely essential to the goal of providing children with the skills they need to become independent learners. Locational skills provide children with the necessary means to secure information and to identify and use appropriate sources of information. The first skill a child must acquire is the ability to *alphabetize.*

Alphabetizing. Children must be able to alphabetize letters and words in order to use dictionaries, encyclopedias, indexes, glossaries, and other reference materials. We suggest that you begin teaching the skill of alphabetizing in a manner similar to the following:

1. Introduce the letters of the alphabet in sequential order.

2. Write the alphabet on the board and ask students to supply the missing letters.

   a, b, ___, ___, e, ___, g, h, ___, ___, ___, l, ___, n, ___,

   p, ___, ___, ___, ___, u, ___, w, x, y, ___.

3. Supply word lists and ask children to alphabetize them by the first letter.

the	we	you
girl	and	day
cat	see	pat
fun	big	red
is	lid	new

4. Supply word lists that will have to be alphabetized by the second letter.

day	fun	lip	set
dog	far	lot	saw

5. Supply word lists that will have to be alphabetized by the third and fourth letters.

bat	gone	hand	pass	them
bang	going	hang	past	these

Dictionaries. Using a picture dictionary is an ideal way in which to reinforce alphabetizing skills while introducing dictionary usage. Single-picture dictionaries arrange words according to some common relationship: animals, clothing, food. Words in the groups may be alphabetized and illustrated with pictures. Numerous dictionaries are available, and children may advance gradually from using simple dictionaries to standard dictionaries. Activity 3 at the end of this chapter is designed to help you to develop very basic alphabetizing and dictionary skills.

Parts of a Book. A child's first lesson in using a book should be through the introduction of the *parts of a book.* During the primary years, children may not need to use *all* the parts of a book, but they need to be aware of the existence of the many components of a book.

Have your students examine the cover of a book and note its title. You might ask such questions as

1. What do you think this book is about?
2. Why do you think the author chose this title?
3. Is there a picture on the cover? If so, what does it show? How do you think this relates to the contents of the book?

After examining the book and discussing the title, the children can be introduced to the *table of contents.* Discuss the author's purpose for including the table of contents and how it can be helpful to the students. You can demonstrate that a table of contents can be used to locate major parts of a book, but it may not contain a complete listing of all headings and subheadings. Explain that the table of contents is in numerical order from beginning to end. Children need to begin finding pages by number as soon as they can read numbers.

The easiest way of helping your students to acquire an understanding of a table of contents is to provide practice in using one. The following table of contents and questions constitutes an exercise that you may want to use with your students.

MUSIC IN AMERICA
TABLE OF CONTENTS

This table of contents provides a vast amount of information about the text. Ask your students to answer the following questions:

1. Where would you look for information about music and art? (Chapter VII)
2. Where would you find an explanation about the contents of the entire book? (Chapter I)
3. If you wanted to sing a sea chantey, where could you find an example? (Chapter II, section B)
4. Where would you look in order to find out what a hammer dulcimer is? (Glossary)
5. How could you tell on what page "On Top of Old Smokey" is located? (Index)
6. Your special assignment is to learn a cowboy song. Where could you find one in this book? (Chapter V, section A)
7. Spirituals were very popular in the South. In what section of the book are spirituals located? (Chapter III, section C)
8. Where would you look to see how many Christmas

songs are printed in this book? (Chapter VI, section B)

9. Farming is very important in the Middle West. If you wanted to sing a song about the corn harvest, where might you find one? (Chapter IV, section C)
10. What is the topic of this book? (American music)
11. How many chapters are in this book? (seven)
12. How could you find out what kind of a song "Mary Ann" is? (Look in alphabetical listing and then turn to that page.)
13. Where could you find out about colonial art? (Chapter VII, section A)
14. Where could you find information about playing an instrument? (Chapter I)
15. Where could you find a Navaho Indian song? (Chapter V, section B, number 2)

Through a class activity such as this, children are able to practice

1. Locating page numbers
2. Finding words, phrases, or sentences in context
3. Using titles and chapter headings

Children benefit from this and similar activities that require them to make decisions about the information contained in a book. You must also be sure that children are always able to support their answers with facts.

The table of contents is the foundation for text usage. Once the students are knowledgeable in using it, they should be introduced to classroom reference materials such as the almanac, atlas, and encyclopedia.

Reference Materials. Young children are naturally curious; you can capitalize on this curiosity by encouraging children to explore atlases, almanacs, and encyclopedias. We recognize that very few primary-level students will be able to use these reference materials independently, but many may be ready to profit from having information read to them. Many children may also be able to read material in some of these references if they have help initially in locating the information. They are capable also of incorporating the terms encyclopedia, atlas, and almanac into their vocabularies. Even the youngest of children should be introduced to these reference tools and encouraged to view them as additional sources of information.

Explaining to the students that most reference books arrange information alphabetically will also serve to reinforce the importance of alphabetizing skills. You may have some children who are ready to explore the use of an index; however, because this is not common, index usage is discussed for intermediate-grade students.

You can introduce your students to classroom reference materials by

1. Discussing the type of information contained in each resource.
2. Comparing and contrasting the purpose of each type of resource.
3. Demonstrating that the text contents appear in alphabetical order.
4. Selecting questions that will provide practice in using the materials. For example,

   a. What is the tallest building in the United States?
   b. Who was the vice president in 1950?
   c. Where might you find a guanaco?
   d. Name a province that borders Alberta, Canada.

5. Surveying materials with the children to determine which is the most suitable for answering each question.

Some teachers may prefer teaching the use of reference materials as part of the library unit; if so, be sure to enlist the aid of your librarian or resource specialist.

Library Skills. It is desirable to introduce children to the library at a very early age. This may encourage children to develop reading habits that will last a lifetime. There are several library skills that the child needs to develop at the primary level: proper care of books, appropriate library behavior, knowledge about types of materials in the library, and a general understanding of the arrangement of library materials.

Instruct the children about appropriate library behavior, emphasizing that such behavior demonstrates respect for the rights of others. Library users are asked to be quiet (not silent) to ensure that everyone in the library can read, work, or study without noisy distractions. Effective instruction on library behavior involves helping children to recognize the type of atmosphere that makes their use of the library most pleasant and

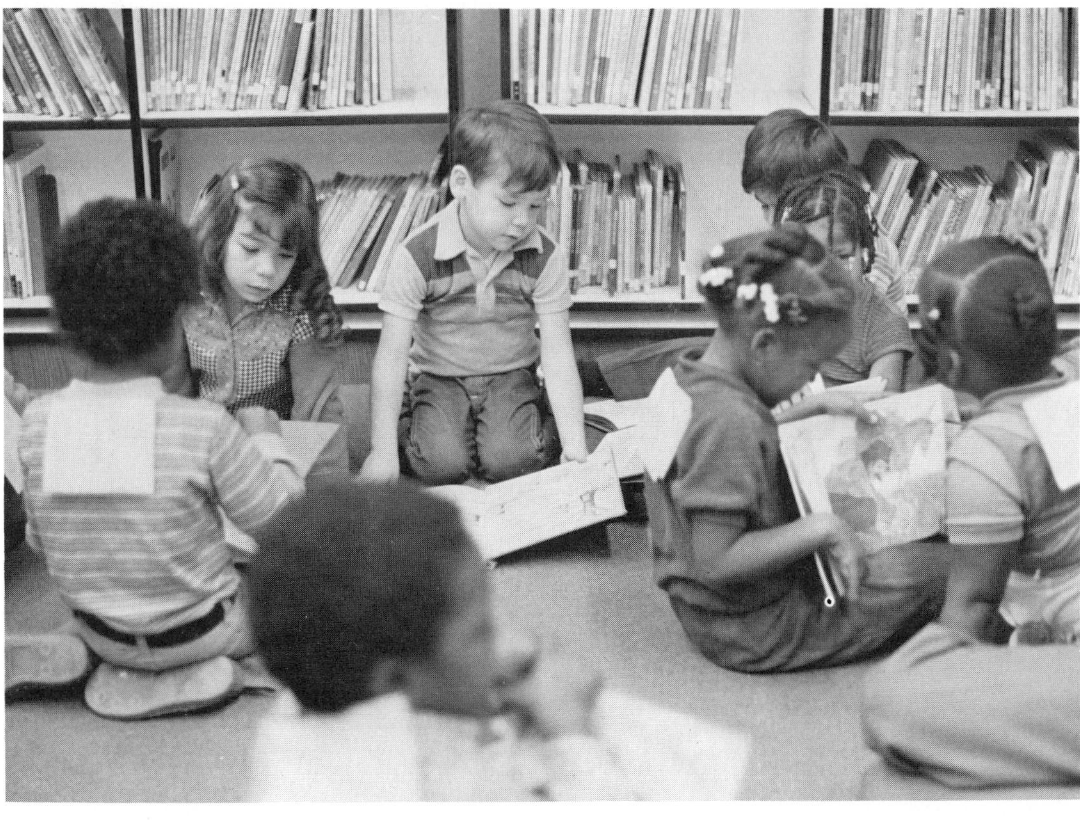

It is desirable to introduce children to the library at a very early age. (Photo by Linda Lungren.)

productive and to realize that they have responsibility for helping to create this atmosphere for others, as well as for themselves.

Once you feel confident that your primary-grade students understand the need for library courtesy and taking care of books and other library materials, you may want to introduce them to the card catalog. Activity 5, at the end of this chapter, will help you to teach this library skill. For more specific information, please refer to a later section of this chapter, "Using a Card Catalog."

Intermediate Years

As we have emphasized throughout this chapter, at the intermediate level the focus is on *expanding* skills developed at the primary level. You can aid students to extend their awareness of locational skills by developing a thorough understanding of the parts of a book.

Parts of Books. Students need to be made aware of the parts of a book, the function of each part, and how to find and choose the material suited to their needs. You can accomplish this best by examining a book with your students and discussing

1. The title (What does it suggest?).
2. The author(s).
3. Name(s) of the person or companies responsible for the production of the book.
4. The copyright date (How current is the information?).
5. The preface (Why did the author(s) write this book?).
6. The acknowledgments.
7. The table of contents (What is the organization of the book?).
8. The index(es).
9. Any appendixes.
10. The glossary.

11. The foreword. (A foreword is an introduction to the book written by someone other than the author. It usually reflects the writer's interpretation of and reaction to the purpose and plan of the book.)

Students need to become competent in using the parts of the book. They must grow to recognize that every part of a book is a potential aid to the student, not merely a "filler."

Using the Index. An excellent way of teaching students about using the index is to contrast it to the table of contents, a book part with which they are already familiar. You can begin by pointing out that a table of contents lists the contents of the book progressively, from beginning to end. An index, however, is arranged alphabetically by topic. The index can provide the reader with more in-depth information about the topical relationships within the text than can be found in the table of contents. The index also synthesizes all references to a single topic by precise page numbers.

Examine and discuss an index with your students. You should explain that some books contain more than one index, for example, a subject index and a name index. By referring to an index similar to the following text excerpt, you can point out that an index usually includes

1. Names of people
2. Events
3. Cross-reference listings
4. Cities, states, and countries
5. Topics

M. Brady and H. Brady, *Idea and Action in American History* (Englewood Cliffs, N.J.: Prentice-Hall, Inc., 1977, p. 535.)

Once your students have an understanding of the purpose of an index and the type of information it includes, you may want to teach the use of an index in the following manner:

1. Provide your students with a set of problems they want to solve.
   a. How did musical instruments originate?
   b. Who is Arthur Fiedler?
   c. Where is the greatest amount of wheat harvested?
   d. Where is the Amazon River located?
2. After developing the problems, encourage the children to delineate the information to be found.
   a. musical instruments, origins
   b. Arthur Fiedler
   c. wheat
   d. Amazon River
3. Have students select a text that may contain the information they are seeking. To answer problems *a* and *b* it may be most helpful to select a music text, whereas for problems *c* and *d* you may select a social studies text.
4. Once the text has been selected, have students survey the index to determine
   a. if entries are listed alphabetically.
   b. if topics, symbols, and names are all part of the same index.
   c. the meanings of any abbreviations.
   d. the purpose of using commas and dashes in entries.
   e. the meaning of words in italics.
   f. if the desired information is included.

Through an activity such as this, children will begin to develop skill in using an index. You may also wish to use activity 6, at the end of this chapter, to provide additional practice in using this locational skill.

Glossary. Frequently, primary-level books do not include glossaries. However, as intermediate-grade students become more involved in reading content area materials, the use of a glossary becomes more important. Students need to realize that a glossary contains words, definitions, and explanations that relate to the special contents of a book.

Nullify To set aside or disobey a law.
Overseer A person who supervised slaves at work.
Pioneer The first person to go into an unsettled land.
Polarization The gradual step-by-step increase in hostility between two groups which moves them further apart.
Popular sovereignty A proposal for letting people in the territories decide for themselves, by voting, whether to permit slavery in their territory.
Preamble An introduction.
Proprietors People to whom the King gave charters to set up colonies in the New World. In return these people gave payments to the King. They were given the right to sell land in their colony and to control the colony's government.
Ratify To give approval.
Reconstruction The period of rebuilding the South after the Civil War.
Referendum A special election in which people vote on certain issues.
Repeal To revoke or cancel.

M. Brady and H. Brady, *Idea and Action in American History* (Englewood Cliffs, N.J.: Prentice-Hall, Inc., 1977), p. 511.

Appendixes. Appendixes are another example of parts of books that are more commonly found in content area texts. Appendixes may have varied content, but their usual purpose is to supply, in a condensed form, supplementary information that is related to the textual content. For example, in a social studies text, you might find any of the following: maps, Declaration of Independence, Bill of Rights, U.S. Constitution, capsulized chronological lists of significant dates, and so on. Appendixes are listed in the table of contents and information included is indexed, as is the other text information. Activity 4, at the end of the chapter, is designed to help you teach the importance of the glossary.

Dictionary Skills. Mastery of dictionary skills should be emphasized continuously at the intermediate level because the ability to use a dictionary correctly to help unlock word meanings and pronunciation is a skill needed by children at every level. In fact, a student's mastery of many skills that are usually categorized as dictionary skills will strongly affect his or her success in using many other reference books. As you attempt to develop this skill, you will need to provide instruction related to the following areas: finding words, word meanings, and word pronunciation.

Finding a Word. There are several skills that a student must possess before being able to use a dictionary successfully to locate a specific word. These are the ability to

1. Recognize letters.
2. Differentiate between letters.
3. Put the letters of the alphabet in the proper sequence.
4. Alphabetize words, by first, second, third, and eventually all letters.

To help students learn to use a dictionary quickly and efficiently, it is desirable to aid students in developing a sense of letter location. You can begin by pointing out that the letter *M* is approximately the middle of the alphabet. Next, have the students open a dictionary in the middle and note which letters are on the pages that fall to the left and right. Then ask them to divide each half so that they can note the letters in each quarter of the dictionary. The students should now be ready to look for the page where a particular letter begins. Ask them to open a dictionary to the place where they anticipate finding the first letter and then going forward or backward to the correct page. Activity 10 at the end of this chapter provides further instruction in this area.

Guide words are valuable tools that can help a student to determine if a particular word is included on a given page. They can also be used to help a child searching for a word determine if he or she should turn forward or backward in relation to the place where the dictionary was opened originally.

SAMPLE ACTIVITY

Guide Words

Say to your class, "Look at the sample dictionary page. The words *poor* and *pork* are printed at the top of the page to the left. These words are called guide words because they tell you whether a word you are looking for is to be found on this page. The word *poor* is the first entry on this page. The word *pork* is the last entry on this page. The words *pop, popcorn,* and *porch* are on this page because they occur in alphabetical order between *poor* and *pork.*" (See page 227.)

After the students have a basic understanding of guide words, you may want to teach them how to find each of these sets of words in their dictionary.

ballet	musical	choreography
gnome	scalawag	hectogram

After they find each word, ask them to write the guide words they find on each page.

The child needs to understand that the guide words point out the first and last words on a page. If the word being pursued is alphabetically between the guide words, then the word should be on that page, if it is included in that particular dictionary. You may want to provide children with a list of words and ask them to supply the order in which they could be found in a dictionary.

____	boy	____	after
____	mansion	____	always
____	plane	____	hurry
____	lava	____	skip
____	apple	____	jump
____	before	____	amble
____	today	____	run
____	yesterday		

Word Meanings. The words children know and use have meaning for them based on their past experiences. Children should be encouraged to use the dictionary to validate the meanings of their language and to encourage vocabulary development.

When children use the dictionary to look up the meaning of a particular word, they will often encounter a variety of information. Sometimes students will have to examine several definitions to select the one that seems to fit the context in which it was used. To help children to understand the meanings of some words, scale drawings are used that students need to interpret. *Synonyms* and *antonyms* are included as part of the definitions of many words; students must understand what synonyms and antonyms are for this information to be helpful in unlocking word meanings.

SAMPLE ACTIVITY

What a Word Means

Start by saying to your class, "You can learn many things about a word from your dictionary. But the question that you will ask most often is, "What does it mean?" That is why we put the meaning right after the entry word itself. The meaning of a word is called its *definition*. When something is definite, it is very clear. The definition is what makes a word clear to you."

"After you find the word you want, you can learn what it means right away. You will not have to read any other information first."

gavel A small wooden hammer. It is used by the person in charge of a meeting or trial to call for order or attention.
gav·el (gav′əl) *noun, plural* **gavels.**

gay Full of joy and fun; merry; cheerful. The children were *gay* at the birthday party. Ruth wore a *gay* dress with many pink ribbons.
gay (gā) *adjective.*

"As you can see from the example for *gavel,* the first part of a definition in your dictionary is short and simple. It is made up of a few words that tell you quickly what you want to know: a *gavel* is 'a small wooden hammer'."

group of people. Dad belongs to a car *pool* in which each person takes a turn driving the others to work. *Noun.*

—To put together for a group to share. The children *pooled* their money to buy a present for their mother. *Verb.*

pool (pōōl) *noun, plural* **pools;** *verb,* **pooled, pooling.**

poor 1. Having little money. She is too *poor* to buy a new dress. 2. Below standard; less than needed; bad. He has *poor* health. The farmer had a *poor* wheat crop. He is a *poor* student. 3. Unfortunate. The *poor* boy lost his pet dog.

poor (poor) *adjective,* **poorer, poorest.**

pop 1. To make or cause to make a short, sharp sound. The balloon will *pop* if you squeeze it. He blew into the paper bag and then *popped* it between his hands. 2. To move or appear quickly or without being expected. Aunt Mary *popped* in to see us. He *popped* his head out the window. *Verb.*

—1. A short, sharp sound. The firecracker exploded with a loud *pop.* 2. A soft drink. Jean drank a bottle of *pop. Noun.*

pop (pop) *verb,* **popped, popping;** *noun, plural,* **pops.**

popcorn A kind of corn having kernels that burst open with a pop when heated. The kernels become white and fluffy, and can be eaten.

pop·corn (pop′kôrn′) *noun.*

pope The head of the Roman Catholic Church.

pope (pōp) *noun, plural* **popes.**

poplar A tall, fast-growing tree. It has wide leaves and long, hanging stalks of flowers. The wood of the poplar is soft and is used to make pulp for paper and cardboard.

pop·lar (pop′lər) *noun, plural* **poplars.**

poppy A plant with round, red or yellow flowers. Opium comes from one kind of poppy.

pop·py (pop′ē) *noun, plural* **poppies.**

Poppy

popular 1. Pleasing to very many people. Baseball is a *popular* sport. The beach is a *popular* place to go on summer afternoons. 2. Having many friends; well-liked. Bill is *popular* at school. 3. Of or for the people. Our country has a *popular* government. 4. Accepted by many people; widespread. It is a *popular* belief that a four-leaf clover will bring good luck.

pop·u·lar (pop′yə lər) *adjective.*

popularity The state of being popular. Gail's *popularity* at school was due to her friendly, happy nature.

pop·u·lar·i·ty (pop′yə lar′ə tē) *noun.*

population 1. The number of people who live in a place. What is the *population* of your city? 2. People. The entire *population* was forced to leave the town because of the flood.

pop·u·la·tion (pop′yə lā′shən) *noun.*

populous Having many people. New York is a *populous* city.

pop·u·lous (pop′yə ləs) *adjective.*

porcelain A kind of pottery. It is very hard, and is thin enough to see through when held to the light. Cups, plates, and other dishes are sometimes made of porcelain.

por·ce·lain (pôr′sə lin) *noun.*

porch A roofed area built onto a house. Grandmother's house has a large front *porch.*

porch (pôrch) *noun, plural* **porches.**

porcupine An animal whose body is covered with sharp quills.

por·cu·pine (pôr′kyə pīn′) *noun, plural* **porcupines.**

Porcupine

The word **porcupine** was made from two Latin words that meant "pig" and "thorn."

pore[1] A very small opening in the skin or other surface. Perspiration passes through the *pores* in our skin. ▲ Another word that sounds like this is **pour.**

pore (pôr) *noun, plural* **pores.**

pore[2] To look at, study, or think about carefully. John *pored* over his homework. ▲ Another word that sounds like this is **pour.**

pore (pôr) *verb,* **pored, poring.**

pork The meat of a pig used as food.

pork (pôrk) *noun.*

How to Learn About a Word from a Picture

Say to your class, "A picture is worth a thousand words." That is an old saying. But even in a dictionary, which is a book of words, a picture can be very important. There are about 30,000 entry words in this book, and more than 1,000 pictures—that is, one picture for every 30 words.

"Why does a book about words need pictures? Many times a picture can tell you more about something than a definition in words can. Prove this to yourself. Read the following definitions."

metamorphosis The series of changes in shape and function that certain animals go through as they develop from an immature form to an adult. Caterpillars become butterflies and tadpoles become frogs through metamorphosis.
met•a•mor•pho•sis (met´ə mor´fə sis) noun, plural **metamorphoses.**

bagpipe A musical instrument made of a leather bag and pipes. A person makes music by blowing air into the bag and then pressing the bag so that the air is forced out through the pipes. The bagpipe is often played in Scotland.
bag•pipe (bag´pip´) noun, plural **bagpipes.**

balance **1.** The condition of having all the parts of something exactly the same in weight, amount, or force. The two children kept the seesaw in *balance* **2.** A steady position. He lost his *balance* and fell down the stairs. The tightrope walker kept her *balance.* **3.** An instrument for weighing things. The chemist weighed some powder on the *balance.* **4.** The part that is left over. He still has the *balance* of his homework to do after supper. Noun.
bal•ance (bal´əns) noun, plural **balances**; verb, **balanced, balancing.**

"What happens in *metamorphosis?*
How do you play the *bagpipe*?
What is *balance*?

"Now look at the picture. Then go back and read the questions over again. Do you have a better idea now of how to answer them?

"Here are the pictures of the words."

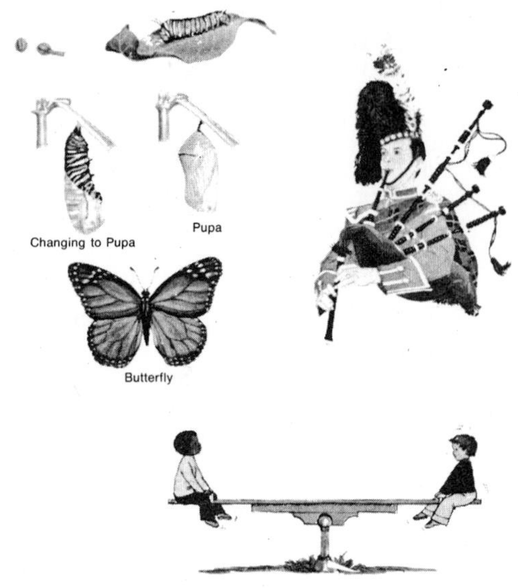

You may also help children to understand word meanings by planning lessons on (1) synonyms, (2) antonyms, and (3) words with multiple meanings. Activities 7 through 9 at the end of this chapter are designed to help develop these skills.

Pronunciation. One of the major functions of a dictionary is to provide a key to interpreting spoken language. For students to use the dictionary effectively for this purpose, they need to have an understanding of syllabication and phonics.

In most dictionaries, the pronunciation of a word is included as part of the dictionary entry. Students need instruction in using a *pronunciation key* in order to develop pronunciation skills. Your lessons on how to use a pronunciation key should include

1. Phonetic respellings
2. The use of accents
3. Diacritical markings
4. Syllabication
5. the *schwa* (ə)

"In dictionary pronunciations each pronunciation symbol stands for one sound. To find out which sound each symbol stands for, turn to the full pronunciation key. This key is at the front and at the back of this dictionary.

"Look at the symbol *a* and at the two words that follow it. The words *hat* and *cap* are called key words because they tell which sound the symbol a stands for, the vowel sound heard in *hat* and *cap*. Perhaps you have learned to call this sound the short *a* sound.

"Now look at the symbols *e, i, o,* and *u*. What vowel sound does each of these symbols stand for? How do you know?

"Look at the symbol *b*. What key words are given for this symbol? Where do you hear the *b* sound in *bad*? in *rob*? Look at the symbols *d, f, g,* and *h*. What consonant sound does each of these symbols stand for? How do you know? Look at the rest of the single letters that stand for consonant sounds. How can you tell which consonant sound each one stands for?

"If you turn to the entry word *yacht* in your dictionary, you will see the pronunciation (yot) after it. How is *yacht* pronounced?

"Below are the pronunciations of fifteen words. Write the numerals 1 through 15 on a piece of paper. Then say each word from its pronunciation, using the full pronunciation key if you need to. Write the spelling of that word after the numeral. The spellings are given in alphabetical order at the right. Do it this way: 1 half"

1 (haf)	9 (nit)	does	laugh
2 (rek)	10 (jim)	fear	lock
3 (fuj)	11 (hav)	fudge	odd
4 (laf)	12 (duz)	gym	ridge
5 (rij)	13 (hil)	half	rough
6 (sez)	14 (ruf)	have	says
7 (fir)	15 (od)	hill	wreck
8 (lok)		knit	

From *Thorndike Barnhart Beginning Dictionary*, Fifth Edition by E. L. Thorndike and Clarence L. Barnhart. Copyright © 1964, 1962, 1959, 1952, 1945 by Scott, Foresman and Company. Reprinted by permission.

An understanding of prefixes, suffixes, and plurals is also important to the development of pronunciation skills. We urge you to include these in your lessons on pronunciation skills. Activities 11 through 14 are included at the end of the chapter to help you teach pronunciation skills.

Library Skills. At the intermediate level, students need to learn additional library skills. These include (1) library organization, (2) use of the card catalog, and (3) extended knowledge and use of reference materials.

Library Organization. Because libraries may have different types of organization, it may be appropriate to gear your lessons to your own school library. Some common organizational patterns include arranging books according to

1. Fiction (These books may be subdivided further. For example, picture books may be separate from other fiction books. Frequently, paperback books are separate from hardback books.)
2. Nonfiction
3. Biographies
4. Reference books
5. Periodicals (magazines and newspapers)

Explain to your students how the books are filed within each section. Fiction is arranged alphabetically by the *author's* last name. Biographies are usually filed alphabetically by the last name of the person about whom the book is written. Frequently, there is no special arrangement of periodicals, although they, too, may be in alphabetical order by title. Reference books may be shelved according to the *Dewey decimal system*, or they may simply be grouped together in one area.

Since most schools still use the Dewey decimal system of classification for nonfiction books, you must explain the system to your students. In this system, all subject matter is divided into ten main classes and assigned particular numbers. Books are filed *numerically* according to content.

000–099	General Works
100–199	Philosophy
200–299	Religion
300–399	Social Studies
400–499	Linguistics
500–599	Pure Science
600–699	Applied Science
700–799	Arts and Recreation
800–899	Literature
900–999	History

Each class can be subdivided several more times according to the contents of a book. For example,

700–799	Arts and Recreation
790	Recreation
796	Athletics and Sports
796.52	Mountain Climbing

Have your students think of a topic and try to decide into which of the ten main classes their topic would likely fall. This will provide an opportunity for you to introduce the use of the *card catalog.*

Using a Card Catalog. Children must be taught that the card catalog is like the index of a book and that books are located in three ways in most card catalogs: the *author card,* the *subject card,* and the *title card.* Students need to learn how to read each of these types of cards and to develop an awareness of the type of card to look for, depending on the information they have or need.

Visiting the library and actually using the card catalog will enable children to understand that

1. Cards are arranged alphabetically by author, subject, or title.
2. Subject, title, and author cards all contain the same information.

You may want to give students examples similar to the following:

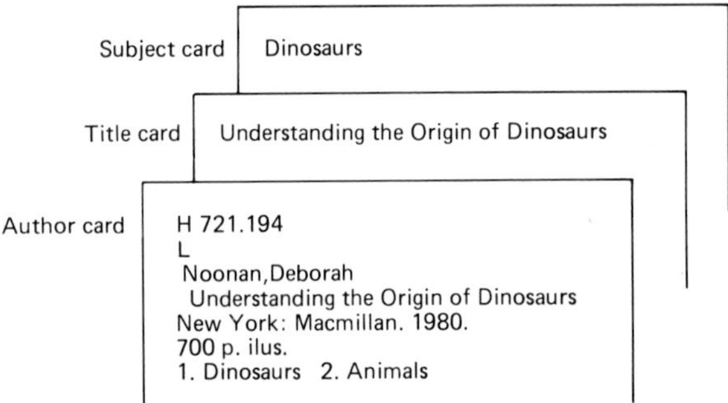

To help the students understand these cards, you should explain

1. How to read each kind of card.
2. How to determine what type a card is.
3. How to determine differences among the cards.
4. When to use each type of card.
5. To what the numbers and letters in the left-hand corner refer.

Reference Materials. Teachers can encourage students to use reference resources by the type of lessons and activities they plan. For example, students can use reference books to acquire additional information on topics being studied currently. You should attempt to ask questions that encourage children to consult many sources. ("What were some of the effects of the 1906 San Francisco earthquake?")

Students need to acquire an understanding of how to match a particular general reference book with the information they are seeking. To find the pronunciation and definition of a word, a dictionary can be used. If an extensive explanation of a particular word is desired, an encyclopedia may be the desired reference. If the student needs more specialized information related to a geographic area, a type of plant, or a scientific phenomenon, a specialized reference book is needed. To help children learn to use reference books, activities 15 and 16 at the end of this chapter should be part of classroom instruction.

Intermediate-grade students often need extended library skills to pursue an area of interest or to research information for a paper or a report. Students should be encouraged to use the *Reader's Guide to Periodical Literature* to locate current magazine articles to supplement material from other sources. The *Reader's Guide* provides references to 175 periodicals; its entries are arranged alphabetically according to topics, similar to an index.

NATIONAL Intercollegiate Flying Association Instrument check ride. R. L. Collins. il Flying 108:92 Ag '81
NATIONAL Lead Company. See NL Industries, Inc
NATIONAL Museum of American History. See Smithsonian Institution—National Museum of American History
NATIONAL parks and reserves

Northwest Territories, Canada

Nahanni: Canada's wilderness park. D. H. Chadwick. il por maps Nat Geog 160:396–420 S '81

Switzerland

Swiss rule . . . stay on the trail [Swiss National Park] il Sunset 166:56 Je '81

Tanzania

Canning of Africa [Serengeti National Park] N. Myers. il map Sci Digest 89:70–5+ Ag '81
NATIONAL Public Radio Can this man's radio network survive? Stay tuned [F. Mankiewicz] V. Warren. il por 50 Plus 21:82–3 S '81
NATIONAL Railroad Passenger Corporation Amtrak in the West this summer

. . . new equipment, future uncertain. il Sunset 166:44+ Je '81
NATIONAL Sea Grant Program. See United States—National Oceanic and Atmospheric Administration—Appropriations and expenditures
NATIONAL Sea Products Ltd
Little game of five-card cod? [layoff of workers] R. Joyce. il Macleans 94:32 Ag 24 '81
NATIONAL symbols on postage stamps. See Postage stamps
NATIONAL Urban League
Back to basics for black people [address. July 19, 1981] V. E. Jordan, Jr. Vital Speeches 47:659-63 Ag 15 '81
NATIVE races *See also* Survival International (organization)
NATO
British propose new missile. il Aviation W 115: 57 Jl 27 '81
Deadly logic [neutron bomb deployment] Nation 233: 132 Ag 22-29 '81
Disarming tactics. B. Crozier. Nat R 33:949 Ag 21 '81
Foreign defense investment restrictions studied, E. Kozicharow. Aviation W 115: 20-2 Jl 27'81
Global minefields Reagan faces next. S. W. Sanders. il Bus W p52 Ag 24 '81

Reader's Guide to Periodical Literature 81 (New York: The H. W. Wilson Company, October 10, 1981), p. 93.

Students will need instruction on how to read each entry and how to interpret the abbreviations. Point out to them that in the front of each *Reader's Guide* there is a page that explains all abbreviations used in the entries. Once having located a particular magazine article, the student's success in interpreting the material will depend to some degree on his or her reading flexibility.

Reading Flexibility. At the intermediate level, there is a slight shift in the focus of reading instruction. The reading program must still emphasize the development of word-recognition and comprehension skills (*learning to read*). In addition, content area reading instruction (*reading to learn*) should encourage the development of flexible reading techniques.

Students need to know

1. When to read slowly and carefully.
2. When to read quickly.
3. How to skim materials.
4. How to scan materials.

You can help children to become flexible readers by encouraging them to always examine their *purpose* for reading before they begin reading. The purpose for reading determines the appropriate *rate* of reading. For example, when students are reading to learn, they are attempting to

1. Comprehend the author's message.
2. Answer questions.
3. Synthesize information.
4. Make generalizations.
5. Identify important facts and supporting details.

With these goals in mind, students must read more slowly and carefully than if they were reading for recreation or enjoyment.

To help students to adapt their reading rates to the purpose for reading, present them with factual text excerpts and several purposes for reading: (1) for enjoyment, (2) to determine the general study topic, and (3) to find a specified bit of information. After covering these area, discuss how the students have altered their reading rates and techniques according to each new purpose.

Skimming is a technique that students should use when their reading purpose is to acquire a general impression of the material content. When a student skims a passage, he or she should be encouraged to note headings, subheadings, and topic sentences. Skimming is a very selective reading process; if the student needs more detailed information to answer questions, skimming may not be appropriate.

Flexible readers must also develop the ability to scan. Hoffman (1979) notes that the objective of scanning "may be to locate specific information in a body of text without attempting to deal with the content as a whole" (p. 324). Students should be encouraged to look for clue words or phrases that may indicate the location of the answer the student is seeking.

You can help your students to develop the ability to scan by providing practice activities. You might begin by asking them to determine answers to very simple questions:

1. *Where* was the meteorite discovered?
2. *When* did the volcano erupt?
3. *Which* world leaders attended the Yalta Conference?

After posing the questions, refer the students to the passage containing the information. Ask the students to

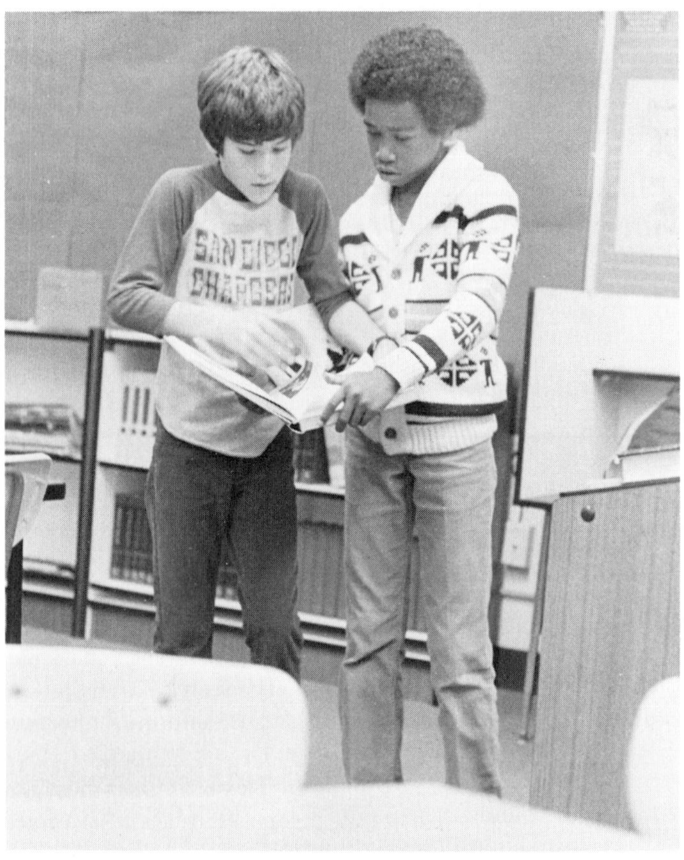

You can help children become flexible readers by encouraging them to always examine their purpose for reading before they begin reading. (Photo by Linda Lungren.)

move their eyes quickly across each line of text until the clue word for their answer becomes obvious.

1. place, meteorite
2. date, volcano
3. names, Yalta Conference

After the students locate the information, encourage them to read the sentences immediately preceding and following the one in which they found their answer. These sentences may contain information that will add exactness to the information being sought.

The key to developing skimming and scanning skills is *practice* with a *purpose*. Proficiency in using these skills frequently has a valuable by-product: increased reading rate. Flexibility in reading allows students to increase reading rates naturally.

Following Directions. One of the most common tasks we ask schoolchildren to perform is *following directions*. Yet, too often, teachers expect children to be able to follow directions even though the students may not have received instruction in this area.

Young children have some maturational limitations

that affect their ability to follow directions. In the early years, the maxim "Keep it short and simple" is appropriate. Directions involving a long string of instructions can only lead to confusion. At the primary level, most directions are given orally; therefore, it is advisable to concentrate on developing effective listening skills. (You may find some of the activities at the end of Chapter 3 helpful in developing these skills.) Be aware, also, that children soon recognize and respond to the teacher's patterns for giving directions. The teacher who habitually repeats directions three times may soon find that children tune in on round three, if at all, and even then they may listen very ineffectively.

Intermediate-grade students are required to follow both oral and written directions. Due to their increased maturational level, these students can recall a longer list of directions for a longer period of time. At these levels, increased ability to reason and see relationships should enable students to make mental connections that facilitate the ability to follow directions.

You can help your students to develop skill in following directions by organizing directions as clearly and concisely as possible. When you are planning instruction that will help children learn to follow directions, remember to do the following:

1. Start by giving one-step directions:
   a. Circle the correct picture.
   b. Number each item.
2. Move to two-step directions only after the child has mastered the concept of one-step directions:
   a. Underline all nouns and circle all verbs.
   b. Review the information in the text and then develop a graphic aid to illustrate the data.
3. Introduce three-step directions only after the child has mastered the concept of two-step directions:
   a. Read the story, draw a picture to illustrate it, and share the story and illustration with a friend.
   b. Eat your lunch, clean up the classroom, and go out to play.
4. Introduce activities that involve multistep directions:
   a. Assemble the model.
   b. Complete the experiment.

Students need instruction and practice to master techniques and skills that will help them be successful when they read for study purposes. Such skills have limited value in isolation; they are, however, significant in relation to their overall effect on a child's academic success. These skills are of a developmental nature. Each child deserves to be introduced to them and to be helped to recognize their purpose and value. Each child also needs multiple opportunities to develop and refine his or her command of them. Most of these opportunities will be developed through learning pursuits that interrelate study skills with such content areas as math, science, and social studies.

TEACHING STRATEGIES

In this chapter, we have suggested various student activities, exercises, and sample teaching activities that are designed to help you guide your students in developing reading study skills. In addition, we would like to suggest that an altered form of a *directed reading activity* (DRA) may be a valuable tool for teaching reading study skills.

The Directed Reading Activity

The directed reading activity, as explained in the previous chapter, is a strategy or approach to planning and conducting instruction. In many ways, it is similar to the SQ3R technique discussed earlier in this chapter. However, whereas SQ3R is a technique used by students, a DRA is a strategy for teachers to employ.

As it is usually presented, a DRA has five steps:

1. *Background and Motivation.* The teacher provides *background* information on the topic under study and attempts to relate this information to the students' knowledge and experiences. By relating this information to the students' life experiences, the teacher also *motivates* the students to want to learn more about the topic.
2. *Vocabulary.* Prior to having students read a selection, the teacher identifies and preteaches any vocabulary words that may cause the students difficulty. Through this process, the teacher frees the students to concentrate solely on the content, without having to struggle with decoding vocabulary words.

3. *Springboard Questions.* Springboard questions are given to the students prior to reading to provide them with a purpose for reading. Such questions help guide the students' reading and focus attention on the important facts in the reading selection.
4. *Silent Reading.* Traditionally, at this point, the students are asked to read a passage from a textbook. This step presupposes that students will always have printed material to read when the teacher plans to use a DRA. In the altered form of a DRA, teachers can delete this step when printed text is unavailable or unnecessary, as in the case of an oral teaching lesson.
5. *Follow-up Questions.* These questions help the teacher assess a student's comprehension of the material that was read or the lesson that was presented. Follow-up questions should parallel the springboard questions closely; this will reinforce the fact that the students did indeed have a specified purpose for reading.

When you are teaching your students reading study skills, your lessons will usually be oral, using supplemental materials, demonstrations, and activities to complement your instruction. It is unlikely that students will be asked to read a selection on, for example, how to outline a passage from a book. We recommend that you use the altered form of a directed reading activity to teach reading study skills in this manner:

1. Introduce the study skill you are planning to teach by defining it and explaining its purpose. By explaining how the acquisition of the particular skill will benefit the student's learning, you can motivate the student to want to learn the skill.
2. Discuss terminology or vocabulary that you will be using in your lesson. Make sure that students understand such terms as *topic sentences, reference materials,* and *survey.*
3. *Do* provide students with a purpose for learning by posing questions that they will be expected to answer after the lesson. These questions should focus the students' attention on
   a. What is the nature of the skill?
   b. How do I use the skill?
   c. How will this skill be valuable to me?
   d. When is it appropriate to use this skill?
4. At this point, you can implement your lesson. A "hands-on" approach to teaching study skills is very beneficial to students. *Demonstrate* techniques; allow students to *examine* materials; *involve* students in discussions and activities. Be certain that your lesson includes the answers to the questions that are giving students their purpose for learning.
5. At the conclusion of the lesson, ask questions and plan activities that will allow the students to demonstrate that they have acquired an understanding of and an ability to use reading study skills.

In Chapter 9, we discuss how to use a DRA in content area subjects such as science, mathematics, and social studies.

ACTIVITIES TO DEVELOP STUDY SKILLS: ORGANIZATIONAL SKILLS

1. Out of Order

Goal: Developing outlining skills

Grade Level: 1-3

Construction: Print a simple outline on oak tag or cardboard. Include at least two main headings and four or five supporting details. Cut each line into strips and attach felt tape to the back of them.

Utilization: The student puts the outline back together in the proper order, using a felt board.

2. Where Do I Belong?

Goal: Developing classifying skills

Grade Level: K-3

Construction and Utilization: Students can work with the teacher to design a bulletin board display on a particular theme or topic. For example, using the theme "Modes of Transportation," divide the bulletin board into four sections: Land, Air, Water, and Space. Examples for each category might include

land: cars, buses

air: airplanes, helicopters

water: ships, submarines

space: rockets, space shuttles

Have the students look for magazine pictures to illustrate each form of transportation. You may also want to have students draw pictures to include in the display.

ACTIVITIES TO DEVELOP STUDY SKILLS: DICTIONARY AND ALPHABETIZING SKILLS

3. Make a Class Directory

Goal: Alphabetizing and utilizing guide words

Grade Level: 2–4

Construction: Design a telephone directory by folding a piece of oak tag or construction paper in half and stapling in white paper for the desired number of pages.

Utilization: Have a group of children design a class telephone directory that includes the name, address, and telephone number of each student. The last names of the students must be placed in alphabetical order. Guide words for a page would be the surnames of the first and last student appearing on each page.

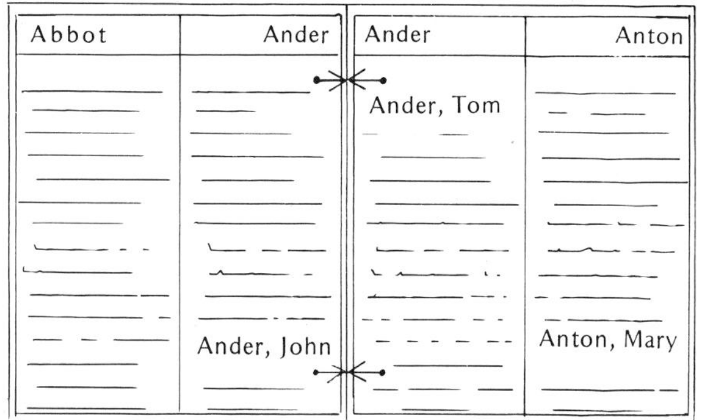

Children need to be introduced to dictionaries at this level also.

ACTIVITIES TO DEVELOP STUDY SKILLS:

USING A GLOSSARY

4. Creative Vocabulary

Goal: Understanding the purpose of a glossary

Grade Level: 4–9

Construction: You can use this activity during a group storytelling activity or as part of a creative writing activity. In either case, have the students make up words that "fit" in their story, no matter how ridiculous.

Utilization: Have the students write a glossary for the "new" or "unfamiliar" words. Students can then exchange these glossaries and compare and discuss "definitions."

USING A CARD CATALOG

5. Cards, Cards, Cards

Goal: Using a card catalog

Grade Level: 1–3

Construction: This activity can be done in the library or classroom. There should be a good supply of books labeled with call numbers as well as a card catalog, which can be constructed by the teacher, if necessary. Put the call number, title, author, number of pages, and a short description on the cards. Prepare duplicate cards so that the student can locate the book using the title, author, or subject. In a grab bag, put index cards that say "Find me a book written by . . ." or "Find me a book about . . .".

Utilization: Students must use the catalog and then present the books to the storekeeper, who gives five points for each card done correctly. The first person to complete five cards correctly wins.

USING AN INDEX

6. Indexed Answers

Goal: Using an index

Grade Level: 4–9

Construction and Utilization: The student can choose any book, magazine, or comic book and make up an index for it. He then asks a classmate to answer questions that require the use of the index. Classmates score two points for each question answered correctly (the index maker is the judge), and the first to score ten points wins.

ACTIVITIES TO DEVELOP STUDY SKILLS: EXTENDED DICTIONARY SKILLS

7. The Great Match-up

Goal: Reinforcement of word meanings

Grade Level: 4–6

Construction: Cut out a piece of cardboard, oak tag, or construction paper approximately 12 x 18 inches. In one column, write several words that are unfamiliar to the student; in a second column, list short definitions of the words. Do not write the correct definition directly across from the word. Punch holes along the right side of each word and on the left side of each definition. Attach a long shoestring or piece of yarn to each hole on the word side.

Utilization: The child threads the yarn into the holes on the definition side, matching the word with the correct definition.

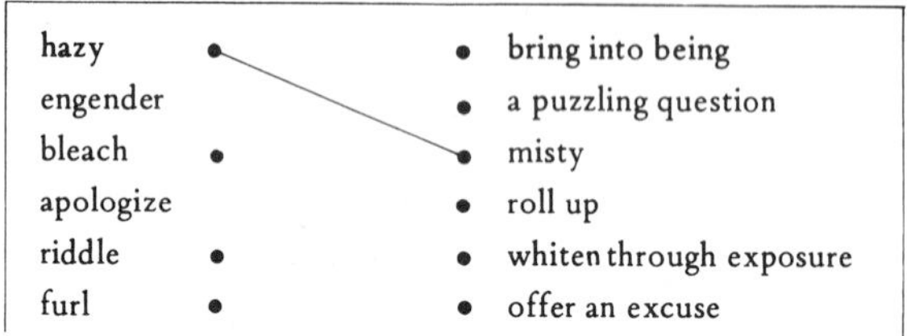

8. Word Toss

Goal: Using guide words

Grade Level: 1-3

Construction: Use a three-walled board with small wooden pegs or large nails inserted in it. On each peg, hang a small card with a word beginning with *n* (or any other letter) written on it. Get small plastic loops (drapery or shower curtain hangers) for a ring-toss game.

Utilization: Players, in turn, toss rings around two words and then must name five words that come between those words in a dictionary. Score one point for each correct word. The first player to reach one hundred wins.

9. What's in a Name?

Goal: Locating words and finding definitions in a dictionary

Grade Level: 4-6

Construction: The teacher should write questions containing unfamiliar words on 3" X 5" cards. For example, "What does an *onager* look like?"

Utilization: Children are grouped into two teams. Team A begins by selecting a card, reading it to team B, and asking "Can you answer that?" Team B must look up the unfamiliar word in a dictionary, answer the question, and state the two guide words taken from the dictionary page on which the answer was found.

10. Eureka!

Goal: Developing skill in using the dictionary

Grade Level: 3-6

Construction: Choose a volunteer who looks up ten to fifteen words in the dictionary and notes the page, column number, and guide words.

Utilization: Have a contest to see who can look up words the fastest. The MC calls out a word and the first person in the group to find the word shouts "I've got it!" and reads the page number, column, and guide words he or she used. The student who finds a word the fastest scores one point. When all the MC's words have been used, the person with the highest score wins.

11. Spelling Twins

Goal: Utilizing accents to aid in word pronunciation

Grade Level: 4-6

Construction: Make 7" x 4" word cards containing words that are spelled the same but are pronounced differently (heteronyms). Be sure to include the accent marks for each word.

present´ ad´dress

pre´sent address´

Utilization: Flash the cards and have the students write sentences using each word correctly.

12. Mail Delivery

Goal: Classifying words according to vowel sounds

Grade Level: 4-6

Construction: Place a cardboard box with dividers that hold large bottles on one side and label each slot with either ă, ā, ĕ, ē, ĭ, ī, ŏ, ō, ŭ, or ū. Make word or picture cards of one-syllable words with long or short vowel sounds.

Utilization: Each child sorts the mail by putting the word or picture cards in the proper slots, according to the vowel sound in the word.

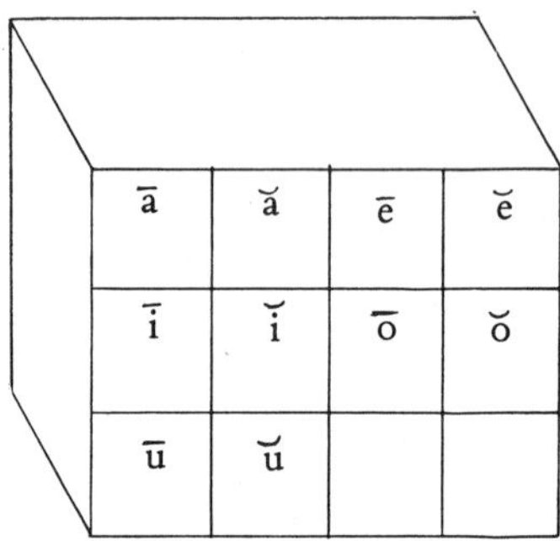

13. Student Translators

Goal: Pronunciation using diacritical markings

Grade Level: 4–6

Construction: Write jokes, stories, or sentences using only diacritical marks.

Utilization: The child translates the joke, story, or sentence and then copies the translation on paper or records it on tape. Examples:

the flōu´ər blooms	The flower blooms.
thē skī iz sun´ē	The sky is sunny.
it iz spri͡ng	It is spring.

14. Please Feed the Bear

Goal: Classifying vowel sounds according to pronunciation keys

Grade Level: K–3

Construction: Put a picture of a bear on the bulletin board. Next, secure three paper plates. Cut one plate in half. Staple one half on each of the other paper plates to form pockets on both of the two remaining paper plates. On the front of one plate write "I like to eat long vowels"; on the second plate write "I like to eat short vowels." Now design one-syllable word cards, utilizing words that are not part of the child's sight vocabulary.

Utilization: Each child selects a card and checks the pronunciation key in the dictionary to determine where to place the card. If it is a short-vowel word, the child places it in the short-vowel pocket, and if it is a long-vowel word, the child places it in the long-vowel pocket.

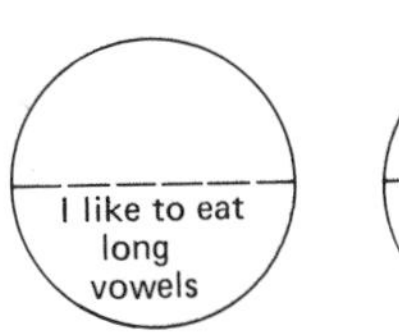

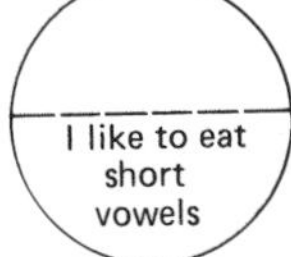

15. In Other Words . . .

Goal: Reinforcement of word meanings and utilization of a thesaurus

Grade Level: 4–6

Construction: You will need at least one copy of a thesaurus, preferably in dictionary form.

Utilization: Give each child a simple sentence or one containing new vocabulary words. The child, using the thesaurus, must rewrite the sentence in several different ways, keeping the original meaning.

Mary walked through the park.
Mary strolled through the park.
Mary ambled through the park.
Mary sauntered through the park.

QUESTIONS AND RELATED READINGS

If you feel that you have not attained adequate knowledge to answer the following questions successfully, we suggest additional related readings.

1. What are the reading study skills students need to master?
2. How will the acquisition of reading study skills enhance students' learning?
3. How might study skills be taught so that students recognize their value and incorporate them into daily study practices?

Goal 1: To help the reader to acquire an understanding of reading study skills.

Question 1: What are the reading study skills students need to master?

Laffey, J. L., ed. *Reading in the Content Areas.* Newark, Del.: International Reading Association, 1972.

Lamberg, W., and C. Lamb. *Reading Instruction in the Content Areas.* Chicago: Rand McNally College Publishing Company, 1980, pp. 87–115.

Shepherd, D. *Comprehensive High School Reading Methods.* 2nd ed. Columbus, Ohio: Charles E. Merrill Publishing Company, 1978, pp. 111–36.

Goal 2: To help the reader to understand the importance of reading study skills.

Question 2: How will the acquisition of reading study skills enhance students' learning?

Brown, A., J. Campione, and J. Day. "Learning to Learn: On Training Students to Learn from Texts." *Educational Researcher* 10 (February 1981), 14–21.

Rickards, J. "Notetaking, Underlining, Inserted Questions, and Organizers in Text: Research Conclusions and Educational Implications." *Educational Technology* 20 (June 1980), 5–11.

Tonjes, M., and M. Zintz. *Teaching Reading/Thinking/Study Skills in Content Classrooms.* Dubuque, Iowa: William C. Brown Company, Publishers, 1981, pp. 203–6.

Goal 3: To help the reader to recognize and implement instructional strategies appropriate to students' grade level and abilities.

Question 3: Explain how study skills might be taught so that students recognize their value and incorporate them into daily study practice.

Estes, T., and J. Vaughan, Jr. *Reading and Learning in the Content Classroom.* Boston: Allyn & Bacon, Inc., 1978, pp. 207–31.

Herber, H. *Teaching Reading in Content Areas*, 2nd ed. Englewood Cliffs, N.J.: Prentice-Hall, Inc., 1978, pp. 213–33.

Vacca, R. *Content Area Reading.* Boston: Little, Brown and Company, 1981, pp. 29–43.

BIBLIOGRAPHY

Brady, M., and H. Brady. *Idea and Action in American History.* Englewood Cliffs, N.J.: Prentice-Hall, Inc., 1977.

Brown, A., J. Campione, and J. Day. "Learning to Learn: On Training Students to Learn From Texts." *Educational Researcher* 10 (February 1981), 14–21.

Bruner, J., et al. *Studies in Cognitive Growth.* New York: John Wiley & Sons, Inc., 1967.

Chambers, D., and H. Lowry. *The Language Arts.* Dubuque, Iowa: William C. Brown Company, Publishers, 1975, p. 75.

Courtney, L. "Recent Developments in Reading in the Content Areas." *Conference on Reading* 27 (1965), 134–44.

Estes, T. "Reading in the Social Studies: A Review of Research Since 1950." In *Reading in the Content Areas*, ed. by James L. Laffey. Newark, Del.: International Reading Association, 1972, pp. 177–87.

Estes, T., and J. Vaughan, Jr. *Reading and Learning in the Content Classroom.* Boston: Allyn & Bacon, Inc., 1978.

Fay, L., T. Horn, and C. McCulloguh. *Improving Reading in the Elementary Social Studies.* Bulletin no. 33. Washington, D.C.: National Council for the Social Studies, 1961.

Friedland, J., and R. Kessler. "A Top (to Bottom) Drawer Way to Teach Outlining." *Teacher* 98 (September 1980), 110–11.

Hawkins, M. *Graphing: A Stimulating Way to Process Data.* How to Do It Series, Series 2, No. 10. Washington, D.C.: National Council for the Social Studies, 1980.

Hoffman, J. "Developing Flexibility Through ReFlex Action." *The Reading Teacher* 33 (December 1979), 323–9.

Lamberg, W., and C. Lamb. *Reading Instruction in the Content Areas.* Chicago: Rand McNally College Publishing Company, 1980.

Reader's Guide to Periodical Literature, 81. New York: The H. W. Wilson Company, October 10, 1981.

Reeves, R. *The Teaching of Reading in Our Schools.* New York: Macmillan Publishing Co., Inc., 1966.

Rickards, J. "Notetaking, Underlining, Inserted Questions, and Organizers in Text: Research Implications." *Educational Technology* 20 (June 1980), 5–11.

Russell, D. *Children Learn to Read.* Lexington, Mass.: Ginn and Company, 1961.

Shepherd, D. *Comprehensive High School Reading Methods*, 2nd ed. Columbus, Ohio: Charles E. Merrill Publishing Company, 1978.

Tonjes, M., and M. Zintz. *Teaching Reading/Thinking/Study Skills in Content Classrooms.* Dubuque, Iowa: William C. Brown Company Publishers, 1981. Chapter opening quotation appears on page 210.

Truman, D. "The Effects of Pictorial Aids on Inferentially Produced Interference in Younger and Older Children's Sentence Learning." Unpublished doctoral dissertation, University of Wisconsin, Madison, 1981.

Vacca, R. *Content Area Reading.* Boston: Little, Brown and Company, 1981.

Witt, M. "Developing Reading Skills and Critical Thinking." *Social Education* 25 (May 1961), 239–41.

CHAPTER 9

Reading: The Key to Content Area Learning

Logical reasoning about reading instruction in the content subjects points to the fact that the teacher, who has a background and expertise in a specific subject, is the one best qualified to adapt the reading skills to it.

D. L. Shepherd, 1978

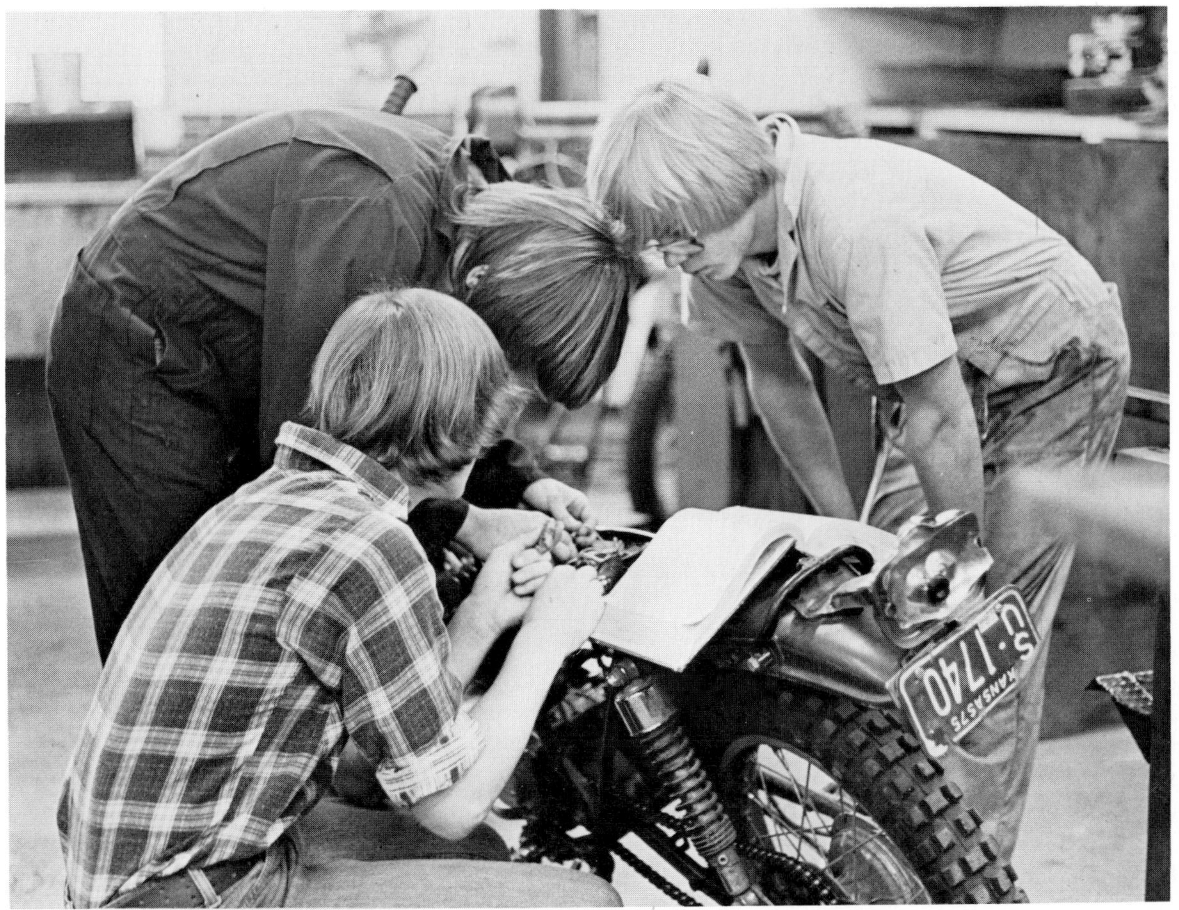

Reading is part of every subject. (Photo by Linda Lungren.)

GOALS: To help the reader to:

1. Understand the role of reading in the learning process.
2. Comprehend the processes involved in the act of reading.
3. Understand the concept of thematic teaching.
4. Learn the importance of reading in social studies.
5. Learn the importance of reading in science.
6. Recognize the importance of reading in mathematics.
7. Appreciate the importance of reading in music and art.

THE CORNERSTONE OF LEARNING IS READING

For decades teachers have been encouraged to teach reading in the content areas. Part of the rationale for this movement is the premise that reading has *no* specific content; it is, however, basic to the mastery of *all* content areas. Jenkinson (1973) reminds us that "reading is not a subject. Since it has no specific content it cannot be taught separately as are most other subjects of the curriculum. It is part of every other subject" (p. 39). Despite the advice of reading experts on this subject, reading is frequently taught only in the content of a basal reading program.

Given this information, it may be appropriate to question the role of university teacher-training programs. The dichotomy between universities espousing teaching reading in the content areas without providing *models* for teaching content area reading skills was the subject of a study by Lapp et al. (1978). They found that preservice teachers were able to implement instructional strategies relating to reading in the content areas only when the cooperating teacher served as a model to demonstrate the implementation of these strategies. Some universities have attempted to correct this deficiency by emphasizing models of teaching in which reading is viewed as a *process* that is needed to master all content area learning. These models of teaching are built upon a philosophy of thematic teaching.

Thematic Teaching

Thematic teaching has been developed from an earlier teaching strategy, unit teaching. Unit teaching stressed the importance of teaching children to read in one specific content area, such as reading in social studies. Thematic teaching presents reading as an integrated, continuous process rather than as a single, static, isolated forty-five-minute-per day basal series activity. In thematic teaching, reading becomes the integrated base of all content area learning.

Thematic teaching is based on a very natural phenomenon, reading about a particular theme. It expands the concept of reading in the content areas by integrating several content areas with reading skills. For example, a teacher may introduce a lesson on train transportation in Boston. During the course of this unit, the students might have required readings that incorporate aspects of the following content areas:

Reading	Content Area
Time schedules	Functional literacy
Price lists	Mathematics
Historical monuments	Social studies
Ethnicity of neighborhoods	Social studies
Maps	Geography
Construction of trains	Science
Mechanics of engines	Science

Throughout this chapter, when we refer to reading in the content areas, we are referring to the concept of thematic teaching.

The Basal Reader and Content Area Teaching

Even as you engage in thematic teaching, we encourage you to retain the successful word-recognition and comprehension teaching strategies commonly identified with the majority of basal reading programs. These are necessary skills for the student who is encountering content area texts. Word-recognition skills enable the student to recognize and analyze new lexical items. Whether the material is narrative (as in most basal readers) or expository (as in most content area texts), comprehension skills are needed for students to recognize literal facts, infer unstated meaning, and evaluate author intent. These basic skills are acquired through basal reading in the primary grades and continue forward to help the intermediate and advanced reader encountering new content area materials.

Content area texts can be incorporated into a classroom curriculum as soon as a child has demonstrated mastery of such readiness skills as letter and sight-word recognition. These content area materials should be considered a *supplement* to, not a replacement for, the basal reader. A basal reading program includes practices that prepare the student for and support content area learning. However, it is not safe to assume that there will be a transfer of learning from the largely narrative basal to a fact-specific content area text without instructional aid.

While factual stories are beginning to appear in basal readers, most of the reading material in the primary grades is narrative. Not surprisingly, this type of reading is not adequate preparation for content area reading. Many times intermediate-grade students who have exhibited little, if any, difficulty with narrative materials demonstrate a limited understanding of content area materials. These students are experiencing problems in making a transition between narrative texts and materials that contain synthesized facts and a concisely stated, often terse, style of writing.

The following excerpts, taken from intermediate texts, illustrate the differences in content and writing styles that are encountered by the intermediate-age student who is required to read narrative and factual materials. Both excerpts deal with the topic of weather and seasonal changes.

> "Oh boy! It'll snow! And tomorrow is Christmas!" Eddie flipped his furry cap into the air, missing Mom's reading lamp. It landed among the potted plants Willa Mae was watering.
>
> "Cut it, Ed!" she cried. "And be sure to stay right with Jason. Mom said for you boys to be home before the snow gets bad."
>
> "Okay, we'll make it home" Jason promised. "It isn't snowing yet. Come on, Eddie, I've got our money all counted."
>
> Eddie slammed the front door. They clattered down the stairs fast.
>
> "Is there enough money for the lamp shade, Jay?" Eddie asked to make sure. "And what will we get for Willa Mae?"
>
> "We'll find something. There'll be enough."
>
> It wasn't long before they caught their first sight of the fountain in the park.
>
> "It's frozen!" Eddie gasped. He pulled Jason toward it. The water in the fountain must have frozen while it was still bubbling down. Now the statue animals—the turtles, frogs, and swans—had frozen into strange, icy shapes. It was lovely, like fairyland.
>
> "Hm . . . snow's starting," Jason said, sniffing the air. A few flakes were blowing lightly over the ice. He looked up at the gray, tumbling sky. "We'd better get downtown for our shopping," he said.
>
> (Clymer, 1970, p. 42)

> If you live in a place where the leaves change color, you probably have noticed that the color display is never quite the same from one year to the next. One year the leaves may be very colorful, but the next year their colors may be dull. Several things seem to affect how bright or how dull the color change will be—the amount of water in the ground during the summer, the amount of nitrogen in the soil, the amount of light reaching the leaves, the amount of sugar stored in the leaves, and the night temperatures during autumn. Strong light and cold nights, for example, seem to help certain pigments form in leaf cells.
>
> In some way we do not yet fully understand, toward the end of summer the chlorophyll pigment of the leaf cells begins to break down. As more and more chlorophyll is broken down, the yellow and orange pigments are unmasked. At the same time, new yellow and orange pigments are being made. The leaves begin to change color.
>
> Meanwhile, other pigments are being made in the leaf cells. How much they show up depends partly on weather conditions during the summer. It also depends partly on weather conditions while the leaves are changing. Brown pigments begin to form when the chlorophyll breaks down. So do the flaming red, blue, and purple pigments. When the brown pigments form, they blend with orange and yellow and give oak leaves their typical orange-brown color. The red pigments seem to reach their peak when the outflow of sugar made in the leaves slows down and the sugar then collects in the leaves.
>
> (Gallant and Asimov, 1973, pp. 33–4)

Which passage do you think would be more difficult for a fourth- or fifth-grade student to read and comprehend? The selections are approximately equal in length, and both deal with the same topic. The second passage, however, contains more difficult, more technical vocabulary than the first (e.g., pigment, chlorophyll). Another vocabulary stumbling block may be the use of familiar words in unfamiliar ways (e.g., color, leaves). Even competent adult readers would admit that the storylike writing style of the first passage is easier to comprehend than is the terse style of writing in the second selection. Reading either passage requires the use of word-recognition and comprehension skills; however, like most content area materials, the second selection also requires the student to be competent in several of the following general study skills:

1. Establishing a purpose for reading.
2. Locating and verifying information from multiple sources: almanac, atlas, encyclopedia, and *Reader's Guide to Periodical Literature*.
3. Considering alternative sources and applying methods of cross-checking.
4. Noting simple clues to organization of selection: definitions, context, numbered ideas, cue words indicating order.
5. Skimming for general concepts.
6. Scanning for minute details.
7. Differentiating fact from opinion.
8. Recognizing main ideas.
9. Interpreting charts, diagrams, and maps.
10. Using dictionaries, glossaries, and footnotes to determine meaning.
11. Utilizing newspapers as a source of current information and opinion.
12. Organizing and summarizing material through outlining.
13. Adjusting reading rate to suit reading purpose and type of material.
14. Classifying information presented from several points of view.

Study Skills

Let us examine the development of study skills by continuing to use the preceding passages. One way in which to foster readiness for reading content-specific material would be to present a narrative story about weather information along with a factual-type story format. Through questions and discussions, the teacher can guide the students in recognizing that topical material can be presented in a variety of genres.

Younger students often need instruction and practice in differentiating fact from opinion. The language experiences of your students can provide an excellent opportunity for teaching this study skill. After eliciting several *opinion* statements from the students, the teacher can encourage and assist the students in changing these to *factual* statements. For example,

Opinion	Fact
Linda: "My dog is very pretty."	"I have an Irish Setter."
Norm: "My sister is really smart."	"My sister is a straight A student."
Lynne: "I like to ride horses."	"I went horseback riding yesterday."

Children can be given additional practice in differentiating fact from opinion by surveying newspapers, magazines, classroom texts, and other classroom reading materials.

For a more comprehensive examination of study skills, refer to Chapter 8.

THE PROCESS OF READING

> Reading *is* a complex process, one that involves perceiving graphic symbols, interpreting their meanings, reacting and applying them to the life situation. It is an active thinking process that demands meaning.
>
> (Tonjes and Zintz, 1981, p. 361)

While not occurring hierarchically, reading is at least a three-part interaction that takes place between the reader and the text. This interaction involves *perception*, *interpretation*, and *application and evaluation*. Before we examine the *process* of reading in relation to the content areas, let us consider each of these components of the reading interaction.

Perception

Perception involves determining the relationship between textual symbol and sound. The reader perceives a letter or word *symbol*, cognitively compares the symbol to other known symbols, and, finally, associates a sound with the symbol. Perception is the base of reading; however, if it is viewed in isolation, it is a very limited skill. The reader must have already acquired the concept that is represented by the symbol, thereby enabling the interpretation of the symbol.

Interpretation

> Readers should not only associate sound with the symbol but also associate meaning with the symbol, drawing on ideas they have developed in relation to the symbol. If the symbol is a word, they associate it with an experience they have had—real or vicarious—in connection with it. That is the meaning for the symbol. If the symbol is other than a word—perhaps a formula, an equation, a sentence, or a paragraph—the process is the same; only the degree of complexity differs.
>
> (Herber, 1978, pp. 9–10)

Herber's discussion of *interpretation* is so cogent it needs no further explanation. Therefore, we may proceed to a discussion of the application and evaluation of the author's message.

Application and Evaluation

As the reader perceives and interprets the material, another very important stage of the reading process occurs that involves the application or evaluation of the text. This process requires reader reaction to the material. Such reaction is based on one's experience and ability to apply what has been read to real-life situations.

The *evaluation* of material is often referred to as critical thinking. The reader is comparing the material being read either with what he or she knows from past experience or with information from another source. The reader is being called upon to make a judgment. A sound topical knowledge base is necessary for evaluative reading to occur. Often, the content area teacher must supply this background information before the student is able to begin an interaction with the text.

Many of the instructional processes involved in enabling the student to perceive, interpret, and evaluate narrative texts have already been discussed in previous chapters. In this chapter, information will be provided (1) to enable you to gain an understanding of the processes involved in transferring these skills to the reading of fact-specific content materials and (2) to develop a thorough understanding of content area reading skills.

STUDY SKILLS IN CONTENT AREA READING

The key to successful content area reading is the application and extension of study skills. Study skills were discussed in depth in Chapter 8. We focus now on specific processes and activities designed to integrate study skills and content area reading. We also provide the basic strategies needed to develop a thematic teaching unit.

Lamberg and Lamb (1980) state that "study skills can and should be taught in the context of content learning, and in fact, many educators see study skills as synonymous with learning skills" (p. 88). Teachers of all grades must be concerned with study skills, because it cannot be assumed that all the skills will be developed and refined in any one grade. The early school years focus on instruction in basic reading skills. Reading instruction in the intermediate grades emphasizes

1. *Refining* basic reading skills.
2. *Extending* comprehension skills.
3. *Expanding* reference study skills.
4. *Exploring* specific content area materials to extend concepts and to clarify generalizations.

PLANNING: STUDENT AND TEACHER CONSIDERATIONS

> The teachers today just go on repeating in rigamarole fashion, annoying the students with constant questions and repeating the same things over and over again. They do not try to find out what the student's natural inclinations are, so that the students are forced to pretend to like their studies; nor do they try to bring out the best in their talents. As a result, the students hide their favorite readings and hate their teachers, are exasperated at the difficulty of their studies, and do not know what good it does them. Although they go through the regular course of instruction, they are quick to leave when they are through. This is the failure of education today.
>
> (Confucius, c. 551–479 B.C.)

As educators, we must make every effort to alter the instructional conditions described by Confucius nearly twenty-five hundred years ago. The following principles can be used as guidelines when you plan for reading in any content area lesson.

Children

1. Children need to have a purpose for learning. This

purpose should be related to the concerns and interests of the students. Shepherd (1978) suggests that "effective classroom procedure will elicit purposes for reading from the students as you preview the material together, discuss their background knowledge and as the students air their opinions and impressions about the topic" (p. 139).
2. Children need to be motivated to learn. "Attentive, involved students will learn more, remember longer, and usually make better use of their learning" (Tonjes and Zintz, 1981, p. 27). Many of the activities at the end of this chapter can be used as motivational devices.
3. Children learn most effectively when they have a positive attitude. Children who have a purpose for learning and who are presented with interesting, challenging activities develop positive attitudes.
4. Children comprehend by relating their school experiences with their life experiences. Roe et al. (1978) state that "the more experience a student has that relates to a topic, the better that student will be able to understand the reading content" (p. 145). The teacher must determine how much a child knows about a particular topic. Instruction should then begin at the student's level of readiness.
5. Children need word-recognition, comprehension, and study skills to learn through reading.
6. Children learn in many ways. Some children learn best through activities that involve listening; other children thrive on reading, writing, and language activities. By offering a variety of learning activities, you will be able to meet the needs of *all* your students.
7. Children learn at different rates. Setting a time limit can be counterproductive unless your purpose is to measure rate.
8. Children need to be active participants in the learning process, for learning is not a passive process. Activities that involve children in planning, as well as participating, are suggested throughout this chapter.

Teachers

1. Teachers must have a thorough understanding of the material they are teaching (refer to Chapter 15).
2. Teachers must have some knowledge about the students they are teaching (refer to Chapter 11).
3. Teachers need to plan activities that will encourage growth of *all* students (such activities are included throughout this text).
4. Teachers must have a thorough understanding of the various methods designed to teach reading through content area subjects (refer to Chapter 10).
5. Teachers should make proper adjustments for word-recognition, comprehension, and study skills application for effective teaching of reading in any content area (as discussed throughout this chapter).
6. Teachers need to understand the practical application of learning theory, for example, How do children learn? Does their rate of learning coincide with their physical and social growth? (refer to Chapter 2).
7. Teachers should be well versed in evaluative techniques (refer to Chapter 15).
8. Teachers must remember that there is no set of unique skills related to learning a specific content area (as discussed throughout this chapter).

IMPLEMENTING THEMATIC INSTRUCTION

Once you have decided to plan a thematic teaching unit, there are three steps you must follow: (1) selecting a theme or themes, (2) identifying content area skills and reading objectives to incorporate within the theme, and (3) planning the lessons.

Selection of a Theme. To make the classroom instruction as relevant as possible, allow your students to have a voice in selecting the theme or themes around which you will plan your instruction. Themes should reflect the interests of students and should be broad enough to allow you to incorporate into them the skills and information required for a specific grade level. More than one theme can be operating simultaneously in your classroom.

Examples of themes that can be explored in the early elementary grades are

1. TV characters
2. Pets
3. Families

Examples of themes that may be appropriate throughout the intermediate grades are

1. Careers
2. American heroes
3. Consumer affairs

Identification of Content Area Skills. Some classroom teachers avoid thematic teaching because they are skeptical about covering content area skills. This concern can be alleviated by carefully identifying the skills you would like to cover from each of the content areas.

Planning Lessons. Once you have selected your themes and have identified the content area skills you will cover through these themes, you can begin to develop lessons. A detailed example of thematic teaching is included in Chapter 15. Please refer to it to obtain a more complete understanding of the planning and evaluative techniques involved in thematic teaching.

The next part of this chapter includes suggestions for the teaching of reading in three key curricular areas: social studies, mathematics, and science. It is extremely important for teachers to understand the basic structures that are used in the written discourse of these three curricular areas.

Reading in Social Studies

Roe et al. (1978) state that "one of the goals of schools in the United States is to perpetuate the principles of democratic government; therefore, social studies are [sic] the core of the overall curriculum" (p. 237). Social studies draws its content from several fields including anthropology, economics, civics, geography, sociology, and psychology.

Note that the following selection, taken from an elementary social studies text, incorporates history, geography, government, sociology, and language:

> Egyptian Civilization developed in the valley of the Nile River. The civilization which merged with it was brought to the area by Alexander the Great in 331 B.C. Alexander was a Greek; but when he conquered Egypt, he went to the temple of Amun and was recognized as the successor to the Pharaohs. As a result of his conquest, Egyptian Civilization and Greek Civilization blended.
>
> The city called Alexandria, which Alexander built at the mouth of the Nile, became a marketplace for the exchange of goods and learning. Alexander loved Alexandria and asked to be buried there. It was the center of trade and culture for all the countries that bordered the Mediterranean Sea. In 200 B.C., it was the largest city in the world.
>
> If we look at a map of Alexander's empire, it is not hard to see how Alexandria achieved its importance. It was set on the point where the Nile meets the sea. It had good harbors and was connected with overland trade routes across the desert. Alexander's empire spread from Greece to India and included North Africa. Alexandria was its center.
>
> Egyptian and Greek culture flourished in Alexandria. An enormous library was built, and scholars went there to study. Learning was so highly prized that ships that sailed into port were forced to surrender the manuscripts which they carried. The library at Pergamum, in Asia Minor, was brought to Alexandria and housed there, as well. The city was known as the "Capital of Learning."
>
> Two harbors served Alexandria, one on the Nile and one on the Mediterranean. Traffic was heavy. Barges came down the Nile loaded with papyrus and corn for export. Gold, spices, pears, and ivory were brought overland from the Red Sea. Timber, olive oil, slaves, and horses were unloaded from foreign vessels and sold in Egypt.
>
> Alexandria held its position of influence and power for several centuries. The last ruler of Egypt under the successors of Alexander was a queen named Cleopatra. Cleopatra was bold. She was both loved and feared by young Roman leaders who wanted control of her country. When she felt she was no longer in a position to influence those leaders, she killed herself. Egypt then became a Roman province.
>
> (Kenworthy, 1972, p. 177)

It is quite common to find passages with information integrated from several disciplines in social studies texts. Social studies stresses the role of the *individual* in society and encourages the study of the interactions of people.

For your students to explore the vast amount of knowledge included in social studies successfully, they will need to learn not only the factual content but also the skills that are needed to become independent learners of this information. In the following pages, we provide you with a thorough understanding of the skills relating to reading in social studies and discuss the processes for implementing these skills in the classroom.

Social Studies Vocabulary. Reading a social studies text requires students to read and comprehend ideas and concepts that may be new or unfamiliar to them. The problem is complicated further by the different types of vocabulary the student will encounter. Shepherd (1978) explains the relationship between *concepts* and *vocabulary* in this way: "A concept is a mental construct which the student develops, or rather evolves. It grows and is refined by experience and the acquisition of factual knowledge which bears upon the idea. Vocabulary in the social studies represents the concepts by labeling them" (p. 206). Marksheffel (1966) also noted that those who write textbooks "understand so well the materials about which they write that they appear to forget that the student has but a meager knowledge of the vocabulary and concepts necessary for understanding" (p. 174).

The potential vocabulary difficulties in social studies are common to all content areas. They are (1) technical vocabulary (words unique to the content area), (2) specialized vocabulary (common words that have a specific meaning in the content area), (3) words with multiple meanings, and (4) acronyms and abbreviations. Examples of these vocabulary problems include the following:

Vocabulary	Examples
1. Technical vocabulary	socialism, republic
2. Specialized vocabulary	court, Third World
3. Multiple meanings	state, cycle
4. Abbreviations and acronyms	sq. mi.; NATO

Following are several suggestions to help you develop the language/reading skills necessary to master social studies vocabulary.

TEACHING SOCIAL STUDIES VOCABULARY

1. Discuss word derivations and forms of words. For example, *democracy* comes from two Greek roots (*demos*, meaning people and *kratos*, meaning rule) and has several forms: Democrat, democratic, democratization, democratically.
2. Examine new words as they appear in the text. The students can learn the meanings of such words through contextual analysis, using the glossary, or using a dictionary.
3. Use supplementary materials such as pictures, maps, globes, models, films, recordings, and exhibits to demonstrate and reinforce vocabulary and concepts.
4. Introduce social slogans, figures of speech, and slang.
   a. End the Draft!
   b. Uncle Sam Wants You!
   c. It's a bummer.
5. Have the students categorize words according to historical periods, for example, Whigs, carpetbaggers, pharoahs.
6. Develop word histories of key words to use as mnemonic devices. A mnemonic device is an aid that helps you to remember something. It is derived from Mnemon, a companion of Achilles who functioned as Achilles' memory.
7. Point out words that involve the concepts of distance, space, or time: beyond and age, for example.

Comprehending Pictorial Data. Social studies facts and information are frequently supplemented by or explained through maps, diagrams, pictures, charts, graphs, and time lines. Too often, teachers assume that these graphic aids are self-evident, when in fact they frequently require instruction for the student to be able to comprehend them. You are likely to encounter illustrations similar to those on the following pages.

1. **Maps**

From *History and Life: The World and Its People* by T. Walter Wallbank, Arnold Schrier, Donna Maier-Weaver, Patricia Gutierrez

2. Diagrams

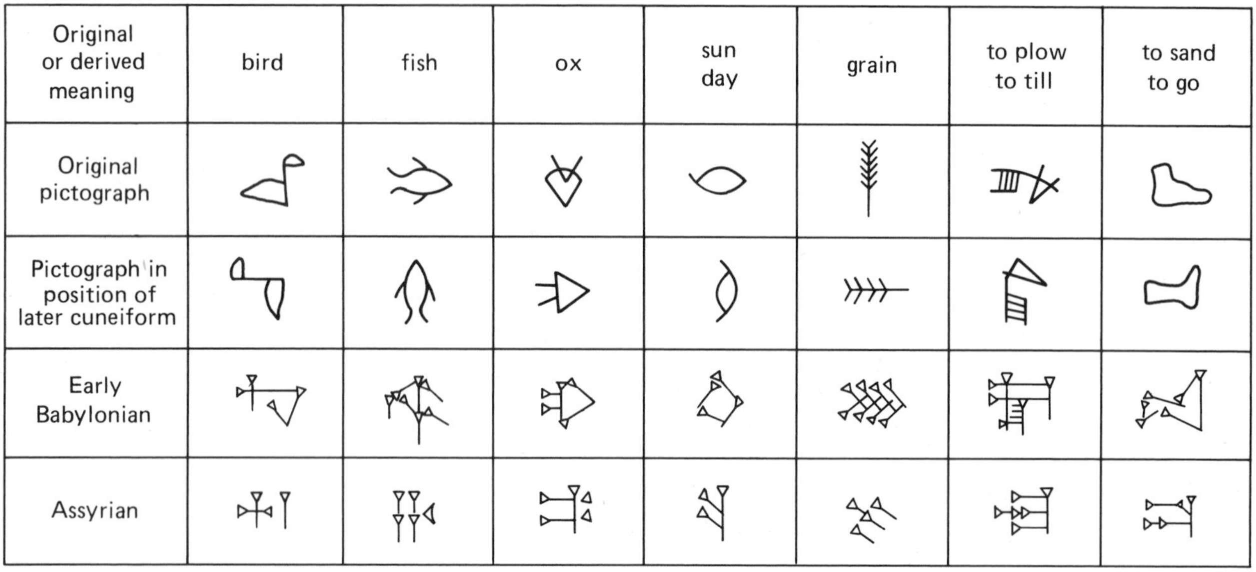

Original or derived meaning	bird	fish	ox	sun day	grain	to plow to till	to sand to go
Original pictograph							
Pictograph in position of later cuneiform							
Early Babylonian							
Assyrian							

B. Linder, E. Selzer, and B. Berk, *A World History* (Chicago: Science Research Associates, 1979), p. 22.

3. Charts

COMPARISON OF HOW LONG A WORKER IN WASHINGTON, D.C., AND A WORKER IN MOSCOW HAD TO WORK IN 1976 TO BUY CERTAIN GOODS

Items	Washington, D.C.	Moscow
Food		
Beef, roast (lb.)	30 min.	65 min.
Chicken, frozen (lb.)	12 min.	98 min.
Ground beef (lb.)	15 min.	94 min.
Fish sticks, frozen (lb.)	20 min.	40 min.
White bread (lb.)	10 min.	9 min.
Sugar, granulated white (lb.)	4 min.	29 min.
Margarine (lb.)	13 min.	59 min.
Milk (quart)	7 min.	21 min.
Eggs (dozen)	12 min.	116 min.
Potatoes (lb.)	4 min.	3 min.
Apples (lb.)	11 min.	23 min.
Clothing, personal needs		
Man's suit	25 hr.	106 hr.
Nylon stockings, pair	16 min.	144 min.
Toilet soap, bar	5 min.	72 min.
Lipstick	31 min.	469 min.
Cigarettes, 20	10 min.	23 min.

Items	Washington, D.C.	Moscow
Household items		
Refrigerator, 4.8 cu. ft.	47 hr.	168 hr.
Washing machine	52 hr.	432 hr.
Color TV	86 hr.	780 hr.
Light bulb, 100 watts	8 min.	30 min.
Apartment rent, unfurn., month	46 hr.	10 hr.
Household gas, monthly bill	7 hr.	1 hr.
Telephone, monthly bill	3 hr.	3 hr.
Transportation		
Compact car	6.9 mo.	37.5 mo.
Gasoline, regular, 10 gal.	91 min.	190 min.
Bus fare, 12 miles	6 min.	4 min.
Air fare, 185 miles, economy	547 min.	505 min.
Services		
Postage, first class	2 min.	3 min.
Man's haircut	51 min.	36 min.
Woman's shampoo and set	97 min.	360 min.
Movie, suburban theater	44 min.	36 min.
Launderette use, 1 load	8 min.	26 min.

B. Linder, E. Selzer, and B. Berk, *A World History* (Chicago: Science Research Associates, 1979), p. 460.

4. Graphs

Average income of men and women workers
(same age, same number of years on the job, same education, about 1971)

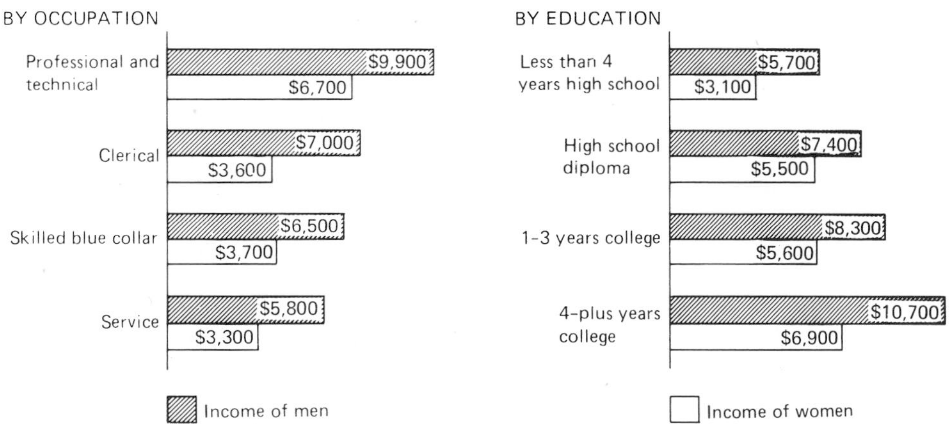

J. Jarolimek and O. L. Davis, "Web of the World," from *Social Studies in the Elementary School* (New York: Macmillan Publishing Company, 1973), p. 154.

5. Relative Percentages (Pies)

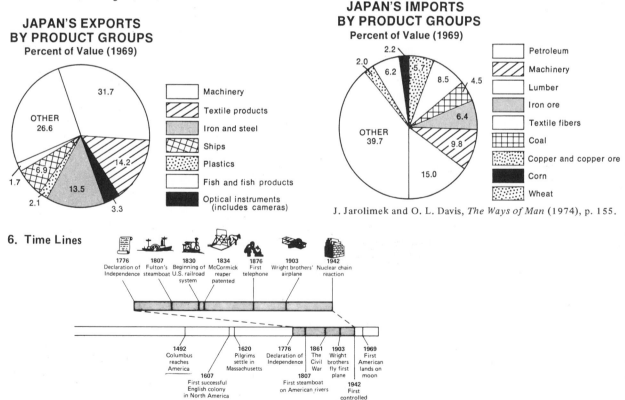

JAPAN'S EXPORTS BY PRODUCT GROUPS
Percent of Value (1969)

31.7
OTHER 26.6
14.2
13.5
6.9
1.7
2.1
3.3

Machinery
Textile products
Iron and steel
Ships
Plastics
Fish and fish products
Optical instruments (includes cameras)

JAPAN'S IMPORTS BY PRODUCT GROUPS
Percent of Value (1969)

2.2
2.0
6.2
5.7
8.5
4.5
6.4
OTHER 39.7
9.8
15.0

Petroleum
Machinery
Lumber
Iron ore
Textile fibers
Coal
Copper and copper ore
Corn
Wheat

J. Jarolimek and O. L. Davis, *The Ways of Man* (1974), p. 155.

6. Time Lines

1776 Declaration of Independence
1807 Fulton's steamboat
1830 Beginning of U.S. railroad system
1834 McCormick reaper patented
1876 First telephone
1903 Wright brothers' airplane
1942 Nuclear chain reaction

1492 Columbus reaches America
1607 First successful English colony in North America
1620 Pilgrims settle in Massachusetts
1776 Declaration of Independence
1807 First steamboat on American rivers
1861 The Civil War
1903 Wright brothers fly first plane
1942 First controlled nuclear chain reaction
1969 First American lands on moon

From *Exploring World Regions: Western Hemisphere* by H. Gross et al. Copyright © 1975 by Follett Publishing Company. Used by permission of Follett Publishing Company.

Many texts present graphics but do not require students to use them or fail to explain them sufficiently so they can be used. You should point out to your students that graphics can help them to understand concepts and facts presented in the text. To ensure that each student is able to analyze the information being presented, ask the following questions about each illustration:

1. What is being illustrated?
2. What is the purpose of the illustration?
3. What information is provided by the caption?
4. What information is provided through the key, symbols, or scales?

Maps are probably the graphic aid most frequently found in social studies texts; therefore, we examine map skills very carefully.

Map Skills. To read a map, students must be taught to

1. Determine the author's purpose for including it.
2. Use the scale and key.
3. Determine latitude and longitude.
4. Determine how directions are portrayed.
5. Compare distances.

In an attempt to help your students further in the development of skills that are necessary for interpreting maps, you should

1. Have the students analyze the parts of the map:
   a. Type of map
   b. Dates
2. Provide activities that require the students to analyze climates, trade routes, currents, and topography.
3. Ask students to compare information from two (or more) maps and to note relationships.
4. Plan activities that require the students to utilize maps and to demonstrate their understanding of the parts of a map.
5. Discuss the importance of captions.

When reading social studies materials, the child is required to draw heavily on several comprehension skills such as understanding cause and effect relationships, making comparisons, detecting propaganda, differentiating fact from opinion, sequencing, and conceptualizing time, space, and place relationships.

Cause and Effect. Facts, events, and interactions in social studies texts are often depicted through cause and effect relationships. Children need to be taught to recognize cause and effect relationships and to identify the cause(s) and the effect(s). The following suggestions and activities can help you to develop these skills in your students:

1. Have your students list causes and effects from social studies reading.

Cause	Effects
Attack on Pearl Harbor	Destruction Death Declaration of war

2. Prepare charts for key events listing causes and effects.
3. Discuss current events or news items in terms of cause and effect.
4. Make discussions relevant to the students. Topics may come from classroom rules, school policy, or student activities. For example, students from other schools have been attending school dances (cause); students must now show a school I.D. card to be admitted to a school dance (effect).
5. After discussing an event in terms of cause and effect, have a class discussion on
   a. Alternative effects that could have occurred.
   b. Alternative causes that could have resulted in this effect.

Activity 1 at the end of this chapter is designed to help you teach cause and effect relationships.

Propaganda. Students are generally taught to recognize propaganda in English and social studies classes. As we discussed in Chapter 7, children may be greatly influenced by many types of propaganda. Students must be made aware that not all propaganda is as obvious as that found in advertisements, political speeches, and historical slogans. Subtle uses of propaganda in writing that appears to be more informative than persuasive are more difficult to detect. Social studies materials can be used to encourage students to

1. Examine an author's purpose.
2. Determine key words used to introduce propaganda.
3. Note the use of persuasive words.
4. Evaluate the facts provided by an author to convey an issue.
5. Evaluate historical slogans as to their origins, application, and persuasive appeal.

Children should be urged to look for propaganda in both written and oral forms. Activity 7 at the end of this chapter can be used as a propaganda-detection activity for your classroom.

Comparison. Social studies materials are well suited to having students learn by making comparisons. Children should be encouraged to make comparisons between governments, countries, customs, policies, land formations, languages, climates, religions, and people. Have your students look for similarities *and* differences in the materials they read. Plan classroom activities that will help your students to become accustomed to making comparisons. Some of these activities might include the following:

1. Have the students compare the customs, culture, and language of several different countries.
2. Have the students compare historical documents from different countries. For example, you may want the students to compare the Magna Carta with the Bill of Rights.
3. Have the students compare the educational systems of various cultures.
4. Have the students compare current modes of transportation with a specific era from the past.
5. Have the students compare the governments of two or more countries.

Activity 4 at the end of this chapter is one that will encourage students to compare the traits of people campaigning for public office.

Sequencing. Shepherd (1978) notes that "history evolves chronologically with the passing of time. One of the understandings students will need to acquire is the large movements of history and the overlap of historical movements" (p. 216). By using activities at the end of this chapter, you can continuously encourage children to develop a choronological perspective by

1. Discussing present-day occurrences while identifying historical factors.
2. Developing historical time lines.
3. Reviewing historical occurrences that have repeated themselves more than once in history: assassination, war, treason. What is the nature of man that he continues to perpetuate these behaviors? What societal factors contribute to his nature?

Differentiating Fact from Opinion. Being able to differentiate fact from opinion is an important reading skill for students of all ages in all content areas. To develop the concept of fact versus opinion initially, have the students analyze each other's statements in any class discussion. Demonstrate how an opinion can be strengthened when it is supported by facts.

Separating fact from opinion is an important skill that must be developed by students to enable them to become wise consumers and independent decision makers. Too often, children have the notion that, if an adult makes a statement or if something can be found in printed material, "it must be true." Students should be encouraged to evaluate supporting premises.

Some ways by which you can help your students to differentiate fact from opinion are the following:

1. Help students become aware that such words and phrases as *perhaps*, *think*, *in my opinion*, *maybe*, *one possibility*, or *my beliefs suggest* often indicate statements of opinion.
2. Have students use reference materials to verify the accuracy of information that may be based fully or partially on opinion or conjecture.
3. Provide paragraphs or short selections that the students can use to practice distinguishing fact from opinion.
4. Encourage students to examine the author's point of view.

Activity 2 at the end of this chapter can be used to

alert children to the need to critically analyze printed information.

Conceptualizing Relationships. To understand and appreciate social studies information, students must be able to conceptualize *time*, *space*, and *place* relationships. You may help your students to develop an understanding of these concepts by instituting such activities as

1. Having students compare different aspects of their city today with how it was fifty or one hundred years ago.
2. Discussing the implications of advanced technology with respect to transportation and communication.
3. Illustrating variations in life-span expectancy and world-time evolution.
4. Having students compare old and ancient maps of regions with modern maps.
5. Having students develop a time line showing important dates and events in their lives.

Activity 5 at the end of this chapter will assist your students in understanding time, space, and place relationships.

Teaching Social Studies. Both the activities suggested in this text and those at the end of the chapter will help you to help your students acquire an understanding of and an appreciation for social studies.

In Chapters 7 and 8, we discussed the directed reading activity (DRA). The following is a sample social studies DRA about the start of Mohammedanism. It was developed under a basic skills grant at San Diego State University in 1981.

DIRECTED READING ACTIVITY

I. Background and Motivation

Most of you know that there are many different religions with different beliefs. But, at least in this country, most people worship one God. There was a time when people worshiped other things. Look at this stone. (Show students a small black stone.) This is similar to a stone that people once worshiped in Arabia. A meteorite had fallen to the earth in Mecca, Arabia. The people put this stone in a temple called the Kaaba. Around the Kaaba were 360 idols (religious objects) that the people also worshiped. The people of Arabia (Arabs) came to think of Mecca as a holy place.

Can you think of any reasons why a meteorite might have been worshiped by the Arabs? (People didn't know what it was; it came from the sky, the "heavens"; there were no other stones like it—unique.)

II. Vocabulary

A. Peninsula—A peninsula is an area of land that is almost completely surrounded by water. Peninsula comes from two Latin words: paene, meaning almost, and insula, meaning isle or small island. Can you think of any areas close to us that could be called a peninsula? (Coronado, Baja California)

B. Meteorite—A meteorite is a piece of stone or metal that has fallen down to earth from space. As a matter of fact, the word comes from the Greek word metéōron, meaning a thing in the air. Most meteorites never make it to earth—they burn up or disintegrate in space before they get here. You might be interested to know that the largest meteorite ever found on earth weighs about 132,300 pounds. This meteorite is in Africa. You can be glad you weren't standing around when that one hit!

C. Caravan—A caravan is a group of people traveling together for safety, usually through the desert. You might also think of it as a convoy. (Remember the movie and/or the song Convoy? There were many trucks traveling together.) One little trick to remember it might be car and van in caravan. These word parts don't really mean car and van, but you know that car and van have to to do with traveling. This will help you remember the meaning of the word.

D. Idol (on board: The Who, ABBA, Cars, Cheap Trick, Van Halen, Ted Nugent)—An idol is something used as an object of worship. (Remember the stone we saw earlier?) It usually is a picture or an image of a religious person or object. Actually, the word idol means image (from the Latin, idolum).

Today, idol doesn't always have a religious meaning. It can mean anyone or anything that many people greatly admire or adore. Look at the names on the board. Some people call them "teenage idols" or "rock idols." What do you think this means? (You may have them add or delete names or just discuss in terms of definition generally.)

E. Persecuted—Did you ever feel as if someone was picking on you or was really out to get you for something? If you did, you felt persecuted. To persecute is to harass constantly. Suppose your favorite color was red and you wore a lot of red clothes. Now suppose that I hate red. Every time you wore a red shirt, I either tried to rip it off of you or color it green with my pen. I also follow you around calling you the Red Menace and laughing at you. You'd be absolutely correct if you said I was persecuting you. Being persecuted isn't much fun.

F. Ministry (on board: minister, administer, administration)—You've probably all heard the word minister, a religious person. Ministry is the job or profession of a minister. You may not know that both words come from the Latin word minis, meaning servant. A minister is a servant of God and a servant of the people. Ministry could then be defined as the job or profession of a person who is a religious "servant." (You might also point out that someone who administers first aid is serving someone. An administration is the people who manage or serve an organization—the administration of your school, President Reagan's administration.)

G. Vision (on board: television, (in)visible, visit)—You can see that many English words come from Greek or Latin words. For example, vis in Latin means has seen. All these words have to do with seeing. (You see television, visible or invisible is able or not able to be seen, visit is to go see someone). When a person has a vision, he or she sees something or someone that is not really there—other people can't see it usually. Some people may think of it as a powerful dream while you're awake or hallucinating.

III. Springboard Questions

1. Why did Mohammed start a new religion?
2. What is the most important city to Moslems? Why?
3. Why is the Battle of Tours important?
4. Why is the city of Bagdad important?

IV. Silent Reading

V. Comprehension Questions

1. What events persuaded Mohammed to start a new religion?
2. Why is Mecca an important city to the Moslems?
3. Explain why Mohammed had to leave Mecca.
4. How did Moslems try to spread Islam?
5. Explain why the Battle of Tours is significant.
6. What was the name of the Frankish leader at the Battle of Tours?
7. What city did the Arabs build on the Tigris River?
8. The Franks and the Moslems both conquered many people in many lands. What was different about the effects of their conquests? (Hint: Remember, the Franks were barbarians.)
9. The Kaaba is ______________________.
10. The Koran is ______________________.

VI. Optional Activity

This activity can be used to demonstrate how word parts can be used to form common words that the students already know. Draw a tree on the board. On the trunk of the tree put a common root word. Students fill in the branches with words from the root word. Example: ped, from the Latin, meaning foot.

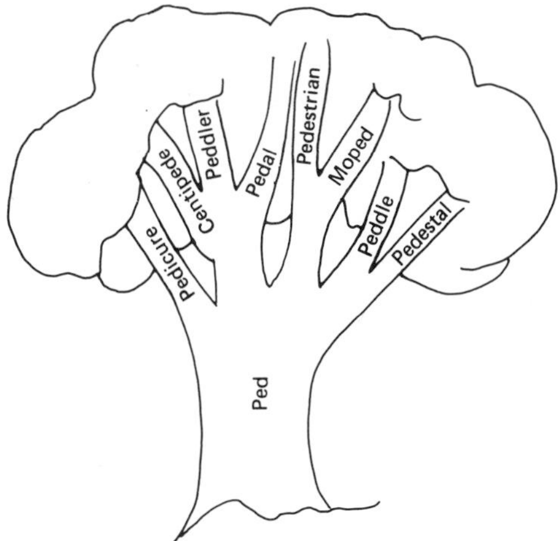

Other possible root words are

graph, graphy (from the Greek), meaning write: photograph, photography, phonograph, autograph, biography, stenographer, geography, bibliography, paragraph, lithograph, telegraph.

tele (from the Greek), meaning far, distant: telegram, telegraph, telephone, telephoto, telescope, television.

Through a lesson such as this you can integrate reading with social studies materials. This DRA (1) included unusual and interesting facts relevant to the material, (2) discussed vocabulary by relating it to the students' lives, (3) offered examples of structural analysis and word derivations, (4) used visual aids, and (5) included a follow-up or optional activity.

One of your primary goals as a classroom teacher should be the integration of reading into the content area curriculum. By emphasizing the various aspects of social studies texts discussed in this section, you can foster and nurture this integration of skills.

Reading in Mathematics

Mathematics is a great deal more than basic computation. The reading and studying of mathematics require

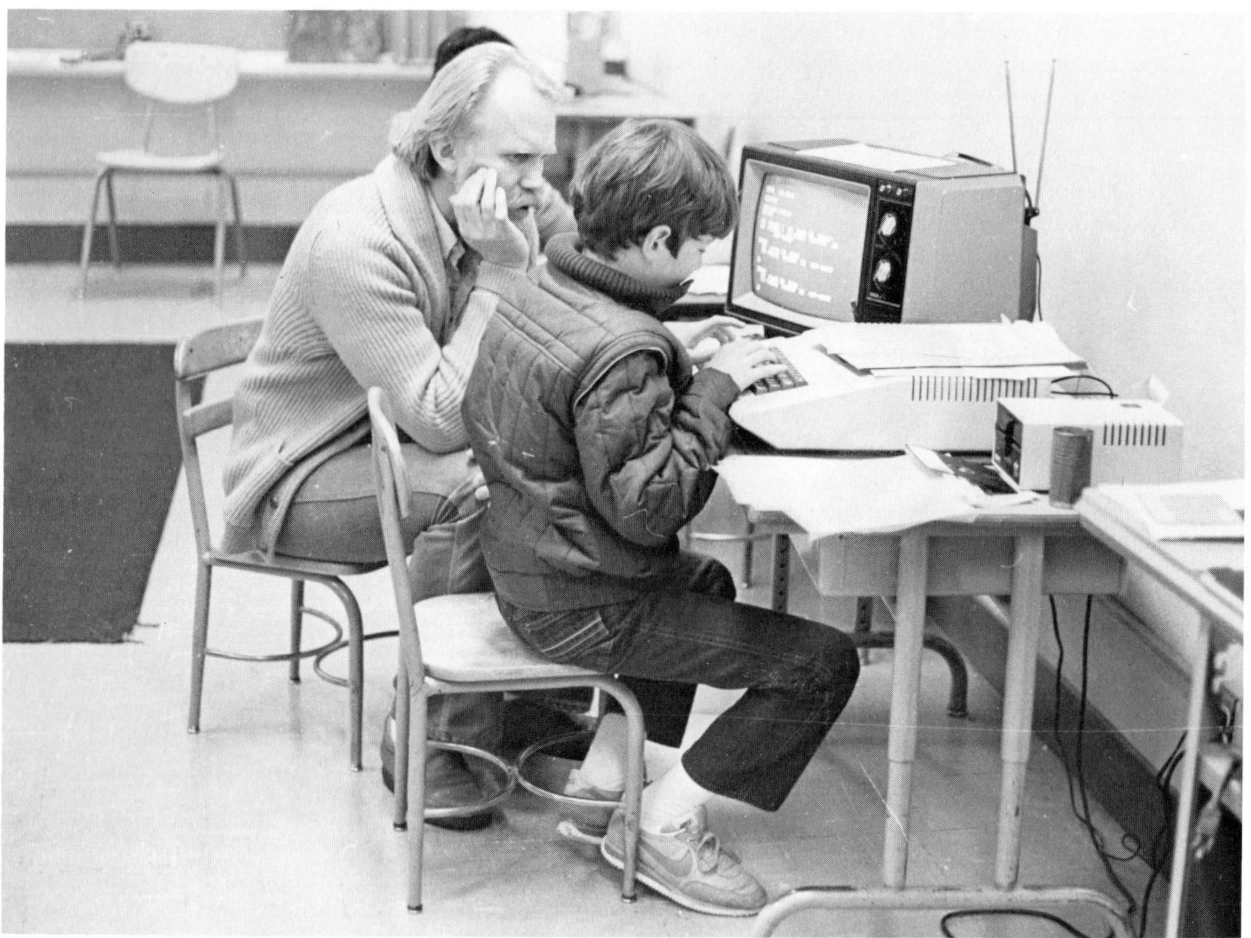

The Language of mathematics is composed of words, numbers, symbols, signs, and abbreviations. (Photo by Linda Lungren.)

both an understanding of and a development of specific concepts and principles. Mathematics instruction should have a twofold purpose:

1. To enable the child to develop an understanding of the patterns that are used to formulate concepts and principles.
2. To enable the child to solve problems.

The accomplishment of these objectives will ensure *both* problem mastery and conceptual understanding.

Mastery of the language of mathematics is essential to accomplishing these objectives. The language of mathematics is composed of words, numbers, and symbols. Roe et al. (1978) point out that "the reader of mathematics must be able to read symbols, signs, abbreviations, exponents, subscripts, formulae, equations, geometric figures, graphs, and tables as well as words" (p. 264). As in the mastery of any other language, the child hears, explores, discusses, experiments, uses, and tests words that might be part of the conceptual framework of this language.

To meet the dual objective of *understanding* and *solving*, a child must have some competence in reasoning, a process that involves a student's ability to reorder known data in an attempt to derive new relationships. *Reasoning* is closely related to *comprehension* because both entail ability to detect problematic clues, to hypothesize, and to evaluate conclusions. Finally, in an attempt to accomplish the specified objective of understanding and to solve problems, the child must be able to estimate and to compute.

A review of reading/mathematics literature suggests that

1. Certain intellectual capabilities are essential for mathematical achievement. According to Piaget, these are competence with the concept of conservation of number, quantity, length, volume, and weight; the achievement of the concept of reversibility; and the maturation of logical abilities. Piaget stated that a child must be able to comprehend the fact that a number is the synthesis of two logical entities, class and asymmetrical relations, before he can achieve in mathematics. He contended that these capabilities are achieved when a child has matured sufficiently to comprehend them.

   Bruner, while accepting a developmental sequence in mathematical capability, contended that a child's environment can be changed so that it is consistent with his intellectual development. Piaget allowed considerable age-range for the development of the intellectual behaviors of children, and Bruner believed that environmental factors modify the learning rate of a child. Perhaps these amount to the same concept. In any event, both maturation and environment should be considered by teachers of elementary mathematics.
2. Certain reading skills are necessary for success in solving verbal arithmetic problems. According to Corle and Coulter (1964), the three most important reading skills are vocabulary development, literal interpretation of the problem, and selection of the proper solution process (reasoning). It is also noted that listening skills seem to be related to mathematical ability, primarily through their relationship to reading achievement.
3. Success in mathematical problem solving is greatly influenced by certain mathematical prerequisites and reading skills, but it is also affected by other variables. Among these are motor abilities, verbal abilities, personality characteristics, and physical conditions. It is also influenced by the arrangement of data within a mathematics problem.
4. Textbook readability is a major consideration in a child's mathematical success because in many classrooms textbooks are the only resource provided for mathematics instruction. Therefore, the vocabulary, both general and quantitative, the difficulty of non-verbal items such as symbols and graphs, and the interest level of the text should be evaluated carefully to insure that the material is suitable to the child's ability and grade level.

From "Reading in Mathematics: A Review of Recent Research," Clyde G. Corle in James L. Laffey (Ed.) *Reading in the Content Areas*, IRA, 1972, pp. 87–88. Reprinted with permission of Clyde G. Corle and the International Reading Association.

Mathematical Language. Reading a mathematics text requires the interpretation of two types of language. The first involves an understanding of the printed word, through which mathematical concepts are explained. The second involves interpretation of signs and symbols.

Shepherd (1978) identifies four types of vocabulary within the printed language of mathematics:

Vocabulary Types	Examples
1. Technical words peculiar to some area of mathematics	Geometry: arc Algebra: polynomial
2. General words with mathematical meanings	prime, radical, square
3. Words which signal a mathematical process	times, difference, subtract
4. General words which can determine a student's comprehension	after, compare, over each, than

It is important for children to learn to recognize and understand various mathematical terms. You can facilitate this process by

1. Providing concrete *and* abstract illustrations.
2. Defining terms.
3. Discussing concepts.

This understanding of the printed word is necessary as the child encounters story or word problems.

Quite often children have difficulty solving word problems, even if they have previously exhibited competence in mathematical computations. Children should be taught to *analyze* word problems and should be encouraged to

1. Read the problem carefully and begin to conceptualize.
2. Reread to decide what problem is posed.
3. Reread to detect the clues given for solving the problem.
4. Determine procedures for solving the problem.
5. Solve the problem.
6. Check the results.

These steps are illustrated in the following problem:

Bob is two years older than Carol. Carol is 9 years old. How old is Bob?

1. Ages? (Problem conceptualization)

   Carol (nine years old)
   Bob (two years older)

2. How old is Bob? (Problem posed)
3. 9 years old (Clues)
   9 years old + 2
4. Addition (Procedure)
5. 9 years old (Solve)
   + 2
   11 years old
   Bob is 11 years old.
6. 11 (Check)
   − 2
   9

In addition to vocabulary words and story problem concepts, the student of mathematics encounters the symbols and signs =, ×, +, −, ÷ that represent words such as equal, times, plus, minus, and divide.

Reading Tables, Graphs, and Pictorial Data. The study of mathematics often requires students to read and interpret tables, graphs, and other pictorial data. On the following pages are some examples of types of visual representations that might be found in mathematics texts.

To understand and develop representations such as these, the child must understand that formulas, equations, and symbols are forms of mathematical shorthand. When attempting to read and study these representations, children should be encouraged to

1. Read descriptive phrases that tell what the table or graph represents.
2. Carefully study any given numbers or letters or words to determine what has been measured.
3. Read any column of data presented to gain a clearer understanding of what is being represented.
4. Analyze any pictorial representations and convert them to numbers.
5. Compare and draw conclusions, if requested.

Students will have a better understanding of bar, line, circle, and picture graphs and tables and histograms if they analyze them using the five preceding steps.

Teaching Mathematics. For your students to acquire the mathematical knowledge and concepts required of them, we recommend the following teaching practices:

Data Given by Graphs

A geography class made this pictograph. It shows the areas of the five largest states. Each area is rounded to the nearest 100,000 square kilometers (Km^2). In the pictograph each ■ represents 100,000 km^2.

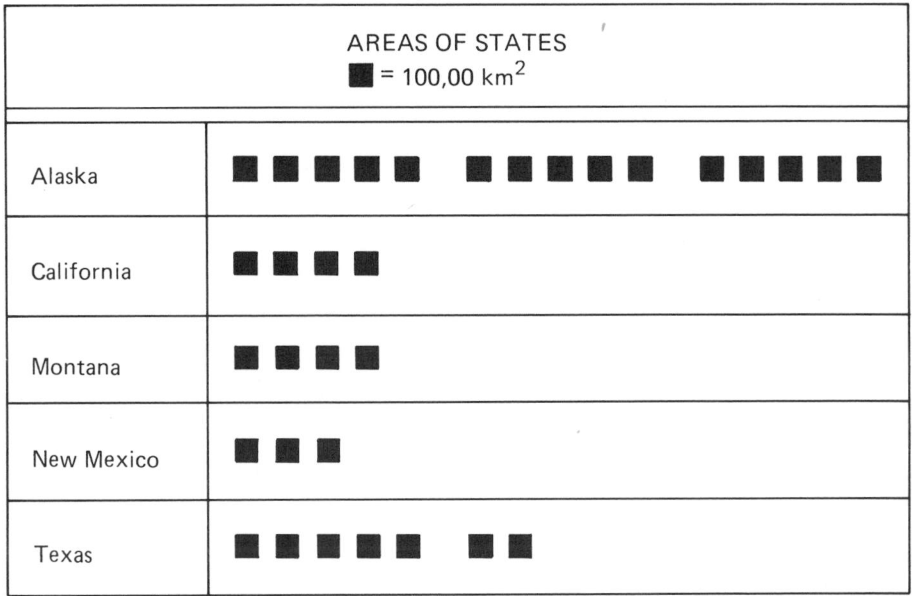

J. Forbes, T. Thoburn, and R. Bechtel, *Macmillan Mathematics*, Book 7 (New York: Macmillan Publishing Co., Inc., 1982), p. 388.

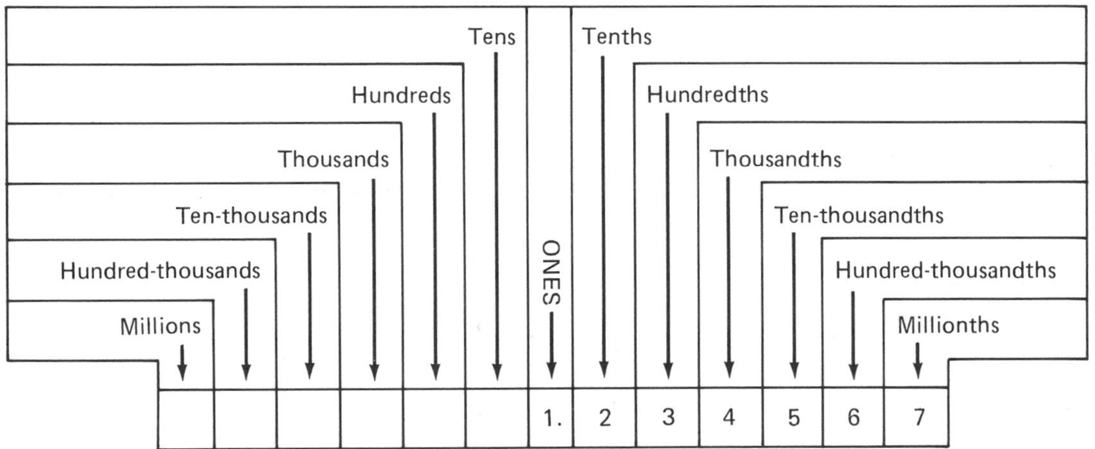

J. Forbes, T. Thoburn, and R. Bechtel, *Macmillan Mathematics*, Book 8 (New York: Macmillan Publishing Co., Inc., 1982), p. 68.

Problem Solving: Using Number Scales

A **number scale** can be used to show numbers that are measures. An important time or position is labeled "zero" and other measures are given as "below or before zero" and "above or after zero."

Example 1

A countdown started 13 minutes before lift-off. It continued for 25 minutes. How long after lift-off did the countdown stop?

A number scale can be used to show times before and after rocket lift-off.

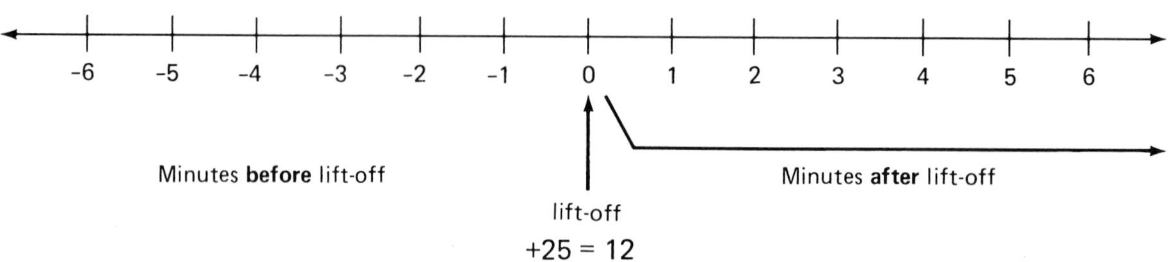

+25 = 12

The countdown stopped 12 minutes after lift-off.

(J. Forbes, T. Thoburn, and R. Bechtel, *Macmillan Mathematics*, Series M, Book 7 (New York: Macmillan Publishing Co., Inc., 1982), p. 362.

1. Children need intense practice in *reading*, *speaking*, and *computing* the succinct language of words and symbols in mathematics.
2. Activities need to be designed to reinforce the technical terms, labeling processes, and symbol representations of mathematics.
3. Children must be encouraged to *read for the purpose* of the problem. Careful reading must be encouraged because the purpose of the problem is intrinsic to solving it.
4. Children must be encouraged to view symbols as mathematical shorthand. Begin by asking children to write formulas in longhand and to restate them in symbols.
5. Children must be encouraged to employ both *analytical* and *computational* processes in solving story problems. Encourage children to read a problem and picture it in their minds. Then ask them to reread the last sentence to determine what they are being asked to do. Next, have them reread and determine the process, estimate an answer, and then attempt to solve the problem.
6. Practice and opportunity must be given children to design tabular, graphic, and pictorial representations. Encourage your children to read the table or graph and determine its purpose. Next, they should analyze the vertical columns to determine their meaning. Finally, they should read all bindings and additional notes. If they are reading a graph instead of a table, they will need help in noting the quantity or units of measurement.
7. Children must be given practice in following directions. Ask children to read or listen to the directions to gain an overview of the task. Next, have them reread each separate phase of the directions while thinking about the exact application. Then, they synthesize or combine all parts of the directional task and proceed.
8. Practice in reasoning, estimating, generalizing, and computing are part of a successful math program.

In Chapters 7 and 8 we discussed the directed reading activity as one type of teaching strategy. The following DRA was developed under a basic skills grant at San Diego State University in 1981. As you read it, note how the background section makes the concept (addition of fractions) relevant to the students, the vocabulary is isolated and pretaught, and the springboard questions give the students a purpose for reading.

DIRECTED READING ACTIVITY

Addition of Fractions

I. Background and Motivation

You know you can ride your bike 10 miles in 1 hour. Your friend lives quite a distance away. You wonder if you could reach his home in one hour. You will travel $4\frac{1}{2}$ miles east. Turn north for $3\frac{1}{6}$ miles. Then turn west for $2\frac{1}{4}$ miles. Could you reach his home in 1 hour?

When you review all the fraction ideas in this lesson, you will have the information you need to solve the above problem.

II. Vocabulary

Numerator: The whole number named by the symbol A in any fraction $\frac{A}{B}$.
Example: In the fraction $\frac{2}{3}$, the 2 is the numerator.

Denominator: The whole number named by the symbol B in any fraction $\frac{A}{B}$.
Example: In the fraction $\frac{2}{3}$, the 3 is the denominator.

Factors: Any number multiplied to give a product.
Example: $1 \times 12 = 12$; $2 \times 6 = 12$; $3 \times 4 = 12$. All the factors of 12 are 1, 2, 3, 4, 6, 12.

Prime: A number that can be divided evenly by 1 and itself and by no other number.
Example: $7 \div 1 = 7$; $7 \div 7 = 1$. The only numbers to divide 7 evenly are 1 and 7. Seven is a prime number.

Prime factors: Prime numbers only, multiplied together to give a product.
Example: $2 \times 6 = 12$. Two is prime. Is 6 prime? No, $2 \times 3 = 6$. Therefore, the prime number factors of 12 are $2 \times 2 \times 3 = 12$.

Equivalent: Being equal. Two names for the same amount.
Example: In discussing units of money, we say two quarters or a half dollar, two names but the same amount. In fractions, $\frac{2}{4}$ and $\frac{1}{2}$ are two names for the same amount. They are equivalent fractions.

Lowest terms: A fraction with a numerator and a denominator that cannot be divided by the same number.
Example: $\frac{3}{4}$. There is not any number, except 1, that can divide both numbers. $\frac{6}{8}$ can be divided by 2. Doing so gives you $\frac{3}{4}$, which is then in lowest terms. Six eighths is not in lowest terms.

Simplifying: Naming the fraction in the lowest terms possible.
Example: Two quarters equal a half dollar. The half dollar is simpler (one coin) than two quarters: $\frac{2}{4} = \frac{1}{2}$. The $\frac{1}{2}$ is a simpler fraction.

Mixed number: A whole number and a fraction together.

Example: $2\frac{3}{5}$. Two is a whole number; $\frac{3}{5}$ is a fraction; $2\frac{3}{5}$ is a mixed number.

Improper fraction: When the numerator names a number greater than the denominator, the fraction is called improper.

Example: $\frac{24}{4}$. The number 24 is greater (names a greater amount) than the 4. This is called an improper fraction. Since the numerator, 24, can be divided by the denominator, 4, evenly, that is what is usually done: $24 \div 4 = 6$.

III. Springboard Questions

1. How are fractions with like denominators added?
2. How is an answer stated in lowest terms?
3. How can fractions with unlike denominators be added?
4. How are missed numbers added?

IV. Silent Reading

V. Follow-up Questions

1. Add the following fractions:
   a. $\frac{2}{8} + \frac{3}{8} =$ ______
   b. $\frac{3}{4} + \frac{1}{4} =$ ______
   c. $\frac{1}{6} + \frac{2}{6} =$ ______
   d. $\frac{3}{2} + \frac{1}{2} =$ ______
   e. $\frac{7}{12} + \frac{2}{12} =$ ______
2. Reduce the following fractions to lowest terms:
   a. $\frac{4}{8} =$ ______
   b. $\frac{6}{9} =$ ______
   c. $\frac{2}{12} =$ ______
   d. $\frac{3}{9} =$ ______
   e. $\frac{2}{10} =$ ______
3. Add the following fractions:
   a. $\frac{2}{6} + \frac{1}{3} =$ ______
   b. $\frac{4}{7} + \frac{3}{4} =$ ______
   c. $\frac{2}{4} + \frac{1}{6} =$ ______
   d. $\frac{5}{8} + \frac{2}{3} =$ ______
   e. $\frac{3}{6} + \frac{7}{9} =$ ______
4. Add the following mixed numbers:
   a. $1\frac{2}{3} + 2\frac{7}{8} =$ ______
   b. $3\frac{3}{4} + 1\frac{1}{2} =$ ______
   c. $7\frac{3}{4} + 4\frac{2}{3} =$ ______
   d. $5\frac{2}{9} + 3\frac{1}{7} =$ ______
   e. $4\frac{1}{6} + 5\frac{3}{5} =$ ______

Reading in Science

Elementary science texts include information from all the sciences—geology, biology, physical science, botany, and chemistry. The emphasis is on *involvement* through observation, inquiry, and discovery. You can help your students to discover the world of science by presenting information through many types of media, including films, pictures, observations, models, and a variety of reading materials. Whenever possible, plan activities that will allow students to *experience* scientific phenomena through all the senses in addition to listening, talking, and reading.

Language and reading skills are essential to a child's mastery of science materials. Students use these skills to *discover* scientific data, *interpret* factual material, and *formulate* generalizations. You must guide your stu-

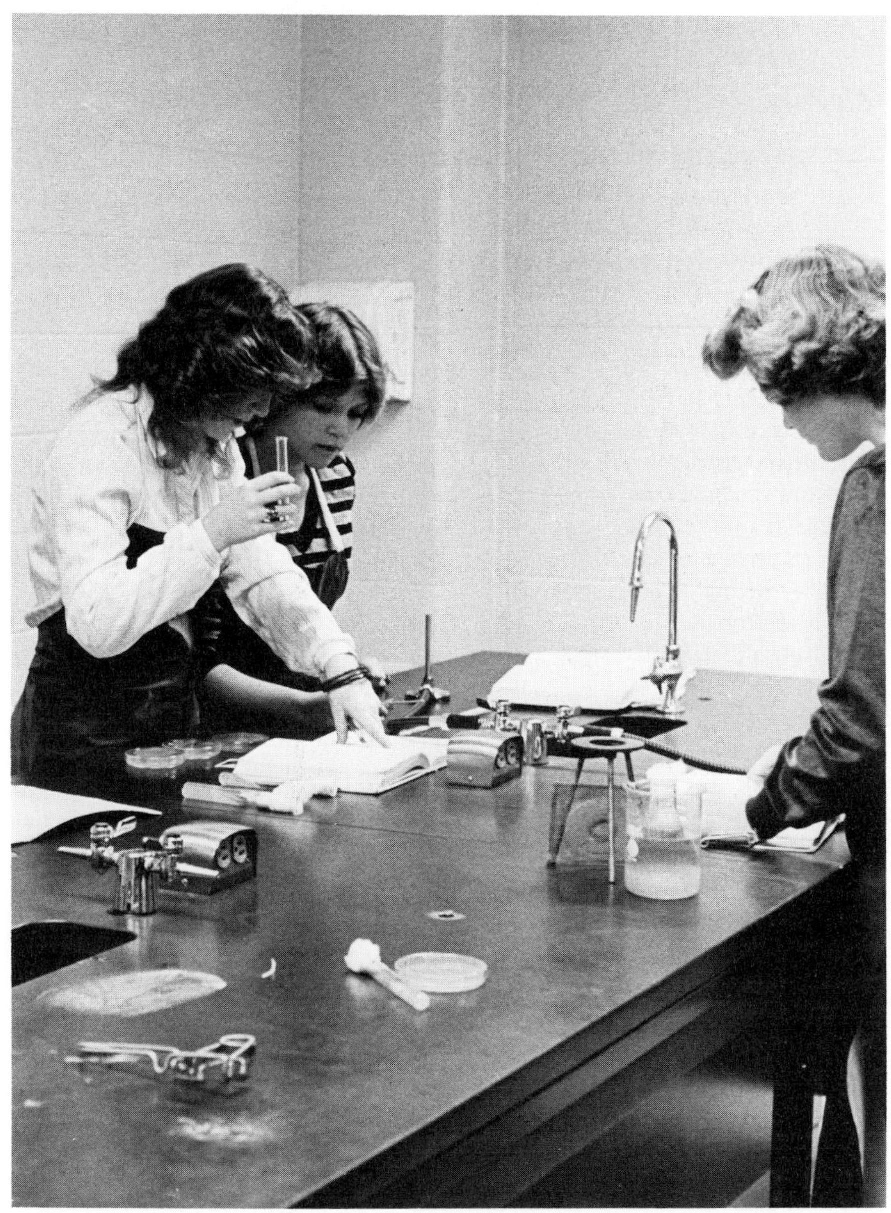

Science texts include information from all of the sciences—geology, biology, physical science, botany, and chemistry. The emphasis is on involvement through observation, inquiry, and discovery. (Photo by Linda Lungren.)

dents in developing the language and reading skills that will enable them to read their science materials. Be aware that scientific writings contain

1. A terse style of writing.
2. An extremely high readability level.
3. A density of facts and details.
4. A multitude of difficult concepts.

Many of the skills required to read science texts successfully are also common to other content areas. This makes it possible to reinforce the common reading and study skills through a variety of content material. In a science classroom specifically, your instruction should enable students to

1. Understand scientific language.
2. Synthesize their rates of reading with their purpose for reading.
3. Utilize the parts of their texts.
4. Understanding and utilize scientific formulas.
5. Read graphic aids.
6. Follow directions.
7. Evaluate data.
8. Make generalizations.
9. Apply new data to solve problems.

Scientific Language. The vocabulary of science is so vast that it is sometimes overwhelming to a student. In recognition of this fact, a "hands-on" approach to science has been used in many schools in an attempt to develop basic concepts before children confront the technical language of science. By using this type of approach, teachers hoped to develop in their students a positive attitude toward the study of science. Before this experience-based approach was used, it was found that the vocabulary of science often negatively affected children's listening comprehension. Children were unfamiliar with both the *technical* and *nontechnical* language. A similar problem occurred when children read scientific materials. Mallinson (1972) suggested that this was true for the following reasons:

1. The level of reading difficulty of many textbooks in science was found to be too high for the students for whom the textbooks were designed.
2. The differences between the levels of reading difficulty of the easiest and the most difficult textbooks analyzed in all the studies were both statistically significant and consequential.
3. In some science textbooks, whose average level of reading difficulty seemed satisfactory, there were passages that would have been difficult even for some college students.
4. Many science textbooks contained nontechnical words that could have been replaced by easier synonyms.
5. Little cognizance seemed to have been taken of growth in reading ability during the school year, since the earlier portions of some of the textbooks were difficult, whereas the latter portions were easier (p. 139).

The following excerpts from elementary science materials illustrate the extent of this language complexity.

About half a billion years ago, one kind of creature very slowly developed something quite unusual. Instead of a shell outside the body, a stiff rod formed inside the body. The rod ran along the creature's back just underneath the nerve cord that carries messages to all parts of the creature's body and keeps the various parts working together.

The rod called the notochord (no tə kord) is present, at some time, in the development of chordates (cor dat'), a large group of animals an early stage in their development—when they are embryos.

(Asimov and Gallant, 1973, p. 55)

This material might even be difficult for a competent adult reader. However, if that were the case, the reader would probably have the dictionary skills necessary to add meaning to this passage. An intermediate-aged child may not possess the study skills necessary to interpret and comprehend this passage.

Let us examine a second excerpt:

The garbage collectors of the sea are the decomposers. Day and night, ocean plants and animals that die, and the body wastes of living animals, slowly drift down to the sea floor. There is a steady rain of such material that builds up on the sea bottom. This is especially true on the continental shelves, where life is rich. It is less true in the desert regions of the deep ocean.

As on the land, different kinds of bacteria also live in the sea. They attack the remains of dead plant and animal tissue and break it down into nutrients. These nutrients are then taken up by plant and animal plankton alike. Among such nutrients are nitrate (ni' trat), phosphate (fos' fāt), manganese (mang' ga nes), silica (sil k), and calcium (kal se m).

(Asimov and Gallant, 1973, p. 155)

Although this is a relatively short selection, it contains many difficult vocabulary words (*decomposers*, *nutrients*, *plankton*) that may interfere with a child's comprehension.

Science texts are replete with fact-specific data. However, many children experience difficulty with this type of subject matter because they lack the skills necessary to *perceive*, *interpret*, and *evaluate* it. As in the previous examples, writers of science texts frequently attempt to include contextual clues as an aid to reading. The student, however, must have some experiential background for the concepts and vocabulary to derive meaning from the reading.

Some children experience problems making the transition from reading largely narrative basal readers to reading factual material with a high concept load. One scientific selection may introduce several new concepts. The student must learn to perceive the necessary relationships, classifications, and relevance of the material. Readers of science materials are also expected to derive information from the interpretation of pictures, maps, graphs, charts, tables, and formulas—a process that may create further difficulties for a child. You can reduce the possibility of language and conceptual difficulties by planning activities with the focus on firsthand observation. Such activities might include field trips, experiments, films, models, and pictures. Following are some additional suggestions for your classroom:

1. Discuss the scientific concept before adding the technical label.
2. Define new words with your students. Encourage them to use the glossary or dictionary.
3. Have students analyze word parts and provide them with lists or charts showing common word part meanings.

   cyto cell, hollow
   logy science, study of
   hemo blood
   poly many, much
4. Substitute common terms for technical terms. For example, *balance* may be an acceptable substitute for *equilibrium*.
5. Discuss the multiple meanings of scientific words. For example, *mass*, *core*, and *cell* all have multiple meanings.
6. Use visual aids to help students understand abstract concepts.
7. Encourage the students to use context clues to help "unlock" the meaning of new words.
8. Develop scientific word charts that clarify and/or classify scientific terms.

   Heat

   radiation
   conduction
   convection

   Or have students classify materials as liquids, solids, or gases.

When presenting new material, it is important to introduce the new vocabulary and concepts that will be encountered in the selection. Many words have multiple meanings and each subject area contains a unique vocabulary. As a classroom teacher, you must teach the vocabulary upon which the key concepts rest.

The following directed reading activity was prepared under a basic skills grant at San Diego State University in 1981. As you read it, note how it incorporates many of the preceding suggestions into the lesson.

DIRECTED READING ACTIVITY

Inside a Plant Cell

I. Background and Motivation

Have you ever wondered what it would be like to be inside a plant cell? Suppose that you are part of a scientific team. Your mission is to explore the inside of a plant cell. To prepare you for this mission you will be given a special injection. The injection will make you small, much smaller than a drop of water. You'll be able to travel in the cell without disturbing anything.

Before you begin your journey, we will "brief you" on the special structures you will find in a plant cell.

II. Vocabulary

The new terms you will need to know for this section are

cell wall
chloroplast
chlorophyll
plastids

Let's look at each one separately.

cell wall

Have you seen the show Barney Miller on television? If so, you probably remember the jail cell. A jail cell has walls to hold in the prisoner. A plant cell has a cell wall that holds in and protects the liquid in the cell.

chloroplast

If we break the word "chloroplast" apart, we have

chloro / plast chloro meaning green.
plast meaning form.

So a chloroplast is a "green form." Chloroplast is an oval-shaped form, or structure, inside the plant cell. If, as you learned earlier, cytoplasm is the "soup of the cell," chloroplasts are the green "lima beans." Chloroplasts contain chlorophyll.

chlorophyll

chloro / phyll

We already know that chloro means green. Phyll means leaf. Chlorophyll is the green material in plant cells that makes leaves and plants green. This green material, chlorophyll, is important because it uses sunlight to make food for plants.

When you see the word part chloro, remember that it means green. A chloroplast is a green form. Chlorophyll means green leaf. In fact, if you buy Clorets, look at the ingredients on the label. Clorets contain chlorophyll. Chlorophyll is used to add green coloring to Clorets and some deodorants and cosmetics.

plastids

We already know that chlorophyll in plant cells makes leaves green. But flowers are part of plants and they aren't green. Carrots, tomatoes, and beets aren't green. Plastids give flowers and vegetables their color. Plastids are tiny grains of color. They are scattered throughout the cytoplasm of most plant cells. Think for a moment about the colors in a plant cell. Cytoplasm, "the soup of the cell," is a grayish color. Chloroplasts add green color to the soup. Then plastids add the tiny specks of bright color—red, orange, yellow, and blue.

Plastids are also the reason why some leaves turn color. In some leaves, chlorophyll breaks down in the fall. Then the bright colors of the plastids show through. So fall leaves turn bright oranges, reds, and yellows.

III. Springboard Questions
   1. How are animal and plant cells different? How are they alike?
   2. What do the special parts of a plant cell do?

IV. Silent Reading

V. Follow-up Questions

   Literal Questions
   1. Which has larger vacuoles—a plant cell or an animal cell?
   2. What does the plant cell wall do?
   3. What are the most important differences between plant and animal cells?
   4. What are chloroplasts?
   5. What part of a plant cell allows a plant to make its own food?
   6. Do all cells of green plants have chlorophyll?
   7. What structures do plant cells and animal cells both have?
   8. What are plastids?

   Interpretive Questions
   9. How is wood formed?
   10. Why do the leaves of some trees turn color in the fall?

Remember that a successful reader can interpret as well as perceive the printed symbol. Activities 16–22 at the end of this chapter are designed to aid you in teaching children to understand and read the language of science.

Comprehending Scientific Data. Young children are naturally curious; therefore, many children in the primary grades are very interested in science. This interest sometimes wanes during the intermediate school years because of the difficulties students encounter in reading printed scientific material. As a classroom teacher, you may be able to lessen these difficulties by following these suggested procedures when you are introducing and implementing a unit of scientific study:

A. Planning for unit implementation
   1. Begin by surveying the unit of study to identify potentially difficult vocabulary.
      a. Which words contain the stems of other words?
      b. Which words may cause multiple-meaning difficulty?
      c. Which words present entirely unexplained concepts?
      d. Which words can be associated with objects?
      e. Which words draw on the experiences of your students?
   2. Determine which of these words contain key bits of understanding.
   3. Categorize all of the remaining terms under key terms.
B. Implementing the unit
   1. List the key terms on the board or on a wall chart.
   2. Present an illustration for each word. Illustrations may be made through *pictures*, *live specimens*, and *slides*.

3. Ask questions that will help youngsters to use the new words.
4. As the unit progresses, introduce other categories of terms in the same manner.
5. Utilize magazines, newspapers, and trade books to supplement textbook reading.
6. Actively involve students in the unit by having them
   a. Collect specimens or pictures of specimens.
   b. Label specimens or picture displays.
   c. Draw charts.
   d. Develop models.
   e. Perform experiments.
   f. Plan field trips.

It is important for students to master the skills of locating information, interpreting formulas, and understanding graphic representations. Through these study skills, the student can collect adequate data to make evaluative judgments. As you know, mastery of these skills is a key element in content area reading. Let us now examine how they relate specifically to the teaching of science.

TEACHING SCIENCE

Locating Information. One of the steps toward implementing your reading/science curriculum is to provide your students practice in locating information and in using supplementary sources of information. Developing this library study skill is particularly valuable as it relates to *scientific inquiry* because many content area science programs are based on this approach.

Spend some time in class discussing the parts of a book and the purpose of each part. Students should become familiar with using the table of contents, glossary, indexes, appendixes, headings, pictures, and graphs. After the child has developed basic competency in using these aids, introduce a variety of science resource materials. These may include encyclopedias, journals (e.g., *Scientific American*), trade books, government publications, and scientific bulletins. Dole and Johnson (1981) also recommend using fiction books with a scientific theme because "these books can provide needed background for science concepts covered in class, and they can help relate these concepts to students' everyday lives" (p. 579).

After students have located a source of information for the topic being investigated, encourage them to *survey* the material to determine the main idea and to take note of all important details. When the specific information being sought has been located, students will be able to continue their study. The location of new scientific data may call for the interpretation of formulas.

Interpreting Formulas. Formulas are part of the vocabulary of science that sometimes interfere with a child's comprehension of material. Children must be taught that formulas are types of sentences that represent thoughts or ideas. The symbols within the formula can be viewed as words.

The sentence, "Centripetal *force* is equal to the *mass* times the *velocity* squared divided by the *radius* of a circle" can be represented as:

$$F = \frac{MV^2}{R}$$

The sentence equals the formula. Now let's examine each symbol, or word, within the formula:

F = force
M = mass
V = velocity
R = radius

After *interpreting* the symbol and the meaning, the reader is ready to evaluate the message. Activity 20 at the end of this chapter encourages this development.

Understanding Graphic Representations. Most scientific materials supplement the printed text with visual aids or graphics. These graphic aids can be valuable in discussions of abstract concepts and are a great help for students who have difficulty interpreting the printed text. Students should be encouraged to note titles and other identifying or explanatory information, as well as the elements of the illustration, when they encounter graphics. Children need instruction in interpreting graphic symbols because many elementary science materials contain the following types of graphic representations:

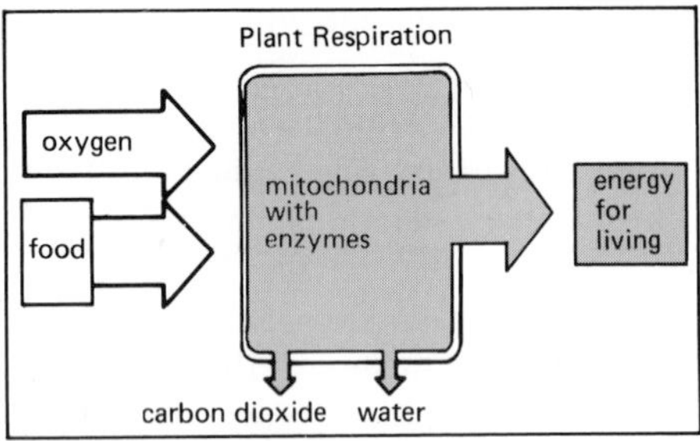

A. Stone and L. Sherman, *Spaceship Earth: Life Science* (Boston: Houghton Mifflin Company, 1975),p. 169.

Calcite	Dilute hydrochloric acid		Calcium chloride	Calcium dioxide	Water
$CaCO_3$ +	2HCl	→	$CaCl_2$ +	CO_2 (bubbles)	+ H_2O

R. Bisque, H. Pratt, and J. Thompson. *Earth Science: Patterns in Our Environment* (Englewood Cliffs, N.J.: Prentice-Hall, Inc., 1975), p. 116.

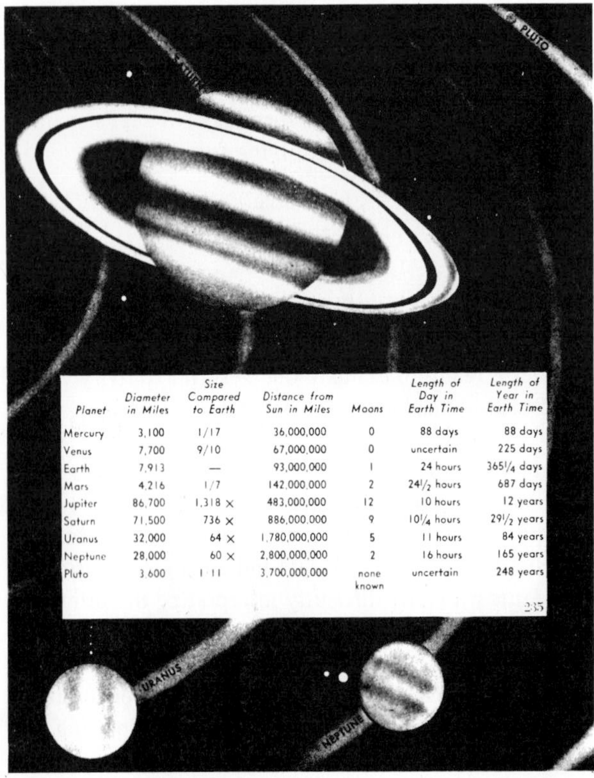

Planet	Diameter in Miles	Size Compared to Earth	Distance from Sun in Miles	Moons	Length of Day in Earth Time	Length of Year in Earth Time
Mercury	3,100	1/17	36,000,000	0	88 days	88 days
Venus	7,700	9/10	67,000,000	0	uncertain	225 days
Earth	7,913	—	93,000,000	1	24 hours	365¼ days
Mars	4,216	1/7	142,000,000	2	24½ hours	687 days
Jupiter	86,700	1,318 ×	483,000,000	12	10 hours	12 years
Saturn	71,500	736 ×	886,000,000	9	10¼ hours	29½ years
Uranus	32,000	64 ×	1,780,000,000	5	11 hours	84 years
Neptune	28,000	60 ×	2,800,000,000	2	16 hours	165 years
Pluto	3,600	1/11	3,700,000,000	none known	uncertain	248 years

235

K. Barnard et al., *Science: A Search for Evidence* (New York: Macmillan Publishing Co., Inc., 1966), p. 235.

Yeast cells, magnified 1000 times. Within four hours after the cell farthest left had begun to bud, there were eight cells.

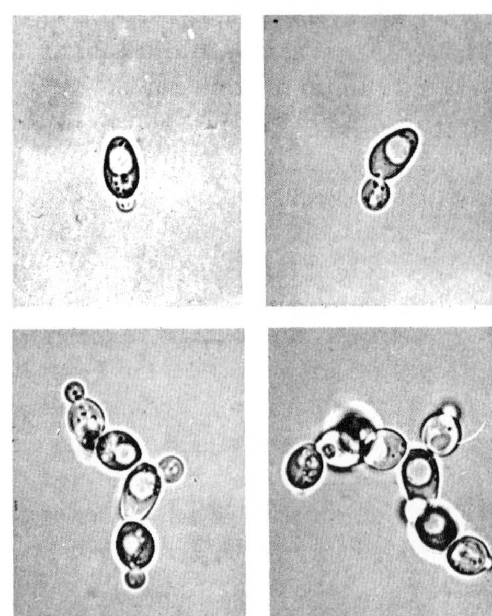

K. Barnard et al., *A Study for Evidence* (New York: Macmillan Publishing Co., 1966), p. 375.

You will find graphic representations similar to these in most scientific materials. They are intended to supplement the printed text by providing clues. Some children may find them difficult to read unless they are given careful instruction. Other children may never grasp the importance of such representations unless they are alerted to their functional value. Activity 24 at the end of this chapter is designed to encourage children to comprehend and use graphic representations as an aid to comprehending the scientific language of their text.

All study skills are vital to the competent reading of all content area subjects. Throughout this chapter we have attempted to enable you to understand clearly the application procedures necessary for implementing these integrated processes within the context of your classroom. Mathematics, science, and social studies have been given special consideration because they are the content areas in which children seem to have the most difficulty.

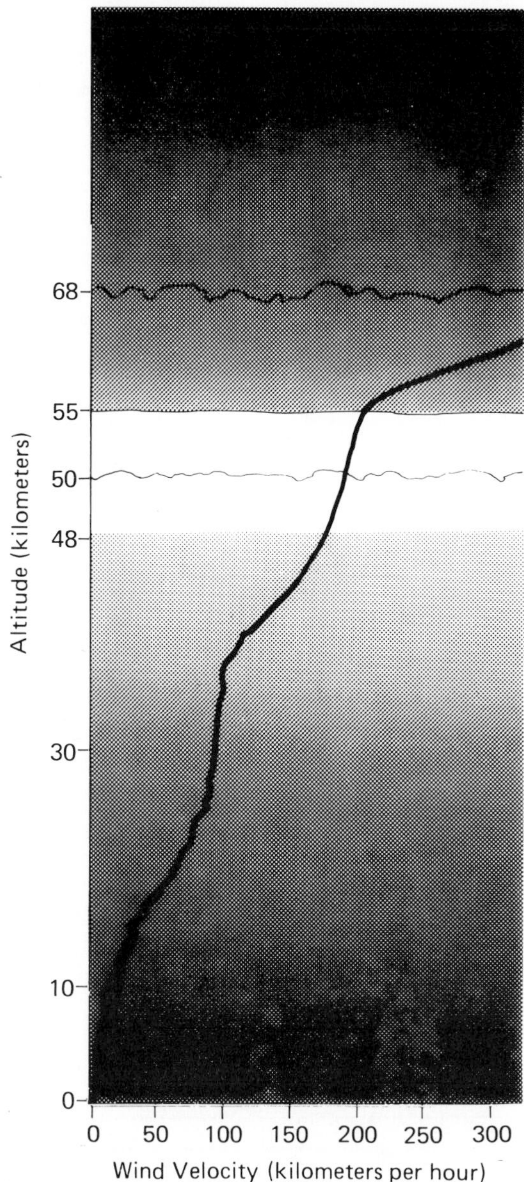

The winds of Venus vary with altitude. Upper clouds whip by at 360 km an hour. But a slow breeze at the surface moves no faster than a walk. Venus is a forecaster's dream; its weather scarely varies.

R. Gallant, *National Geographic Picture Atlas of Our Universe* (Washington, D.C.: National Geographic Society, 1980), p. 88.

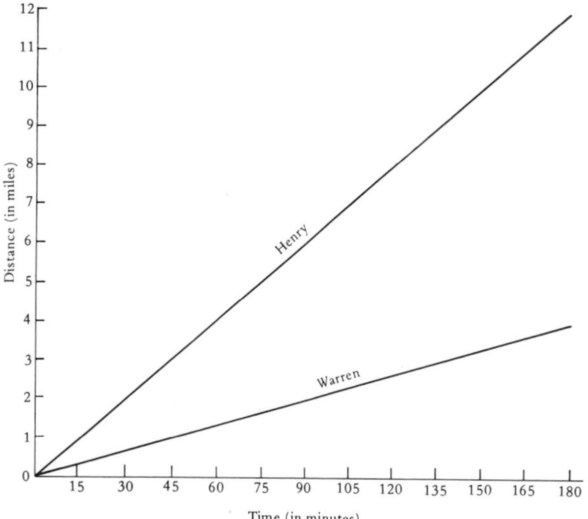

K. Barnard, and C. Lavatelli, *Science Measuring Things* (New York: Macmillan Publishing Co., Inc., 1970), p. 35.

As a teacher in a self-contained classroom, you may find yourself responsible for teaching art and music. Let us briefly explore the relationships between reading and the arts.

Reading and the Arts

Music and art should be a part of every classroom, even when a school is fortunate enough to have music and art specialists as part of the staff. Some teachers underrate the role of the humanities in a school curriculum and fail to incorporate these areas into content area subjects.

We urge you to provide both art and music activities that will foster lifetime interest, enjoyment, and pursuit of these arts in your students. The integration of reading and the arts is similar to that of other content areas. We examine each of these areas briefly.

Music. Although young children do not become involved with in-depth studies of musical theory, they do encounter new vocabulary and symbols that must be read and interpreted. Music has a technical vocabulary, as do other content area subjects, and an array of musical symbols that have specific meanings. Music texts often contain materials similar to the following:

DYNAMICS

You might try the following.

Term	Sign	Meaning
f	forte	loud
p	piano	soft
<	cresendo	gradually getting louder
>	decresendo	gradually getting softer

M. Marsh, et al., *The Spectrum of Music with Related Arts,* Book 5 (New York: Macmillan Publishing Co., Inc., 1980), p. 15.

What kinds of repetition are used in "Come and Dance"? What keeps the repetition in the verse from becoming monotonous?

Listen to each phrase of the verse. Where do you hear contrast?

M. V. Marsh, et al., *The Spectrum of Music with Related Arts,* Book 5 (New York: Macmillan Publishing Co., Inc., 1980), p. 124.

Music has a technical vocabulary, like other content area subjects, and an array of musical symbols that have specific meanings. (Photo by Linda Lungren.)

LEARNING STEP PATTERNS

Here is a picture of part of a keyboard. ▶

A half step is the distance from any key to its nearest neighbor. Play this half step. Listen to its sound. Then play other half steps. ▶

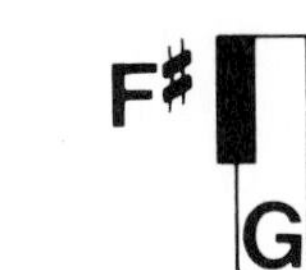

A whole step is the distance of two half steps. Play these whole steps. Listen to their sounds. Play other whole steps. ▶

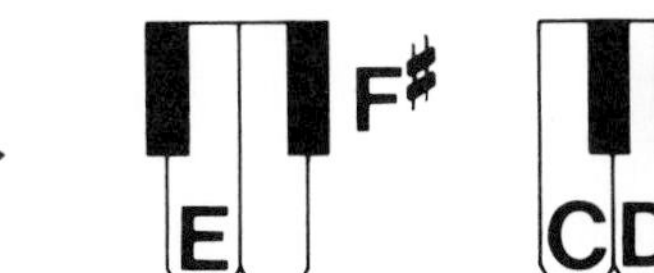

You may remember that you can play a major scale beginning on any key of the piano or any bell, by using these whole (W) and half (½) step patterns.

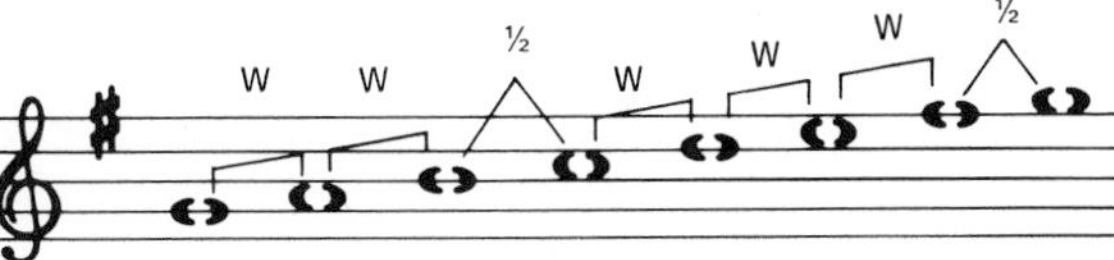

Begin on G. Play the G major scale. It has one sharp. Which note has the sharp?

M. V. Marsh, et al., *The Spectrum of Music with Related Arts,* Book 5 (New York: Macmillan Publishing Co., Inc., 1980), p. 88.

As you attempt to integrate music and reading, remember that children must be helped to

1. Perceive the technical terms and symbols.
2. Interpret and understand the symbols.
3. Follow performance directions.
4. Evaluate music criticisms.

Activities 26 through 29 at the end of this chapter will help you incorporate reading and music into your curriculum.

Art. Elementary school children rarely have art textbooks per se; rather, they often encounter reproductions of art works in content areas texts, such as in social studies. These opportunities can be used to encourage children to compare artistic styles and trends and to show how art works are often a reflection of the times.

Reading skills are related to art in that there is a technical vocabulary (e.g., *relief*, *fresco*, *chroma*) and also because *following directions* is very important in art instruction. For example, students must follow directions in mixing paints or other art materials. Students are also often asked to *evaluate* works of art. As you can see, the relationship between reading and art is very similar to other content area subjects.

Activities 26 and 29 at the end of this chapter will help you incorporate art and reading into your curriculum.

FUNCTIONAL LITERACY

One of the primary goals of *all* teachers on all levels is to make students functionally literate. As you prepare children to analyze content area materials critically, you need to include such items as job application forms, newspaper classified ads, labels on cans, tax forms, bank loan applications, insurance policies, and bank statements. Including such literacy materials in your curriculum is both desirable and legitimate because students who can use critical communication skills to meet their basic daily needs are functionally literate.

In recent years, some criticisms have been levied against the educational system because some adults seem unprepared to meet the challenges of daily life in a literate society. Functional literacy, therefore, has become a major thrust in educational literature. It has also become the basis of many educational programs because students as adults often encounter difficulty when applying for schooling, housing, health care, and employment. By exploring some of these situations and materials, middle-school-aged children often become aware of the reading/language criteria needed for future success in these encounters.

The age of your students will determine what type of activities and materials are appropriate in your classroom. For example, in elementary classrooms you may have your children "play store" to learn the value of comparative shopping. A Boy Scout or Girl Scout manual may be of interest to intermediate-grade children, whereas older students may prefer reading the *Drivers' Educational Manual* or examining job application forms.

The inclusion of functional literacy programs can be viewed as a first step toward building positive educational experiences for students of all ages. A well-planned functional literacy curriculum should provide the study of topics and skill areas that will be of value in encounters outside of school and in school-related activities. Being able to read and follow recipe directions, for example, may spark interest and competency in projects related to content area knowledge, such as the reading of graphs and measurement techniques.

Functional literacy skills should be included as an integral part of your total curriculum and should *not* be viewed as a separate "subject." The functional literacy component should extend reading, writing, speaking, and listening skills through a well-planned unit of thematic instruction. For example, as you study "Our Community" with a group of second-graders, you may want to discuss the procedures their parents engaged in when they bought a house or rented an apartment. A question such as the following may be all that is needed to spark a lively conversation: "How did your parents find out that your home or apartment was for rent or sale?" Simulated activities, such as visiting and interviewing a bank teller or a rental agent, may provide all the understanding needed by that age group.

You can implement a functional literacy program by making it *relevant* to all aspects of daily life and by *integrating* it into content area units of study.

TEACHING ACTIVITIES THAT INTEGRATE READING AND SOCIAL STUDIES

1. The Nightly Cause and Effect Show

Goal: Understanding cause and effect relationships

Grade Level: 4–9

Construction: Have one group of students prepare a radio script or newscast to be presented to the class. The news can be of a serious or a humorous nature. Possible topics might include upcoming school events, student elections, or fictional stories about students or teachers, or the news items may reflect current events. A microphone from a tape recorder or even a tin can may be used for the radio microphone.

Utilization: The audience listens to the newscast and makes a cause and effect chart noting five effects of five causes. The team of newscasters determines if they are correct.

2. Just the Facts, Please

Goal: Differentiating fact from opinion

Grade Level: 2–9

Construction: Have the students listen to and observe television, radio, and newspaper advertisements for one week. (Older students could take notes on a particular number of advertisements.)

Utilization: Have the students make a list of the words, techniques, or devices used in the advertisements that were opinion or hearsay, but not facts. Then have them try to write their own advertisements, using only facts, and present them to the class.

3. Learning Stations—Intermediate Grades and Above*

Goal: To increase proficiency in map reading; to develop alphabetizing; to develop understanding of directionality used in maps.

Grade Level: 4–6

Construction: Map of midtown New York City

Numbered index of restaurants in midtown Manhattan.

Written directions.

Activity cards with outlined task and answer key.

Utilization: Provide a map of restaurants, a restaurant index, written instructions, activity cards, and worksheets. Allow students to choose one of five activity cards. Have them read the task outlined on the card and, using the given map and index as references, record the number of the activity card and complete the assignment on the worksheet provided. Upon completion, check their answers by lifting the flap on the activity card.

Sample Activity Card Tasks

Activity Card A. You are at Rockefeller Plaza between W. 48th St. and W. 51st St. and would like to examine the five restaurants in that immediate vicinity. Locate each of them on the map and list their names and numbers on your paper in alphabetical order.

Activity Card B. Number and list alphabetically all the restaurants you would encounter on your left-hand side as you stroll on Second Ave. from E. 65th St. to E. 46th St.

Activity Card C. In touring *only* those streets between 59th and 65th running from west to east as you leave Central Park, number and list alphabetically only those restaurants you would *directly* encounter along the way.

Activity Card D. Facing west at E. 49th and Second Ave., walk a complete rectangle back to your starting point, listing alphabetically all the restaurants you would pass on either side along the way.

4. Compare First, Vote Later

Goal: Making comparisons in social studies

Grade Level: 3–8

Construction: Have two or more volunteer students from the class run for political office, assuming the identities of prominent people currently campaigning for president, senator, mayor, or city council. The campaigning students must research their platform, using newspapers, radio, television, or the campaign headquarters.

Utilization: The class develops a record of the collected information, making a chart of each candidate's positive and negative aspects. At the end of an alloted time period, the class votes on the basis of the charted information, identifying statements of fact and opinion and propaganda, for example.

5. A Different Perspective

Goal: Conceptualizing time, space, and place relationships

*Developed by Diane Scatasi for the Wellesley School District, Wellesley, Mass.

Grade Level: 4-8

Construction: Have students make a three-dimensional model of the neighborhood surrounding the school. First, if possible, have drivers take groups of students to survey the area and make general maps of the area showing streets, buildings, and landmarks.

Modeling Mixture for Relief Maps

2 c. salt (500 gr) 1 c. water (250 ml)
1 c. flour (150 gr)

Mix the ingredients until they are smooth and pliable. On a piece of plywood, draw the outline to be molded. Apply a thin layer of modeling mixture of no more than one fourth of the thickness to the entire surface. Depress the clay where there are to be rivers and lakes and add additional clay to form mountains.

Away from a radiator the clay takes one week to dry. Paint with temperas and run strings to pinpoint specific locations.

Utilization: The class can then make a three-dimensional model of the area using salt clay or regular modeling clay (see recipe). Mark buildings, the students' homes, and the school with small flags, using toothpicks and construction paper. If desired, the students can also make charts stating the number of miles or blocks between two points and how long it takes to travel between the points by walking and by car.

6. The Order Is the Thing

Goal: Sequencing chronological events

Grade Level: 3-9

Construction and Utilization: Have students follow a newspaper story for a period of a week or more and make a time line of the events that occur. The time line could be prepared individually or as a class project. Hang a clothesline across the classroom on which events can be hung on cards and chronically sequenced. Trials, investigations, or journeys by world leaders provide many places, people, dates, and events to keep in order. Students could also take one complex article or television show and make a time line of its events.

7. Such a Deal!

Goal: Detecting propaganda

Grade Level: 3-9

Construction: A student chooses a topic or item to convince, sell, or persuade other students. After a selection has been made, an oral presentation is given to the class.

Utilization: The class then discusses what motions, words, and propaganda devices the student used. They can vote on which devices were most convincing.

8. Eyewitness Reports

Goal: Sequencing and making comparisons

Grade Level: 5-8

Construction: Arrange with two or three students or members from another class to stage a one-minute totally unexpected event in the classroom. For example, the group could run in, say a few words to each other, pantomime a crime, and run off. Later, have a few members of the class write down exactly what happened in the correct order.

Utilization: Compare the reports with the class and discuss discrepancies in what was seen. Draw a parallel between this experience and that of witnesses at trials.

TEACHING ACTIVITIES THAT INTEGRATE READING AND MATHEMATICS

9. Student Tycoons

Goal: Interpreting information portrayed through graphs.

Grade Level: 4-8

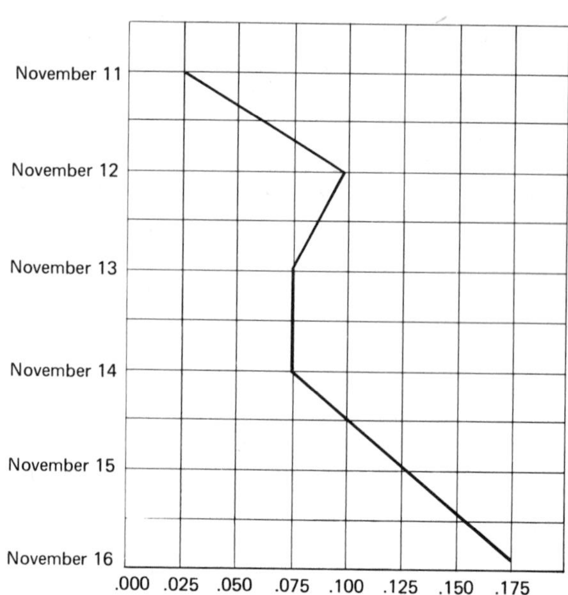

Construction: Assist students in choosing a particular kind of stock and aid them in keeping track of its losses and gains by reading the newspaper.

Utilization: Students can graph the daily fluctuations by putting the date on the X axis and the losses or gains on the Y axis. The class might also want to have a bake sale or car wash and buy a small share of their own stock.

10. Getting There Prepared and on Time

Goal: Reading representational information and organizing schedules

Grade Level: 4–9

Construction and Utilization: Make arrangements for the class to go on a field trip. The class is responsible for arranging the transportation, reservations, meals, supplies, and equipment. A different group could be responsible for each aspect of the preparation. This would involve reading bus or train schedules, lists, and tables of the hours museums are open. Another activity that would involve using tables is figuring the expenses involved.

11. Word Hunt

Goal: Developing an understanding of mathematical language

Grade Level: 3–6

Construction: Design and mimeograph a chart of math terms placed vertically, diagonally, and horizontally in rows and columns. Extra, nonfunctional letters can be placed in the chart. On a laminated card give definitions of mathematical terms.

Utilization: After reading a definition, the student circles the correct term in the puzzle. Words can be circled horizontally, vertically, or diagonally.

D	N	U	M	B	E	R	I	U
I	J	C	O	L	P	J	N	R
V	A	C	D	E	R	A	T	E
I	B	D	I	V	I	D	E	V
D	O	M	D	N	M	U	G	E
E	L	C	S	I	E	G	E	N
W	G	H	M	A	T	H	R	P
R	A	A	X	N	R	I	Q	Y
E	R	L	T	O	G	B	O	U
T	C	F	I	V	E	H	T	N

12. Treasure Clues

Goal: Following directions in mathematics

Grade Level: 3–8

Construction: Hide a small "treasure" somewhere in the room. Plant clues around the room that describe tasks to be completed in order to find the object. The clues could say "measure 82.5 meters from the desk" or "multiply 6 $\times$ 6 and walk that number of centimeters." Make a different set of clues for each player.

Utilization: The first person to find the object according to his clues wins.

13. Say What?

Goal: Developing an understanding of the language of symbols

Grade Level: 2–4

Construction: Write sentences replacing words with mathematical symbols. Example: $\div$ the pie in 1/2. Two wrongs do not = a right.

Utilization: The student rewrites the sentence substituting the correct word for the symbol. Depending on grade, other symbols may be substituted.

14. Our Favorite Things

Goal: Constructing math histograms.

Grade Level: 5–8

Construction: Prepare dittos divided into small squares or give each child a piece of graph paper.

Utilization: Have one student ask one question of other members of the class. Example:

What is your favorite color?
What is your favorite TV show?
In what month were you born?

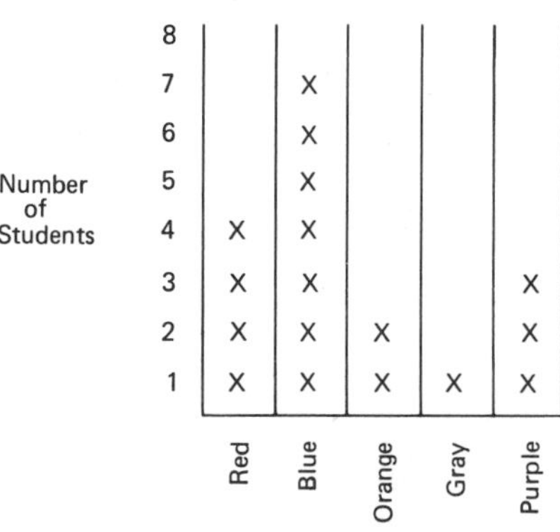

On the paper, the student labels the *X* and *Y* axis according to the topic (as shown). He then marks an *X* in the appropriate square to show the person's response. A short summary of the results should be written.

15. Our Community

Goal: Understanding picture graphs

Grade Level: 5–8

Construction: Assist students in collecting data about the surrounding areas of their homes or school. From the library, chamber of commerce, weather stations, or state house, they can find amount of rainfall in the different areas, location of natural resources, or elevations, for example.

Utilization: From the information gathered, students should choose a color code representing various levels, amounts of rainfall, and so on. Using the color code, the students could design a picture map showing the different elevations or the amounts of rainfall of the selected geographical area.

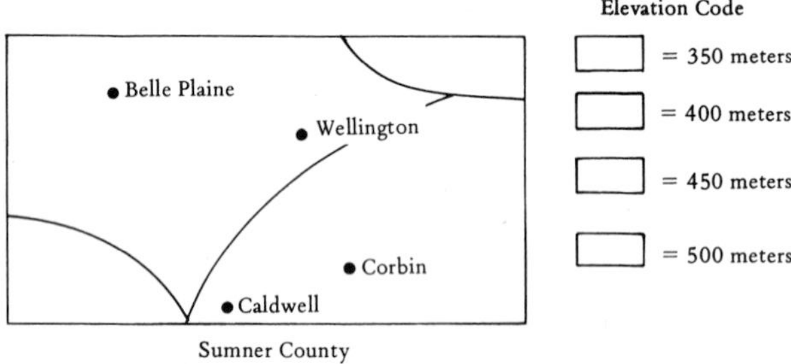

Sumner County

TEACHING ACTIVITIES THAT INTEGRATE READING AND SCIENCE

16. Matched Pairs

Goal: Understanding science vocabulary

Grade Level: 3–8

Construction: Make paired sets of index cards so that one card is a science vocabulary word and one is a short definition of that word.

Utilization: Cards are scrambled and placed face down in rows. The players take turns turning over two cards. If the word and the definitions match, the player retains them and takes another turn. If they do not match, the cards are turned back over and the other player takes his turn. Whoever has the most pairs when all the cards have been matched wins the game.

17. Scrambled, but Not Eggs

Goal: Understanding science vocabulary

Grade Level: 1–2

Construction: Divide a sheet of laminated paper in half. Label one side "carnivores" and the other "herbivores." Under each heading write the names of appropriate animals, but scramble the letters. Underneath each word, draw small boxes in which students can write the unscrambled words.

Utilization: The students should first try to think of animals that are plant or meat eaters, and then they should try to unscramble the letters. The headings can be changed to reinforce any vocabulary words: reptiles and amphibians, conductors of electricity and nonconductors, and so on.

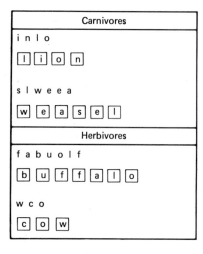

Carnivores

i n l o

l i o n

s l w e e a

w e a s e l

Herbivores

f a b u o l f

b u f f a l o

w c o

c o w

18. Science Ups and Downs

Goal: Understanding science vocabulary

Grade Level: 4–8

Construction: Make up a crossword puzzle on a laminated sheet of paper or dittos. If desired, give a list of words to choose from at the bottom of the page. The clues should be worded so that they give a definition or provide context clues.

Utilization: Students complete the puzzle by finding the proper word and writing it in the correct puzzle square.

19. Meaning, Meaning

Goal: Developing science vocabulary

Grade Level: 1–8

Construction: On a large piece of cardboard or oak tag, draw circles with scientific vocabulary written in each.
Examples:
mass, energy, work, heat, standard, substance, power

Utilization: The board is placed on a table and players sit about 1 meter away. Using small plastic or cardboard disks, the player aims for any word. For whatever word the disk lands on, he must give both the technical and nontechnical meaning. A student judge decides if the definitions are acceptable. The players receive five points for each acceptable definition—five points if he only knows one meaning, ten if he knows both. The game ends when each word has been given both a technical definition and a nontechnical definition. No word can receive more than one technical definition and one nontechnical definition.

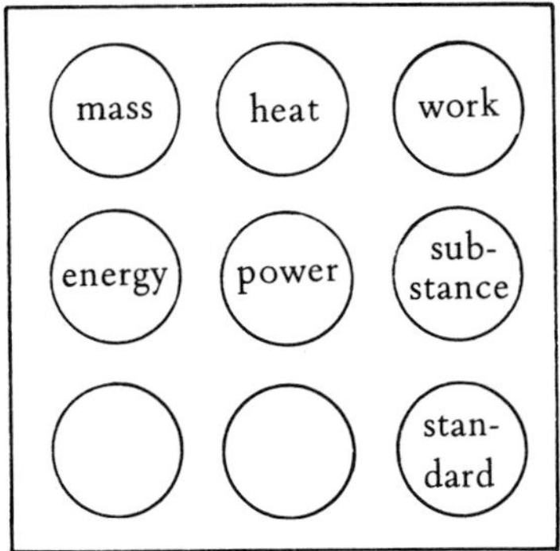

20. Moon Landing

Goal: Interpreting scientific formulas

Grade Level: 4–8

Construction: Make a large board game with a path of squares to follow. The beginning square should be labeled "Blast Off," and the ending square should contain a picture of the moon. The remaining squares should be blank or labeled with "Draw a card," "Lose a turn," "Go back three spaces," and so on. For "Draw a card" construct small oak-tag cards stating a scientific formula. One die or two dice should be secured for the player.

Utilization: Each player is given four playing pieces. The object of the game is to land all four playing pieces on the moon. Each player rolls one die, moves one of his four playing pieces the specified number of squares, and then follows the instruction on the square. If a player lands on a space that says "Draw a card," he must draw a card and interpret the formula correctly or else lose his turn. The first person to land all four playing pieces on the moon wins the game.

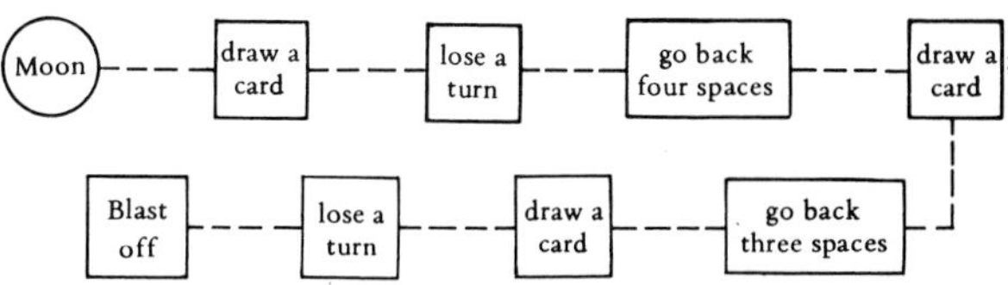

21. Solitaire Roots

Goal: Analyzing word roots (science)

Grade Level: 5–8

Construction: Choose four different root words for which there are twelve other words or word combinations. Example:
oat, oats, oat cake, oat like, wild oats, oaten, oatmeal, rolled oats, oat grass, oatmeal cookies, Quaker Oats, Mother's Oats

Make fifty-two playing cards with words on them from the four different roots. Number the cards from ace to king (Q, J, 10, 9, . . .) with the aces being the root words.

Utilization: Any solitaire rules can be used, with the goal being to get the king through ace all in the same row for each root category.

22. Science Tic-Tac-Toe

Goal: Understanding science vocabulary

Grade Level: 3-5

Construction: Twelve students can play this game. One student is the MC, two are contestants, and the remaining nine represent a tic-tac-toe board, sitting in three rows of three each. Write words from the science vocabulary on index cards with the definitions on the reverse side and give them to the MC. Write an X on nine large cards and an O on nine large cards. Each of the nine students representing the tic-tac-toe board is given one X card and one O card.

Utilization: One contestant is assigned X and the other contestant is assigned O. The MC reads a science vocabulary word for the first contestant. The contestant selects a student on the tic-tac-toe board to provide a definition. The contestant then states whether he agrees or disagrees with the given definition. To determine if the contestant received his letter, see the chart.

Student on Playing Board	Contestant	Scores an X or O
Gives correct definition	Agrees	Yes
Gives correct definition	Disagrees	No
Gives incorrect definition	Agrees	No
Gives incorrect definition	Disagrees	Yes

If the contestant scores the X or O, the student on the tic-tac-toe board holds the appropriate letter in front of him. Whoever is the first to score three Xs or three Os in a vertical, horizontal, or diagonal row wins.

23. Science Between Grades

Goal: Developing location skills involving the glossary

Grade Level: 5-8

Construction and Utilization: Have students write a short article concerning any area in science for someone in a lower grade. At the end of the story, the student-author should provide a glossary of the more difficult terms. Perhaps after the younger student has read the article, he can discuss it with the student-author, reviewing the terms in the glossary.

24. A Picture Is Worth . . .

Goal: Utilizing graphic representations as an aid to understanding scientific language

Grade Level: 4-8

Construction and Utilization: Have students make up a simple experiment. When possible, encourage the use of picture diagrams as a substitute for vocabulary. After attempting the experiment, the student should reexamine the diagrams illustrating the aids to understanding unfamiliar scientific language. A diagram is then exchanged with another student. After a second person has performed the experiment, the results should be compared, noting any changes that need to be made in the diagram. A modification of this activity could involve taking something apart that is not too complex and using diagrams to explain how to put it together.

25. Domino Demons

Goal: Analyzing word derivations

Grade Level: 5-8

Construction: Make a domino game using derivatives of scientific words. Cut rectangle dominoes measuring 5 cm by 8 cm from stiff cardboard. On one domino write two derivatives of the same word on both ends. This double derivative is to be used as the starting domino. For the rest, write two words of different derivatives on each domino.

Utilization: Play begins by turning all the dominoes face down with each player drawing five dominoes. Whoever has the double domino puts it out. If no one has the double domino, all the dominoes are returned face down to the middle, and players draw again. In turn, players try to match one end of their domino to an open end of another domino already played. If a player cannot make a match, he draws up to five dominoes from those remaining, and if he still cannot make a match, he loses his turn. The game ends when one player has used up all his dominoes or no one can play. In this case, the player with the fewest number of dominoes is the winner.

Examples:

mitotic	analyze	hydrolosis	evaporate
mitosis	analysis	hydrate	vaporize
osmosis	analytic	dehydrate	vaporous
osmotic			

TEACHING ACTIVITIES THAT INTEGRATE ART AND MUSIC

26. Socks Talk

Goal: Incorporating reading and art activities

Grade Level: 5–8

Construction: Students choose a play they want to perform with puppets. If they cannot decide on a particular play, assist them in rewriting a favorite story in dialogue form. Make puppets out of old socks with buttons and other pieces of material sewn on for facial features. If desired, paper bags can be used instead of socks. Decorate with yarn and construction paper.

Utilization: Students present the puppet show to the class, reading from the prepared script during practices. If possible, the students should be encouraged to memorize the lines for the final production.

27. Singing Syllables

Goal: Developing reading skills through singing

Grade Level: K–3

Construction and Utilization: Simply learning a song is an excellent way to practice rote memorization, rhythm, and proper inflection, accenting, and syllabication. For syllabication, in particular, have a group walk and clap the beat of a song, separating the words into correct syllables. Next, just have them sing part of the song, leaving out certain syllables, words, or phrases to develop a hearing for the proper separation of words.

28. Secret Word

Goal: Applying the skills needed to read music textbooks

Grade Level: 2–6

Construction: Instruct students in the basics of music reading—in particular, how to tell if a note is a C, B, or G, for example, by the line the note is standing on. Prepare laminated music sheets, placing notes in such a position that, when interpreted into letters, they will spell out a word or message.

Utilization: Students write the correct letter next to the note and read the secret word or message.

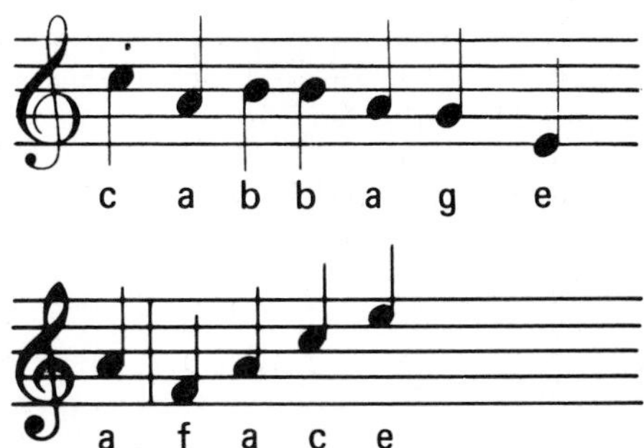

29. The Greatest Show on Earth

Goal: Combining reading/art/music skills

Grade Level: 3–8

Construction and Utilization: Assist the class in planning a small-scale musical. First they must select a play or write their own show about the people or events in school. After the script has been chosen or written, parts should be assigned including those of actors, stage crew, scenery painters, prop collectors, and costume makers. Next, the music for the show should be selected from contemporary songs on radio or TV, or just songs that everyone knows. Everyone should have the chance to help paint the scenery, practice the music, and perform for other classes.

QUESTIONS AND RELATED READINGS

If you feel that you have not attained adequate knowledge to answer the following questions successfully, we suggest additional related readings.

1. What is the role of reading in the learning process?
2. What processes are involved in the act of reading?
3. How are reading skills taught through thematic teaching units?
4. How is reading related to the study of social studies?
5. How is reading related to the study of science?
6. How is reading related to the study of mathematics?
7. How is reading related to the study of music and art?

Goal 1: To help the reader to understand the role of reading in the learning process.

Question 1: What is the role of reading in the learning process?

Carroll, J. "Words, Meanings, and Concepts." In *Thought and Language/Language and Reading*, ed. by M. Wolf, M. McQuillan, and E. Radwin, Cambridge, Mass.: Harvard Educational Review, 1980, pp. 26–50.

Smith, C., S. Smith, and L. Mikulecky. *Teaching Reading in Secondary School Content Subjects: A Bookthinking Process*. New York: Holt, Rinehart and Winston, 1978, pp. 24–51.

Tonjes, M., and M. Zintz. *Teaching Reading/Thinking/Study Skills in Content Classrooms*. Dubuque, Iowa: William C. Brown Company, Publishers, 1981, pp. 5–24.

Goal 2: To help the reader to comprehend the processes involved in the act of reading.

Question 2: What processes are involved in the act of reading?

Herber, H. *Teaching Reading in Content Areas*. 2nd ed. Englewood Cliffs, N.J.: Prentice-Hall, Inc., 1978, pp. 1–13.

Petty, W., and J. Jensen. *Developing Children's Language*. Boston, Mass.: Allyn & Bacon, Inc., 1980, pp. 206–12.

Sullivan, J. "Receptive and Critical Reading Develops at All Levels." *The Reading Teacher* 27 (May 1974), 796–800.

Goal 3: To help the reader to understand the concept of thematic teaching.

Question 3: How are reading skills taught through thematic teaching units?

Lamberg, W., and C. Lamb. *Reading Instruction in the Content Areas*. Chicago: Rand McNally College Publishing Company, 1980, pp. 297–311.

Roe, B., B. Stoodt, and P. Burns. *Reading Instruction in the Secondary School*. Rev. ed. Chicago: Rand McNally College Publishing Company, 1978, pp. 73–76.

Shepherd, D. *Comprehensive High School Reading Methods*. 2nd ed. Columbus, Ohio: Charles E. Merrill Publishing Company, 1978, pp. 149–150.

Goal 4: To help the reader to learn the importance of reading in social studies.

Question 4: How is reading related to the study of social studies?

Carpenter, H., ed. *Skill Development in Social Studies*. Thirty-third Yearbook. Washington, D.C.: National Council for the Social Studies, 1963.

Johnson, R., and E. Vardian. "Reading Readability and Social Studies." *The Reading Teacher* 24 (February 1973), 483–8.

Roe B., B. Stoodt, and P. Burns. *Reading Instruction in the Secondary School*. Chicago: Rand McNally College Publishing Company, 1978, pp. 237–53.

Goal 5: To help the reader to learn the importance of reading in science.

Question 5: How is reading related to the study of science?

Bechtel, J., and B. Franzblau. *Reading in the Science Classroom*. Washington, D.C.: National Education Association, 1980.

Dole, J., and V. Johnson. "Beyond the Textbook: Science Literature for Young People." *Journal of Reading* 24 (April 1981), 579–82.

Shepherd, D. *Comprehensive High School Reading Methods*. 2nd ed. Columbus, Ohio: Charles E. Merrill Publishing Company, 1978, pp. 231–71.

Goal 6: To help the reader to recognize the importance of reading in mathematics.

Question 6: How is reading related to the study of mathematics?

Aaron, I. "Readings in Mathematics." *Journal of Reading* 8 (May 1965), 391–5.

Collier, C., and L. Redmond. "Are You Teaching Kids to Read Mathematics?" *The Reading Teacher* 27 (May 1974), 804–8.

Sochor, E. "Special Reading Skills Are Needed in Social Studies, Science, Arithmetic." *The Reading Teacher* 6 (March 1953), 4–11.

Goal 7: To help the reader to appreciate the importance of reading in music and art.

Question 7: How is reading related to the study of music and art?

Gump, P., and R. Muller. "Using Art and Imagery in a Multimedia Center." *The Reading Teacher* 25 (April 1972), 657–62.

Marsh, M., et al. *The Spectrum of Music with Related Arts*. New York: Macmillan Publishing Co., Inc., 1980.

Vawter, G. "Music Attuned to Reading." *School and Community* 51 (November 1964), 21.

BIBLIOGRAPHY

Artley, A. S. *Trends and Practices in Secondary Reading.* ERIC/CRIER Reading Review Series. Newark, Del.: International Reading Association, 1968, p. 108.

Asimov, I., and R. G. Gallant. *Ginn Science Program: Intermediate Level C.* Lexington, Mass.: Ginn and Company, 1973.

Austin, M. C. "Improving Comprehension of Mathematics." In *Reading in the Secondary Schools*, ed. by M. J. Weiss. Indianapolis, Ind.: The Odyssey Press, 1961, pp. 391–6.

Austin, M., and C. Morrison. *The First R.* Cambridge, Mass.: Harvard University Press, 1963, p. 50.

Barnard, K., and C. Lavatelli. *Science: Measuring Things.* New York: Macmillan Publishing Co., Inc., 1970.

Barnard, K., et al. *Science: A Search for Evidence.* New York: Macmillan Publishing Co., Inc., 1966.

Bilodeau, E. A. *Acquisition of Skill.* New York: Academic Press, Inc., 1966.

Bisque, R., H. Pratt, and J. Thompson. *Earth Science: Patterns in Our Environment.* Englewood Cliffs, N.J.: Prentice-Hall, Inc., 1975.

Bruner, J. S., "On Perceptual Readiness." *Psychological Review* 64 (1957), 123–52.

______ . *On Knowing.* Cambridge, Mass.: Harvard University Press, 1962.

Bruner, J. S., et al. *Studies in Cognitive Growth.* New York: John Wiley & Sons, Inc., 1967.

Chambers, D. W., and H. W. Lowry. *The Language Arts.* Dubuque, Iowa: William C. Brown Company, Publishers, 1975, p. 75.

Clymer, T. *Ginn 360, 720.* Lexington, Mass.: Ginn and Company, 1970, p. 76.

Corle, C. G. "Reading in Mathematics: A Review of Recent Research." In *Reading in the Content Areas*, ed. by J. L. Laffey. Newark, Del.: International Reading Association, 1972, pp. 75–94.

Corle, C. G., and M. L. Coulter. *The Reading Arithmetic Skills Program–A Research Project in Reading and Arithmetic.* University Park: The Pennsylvania School Study Council, 1964.

Courtney, L. "Recent Developments in Reading in the Content Areas." *Conference on Reading* 27 (1965), 134–44.

Davis, F. B. "Research in Comprehension in Reading." *Reading Research Quarterly* 3 (Summer 1968) 499–545.

Dechant, E. V. *Improving the Teaching of Reading.* Englewood Cliffs, N.J.: Prentice-Hall, Inc., 1964.

Dole, J., and V. Johnson. "Beyond the Textbook: Science Literature for Young People." *Journal of Reading* 24 (April 1981), 579–82.

Early, M. J. "The Interrelatedness of Language Skills." In *Developing High School Reading Programs*, ed. by M. H. Dawson. Newark, Del.: International Reading Association, 1967, p. 101.

Estes, T. H. "Reading in the Social Studies: A Review of Research Since 1950." In *Reading in the Content Areas*, ed. by J. L. Laffey. Newark, Del.: International Reading Association, 1972, pp. 177–87.

Fay, L., T. Horn, and C. McCullough. *Improving Reading in the Elementary Social Studies.* Bulletin No. 33. Washington, D.C.: National Council for the Social Studies, 1961.

Forbes, J., T. Thoburn, and R. Bechtel. *Macmillan Mathematics*, Books 7 and 8. New York: Macmillan Publishing Co., Inc., 1982.

Gallant, R. *National Geographic Picture Atlas of Our Universe.* Washington, D.C.: National Geographic Society, 1980.

Gallant, R., and I. Asimov. *Ginn Science Program: Intermediate Level B.* Lexington, Mass.: Ginn and Company, 1973, pp. 33–34.

Gary, Indiana, Board of Education. *Reading and Language in the Elementary School.* Gary, Ind.: Gary Public Schools, 1962.

Gross, H. D., et al. *Exploring World Regions: Western Hemisphere.* Chicago: Follett Publishing Co., 1975.

Herber, H. *Teaching Reading in Content Areas*, 2nd ed. Englewood Cliffs, N.J.: Prentice-Hall, Inc., 1978.

Jarolimek, J., and O. L. Davis. *Social Studies in the Elementary School.* New York: Macmillan Publishing Co., Inc., 1973, 1974.

Jenkinson, M. "Ways of Teaching." In *The Teaching of Reading*, ed. by R. Staiger. Paris: UNESCO, 1973.

Joly, R. W. "Reading Improvement in Subjects Other than English." *High Points* 47 (January 1965), 22–30.

Karlin, R. *Teaching Elementary Reading.* New York: Harcourt Brace Jovanovich, 1971, p. 218.

Kenworthy, L. S. *Eleven Nations.* Lexington, Mass: Ginn and Company, 1972, p. 177.

Lamberg, W., and C. Lamb. *Reading Instruction in the Content Areas.* Chicago: Rand McNally College Publishing Company, 1980.

Lapp, D., and L. Lungren. "Musical Creativity: Exclusively an Elementary School Concept?" *American Music Teacher* 24 (June–July 1975), 21–22.

Lapp, D., A. Lahnston, R. Rezba, and A. Duelfer. "Is It Possible to Teach Reading Through the Content Areas?" *The New England Reading Association Journal* 13:3, 1978, pp. 20–26.

Linder, B., E. Selzer, and B. Berk. *A World History.* Chicago: Science Research Associates, Inc., 1979.

Mallinson, G. G. "Reading in the Sciences: A Review of the Research." In *Reading in the Content Areas*, ed. by J. L. Laffey. Newark, Del.: International Reading Association, 1972, pp. 127–52.

Marksheffel, N. D. *Better Reading in the Secondary*

School. New York: The Ronald Press Company, 1966, p. 174.

Marsh, M., et al. *The Spectrum of Music with Related Arts.* New York: Macmillan Publishing Co., Inc., 1980.

National Society for the Study of Education. *Reading in the Elementary School.* Forty-eighth Yearbook. Chicago: University of Chicago Press, 1962.

Reeves, R. *The Teaching of Reading in Our Schools.* New York: Macmillan Publishing Co., Inc., 1966.

Robinson, H. M. *Dimensions of Critical Reading.* Newark: University of Delaware, Reading Study Center, 1964.

Roe, B., B. Stoodt, and P. Burns. *Reading Instruction in the Secondary School.* Rev. ed. Chicago: Rand McNally College Publishing Company, 1978.

Russell, D. *Children Learn to Read.* Lexington, Mass.: Ginn and Company, 1961, p. 457.

Shepherd, D. *Comprehensive High School Reading Methods.* 2nd ed. Columbus, Ohio: Charles E. Merrill Publishing Company, 1978.

Stone, A., and L. Sherman. *Spaceship Earth: Life Science.* Boston: Houghton Mifflin Company, 1975.

Tirro, F. "Reading Techniques in the Teaching of Music." In *Fusing Reading Skills and Content*, ed. by H.A. Robinson and E. L. Thomas. Newark, Del.: International Reading Association, 1968, pp. 103–7.

Tonjes, M., and M. Zintz. *Teaching Reading/Thinking/Study Skills in Content Classrooms.* Dubuque, Iowa: William C. Brown Company, Publishers, 1981.

Wallbank, T., A. Schrier, D. Maier-Weaver, and P. Gutierrez. *History and Life: The World and Its People.* Glenview, Ill.: Scott, Foresman and Company, 1980.

Wallen, N. E., and R. M. W. Travers. "Analysis and Investigation of Teaching Methods." In *Handbook of Research on Teaching.* Skokie, Ill.: Rand McNally and Company, American Educational Research Association, 1963, p. 453.

Witt, M. "Developing Reading Skills and Critical Thinking." *Social Education* 25 (May 1961), 239–41.

SECTION IV

Your Reading Program

This section introduces you to the concept of a diagnostic-prescriptive reading program so that you may design a similar program for your classroom. Because you will base your entire approach to the teaching of reading on your personal definition of reading, we will continually encourage you to consider and reconsider your ideas about the nature of reading and to attempt to refine, as fully as possible, your definition of the reading process. Toward this end, you are provided with several interpretations and "definitions" of the reading process.

Approaches and methods of teaching reading, along with selected materials, are presented in an historical framework that traces the development of the pedagogy of reading.

You are introduced to formal and informal ways of assessing your students' interests and attitudes and your reading program itself. In each case, the emphasis is directed toward personalized curriculum planning and management. Simulated programs are included to demonstrate the integration of theory and practice.

To help you meet the needs of all your students, two separate chapters are included to help you understand and teach bilingual students and special students who may be mainstreamed into your classroom. A thorough understanding of the nature of the difficulties these children face is essential to an effective reading program.

Too often, classroom teachers are well trained in educational theory but are limited in their knowledge of classroom management procedures. The information in this section is designed to help you to integrate theory and practice into an effective reading program.

CHAPTER 10

Approaches and Methods of Teaching Reading

At the outset, let us state there is no one miracle method that will teach all children to read. Children are individuals and will learn individually, using the approach or approaches most meaningful to them. Thus, the teacher must be familiar with all approaches and materials.

C. Matthes, 1977

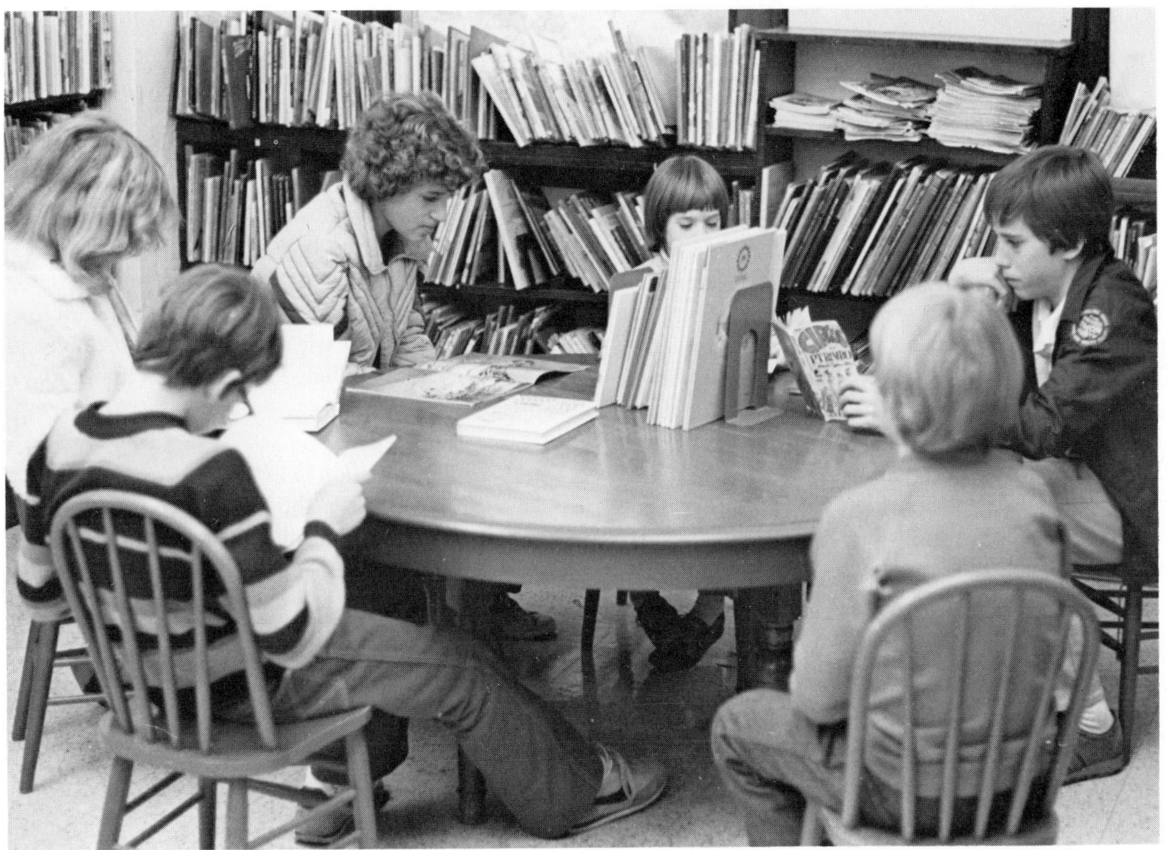

There is no one miracle method that will teach all children to read since children are individuals and will learn individually. (Photo by Linda Lungren.)

GOALS: To help the reader to

1. Appreciate the history of reading instruction in the United States.
2. Understand the various methods of reading instruction.
3. Recognize the strengths of each method studied.
4. Understand the importance of developing a personal definition of reading on which to base an instructional program.

Throughout this text, we have discussed the teacher, the child, the reading process, the components of reading, and related aspects of reading instruction. We turn now to the ultimate goal: teaching children to read. If there were a simple answer to the question "How do I teach a child to read?" there would not exist the great controversy and diversity in evidence in American classrooms today.

As teachers, you will have to make many important decisions in your classroom regarding such issues as instructional approaches to teaching reading, effectiveness of materials, evaluation of students' progress, selection of optional materials, and alternative methods of instruction based on students' needs. To make these decisions effectively requires a great deal of psychological and intellectual preparation on the part of the teacher.

We begin this chapter by presenting a brief overview of the ways in which reading instruction has taken place in the United States, to understand how educators in the past have answered the question "How do I teach a child to read?" These historical insights will help us to understand the advances made in reading instruction as well as the progress that has been made in scientific teaching.

HISTORICAL PERSPECTIVE OF READING INSTRUCTION

In a comprehensive history of American reading instruction, Smith (1965) characterizes the reading instruction of the various eras as follows:

Religious emphasis (1607–1776). During this era, reading instruction was directed toward a single purpose: teaching children to read religious materials (such as the Bible). The early settlers of America were seeking religious freedom, and Smith (1965) points out that "as the religious motive was the all-controlling force in their lives, it is quite natural that one should find it permeating and directing the instruction in their schools" (p. 12).

Nationalistic-Moralistic (1776–1840). Starting at the time of the American Revolution, the emphasis of reading instruction shifted. Politics now replaced theology as the center of intellectual interest, and reading materials began to reflect the patriotism of the times.

Education for Intelligent Citizenship (1840–1880). This era is in some ways almost a natural outgrowth of the preceding one. Patriotism was still very important, but it was recognized that it was not enough. "Educators came to realize that the success of the new democracy depended not so largely upon arousing patriotic sentiment as upon developing the intelligence of the people, whose ballots were to choose its leaders and determine its policies" (Smith, 1965, p. 75).

Reading as a Cultural Asset (1880–1910). This was a tranquil time in American history, and education reflected this serenity. More leisure time and peace of mind encouraged the use of reading as a medium for developing a lifelong interest in books and literature (and other cultural pursuits).

Scientific Investigation (1910–1925). Smith tells us that this time period is the "first truly great breakthrough in American reading instruction" (p. 157). The development of scientific instruments of measurement made it possible to assess the effectiveness of reading methods and materials. This, in turn, promoted reading research and led to the development of standardized reading tests.

Intensive Research and Application (1925–1935). As an expansion of the Era of Scientific Investigation, many new research studies were undertaken, and vigorous applications of this research were made. One of the developments that characterized this period of time was the application of broader objectives in teaching reading; the instruction was now aimed at developing abilities needed for well-rounded living.

International Conflict (1935–1950). This era was marked by national and international unrest. It came as a shock to many to discover that many of the young men in the armed forces could not read well enough to read printed instructions and manuals. This led to a renewed emphasis on systematic reading instruction at all levels.

Expanding Knowledge and Technological Revolution (1950–1965). With the sudden dramatic expansion of knowledge that characterized this era came the recognition that the key to knowledge is education and that the key to education is reading. Teachers were no longer the only ones concerned about reading instruction—it became a national concern and was emphasized heavily in American education.

In an effort to make this accounting current, we offer the following description of the periods since the publication of Smith's book.

Humanistic Influences on Reading (1965–1973). Educators began to emphasize the *individual* in reading instruction and methods and materials reflected this shift in focus. It came to be recognized that instruction must be based on individual needs, and there was a great flurry of activity to personalize instruction.

Reading as Information Processing (1973–Present). In the 1970s and early 1980s, a great deal of research has been directed toward understanding the process of reading. Many believe that effective reading instruction must be based on an understanding of how the reading process occurs, and reading as information processing seems to be the most widely accepted current theory.

We begin our discussion of the history of reading instruction by examining some of the early materials and the instructional emphases that reflected these various eras of American reading instruction.

Early Materials and Instructional Emphasis*

In the colonial period of the United States (which roughly parallels Smith's religious emphasis and nationalistic-moralistic eras), an alphabet spelling system was the methodology used to teach reading. The two sample pages shown here are from Noah Webster's *The Elementary Spelling Book*, which was published in 1800. Instruction was given in single-letter recognition; then combined letter-sound correspondences, such as *ab* and *ac*; then parts of words, such as *tab*; and finally, the whole word, *table*. Reading was almost a totally oral process in these early years because it included intensive instruction in pitch, stress, enunciation, gesticulation, memorization, and recitation. Some examples from Webster's book appear on the next page.

Because of the religious emphasis of the era, instruction was directed toward a single purpose: the reading of prayer books and religious and moral books. Robinson (1977) tells us that "content was considered more important than any methodology directed toward developing independent readers. Oral reading was promoted as *the* reading procedure for social and religious needs" (p. 46). Because the goal of reading instruction was solely to enable people to read religious materials, it was an extremely simplified process. Only a limited number of people were actually taught to read. Most children learned letters of the alphabet from the *Hornbook* and the *New England Primer*, which were among the earliest readers in the United States.

Horace Mann, an educational pioneer, was instrumental in introducing the whole-word method of reading instruction in American schools. He advocated memorizing entire words before analyzing letters and letter patterns. His approach stressed silent reading and emphasized reading for comprehension. About this time, the *McGuffey Eclectic Reader*, which emphasized a controlled repetition of words, was introduced. Children were beginning to be taught to read through the use of stories, parables, moral lessons, and patriotic selections in an attempt to develop "good" citizens. Although the *McGuffey Readers* did not have the most interesting narrative stories, they were an improvement over the existing texts because of their organizational scheme: sentence length and vocabulary were controlled to match the students' current developmental level.

On pages 288-90 are sample selections from the primer and the sixth reader of the *McGuffey Eclectic Readers* (1881, 1879). They are included in order to demonstrate the differences between the early and more advanced readers. Note the differences in print size, vocabulary, syntactic control, and content. Smith (1965) suggests that "McGuffey must be given the credit

*From the period of Religious Emphasis to the Era of Intensive Research and Application.

8 THE ELEMENTARY

ANALYSIS OF SOUNDS

IN THE ENGLISH LANGUAGE.

The Elementary Sounds of the English language are divided into two classes, ***vowels*** and ***consonants.***

A *vowel* is a clear sound made through an open position of the mouth-channel, which molds or shapes the voice without obstructing its utterance; as *a* (in *far*, in *fate*, etc.), *e*, *o*.

A *consonant* is a sound formed by a closer position of the articulating organs than any position by which a vowel is formed, as *b*, *d*, *t*, *g*, *sh*. In forming a consonant the voice is compressed or stopped.

A *diphthong* is the union of two simple vowel sounds, as *ou* (äŏŏ) in *out*, *oi* (a̤ĭ) in *noise*.

The English Alphabet consists of twenty-six letters, or single characters, which represent vowel, consonant, and diphthongal sounds—a, b, c, d, e, f, g, h, i, j, k, l, m, n, o, p, q, r, s, t, u, v, w, x, y, z. The combinations *ch*, *sh*, *th*, and *ng* are also used to represent elementary sounds; and another sound is expressed by *s*, or *z*; as, in *measure*, *azure*, pronounced *mĕzh'yoor*, *ăzh'ur*.

Of the foregoing letters, *a*, *e*, *o*, are always simple vowels; *i* and *u* are vowels (as in *in*, *us*), or diphthongs (as in *time*, *tune*); and *y* is either a vowel (as in *any*), a diphthong (as in *my*), or a consonant (as in *ye*).

Each of the vowels has its regular long and short sounds which are most used; and also certain *occasional* sounds, as that of *a* in *last*, *far*, *care*, *fall*, *what*; *e* in *term*, *there*, *prey*; *i* in *firm*, *marine*; *o* in *dove*, *for*, *wolf*, *prove*; and *u* in *furl*, *rude*, and *pull*. These will now be considered separately.

A. The regular long sound of *a* is denoted by a horizontal mark over it; as, ān'cient, pro-fāne'; and the regular short sound by a curve over it; as, căt, păr'ry.

SPELLING BOOK. 9

Occasional sounds.—The Italian sound is indicated by two dots over it; as, bär, fä'ther;—the short sound of the Italian *a*, by a single dot over it; as, fȧst, lȧst;—the broad sound, by two dots below it; as, ba̤ll, sta̤ll;—the short sound of broad *a*, by a single dot under it; as, wha̩t, qua̩d'rant;—the sound of *a* before *r* in certain words like *care*, *fair*, etc., is represented by a sharp or pointed circumflex over the *a*, as, câre, hâir, fâir, etc.

E. The regular long sound of *e* is indicated by a horizontal mark over it; as, mēte, se-rēne'; the regular short sound, by a curve over it; as, mĕt, re-bĕl'.

Occasional sounds.—The sound of *e* like *a* in *care* is indicated by a pointed circumflex over the *e*, as in thêir, whêre; and of short *e* before *r* in cases where it verges toward short *u*, by a rounded circumflex, or wavy line, over it; as, hẽr, pre-fẽr'.

I, O, U. The regular long and short sounds of *i*, *o*, and *u* are indicated like those of *a* and *e* by a horizontal mark and by a curve; as, bīnd, bĭn; dōle, dŏll; tūne, tŭn.

Occasional sounds.—When *i* has the sound of long *e* it is marked by two dots over it; as, fa-tïgue', ma-rïne';—when *o* has the sound of short *u*, it is marked by a single dot over it; as, dȯve, sȯn;—when it has the sound of ōō, it is marked with two dots under it; as, mo̤ve, pro̤ve;—when it has the sound of ŏŏ, it is marked with a single dot under it; as, wo̩lf, wo̩'man;—when it has the sound of broad *a*, this is indicated by a pointed circumflex over the vowel; as, nôrth, sôrt;—the two letters *oo*, with a horizontal mark over them, have the sound heard in the words bōōm, lōōm;—with a curve mark, they have a shorter form of the same sound; as, bŏŏk, gŏŏd;—when *u* is sounded like short *oo*, it has a single dot under it; as, fu̩ll, pu̩ll; while its lengthened sound, as when preceded by *r*, is indicated by two dots; as in rṳde, rṳ'ral, rṳ'by.

NOTE.—The long *u* in unaccented syllables has, to a great extent, the sound of *oo*, preceded by *y*, as in *educate*, pronounced ĕd'yoo-kāte: *nature*, pronounced nāt'yoor.

24 THE ELEMENTARY

BÄR, LȦST, CÂRE, FA̤LL, WHA̩T; HẼR, PREY, THÊRE; GET; BĪRD, MARÏNE; LIŅK;

ăpt	eärt	stärt	hûrt	pȧst	jĕst
chăpt	dart	pĕrt	shĭrt	vast	lest
kĕpt	hart	vert	flirt	dĭdst	blest
slept	chart	wert	eȧst	midst	nest
erept	mart	shȯrt	fast	bĕst	pest

No. 25.—XXV.

rĕst	quĕst	mĭst	eŏst	thĭrst	lŭst
erest	west	grist	fĭrst	bŭst	must
drest	zest	wrist	bûrst	dust	rust
test	fĭst	wist	eurst	gust	erust
vest	list	lŏst	durst	just	trust

Fire will burn wood and coal.
Coal and wood will make a fire.
The world turns round in a day.
Will you help me pin my frock?
Do not sit on the damp ground.
We burn oil in tin and glass lamps.
The lame man limps on his lame leg
We make ropes of hemp and flax.
A rude girl will romp in the street.
The good girl may jump the rope.
A duck is a plump fowl.
The horse drinks at the pump.
A pin has a sharp point.
We take up a brand of fire with the tongs.
Good boys and girls will act well.
How can you test the speed of your horse?
He came in haste, and left his book.
Men grind corn and sift the meal.
We love just and wise men.
The wind will drive the dust in our eyes.
Bad boys love to rob the nests of birds.
Let us rest on the bed, and sleep, if we can.
Tin and brass will rust when the air is damp.

SPELLING BOOK. 25

MO̤VE, SȮN, WO̩LF, FŎŎT, MŌŌN, ÔR; RṲLE, PU̩LL; EXIST; €=K; Ġ=J; Ș=Z; ÇH=SH.

No. 26.—XXVI.

WORDS OF TWO SYLLABLES, ACCENTED ON THE FIRST.

bā' ker	trō ver	sō lar	wō fu̩l	pā pal
sha dy	elo ver	po lar	po em	eō pal
la dy	do nor	lū nar	fo rum	vī al
tī dy	vā por	sō ber	Sā tan	pē nal
hō ly	fa vor	pā çer	fū el	ve nal
lī my	fla vor	ra çer	du el	fī nal
sli my	sa vor	grō çer	eru̩ el	ō ral
bō ny	ha lo	çī der	gru̩ el	ho ral
po ny	sō lo	spi der	pū pil	mū ral
po ker	hē ro	wā fer	lā bel	nā ṣal
tī ler	ne gro	ea per	lī bel	fa tal
eā per	tȳ ro	tī ġer	lō eal	na tal
pa per	out go	mā ker	fo eal	ru̩ ral
ta per	sā go	ta ker	vo eal	vī tal
vī per	tū lip	ra ker	lē gal	tō tal
bi ter	çē dar	sē ton	re gal	o val
fē ver	brī er	ru̩ in	dī al	plī ant
ō ver	fri ar	hȳ men	tri al	ġi ant

Bakers bake bread and cakes.
I like to play in the shady grove.
Some fishes are very bony.
I love the young lady that shows me how to read.
A pony is a very little horse.
We poke the fire with the poker.
The best paper is made of linen rags.
Vipers are bad snakes, and they bite men.
An ox loves to eat clover.
The tulip is very pretty, growing in the garden.
A dial shows the hour of the day.
Cedar trees grow in the woods.
The blackberry grows on a brier.

Noah Webster, *The Elementary Spelling Book* (New York: American Book Company, 1800), pp. 8–9, 24–25.

of being the first author to produce a clearly defined and carefully graded series consisting of one reader for each grade in the elementary school" (pp. 105–6).

The next "innovation" in reading instruction occurred during the latter half of the nineteenth century. It was a phonetics method, a synthetic phonics system, similar to the programs that were discussed in detail in Chapter 5. Teachers became dissatisfied with this method because too much attention was placed on word analysis and too little attention was given to comprehension. This method was temporarily abandoned, being replaced sometime around 1910 with the new "look-and-say" method. The look-and-say method also lost favor with many teachers because the child had to learn every word as a sight word, and children made little progress in learning to read.

The rise of the silent reading method began around 1920, the era in which scientific research was dominant in education. This method was much like the earlier program Horace Mann had advocated. Teachers were now urged to abandon all oral methods of instruction and testing. Robinson (1977) states that "there were increasing demands placed on reading for meaning, instead of on oral exercise, in order to meet the varied needs of society" (p. 50). In addition, the scientific era marked the advent of intelligence testing and educational measurement and "research reports began to show the superiority of silent reading over oral reading for both fluency and comprehension" (Robinson, 1977, p. 50). A great deal of reading research was widely conducted (Gray, 1925–1932; Good, 1923–1953), the results of which gave rise to the extremely popular method that followed—the basal reading method—launched throughout the United States in the early 1930s.

From Basal Readers to the Present

From the 1930s onward, due largely to the earlier emphasis on research and scientific investigation, the basal reading method was at the core of most reading instruction. The basal reading program included a student text and teacher's manual as the base of the reading program. Each basal presented a controlled vocabulary and introduced levels of syntactic complexity that paralleled children's development. The basal method was dominant over other methods until the 1950s and 1960s, when there was a return to *phonics*. This occurred because teachers were dissatisfied with the basal as the *only* form of reading instruction. Phonics strategies such as ITA and Words in Color (which will be explained later in this chapter) were used to supplement basals. Many basal series now contain a strong phonics emphasis.

In the 1960s, when the period of humanistic influences began, educational efforts were focused on meeting the individual needs of children. Techniques for *individualizing reading instruction* were encouraged, and *programmed materials* were developed to provide better classroom management techniques.

During this era, the language-experience method, an updating of an earlier practice, was promoted as an effective teaching method. From the late 1960s until the present, linguistic points of view have influenced the structure of many basal readers. Linguists have promoted the teaching of reading through patterned word units, for example,

Nan ran to the man.

Very few educators would argue against the theory of a personalized reading program for each child; however, the major problem with this approach was perceived to be a time constraint. Creating an efficient, well-organized system to manage twenty-five or thirty different personalized programs daily seemed like an overwhelming task, even to some excellent teachers. This situation occurred because teachers were not trained in flexible grouping techniques, personalized contracts, and classroom management processes.

These selections appeared in the primer of the *McGuffey Readers*:

LESSON XIV.

hōlds̤ tọ

blīnd Mā′rȳ

hănd kīnd

ā ọ k ȳ

This old man can not see. He is blind.

Mary holds him by the hand.

She is kind to the old blind man.

LESSON XV.—REVIEW.

I see ducks on the pond; Tom will feed them.

Tom is blind; he holds a box in his hand.

Nell is kind to him.

This old hen has a nest.

Mary will run and get the eggs.

LESSON XVI.

Sūe dŏll drĕss new hẽr

lĕt

ẽ

ū

ew

Sue has a doll.

It has a new dress.

LESSON XXXVI.

Mĭss wạnts wọuld tĕlls̤

rụle

kēep

gŏŏd

thăt

ēach

ụ

The girls and boys all love Miss May; she is so kind to them.

Miss May tells them there is a rule that she wants them to keep. It is, "Do to each one as you would like each one to do to you."

This is a good rule, and all boys and girls should keep it.

LESSON XXXVII.

schōōl child

chûrch whĕn

bŏŏks

slātes

What kind of house is this? Do you think it is a schoolhouse, or a church?

It looks like a church, but I think it is a schoolhouse.

These selections are taken from the sixth reader of the *McGuffey* series:

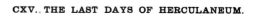

SIXTH READER. 401

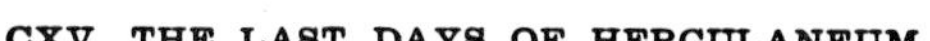

CXV. THE LAST DAYS OF HERCULANEUM.

Edwin Atherstone, 1788–1872, was born at Nottingham, England, and became known to the literary world chiefly through two poems, "The Last Days of Herculaneum" and "The Fall of Nineveh." Both poems are written in blank verse, and are remarkable for their splendor of diction and their great descriptive power. Atherstone is compared to Thomson, whom he resembles somewhat in style.

THERE was a man,
A Roman soldier, for some daring deed
That trespassed on the laws, in dungeon low
Chained down. His was a noble spirit, rough,
But generous, and brave, and kind.
He had a son; it was a rosy boy,
A little faithful copy of his sire,
In face and gesture. From infancy, the child
Had been his father's solace and his care.

Every sport
The father shared and heightened. But at length,
The rigorous law had grasped him, and condemned
To fetters and to darkness.

The captive's lot,
He felt in all its bitterness: the walls
Of his deep dungeon answered many a sigh
And heart-heaved groan. His tale was known, and touched
His jailer with compassion; and the boy,
Thenceforth a frequent visitor, beguiled
His father's lingering hours, and brought a balm
With his loved presence, that in every wound
Dropped healing. But, in this terrific hour,
He was a poisoned arrow in the breast
Where he had been a cure.

6.—26.

V. THE VOICE.

PITCH AND COMPASS.

The **natural pitch** of the voice is its keynote, or governing note. It is that on which the voice usually dwells, and to which it most frequently returns when wearied. It is also the pitch used in conversation, and the one which a reader or speaker naturally adopts — when he reads or speaks — most easily and agreeably.

The **compass** of the voice is its range above and below this pitch. To avoid monotony in reading or speaking, the voice should rise above or fall below this keynote, but always with reference to the sense or character of that which is read or spoken. The proper natural pitch is that above and below which there is most room for variation.

To strengthen the voice and increase its compass, select a short sentence, repeat it several times in succession in as low a key as the voice can sound naturally; then rise one note higher, and practice on that key, then another, and so on, until the highest pitch of the voice has been reached. Next, reverse the process, until the lowest pitch has been reached.

EXAMPLES IN PITCH.

High Pitch.

NOTE.—Be careful to distinguish *pitch* from *power* in the following exercises. Speaking in the open air, at the very top of the voice, is an exercise admirably adapted to strengthen the voice and give it compass, and should be frequently practiced.

1. Charge\`! Chester\`, charge\`! On\`! Stanley, on\`!
2. A horse\`! a horse\`! my kingdom\` for a horse\`!
3. Jump far out\`, boy\`, into the wave\`!
   Jump\`, or I fire\`!

4. Run\`! run\`! run for your lives!
5. Fire\`! fire\`! fire\`! Ring the bell\`!
6. Gentlemen may cry peace′! peace′! but there is no peace!
7. Rouse\`, ye Romans! rouse\`, ye slaves\`!
   Have ye brave sons′? Look in the next fierce brawl
   To see them die\`. Have ye fair daughters′? Look
   To see them live, torn from your arms\`, distained\`,
   Dishonored\`, and if ye dare call for justice′,
   Be answered by the lash\`!

Medium Pitch.

NOTE.—This is the pitch in which we converse. To strengthen it, we should read or speak in it as loud as possible, without rising to a higher key. To do this requires long-continued practice.

1. Under a spreading chestnut tree,
   The village smithy stands\`;
   The smith, a mighty man is he,
   With large and sinewy hands\`;
   And the muscles of his brawny arms
   Are strong as iron bands.

2. There is something in the thunder's voice that makes me tremble like a child. I have tried to conquer\` this unmanly weakness\`. I have called pride\` to my aid\`; I have sought for moral courage in the lessons of philosophy\`, but it avails me nothing\`. At the first moaning of the distant cloud, my heart shrinks and dies within me.

3. He taught the scholars the Rule of Three′,
   Reading, and writing, and history\`, too\`;
   He took the little ones on his knee′,
   For a kind old heart in his breast had he′,
   And the wants of the littlest child he knew\`.
   "Learn while you 're young\`," he often said′,
   "There is much to enjoy down here below′;
   Life for the living′, and rest for the dead\`,"
   Said the jolly old pedagogue\`, long ago\`.

In recognition of the need for a personalized reading program, without time or management constraints, several book publishers "rose to the occasion" in the 1970s and 1980s with managed language/reading method materials. These materials include elaborate record-keeping systems, basal readers, teacher's manuals, and criterion-referenced and norm-referenced tests. These tests are explained in detail in Chapter 12.

This brief historical overview of reading instruction practices in the United States may shed some light on important considerations that you will have to examine before selecting the best methods of instruction for your students.

The following chart summarizes the changing focus of reading instruction:

Approximate Date	Learning System	Materials	Characteristics
1600–1800	Alphabet spelling system	*Hornbook* *New England Primer*	Oral reading Memorization Recitation
1800s	Whole-word method		Silent reading Oral reading Reading for comprehension
	Controlled repetition	*McGuffey Eclectic Readers*	Silent reading Controlled repetition of words
Late 1800s	Artificial phonics system	Basic readers containing tales and excerpts from classics	Word analysis emphasis
Early 1900s	Look-and-say		Sight-word emphasis Testing initiated
	Silent reading method		Elaborate testing and measurement Silent reading emphasis
1930s	Basal method	Student and teacher workbooks *Dick and Jane* *Alice and Jerry*	Controlled vocabulary Oral and silent reading, phonics influence
1950s and 1960s	Phonics strongly emphasized Words in Color Individualized instruction Programmed instruction Language experience method	SRA materials	Individualization Individual language patterns Personalization
Late 1960s	Linguistic influence	*Let's Read*	Patterned word units
Mid-1970s to present	Managed language/reading	Use of a variety of methods and materials *Ginn 720* *Macmillan R*	Personalization Individualization Sequential organization

Philosophy of Approaches

If you examine the historical information we have presented in light of the social trends that reflected each era, it becomes apparent that *two* different philosophies of reading instruction have existed throughout the history of teaching reading. (Look at the accompanying time line carefully.) We refer to the first of these philosophies as a *sequential reading approach*, which encourages the use of materials that are systematically designed according to the developmental stages of children. In the following diagram, application of this philosophy is labeled *A*. The second philosophy may be referred to as the spontaneous reading approach, which encourages the development of materials related to the organic interest of the child. In the diagram, application of this philosophy is labeled *B*.

The goal of any approach, method, or philosophy has always been teaching children to read. In this respect, these philosophies are not entirely opposed to one another. However, the process of implementation is quite different for each philosophy. It may be productive to think of these two philosophies as existing in a continuum because they encompass almost all the existing methods and influences of teaching reading.

Every approach to reading instruction is contained within these two philosophies. Under a variety of titles, these two philosophies exist today, and both are probably in operation in every school. We refer to these two philosophies as the basic approaches to reading instruction that have existed at various points in the educational history of the United States.

Because of the emphasis on personalizing reading instruction, it would seem that the managed language/reading system is the most effective method of teaching reading. However, it should be noted that teachers' personal preferences and experiences sometimes dictate the use of a different method. Most teachers do, in fact, use a variety of methods in their classrooms in order to personalize each child's instructional program.

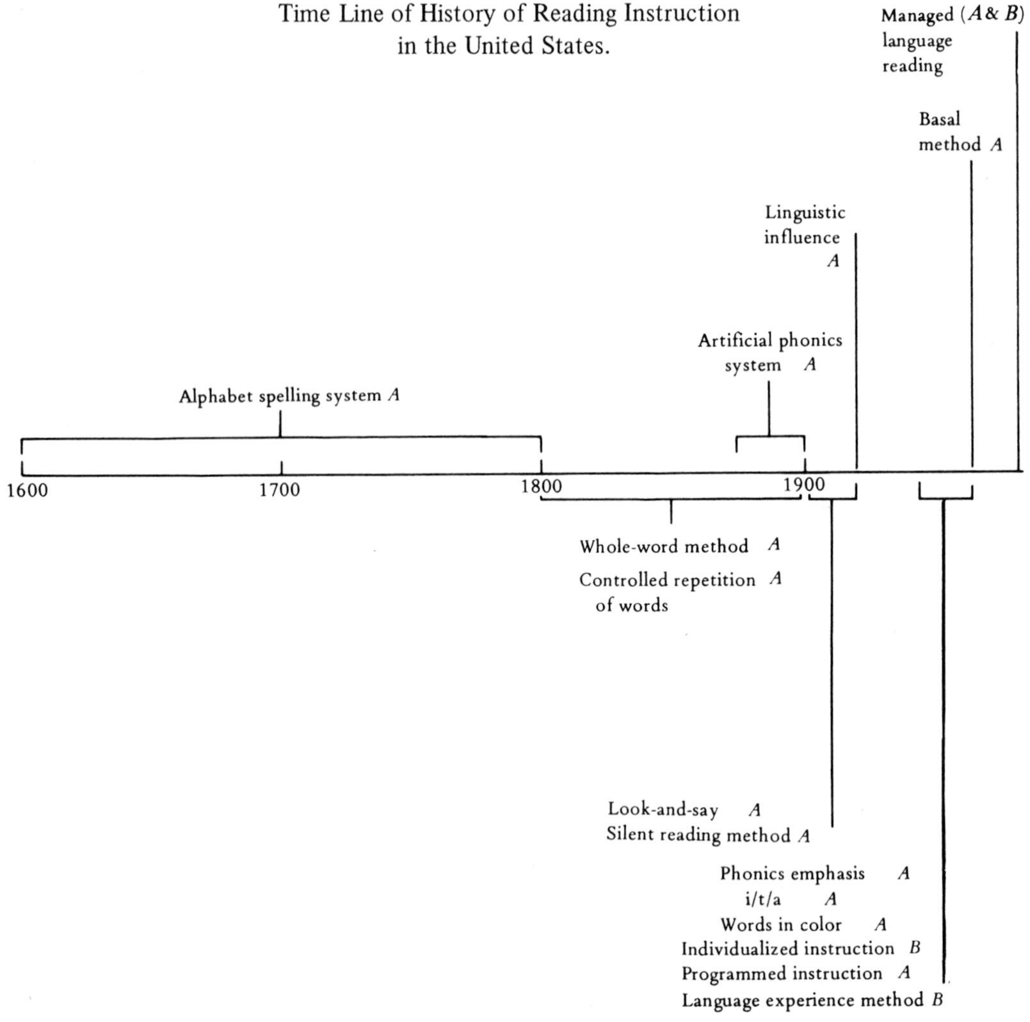

The following diagram illustrates the embedding of existing methods of teaching reading within the sequential and spontaneous reading approaches. The *sequential* reading approach is exemplified in *phonics* and *linguistic basals* and *programmed instruction*. As these methods clearly demonstrate, the sequential development approach emphasizes *decoding* followed by comprehension. The *spontaneous reading approach* is characterized by *language experience* and *individualized instruction.* Reading for meaning from the initial stages of reading instruction is the major emphasis of this program. The diagram also shows the origins of the current *managed language/reading approach*, which integrates the strengths of both the sequential and spontaneous developmental approaches.

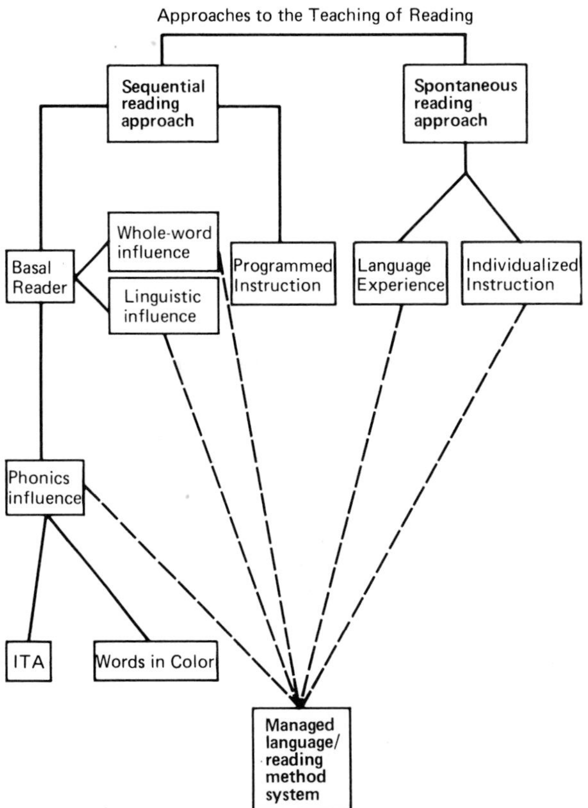

The strengths and weaknesses of each of the two basic approaches are readily apparent, and they can be explained in the following way:

Approaches	Sequential Reading Development	Spontaneous Reading Approach
Strengths	Prepared materials Logically organized	Personalized Emphasizes language base
Weaknesses	Lack of personalization	Too time-consuming Lack of manufactured materials Elaborate record keeping

Current educational philosophy has led to the development of managed language/reading systems that capitalize on the strengths of the system and rectify any weakness of the system. Creators of these new systems acknowledge the logical developmental stages of children, yet provide management systems that encourage the incorporation of spontaneous development. The creators fully realize that such systems cannot be implemented effectively without the classroom teacher. They strongly encourage the teacher to use the spontaneous language development of the child as the base of the reading program. The application of the managed language-experience approach is thoroughly explained in Chapter 15.

APPROACHES/METHODS/MATERIALS

In the following section of this chapter, we explore several of the methods of teaching reading illustrated in the preceding diagram. These methods provide the basis for most of the programs currently available for classroom use.

We use the following outline in presenting the various methods and their programs:

I. Sequential reading approach
   A. Basal reading instruction
      1. Whole-word influence
      2. Phonics influence
         a. ITA
         b. Words in Color
      3. Linguistic influence
   B. Programmed instruction

II. Spontaneous reading approach
   A. Language experience
   B. Individualized instruction
III. Managed language/reading systems

Sequential Reading Approach

The characteristics of the sequential reading approach dictate that the content to be conveyed is organized in an objective, tightly structured, and logically ordered manner. The primary focus of this material is directed toward the intellectual dimensions of the student. As suggested in the preceding time line, the earliest attempts to develop criteria for this approach occurred in early Puritan times. A Massachusetts law of 1642 extended this practice when it mandated that all children be taught to read.

Many basal reading series and some programmed instructional materials emphasize a sequential reading approach. The philosophical parameters of this approach rely heavily on the validity of premises similar to Bruner's idea that "knowledge is a model we construct to give meanings and structure to regularities of experience" (1960, p. 31), and on other similar theories of learning.

Basal Reading Instruction. The premise underlying the basal reading method is that reading is a developmental task involving the acquisition of major skills and that each of these major skills is comprised of many subskills. These subskills vary in difficulty and complexity and, therefore, need to be introduced to the reader in a logical, prescribed order. Not only do the subskills in each major skill area need to be ordered, but plans need to be made for integrating them into an instructional program so that the reader can begin to interrelate them. If this is successfully managed, reading becomes an integrated, meaningful whole.

Most basal series are generally developed for the elementary school, grades one through six, although some extend to the eighth-grade level. Traditionally, they include stories for reading levels from readiness through sixth (or eighth) grade or the equivalent subdivisions used by various school systems. The materials of a basal program generally include a collection of reading readiness materials, two or three preprimers, a primer, a first reader, two texts for the second grade, two texts for the third grade, and one text for each of the upper grades. At every level skill workbooks, dittos, worksheets, films and filmstrips, records, and supplementary readers may be included in the package. At the beginning levels, large charts or large editions of the child's book are available.

A detailed teacher's manual is provided for each text in the program. In these manuals, publishers usually include a statement of the philosophy basic to the particular program, a series of story-lesson plans, unit tests, lists of supplementary materials, and other related information.

A salient feature of a basal reading program is a controlled vocabulary. The program identifies and introduces a controlled vocabulary, new words in isolation and in context. This is followed by silent and oral reading and interpretation of the material that the child has read. Subsequent activities usually involve further skill development (word-recognition, comprehension, and study skills) and enrichment activities designed to relate the topic of the lesson to art, music, dance, or literature.

In a typical basal series, an effort is made to adjust the material to the maturity level of the reader. In beginning materials, only a limited number of words are introduced, and they are reinforced through *repetition*. These words are used repeatedly in the sentences on the subsequent pages and continue to appear throughout the book. As the child moves upward throughout the series, more words are introduced at each level with fewer repetitions. Some teachers' manuals explain the ratio of new words per page and the number of repetitions planned for each new word. The purpose behind controlled vocabulary and planned repetition is easily understood: too many new words introduced at once, and too few exposures to the word, lead easily to reading difficulties.

If you examine a basal reading series, you will also note an adjustment in print size and spacing between letters, words, and lines. These adjustments are designed to help the child who is learning to move his or her eyes from left to right and swing back to the beginning of the next line on the left.

Most basal readers, particularly those at the lower levels, are replete with pictures and illustrations. Durkin

(1976) suggests two reasons for the inclusion of pictures and illustrations: "One is that they add interest to a book; the other is the need for pictures to tell the story when limitations in the children's reading ability make a simple text mandatory" (p. 262). In addition, most basals adjust the ratio of illustration space to print space. At lower levels, illustrations often appear on every page or every other page. These are usually large pictures that are controlled for salient features. By the higher grades, illustrations may be more sparse, smaller, and more detailed. Samples of contemporary basals are presented here. The first two selections are taken from the primary-level 5 basals (grade one) of the *Ginn 720* series. Note the print size, the illustrations, the repeated vocabulary items, and the controlled syntax.

ISABEL

"You can't guess where we are going," said David Yee.

"It's going to be a surprise."

"I like surprises," said Isabel.

"I'll let you guess where we are all going," said David.

This selection is taken from level 13 (grade six) of the *Ginn 720* series. Note the print size, the sophistication of the illustrations, the advanced vocabulary—for example, sullenly—and the complex syntax.

FANTASTIC VICTORY

HAVE YOU EVER FOUND it difficult to start a writing assignment because you couldn't think of anything to write about? When Victory Benneker finally succeeds in starting her composition, she discovers something about herself.

"All right, class," Mrs. Friedman said, "your homework for the weekend is—"

"Aww," everybody groaned. Homework on a weekend is one of the crummiest ideas teachers have. Homework on a week day is bad enough, but at least it only louses up one evening. On a weekend it louses up three nights and two days, because if you don't do it right away Friday afternoon (and who wants to come home Friday afternoon and do homework?) you *think* about having to do it all through Friday night, Saturday and half of Sunday, and it ruins whatever else you're doing while you're not doing the homework. And when you finally *do* get to it, on Sunday night, your parents stand over you and say, "Why do you always leave things for the last minute? You had *all weekend* to do it. . . ." At least mine say that.

64

"Your assignment for the weekend," continued Mrs. Friedman, ignoring the groans, "is to write a composition—"

"Yucch," said Kenny Clark.

"—about one of these qualities."

She turned to the blackboard—which is not black, but green, and you're supposed to call it the chalkboard, but only Mrs. Friedman calls it that—and wrote:

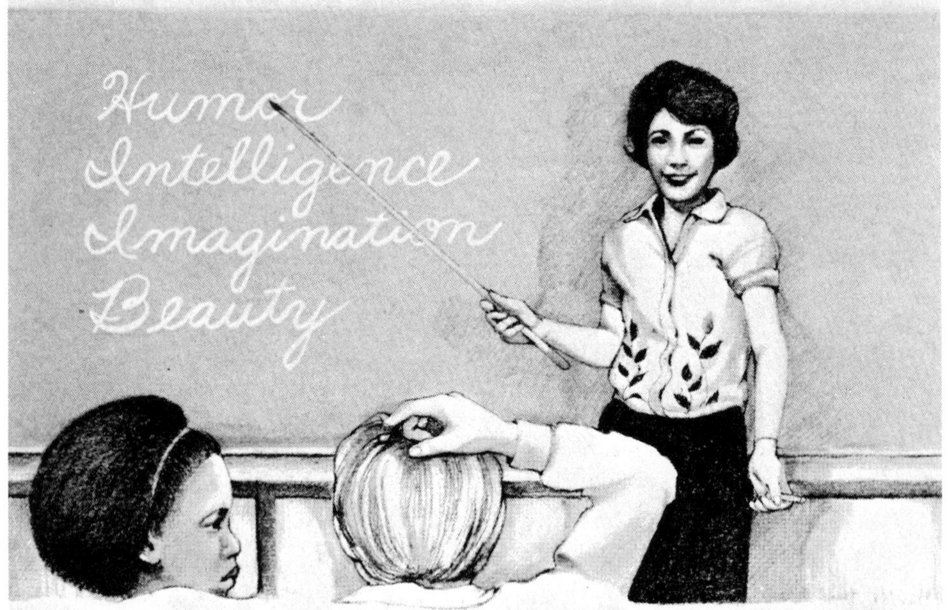

"Now what I want you to do is pick the quality that you think is most important, and tell me why."

"I don't get it," Kenny Clark said sullenly. "Most important for what?"

"For whatever you want," Mrs. Friedman replied. "That's up to you to decide."

"I still don't get it."

Basal Reading Series. Yarington (1978) states that basal readers are "used in 95 percent of the schools in the United States as the major component of the reading program" (p. 7). In recent years, basal series have been the focus of much of the criticism directed toward reading programs. It is not at all unusual to hear people speak critically of reading instruction and hurl disparaging remarks toward Dick and Jane, those characters found in the basal series that, at its peak, probably had been purchased and used more widely than any other series ever produced. Poor Dick and Jane became the symbols of the boy and girl found in all beginning materials and, therefore, had to suffer the insult and injury aimed at many similar basal series.

Many criticisms have been leveled at basal reading series. The most prominent of these criticisms include

1. The vocabulary and sentence patterns do not match the spoken language of the children.
2. The content is not interesting to children.
3. The books are developed for graded levels and the child is forced to read in the book for his or her grade level.
4. The manual is looked upon as the last word in instructional guidance and must be followed to the letter. As a result, the program is not adjusted to individual needs, and instruction often becomes sterile and uncreative.
5. Use of a basal leads to a uniform three-achievement-level grouping plan.
6. Children are asked to do workbook pages that they have mastered.
7. The basal reader provides the sole source of material used in teaching reading skills to children.
8. Basals do not provide for different learning styles or different modes of instruction.
9. Basals are not based on a sound theory of learning.
10. Basal series do not provide instructional procedures.
11. The content often furthers sexual and class stereotypes.

Undoubtedly, there is justification for some of these criticisms. However, we urge you to re-examine these criticisms in the context of these questions:

1. How many are actual criticisms of basal series?
2. How many are critical of the manner in which the basal series were *used*?

Many beginning readers possess an extensive oral vocabulary; it is true, however, that the content of beginning levels of basal series frequently does not reflect children's language and language patterns. Smith et al. (1978) say that since the mid-1970s some basals "have undergone a noticeable shift in content," part of which is "a more natural language, the kind of language people speak" (pp. 41-2).

Although there seems to be a need to loosen the control of the vocabulary in the content of the series, an attempt to match the extensive lexical diversity of the majority of beginning readers may not be possible or desirable when teaching a child to *read*. In answer to the criticisms that basals have had too strict control over vocabulary, Harris and Jacobson (1972) have found that

> A much less stringent control over vocabulary than formerly is characteristic of some of the new basal reading programs. . . . Thus it may be anticipated that a word list based on readers popular in 1930 may reflect this trend toward less exacting control over basal reader vocabularies. (p. 227)

As a teacher, you must be ready to personalize reading instruction to facilitate the language development of your students. No publisher can print a series that will reflect the oral vocabulary of every child in the United States. As a teacher, you will need to supplement the basal series with the experience of the children you are teaching. Remember, the basal series was designed to be only the base of your program rather than the entire program.

One of the most positive components of basal reading

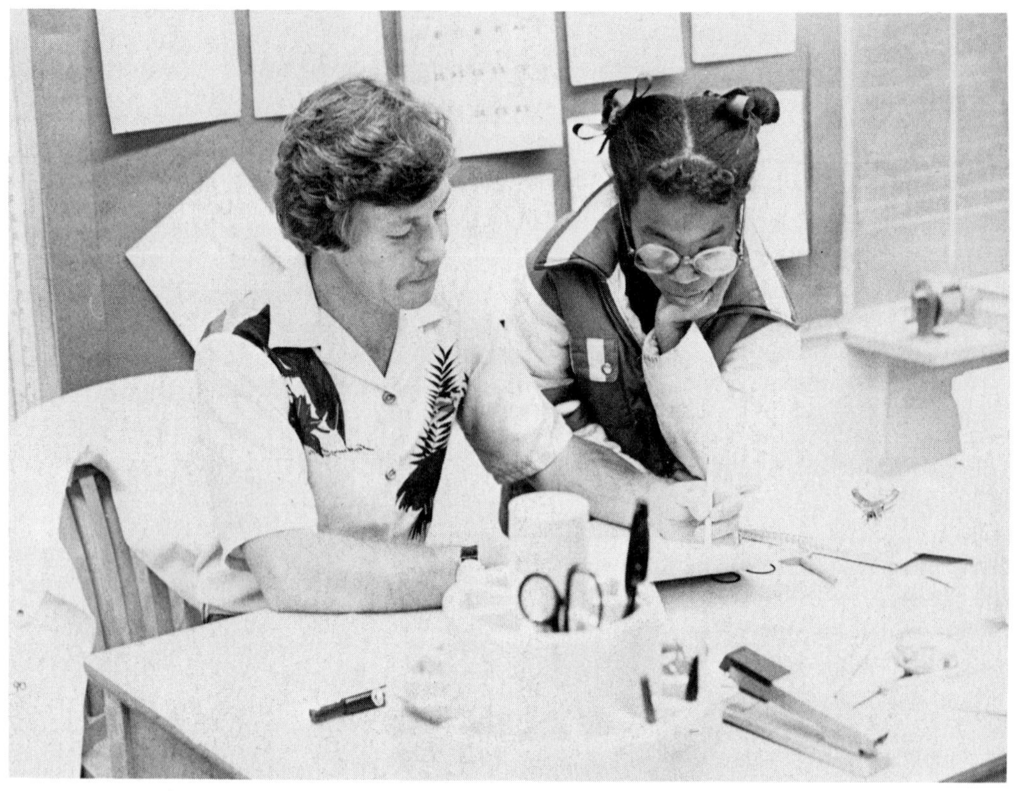

As a teacher, you must be ready to personalize reading instruction to facilitate the language development of your students. (Photo by Linda Lungren.)

series is the teacher's manual. These manuals provide continuity for the program as well as security and assistance for beginning teachers. Misuse of the teacher's manual occurs when a teacher depends entirely on the manual or guide for classroom instruction. As Matthes (1977) cautions, "a good teacher uses the guide as a guide—supplementing, enriching, and creating other experiences as the child's needs so warrant" (p. 16).

Today, all basal series are not the same. There are some (*Economy*, 1975) that provide a strong phonics program; others (*Macmillan R*, 1980; *Ginn 720*, 1976) purport to be more creative than the average in their content and managed enrichment activities; still others are developed around classical literature for children. The authors and producers of every series have attempted to build into their program activities that give the series unique characteristics. In the 1970s, some series attained uniqueness by shifting from graded to ungraded levels. Durkin (1976) cites the reason for this change as "an attempt to counteract criticism of the traditional graded approach to instruction" (p. 221). Publishers indicated increased difficulty of material through consecutive letters and numbers, for example, J, K, L, M, N. This shift is now a trend among all basal series.

In an attempt to counter the criticism that basals tend to reflect the values and mores of white middle-class families, educators have developed *The Chandler Language Experience Readers* by Carillo et al. and *The Bank Street Readers* by Black. While both series deal with multiethnic urban environments and contain many illustrations to motivate readers, criticisms have also been raised against them because they illustrate only the mores of one culture: the black inner-city culture. In an attempt to rectify the sociological narrowness of a one-culture text, *Ginn 720*, *Macmillan R*, the *Laidlaw Reading Series*, and many others have attempted to present a culturally diverse content.

These following examples are taken from *The Bank Street Readers*.

But one thing the boys and girls did wish for. They had never seen snow. They wished it would snow.

It did!

Snowflakes fell from the dark sky. They fell slowly at first, then faster and faster.

Cold white flakes of snow fell on the buildings. They fell on the trees. They fell on the streets. Soon the city was white with snow.

Snow was in the parks and on the buildings. Car wheels threw wet snow up on the sidewalks and up on the people. The policeman at the corner looked like a snowman. There was snow on everything.

132

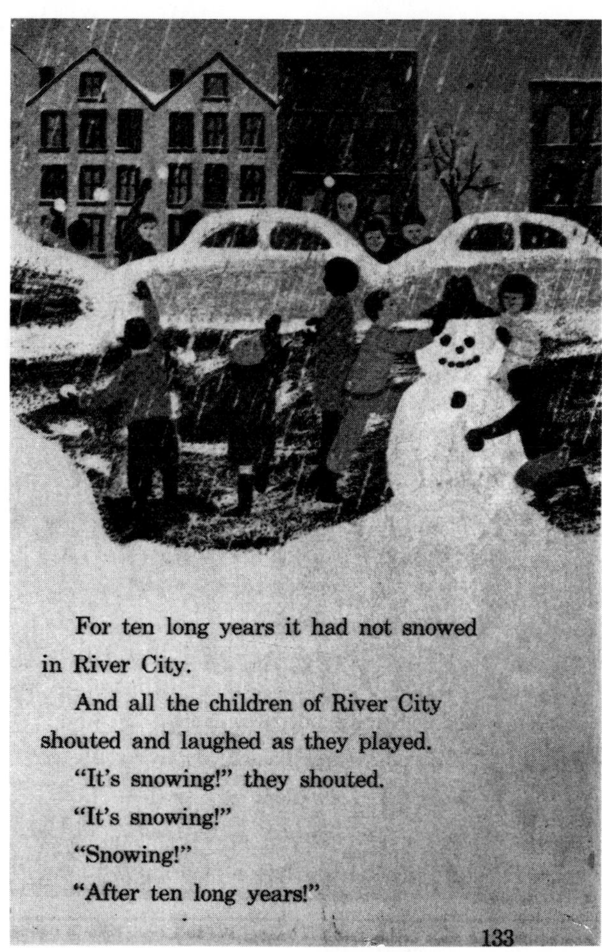

For ten long years it had not snowed in River City.

And all the children of River City shouted and laughed as they played.

"It's snowing!" they shouted.

"It's snowing!"

"Snowing!"

"After ten long years!"

133

From *My City*, Bank Street Readers, Grade 2, Level 5, Bank Street College of Education, Irma Simonton Black, Senior Editor. (Copyright © 1972 Macmillan Publishing Co., Inc., 1966), pp. 74, 75, 132–3.

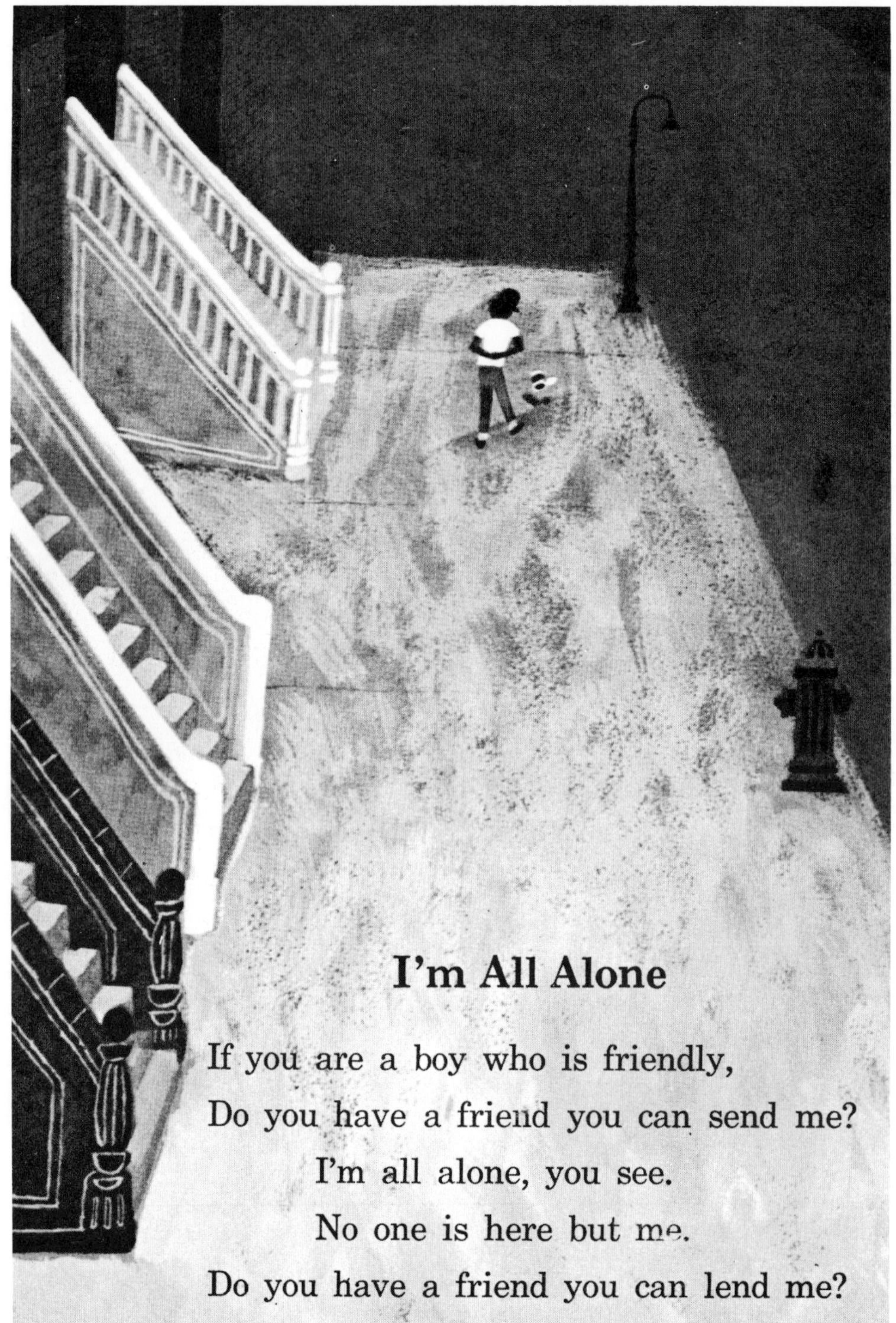

I'm All Alone

If you are a boy who is friendly,
Do you have a friend you can send me?
I'm all alone, you see.
No one is here but me.
Do you have a friend you can lend me?

Always Arthur

There was Arthur. He was always there.

Every day when David came home from school, Arthur was there, waiting for him.

Arthur was only four. He lived in the apartment next to David. He waited for David every day.

Some days he waited on the steps of the house. Some days he came to the door of David's apartment. But every day he was there, waiting for David.

75

The following pages provide sample selections from contemporary basals. The first two are taken from level 6 (grade one) of the *Laidlaw Reading Program*; the others are from levels 19–24 (grade four) of the *Macmillan R* series. (See pages 304–309.) Compare the differences in print size, spacing between lines, vocabulary, syntax, and illustrations. You will also note the *Macmillan R* selection reflects the efforts of authors and publishers to include culturally diverse material.

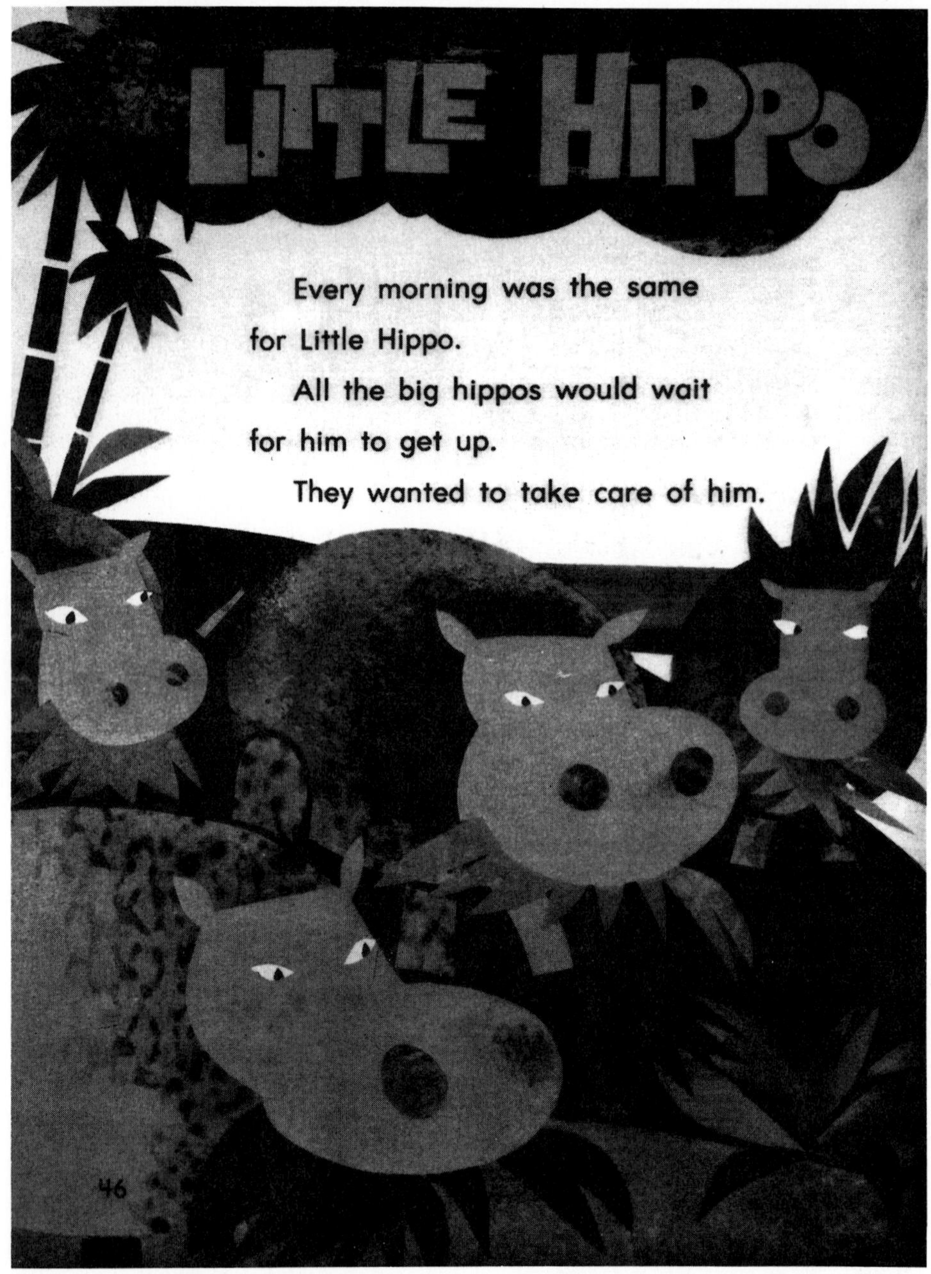

By permission of LAIDLAW BROTHERS, a Division of Doubleday & Company, Inc.

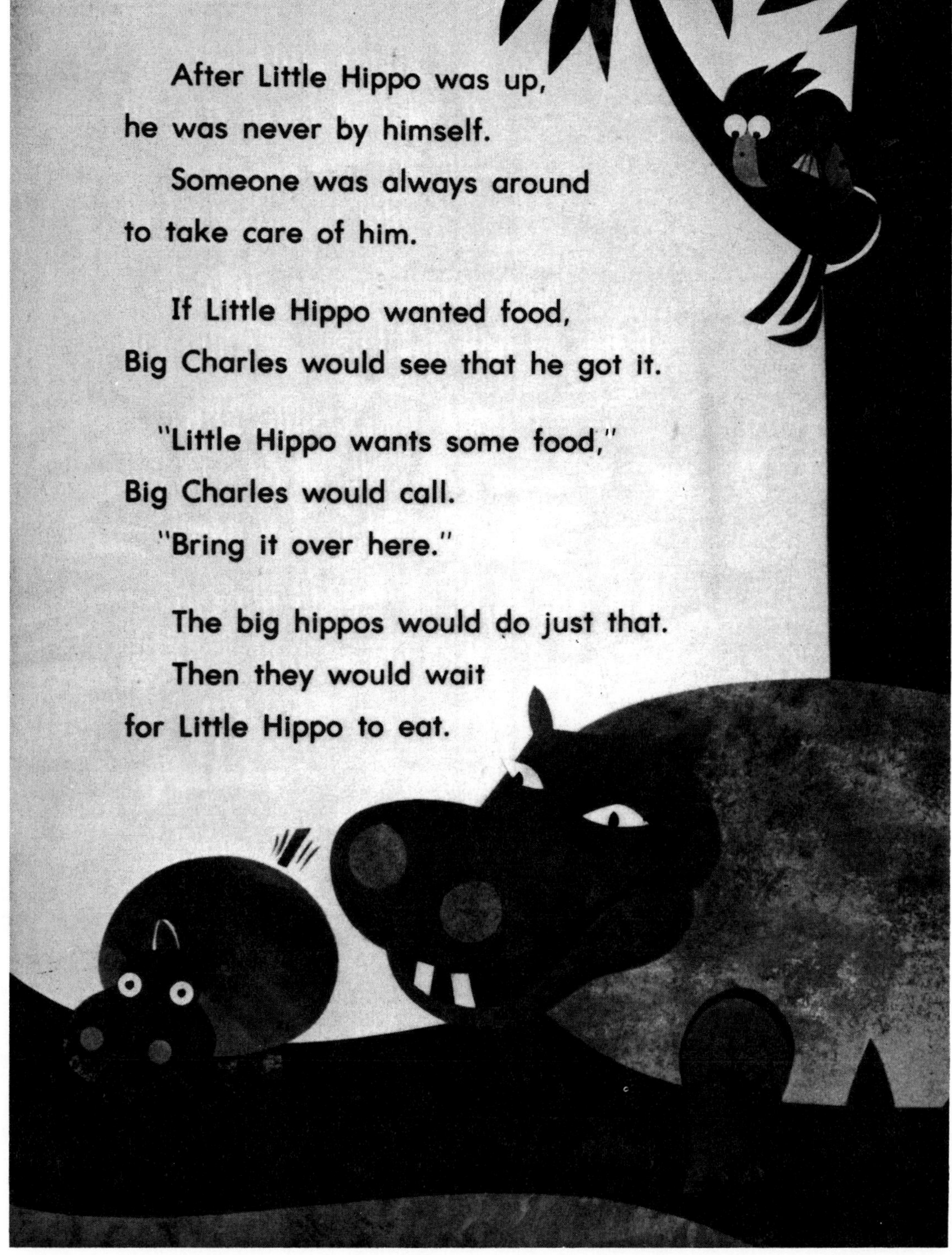
After Little Hippo was up,
he was never by himself.
Someone was always around
to take care of him.
If Little Hippo wanted food,
Big Charles would see that he got it.
"Little Hippo wants some food,"
Big Charles would call.
"Bring it over here."
The big hippos would do just that.
Then they would wait
for Little Hippo to eat.

KNOTS, BEADS, AND BEATS

Mary Lee Johansen

When you write, you communicate with special signs. These signs are the letters of our alphabet. You put the letters of the alphabet into groups called words. Each word sends a special message. But what if we didn't have an alphabet? How could we communicate?

What if one day in the mail you got a piece of knotted string? You might think someone was playing a trick on you. But the Incan Indians of Peru used knotted strings to keep records and to send messages.

These knotted strings were called **quipus.** The knots stood for numbers. The Inca used quipus to keep records of how many sacks of grain they had to sell. They also used quipus to keep track of how many children were born in a village. The Inca also sent quipus messages to other villages. The knots could tell how many days there were until a feast. They could also tell how many people were invited.

Rhymes and Reasons, Carl B. Smith and Ronald Wardhaugh, senior authors. Series r: MACMILLAN READING, 1980, Grade 4, Levels 19–24.

The American-Indian tribes of the northeastern United States used wampum belts to send messages. On these belts, white and purple shells were woven in patterns. The patterns were a language. Wampum belts were used to call tribes together for meetings. New settlers and American Indians also talked to each other with wampum belts. Through these shell messages, each knew what the other wanted to trade.

Some African tribes used beads on cords to send messages. For messages about food or work, they used black and white beads. They saved their brightly colored beads for love letters.

Today, in parts of Africa, drums are an important way of sending messages. Drums announce the arrival of visitors. Drums are often the fastest way to send news.

People who live on islands near China and Japan also use drums to send messages. Scientists who work on these islands find drums very useful. Once a doctor in a hurry needed someone to take him across a river. But all the people of the village were working some distance away. The doctor quickly beat out this message on a drum: "I need someone with a boat to take me across the river." In a short time, several men came paddling down the river in their boats.

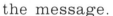

Scientists studying the birds and plants of these islands use drums, too. They beat out messages to tell people far away what kinds of birds or plants they want for their studies. They always tell how much they will pay for what they need.

Quipus and wampum belts are two of the ways people communicated years ago. Drums are one way in which people still send messages today. But one thing is sure. No matter what system people use for communicating, a person has to know what the drumbeats, the knots, or the shell or bead patterns mean in order to get the message.

It is likely that basal series will always have their critics; however, remember that basals can be an asset to you as a classroom teacher when used *properly*. In recent years, publishers have made serious efforts to include relevant stories and to provide technical assistance for teachers. Individualized instruction and using basal readers need not be diametrically opposing methods of teaching reading. We urge you to examine a basal series for yourself and then decide if it is useful for your purposes. In doing so, you will find that basals used properly will aid you in the process of individualizing and personalizing your curriculum.

Whole-Word Methodology. Whole-word instruction is a method of teaching unfamiliar vocabulary. It is often referred to as the look-and-say method, which Cheek and Cheek (1980) define as "the development of the reading skills necessary to remember words that occur most frequently in reading and that are not easily analyzed through other procedures" (p. 265). When a child encounters an unfamiliar vocabulary word, he or she can "attack" it in one of three ways.

1. *Phonics*: Letter-by-letter, sound-by-sound analysis.
2. *Structural Analysis*: Word part (prefix, root, suffix) analysis.
3. *Whole Word*: "What does that say?"

Similarly, since the whole-word method involves instant identification of the whole word, each time you turn to your students and say, "What does that word say?" you will be using the whole-word method of instruction.

The whole-word method is commonly used in basal readers because children need to learn basic sight words such as *saw*, *was*, *they*, *under*, *over*, *it*, *them*, and because children may not have acquired word attack skills yet. The whole-word method of instruction is also necessary because the English language is not a perfectly alphabetic language. Twenty-six letters in the English alphabet represent approximately forty-four sounds. In many instances, it is difficult to predict through phonetic analysis the sound patterns of many irregular words. Common words such as *walk*, *talk*, *through*, *although*, and *lamb*, as well as words derived from other languages—*chamois*, *hors d'oeuvre*, *depot*, *choir*, *vein*, *suite*—are taught more easily through the whole-word method. It may also be useful when teaching *homographs*

Bow your head down.

Paul has a bow and arrow.

The captain of the ship is on the bow.

I read before I go to bed.

Larry read the directions twice.

or *homophones*

The weather vane is crooked.

Myra is vain about her pretty coat.

The nurse drew blood from the vein in my arm.

Lynn put sand in the pail.

Jan looks a little pale today.

It seems obvious that knowing such words on sight would certainly be more productive to the reader than engaging in an analysis of letter-sound relationships.

As you can see, when you teach children whole words, you are relying heavily on their visual discrimination ability. This topic was discussed in Chapters 3 and 5; however, let us re-emphasize that many studies (Durrell, 1958; Barrett, 1965; Silvaroli, 1965; Samuels, 1972) suggest that the major visual discrimination skill associated with reading success is the ability to discriminate letters of the alphabet. The necessity of this skill becomes quite obvious when you are teaching whole words; for example,

This word is pat.
It looks like bat, except
pat begins with p and
bat begins with b.

After several exposures to these words, they will become part of students' whole-word sight vocabulary. You may recall that this is the same procedure used when introducing students to the basic sight words of the Dolch Sight Vocabulary list found in Chapter 6.

Phonics Influence. The phonic approach is another

method for teaching word recognition, the goal of which "is to give the child a key to independently unlock unfamiliar words" (Matthes, 1977, p. 44). It has been used widely since the late 1800s when educators recognized the value of letter-sound relationships as an aid to identifying unfamiliar words. Although the importance of such a process is quite obvious, it is equally important to realize that phonics can only be a partial word analysis process because the English language contains twenty-six letters representing approximately forty-four sounds. The English language, which frequently borrows words of foreign origin, does not have an exact one-to-one sound symbol correspondence. Even though such limitations are a reality, phonics instruction is quite important and has for decades been part of basal materials. (See Chapter 5 for an in-depth discussion of the content of phonics as well as classroom application strategies.) Over the years, attempts have been made to develop teaching materials that would alleviate phonic inconsistencies. We examine two such attempts, *ITA* and *Words in Color*.

ITA. ITA, the initial teaching alphabet, was devised by an Englishman, Sir James Pitman, in 1964. His augmented alphabet was designed to alleviate some of the confusion caused by the fact that some graphemic symbols must represent more than one sound and that several sounds can be represented by multiple spellings. The ITA, an artifical orthography, has forty-four symbols. In formulating this alphabet, an attempt was made to illustrate the upper half of the alphabetic letter as it was illustrated in the traditional roman alphabet. This was an attempt to aid the student who would eventually have to transfer to the traditional orthography. It was believed that such illustrations would make the transition easier.

The ITA is not a method of reading instruction; rather, it is a tool that can be integrated into any method of instruction. The Early-to-Read program (1966) has been circulated throughout America and used in a number of school systems in beginning reading programs. ITA can be used readily in a language-experience program. Using the ITA, however, can have many disadvantages.

Researchers have discovered that children who begin reading through an ITA method often have difficulty transferring their reading skills to texts that use traditional orthography. A second criticism of the ITA method is the difficulty that many children experience with learning to spell. Additionally, use of the ITA represents a large capital investment in new reading books and library books. Pitman's alphabet is shown here.

æ face · b bed · c cat · d dog · ee key
f feet · g leg · h hat · ie fly · j jug · k key
l letter · m man · n nest · œ over · p pen · r girl
r red · s spoon · t tree · ue use · v voice · w window
y yes · z zebra · z daisy · wh when · ch chair
th three · th the · sh shop · ʒ television · ng ring
a father · au ball · a cap · e egg · i milk · o box
u up · ω book · ω spoon · ou out · oi oil

James Pitman's forty-four symbol alphabet.

WORDS-IN-COLOR. Words-in-Color was developed by Gattegno (1962) to help children in phonics analysis. A color is used to represent an English speech sound, regardless of which letter or combination of letters represents the sound. The material consists of charts with words, letters, and sounds represented by forty-seven distinctive colors.

Twenty-one charts contain word illustrations, while letters and letter combinations are presented on six phonic-code charts. For example, the following phonic codes are presented to represent the sound of long $\bar{A}$.

a – able	eigh – weigh
ey – they	aigh – straight
ay – hay	ea – great
ai – mail	

Whether you pronounce each of these words as a long $\bar{A}$ sound depends upon your dialect. Each time any of these long $\bar{A}$ sounds appear in the word, they are coded *green*. Each time the short $\breve{a}$ sound appears in a word, it is coded white. All letter combinations representing the sound of long $\bar{E}$ are colored vermillion. Color codes are presented for forty-seven English sound combinations.

Words-in-Color may limit children in their selection of reading materials because very few other materials are prepared with this color-sound code. These materials also rely heavily on phonics instruction, and as with any phonics program, children rely heavily on letter sounds and word parts rather than on letter names and whole words. Children may also have difficulty with the visual discrimination of colors because the exactness of color is not significant. For example, when observing one series of color shades (dark green, olive green, yellow green, light green, emerald green, and leaf green), potential discrimination problems become obvious.

Linguistic Influences. Linguistics is the scientific study of language, and its influence on basal reading instruction is relatively new. Linguistics focuses on the sounds used in language, the words that result from a combination of sounds, and the meanings attached to these sounds. It also involves the structuring of words into meaningful units. Among the linguistic reading programs developed, the influence of the structural linguists seems strongest at the present time.

Since the appearance of the first linguistic series to be developed, *Let's Read* (Bloomfield and Barnhart, 1961), a number of other linguistic reading programs have appeared: *Merrill Linguistic Readers,* the *Miami Linguistic Reading* program, and the *Palo Alto Linguistic Program*. These series use strict vocabulary control in beginning materials to facilitate the teaching of certain phonic principles. Students learn the sound-symbol relationships for specified consonants and the short sound of one or two vowels. Then, as many different words as possible are made from the combination of these letters. The following set of sentences illustrates the type of content characterizing the beginning levels of these programs:

Dan has a fan.

The fan is tan.

Dan's fan is tan.

Some series do not include pictures or illustrations with their stories. This is because some authors support the theory that pictures are an unnecessary crutch and should be avoided. Other authors achieve a compromise between stark reading materials and ordinary illustrations by using very simple illustrations involving one or two colors.

Some linguists criticize basal reading programs because the language patterns used are unnatural, for example, "Oh, oh, oh. See Spot run." However, it is also difficult to consider sentences about "Dan, the fan man" to be reflective of natural expression. It is true, though, that as linguistic programs move to more advanced levels, sentence patterns reflect ordinary language usage. In addition, when they are compared with other basal materials on an equivalent level, the sentences in the linguistic readers often appear more complex. (The following example is taken from the *Palo Alto Reading Program*, Book 20.)

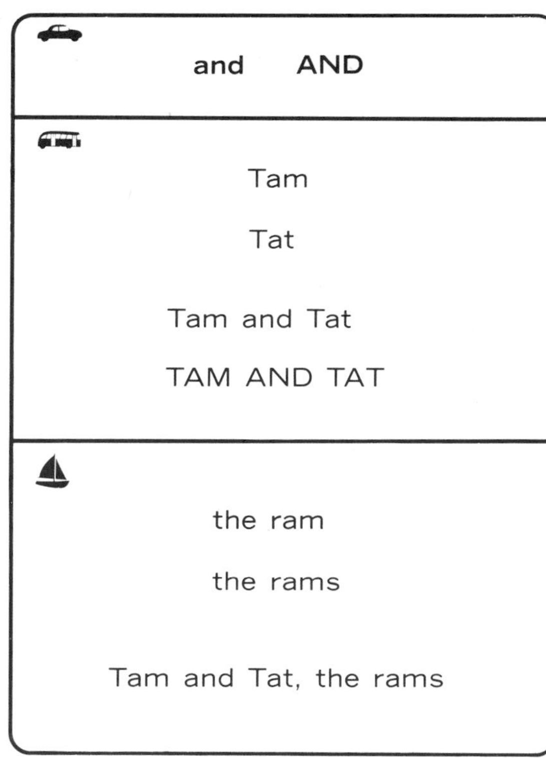

and AND

Tam

Tat

Tam and Tat

TAM AND TAT

the ram

the rams

Tam and Tat, the rams

TAM AND TAT

I see Tam.
I see Tat.

I see Tam and Tat.

I see Tam, the ram.
I see Tat, the ram.

I see Tam and Tat, the rams

Ham for Nat

Dad had a tin can.
The can had bits of ham in it.
The ham is for Nat.
Dad had to fit the bits of ham
into Nat's tin pan.

Nat ran to look.
He had a bit of ham.

Ham for Dan

A bit of ham is in a tin can.
It's for Dan.

Dan looks into the can.
Rags looks at Dan.
He sits and wags for the ham.

Ham fat is bad for Rags.
The ham in the can is Dan's.

The Dragon That Laughed

Long ago, in the days of King Arthur, there lived a terrible dragon. It lived in a cave in the forest. It was unlucky for any person to be in the forest at nighttime. The terrible dragon might be roaming about looking for victims. Fire and smoke came from its nostrils. Chilling roars came from its mouth. Its long claws tore up the ground. Its huge tail snapped the trees as if they were twigs. Indeed, it was a terrible dragon. And all who lived in King Arthur's kingdom feared the terrible dragon—all but one person, Sir Dunton the Terrible.

It was said that the terrible dragon was once a relative of Sir Dunton. It was said that was why they understood each other. Sir Dunton plotted with the

Charles E. Fries et al., *Merrill Linguistic Readers*. Reader 2. Columbus, Ohio: Charles E. Merrill Publishing Company, 1966, pp. 16–17. Reprinted by permission.

Criticisms of linguistic reading programs include the following:

1. There is no *one* linguistic approach to reading instruction.
2. The controlled vocabulary does not take into account the vocabulary of the children.
3. Decoding is overemphasized and comprehension is underemphasized.
4. Word-by-word reading is encouraged.
5. Only words with regular spelling patterns are taught initially.
6. Pictures, which may stimulate interest or help with decoding unknown words, are often omitted.

The aspect of linguistic programs that has provoked the most unfavorable reactions is the rather monotonous content that results from the patterns of letter substitution and morpheme substitutions. Some teachers find it extremely difficult to generate enthusiasm for "Dan, the fan man." Other teachers, however, feel that content is of little significance in the initial stages of reading and that the security that children gain from the contact with these dependable sound-symbol patterns more than compensates for the lack of content substance. This pattern generates dependability and its concomitant success generates its own success.

The selections on pages 313–314 are from different programs illustrating the variety in linguistic reading programs.

Programmed Instruction

Programmed instruction is another example of the sequential reading approach. Programmed instruction is a systematic effort to take a specific block of information and divide it into small units that are organized for logical, sequential learning. The organization of programmed instruction may either be branched or linear.

In a branched program, one unit (frame) of information is presented to the learner for response. If the response is correct, the student may bypass several frames. This allows for some differentiation of instruction.

No frames are bypassed in a linear arrangement. The student using the program proceeds step-by-step through each frame. Individualization is achieved through the rate at which the student moves through the program.

One of the most significant aspects of programmed instruction is its immediate feedback, positive reinforcement of correct responses, and instant correction of errors. With programmed instruction, the learner usually completes one frame, or small block, of the program and checks to determine the correctness of his or her response before moving to the next frame. If the response is erroneous, the learner is corrected at once, so that he or she need not continue thinking and using incorrect data.

The format of a program may be a workbook, teaching machine, or computer. There may also be some variety in the mode of response. Whatever the variations, the programs are designed to require individual response, immediate feedback with reinforcement (answer correct), or correction (answer wrong).

The following is an example of a child using programmed instruction.*

Eric Michaels entered his nongraded school and took his seat at a learning carrel. He keypunched his name onto the empty computer spaces.

Good morning—The punching of his name alerted the computer to the fact that Eric was ready to begin study of the program his teachers had earlier prepared for him.

As the first frame appeared,

> 1. Programmed instruction is a learning experience in which a program replaces a tutor. The student is led through the program by a sequence of learning sets that are structured to teach the student a desired skill.
>
> ________ ________ is a learning experience that replaces a tutor.

Eric remembered that earlier in the week Ms. Roser, one of his instructors, had mentioned that Eric was interested in computers and that he might enjoy learning about programmed instruction. Eric keypunched the words *programmed instruction* and smiled as Frame 2 appeared.

> 2. Good work, please continue.
> The program, which may be presented to the student in the form of a teaching machine or a programmed textbook, consists of statements, facts, and questions to which a student is asked to respond. The response may be made by filling in short answers or selecting an answer from multiple choices. Correct program responses are made available for the student to compare with his own. Frame 1 of this program asked you to respond by
>
> A. filling in a short answer.
> B. selecting from multiple choices.
> ________ C. leaving the space blank.

Eric hesitated and then punched A and B. Frame 3 appeared.

> 3. Very good thinking, please continue.
> In programmed instruction, large subject areas are divided into smaller thought sequences called frames. Material presented in one frame is related to material presented in preceding frames. Material contained in a frame is brief, with generally one question being asked about the material. In many programs, the ability of the student to answer the questions is a prerequisite for proceeding to the next frame. The above discussion of a programmed instruction frame is in itself a ____.

While very interesting to Eric, this was somewhat difficult. He read the frame again and keypunched the word *frame*. Immediately Frame 4 appeared.

> 4. Excellent, please continue.
> B. F. Skinner's demonstration of a practical learning device based on reinforcement drew attention from academicians who began to discuss the educational possibilities of programmed instruction.
>
> Programmed learning was early applauded by ____.

Easy, thought Eric as he punched *Skinner*. Frame 5 appeared.

> 5. Well done, please continue.
> While the idea of programmed instruction may have originated with the Elder Sophists of Ancient Greece, Maria Montessori may have been the first to attempt to apply a mechanism to a psychological theory of child development.
>
> The first person to attempt to apply a theory to a mechanism was________ ________ .

Eric punched *Maria Montessori* and wondered who she was.

> 6. Good work, please continue.
> At the American Psychological Association Convention in 1926, Sidney Pressey, a psychologist from Ohio State University, exhibited a teaching machine.
>
> Sidney Pressey presented a____in 1926.

*D. Lapp et al., *Teaching and Learning: Philosophical, Psychological, Curricular Applications* (New York: Macmillan Publishing Co., Inc., 1975), pp. 95–101.

Eric punched *teaching machine* and thought about those in his classroom: television, filmstrip projectors, slide projectors, record players and earphones, talking typewriters, and books with recorded stories. He smiled and thought about the fun he had working with the teaching machines. Frame 7 appeared.

> 7. Very well done, please continue.
> Industry has also adopted the programmed instruction for many one-the-job training situations. This occurred because programmed instruction could often accommodate daily scheduling better than traditional lectures. Having two or three trainees using machines at one setting seems more practical in industry than stopping production to have the entire office attend one lecture.
>
> For job-training economy, ______ adopted programmed instruction.

As Eric keypunched the word *industry*, he wondered how many other people were learning through computer-assisted instruction at that exact moment. As Frame 8 appeared, Ms. Roser put her arm around Eric and asked if he needed any help. He told her his thoughts. She smiled and reminded him that computers were involved in sending people to the moon, in developing new energy systems, and in eliminating disease and famine. She also explained to him that someday he wouldn't have to read to acquire information but that any knowledge he might desire could be obtained from an electronic bank where the information could be transmitted directly to his nervous system by means of coded electronic messages. These several uses of computers made Eric anxious to learn more about his nervous system. As he listened he thought of all the things he would like to learn without reading. Ms. Roser asked if she could listen to Eric read and answer Frame 8. Eric began:

> 8. Well done, please continue.
> While programmed instruction in many instances successfully supplements both business and educational programs, research suggests that the success of this supplement is dependent on the acceptance level of both instructor and trainee. One weakness of programmed instruction seems to be that students are rewarded when their thinking positively correlates with that of the programmer.
>
> In some instances programmed instruction is a ______ to both business and educational programs.

Eric keypunched *supplement*, and Ms. Roser smiled as Frame 9 appeared.

> 9. You are doing a fine job, please continue.
> The program is the most important part of programmed instruction. One type of program that offers the student many answer clues is linear programming. In such a program the student is required to recall information presented to him in a frame by either filling in an answer or selecting one answer from a series of multiple choices. When the child obtains the correct answer, he is positively reinforced as he continues to the next frame. All students working the same program proceed through the frames in the same order.
>
> This frame on programmed instruction has thus far been a ______ program.

Eric keypunched *linear* and proceeded to Frame 10.

> 10. You are doing very well, please continue.
> The second major type of programmed instruction program is called intrinsic. Incorrect responses are corrected through a system known as branching. The sequence of frames that the student views is determined by his response to the questions. An incorrect response generally directs the student toward additional frames dealing with the subject with which the student experienced difficulty. A correct response directs the student to skip the additional frames. If you think the above frame is linear, turn to frame eleven. If you believe this frame is intrinsic or branching, turn to Frame 13.

Although Eric realized the answer was intrinsic, he pushed number 11 to see exactly what happened with incorrect answers.

11. Frame 10 is intrinsic because the direction that you took in your program depended on your response. The basis of the intrinsic or branching system is the computer's ability to record performance data and select sequential program frames on the results of previous performance. Branching provides for the individuality of the respondent by designing a program from his correct replies.

    A program in which the direction of the program is determined by your response is called an _____ or _____ program.

Eric keypunched *intrinsic* and *branching* and continued to Frame 12.

12. Good work, please continue.
    A linear program is one in which your response does not alter the frame sequence. All frames are viewed by all students.

    A program in which all students following the same frame sequence is called a _____ program.

Eric keypunched *linear* and Frame 13 appeared automatically.

13. Good, please continue.
    A third type of program is the combination program. In the combination program, some of the frames are linear while others are intrinsic.

    A _____ program combines aspects of both linear and intrinsic programs.

As Eric keypunched the word *combination*, Mr. Lee, his other instructor, approached and asked if he was enjoying the programmed instruction program. Mr. Lee and Ms. Roser were team instructors who believed that their major function was to work individually with their students. Mr. Lee suggested when Eric finished his program he might like to join with Mr. Lee and four other students to discuss how computers are programmed. Eric agreed, since he had been discussing this concept with Mr. Martin, the teacher aide, only yesterday. Mr. Lee watched as Eric began Frame 14.

14. Well done, please continue.
    A teaching machine is a device that presents a program. The basic function of all teaching machines is to teach a program frame by frame. Some programs, such as yours, are connected to a computer.

    A teaching machine may serve as a _____ when it presents a program.

Eric hesitated. Mr. Lee reread the frame with Eric and suggested that the teaching machine is often the *teacher*. Eric laughed and keypunched teacher. Frame 15 appeared.

15. Good work, please continue.
    A program must be reliable. To establish such reliability the program must be administered to students and revised according to their responses. Without this data one cannot be sure that the program teaches what it was designed to teach.

    The _____ of the program is important to determine if it teaches what it was designed to teach.

As Eric keypunched *reliability*, he and Mr. Lee reviewed the term, since they had discussed it early that year. Mr. Lee moved to another student as Eric began Frame 16.

16. Very good, please continue.
    The final step in developing a good program is the development of a multiple-choice or fill-in-test that measures student knowledge of the presented material. Success on the test is determined by initial program objectives. If the main points of the program are not learned, the program may be revised through evaluation.

    At this time you are to group with Mr. Lee, who will determine through discussion with you the degree of program competency. Thank you, you did very well.

In the first part of the chapter, we discussed and presented teaching methods and programs that exemplified the sequential reading approach. In the following section, you will find several methods that can be used to implement the spontaneous reading approach.

Spontaneous Reading Approach

The spontaneous reading approach integrates the cognitive and affective dimensions of students; that is, it relates to their interests as well as to their needs. As is the case for the sequential reading approach, the spontaneous reading approach is organized sequentially to levels of cognitive development; however, it is also highly dependent on the affective domain. By developing a curriculum that is of interest to children, you will be able to strengthen their competencies while you remediate their needs.

The spontaneous reading approach occurred through happenstance in the early decades of reading instruction. Throughout American educational history, attempts to focus instruction on the competencies as well as on the interests of children have met with little success. This limited success can be attributed in part to a lack of understanding about classroom management procedures.

The two most common methods through which teachers have attempted to personalize reading instruction are language-experience and individualized instruction. Philosophical parameters of these methods rely heavily on the validity of such premises as Dewey's famous statement (1916) "to learn from experience is to make a backward and forward connection between what we do to things and what we enjoy or suffer from things in consequence" (p. 125) and Jenkins' (1955):

> Children work hard and long when they choose their own jobs. They move ahead when they have the opportunity to set their own goals. They read with greater enjoyment when they choose the material. In self-selection the teacher works with the individuals and knows their interests and needs more adequately than when a group works on a single book chosen by the teacher. (p. 125)

Language Experience. The language-experience approach to teaching reading is a relatively recent program that typifies the spontaneous reading approach. It uses the already existing language of the child to develop reading, writing, and listening skills. This is not to suggest, however, that training in structural analysis, contextual analysis, or phonics analysis is unnecessary.

Smith et al. (1978) remind us that " the average child of six has . . . learned to hear and respond to a large number of words, perhaps as many as twenty thousand. Thus personal language is an excellent base for successful growth in school" (p. 47). The language experience approach is designed to capitalize on these listening and language skills. Proponents of the language experience approach believe that it has merit because it builds upon the interest of the child and the language that the child has already mastered. Veatch et al. (1979) also point out that a language-experience approach, by using a child's own language, "provides experiences that are closely related to the child's personal and social needs" (p. 12). Perhaps, more strongly than any other approach, it emphasizes the relationships among thought, oral language, and written language.

Allen (1976) discusses the language experience approach in terms of "truths about self and language."

1. I can think about what I have experienced and imagined.
2. I can talk about what I think about.
3. What I can talk about I can express in some other form.
4. Anything I record I can recall through speaking or reading.
5. I can read what I can write by myself and what other people write for me to read.
6. As I talk and write, I use some words over and over and some not so often.
7. As I talk and write, I use some words and clusters of words to express my meaning.
8. As I write to represent the sounds I make through speech, I use the same symbols (letters) over and over.
9. Each letter of the alphabet stands for one or more sounds that I make when I talk.
10. As I read, I must add to what an author has written if I am to get full meaning and inherent pleasure from print. (pp. 50–55)

These points are in some sense an elaboration of Allen's (1961) often-quoted statement:

> What I can think about, I can talk about.
> What I can say, I can write.
> What I can write, I can read.
> I can read what I write and what other people can write for me to read. (p. 880)

Some advocates of the language-experience approach encourage teachers to stress to children that reading (or written material) is "talk written down." Although it is desirable to help children make the connection between speech and reading, this is not a totally accurate conception of the relationship. There are some aspects of speech, such as voice inflection and rate of speaking, that will not be recorded when "talk is written down." Therefore, even though it seems highly desirable to help children relate reading to talking, it does not seem desirable to use the idea of "talk written down" in isolation because you will not be dealing with the entire process of reading.

Since the language-experience approach was meant to grow out of the oral expressions of children, it does not rely heavily on published materials. On the following pages you will find an example of material that has been developed and published in an attempt to encourage language-experience programs. The example on page 320 reflects one type of lesson or series of lessons that might be used in a language-experience reading program.

The language experience approach to teaching reading uses the already existing language of the child to develop reading, writing, and listening skills. A trip to the zoo provides a stimulus for many language arts activities. (Photo by Linda Lungren.)

Page 5
Zoo Animals and Me

Suggested time: 3–4 days

Concept to be developed

• The use of comparisons (similes) helps other people picture our thoughts.

Activities with the pupil book

30–40 minutes per day

1. Play a recording, read a story or poem, or show a film about zoo animals.

Let children engage in dramatic play to show movements and sounds of animals.

If possible, play the record "The Carnival of the Animals" by Saint-Saens (Leonard Bernstein and the New York Philharmonic Orchestra, Columbia Masterworks, ML 5768). On the record Mr. Bernstein explains each portion of this wonderful musical trip to the zoo. As the record is played, have children seated on the floor or in a circle of chairs so that they will have ample space to act out movements and sounds of the animals. Since the record is too long for one listening session, choose an actively animated portion of the record or have more than one listening session.

"Let's Go to the Zoo" by Ed Lewis (Magic Key Record, MK-12) is another good record for the study of zoo animals. Some children may be able to bring records from home.

If suitable records are not available, stimulate dramatic play by reading stories and poems about wild animals. A film is also a good way to introduce the topic and invite dramatic play. It is important to show a film to children who have never had an opportunity to see zoo animals.

The following are just a few of the many good poems about wild animals.

SUPPER FOR A LION

Dorothy Aldis

Savage lion in the zoo,
Walking by on padded feet,
To and fro and fro and to,
You seem to think it's time to eat.

Then how about a bowl of stew
With jello for dessert? Or would
A juicy bone be best for you?

Oh, please don't stare as though you knew
That I'd taste good!

IF YOU SHOULD MEET A CROCODILE

If you should meet a Crocodile
Don't take a stick and poke him;
Ignore the welcome in his smile,
Be careful not to stroke him.
For as he sleeps upon the Nile,
He thinner gets and thinner;
And whene'er you meet a Crocodile
He's ready for his dinner.

THE KANGAROO

Old Jumpety-Bumpety-Hop-and-Go-One
Was lying asleep on his side in the sun.
This old kangaroo, he was whisking the flies

("Supper for a Lion," reprinted by permission of G. P. Putnam's Sons from ALL TOGETHER by Dorothy Aldis. Copyright 1925, 1926, 1927, 1928, 1934, 1952 by Dorothy Aldis.)

(The author of "If You Should Meet a Crocodile" is unknown. Reprinted from THE SOUND OF POETRY, by Mary C. Austin and Queenie B. Mills, Allyn and Bacon, Inc., 1963.)

(The author of "The Kangaroo" is unknown. Reprinted from THE SOUND OF POETRY, by Mary C. Austin and Queenie B. Mills, Allyn and Bacon, Inc., 1963.)

Zoo Animals and Me
Name
I can run
as fast as
I can eat
as much as
5

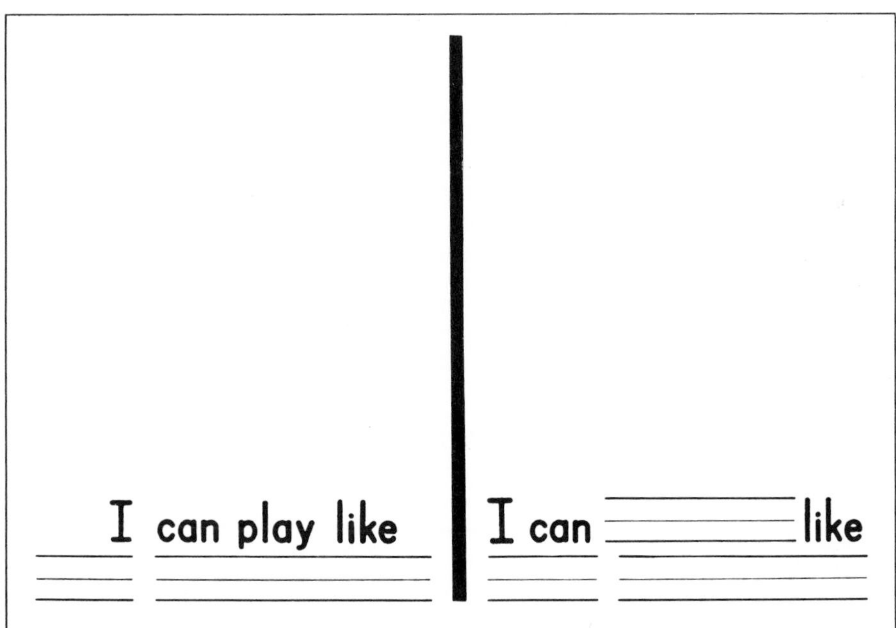
I can play like
I can
like

(8)

(With his long glossy tail) from his ears and his
eyes.
Jumpety-Bumpety-Hop-and-Go-One
Was lying asleep on his side in the sun,
Jumpety-Bumpety-Hop!

2. Let children who have visited a zoo or circus tell something about their visit. List animals they saw there.

bear	tortoise
lion	sea lion
tiger	penguin
elephant	deer
giraffe	fox

Ask the children, "What can *you* do like one of these animals? Can you compare something you know to these animals by saying that something is as ______ as a ______?"

3. Explain to the class that we can say we act or sound like a particular animal in order to help our listeners and readers know better what we mean.

Talk about ways in which we compare our own actions with those of animals. Add the comparisons to the list of animals on the board.

as tall as a giraffe
as big as an elephant
as slow as a tortoise
as sly as a fox
growl like a bear
roar like a lion
swim like a sea lion
jump like a kangaroo
strut like a peacock
soar like an eagle

The words *as* and *like* are used many times in speech and writing. Their use needs to be understood by children although you do not need to use the term *simile*. Your object is to help the children realize that they already use these forms of comparison in their speech and that the same forms are useful in writing.

4. Each child chooses one zoo animal to illustrate with a paper cutout or a crayon drawing.

Help each one select an appropriate simile to write or dictate at the bottom of the picture. Make a bulletin board display of these animal posters (8).

Choose a few of the similes for dramatization. All the children can participate in the dramatization or you can select a few at a time until all children have participated. They can, for example, leap like a kangaroo, growl like a bear, strut like a peacock.

5. Give children Page 5 of the pupil book and help them read the sentences on the front and back of the page.

Direct children to resources in the classroom to help them spell the words they want to complete the sentences. After the children have spelled and written the words correctly, have them do the illustrations to complete both sides of the page.

6. Combine the pages into books.

Read the books with groups of children, helping them read the sentences with meaningful expression. Work to build a sight vocabulary of animal names.

7. Provide animal stories and books for children to read, especially stories about wild animals. Read with a few children each day.

The following example illustrates how the language-experience approach can be used in the classroom:

Mrs. Fredericks, a beginning-level reading teacher, is working with a group of five children who came to school very excited about a television program they had watched the previous evening. The program had followed a particular bird family from the nest-building stage through the leaving-the-nest stage. Mrs. Fredericks decided to take advantage of their interest and excitement and develop a reading story. She called the group together in one corner of the room near the chalkboard. She invited the children to think of one thing they would like to say or ask about the birds. They knew from previous experience that she would write the things they said. She recorded the following:

> The two birds worked hard to build the nest.
> They used grass and real little sticks.
> The nest was high up.
> Little birds hatched.
> The big birds fed them.
> The big birds pushed the babies out of the nest.

As Mrs. Fredericks recorded each sentence, she repeated what the speaker had said. Then she asked the child to repeat the sentence looking at the written form while the others looked also. She swept her hand from left to right to help the readers follow. When composing had been completed, the group reread the story. Then individual children volunteered to read different sentences. They discussed a name for the story and chose "The Bird Family."

Children in the group already knew some of the words: *the, was, of, to, birds,* and *big*. Mrs. Fredericks asked them to identify some words they would like to add to their word banks. (These were individual word files that the children kept. Each file had two compartments: one for words already learned and one for words the child wanted to learn.) Children took turns telling Mrs. Fredericks three words they wanted to put in their files. She wrote the words on individual cards for them. After each child's words were written, the child looked at the words and pronounced them. It was understood by each child that he or she would say the words for her again later in the day.

Each child in the group also made an independent copy of the story to put in his or her personal story book. Having finished copying the story, the child took his or her copy for Mrs. Fredericks's examination and read the story to her from the copy. If any significant errors had been made in copying, the child corrected this work before putting the story in the book folder.

Mrs. Fredericks made two chart copies of the story. One copy she put on a chart board where children who wished might read or refer to it. She asked each child to draw an illustration for the sentence he or she had contributed to the story. These were placed around the chart as they were completed.

During her next session with this group, Mrs. Fredericks used sentence strips from the second copy of the story. These were distributed to different children who read their sentences to the class. Then they stood in line according to the sentence order in the story. In addition, each child read the words from the "to learn" compartment of his or her word file to Mrs. Fredericks. When a word had been identified without help during three different reading sessions, it could be filed in the "learned" compartment. Soon Mrs. Fredericks hoped to advance to the individual composition of stories. The words in the word files could be used independently in these stories.

Mrs. Fredericks uses a procedure, or pattern, common to many language-experience programs. She encourages oral expression and tries to help children to be more aware of new words they hear and may pick up. She moves into group composition, and then, as children are able, she moves them into individual composition.

As she works with children, she learns their interests and selects trade books to bring from the library into the classroom. She reads books to children and encourages them to look at and, if possible, read these books. She also encourages and provides opportunities for children to read their own stories to others.

Mrs. Fredericks recognizes two potential problems in a language-experience program. One relates to the teaching of word-recognition skills. Mrs. Fredericks tries to use words that occur in children's stories as a basis for teaching as many phonic principles as possible. She does realize the danger inherent in such a program of limited development of phonics skills.

She also realizes that some children have a wealth of background experiences from which stories can be generated, whereas others have limited story resources. She tries to provide many new and appropriate experiences for her children. She also realizes the necessity of pulling in new vocabulary through these experiences. She encourages children to use new words in communication through conversation and writing.

Mrs. Fredericks is well aware of the factors that need to be developed in an effective reading program. She is adept at learning children's interests and concerns and at getting them to express themselves verbally. She also views the language-experience reading program as a stepping stone to another type of program and works to integrate other reading materials into the program. She does not recommend that the language-experience approach be used as the major plan for helping children learn to read after the primary levels. She does feel that it can be used well in conjunction with some other approach in the intermediate levels. Perhaps at those levels the emphasis in its use should shift to creative and informative writing rather than reading instruction.

One concern of teachers using the language-experience approach to reading instruction is "Should I edit children's oral contributions?" There is no one universally accepted answer to this question. Durkin (1976) suggests: "Take down whatever children say, spelling correctly whatever is offered . . .. Once materials enter into the teaching of reading, another guideline takes over because children are in school to learn to read standard English. . . . Materials for teaching reading, whether commercial or homemade, should be written in standard English" (p. 242). Similarly, Spache and Spache (1973) provide this description of the teacher's role: " The teacher discusses word choice, sentence structure, the sounds of letters and words. But he does not censor or elaborate" (p. 245). Veatch et al. (1979), however, allow that "some editing is needed: pupil dictation with wrong usage is altered, and the wrong word is found and changed" (p. 46).

Perhaps there is no right answer to this question because children are unique. Cautious editing may have no effect on one child, whereas another student may perceive a "criticism" of his *language* as a criticism of *himself*. You will each have to decide what is appropriate for your classroom. It may be helpful to consider these questions:

1. Does the form of expression used by the child reflect that used by the group? Do others understand what the child is saying?
2. Do you consider the change you would like to be mechanical, an inaccurate choice of words, or a crude or rude expression?
3. Can the child's wording be changed without diminishing the child?

It may be that the answer lies in adjusting to the needs of the individuals in a group. It is a wise teacher who keeps in mind that language versatility is a goal to seek. Your aim should not be to erase one language style just to develop another, more acceptable one in its place but, rather, to build on the personal language patterns the child has already acquired.

You can plan a language-experience program that interrelates visual, oral, auditory, and kinesthetic experiences by beginning with what each child brings to school–his or her *language*. Ordinary school activities such as class projects, recess games, field trips, and art activities, as well as events and experiences from children's daily lives, can provide the basis for oral language experiences. Children's *interest* is the key.

Developing Skills Through Language Experience. An understanding of oral language, or the listening-spoken vocabulary, is the foundation on which children build a reading vocabulary. When you tape record or make a script of children's statements, children see written and oral language come together. After you have recorded the spoken text of your children, you transcribe these same reactions onto large sheets of lined chart paper. While reading these statements orally to your children, you might incorporate some of the activities suggested in Chapters 5 and 6, which are designed to aid the development of phonics skills, thereby using their language to develop basic word-recognition competencies. This will aid you in integrating the sequential and spontaneous approaches to the teaching of reading. We must remember that a word-recognition program is a program involving language. Most children come to school with spoken vocabularies of approximately 1,500 to 2,000 words. Children have learned a great many of these words through interaction with people in their environment. This vocabulary can be expanded through the language-experience method. Through this method you can capitalize on the spoken language of the child, while using the word-recognition skills needed to develop both a sight and meaning vocabulary. The central theme of

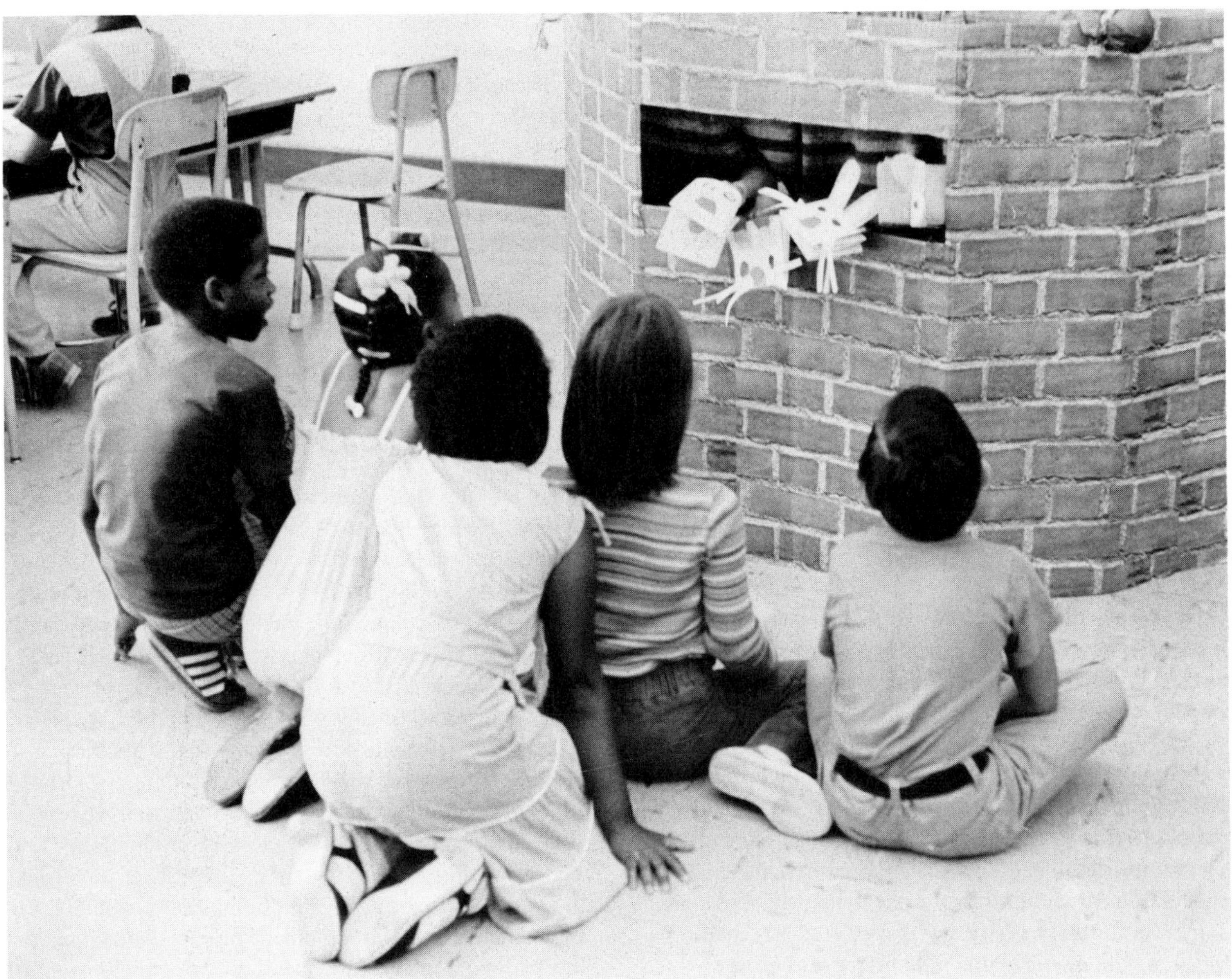

An understanding of oral language, or the listening–spoken vocabulary, is the foundation on which children build a reading vocabulary. (Photo by Linda Lungren.)

this process becomes one of communication, with your charting of the children's expressed ideas. Through the development of these charts, the child sees his or her language turn to print. Perhaps equally important, you have made reading both *meaningful* and *fun* for the children.

When you are teaching beginning readers from a language-experience approach, start by stressing the importance of sound-symbol correspondence. In this way, children begin to see that print represents ideas and that through reading, they can share these ideas. Children begin to build a sight vocabulary because the words they see and hear are *their* words, their language. With this foundation, you can begin to introduce phonics and other word-attack skills to help children identify unknown and different words. Through this approach, word-attack skills are not being learned in isolation; rather, they are acquired more naturally through reading activities utilizing a child's own language. In this way, sequential and spontaneous approaches to reading instruction begin to be integrated.

The strength of an eclectic or integrated language/reading program is in the incorporation of all methods of teaching the language arts within one program.

> Developing and acquiring a sight vocabulary can be done in a circumstance that rightly simulates the learning to talk stage. Sound and sight are not divorced. Rate of "new" word learning is not paced by some artificial, illogical plan of one or two words per page or one or two words per basic reader "story," even though there are no "stories" in preprimers.
>
> (Stauffer, 1965, p. 259)

By implementing this approach, children continually expand their sight vocabularies. In addition, we encourage you to help children note beginning word differences and similarities. Studies of eye movement and miscues have indicated that readers concentrate more on initial and ending portions of words than on medial positions.

Initial letters: tall, tag, ten
Ending letters: bat, sat, cat
Medial letters: were, table, book

There are many ways by which you can extend basic lessons through language experience. For example, you may give each child a typed copy of his or her reaction to an experience. Each child is asked to cut the story into words and phrases. The child thus begins to realize that stories consist of words and phrases that can be spoken. The child is now asked to match these isolated units with the sentence in its complete form. You might ask the children to name and spell particular words as they paste them onto a second copy. As another activity, give paired students envelopes containing the words and phrases of their reactions and ask them to reconstruct their stories for their partners to read. Throughout this experience you may want to stress story punctuation. Ask children to consult a dictionary (with your help) to determine word meanings, pronunication keys, and word histories.

Another lesson in this series might involve the child perfecting his or her writing ability. Have the child lie on a large piece of craft paper while you trace his form. Then ask the child to cut out his form and color in any parts he chooses. He might also paste a photograph of himself onto the form. Now give each child a typed copy of his earlier writing contribution that he will edit. When he is satisfied with his piece of writing, he may paste it onto his self-portrait or copy it onto his silhouette. You will find that you can also use many of the activities contained in this text to further this language experience.

Through these language experiences, children begin to acquire

1. Important phonics generalizations
2. Basic study skills
3. Extended reading vocabularies

Because they are introduced in the context of the child's own language, rather than as isolated processes, learning becomes a unified experience.

Too often children are required to spend twenty minutes on dictionary skills, thirty minutes learning new vocabulary words, forty-five minutes on phonics, and thirty minutes reading their basals. Although all these experiences may be necessary, a synthesis of learning never seems to occur because we tend to ignore the language of the children rather than use it as a base foundation. Through a language-experience method, you can provide the child with an opportunity for synthesizing the independent skills of the reading/thinking process.

In addition to furthering skill development, we encourage you to also ask the children to discuss their individual reactions to their experiences. Often, we become so involved with the group *product* that we lose sight of the individuals involved in the production.

Throughout these experiences, the teacher is obliged to continue helping *each* child's phonics, vocabulary, and comprehension development through *individual* or small-group activities using personal story booklets, basal readers, or other materials of interest to the children. As the speaking, reading, listening, and writing abilities of the children become more complex, so will your language-experience program.

A great deal of research (Allen, 1961; Goodman, 1965; Stauffer, 1965; Serwer, 1969; Shuy, 1969; Hall, 1975) supports the language-experience approach because

A. Children realize through observation that printed text is their language written down.
B. It develops
    1. Left-to right reading.
    2. Auditory discrimination.
    3. Visual discrimination.

4. Auditory-visual discrimination.
5. Hand-eye coordination.
6. Development of cooperation.
7. Expansion of attention span.
8. Oral language usage.
9. Word recognition.
10. Alphabet recognition.
11. Punctuation.
12. Pronunciation.
13. Word meanings.
14. Word histories.
15. Dictionary skills.
16. Group discussion.
17. Social encounters with peers.

Smith et al. (1978) also point out that "the marvelous advantage to the educator of using the student's own language is that it gives him a success base from which to build. It is akin to saying, 'Your language is good. Start with your language and learn how to improve it'" (pp. 47–48). Using this formula for success, there are many profitable experiences that result from the language-experience approach. However, we caution you to use this language structure only as a curriculum base. Do not fall into the same kind of faulty, repetitious, uncreative patterns that many teachers do when they misuse a basal reader program. Be careful to incorporate the spontaneous expressions of your children in the initial lessons. Grammar, usage, and punctuation may be the focus of supplementary lessons.

We also urge you to move a child into basals and trade books smoothly. The transition should be made in conjunction with topics that the child is interested in discussing. For example, if the class is discussing salads, you could introduce supplementary material on the origin of salads. Language-experience charts, which may cover a wide variety of topics, can still be of service to your program after your children have begun to explore the topic in texts. Children are a storehouse of ideas, many of which can become language-experience charts.

The following lesson plan is an example of one that you might use in your classroom.

Content: Directions for making a Waldorf salad

Grade Level: K–3

Objective: To help students write and read a recipe after they have made a Waldorf salad in class.

Activity:

Step 1: Have a group of students make a Waldorf salad.

Step 2: Have a student copy the steps of the recipe and print them on a large sheet of tag board.

Step 3: Place the recipe on the board and ask students in a second group to make a Waldorf salad following the recipe directions.

Recipe for Waldorf Salad

1. Cut up a head of lettuce.
2. Slice three celery stalks into ½-inch pieces.
3. Slice one large green pepper into ¼-inch pieces.
4. Core three apples and slice them into ½-inch pieces.
5. Sprinkle the salad gingerly with walnut pieces.

Individualized Instruction. In recent years, a great deal of emphasis has been placed upon *individualizing* reading instruction. Matthes (1977) suggests this is because "educators have agreed that children must develop at their own pace rather than be limited to group grade-leveled expectations" (p. 26). As such, individualized instruction is the base of the spontaneous reading approach.

The two key aspects of the individualized reading method are that the student establishes an independent pace and sequence for reading instruction, and the student selects independent reading materials. By allowing students to substitute interesting reading materials for the sometimes uninteresting content of basals, you can see that a definition of reading is embedded in the individualized reading method.

Within the framework of the spontaneous reading approach, reading has been described as an individualized set of process skills that are learned in social settings. Children work alone or in groups using a wide variety of materials. In this type of individualized/personalized program, children read materials of their choice, related to their interests. It is the intent of these programs to allow children to set their own pace for progress in materials that they have selected.

As a teacher using an individualized method, you will need to provide your students access to a wide variety of materials. These materials must span the range of reading levels and abilities appropriate for your classroom. It is recommended that you have three to five choices available for each child at all times. If your school library does not have an adequate supply of texts, you may be able to secure materials from the public library for an extended period of time. After the selections have served their purpose, exchange them for additional books.

To implement an individualized program, you will need to be familiar with

1. The reading process.
2. Organizational skills.
3. Sequential skill development.
4. Assessment techniques.
5. Reading materials.
6. Classroom management procedures.

In the following paragraphs we have included a description of the way one teacher went about acquiring these areas of knowledge and setting up an individualized reading program.

Ms. Silver decided to begin the school year with an individualized reading program. She read chapters in several texts describing the approach and added to her mental outline of the requirements for a good individualized program several notes from her own experience. Still feeling unsure about some points, she obtained permission to visit and observe in classrooms where individualized reading programs were being conducted. With this preparation, she still felt there were some questions that would simply have to be answered as her program evolved.

As soon as Ms. Silver was able to learn which students she would have for reading instruction, she obtained their records and studied them to learn as much as possible about their reading achievement and to gain some insight into their interests. She was fortunate in finding interest inventories that had been completed by a number of the children. These proved very helpful as she tried to anticipate books and materials that children in her class might find intriguing.

After studying the records available to her, she felt that she was able to estimate the range in reading levels that would be represented in her class. Had this not been true, she had planned to administer a reading survey (reading achievement test) soon after school began. She had also planned to choose books on what appeared to be an appropriate instructional level for each child. She planned to hear each child read orally from material on his or her estimated level. This she felt would either confirm her original estimate or give her a sound basis for re-estimating. She felt that this would still be a good procedure to follow, even though she no longer needed to administer the reading test.

Her next step was to purchase multiple copies of workbooks designed for independent use rather than being tied to any specific program content. She went through these materials, taking them apart and reorganizing them so that she had different categories of exercises for developing word-recognition skills, comprehension skills, and some study skills. Feeling that in some areas her supply of work sheets was inadequate, she developed some additional ones herself. She prepared an index for these exercises so that a worksheet for almost any aspect of reading with which the child might need help could be found quickly.

Her next step was an extensive study of the library to determine holdings on the levels needed at the beginning of school and the levels that would most likely be needed by the end of the term. Because her town had a good children's division in its public library, she also surveyed the holdings there. Not only did she check for books of fiction, but she also checked on reference books, magazines, and brochures.

Ms. Silver then consulted her principal and found that it would be possible to subscribe to two daily newspapers published in the area. She would have some money allocated for the purchase of instructional materials and decided to purchase some reading games and records that could be used for additional skill development by individuals or groups.

Prior to the beginning of school, she selected books representing the interests and reading levels in her group. These she organized in her room by topic, not level of difficulty.

Once school began, she introduced the new program to the class. They worked out a schedule whereby Ms. Silver would have individual conferences with five or six of the twenty-five students in her class each day. A block of time was left to work with any students who needed and requested help. This made it possible to request interruption-free conference time.

During conference, the student would talk with her about the material he was reading, expressing his reaction to it. He would also read aloud to her. Sometimes she would choose the portion to be read. At other times, the student would make the selection. While this took place, the rest of the class would read independently or work on skill development activities.

Ms. Silver showed the class the checklist she had developed and would use to keep record of the progress each individual made in reading from conference to conference. On it she had outlined all the skills she hoped to help them develop. On this checklist she could quickly indicate strengths and areas needing extra work. She could also make notes of worksheets or other activities to which the child was being referred. All of this would give her something to refresh her memory and to build on as she gave the individual needed help. The student was invited to refer to his list whenever he felt it would be helpful.

In addition to keeping records herself, Ms. Silver urged each child to keep a record of the things he or she had read throughout the program. She worked with the class developing a list of types of literature and general topics in which they were interested. Each child took a copy of this and was encouraged to read at least one selection for each category during the year.

Ms. Silver kept careful records not only for each child, but on the total program also. As time passed, she felt that some group activity would be helpful. Because sharing what one has read often enhances the reading, she arranged for children who were reading on the same topic to get together to discuss their books and share portions of them through oral reading. When she first initiated the group discussion-sharing sessions she remained with the group to help them get organized and use their time well. Later, she felt the groups were able to work satisfactorily without her participation. This allowed her to work with others while tuning in occasionally to the group's activities. In addition, she organized a similar type of group activity where individuals who had completed a selection might get together. She felt that this could lead children to develop new interests, if those having read the materials handled them with enthusiasm. As need occurred, she organized groups to work on a common problem. She felt that an economic use of time required this.

Finding still some further need for group involvement, she selected some plays for children to read in a group. Choral reading was worked into some group session.

The class with which Ms. Silver was working was at a level roughly equivalent to fifth grade. Many of the things she tried out with these children could not have been done with younger children, or if done, they would have required a different approach on her part. The individualized reading approach is not recommended as a beginning reading plan. However, as children begin gaining some independence in reading, it surely can be used in conjunction with other approaches. The teacher wishing to do so must gradually phase out the other approach.

From this description, you can see that one of the strongest arguments for using this method is that only by self-selection would two students be reading the same material at the same time. This dramatically reduces the likelihood of achievement comparisons. The other major advantages of this program are that children select their own materials and set their own rate of progress. The obvious disadvantage of this method is that you may experience some initial problems with classroom management procedures. This may occur because some children move at a snail's pace when they are allowed to set their own course and rate. Occasionally, there is the child who is an enthusiastic selector but a reluctant finisher. You must deal with each of these problems on an individual basis. Chapter 15 is designed to help you to develop techniques you will need to implement a successful individualized reading program.

Next we present the most current system for teaching reading, the managed language/reading system, which has attempted to incorporate the best features of the sequential reading approach and the spontaneous reading approach.

Managed Language/Reading System. The managed language/reading system has evolved from the need to provide classroom teachers with a manageable program. The system capitalizes on the strengths of both the sequential and spontaneous reading approaches. Its content, while organized logically, emphasizes an individual format of instruction. Many of the "new" programs include basals with stories that are relevant and interesting to students. Many of these systems include filmstrips and tapes of the stories, worksheets, teacher guides and manuals, criterion-referenced tests, and elaborate easy-to-manage record-keeping systems. Each of these additions to the basic program is intended to help teachers individualize their program.

To provide teachers with the opportunity to individualize instruction, and also to meet the needs of each child, these new programs include intensive management systems. These management systems help the teacher to *diagnose*, *prescribe*, and *evaluate* the program for each child.

The following description of a management system has been taken from Ginn's *Reading 720*. Other programs (by Macmillan, 1981; Economy, 1980, and Laidlaw, 1980) parallel this description.

The management system for an instructional program is neither the content of that program nor the teaching method by which content is presented to pupils. Rather, it represents a kind of framework or pattern by means of which content and teaching methods can be organized to assure that some specific outcomes occur. Usually, the desired effects of managing instruction are as follows: (1) that pupils are systematically taught at least a core set of specified educational objectives, with the exception of those pupils who have previously become proficient in certain of these objectives, (2) that evidence is generated to show whether pupils learn these objectives at a level of proficiency prespecified as desirable, (3) that provision is made for systematic reinstruction of pupils on any of the objectives for which they have failed to demonstrate proficiency, and (4) that teaching pupils to acceptable proficiency on this set of core objectives is accomplished in the minimum reasonable time.

When the core strands of Reading 720 are taught in the management mode, the foregoing outcomes can be realized. Using a management system, the teacher may select from the rich pool of hundreds of objectives, those specific ones that represent the core skills of Reading 720, drawn from the comprehension, vocabulary, and decoding strands. The teacher may then build lesson plans emphasizing, or even restricted to, these core objectives and teach those children known to need them. Additional Reading 720 components allow the teacher to evaluate with precision the proficiency of pupils on the core objectives. Other Reading 720 resources can then be used to reteach missed objectives to just those pupils who need reinstruction. Because managed instruction focuses so tightly on core essentials and attempts to limit instruction within the core strands to that demonstrably required, whether initial or reteaching, it moves pupils with maximum efficiency toward attainment of the desired outcomes.

Implementing a management system in teaching Reading 720 aids the teacher in the following ways:

in helping to select what pupils are to learn

in systematic planning for and provision of supplementary instruction

in individualizing instruction according to pupil needs

in establishing an instructional pace that is efficient yet accomplishes desired goals

The components of a successfully managed language/reading system are integrated into the existing basal program. The following example and materials, taken from Ginn's *Reading 720*, emphasize such integration.

Components of Reading 720 Management System

A management system is integrated or built into Reading 720. All the directions needed for managing core skills instruction are found in this Teacher's Edition. Instructions will be found placed sequentially, as needed, throughout the various sections of the lesson plans and in the manuals accompanying the various components that are essential to managing instruction in Reading 720. All such manuals are supplied with these components when purchased separately, and are also reproduced in this section of the Teacher's Edition.

The following are necessary for managing the instruction of the core skills. These items are also available as separate components.

Activities in Part 4 of the Lesson Plan

Activities in Part 4 of each plan are designed to introduce and give practice reinforcement of objectives taught in unit.

Unit Criterion Exercises

The Unit Criterion Exercises may be used to assess pupil proficiency on the specified core skills of a unit. Pupils scoring at or above Suggested Criterion Score (SCS) are assumed to have attained acceptable proficiency on the tested objective. The rationale for establishing the SCS is described in the Criterion Exercise manual.

Criterion Exercise Record Sheets (CERS)

The CERS are forms for recording and organizing groups of pupils' Unit Criterion Exercise scores and referencing them to specific supplemental instruction or enrichment resources. The CERS for each unit are found on pages 265–267.

Booster Activities

Paper-and-pencil instructional activities are designed to give practice or reinforcement to pupils scoring below Suggested Criterion Score on any of the objectives tested in a Unit Criterion Exercise. All the Booster Activities for Level 5 are found on pages 271–280 and the manual of directions for their use is on pages 268–270. Instructions for selecting the proper Booster Activity are found in the manual. It is important to note that Booster Activities "boost" marginally performing pupils to an acceptable level. When pupils score *very* low on an ob-

Reading 720 Initial Placement Test

CLASS WORK SHEET

Teacher's Name

School Date

City Grade

PUPIL'S NAME	IPT Level	Initial Assigned Level	Assigned Level After 2 Weeks	COMMENTS
1.				
2.				
3.				
4.				
5.				
6.				
7.				
8.				
9.				
10.				
11.				
12.				
13.				
14.				
15.				
16.				
17.				
18.				
19.				
20.				

jective, especially if they get none of the items right, they need reteaching. After reteaching has been accomplished, the Booster or the other practice activities may be given.

Use of the following component, while not essential, is strongly recommended.

Reading Achievement Card

The Reading Achievement Card is a chart for recording and organizing all of an individual pupil's criterion exercise scores for one level. This component is reproduced in this Teacher's Edition. It is also found on the last two pages of each Unit Criterion Exercise booklet, and, in addition, is available separately printed on tag board.

Several other Reading 720 components are optionally usable with management mode instruction and, except for the Informal Reading Inventory, do not appear in this Teacher's Edition. Each has its own manual or other directions describing its use. These components include the following:

Reading 720
Reading Achievement Card
Level 2

Pupil's Name________
School________

Key: Total = Number of Items; SCS = Suggested Criterion Score; PS = Pupil's Score

Directions: Record in the appropriate box the pupil's score on each part of the Criterion Exercise. At the end of a level, sign and date the card.

Unit	Skill	Total	SCS	PS	Notes
Unit 1	DECODING initial consonants /b/b, /l/l, /r/r, /h/h	12	10		Notes:
	VOCABULARY Word Recognition	8	6		
Unit 2	DECODING initial consonant /ǰ/j	4	3		Notes:
	VOCABULARY Word Recognition	10	8		
Unit 3	DECODING initial consonant /k/c	4	3		Notes:
	VOCABULARY Word Recognition	12	10		
Unit 4	DECODING initial consonants /f/f, /y/y, /n/n	9	7		Notes:
	VOCABULARY Word Recognition	10	8		

Initial Placement Test

The Initial Placement Test aids in determining the level in which to start pupils new to Reading 720.

Informal Reading Inventory

The Informal Reading Inventory helps in making initial individual placement decisions or in post-instruction diagnosis as a supplement to the Unit Criterion Exercises.

Unit Decoding Pretests

The Pretests are an aid in determining which decoding skills pupils already know before they start a unit.

Level Mastery Tests

Level Mastery Tests may be used for surveying pupil achievement on an entire level, or for providing a cumulative, final check on pupil proficiency on the level's objectives.

Reading Progress Card

The Reading Progress Card serves as a device for recording cumulative reading achievement test and other data for all thirteen levels. It is available in file-folder format.

The following exercise is a comprehension measure found in Ginn's *Reading 720.*

Read the following selection and circle the correct answer to the questions. Continue until you have answered all the questions.

Eddie slammed his locker shut, picked up his jacket and books, and walked sullenly toward the subway. His sixth grade class had just had an assembly to discuss graduation to the junior high school. The assembly had had a big impact on Eddie. He had learned that the work would be intensified in junior high and that there would be many more students. He didn't want to leave his school. Here he was one of the oldest pupils. Everyone knew him and looked up to him. He was a good baseball player, strong and agile. Besides that, he knew he did well on his schoolwork. The more Eddie thought about it, the less he wanted to go to a school full of strangers where he would be one of the youngest. No one there would know how good he was.

Eddie brooded as he walked along, trying to think of a way out. "I just won't go," he thought. "I'll defy them all. They can't make me do what I don't want!" He began to scheme and think of ways to stay in the sixth grade. Suddenly, he knew what he would do. He would fail his schoolwork! If he didn't pass his courses, then they would have to keep him back.

Eddie began his campaign the next day. He showed up late for school and he did not prepare his lessons. In the weeks that followed, his work went steadily downward. He stopped answering questions in class and didn't turn in his homework. His customary enthusiasm was gone. Eddie's conscience was bothering him and he became shiftless and irritable.

Mr. Panco, Eddie's teacher, became worried about Eddie's strange behavior and one day asked him to stay after school. When Mr. Panco confronted Eddie with his poor performance record, Eddie was reluctant to say anything. He didn't want to tell the teacher he was scared. But Mr. Panco persuaded Eddie to tell him what was wrong. They talked for a long time, and the teacher reassured Eddie that in junior high school things would not change so much. "A lot of your friends are going with you, so you won't be alone," Mr. Panco pointed out. "You can still play baseball too. The junior high has a team. If you just continue to do all the things you've always done, everything will be fine."

After their talk, Eddie felt better about his future. He caught up on all the work he had not done and even began to enjoy the thought of the coming graduation ceremony. By the time June rolled around, Eddie was looking forward to the fall.

1. What two things caused Eddie to be upset?
   He wasn't able to do his schoolwork.
   He was afraid of leaving his school.
   His conscience bothered him.
   He disliked his teacher.
2. What would Eddie probably have done if he hadn't talked with Mr. Panco:
   Failed all his courses?
   Transferred to another school?
   Stayed home?
3. Which statement describes the theme of this story?
   People sometimes fear the unknown.
   Junior high schools are frightening places.
   It pays to be shiftless.
4. Which of the following is an example of an opinion?
   Eddie will not do well in junior high school.
   Eddie does his sixth grade work well.
   The idea of going to junior high upset Eddie.
5. Which phrase describes Mr. Panco:
   Uppity and conceited?
   Concerned and reassuring?
   Sneering and defiant?
6. The main idea of the second paragraph is that Eddie began to scheme about how he could stay in the sixth grade. Which of the following is a detail that might be added to support the main idea?
   Eddie is liked by his peers.

Eddie's parents want him to succeed in school.
Eddie thought he might bribe his teachers.

7. Which of the following is an example of a fact?
"No one there would know how good I was."
"Here he was one of the oldest pupils."
"They can't make me do what I don't want."
8. At the end of the story, how are Eddie and Mr. Panco alike?
They are optimistic about Eddie in junior high school.
They agree that junior high school will be a disaster.
They think Eddie should stay in sixth grade.
9. Why did Mr. Panco talk with Eddie?
He was angry about Eddie's misbehavior.
He didn't want Eddie to fail sixth grade.
He wanted to help Eddie to be a better ballplayer.
10. What was the effect of Mr. Panco's discussion with Eddie?
Eddie became more agitated than he was before.
Eddie decided to drop out of baseball.
Eddie overcame his fears about junior high school.

At the completion of this activity the classroom teacher is better able to assess the strengths and needs of the reader in the area of comprehension.

Reading: How Do You Define It? In this chapter we have examined major approaches to the teaching of reading and the various methods that have evolved from these philosophical points of view. The program that *you* decide to implement in your classroom will depend largely on your personal definition of reading. You must ask yourself these questions: "What do I think reading is?" "What are my objectives in teaching a child to read?"

To help you formulate your personal definition of reading, we offer several definitions of reading that reading research specialists have devised. We also provide some examples of "reading instruction in action," which you can use to infer definitions of reading.

What the Experts Say. Smith and Dechant (1961) call attention to the fact that the vantage point from which one attempts to define reading strongly affects its definition:

> The psychologist is interested in reading as a thought process. The semanticist is concerned with meaning and considers the printed page to be the graphic representation of speech. The linguist concerns himself with the relationships between the sounds of language and its written form. The sociologist studies the interaction of reading and culture, and the litterateur reacts to the artistic nature of the production before him. (p. 21)

They point out that reading includes more than recognition of graphic symbols:

> Effective reading includes experiencing, learning, and thinking. It frequently requires reflection, judgment, analysis, synthesis, selection, and critical evaluation of what is being read. The reader is stimulated by the author's printed words, but in turn he vests the author's words with his own meaning. And frequently the reader must select one specific meaning from numerous meanings that he has acquired. (p. 22)

Robinson (1966), completing a refinement of a definition of reading that William S. Gray had begun prior to his death, identified five major components of reading: word perception, comprehension, reaction, assimilation, and rate, a dimension that Gray had not previously included in his analysis of major components of reading. According to the Gray-Robinson definition, or model, of reading, word perception includes word recognition and the association of meanings with words. The second dimension, comprehension, involves two levels of meaning, literal and implied. The third aspect, reaction, involves intellectual judgments and emotional responses. Assimilation, the fourth aspect, involves fusion of old ideas with new ideas which now have been obtained through reading. Rate, the fifth dimension, is recognized as varying speeds depending on load of new words, the length of the lesson or time one is expected to read, and the concept load of material to be read.

Gray and Reese's (1963) definition examines the importance of reading in life. They maintain that reading is an aid to meeting everyday needs, a tool for vocation, a pursuit for leisure time, an aid to enrichment of experience, a tool of citizenship, and a source of spiritual refreshment.

Spache and Spache (1973), taking a somewhat similar approach to the definition of reading, focus on the process rather than the use of reading. They define reading as skill development, a visual act, a perceptual act, a reflection of cultural background, a thinking process, an information process, and an associational learning process.

Tinker and McCullough (1968) believe that reading:

> involves the identification and recognition of printed or written symbols which serve as stimuli for the recall of meanings built up through past experiences, and further the construction of new meanings through the reader's manipulation of relevant concepts already in his possession. The resulting meanings are organized into thought processes according to the purposes that are operating in the reader. Such an organization results in modifications of thought, and perhaps behavior, or it may even lead to radically new behavior which takes its place in the personal or social development of the individual. (p. 8)

Frank Smith's model (1971, 1978) of reading describes the process from the printed words to comprehension as follows:

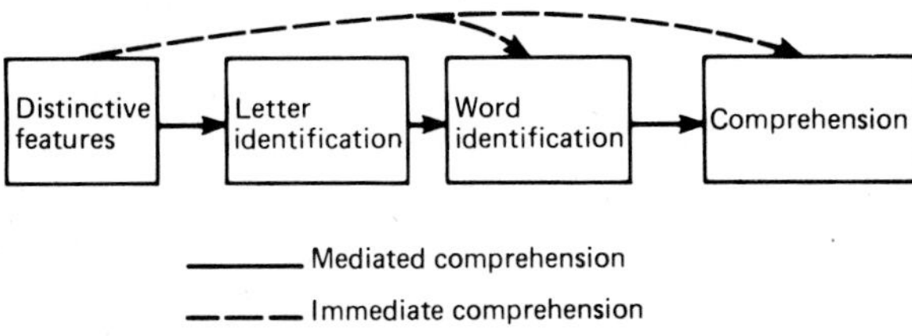

Harris (1972) discusses the nature of reading, pointing out that reading is an extension of oral communication that must have listening and speaking skills as its foundation. He says that reading may be defined "as the act of responding with appropriate meaning to printed and written verbal symbols" and that "the reasoning side of reading becomes increasingly important as recognition is mastered" (pp. 3, 10).

J. Smith (1973) emphasizes the creative aspect of reading in his definition:

> Reading is the ability to recognize and understand the printed symbols of the child's spoken vocabulary. Printed words, as well as spoken ones, are meaningful to the young child only insofar as his field of experience overlaps that of the author of the printed text. The old cliché, "You can take from a book only what you bring to it" is, in essence, true. The reader learns from a book only if he is able to understand the printed symbols and rearrange them into vicarious experiences in his mind. His ability to think, to reason, and to conceptualize makes it possible for him to receive new ideas from a printed page without actually experiencing the new idea, *but he must have experienced each symbol that helps him make up the new idea.* (pp. 31–2)

Rumelhart (1976) stresses the interactive nature of the reading process:

> Reading is the process of understanding written language. It begins with a flutter of patterns on the retina and ends (when successful) with a definite idea about the author's intended message. Thus, reading is at once a "perceptual" and a "cognitive" process. It is a process which bridges and blurs these two traditional distinctions. Moreover, a skilled reader must be able to make use of sensory, syntactic, semantic and pragmatic information to accomplish his task. These various sources of information appear to interact in many complex ways during the process of reading. A theorist faced with the task of accounting for reading must devise a formalism rich enough to represent all of these different kinds of information and their interactions. (p. 1)

C. Smith (1978) also views reading as an interactive process, that is, as an interaction between reader and author:

> Reading then can be defined as an interaction, a communication in which the author and the reader each brings his background language, and a common desire to reach the other person. No matter how else one defines reading, it must involve ideas, backgrounds, common language, common interest, and a mutual point of departure. (p. 28)

Now that you have considered some of these formal definitions of reading, you should attempt to formalize your own personal definition of reading and try to establish an effective reading program that follows logically from your definition. In the next few pages, we describe four classroom situations. As you read each of these, try to determine the definition and the method of reading instruction which each teacher is using.

The four situations that follow may occur in any classroom. Read each of the situations, and answer these questions:

1. What is this teacher's definition of reading?
2. What method of reading instruction is this teacher using?
3. To which earlier definition is the teacher's definition most similar?

Situation 1

Mrs. Bellus teaches a class of children who are nine to ten years old. If you are grade-level oriented in your thinking, these children would probably be fourth-graders.

Mrs. Bellus' class has expressed a strong interest in the theme of cowboys as an outgrowth of a television program that many of the children watched. After a class discussion, the children voted to do an extended study on *cowboys throughout the world*. It was decided that much of the information being gathered would have to come from printed material.

Mrs. Bellus is a resourceful teacher who has a good working relationship with both the school and public librarian. She has stocked her classroom with many books, pamphlets, magazines, encyclopedia volumes, some records, and filmstrips (on varying levels of difficulty because the reading levels of students in her class is 2.4 through 8.8).

The selection of nontextbook materials suggests that Mrs. Bellus believes that any material that displays a written word or idea related to the topic of study is to be viewed as an "instructional material." Instructional materials can be defined as any material that motivates children to read. Such materials are often those related to the private and social lives of children (cartoons, games, magazines).

High-interest, easy-vocabulary books are also found in this classroom. These materials explore topics of interest to older children but contain vocabulary that can be easily read by a child who is having difficulty with grade-level reading. The following references serve as high-interest, easy-vocabulary text sources:

Geisel, T. Seuss. *The Cat in the Hat.* New York: Random House, Inc., 1952.

_____ . *The Cat in the Hat Comes Back.* New York: Random House, Inc., 1958.

Because many of these materials are ungraded, she has to use a readability formula to determine the approximate grade level of the materials. *Readability* refers to the difficulty of the material as measured through the use of a simple mathematical formula. Although many formulas are available (Gray, 1935; Lorge, 1944; Flesch, 1943; Dale-Chall, 1948; Spache, 1973), we believe the simplest one to use is Fry's (1969).

When selecting materials, Mrs. Bellus keeps the following purposes in mind. She wants to be sure that she has a basic understanding of the concepts that the children will be learning; she feels that she should have some idea of the vocabulary they will encounter in the books. She wants to keep children motivated and at the same time lead follow-up discussions, after children have completed reading their books. Mrs. Bellus hopes that these discussions will not only develop awareness of information but also will provide students with experiences that encourage the development of comparative and evaluative thinking skills. She hopes to encourage her students to question the information they find and to question the qualifications of the authors providing the information. Finally, Mrs. Bellus hopes to help the class synthesize the information they have obtained in an attempt to develop a view and appreciation of cowboys (or their counterparts) that reach beyond what they may have developed through hours of TV viewing of Western movies or programs.

When planning for *some* groups, Mrs. Bellus plans to introduce *some* vocabulary with which she feels *some* children may have difficulty. She plans to present the written words and then help individual children needing it with the pronunciation of the words. Other words will be analyzed phonetically from the regular spelling, and yet other words that do not adhere to the general phonetic principles of the English language will be introduced through context clues or dictionary aids. Mrs. Bellus views the development of word analysis skills as an important step toward helping children feel comfortable when they meet the words in print. She believes this word knowledge will help with comprehension and rate of reading. She also suspects that it may be helpful in sustaining student interest, because some children are easily discouraged when they meet many unfamiliar words in printed material.

After potentially troublesome vocabulary has been studied, Mrs. Bellus encourages individuals to return to their reading. She circulates among them to note who is reading what and whether anyone seems to be having difficulty. She pauses here and there to help with a word or to check on an individual's comprehension of whatever he or she has read. She also makes some mental notes of how rapidly children seem to be reading.

After several periods have been spent reading, the group comes together to share some findings. Individuals in the group are encouraged to respond to what others relate. Mrs. Bellus, too, inserts questions that cause students to relate their findings to those of others. She encourages critical evaluation rather than unquestioning acceptance of what is read.

As summarizing or concluding activities, students have an opportunity to compare new images of a cowboy with former images, while explaining the change. This is followed by an enrichment activity that allows students to relate their images of cowboys through art, drama, and music. Children progress through all activities at their own individual rate.

1. What is the teacher's definition of reading?
2. What method of reading instruction is this teacher using?
3. To which earlier definition is this teacher's definition most similar?

Let's see if we agree: we believe that situation 1 seems to be reflective of the Gray-Robinson definition or model of reading. It gives attention to word recognition, comprehension of words and groups of words, reaction to ideas, fusion of new and already held ideas, and the rate at which some of this can occur.

It seems quite likely that Gray and Reese, Spache and Spache, Harris, Smith and Dechant, Tinker and McCullough, James Smith, and Frank Smith could find their concepts of reading being dealt with in this situation. While each would probably change part or all of the situation or shift some emphasis if he were Mrs. Bellus, each seemingly could accept the situation.

Situation 2

The setting for this situation is a first-year reading group. Children in this group have been taught the names of many of the letters. In some cases, they have also been taught the sound the letter represents. They have mastered the learning of sounds, associated with phonograms, such as *at*, *an*, and *am*. They have had experience in blending initial sounds with the sounds represented by these phonograms, so that they have worked with a number of words involving one phonogram: bat, cat, fat, hat, mat, nat, pat, rat, sat, tat, and vat. They have also been introduced to a number of sight words. This was repeated until the word was immediately recognized on sight.

Mr. Kavanaugh is the teacher of this group. He believes that his method of reading instruction gives children the key to unlocking words (decoding) and that repeated practice with a phonetic unit helps the child master sound-symbol combinations. He argues that this helps children to develop security in reading.

The phonogram to which the class is now being introduced is *ad*. They begin with the following list of *ad* words:

bad	had	pad	dad	tad
lad	sad	fad	mad	cad

The phonogram *ad* is examined and discussed; its sound is identified. The blending process is used to add the beginning sounds for the words listed here. Mr. K. spends time with the pronounciation of each of these words. Then the following story is read silently and orally. Mr. Kavanaugh encourages use of correct intonation to indicate statements and questions.

Tad has been bad.
He had a pad.
The pad was Dad's.
Dad wanted the pad.
Tad was a sad lad when Dad found the pad.
Was Tad a bad lad to get Dad's pad?
Was Dad mad at Tad?

After the story has been read, the students are given copies of the following worksheet and asked to put the right letter in the blank.

_ad had Dad's _ad.
Dad was _ad.
He was made at _ad.
_ad found the pad.

The worksheets are collected and checked by Mr. Kavanaugh. Some children who missed specific items are required to take a second round of similar instruction.

1. What is this teacher's definition of reading?
2. What method of reading instruction is the teacher using?
3. To which of the earlier definitions is the teacher's definition of reading most similar?

We found that situation 2 reflects the kinds of programs linguists have developed. There is definite emphasis on the recognition or association of sound and symbol. Special attention has been given to one linguistic element, the phonogram. It can also be noted that little stress is placed on the comprehension of ideas. This situation reflects the philosophy of Fries, which emphasized decoding over meaning in beginning reading instruction.

Situation 3

Mr. Hill has an upper-primary class. These children are involved in many exercises designed to sharpen the senses. They frequently have tasting or "sniffing" parties where they try to identify things by flavor and scent.

Today Harold brought some brightly colored leaves that he picked on the way to school. Examination and discussion of these led Mr. Hill to suggest that the entire class go outdoors to examine and enjoy other evidences of the approach of fall. Once outdoors, they noted other types and coloring of leaves and compared shapes, sizes, textures, and shades. They also discussed how the very air seemed to have a softer, gentler feeling than in the past few weeks. Many plants that had previously blossomed now had pods that were bursting and scattering seeds.

Upon returning to the classroom, Mr. Hill and the children discussed the things they saw, heard, felt, and smelled when they were outdoors. Then Mr. Hill gave each child a copy of a poem entitled "Fall" and a story entitled "The Cricket, the Fall, and Me." He read the poem to the children, inviting them to follow along, and then he suggested that they read it with him. Next he called attention to the "word pictures" in the poem. After they had completed this reading, they read the story and looked for "word pictures." When this was over, they were asked to keep their eyes, ears, noses, and sense of touch alert as they went home in the afternoon. The impression that they gathered would be used for discussion and story writing the following day.

1. What is this teacher's definition of reading?
2. What method of reading instruction is this teacher using?
3. To which of the earlier definitions is the teacher's definition of reading most similar?

Situation 3 certainly leaves one wondering about how and when children will get to the business of learning to recognize words. There is ample evidence of sensitizing students to the world through their senses, but it is difficult to understand how and when the teacher gets to the business of recognition of words and the ability to locate information. This situation reflects the rudiments of a language-experience method. However, Mr. Hill has not yet attempted to deal with each child's needs.

Situation 4

Mrs. DeLeo has a class of eight-year-olds. These might be classified roughly as second-to-third-graders. These students have been introduced to many of the alphabet letters and taught the sounds they represent singly and in clusters. They have also discussed some of the different sounds vowels represent under different circumstances. For example, a vowel in a word that ends with an *e* can be expected to represent its long sound, whereas a vowel in the middle of a word that ends with a consonant can be expected to represent its short sound.

Today Mrs. DeLeo is working on review and extension of those two vowel "rules." She is using the following list of words:

dim–dime	kit-kite
Tim–time	mill-mile

Each word is analyzed letter by letter and sound by sound.

Situation 4 has some similarity to situation 2 in its emphasis on sound-symbol relationhip, but there is a difference in approach. It reflects most of the ideas one would employ when using a synthetic approach to phonics. Sounds are analyzed and then blended into words. Flesch (1943) would probably endorse this particular situation and would feel that reading had been satisfactorily achieved when students could "sound and blend" to arrive at pronunciations.

A Final Definition

Reading, as it has been considered in this text, is the process of perceiving, interpreting, and evaluating printed material. It is one of the four major tools of communication: listening, speaking, reading, and writing. It is usually silent, and it is receptive in nature. Foundations for success in reading lie in the individual's development of skill in listening and speaking.

Reading requires the development of a meaningful vocabulary and a multiplicity of skills. The reader must be able to perceive and recognize written symbols as well as to associate concepts with written symbols. The reader must be able to understand both concrete and abstract ideas as they are presented in written form.

The effective reader questions that which has been read. The reader may approach written material on a literal basis, but he or she must progress to levels of interpretation and critical evaluation. The ability to locate needed material or information and the ability to select materials pertinent to the topic on which one reads are two very important skills in reading. In addition, the effective reader is one who can adjust rate of reading to the purpose for which reading is done.

As you continue to read and think about each of the definitions of reading that have been presented, we hope that you will be able to answer more specifically the probing questions about your individual goals as a teacher of reading. We also hope that you will generate more questions about the specific operations within each definition. Only in this way will you be able to establish an effective, managed language/reading program within your own classroom.

QUESTIONS AND RELATED READINGS

If you feel that you have not attained adequate knowledge to answer the following questions successfully, we suggest additional related readings.

1. What are the historical trends in reading instruction?
2. Why is it important for teachers to understand several methods of reading instruction?
3. What are the strengths of each of the methods discussed in this chapter?
4. Why is there a need for you to develop a personal definition of reading?

Goal 1: To help the reader to appreciate the history of reading instruction in the United States.

Question 1: What are the historical trends in reading instruction?

Chall, J. *Learning to Read: The Great Debate.* New York: McGraw-Hill Book Company, 1967.

Robinson, H., ed. *Reading and Writing Instruction in the United States: Historical Trends.* Urbana, Illinois: ERIC Clearinghouse on Reading and Communications Skills, and Newark, DE: International Reading Association, 1977.

Smith, N. *American Reading Instruction.* Newark, Del.: International Reading Association, 1965.

Goal 2: To help the reader understand the various methods of reading instruction.

Question 2: Why is it important for teachers to understand several methods of reading instruction?

Cheek, M., and E. Cheek. *Diagnostic-Prescriptive Reading Instruction.* Dubuque, Iowa: William C. Brown Company, Publishers, 1980.

Tierney, R., et al. *Reading Strategies and Practices: Guide for Improving Instruction.* Boston: Allyn & Bacon, Inc., 1980.

Veatch, J., et al. *Key Words to Reading: The Language Experience Approach Begins.*, 2nd ed. Columbus, Ohio: Charles E. Merrill Publishing Co., 1979.

Goal 3: To help the reader recognize the strengths of each method studied.

Question 3: What are the strengths of each of the methods discussed in this chapter?

Barrett, T., and D. Johnson. *Views on Elementary Reading Instruction.* Newark, Del.: International Reading Association, 1973.

Hunt, L., ed. *The Individualized Reading Program: A Guide for Classroom Teaching.* Proceedings of the

Eleventh Annual Convention of the International Reading Association. Vol. II, Part 3. Newark, Del.: International Reading Association, 1967.

Matthes, C. *How Children Are Taught to Read*. 2nd ed. Lincoln, Neb.: Professional Educators Publications, Inc., 1977.

Goal 4: To help the reader understand the importance of developing a personal definition of reading on which to base an instructional program.

Question 4: Why is there a need for you to develop a personal definition of reading?

Durkin, D. *Teaching Young Children to Read*, 2nd ed. Boston: Allyn & Bacon, Inc., 1976, pp. 43-61.

Smith, F. *Understanding Reading*, 2nd ed. New York: Holt, Rinehart and Winston, 1978, pp. 175-95.

Spache, G., and E. Spache. *Reading in the Elementary School*. 3rd ed. Boston: Allyn & Bacon, Inc., 1973, pp. 1-17.

BIBLIOGRAPHY

Allen, R. *Report of the Reading Study Project*, Monograph No. 1. San Diego, Calif.: Department of Education, San Diego County, 1961.

_____. *Language Experiences in Communication*. Boston: Houghton Mifflin Company, 1976.

Aukerman, R. *Approaches to Beginning Reading*. New York: John Wiley & Sons, Inc., 1971.

Barrett, T. "Predicting Reading Achievement Through Readiness Tests." In J. A. Figurel *Reading and Inquiry. Proceedings of the International Reading Association Conference*. Newark, Del.: International Reading Association, 1965, pp. 26–28.

Black, I. *The Bank Street Readers*. New York: Macmillan Publishing Co., Inc., 1966.

Bloomfield, L., and C. Barnhart. *Let's Read: A Linguistic Approach*. Detroit: Wayne State University Press, 1961.

Bruner, J. *The Process of Education*. Cambridge, Mass.: Harvard University Press, 1960.

Buchanan, C., and Sullivan Associates. *Programmed Reading*. St. Louis, Mo.: Webster Division, McGraw-Hill Book Company, 1966.

Burmeister, L. "Content of a Phonics Program." In *Reading Methods and Teacher Improvement*, ed. by N. Smith. Newark, Del.: International Reading Association, 1971, pp. 27–33.

Calvin, A. "How to Teach with Programmed Textbooks." *Grade Teacher* 84 (February 1967), 81.

Carillo, L., and D. Bissett. *The Chandler Language Experience Readers*. San Francisco: Chandler Publishing Co.

Cheek, M., and E. Cheek. *Diagnostic-Prescriptive Reading Instruction*. Dubuque, Iowa: William C. Brown Company, Publishers, 1980.

Clymer, T. "The Utility of Phonic Generalizations in the Primary Grades." *The Reading Teacher* 16 (1963), 252–8.

Clymer, T., et al. *Ginn 720 Reading Program*. Lexington, Mass.: Xerox Corporation, 1976.

Dale, E., and J. Chall. "A Formula for Predicting Readability." *Educational Research Bulletin* 27 (January 1948), 11–20.

Dallman, M., L. Rouch, L. Chang, and J. DeBoer. *The Teaching of Reading*, 4th ed. New York: Holt, Rinehart and Winston, 1974.

Dewey, J. *Democracy and Education*. New York: Macmillan Publishing Co., Inc., 1916.

Durkin, D. *Teaching Them to Read*. 2nd ed. Boston: Allyn & Bacon, Inc., 1974.

_____. *Teaching Young Children to Read*, 2nd ed. Boston: Allyn & Bacon, Inc., 1976.

Durrell, D. "Success in First Grade Reading." *Boston University Journal of Education* 140 (February 1958), 2–47.

Eller, W., et al. *Laidlaw Reading Program*. River Forest, Ill.: Laidlaw Publishing, 1980.

Fisher, J. "Dialect, Bilingualism and Reading." In *Reading for All*, ed. by R. Karlin. Proceedings of World Congress of IRA, Buenos Aires, Argentina, August 1974.

Flesch, R. *Marks of Readable Style: A Study of Adult Education*. New York: Bureau of Publications, Teachers College Press, Columbia University, 1943.

Fries, C. *Linguistics and Reading*. New York: Holt, Rinehart and Winston, 1962.

_____. *Reading in the Elementary School*. Boston: Allyn & Bacon, Inc., 1964.

Fries, C., et al. *Merrill Linguistic Readers*. Columbus, Ohio: Charles E. Merrill Publishing Company, 1966.

Fry, E. "Programmed Instruction and Automation in Beginning Reading." In *Elementary Reading Instruc-*

tion, ed. by A. Beery et al. Boston: Allyn & Bacon, Inc., 1969, pp. 400–13.
Gattegno, C. *Words in Color.* Chicago: Learning Materials, Inc., 1962.
Good, C. "Doctoral Studies Completed or Underway." *Phi Delta Kappa.* 1923–1953.
Goodman, K. "Dialect Barriers to Reading Comprehension." *Elementary English* 42 (December 1965), 852–60.
_____, ed. *The Psycholinguistic Nature of the Reading Process.* Detroit: Wayne State University Press, 1968.
Goodman, Y. "Using Children's Reading Miscues for New Teaching Strategies." *The Reading Teacher* 23 (February 1970), 455–9.
Gray, L. *Teaching Children to Read*, 3rd ed. New York: Ronald Press Company, 1963.
Gray, W. "Summary of Investigations Relating to Reading." *Elementary School Journal*, 1925–1932.
_____ and B. Leary. *What Makes a Book Readable.* Chicago: University of Chicago Press, 1935.
Hafner, L., and H. Jolly. *Patterns of Teaching Reading in the Elementary School.* New York: Macmillan Publishing Co., Inc., 1972.
Hall, M. *Reading as a Language Experience.* Columbus, Ohio: Charles E. Merrill Publishing Company, 1975.
Harris, A. *How to Increase Reading Ability*, 5th ed. New York: David McKay Co., Inc., 1970.
Harris, L., and C. Smith, eds. *Individualized Reading Instruction: A Reader.* New York: Holt, Rinehart and Winston, 1972.
Harris, T., et al. *The Economy Company Readers.* Boston: The Economy Company, 1972.
Harris, T., and M. Jacobson. *Basic Elementary Reading Vocabularies.* The First R Series. New York: Macmillan Publishing Co., Inc., 1972.
Jenkins, M., ed. "Here's to Success in Reading Self Selection Helps." *Childhood Education* 32 (November 1955), 124–31.
Karlin, R. *Teaching Elementary Reading: Principles and Strategies.* New York: Harcourt Brace Jovanovich, 1971.
Lapp, D., et al. *Teaching and Learning: Philosophical, Psychological, Curricular Applications.* New York: Macmillan Publishing Co., Inc., 1975.
Lorge, I. "Predicting Readability." *Teachers College Record* 45 (March 1944), 404–19.
Matthes, C. *How Children Are Taught to Read*, 2nd ed. Lincoln, Neb.: Professional Educators Publications, Inc., 1977, p. 9.
Mazurkiewicz, A., and H. Tanzer. *Early to Read Program, Revised Phases 1, 2, 3.* ITA, 1965–66.
McKim, M., and H. Caskey. *Guiding Growth in Reading*. 2nd ed. New York: Macmillan Publishing Co., Inc., 1963.
Pitman, Sir J., A. Mazurkiewicz, and H. Tanzer. *The Handbook on Writing and Spelling in i/t/a.* New York: i/t/a Publications, 1964.
Robinson, H., ed. *Reading: Seventy-five Years of Progress.* Supplementary Educational Monographs, No. 96. Chicago: University of Chicago Press, 1966.
____, ed. *Reading and Writing Instruction in the United States: Historical Trends.* Urbana, Illinois: ERIC Clearinghouse on Reading and Communication Skills and Newark, Del.: The International Reading Association, 1977.
Rumelhart, D. *Toward an Interactive Model of Reading.* Center for Human Information Processing, Technical Report No. 56. La Jolla: University of California, San Diego, 1976.
Samuels, S. "The Effect of Letter-Name Knowledge on Learning to Read." *American Educational Research Journal* 9 (Winter 1972), 65–74.
Sartain, H. "The Place of Individualized Reading in a Well Planned Program." In *Readings on Reading Instruction*, ed. by A. Harris and E. Sipay. 2nd ed. New York: David McKay Co., Inc., 1972, pp. 193–9.
Savage, J. *Linguistics for Teachers.* Chicago: Science Research Associates, Inc., 1973.
Schulwitz, B., ed. *Teachers, Tangibles, Techniques: Comprehension of Content in Reading.* Newark, Del.: International Reading Association, 1975.
Serwer, B. "Linguistic Support for a Method of Teaching Beginning Reading to Black Children." *Reading Research Quarterly* (Summer 1969), 449–67.
Shuy, R. "Some Considerations for Developing Beginning Reading Materials for Ghetto Children." *Journal of Reading Behavior* 1 (Spring 1969), 33–44.
Silvaroli, N. "Factors in Predicting Children's Success in First Grade Reading." In *Reading and Inquiry, Proceedings of the International Reading Association*, Newark, Delaware 1965, pp. 296–8.
Smith, C. *The Macmillan R.* New York: Macmillan Publishing Co., Inc., 1975.
Smith, C., et al. *Teaching Reading in Secondary School Content Subjects: A Book-Thinking Process.* New York: Holt, Rinehart and Winston, 1978.
Smith, C., and R. Wardhaugh. *Macmillan Reading, Series R.* New York: Macmillan Publishing Co., Inc., 1980.
Smith, F. *Understanding Reading*, 2nd ed. New York: Holt, Rinehart and Winston, 1978.
Smith, H., and E. Dechant. *Psychology in Teaching Reading.* Englewood Cliffs, N.J.: Prentice-Hall, Inc., 1961.
Smith, J. *Creative Teaching of Reading in the Elementary School,* 2nd ed. Boston: Allyn & Bacon, Inc., 1973.
Smith, N. *American Reading Instruction.* Newark, Del.: International Reading Association, 1965.

Spache, G. "Psychological and Cultural Factors in Learning to Read." In *Reading for All*, ed. by R. Karlin. *Proceedings of the Fourth IRA World Congress on Reading*. Newark, Del.: International Reading Association, 1973, pp. 43–50.

Spache, G., and E. Spache. *Reading in the Elementary School*, 3rd ed. Boston: Allyn & Bacon, Inc., 1973.

Stauffer, R. "The Language Experience Approach." In *First Grade Reading Programs*, ed. by J. Kerfort. *Perspectives in Reading*, No. 5. Newark, Del.: International Reading Association, 1965, 86–118.

_____. *The Language-Experience Approach to the Teaching of Reading*. New York: Harper & Row, Publishers, 1970.

_____. *Directing the Reading-Thinking Process*. New York: Harper & Row, Publishers, 1975.

Strickland, R. "The Language of Elementary School Children: Its Relationship to the Language of Reading Textbooks and the Quality of Reading in Selected Children." *Bulletin of the School of Education* 38 (1962), 4.

Strang, R. *Diagnostic Teaching of Reading*. New York: McGraw-Hill Book Company, 1964.

Tinker, M., and C. McCullough. *Teaching Elementary School*, 3rd ed. New York: Appleton-Century–Crofts, 1968.

Veatch, J., et al. *Key Words to Reading: The Language Experience Approach Begins*, 2nd ed. Columbus, Ohio: Charles E. Merrill Publishing Company, 1979.

Wardhaugh, R. "Is the Linguistic Approach an Improvement in Reading Instruction?" In *Current Issues in Reading*, ed. by N. Smith. Newark, Del.: International Reading Association, 1969, pp. 254–67.

Yarington, D. *The Great American Reading Machine*. Rochelle Park, N.J.: Hayden Book Company, Inc., 1978.

CHAPTER 11

Developing a Student's Interest in Reading

Teachers have the dual responsibility of developing in their students both reading skills and positive attitudes toward reading: and the two are more interdependent than independent. That is, no one can learn to value reading without having many satisfying reading experiences: and no one can become a facile reader without valuing reading enough to spend many hours learning and strengthening the requisite skills.

R. Smith and D. Johnson, 1976

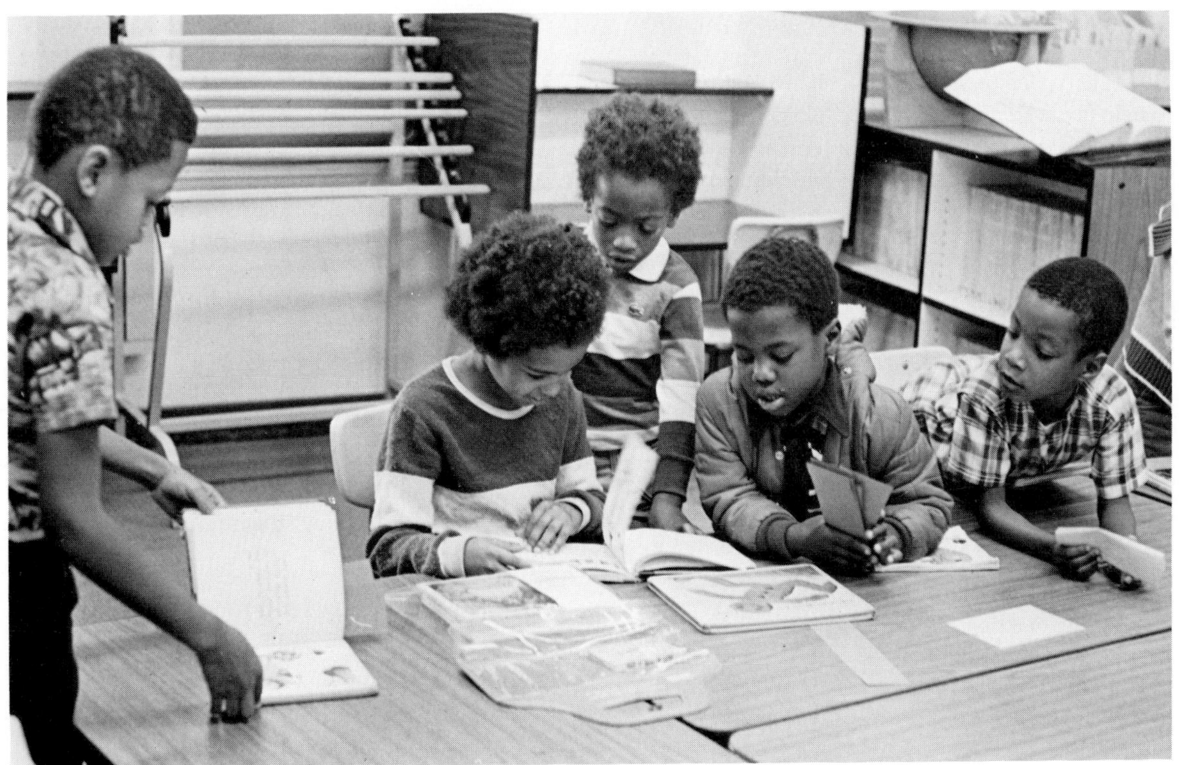

Helping students develop a positive attitude toward reading is very important. As teachers, you must plan curricula that will excite students to read while enabling them to gain an understanding of the worth of reading. (Photo by Linda Lungren.)

GOALS: To help the reader to

1. Understand and assess children's attitudes toward reading.
2. Utilize children's reading interests to encourage reading.
3. Understand how teachers and parents can motivate children to read.
4. Assess children's most effective style of learning.
5. Choose stimulating and appropriately motivating reading materials for students.

THE NEED TO READ

In today's society, it is becoming increasingly difficult to show children (and some adults) that there are important reasons for reading. Relatively free access to video recorders, video tapes, television, movies, recordings, filmstrips, and radio all *seem* to downplay the importance of reading.

As teachers, one of your most challenging goals will be to help children understand how books and other printed materials can enrich their lives. The greatest gift you can give to your students is a lifelong love of books and reading.

REASONS FOR READING

If you were to examine some of the most common reasons why people read, your list would probably include

1. Learning how to do something.
2. Acquiring an understanding of a concept.
3. Proving a point.
4. Learning more about a person or place.
5. Satisfying one's curiosity.
6. Gaining information.
7. Entertaining oneself.
8. Enjoying vicarious experiences.
9. Relaxing.
10. Filling time.

As you can see, there are essentially two reasons why people read: for *information* and for *enjoyment*.

As teachers, you must plan curricula that will excite students to read while enabling them to gain an understanding of the worth of reading. As Russell (1961) points out

> The acid test of any reading program is whether or not the children in it or graduated from it read for themselves. There is little value in developing competent reading ability unless it is voluntarily put to use. One of the aims of any modern program . . . is the development not only of skills but of habits of reading and positive attitudes toward it. The best means of evaluation of the success of a school program is not a score on a standardized test, but rather the amount and quality of the materials children read. The development of worthwhile interests and tastes may be regarded as the crowning achievement of any reading program. A good program creates the desire to read and develops habits of reading not only for recreation but as a means of personal development.
>
> The development of a permanent interest in reading seems to have a number of social and personal values. . . . the health of a democracy is dependent upon a citizenry equipped with some knowledge of the problems faced by the total group. Unless these problems are known to all, and unless possible solutions are communicated through the printed word, without this unifying influence the democracy may become an oligarchy, an anarchy, or a fascist state. One of the personal values in the habit of wide reading during the school years is the favorable effect on reading ability itself. One of the best ways of becoming a competent reader, as measured by a standardized test or any other instrument, is to do much reading of different kinds of materials. Probably more important, the habit of reading can contribute to the child's knowledge of himself, his acquaintance, and his world in a way few other activities can. (pp. 362–3)

In the following play, a king is convinced of the value of reading, and that reading can be fun; similarly, an intuitive teacher can show students how books can contribute to their lives in a personal and exciting way.

THE PUNCTUATION PROCLAMATION

Characters

HARK } HERALDS
HO }

ROYAL TREASURER
ROYAL COOK

KING PISH-POSH
ROYAL TUTOR
ROYAL STORYTELLER
ROYAL SCRIBE
TWO BOY COURTIERS
TWO GIRL COURTIERS
OTHER COURTIERS

SETTING: *The throne room of* KING PISH-POSH, *in the kingdom of Bosh.*

AT RISE: KING PISH-POSH *is snoring noisily on his throne.* HARK *is patrolling the stage from right;* HO *is patrolling from left, and they meet at center.*

HARK: Come on, now. It's your turn to waken him, HO.

HO: Oh, no. I distinctly remember that I woke him the last time, HARK.

HARK: Go on. It's half past the hourglass. He'll miss his reading lesson.

HO: That reading lesson! He's always in such a fearful temper when he has to read. Here, let's toss a coin. (*He takes coin from pocket, tosses and catches it and puts it on the back of his hand.*)

HARK: Heads.

HO: Tails. (*Looks at his hand*) Whew! It's tails. Go ahead, HARK. I'll stay right behind you to catch you when he flattens you. (ROYAL TUTOR *enters timidly from left, with easel, large lesson pad, and book.*)

HARK: Wait. Here's the ROYAL TUTOR. Let him have the honor of telling the KING it's time to read. HERALDS *tiptoe down right, sit on stools, and watch.*

TUTOR *places easel, with lesson pad on it, up left, near throne. He opens book, crosses to throne, and pulls gently at* KING's *sleeve.*)

TUTOR: Your Majesty.

KING: (*Snoring*): Bluhuhuh

TUTOR (*A little louder*): It is time for your daily reading lesson, KING PISH-POSH. (KING *sits bolt upright.*)

KING: Humph! Reading, is it? I knew there was some reason why this was a bad day.

TUTOR: If Your Majesty would only relax. Reading is fun.

KING: Fun! I'd rather be boiled in green, gurgling oil. All those letters huddling together, staring at me like black cats—

TUTOR: The letters are trying hard to mean something to you, Sire. Here— (*He uncovers sentence written on the lesson pad. It reads "I am the King."*) Here is the sentence we have been trying to read for the last three months. Do let us see now how well you can read it.

KING (*Scowling*): TUTOR, that sentence is too hard. There are (*counts on fingers*) ten letters in that sentence. Why can't I have a sentence with *one* letter? I could read that.

TUTOR (*Sighing*): Impossible, Sire. Come now, please. I know you can read this. I beg you to try.

KING: Botheration! (*He thrusts out his lip as he glares at sentence.*) Um-um-um.

TUTOR: The first word is—(*Points to himself*)

KING: The first word is "you." There, I read a word.

TUTOR: No, no, Majesty. The word is "me"—I mean, "I."

KING: I knew that. I was jesting with you. Let me read it, now. "I"—

TUTOR: Sound it out, Gracious Highness.

KING: A-M. A-M. Aha! I have it. LALLAPALOOZA!

TUTOR (*Throwing up his hands*): No, Sire—"am." Now, try the next word. And I suggest that you really *look* at the word.

KING: You never let a poor king rest, do you? Very well, I'll look. I'll stare a hole through the paper. (*He stares at easel. He rises, takes a step closer, and stares again. Then he goes up and tries to brush the period off the paper.*)

TUTOR: What is the matter, Majesty?

KING: There is some sort of beetle on the paper. (*Slaps easel*) There! I got it! No, I didn't. He's still there.

TUTOR (*Coming to easel*): Let me see. Oh, I beg to differ with you, Sire. That is not a beetle. That is a "period."

KING (*Walking back to throne):* I don't care what kind of insect it is. It doesn't belong in my nice, neat palace. (KING *sits on throne*)

TUTOR: But a period is a punctuation mark. It is part of the sentence.

KING: What? Do you mean to tell me that, in addition to twenty-six letters of the alphabet, I shall have to remember an inky blob?

TUTOR: There are many punctuation marks, Sire. There are commas, exclamation marks, question marks, colons, and apostrophes.

KING (*Holding his ears*): Enough! Stop! I won't have it. No. Twenty-six letters are troublesome enough.

TUTOR: But there is nothing I can do, Sire. Punctuation was part of the language before we were even born.

KING: Well, *I* can do something about it. I shall abolish it.

TUTOR (*Wringing his hands*): That is not possible!

KING: Am I, or am I not the King? I am the King! (*Pompously*) There. That's a good sentence. You ought to have that sentence on the easel: "I am the King." I can abolish anything I wish. (*To the heralds*) Heralds! Heralds! (*They rise and run to* KING.)

HARK: Front and center, Sire!

HO: At your service, Majesty!

KING: Draw up a proclamation of abolishment. (*Heralds cross to table with scrolls and quill pens, and prepare to write proclamation.*—Ahem. (KING *dictates.*) "His Royal Highness, King Pish-Posh, of the kingdom of Bosh—" Do you have that?

HARK: Yes, Sire.

KING: "Hereby proclaims that all punctuation marks shall be abolished throughout the land, forever and ever and a day." Seal it with the Royal Seal, and proclaim it immediately.

HO: Immediately, Your Majesty. (HERALDS *bow and exit with scrolls,* HARK *at left,* HO *at right.*)

KING: There. That is that. Now, let us be done with reading. It is time for the court to assemble. TUTOR, bid my courtiers and the STORYTELLER enter. (*The* TUTOR *goes off right and returns with* COURTIERS.) Now, we must have a jolly story. Where *is* my STORYTELLER? (COURTIERS *sit on chairs to left and right of throne.* ROYAL STORYTELLER *runs in from right with large book under his arm.*)

STORYTELLER: The ROYAL STORYTELLER begs to announce his presence in the court of KING PISH-POSH.

KING: Humph. Very good, Let us have a story.

TUTOR (*Aside*): I do hope it isn't "Goldilocks and the Three Bears" again.

COURTIERS (*Groaning*): Oh, no!

1ST BOY COURTIER: Please, Sire, not that story today.

1ST GIRL COURTIER: Please, Sire, we have heard that story three hundred sixty-five times.

KING: Humph. I suppose it is the fashion to be democratic. Very well. What other story would you like to hear?

2ND BOY COURTIER: Might we hear about Robin Hood?

COURTIERS: Yes, yes!

KING: Robin Hood? That's a frightful story. Think what that outlaw did to good King John. Some other tale, think of some other tale.

2ND GIRL COURTIER: Then, Your Majesty, may we hear the story of Sleeping Beauty? We ladies would enjoy it so much.

KING: Would you?

GIRL COURTIERS: Yes, yes!

KING: Does it have a bad fairy in it?

2ND GIRL COURTIER: Oh, yes. She is most dreadfully wicked.

KING: Then we shan't have it. Bad fairies make me nervous.

GIRL COURTIERS (*Sadly*): Oooh.

KING: It is my turn. ROYAL STORYTELLER, open your book to the story of Goldilocks and the Three Bears. (*As* STORYTELLER *opens book,* HO *enters from right, and* HARK *enters from left, to announce proclamation. They read from scrolls.*)

HO: Hear ye! Hear ye! His Royal Highness, King Pish-Posh, of the kingdom of Bosh, hereby proclaims—

HARK: That all punctuation marks shall be abolished throughout the land, forever and ever and a day. (HERALDS *exit,* HARK *left and* HO *right.*)

STORYTELLER: What? No more punctuation?

KING: Never mind. It doesn't concern you. Continue.

STORYTELLER: Very well, Your Highness. (*He begins to read in a singsong fashion with no pauses. As he reads the* COURTIERS *yawn, and fall asleep, and the* KING *grows more puzzled.*) "Once upon a time there lived a little girl named Goldilocks she was an adventurous child she lived in a great wood her parents said do not go into the forest alone but she said pooh pooh I am old enough to take care of myself—"

KING: Stop!

STORYTELLER: This is impossible, Your Majesty. There are no commas or periods. It is like being in a wilderness with no signposts.

KING (*To* TUTOR): Is this true?

TUTOR: It is true, Sire. I tried to warn you. (HARK *enters from left with* ROYAL SCRIBE *and* ROYAL COOK, *who carries large menu and wooden spoon.* HO *enters from right with* ROYAL TREASURER, *who carries small abacus.*)

HARK: Your Highness! There is terrible chaos in the land. The people clamor for you to restore punctuation. Thousands of requests are pouring in. The ROYAL SCRIBE is desperate.

SCRIBE (*Bowing*): Honored King, the records of the kingdom are snarled and confused. We need our apostrophes urgently. With apostrophes we do not know what belongs to whom, or whose things are which.

HO: The ROYAL TREASURER is in a tizzy. He cannot figure out the taxes.

TREASURER (*Bowing*): Moneyed Majesty, I must have periods in abundance. We use them by the carton for decimal points. (*Holding up abacus*) I cannot tell now whether you have one million gold ducats or only one millionth of a ducat.

KING: My treasury is in danger? This *is* serious.

HARK: What's more, Your Majesty, the ROYAL COOK is frantic.

COOK (*Tartly*): Highness, I demand that you put commas back.

KING: Humph. I see no need for commas. I don't eat commas.

COOK (*Advancing to* KING *and thrusting menu under his nose*): Look at this menu. Does this sound appetizing? Beef soup salad creamed chicken ice cream coffee cigars.

KING: Coffee cigars? Blah. Very well. I declare a state of emergency. I seem to have made a mistake. Kings do make mistakes.

TUTOR: Sire—

KING: You shouldn't interrupt in the middle of my mistake.

TUTOR: But, I merely wanted to tell you that you *can* put things right again. (*In stage whisper, as he points to heralds*) The HERALDS.

KING: I can? Yes, yes, of course I can. HERALDS. (*They bow.*) Punctuation is in again. Go spread the word.

ALL: Hooray! (HERALDS *exit.*)

KING: And now we can get on with our story.

ALL: UGH.

KING: On second thought, ever since I heard that story without punctuation, I am not nearly so fond of it. (*To* 2ND GIRL COURTIER) What was the title of that tale you declared was so interesting?

2ND GIRL COURTIER: "Sleeping Beauty," Your Majesty.

KING: "Sleeping Beauty" it shall be, then. After all—(*He stares at the easel.*) I-AM-THE-KING. Period! I read it. I read the sentence. There was nothing to it. It was fun!

ALL: Hooray for King Pish-Posh!

KING: I'm a Royal Reader! What didn't someone tell me it was fun?

TUTOR: We tried, Sire. We certainly did try! (*curtain*)

The End

ATTITUDES

Alexander and Filler (1976) state that "a universal goal of reading instruction should be the fostering of positive attitudes toward reading" (p. 34). It is important, therefore, to examine what an *attitude* is, and how attitude relates to reading.

Attitude has been defined by Thurstone (1928) as the "sum total of man's inclinations and feelings, prejudice or bias, preconceived notions, ideas, fears, threats, and convictions about any specific topic" (p. 531). Allport (1935) defined attitude in both cognitive and physioneural terms as "a mental and neural state of readiness, organized through experience, exerting a direct or dynamic influence upon the individual's responses to all objects and situations in which he is related" (p. 798). Dobbs (1947) defined attitude as a predisposition to respond to a specified object. Fishbein (1967), building on these earlier definitions, suggested that the predisposition to respond remains consistent. For example, if a child is predisposed to dislike reading, the child will probably display negative behaviors each time he or she is engaged in the act of reading. While these reactions may demonstrate a negative attitude toward the act of reading, only the behaviors, not the attitude, would be visible to the observer. Since attitudes cannot be seen or touched, astute teachers must infer their existence from such behaviors.

Epstein (1980), commenting on the many definitions of attitude, cites five common characteristics of the various definitions:

1. An attitude is a mental construct.
2. Attitudes are learned.
3. Attitudes center on a focal object.
4. Attitudes predispose individuals to respond toward some object.
5. Attitudes are evaluative in nature. (pp. 14–5)

As teachers, we are most concerned with reading attitudes. Ciccone (1981) maintains that reading attitude is a system of feelings related to reading, influencing a student to approach or avoid a reading situation. Since attitudes are indeed learned, they can be altered or improved upon by a teacher who examines children's reading attitudes and responds to them.

Teacher observation is one of the most valuable ways to assess attitudes (Alexander and Filler, 1976), yet the difficulty of accurate measurement through observation alone is obvious. Thurstone cautioned us about the major problem existing in assessing attitude; one's outward expression and one's actual attitude may not always be congruent. Dobbs (1947) illustrated a second problem in assessing student attitude when he suggested that it may be possible for several people to possess the same unobservable attitude but may not always be possible to recognize this similarity because their behavioral responses may be different. For example, three children in your classroom may have negative attitudes toward reading: one may feign illness, one may misbehave, and the third student, who also has a negative attitude toward the act of reading, may be attentive to reading because he realizes that the act of reading is important to you. As a teacher you may be perplexed. You may wonder what actually determines one's behavioral response. Perhaps it is a combination of the *cognitive* (development of intellect), *affective* (development of emotions or attitudes), and *conative* (development of volition) domains.

Components of Attitude

Several theories have proposed that attitudes consist of three components: cognitive, affective, and behavioral (conative) (Epstein, 1980, p. 16). Since attitude is a mental construct, the significance of the cognitive (thinking) component is obvious. The affective domain is significant in forming attitudes because the affective domain is basic to the learning process. Turner and Alexander (1980) maintain that the way a reader regards the information that he or she is processing affects his or her learning and later use of that information. This "later use" is reflected in Epstein's (1980) remark: "The ultimate success of a reading program's effectiveness shall be judged not solely on the basis of how well students learn to read but also in terms of whether they do in fact read" (p. 8).

Conation is discussed infrequently in educational literature. As defined by McDougall (1911), conation denotes "the active or striving side of our nature, as the equivalent of will in its wildest sense, as comprehending desire, impulse, craving, appetite, wishing, and willing" (p. 325). The conation is the original impulse that "supplies the motive power to all the activities that are only means to the attainment of the desired end. The train of activity, supported by any one of the instinctive impulses, may become indefinitely prolonged and incessantly renewed, it may take the predominantly intellectual form of thinking our means for the attainment of the end" (McDougall, 1921, p. 181). Epstein (1980) states that the "[conative] component [of attitude] concerns itself with the individual's predisposition to respond to, seek out, and to approach the attitude object" (p. 16).

Having examined the definitions of attitude and the components of attitude, let us now examine how attitude relates to achievement in reading.

Attitude and Achievement

Roswell (1967) attempted to determine the relationship between achievement and change in attitudes toward reading of forty elementary and junior high school students, all considered disabled readers. It was discovered that negative attitudes toward reading were related more closely to reading achievement than to other factors, such as socioeconomic status or age. Similar findings were reported by Gardner (1972) and Puryear (1975) when studying the attitudes and achievement of fourth-graders. A follow-up study of remedial reading instruction was reported by Buerger (1968). The focus of this study was an investigation of the effect of remedial reading instruction on long-term progress and attitude. The findings indicated that the remedial reading instruction itself had no significant effect upon mental ability, vocabulary, reading comprehension, or attitudes toward reading.

Ransbury (1973) found that fifth- and sixth-grade children attributed their attitudes toward reading mainly to their ability to read. Neale, Gill, and Tismer (1970) found a positive correlation between attitude toward various subjects, including reading, and achievement in those areas.

Mathewson (1976) points out that studies in the literature that show only a small relationship between attitude and reading achievement may be due to experiments that "measure attitude toward reading as a school course or as a school activity rather than attitude toward preferred reading content" (p. 665). This would seem to be borne out by Groff's (1962) conclusion that "the reading comprehension of an individual child as he reads is influenced to a degree by his attitude toward content type of material being read" (p. 314).

The data on the relationship between attitude and achievement are inconclusive. However, if further research is to provide greater insights, educators need to construct useful instruments that measure attitudes. An example of such an inventory was constructed by Ransbury (1971). Refer to page 359 to view Ransbury's Reading Attitude Inventory. The Reading Apperception Test, developed by O'Connor (1968), explored relationships between attitude toward reading and reading achievement. He concluded that attitude toward reading was related to reading ability within a specific reading situation.

These studies have been included to offer some insight into the relationship between attitude development and reading. They do not offer any explanations, however, as to why some students have negative attitudes toward reading. It may be that some students (1) are very much like the king in the preceding play, in that they are uninterested in reading, and (2) are unaware of a reason for reading. If the second reason appears to be a prime factor, American children may be like *The Little Old Man Who Could Not Read*.

THE LITTLE OLD MAN WHO COULD NOT READ
by Irma Simonton Black*

Once there was a little old man who could not read. He just never wanted to learn. His wife went to the store and bought the food but the little man stayed home and made beautiful toys out of wood. Children all over the world loved his toys, and many wrote to tell him so. But still the little old man never wanted to learn to read. One day his wife decided to go on a visit. "You will need to go to the store," she said. "Get a can of soup, and a big can of spaghetti sauce and some spaghetti. Get some sugar and some milk and some oatmeal. Eat well!" And she kissed the old man and left. The old man went to the store. There were rows and rows of cans with pictures on them. And there were rows and rows of cans and boxes without pictures. What were they? The little man did not know, and he didn't like to ask. He bought a middle-sized can. It looked like the cans of soup his wife brought home. He bought a long box that looked like the spaghetti box and a big can that looked like a spaghetti sauce can. He bought a blue box that looked like a sugar box. He bought a round box that looked like an oatmeal box. And, last of all, he bought a square carton. It looked like the milk cartons his wife brought home. "Ah!" said the little old man when he got home. "That walk made me hungry. I shall have some hot soup for lunch." He opened the middle-sized can. It was onion soup. The little old man hated onions of any kind—and onion soup worst of all. "Fiddle," he said. "Onion soup. I shall save it for my good wife." At dinnertime, the little old man rubbed his hands with pleasure and took down the long box that looked like a spaghetti box and the great big can that looked like a spaghetti sauce can. Beaming, he opened the long box. But the box did not have spaghetti in it. It had waxed paper. "Fiddlesticks and fish fur!" said the little old man. "Who wants to eat waxed paper—even with sauce on it? Not I, for one. But I can eat the sauce all by itself." He reached for the big can. For the first time, he noticed that it had a plastic top on it, so he took that off. "That's funny," he said to himself. "I never saw a

*Reader's Digest Services, Inc., Pleasantville, N.Y., 1968.

plastic top on a sauce can. I do hope this isn't a coffee can!" He opened the big can. It *was* a coffee can. The coffee smelled delicious, but it wasn't much good for a hungry little old man. "Shall I have my oatmeal and milk and sugar instead?" he asked himself. Then he answered himself. "No, I'll have a cup of coffee and go to bed. In the morning, I'll have a nice big breakfast." By the next morning, he was very, *very* hungry. "Oatmeal!" said the old man as he jumped out of bed. "I shall put lots and lots of milk and sugar on it. Ah!" The little old man got the round box and the blue box and the square carton. He put them all on the table. Then he opened the round box. There was no oatmeal in it. It was full of something grainy and white. The old man tasted it carefully. Salt! "Fiddles and flutes," said the old man. "Who wants milk and sugar on salt?" He opened the blue box and got a spoon to have a sweet taste of sugar. But there was no sugar in the box. It was full of little white flakes. "Soap!" said the old man sadly. "Who wants soap even with milk? Oh, oh, how hungry I am!" He opened the square carton to get a drink of milk. But the milk in the carton smelled funny. It was buttermilk, sour *sour* buttermilk. The old man hated buttermilk, but he was so hungry that he drank every drop of it. The old man hated onion soup. But at noon he was so hungry that he ate onion soup. At night the wife came back. The old man was very glad to see her. "Wife," he said, "I had a bad time." He told her how he got all mixed up with the cans and cartons and boxes. "The long box was not spaghetti. It was waxed paper! The blue box was soap flakes! The round box was salt! Wife, please teach me to read!" "Very well, I shall," said his good wife. First the old man learned to read the word spaghetti. Next he learned to read the word milk. Then he learned to read the words for everything in the big store. And then he learned to read the words for everything in the world. But he still made his beautiful toys out of wood, and now he could read the letters the children sent to him. And he never—no, never—went hungry again.

Students may have attitudes that are similar to the king's (they do not *like* to read), or, like the little old man, they may not see a purpose for reading. In either case, the key to making students *want* to read (the conative domain) may reside in the teacher and in the classroom environment.

THE TEACHER AND THE ENVIRONMENT

Some of the children in your classroom may regard reading as a pleasurable activity, perhaps because of early encounters with books that they have shared with a loved one. But some of these children who enter school having had pleasurable reading experiences find that school reading is an arduous task involving basal readers, worksheets, and constant teacher reprimands. Many of these children quickly develop negative attitudes toward reading. Within this group of children there may be those who view reading as a means of becoming more like the adult they aspire to model, and they may realize that reading is necessary for later pleasure. But there may also be students who are unable to see the purposes of reading and their negative behaviors may manifest this lack of purpose.

Alexander and Filler (1976) remind us that "both the teacher (what he is and what he does) and the general atmosphere of the classroom may have effects on positive attitude development and maintenance" (p. 8). Wilson and Hall (1972) further state that

> The key to developing a personal love of books is a teacher who communicates enthusiasm and an appreciation of literature through his attitude and example. Knowing children and their interests, and knowing literature are of great importance in promoting personal reading. Significant as these are, however, the success or failure of the personal reading program in the elementary school rests with the classroom teacher. In those classrooms where teachers are enthusiastic about books and where stimulating contacts with literature are an integral part of the school experience, children are more likely to become avid readers. (pp. 243–244)

One of the best (and easiest) ways for a teacher to communicate enthusiasm and appreciation for literature is by being a good *model* for students. Ask yourself the following questions:

1. Do I freely choose to spend my spare time reading?
2. Do I read to my students regularly?
3. Do I reach for a book when I need information?
4. Am I knowledgeable enough about children's books to make recommendations based on students' interests and achievement levels?
5. Do I discuss my interest in reading with my students?

6. Do my personal attitudes and my classroom environment demonstrate that I value reading?
7. Am I enthusiastic and positive in my approach to reading?

Your classroom environment also reflects the value you place on books and reading. Is there a reading area that is warm, attractive, and inviting? Are books and magazines displayed prominently? Do the reading materials accurately reflect the students' interests and developmental levels? Do you promote book fairs? Are there posters telling about authors and their books?

The teacher and the classroom environment are important factors that can influence students' attitudes about reading. Together, they may encourage children to read or listen to books so that "any sparks of excitement they give off in response to good books can be fanned into fires of warm enthusiasm toward reading as a meaningful lifelong habit" (Somers and Worthington, 1979, p. 6).

What the Teacher Can Do in the Classroom

One of the best ways through which a teacher can help children enjoy reading is by reading books and sto-

One of the best ways through which a teacher can help children enjoy reading is by reading books and stories to them. (Photo by Linda Lungren.)

ries to them. Dawson (1972) encourages this approach: "Teachers should read to children every day from books that are worthwhile, appropriate in level of interest, but probably too hard for them to read themselves" (p. 37). Commenting on the value of reading to students, Spiegel (1981) also points out that " all the work is being done by the readers; the listeners can just relax and enjoy the story. As a result, children may learn to associate reading with pleasure. Furthermore, teachers are showing the audience that reading is something they enjoy and value" (pp. 29-30). The perceptive teacher will find numerous opportunities to read aloud to children. Many students have been "hooked on reading" through this method. Reading to children provides the teacher with an opportunity to choose and help develop a taste for good literature. The following books are only a sampling of the many materials that you can share with children.

1981 Winners

Newberry

Winner: *Jacob Have I Loved*, Katherine Paterson (New York: Thomas Y. Crowell Company)

Honor Book: *The Fledgling*, Jane Langton (New York: Harper & Row, Publishers), illustrated by Erik Blegvad

Honor Book: *A Ring of Endless Light*, M. L'Engle (New York: Farrar, Straus & Giroux, Inc.)

Caldecott

Winner: *Fables*, written and illustrated by Arnold Lobel (New York: Harper & Row, Publishers)

Honor Book: *The Grey Lady and the Strawberry Snatcher*, Molly Bang (New York: Four Winds Press)

Honor Book: *Mice Twice*, J. Low (McElderry/Atheneum Publishers)

Honor Book: *Truck*, D. Crews (New York: Greenwillow Books)

1980 Winners

Newberry

Winner: *A Gathering of Days*, Joan Blos (New York: Charles Scribner's Sons)

Honor Book: *The Road from Home,* David Kherdian (New York: Greenwillow Books)

Caldecott

Winner: *Ox-Cart Man*, Donald Hall (New York: The Viking Press, Inc.), illustrated by Barbara Cooney

Honor Book: *Ben's Trumpet*, Rachel Isadora (New York: Greenwillow Books)

Honor Book: *The Garden of Abdul Gasazi*, Chris Van Allsburg (Boston: Houghton Mifflin Company)

Honor Book: *The Treasure*, Uri Schnelvitz (New York: Farrar, Straus & Giroux, Inc.)

1979 Winners

Newberry

Winner: *The Westing Game*, Ellen Raskin (New York: E. P. Dutton & Co., Inc.)

Honor Book: *The Great Gilly Hopkins*, Katherine Paterson (New York: Thomas Y. Crowell Company)

Caldecott

Winner: *The Girl Who Loved Wild Horses*, written and illustrated by Paul Gŏble (Scarsdale, N.Y.: Bradbury Press)

Honor Book: *Freight Train*, Donald Crews (New York: Greenwillow Books)

Honor Book: *The Way to Start a Day*, Byrd Baylor (New York: Charles Scribner's Sons), illustrated by Peter Parnall

1978 Winners

Newberry

Winner: *Bridge to Terabithia*, Katherine Paterson (New York: Thomas Y. Crowell

Company), illustrated by Donna Diamond

Honor Book: *ANPAO: An American Indian Odyssey*, Jamake Highwater (New York: Harper & Row, Publishers)

Honor Book: *Ramona and Her Father*, Beverly Cleary (New York: William Morrow & Co., Inc.)

Caldecott

Winner: *Noah's Ark*, Peter Spier (Garden City, N.Y.: Doubleday & Company, Inc.)

Honor Book: *Castle*, David Macaulay (Boston: Houghton Mifflin Company)

Honor Book: *It Could Always Be Worse*, Margot Zemach (New York: Farrar, Straus & Giroux, Inc.)

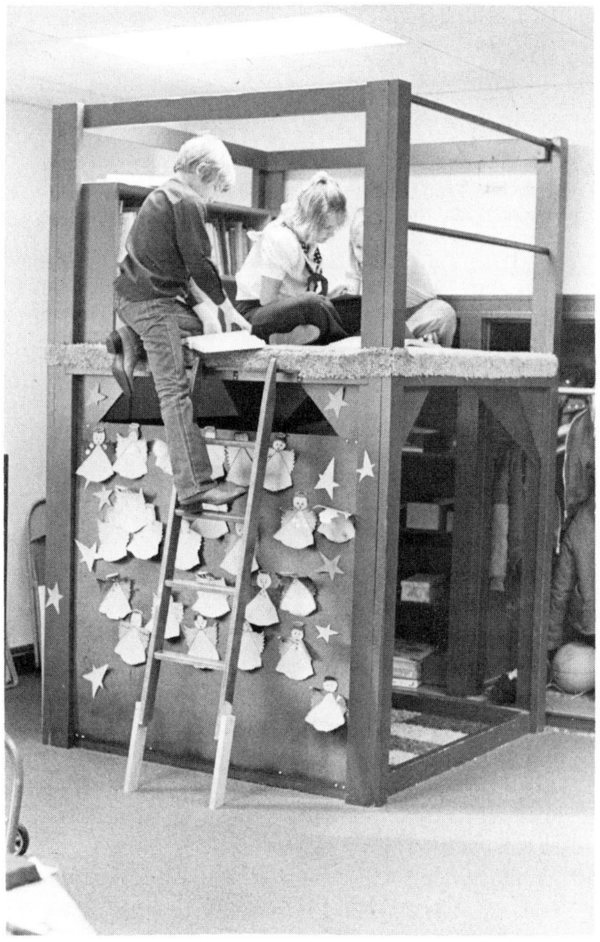

Establish a reading center or corner. It can be simple or elaborate but it is important to make the space warm and inviting. (Photo by Linda Lungren.)

Building Reading Interests

SUGGESTIONS FOR THE TEACHER

1. Set aside a particular time each day to read to your students.
2. Choose materials with a variety of different content to read to children. Try to choose something related to the special interest of each child. This has a two-fold value: reading is enhanced for the child whose interest is tapped as well as for other children because they often discover a new interest.
3. Encourage students to read newspapers and magazines by having classroom subscriptions to them. Frequently, local newspaper publishers or the PTA will donate such subscriptions.
4. Have students share interesting stories or facts they have read in newspapers and magazines. This should not be strictly a current events activity; allow the students to include human interest stories.
5. Establish a reading center or corner. This can be as simple as putting a throw rug in a quiet corner, or it can be an elaborate adventure, depending on the available space and resources. It is important to make the space warm and inviting. Guidelines for the use of the corner should be designed by the teacher and the students together.
6. Encourage children to seek variety in their reading selections. To facilitate this, you may want to have shelves labeled with different types of literature, such as biography, science fiction, history, science, fairy tales, and humor.
7. Have children who have all read the same book dramatize all or part of it. They can do this for their own enjoyment or to share it with classmates.
8. Purchase collections of children's drama and organize a reader's theater for children. The reader's theater approach is discussed in greater detail at the

end of this chapter. Some excellent collections include

Collections

Carlson, B. *Funny-Bone Dramatics*, illustrated by Charles Cox, Nashville, Tenn.: Abingdon Press, 1974.
Chambers, D. W. *Storytelling and Creative Drama.* Dubuque, Iowa: William C. Brown Company, Publishers, 1970.
Durrell, D. D. *Favorite Plays for Classroom Reading.* Boston: Plays, Inc., 1965.
Fontaine, R. *Humorous Skits for Young People: A Collection of Royalty-free Short Plays and Easy-to-Perform Comedy Sketches.* Boston: Plays, Inc., 1965.
Kamerman, S., ed. *Fifty Plays for Junior Actors.* Boston: Plays, Inc., 1966.
Korty, C. *Silly Soup.* New York: Charles Scribner's Sons, 1977.
Olfson, L. *Classics Adapted for Acting and Reading.* Boston: Plays, Inc., 1972.

9. Start a recommended book file. In a small file, place dividers labeled with various types of literature. Invite children to write brief recommendations for books that they have read and enjoyed. The size of the file and the cards included in the file will determine the maximum length of the recommendation. Standards for these recommendations should be set up so that they will adequately help the potential reader get an idea about the book without "giving away" the whole story.
10. Build students' enjoyment of poetry by selecting a variety of poems to read to them. Provide copies for students so that they can participate through choral reading. Have a variety of poetry anthologies available in the classroom for students to read.
11. Allow time occasionally for children to read something they have particularly enjoyed to other children.
12. Expand your classroom library with paperback books. If teachers coordinate the purchase of books, it is often possible to build an elaborate classroom collection through bonus books; the agency from which books are published might contribute free books for every fifteenth or twenty-fifth class purchase.
13. Work cooperatively with the art teacher to plan National Book Week festivities. Children can plan and develop bulletin boards, murals, and paper sculpture to display the books that they have read.
14. Prepare crossword puzzles about books and authors and about the content of a particular book.

Crossword Puzzles

Animal Crossword Puzzles. New York: Wonder, Wonder Treasure Books, Inc., Division of Grosset & Dunlap. For grades 2–3.
Beginner's Crossword Puzzles. Garden City, N.Y.: Doubleday & Company, Inc. For grades 4–9.
Crackerjack Crosswords. Garden City, N.Y.: Doubleday & Company, Inc. For grades 4–9.
Crossword Puzzles. New York: Wonder, Wonder Treasure Books. For Grade 1–2.
Crossword Puzzles. New York: Wonder, Wonder Treasure Books. For Grades 2–3.
Crossword Puzzles. New York: Wonder, Wonder Treasure Books. For Grades 3–4.
Junior Crossword Puzzle Books. New York: Platt, Platt & Munk Publishers, Division of Questor, Educational Products. For grades 4–8.
X-Word Fun. Englewood Cliffs, N.J.: School Book Service, Scholastic Book Services, Division of Scholastic Magazines. For grades 7–9.

15. Devote one week per month to a particular children's book author. Learn and share information that will make the authors familiar to the children.
16. Create riddles about book characters and authors who are familiar to the students. These can be organized so that they can be enjoyed by individuals or they can be played by pairs or teams of players.

Riddle Books

Cricket's Jokes, Riddles & Other Stuff, compiled by M. Leonard and the editors of *Cricket Magazine*. New York: Random House, Inc., 1977.
How Do You Make an Elephant Laugh? by J. Rosenbloom, illustrated by J. Behr. New York: Sterling Publishing Company, Inc., 1979.
Riddle Me, Riddle Me, Ree, by M. Leach. New York: The Viking Press, Inc., 1970.
Tinkerbell is a Ding-a-ling, by R. Doty. Garden City, N.Y.: Doubleday & Company, Inc., 1980.

Suggestions for the Parent. Often, parents want to help their children develop good reading habits, but they are not quite sure what they can do. You should encourage parent-child interactions in reading throughout the elementary school years. Explain to parents that, as the child matures beyond the beginning reading stages, adults can continue to provide the basis for a good attitude toward reading by reading themselves and by making good material available for their children to read. They can encourage children to discuss things they have read, and they can discuss with each other and their children some of the interesting things that they have read.

Nursery rhymes and jingles are particularly enjoyable to young children. In addition, picture books are designed for the young child. Parents can acquaint themselves and their children with the children's division of the library. The young child who visits the library with a parent and watches as the parent selects books for himself or herself is acquiring the "library habit." Magazine and newspapers that are available in the home make a worthwhile contribution to the child's background or foundation for becoming a reader. You may want to share the following suggestions with the parents of your students.

1. Help young children to realize the fun to be found in reading. Select humorous poems, short stories, or magazine articles (on the child's level). Read some of the following books to your child and enjoy the humor with him or her.

Humorous Short Stories and Poems

Blume, J. *The One in the Middle is the Green Kangaroo*, illustrated by A. Aitken. Scarsdale, N.Y.: Bradbury Press, 1981. For grades 3–5.

Fenner, P. R. *Fun, Fun, Fun.* Stories of Fantasy and Farce, Mischief and Mirth, Whimsy and Nonsense, illustrated by J. Zabinski. New York: Franklin Watts, Inc., 1953. For grades 5–6.

Hendra, J., ed. *The Illustrated Treasury of Humor for Children.* New York: Grossett and Dunlap, Publishers, 1980. For grades 3–7.

Riley, J. W. *Joyful Poems for Children*, illustrated by Charles Geer. Indianapolis: The Bobbs-Merrill Co., Inc., 1960. For grades 3–6.

Smith, W. J. *Laughing Time*, illustrated by Juliet Kepes. Boston: Atlantic and Toronto: Little Brown Books, 1953. For Grades K–3.

Wiggins, K. D., and N. A. Smith, *Tales of Laughter.* Garden City, N.Y.: Doubleday & Company, Inc., 1954. For grades 5–8.

2. An excellent way in which a child can begin to expand his or her vocabulary is by choosing books or stories with a reasonable number of unfamiliar words. Have the child tell you when an unfamiliar word is heard. You can record the word and return to it at an appropriate stopping place. At that time, discuss the word and its meaning. Any of the following books may be valuable for vocabulary expansion:

Vocabulary Expansion

Alexander, L. *Westmark.* New York: E. P. Dutton & Co., Inc., 1981.

Bond, F. *Poinsettia and Her Family.* New York: Thomas Y. Crowell Company, 1981.

Bunting, E. *Demetrius and the Golden Goblet*, illustrated by M. Nague. New York: Harcourt Brace Jovanovich, 1980.

Goldsmith, H. *Toto the Timid Turtle*, illustrated by S. Chan. New York: Human Sciences Press, 1980.

L'Engle, M. *A Wrinkle in Time.* New York: Farrar, Straus & Giroux, Inc., 1962.

O'Dell, S. *Island of the Blue Dolphins.* Boston: Houghton Mifflin Company, 1960.

3. Illustrations in picture books can help children to develop an interest in reading. Encourage children to look at the picture and tell the story that the pictures depict. Some appropriate books are the following:

Picture Books

Crews, D. *Light.* New York: Greenwillow Books, 1981.

Freeman, D. *Penguins of All People!* New York: The Viking Press, Inc., 1971.

Lifton, B. *The Many Lives of Cio and Goro.* New York: W. W. Norton & Company, Inc., 1968.

Sendak, M. *Outside Over There.* New York: Harper & Row, Publishers, 1981.

Sharmat, M. *Gila Monsters Meet You at the Airport*, illustrated by B. Barton. New York: Macmillan Publishing Co., Inc., 1980.

Shimin, S. *A Special Birthday.* New York: McGraw-Hill Book Company, 1976.

4. When your child has particularly enjoyed a story, choose characters from the story you can imitate or portray. As you and your child go about your daily routine, act as you think your chosen characters might act in your situation. Here are some useful references:

Play-Acting Books

Bale, J. *Jango.* New York: Delacorte Press, 1965.

Buckley, H. *Too Many Crackers.* New York: Lothrop, Lee & Shepard Company, 1966.

Cowles, G. *Nicholas.* New York: The Seabury Press, 1975.

Duncan, L. *Giving Away Suzanne.* New York: Dodd, Mead & Company, 1963.

Gantos, J. *Aunt Bernice*, illustrated by N. Rubel. Boston: Houghton Mifflin Company, 1978.
Kraus, R. *Mert the Blurt*, illustrated by J. Aruego and A. Dewey. New York: Windmill Books/Simon and Schuster, 1980.
Levitin, S. *Journey to America.* New York: Atheneum Publishers, 1970.
Ness, E. *Do You Have the Time, Lydia?* New York: E. P. Dutton & Co., Inc., 1971.
Newman, R. *Merlin's Mistake.* New York: Atheneum Publishers, 1970.

5. Try to interest your child in some of the following magazines:

Boys' Life
Child Life
Children's Digest
Co-ed
Cricket
Curious Naturalist
Current Events
Daisy
Ebony, Jr.
Highlights for Children
Horn Book
Humpty Dumpty's Magazine for Little Children
Illinois History
Jack & Jill
Junior Scholastic
Kansas School Naturalist
Kids for Ecology
Man & His Music
Maryland Conservationists
Maryland Magazine
Model Airplane News
My Weekly Reader Eye
National Geographic World
Nature Canada
News Explorer
Popular Science
Ranger Rick's Nature Magazine
Read
Roots
Science and Children
Science World
Senior Scholastic
Senior Weekly Reader
Texan Historian
Wee Wisdom
Wee Wish Tree
Wisconsin Trails
World Traveler
Young Miss
Young World
Zoonooz

6. Set aside a family reading time. The type of material read is not as important as the *regularity* of the reading time.
7. Try to acquire, or borrow from the library, some of the following records and "read along" editions of good books for readers.

Read-Along Books

Drummer Hoff by Barbara Emberley (K-3)
Film, Morton Schindel, 1969, 16mm 5 min, color
Filmstrip, Weston Woods, 34 frames, color w/record or cassette
European Folk and Fairy Tales, CMS Records 1968 (K-6)
Evan's Corner by Elizabeth Starr Hill (K-6)
Film, Stephen Bosustow, 16 mm, color
Mother Mother I Feel Sick Send for the Doctor Quick Quick Quick by Remy Charlip (K-3)
Filmstrip, Look/Listen & Learn, 43 frames, b/w
The Mouse That Roared by Leonard Wibberley (7-8)
Film, Columbia, 1959, 16mm color
Record, CMS Records, 1970 (by the author)
Poetry Parade
Record or cassette, Weston Woods, 1967
Where Does the Butterfly Go When It Rains? by Mary Garelick
Filmstrip, Weston Woods, 20 frames, color w/cassette or record
The Wind in the Willows, Kenneth Grahame
Filmstrip (color), record or cassette
Spoken Arts, Inc., 1977
The Wisest Man in the World, retold by Benjamin Elkin (K-6)
Film, Thomas Sand, 1970, 16mm, color
The Witch of Blackbird Pond, Elizabeth George Speare
Record or cassette, Miller-Brody Production, 1970

8. Books make excellent gifts. Ownership has also been found to be one of the most important factors in encouraging reading. Some interesting books for gifts are:

Gift Books

Blue, R. *My Mother the Witch*, illustrated by T. Lewin. New York: McGraw-Hill Book Company, 1980. For grades 4-6.
Byars, B. *After the Goat Man.* New York: The Viking Press, Inc., 1974. For grades 4-6.
Hill, D. *Mr. Pecknuff's Tiny People*, illustrated by A. Daniel. New York: Atheneum Publishers 1981. For grades 1-3.
Mazer, H. *The Island Keeper.* New York: Delacorte Press, 1981. For grades 6-8.
Preston, E. *Squawk to the Moon, Little Goose.* New York: The Viking Press, Inc., 1974. For preschool-grade 1.
Synder, Z. *The Truth About Stone Hollow.* New York: Atheneum Publishers, 1974. For grades 4-7.

Determining a Student's Self-concept

Self-concept may be defined as a student's perception of himself, what he believes he is. According to Quandt (1972), there is strong evidence to suggest that there is a positive correlation between levels of reading achievement and levels of self-concept. Alexander and Filler (1976) also state that "it is possible that there may be interactions among achievement, self-concept, and attitudes toward reading" (p. 6).

Diagnosis of self-concept is difficult because "self-concept is a construct, not a behavior" (Quandt, 1972, p. 11). Several researchers have attempted to present the components of the affective domain of the human intellect in a hierarchical array similar to the taxonomies presented by Bloom (1954) and Barrett (1968). Krathwohl (1969), among others, has attempted to demonstrate the relationship between affective processes and reading ability. The Krathwohl taxonomy is presented here:

1.0 Receiving (attending)
  1.1 Awareness
  1.2 Willingness to receive
  1.3 Controlled or selected attention
2.0 Responding
  2.1 Acquiescence in responding
  2.2 Willingness to respond
  2.3 Satisfaction in response
3.0 Valuing
  3.1 Acceptance of a value
  3.2 Preference for a value
  3.3 Commitment (conviction)
4.0 Organization
  4.1 Conceptualization of a value
  4.2 Organization of a value system
5.0 Characterization by a value or value complex
  5.1 Generalized set
  5.2 Characterization (p. 95)

Many researchers have used Krathwohl's taxonomy to demonstrate a relationship between a child's self-concept and reading ability. Some educators have attempted to develop a child's self-concept in the hope that an increase in positive self-concept would result in increased reading ability.

To determine which students may benefit from an intervention program, it is important to assess the self-concept of each child. Many instruments have been developed to assess self-concepts (see Apendix in Quandt, 1972, pp. 34–35). As an example, the first six items from Gordon's (1966) *How I See Myself Scale* are presented here:

1. Nothing gets me too mad	1	2	3	4	5	I get mad easily and explode
2. I don't stay with things and finish them	1	2	3	4	5	I stay with something till I finish
3. I'm very good at drawing	1	2	3	4	5	I'm not much good at drawing
4. I don't like to work on committees, projects	1	2	3	4	5	I like to work with others
5. I wish I were smaller (taller)	1	2	3	4	5	I'm just the right height
6. I worry a lot	1	2	3	4	5	I don't worry much

Determining a Student's Attitude Toward Reading

It is important that teachers assess students' attitudes toward reading because these attitudes affect the acquisition of reading skills and determine if students continue to read for information and recreation. Epstein (1980) endorses assessing students' attitudes when he says:"If we truly desire to promote positive reading attitudes or at least reduce negative attitudes (feelings), we must be aware of students' present attitudes" (p. 9).

Teacher observation can be a valuable assessment tool; in addition, you may find the following measures helpful in determining your students' attitudes toward reading, the first of which is especially appropriate for young children.

READING ATTITUDE INVENTORY
by Paul Campbell, 1966

Name ____________ Grade ____ Teacher ____________

1. How do you feel when your teacher reads a story out loud?

2. How do you feel when someone gives you a book for a present?

3. How do you feel about reading books for fun at home?

4. How do you feel when you are asked to read out loud to your group?

5. How do you feel when you are asked to read out loud to the teacher?

6. How do you feel when you come to a new word while reading?

7. How do you feel when it is time to do your work-sheet?

8. How do you feel about going to school?

9. How do you feel about how well you can read?

10. How do you think you friends feel about reading?

11. How do you think your teacher feels when you read?

12. How do you think your friends feel when you read out loud?

13. How do you feel about the reading group you are in?

14. How do you think you'll feel about reading when you're bigger?

The following is an alternate form of the first measure.

READING INTEREST/ATTITUDE SCALE

Right to Read Office, Washington, D.C, 1976

Date__________Grade____ Name ________________

Directions: Read each item slowly twice to each child. Ask him or her to point to the face which shows how he or she feels about the statement. Circle the corresponding symbol. Read each item with the same inflection and intonation.

A
Strongly Agree
(Makes me feel good)

B
Undecided
(OK or don't know)

C
Strongly Disagree
(Makes me feel bad)

A B C 1. When I go to the store I like to buy books.
A B C 2. Reading is for learning but not for fun.
A B C 3. Books are fun to me.
A B C 4. I like to share books with friends.
A B C 5. Reading makes me happy.
A B C 6. I read some books more than once.
A B C 7. Most books are too long.
A B C 8. There are many books I hope to read.
A B C 9. Books make good presents.
A B C 10. I like to have books read to me.

This second measure can be used with older students.

You can read some of the following statements to your students in order to assess their attitudes toward reading.

READING ATTITUDE INVENTORY
by Molly Ransbury, 1971

Yes	No	
_____	_____	1. I visit the library to find books I might enjoy reading.
_____	_____	2. I would like to read a magazine in my free time.
_____	_____	3. I cannot pay attention to my reading when there is even a little noise or movement nearby.
_____	_____	4. I enjoy reading extra books about topics we study in school.
_____	_____	5. I would like to read newspaper articles about my favorite hobbies or interests.
_____	_____	6. I feel I know the characters in some of the comic books I read.
_____	_____	7. My best friend would tell you that I enjoy reading very much.
_____	_____	8. I would like to belong to a group that discusses many kinds of reading.
_____	_____	9. I would enjoy spending some time during my summer vacation reading to children in a summer library program.
_____	_____	10. My ideas are changed by the books I read.
_____	_____	11. Reading is a very important part of my life. Every day I read many types of materials.
_____	_____	12. I read magazines for many different reasons.
_____	_____	13. My friends would tell you that I'd much rather watch T.V. than read.
_____	_____	14. When I listen to someone read out loud, certain words or sentences might attract my attention.
_____	_____	15. I would only read a book if my teacher or my parents said I had to.

Yes	No	
____	____	16. Magazines, comic books, and newspapers do not interest me.
____	____	17. I do not enjoy reading in my free time.
____	____	18. I would enjoy talking with someone else about one of my favorite books.
____	____	19. I might go to the library several times to see if a special book had been returned.
____	____	20. I am too busy during vacations to plan a reading program for myself.
____	____	21. Sometimes the book that I'm reading will remind me of ideas from another book that I've read.
____	____	22. If my only reading was for school assignments, I would be very unhappy.
____	____	23. Reading is not a very good way for me to learn new things.
____	____	24. I think reading is boring.
____	____	25. If I see a comic book or magazine, I would usually just look at the pictures.
____	____	26. I sometimes read extra books or articles about something that we have discussed in school.
____	____	27. I enjoy going to the library and choosing special books.
____	____	28. I do not read during any of my vacations from school.
____	____	29. I would not want to help set up a book exhibit.
____	____	30. It would be very, very nice for me to have my own library of books.
____	____	31. I don't try to read many different kinds of books.
____	____	32. If I do not read many things when I'm an adult, I will miss many important ideas about life.
____	____	33. I read because the teacher tells me to.
____	____	34. I read only because people force me to.

Yes	No	
____	____	35. I must shut myself in a quiet room in order to read almost anything.
____	____	36. I never do extra reading outside of schoolwork because reading is so dull.
____	____	37. I only read extra books if my parents say I have to.
____	____	38. Reading certain newspaper articles might make me happy, or sad, or even angry.
____	____	39. I should spend some of my time each day reading so that I can learn about the world.
____	____	40. Before I make up my mind about something, I try to read more than one writer's ideas.
____	____	41. When I read, I sometimes understand myself a little better.
____	____	42. Some characters I have read about help me to better understand people I know.
____	____	43. Reading is a very important part of my life. I read nearly every day in books or newspapers and I enjoy doing so.
____	____	44. I would like to read some of the novels my teacher reads to the class.
____	____	45. I would like to read more books if I had the time.
____	____	46. I might keep a list of the books that I wish to read during the next few months.
____	____	47. My parents force me to read.
____	____	48. If people didn't tell me that I had to read, I would probably never pick up a book.
____	____	49. Sometimes I think ahead in my reading and imagine what the characters might do.
____	____	50. I wish I could buy more books for myself.
____	____	51. Sometimes I wish the author of

Yes	No	
		the book had written the story a different way.
____	____	52. Much of my free time is spent in reading, library browsing, and discussing books.
____	____	53. I read lots of different newspaper articles so that I can learn more about the world.
____	____	54. Reading is as much a part of my life as eating, sleeping, and playing.
____	____	55. A story that I see on television might also be interesting to read in a book.
____	____	56. Even a little reading makes me feel tired and restless.
____	____	57. I try to read many different types of materials in my free time.
____	____	58. I would always rather talk about things than read about them.
____	____	59. I have never wanted to read a book twice.
____	____	60. When I am an adult and work all day, I will not read.
____	____	61. I would feel disappointed if I could not find a book that I was very interested in reading.
____	____	62. I have sometimes told my friends about a really good book that they might like to read.
____	____	63. I look for some main ideas that the writer presents when I read a magazine article.
____	____	64. Reading is a very important part of my life when I am not in school.

This third measure can be used with secondary-level students.

RHODY SECONDARY READING ATTITUDE ASSESSMENT*

*R. Tullock-Rhody and J. Alexander. "A Scale for Assessing Attitudes Toward Reading in Secondary Schools." *Journal of Reading* 23 (April 1980), p. 612.

Directions: This is a test to tell how you feel about reading. The score will not affect your grade in any way. You read the statements silently as I read them aloud. Then put an X on the line under the letter or letters that represent how you feel about the statement.

SD – Strongly disagree
D – Disagree
U – Undecided
A – Agree
SA – Strongly agree

	SD	D	U	A	SA
1. You feel you have better things to do than read.	__	__	__	__	__
2. You seldom buy a book.	__	__	__	__	__
3. You are willing to tell people that you do not like to read.	__	__	__	__	__
4. You have a lot of books in your room at home.	__	__	__	__	__
5. You like to read a book whenever you have free time.	__	__	__	__	__
6. You get really excited about books you have read.	__	__	__	__	__
7. You love to read.	__	__	__	__	__
8. You like to read books by well-known authors.	__	__	__	__	__
9. You never check out a book from the library.	__	__	__	__	__
10. You like to stay at home and read.	__	__	__	__	__
11. You seldom read except when you have to do a book report.	__	__	__	__	__
12. You think reading is a waste of time.	__	__	__	__	__
13. You think reading is boring.	__	__	__	__	__
14. You think people are strange when they read a lot.	__	__	__	__	__
15. You like to read to escape from problems.	__	__	__	__	__
16. You make fun of people who read a lot.	__	__	__	__	__

	SD	D	U	A	SA
17. You like to share books with your friends.	___	___	___	___	___
18. You would rather someone just tell you information so that you won't have to read to get it.	___	___	___	___	___
19. You hate reading.	___	___	___	___	___
20. You generally check out a book when you go to the library.	___	___	___	___	___
21. It takes you a long time to read a book.	___	___	___	___	___
22. You like to broaden your interests through reading.	___	___	___	___	___
23. You read a lot.	___	___	___	___	___
24. You like to improve your vocabulary so you can use more words.	___	___	___	___	___
25. You like to get books for gifts.	___	___	___	___	___

Scoring: To score the *Rhody Secondary Reading Attitude Assessment*, a very positive response receives a score of 5, and a very negative response receives a score of 1. On items 4, 5, 6, 7, 8, 10, 15, 17, 20, 22, 23, 24, and 25, a response of "strongly agree" indicates a very positive attitude and should receive a score of 5. On the remaining items, a "strongly disagree" response indicates a very positive attitude and should receive the 5 score. Therefore, on the positive item, "strongly agree" receives a 5, "agree" receives a 4, "undecided" receives 3, "disagree" receives a 2, and "strongly disagree" receives a 1. The pattern is reversed on the negative items. The possible range of scores is 5 X 25 (125) to 1 X 25 (25).

These are only a few of the many available instruments that purport to measure reading attitudes. Others that may be of interest to you include

Estes, T. H. "A Scale to Measure Attitudes Toward Reading," *Journal of Reading* 15 (November 1971), 135–138. For grades 4–6.

Heathington, B. "Scales to Measure Attitudes Toward Reading," Doctoral Dissertation, University of Tennessee 1975, unpublished. For grades 1–6.

Determining a Student's Interests in Reading

Many reading authorities believe that a student's interests and attitudes are closely related. Witty (1963) defined interest as

> a disposition or tendency which impels an individual to seek out particular goals for persistent attention. The goals may be objects, skills, knowledges, and art activities of various kinds. The behavior patterns in seeking these goals may be regarded as particular interests such as collecting objects or viewing TV. They should be looked upon as acquired, although they are based upon such factors as the constitutional nature of the individual and his personality structure as affected by his unique experiences and his particular environment. (p. 331).

When applied to reading, this definition would suggest that the development of positive student interest may hinge on (1) understanding the child's background and experiences and (2) acquiring some understanding of individual personality. There are several ways in which you can learn about children's interests.

Classroom interactions, both student-teacher and student-student, provide many opportunities for teachers to learn about children's interests. If you talk to children about your interests, hobbies, and activities, many children will share their interests with you. Take note of which kind of things hold a child's interest and attention and which do not. It may also be helpful to assess students' reading interests by collecting information from an informal survey. Three surveys that you may find useful are presented in the following pages. The first was developed for students in middle school, although it can be used or adapted for other levels. It can be helpful in guiding your selection of books and reading materials. The other two surveys will provide you with information on students' interests in general, including reading interests.

READING INTEREST CHECKLIST

Your feelings can be shown by circling the appropriate

number beside each item. For "very little," circle the number 1. For "very much," circle the number 5. If your "likes" are somewhere between, circle the appropriate number.

I like to read about	Very little				Very much
a. adventure	1	2	3	4	5
b. animals	1	2	3	4	5
c. art/music/dance	1	2	3	4	5
d. boys/girls my age	1	2	3	4	5
e. comedy	1	2	3	4	5
f. famous people	1	2	3	4	5
g. food	1	2	3	4	5
h. history	1	2	3	4	5
i. human body/health	1	2	3	4	5
j. make-believe characters	1	2	3	4	5
k. mysteries	1	2	3	4	5
l. romance/love	1	2	3	4	5
m. science	1	2	3	4	5
n. science fiction	1	2	3	4	5
o. space	1	2	3	4	5
p. sports	1	2	3	4	5
q. transportation	1	2	3	4	5
r. war/armed services	1	2	3	4	5

I like to read					
a. comic books	1	2	3	4	5
b. encyclopedias	1	2	3	4	5
c. funnies	1	2	3	4	5
d. hardbacks	1	2	3	4	5
e. library	1	2	3	4	5
f. magazines	1	2	3	4	5
g. newspapers	1	2	3	4	5
h. novels	1	2	3	4	5
i. paperbacks	1	2	3	4	5
j. textbooks	1	2	3	4	5
k. TV guides	1	2	3	4	5

B. Heathington. "What to Do About Reading Motivation in the Middle School." *Journal of Reading* 22 (May 1979), 709–13.

INTEREST INVENTORY

Name____________ Age______

Date____________

1. My favorite day of the week is____________because ____________.
2. The television programs I like the most are ____________.
3. The most fun I ever had was when ____________.
4. The person I would most like to meet is____________because ____________.
5. My favorite course in school is ____________.
6. The one course in school I don't like is____________.
7. I dislike it because ____________.
8. On a sunny day I like to ____________.
9. Reading is ____________.

10. The things I like to read are ______.
11. The best story I ever read was ______.
12. In my spare time I like to ______.
13. The chores I do at home are ______.
14. My brothers and sisters ______.
15. My hobbies are ______.
16. I get really mad when ______.
17. When I grow up I'd like to be ______ because ______.
18. Poetry makes me ______.
19. Music is ______.
20. Places I'd like to visit are ______.
21. My favorite sport is ______.
22. Libraries are ______.
23. During the summer I like to ______.
24. On a winter day I like to ______.
25. I wish my parents would ______.
26. Animals are ______.
27. I'd like to have a ______ for a pet because ______.
28. The best food in the world is ______.
29. My favorite color is ______.
30. Right now I'd like to ______.

The following survey calls for the child to listen as the teacher reads each of these items, and then respond to them orally.

INTEREST INVENTORY

Name ______ Age ____

Date ______

1. What do you like to do when you have free time?
2. How do you usually spend your summers?
3. How much reading do you do on your own?
4. How much television do you watch each day?
5. What are your favorite TV programs?
6. What movies have you seen that you really liked?
7. Do you ever read a book after you have seen the television or movie version?
8. Have you ever visited any of these places?

Art museum	Circus	Theater
Science museum	National park	Library
Concert halls	Zoo	

9. What other countries have you visited or lived in?
10. What other cities or states have you visited or lived in?

Circle the school subjects you like; cross out the subjects you don't like:

Arithmetic	Science	Gym
Spelling	Social studies	Health
Reading	Music	English
Art	Other languages	

Circle the kinds of books and stories you like; cross out the books and stories you don't like:

Adventure	Mystery	Magazines
Animal stories	Motorcycles	Comic books
Hobby stories	Love and romance	Ghost stories
Biography	Science fiction	Family stories
Autobiography	Car magazines	Riddles and jokes
Science	Fables and myths	Horse stories
Western stories	Sports	Humor
Art and music	Religion	Fantasy
Fairy tales	People of other lands	History
Poetry	Newspapers	Geography

11. What is it that you do well?
12. What is it that you do not do well?

Determining Learning Style

Educational researchers direct a great deal of their attention to the learning style of the child. Each of us has a preferred learning style for every task we undertake. Some of us will say, "I'm a graphic-visual learner. I can only study by writing out the information." Others will say, "I'm an auditory learner; I need to have things spoken before I can learn." Although these statements may be true for a specific situation, they probably do not carry over to all situations. In other words, as competent adults we use several different learning styles despite the fact that we have a preferred style.

Your students, however, may not have acquired an array of styles, yet. The following instrument will help you to assess students' perceptions of their "best" style and then decide if you want to teach to this one style or build an array of effective styles.

LEARNING STYLE INDICATOR

Directions: Read each pair of statements and mark the box next to the statement that *most closely* describes you.

1.	I understand things better from a picture.	☐ ☐	I understand things better from someone telling me or reading about them.
2.	I look at charts and diagrams before I read the written part.	☐ ☐	I read the written part before I look at the charts and diagrams.
3.	I memorize things by writing them out.	☐ ☐	I memorize things by repeating them aloud.
4.	I like examples first, rules later.	☐ ☐	I like rules first, examples later.
5.	I usually get more done when I work alone.	☐ ☐	I usually get more done when I work with others.
6.	I enjoy doing a number of things at the same time.	☐ ☐	I prefer doing things one at a time.
7.	I usually ask "why" questions.	☐ ☐	I usually ask about facts.
8.	I prefer working quickly.	☐ ☐	I prefer to work slowly.
9.	I answer questions quickly.	☐ ☐	I answer questions carefully and slowly.
10.	I take chances at making mistakes.	☐ ☐	I try to avoid making mistakes.

High-Interest Materials

Some children acquire negative attitudes about reading because they experience great difficulty with materials written at their *grade level*. It is vitally important that you select reading materials that stimulate children's interest while complementing their level of *reading competency* in order to attempt to reverse negative reading attitudes. The following list includes several resources that can assist you with your text selection.

Booklist. Chicago: American Library Association.
High/Low Report. New York: Riverside Publications.
Sarkissian, A. *High Interest Books for Teens: A Guide to Book Reviews and Bibliographic Sources.* Detroit: Gale Research Co., 1981.
Spache, G. *Good Reading for Poor Readers.* 10th ed. Champaign, Ill.: Garrard Publishing Company, 1978.
White, M., ed. *High-Interest Easy Reading for Junior and Senior High School Students.* 3rd ed. Urbana, Ill.: National Council of Teachers of English, 1979.

The following titles are examples of high-interest/low vocabulary materials you may want to examine (RL = reading level; IL = interest level).

Eisenberg, L. *Tiger Rose.* Chicago: Childrens Press, 1980. RL 1; IL 5–9.
Myers, W. *Brainstorm.* New York: Franklin Watts, Inc., 1977. RL 2; IL 5–10.
Platt, K. *Dracula, Go Home!* New York: Franklin Watts, Inc., 1979. RL 2; IL 7–9.
Rabinowich, E. *Toni's Crowd.* New York: Franklin Watts, Inc., 1978. RL 2; IL 7–9.
Salas, N. *Night of the Kachina.* Childrens Press, 1977. RL 1; IL 7–8.
Sanderlin, O. *Tennis Rebel.* New York: Franklin Watts, Inc., 1978. RL 2; IL 7–10.
Stevenson, J. *Help, Yelled Maxwell,* illustrated by Edwina Stevenson. New York: Greenwillow Books, 1978. RL 3; IL 2–4.

As part of your total reading program, we also recommend that you include high-interest games as part of your classroom materials. Two examples of such games are

Alchoch, D. *Blendograms.* Covina, Calif.: Alcoch Publishing, 1982. RL K–3; IL 3+.
Balinger, W. *You and Your World.* Belmont, Calif.: Pitman Learning, Inc., 1964. RL primary; IL jr. and sr. high.

Astrology

Generally, even people who claim that they "don't believe" in astrology know their own astrological sign. Astrology, like magic, has delighted and involved audiences through the ages. The following list of people born under each of the various signs should produce some interest among your students. This list can be a high-interest motivator for several reading lessons.

Ask your students to (1) determine their sign and (2) "read" about the characteristics of their sign.

Several more advanced reading and reference skills lessons could be developed around the theme of astrological signs. Ask students to find other famous people who were born under their sign.

Capricorn
(Dec. 22–Jan. 20)
Dennis Cunningham
Muhammed Ali
Martin Luther King, Jr.
Joan Baez
Howard Hughes

Aquarius
(Jan. 21–Feb. 19)
Leontyne Price
Ronald Reagan
Clark Gable
Thomas Edison
Hank Aaron

Pisces
(Feb. 20–March 20)
Sidney Poitier
Sly Stone
W. E. B. Dubois
Albert Einstein
Barbara Gordon

Aries
(Mar. 21–Apr. 19)
Pearl Bailey
Robert Frost
Charlie Chaplin
Gloria Steinem
Johann Sebastian Bach

Taurus
(Apr. 20–May 20)
Harry Truman
Willie Mays
Peter Tchaikovsky
Barbara Streisand
Karl Marx

Gemini
(May 21–June 21)
Marilyn Monroe
John F. Kennedy
Paul McCartney
Joe Namath
Bob Hope

Cancer
(June 22–July 21)
Nelson Rockefeller
Arthur Ashe
Bella Abzug
Ernest Hemingway
The United States

Leo
(July 22–Aug. 21)
Neil Armstrong
James Baldwin
Casey Stengel
Jackie Kennedy Onassis
Napoleon Bonaparte

Virgo
(Aug. 22–Sept. 22)
Lyndon Johnson
Queen Elizabeth
Leonard Bernstein
Sophia Loren
Henry Ford

Libra
(Sept. 23–Oct. 22)
Johnny Carson
Pope Paul VI
John Lennon
Dwight Eisenhower
Ed Sullivan

Scorpio
(Oct. 23–Nov. 21)
Chang Kai-Shek
Billy Graham
Robert F. Kennedy
Pablo Picasso
Spiro Agnew

Sagittarius
(Nov. 22–Dec. 21)
Walt Disney
Ludwig von Beethoven
Jane Fonda
Shirley Chisholm
Mark Twain

As part of a cross-cultural unit, you may want to ask students to find out the symbol in the Chinese calendar for the year of their birth. They can also cross-reference people born under their sign with their Chinese character symbol.

Year of the

Rat	Ox	Tiger	Hare	Dragon	Snake
1960	1961	1962	1963	1964	1965
1972	1973	1974	1975	1976	1977

Horse	Sheep	Monkey	Rooster	Dog	Pig
1966	1967	1968	1969	1970	1971
1978	1979	1980	1981	1982	1983

Reader's Theater

Reader's theater has been used successfully by many teachers to encourage and motivate students to read. Reader's theater is the presentation of literature in which the student hears the spoken words but must *imagine* the scenery, action, and characters. Ratliff (1980) tells us that reader's theater may be used to

1. Enhance critical study of literature and language.
2. Explore appreciation and meaning of literature.
3. Bring vitality and relevance to literature.
4. Promote reading, writing, and listening skills.
5. Permit students to display their creative performance talents publicly to an audience of peers or parents.

There are several differences between reader's theater and conventional theater. The major difference is the role of the *audience*; in reader's theater, the audience members are *interpreters*, not merely *observers*. The goal of reader's theater is to establish scenes and *suggest* (not portray) characters, forcing the audience to conjure or imagine the action. In addition, Woodbury (1979) cites five other conventions in reader's theater:

1. Scenery and costumes are not used or they are only selectively employed.
2. Action or physical movement is merely suggested by the interpreter and is visualized in the minds of the audience.
3. A narrator, speaking directly to the audience, usually establishes the basic situation or theme and links the various segments together.
4. A physical script is usually carried by the reader or at least is in evidence somewhere.
5. There is a continuing effort to develop and maintain a closer, more personalized relationship between performer and audience. . . . The emphasis is on aural appeal and the audience's attention is concentrated on the literature. (p. 65)

Reader's theater is an excellent reading activity for many students. First, some students are incapable or reluctant to act out parts in a play. Reader's theater does not demand physical portrayal; it asks for oral interpretation. Second, the student who is part of the audience has to visualize the spoken word. Reader's theater is a good exercise for helping students with their listening skills. Third, less capable readers can become involved in this form of reading because they have the opportunity to prepare the script. In the beginning, they can take the roles that demand less reading.

The experimental nature of reader's theater allows students to be creative. There is no limit to what can happen in the minds of the audience. Reader's theater is dramatic because our imaginations can soar and are not constrained by the actions on stage, as in conventional theater. Extensive rehearsal and memorization usually are unnecessary. But, as with any dramatic presentation, familiarity with the material enhances the production considerably.

Reader's theater can be used effectively in team-teaching situations. A class can research the life of a famous scientist, mathematician, or literary figure and write a biographical reader's theater script about him or her. The script can include sections from the subject's journals, letters, and diaries and news clippings and personal documents.

An added benefit of reader's theater is that children enjoy rewriting literature into dramatic plays. The stories and novels that are best for reader's theater are those in which there is a considerable dialogue. Actions that are visually important, but unspoken, are inappropriate for reader's theater, for example, Desdemona's dropping of the handkerchief.

When you and your students engage in a reader's theater production, it is important for you to stress to the students that their role is that of *interpreter*, not actor. This is often difficult, particularly for young children, because they want to look at each other. It is important to discuss with students that the most important *sense* played to in reader's theater is not the audience's eyes, but their ears, as well as their minds and imaginations.

In reader's theater, part of your classroom becomes the stage. Students can be seated on stools or chairs, holding their script in front of them. A change in scene can be narrated by a student. Entrances and exits are handled by the characters standing or sitting, stepping forward or backward, dropping their eyes, or by any other method that seems appropriate for a particular script. There are no rules in reader's theater, but the audience should not *see* the action on the stage. There should be one guiding principle: make the audience do the work in their minds.

On the following pages are examples of scripts that are useful for reader's theater classroom productions.

A SHIP LIKE THIS*
by B. Carlson

NARRATOR
MRS. NIFFY
MRS.TIFFY
STEWARD

NARRATOR: Two women are on the deck of an ocean liner. One woman is sitting in a deck chair as the second woman approaches.

*Adapted from ***Funny-Bone Dramatics*** by Bernice Wells Carlson. Copyright © 1974 by Abingdon Press. Used by permission.

MRS. TIFFY: Good morning, Mrs. Niffy. How are you today?

MRS. NIFFY: Oh, oh, I just don't know.

MRS. TIFFY: May I sit down?

MRS. NIFFY: Of course! Of course! Do whatever you wish. Anything you do is all right with me.

MRS. TIFFY: Did you sleep well last night?

MRS. NIFFY: No, no, not a wink.

MRS. TIFFY: Were you seasick?

MRS. NIFFY: No, no, I wasn't seasick.

MRS. TIFFY: Well, what's your problem?

MRS. NIFFY: I'm afraid.

MRS. TIFFY: Afraid of what?

MRS. NIFFY: I'm afraid this ship will sink.

MRS. TIFFY: Oh, come now. That's a silly fear. A ship this size doesn't sink.

MRS. NIFFY: Oh, I read about a ship that sank.

MRS. TIFFY: Here comes the steward. Let's talk to him.

MRS. NIFFY: All right.

MRS. TIFFY: Pardon me.

STEWARD: Good morning, ladies. May I help you?

MRS. TIFFY: I hope so. We have a question. Maybe you can answer it and put our minds at rest.

STEWARD: I'll answer if I can.

MRS. TIFFY: Does a ship like this sink very often?

STEWARD: Oh, no! A ship like this sinks only once.

THE MOCK TURTLE'S TALE*
by Lewis Carroll

NARRATOR
MOCK TURTLE
GRYPHON
ALICE

NARRATOR: As Alice is meeting all of the strange characters of Wonderland, the Queen of Hearts discovers that Alice has not yet met the Mock Turtle. The Queen commands the Gryphon to take Alice to the Mock Turtle, to meet him and to hear his story. The Gryphon takes Alice to the Mock Turtle and explains that Alice wants to hear his history.

*Adapted from Carroll, Lewis (Charles Dodgson). *Alice's Adventures in Wonderland* (New York: Avenel Books, n.d.) pp. 140–146.

MOCK TURTLE: Once, I was a real Turtle.

GRYPHON: Hjckrrh!

NARRATOR: These words were followed by a long silence, and Alice begins to wonder if she had already heard the whole story. The Mock Turtle is sobbing, but finally grows calm.

MOCK TURTLE: When we were little, we went to school in the sea. The master was the old Turtle—we used to call him Tortoise—

ALICE: Why did you call him Tortoise, if he wasn't one?

MOCK TURTLE: We called him Tortoise because he taught us; really you are very dull!

GRYPHON: You ought to be ashamed of yourself for asking such a simple question.

NARRATOR: The Gryphon and the Mock Turtle both sat silent and looked at poor Alice, who felt ready to sink into the earth. At last the Gryphon said to the Mock Turtle:

GRYPHON: Drive on, old fellow! Don't be all day about it!.

MOCK TURTLE: Yes, we went to school in the sea, though you mayn't believe it—

ALICE: I never said I didn't!

MOCK TURTLE: You did.

GRYPHON: Hold your tongue!

MOCK TURTLE: We had the best of educations—in fact, we went to school every day—

ALICE: *I've* been to a day-school too; you needn't be so proud as all that.

MOCK TURTLE: With extras?

ALICE: Yes, we learned French and music.

MOCK TURTLE: And washing?

ALICE: Certainly not!

MOCK TURTLE: Ah! Then yours wasn't a really good school. Now at *ours* they had at the end of the bill, "French, music, *and washing*-extra."

ALICE: You couldn't have wanted it much, living at the bottom of the sea.

MOCK TURTLE: I couldn't afford to learn it. I only took the regular course.

ALICE: What was that?

MOCK TURTLE: Reeling and Writhing, of course, to begin with, and then the different branches of Arithmetic-Ambition, Distraction, Uglification, and Derision.

ALICE: I never heard of "Uglification." What is it?

GRYPHON: Never heard of uglifying! You know what to beautify is, I suppose?

ALICE: Yes, it means—to—make—anything—prettier.

GRYPHON: Well then, if you don't know what to uglify is, you *are* a simpleton.

NARRATOR: Alice did not feel encouraged to ask any more questions about it, so she turned to the Mock Turtle and said:

ALICE: What else had you to learn?

MOCK TURTLE: Well, there was Mystery, ancient and modern, with Seaography: then Drawling—the Drawling-master was an old conger-eel, that used to come once a week: *he* taught us Drawling, Stretching, and Fainting in Coils.

ALICE: What was *that* like?

MOCK TURTLE: Well, I can't show it to you, myself: I'm too stiff. And the Gryphon never learnt it.

GRYPHON: Hadn't time. I went to the Classical master, though. He was an old crab, *he* was.

MOCK TURTLE: I never went to him. He taught Laughing and Grief, they used to say.

GRYPHON: So he did, so he did.

ALICE: And how many hours a day did you do lessons?

MOCK TURTLE: Ten hours the first day, nine the next, and so on.

ALICE: What a curious plan!

GRYPHON: That's the reason they're called lessons, because they lessen from day to day.

NARRATOR: This was quite a new idea to Alice, and she thought it over a little before she made her next remark.

ALICE: Then the eleventh day must have been a holiday?

MOCK TURTLE: Of course it was.

Your students may find it amusing to make a comparison of the educational systems described in fantasy works. Learning in the Land of Oz is quite different from what the Mock Turtle experienced—and it is certainly far removed from what your students experience!

140 THE MOCK

So they went up to the Mock Turtle, who looked at them with large eyes full of tears, but said nothing.

"This here young lady," said the Gryphon, "she wants for to know your history, she do."

"I'll tell it her," said the Mock Turtle in a deep, hollow tone: "sit down both of you, and don't speak a word till I've finished."

So they sat down, and nobody spoke for some minutes. Alice thought to herself, "I don't see how he can *ever* finish, if he doesn't begin." But she waited patiently.

"Once," said the Mock Turtle at last, with a deep sigh, "I was a real Turtle."

These words were followed by a very long silence, broken only by an occasional exclamation of "Hjckrrh!" from the Gryphon, and the constant heavy sobbing of the Mock Turtle. Alice was very nearly getting up and saying, "Thank you, sir, for your interesting story," but she could not help thinking there *must* be more to come, so she sat still and said nothing.

TURTLE'S STORY. 141

"When we were little," the Mock Turtle went on at last, more calmly, though still sobbing a little now and then, "we went to school

HOW THE WOGGLEBUG TAUGHT ATHLETICS*
by L. Frank Baum

NARRATOR
PROFESSOR WOGGLEBUG
DOROTHY
OMBY AMBY
AUNT EM
SHAGGY MAN
WIZARD

NARRATOR: After Dorothy and her family move to Oz, they go on a trip with some of their friends to meet the people and see the sights. Along the way, they decide to visit the Royal Athletic College of Oz.

PROFESSOR: Welcome, Dorothy, and welcome to all your friends. We are indeed pleased to receive you at this great Temple of Learning.

SHAGGY MAN: I thought it was an Athletic College.

PROFESSOR: It is, my dear sir. Here it is that we teach the youth of our great land scientific College Athletics—in all their purity.

DOROTHY: Don't you teach them anything else? Don't they get any reading, writing and 'rithmetic?

PROFESSOR: Oh, yes; of course. They get all those, and more. But such things occupy little of their time. Please follow me and I will show you how my scholars are usually occupied. This is a class hour and they are all busy.

NARRATOR: As they walk with the Professor, they see hundreds of young Ozites playing football, baseball, tennis, and golf. Some students are swimming in a pool while others are rowing boats on the river. Still others are playing basketball or cricket, and they see a ring for boxing and wrestling.

PROFESSOR: This college is a great success. Its educational value is undisputed, and we are turning out many great and valuable citizens every year.

DOROTHY: But when do they study?

PROFESSOR: Study?

DOROTHY: Yes; when do they get their 'rithmetic, and jogerfy, and such things?

PROFESSOR: Oh, they take doses of those every night and morning.

*Adapted from Baum, L. Frank. *The Emerald City of Oz* (Chicago: Rand McNally & Co., 1910), pp. 95-99.

DOROTHY: What do you mean by doses?

PROFESSOR: Why, we use the newly invented School Pills, made by your friend the Wizard. These pills we have found to be very effective, and they save a lot of time. Please step this way and I will show you our Laboratory of Learning.

NARRATOR: He led them to a room in the building where many large bottles were standing in rows upon shelves.

PROFESSOR: These are the Algebra Pills. One at night, on retiring, is equal to four hours of study. Here are the Geography Pills—one at night and one in the morning. In this next bottle are the Latin Pills—one three times a day. Then we have the Grammar Pills—one before each meal—and the Spelling Pills, which are taken whenever needed.

DOROTHY: Your scholars must have to take a lot of pills. How do they take 'em, in applesauce?

PROFESSOR: No, my dear. They are sugar-coated and are quickly and easily swallowed. I believe the students would rather take the pills than study, and certainly the pills are a more effective method. You see, until these School Pills were invented we wasted a lot of time in study that may now be better employed in practicing athletics.

OMBY AMBY: Seems to me the pills are a good thing.

PROFESSOR: They are, sir. They give us an advantage over all other colleges, because at no loss of time our boys become thoroughly conversant with Greek and Latin, Mathematics and Geography, Grammar and Literature. You see they are never obliged to interrupt their games to acquire the lesser branches of learning.

DOROTHY: It's a great invention, I'm sure.

PROFESSOR: We live in an age of progress. It is easier to swallow knowledge than to acquire it laboriously from books. Is it not so, my friends?

AUNT EM: Some folks can swallow anything, but to me it seems too much like taking medicine.

WIZARD: Young men in college always have to take their medicine, one way or another; and, as our Professor says, these School Pills have proved to be a great success. One day while I was making them I happened to drop one of them, and one of Billina's chickens gobbled it up. A few minutes afterward this chick got upon a roost and recited "The Boy Stood on the Burning Deck" without making a single mistake. Then it recited "The Charge of the Light Brigade" and afterwards "Excelsior." You see, the chicken had eaten an Elocution Pill.

NARRATOR: They now bade goodbye to the Professor, and thanking him for his kind reception mounted again into the red wagon and continued their journey.

grounds several crews in racing boats were rowing with great enthusiasm. Other groups of students played basket-ball and cricket, while in one place a ring was roped in to permit boxing and wrestling by the energetic youths. All the collegians seemed busy and there was much laughter and shouting.

"This college," said Professor Wogglebug, complacently, "is a great success. It 's educational value is undisputed, and we are turning out many great and valuable citizens every year."

"But when do they study?" asked Dorothy.

"Study?" said the Wogglebug, looking perplexed at the question.

"Yes; when do they get their 'rithmetic, and jogerfy, and such things?"

"Oh, they take doses of those every night and morning," was the reply.

"What do you mean by doses?" Dorothy inquired, wonderingly.

"Why, we use the newly invented School Pills, made by your friend the Wizard. These pills we have found to be very effective, and they save a lot of time. Please step this way and I will show you our Laboratory of Learning."

He led them to a room in the building where many large bottles were standing in rows upon shelves.

"These are the Algebra Pills," said the Professor, taking down one of the bottles. "One at night, on retiring, is equal to four hours of study. Here are the Geography Pills—one at night and one in the morning. In this next bottle are the Latin Pills—one three times a day. Then we have the

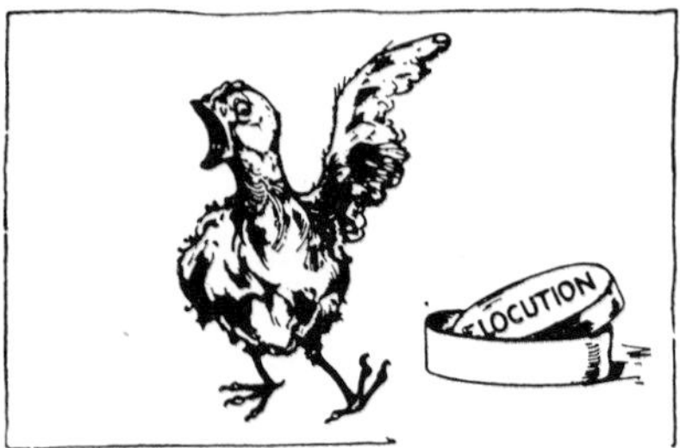

Grammar Pills—one before each meal—and the Spelling Pills, which are taken whenever needed."

"Your scholars must have to take a lot of pills," remarked Dorothy, thoughtfully. "How do they take 'em, in apple-sauce?"

"No, my dear. They are sugar-coated and are quickly

GERTRUDE McFUZZ*
by Dr. Seuss

(Elementary)

NARRATOR 1
NARRATOR 2
GERTRUDE
LOLLA–LEE–LOU

NARRATOR 1: "Gertrude McFuzz."
NARRATOR 2: By Dr. Seuss.
NARRATOR 1: There once was a girl-bird named
GERTRUDE: Gertrude McFuzz.
NARRATOR 2: And she had the smallest plain tail there ever was.
GERTRUDE: One droopy-droop feather.
NARRATOR 1: That's all that she had.
NARRATOR 2: And, oh! That one feather made Gertrude so sad!
GERTRUDE: (echoes "So sad!")
NARRATOR 1: For there was another young bird that she knew.
LOLLA-LEE-LOU: A fancy young birdie named Lolla-Lee-Lou.
NARRATOR 1: And instead of one feather behind, she had
LOLLA-LEE-LOU: Two!
NARRATORS 1 & 2: Poor Gertrude!
NARRATOR 2: Whenever she happened to spy
Miss Lolla-Lee-Lou flying by in the sky,
LOLLA-LEE-LOU: She got very jealous.
NARRATOR 1: She frowned.
NARRATOR 2: And she pouted.
NARRATOR 1: Then one day she got awfully mad
And she shouted.
GERTRUDE: This just isn't fair! I have *one*! She has *two!* I must have a tail just like Lolla-Lee-Lou!
NARRATOR 1: So she flew to her uncle, a doctor named Dake, Whose office was high in a tree by the lake. And she cried.
GERTRUDE: Uncle Doctor. Oh, please do you know
Of some kind of a pill that will make my tail grow?
NARRATOR 2: Tut Tut!
NARRATOR 1: Said the doctor.
NARRATOR 2: Such talk! How absurd!
Your tail is just right for your kind of a bird.
NARRATOR 1: Then Gertrude had tantrums. She raised such a din
Then finally her uncle, the doctor, gave in
And told her just where she could find such a pill.
NARRATOR 2: On a Pill-Berry vine on top of the hill.
GERTRUDE: Oh, thank you!
NARRATOR 1: Chirped Gertrude McFuzz, and she flew
Right straight to the hill where the Pill-Berry grew.
GERTRUDE: Yes! There was the vine!
NARRATOR 2: And as soon as she saw it
She plucked off a berry.
NARRATOR 1: She started to gnaw it.
GERTRUDE: It tasted just awful.
NARRATOR 2: Almost made her sick.
NARRATOR 1: But she wanted that tail, so she swallowed it quick.
NARRATOR 2: Then she felt something happen!
NARRATOR 1: She felt a small twitch
NARRATOR 2: As if she'd been tapped, down behind, by a switch.
NARRATOR 1: And Gertrude looked 'round, and she cheered!
NARRATOR 2: It was true!
GERTRUDE: *Two feathers*!
NARRATOR 1: Exactly like Lolla-Lee-Lou!
NARRATOR 2: Then she got an idea!
GERTRUDE: Now I know what I'll do . . .
I'll grow a tail *better* than Lolla-Lee-Lou!
———— feathers are working just fine.
NARRATOR 1: So she nibbled another one off of the vine!
NARRATOR 2: She felt a new twitch.
NARRATOR 1: And then Gertrude yelled.
GERTRUDE: Whee!
Miss Lolla has only just *two*! I have *three*!
When Lolla-Lee-Lou sees this beautiful stuff,
She'll fall right down flat on her face, sure enough!
I'll show *her* who's pretty! I certainly will!
Why, I'll make my tail even prettier still!
NARRATOR 2: She snatched at those berries that grew on that vine.
NARRATOR 1: She gobbled down four.
GERTRUDE: five,

*Copyright 1950, 1951, © 1958 by Dr. Seuss. Reprinted from *Yertle the Turtle and Other Stories*, by Dr. Seuss, by permission of Random House, Inc.

NARRATOR 2: six,
NARRATOR 1: seven,
NARRATOR 2: eight,
GERTRUDE: nine!
NARRATOR 1: And she didn't stop eating.
NARRATOR 2: Young Gertrude McFuzz,
NARRATOR 1: Till she'd eaten three dozen!
GERTRUDE: That's all that there was.
NARRATOR 1: Then the feathers popped out!
GERTRUDE: *With a zang!*
LOLLA-LEE-LOU: With a *zing*!
NARRATOR 2: They blossomed like flowers that bloom in the spring.
LOLLA-LEE-LOU: All fit for a queen! What a sight to behold!
NARRATOR 1: They sparkled like diamonds
NARRATOR 2: And gumdrops
LOLLA-LEE-LOU: And Gold!

PROLOGUE TO MORNING*
by Dorothea Parfit

(Intermediate 4–8)

EVERYMAN: Watchman, what of the night?
WATCHMAN: The night has no stars and the winds are rising.
EVERYMAN: Watchman, what of the sea?
WATCHMAN: The sea is wild, and the shores are strewn with ships.
EVERYMAN: Watchman—
WATCHMAN: I hear
EVERYMAN: What of the hearts of men?
WATCHMAN: They are as the night, and as the sea.
EVERYMAN: Watchman, I am Everyman, and I am troubled. Where is my hope?
WATCHMAN: Your hope is where it *has* been.
EVERYMAN: Watchman, your answer is dark.
WATCHMAN: To your mind, but not to your heart.
Let the heart
Listen and it will hear.
Though the winds cry and the seas break.

*"Prologue to Morning" is included here by permission of Mrs. Dorothea Parfit, 1207 North Western Avenue, Hollywood, Calif. 90029.

EVERYMAN: My heart is open.
WATCHMAN: What does it hear?
EVERYMAN: Storm.
WATCHMAN: What else?
EVERYMAN: A crying, as of a child lost in the dark.
WATCHMAN: A crying?
EVERYMAN: A fury, as of a child destroying his toys.
WATCHMAN: No more?
EVERYMAN: A Voice.
WATCHMAN: A Voice?
EVERYMAN: A Voice that cries, Think!
WATCHMAN: What else?
EVERYMAN: A Voice that calls, Aspire!
WATCHMAN: What more?
EVERYMAN: A Voice that whispers, Believe!
WATCHMAN: Bow down, and hear!
EVERYMAN: A voice that commands, Dare!
WATCHMAN: Lift up your eyes!
EVERYMAN: Watchman what have I heard?
WATCHMAN: You have heard God speaking to Moses and to Socrates.
To Jesus in the lonely places,
To Isaiah and Amos and Micah,
And Peter and John and Paul and Francis and Joan.
You have heard God speaking to all His saints
Who have fought for the recognition of His glory,
And for liberation, and the expansion of the imprisoned, and the dwarfed spirit.
You have heard God speaking to the men who dared the seas to build a new nation,
To Franklin and Washington and Jefferson
And all the makes of the immortal Declaration
That utters the hunger for life, for liberty and the right of man to be free of the chain, the bars, and the whip.
You have heard God speaking to Abraham Lincoln—
And to you.
EVERYMAN: To me? What am I that the God Who spoke to these
Should speak to me?
WATCHMAN: What does the Voice say, the Voice in the heart?
EVERYMAN: The Voice says, You are of the great succession.
Men have torn down, men have broken, men have destroyed.
It is yours to build, says the Voice, yours to build.

Out of the disaster of hate to bring the miracle of love.
Out of the fury of destruction to bring a new creation.
By men has the world been brought low.
By men shall the world again be lifted up.
By men and the Voice of God.

WATCHMAN: The Voice of God is calling through the world!

EVERYMAN: It is calling to me. I hear!

WATCHMAN: What does the Voice say, the Voice in the heart?

EVERYMAN: The Voice says, Everyman,
I have a burden for you and a splendor.
You are the end of things—
Or a new world.
Think!
Believe!
Aspire!
Dare!

WATCHMAN: What more?

EVERYMAN: The Voice says, Day and night, let your heart listen.

WATCHMAN: What is your answer, Everyman?

EVERYMAN: My heart is listening . . .

WATCHMAN: Then the new world is born.

QUESTIONS AND RELATED READINGS

If you feel that you have not attained adequate knowledge to answer the following questions successfully, we suggest additional related readings.

1. How can you assess children's attitudes toward reading?
2. In what ways can you use children's reading interests to encourage them to read?
3. What can the classroom teacher and parent do to make children want to read?
4. What procedures would you employ to assess the learning styles of your students?
5. How do you select materials that have motivating appeal for children?

Goal 1: To help the reader to understand and assess children's attitudes toward reading.

Question 1: How can you assess children's attitudes toward reading?

Alexander, J., and R. Filler. *Attitudes and Reading.* Newark, Del.: International Reading Association, 1976.

Epstein, I. *Measuring Attitudes Toward Reading.* Princeton, N.J.: ERIC Clearinghouse on Tests, Measurement, and Evaluation, 1980.

Mathewson, G. "The Function of Attitude in the Reading Process." In *Theoretical Models and Processes of Reading*, ed. by H. Singer and R. Ruddell, 2nd ed. Newark, Del.: International Reading Association, 1976, pp. 655–76.

Goal 2: To help the reader to utilize children's reading interests to encourage reading.

Question 2: In what ways can you use children's reading interests to encourage them to read?

Huus, H. "Helping Children Turn to Reading for Information and Enjoyment." In *Development of Lifetime Reading Habits*, ed. by D. Dietrich and V. Mathews. Newark, Del.: International Reading Association, 1968, pp. 14–23.

Newsom, S. "Rock 'n Roll 'n Reading." *Journal of Reading* 22 (May 1979), 726–33.

Olson, A., and W. Ames. *Teaching Reading Skills in Secondary Schools.* Scranton, Penn.: Intext Educational Publishers, 1972, pp. 159–82.

Goal 3: To help the reader to understand how teachers and parents can motivate children to read.

Question 3: What can the classroom teacher and parent do to make children want to read?

Ciani, A., ed. *Motivating Reluctant Readers.* Newark, Del.: International Reading Association, 1981.

Glazer, S. *How Can I Help My Child Build Positive Attitudes Toward Reading*? Newark, Del.: International Reading Association, 1980.

Heathington, B. "What to Do About Reading Motivation in the Middle School." *Journal of Reading* 22 (May 1979), 709–13.

Goal 4: To help the reader to assess children's most effective learning styles.

Question 4: What procedures would you employ to assess the learning style of your students?

Criscuolo, N. *Improving Classroom Reading Instruction.* Worthington, Ohio: Charles A. Jones Publishing Co., 1973, Chap. 8.

Karlin, R., ed. *Perspectives on Elementary Reading.* New York: Harcourt Brace Jovanovich, 1973, Part 8.

Koe, F. "Attitudes Toward Reading." *Elementary English* 52 (March 1975), pp. 342, 366.

Goal 5: To help the reader to choose stimulating and appropriately motivating materials for students.

Question 5: How do you select materials that have motivating appeal for children?

Bingham, J., and G. Scholt. "The Great Glass Slipper Search: Using Folktales with Older Children." *Elementary English* 51 (October 1947), 908–9.

Snyder, G. "Do Basal Characters Read in Their Daily Lives?" *The Reading Teacher* 33 (December 1979), 303–6.

Somers, A., and J. Worthington. *Response Guides for Teaching Children's Books.* Urbana, Ill.: National Council of Teachers of English, 1979.

BIBLIOGRAPHY

Alexander, J., and R. Filler. *Attitudes and Reading.* Newark, Del.: International Reading Association, 1976.

Allport, G. "Attitudes." In *A Handbook of Social Psychology*, ed. by C. Murchison. Worcester, Mass.: Clark University Press, 1935, p. 798.

Arbuthnot, M. H. *Children and Books.* Glenview, Ill.: Scott, Foresman and Company, 1957, p. 2.

Ausubel, D. P. "The Use of Advance Organizers in the Learning and Retention of Meaningful Verbal Material." *Journal of Educational Psychology* 51 (1960), 267–72.

Bandura, A., and A. Huston. "Identification as Accidental Learning." *Journal of Abnormal and Social Psychology* 63 (1961), 311.

Bandura, A., and F. McDonald. "Influences of Social Reinforcement and the Behavior of Models in Shaping Children's Moral Judgments." *Journal of Abnormal and Social Psychology* 67 (1963), 274–81.

Barrett, T. "The Barrett Taxonomy of Cognitive and Affective Dimensions of Reading Comprehension." In "What Is Reading? Some Current Concepts." *Innovation and Change in Reading Instruction*, ed. by T. Clymer. Sixty-seventh Yearbook of the National Society for the Study of Education. Chicago: University of Chicago Press, 1968, pp. 7–29.

Bloom, B. S. "The Thought Process of Students in Discussion." In *Accent on Teaching*, ed. by S. French. New York: Harper & Row, Publishers, 1954.

Boiko, C. *Children's Plays for Creative Actors.* Boston: Plays, Inc., 1967.

Buerger, T. A. "A Follow-up of Remedial Reading Instruction." *The Reading Teacher* 21 (1968), 329–34.

Campbell, P. *Reading Attitude Inventory.* Livonia, Mich.: Livonia Public Schools, 1966.

Ciccone, D. "Reading Attitudes and Interests of Sixth Grade Pupils." Unpublished Masters thesis, Kean College of New Jersey, Union, N.J., 1981.

Combs, A. W., and D. W. Soper. "The Self, Its Derivative Terms, and Research." *Journal of Individual Psychology* 13 (1957), 134–45.

Combs, A. W., D. W. Soper, and C. C. Courson. "The Measurement of Self-Concept and Self Report." *Educational and Psychological Measurement* 23 (1963), 493–500.

Dawson, M. "Developing Interest in Books." In *The Quest for Competency in Teaching Reading*, ed. by H. Klein. Newark, Del.: International Reading Association, 1972, pp. 36–41.

Dole, D. "Instructional Resources." In *The Changing American School*, ed. by J. L. Goodlad. (Sixty-fifth Yearbook of the National Society for the Study of Education, Part II). Chicago: University of Chicago Press, 1966, p. 108.

Dobbs, L. W. "The Behavior of Attitudes." *Psychological Review* 54 (1947), 135–56.

Epstein, I. *Measuring Attitudes Toward Reading.* ERIC/TM Report 73. Princeton, N.J.: ERIC Clearinghouse on Tests, Measurements, and Evaluation, 1980.

Estes, T. H. "A Scale to Measure Attitudes Toward Reading." *Journal of Reading* 25 (1971), 135–8.

Fishbein, M. "Attitude and the Prediction of Behavior." In *Readings in Attitude Theory and Measurement*, ed. by M. Fishbein. New York: John Wiley & Sons, 1967, pp. 477–92.

Gans, R. *Common Sense in the Teaching of Reading.* Indianapolis, Ind.: The Bobbs-Merrill Company, 1962, p. vi.

Gardner, R. C. A. "The Relationship of Self-esteem and Variables Associated with Reading for Fourth Grade Pima Indian Children." Unpublished doctoral dissertation, University of Arizona, Tucson, 1972.

Gordon, I. J. *Studying the Child in School.* New York: John Wiley & Sons, 1966.

Gray, M. J. "Through Printed Page." *Journal of Reading* 22 (May 1979), 698.

Greenwald, A., T. C. Brock, and T. M. Ostrom. *Psychological Foundation of Attitudes.* New York: Academic Press, Inc., 1968.

Groff, P. J. "Children's Attitudes Toward Reading and Their Critical-Type Materials." *Journal of Educational Research* 55 (April 1962), 313–14.

Gruber, J. "Exercise and Mental Performance." Address to the American Association for the Advancement of Science, Dallas, Texas, September 27, 1968.

Hall, M., J. Ribovich, and C. Ramig. *Reading and the Elementary School Child*, 2nd ed. New York: D. Van Nostrand Company, 1979.

Heathington, B. S. "The Development of Scales to Measure Attitudes Towards Reading." Unpublished doctoral dissertation, University of Tennessee, 1975.

______"What to Do About Reading Motivation in the Middle School." *Journal of Reading* 22 (May 1979), 709–13.

Jersild, A. T. *In Search of Self.* New York: Bureau of Publications, Teachers College, Columbia University, 1952.

Krathwohl, D. R., B. S. Bloom, and B. B. Masia. *Taxonomy of Educational Objectives. Handbook II: Affective Domain.* New York: David McKay Co., Inc., 1969.

Labov, W. "The Logic of Non-Standard English." In *Language, Society and Education*, ed. by J. S. DeStefano. Worthington, Ohio: Jones Publishing Company, 1973, p. 18.

McDougall, W. *Body and Mind.* New York: Macmillan Publishing Co., Inc., 1911.

_____. *An Introduction to Social Psychology.* Boston: John W. Luce and Co., 1921.

Mathewson, G. "The Function of Attitude in the Reading Process." In *Theoretical Models and Processes of Reading*, ed. by H. Singer and R. Ruddell, 2nd ed. Newark, Del.: International Reading Association, 1976, pp. 665–76.

Miller, N., and J. Dollard. *Social Learning and Imitation.* New Haven, Conn.: Yale University Press, 1941.

Neale, D. C., N. Gill, and W. Tismer. "Relationship Between Attitudes Toward School Subjects and School Achievement." *Journal of Educational Research* 63 (1970), 232–7.

O'Connor, W. F. "The Reading Apperception Test: An Exploration of Attitudes Toward Reading." Unpublished doctoral dissertation, Oklahoma State University, Stillwater, Okla., 1968.

Peifer, J. E. "The Development of an Attitude Scale to Measure Students' Attitudes Toward Reading in the Secondary Schools." Unpublished doctoral dissertation, Pennsylvania State University, University Park, Penn., 1962.

Puryear, C. "An Investigation of the Relationship Between Attitudes Toward Reading and Reading Achievement." Unpublished doctoral dissertation, University of South Carolina, 1975.

Quandt, I. *Self-Concept and Reading.* Newark, Del.: International Reading Association, 1972.

Ransbury, M. "Critical Factors in the Development of Attitudes Toward Reading as Defined by Individual Perceptions of Students, Their Teachers and Parents." Unpublished doctoral dissertation, Indiana University School of Education, Bloomington, 1971.

_____. "An Assessment of Reading Attitudes." *Journal of Reading* 17 (October 1973), 25–28.

Ratliff, G. "Reader's Theatre: The 'Theatrical' Approach to Teaching Literature." Master's thesis, Montclair State College, Montclair, N.J., 1980.

Roswell, C. G. "Change in Attitude Toward Reading and Its Relationship to Certain Variables Among Children with Reading Difficulties." Unpublished doctoral dissertation, George Peabody College for Teachers, Nashville, Tenn., 1967.

Rotter, J. *Social Learning and Clinical Psychology.* Englewood Cliffs, N.J.: Prentice-Hall, Inc., 1954.

Russell, D. *Children Learn to Read.* Lexington, Mass.: Ginn and Company, 1961.

Schroeder, H., M. Driver, and S. Streufert. *Human Information Processing.* New York: Holt, Rinehart and Winston, 1967.

Skinner, B. F. *Science and Human Behavior.* New York: Macmillan Publishing Co., Inc., 1953.

Smith, J. A. *The Nature of Creative Teaching.* Boston: Allyn & Bacon, Inc., 1975.

Smith, R., and D. Johnson. *Teaching Children to Read.* Reading, Mass.: Addison-Wesley Publishing Co., Inc., 1976. Chapter opening quotation appears on page 343.

Somers, A., and J. Worthington. *Response Guides for Teaching Children's Books.* Urbana, Ill.: National Council of Teachers of English, 1979, p. 6.

Spiegel, D. L. *Reading for Pleasure: Guidelines.* Newark, Del.: International Reading Association, 1981.

Stephens, J. *The Crock of Gold: Irish Fairy Tales.* New York: Macmillan Publishing Co., Inc., 1960.

Thorndike, R. "Children's Reading Interests." In *Readings on Reading Instruction*, ed. by A. J. Harris. New York: David McKay Co., Inc., 1963, pp. 338–71.

Thurstone, L. L. "Attitudes Can Be Measured." *The American Journal of Sociology* 33 (1928), 529–54.

Tullock-Rhody, R., and J. Alexander. "A Scale for Assessing Attitudes Toward Reading in Secondary Schools." *Journal of Reading* 23 (April 1980), 609–14.

Turner, T., and J. Alexander. "Promising Practices for Improving Reading Attitudes." Paper presented at the Annual Meeting of the Southeastern Regional Conference of the International Reading Association, Nashville, Tennessee, February, 1980.

Witty, P., and associates. "Studies of Children's Interests—A Brief Summary." In *Readings on Reading In-*

struction, ed. by A. J. Harris. New York: David McKay Co., Inc., 1963, pp. 330–37.

Woodbury, J. "Choral Reading and Reader's Theatre: Oral Interpretation of Literature in the Classroom." In *Developing Active Readers: Ideas for Parents, Teachers, and Librarians*, ed. by D. Monson. Newark, Del.: International Reading Association, 1979, pp. 65–72.

Yeatts, P. P. *Developmental Change in the Self-concept of Children Grades 3–12.* Gainesville: Florida Educational Research and Development Council Research Bulletin, 1967, 3(2).

CHAPTER 12

Assessing Reading Achievement

Diagnosis is meaningful only to the extent that what it uncovers affects instructional decisions.

D. Durkin, 1976

It is necessary for the teacher to be familiar with what to expect in terms of variety of reading levels in a single classroom. (Photo by Linda Lungren.)

GOALS: To help the reader to

1. Understand the possible spectrum of reading levels in the classroom.
2. Assess readability.
3. Understand factors contributing to reading expectancy levels including the concept of intellectual functioning (IF) scores.
4. Recognize the importance of student diagnosis in the evaluation process.
5. Learn formal and informal student assessment measures.

To begin a reading program based on the competencies and needs of individual students, a teacher must know what these strengths and needs are. Information supplied through educational measurement, including formal and informal tests, and teacher observation provide insight into where to begin a program of reading instruction. It is necessary for the teacher to be familiar with what to expect in terms of variety of reading levels in a single classroom and individual potentials before assembling the materials needed to begin a diagnostic-prescriptive program. Familiarity with readability formulas and their uses makes the selection of material to match specific needs easier.

Evaluation is a continuous process that you will use constantly as you set goals, diagnose student needs, and plan instructional programs. In this chapter, we hope to provide you with the information necessary to make right decisions to select the best possible course of reading instruction for each student in your charge.

From the first reading experience in any classroom, it becomes obvious that not all children in the same grade are reading at the same level. While this fact is common knowledge, due largely to media interest in public school reading achievement, the actual range of reading levels found in students within a single classroom can be astonishing. According to Goodlad (1966), the "broad spread from high to low achiever steadily increases with the upward movement of heterogeneous classes (relatively homogeneous in chronological age) through the school" (p. 34). He estimates that the range in levels is reflected by the number of years delineated by the grade-level number (third grade, three years). Apparently this holds true for the intermediate grades, while in the junior high grades the range may be approximated by taking two thirds of the median chronological age. Goodlad states further that in subject areas that allow for outside development such as language arts and recreational reading, the range broadens to one and one half to two times the number of the grade level.

To demonstrate the significance of Goodlad's finding for the classroom teacher, some examples are provided: in a fourth-grade class, the reading ability range might be computed as follows:

Grade 4

$4 \times 1.5 = 6$	Grade level (4) times a spread of 1.5 for each grade level.
$6 \div 2 \quad = 3$	Dividing spread by 2 determines the spread on either side of the grade level.
$4 + 3 \quad = 7$ (high) $4 - 3 \quad = 1$ (low)	Adding and subtracting spread (3) from grade level (4) determines the range of reading ability and grade level.

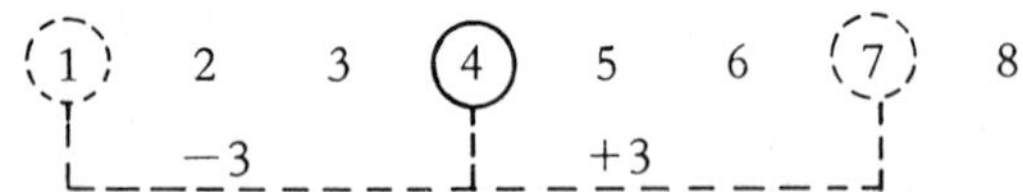

Therefore, in the fourth grade, a teacher might be expected to teach a class of students ranging from first-grade to seventh-grade reading levels.

Now suppose that you are a third-grade teacher and determine the range of reading levels that your children may have.

Grade 3

$3 \quad \times 1.5 = 4.5$	Grade level (3) times a spread of 1.5 for each grade level.
$4.5 \div 2 \quad = 2.25$	Dividing total spread (4.5) by 2 determines the spread on either side of the grade level.
$3 + 2.25 = 5.25$ (high) $3 - 2.25 = \ .75$ (low)	Adding and subtracting spread (2.25) from grade level (3) determines the range of reading ability grade levels.

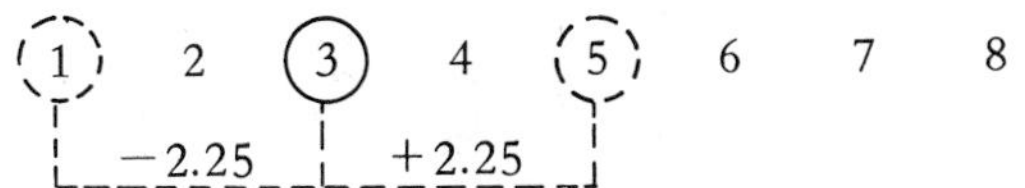

The reading ability range in the third grade might vary from first-grade level to fifth-grade level.

Goodlad's statement also suggests that the range of reading achievement in intermediate classrooms equals two thirds the chronological age (CA). The following chart reflects the CA for each intermediate grade level.

Grade	CA
6.0	11.2
7.0	12.0
8.0	13.2
9.0	14.2
10.0	15.2
11.0	16.2
12.0	17.2

Now suppose that you are an eighth-grade teacher. What range of reading would be possible according to Goodlad's statement?

Grade 8

Grade 8 chronological age = 13.2	Information from the chart.
$13.2 \times 2/3 = \frac{26.4}{3} = 8.8$ or 9	Chronological age times 2/3.
$9 \div 2 = 4.5$	Dividing total spread (9) by 2 determines the spread on either side of the grade level.
$8 + 4.5 = 12.5$ (high) $8 - 4.5 = 3.5$ (low)	Adding and subtracting spread (4.5) from grade level (8) determines the range of reading ability grade levels.

1 2 3 4 5 6 7 8 9 10 11 12

In an attempt to accommodate these reading differences, you will need reading materials that cover an adequate range of readability.

READABILITY: COMPUTATION AND CAUTION

Vocabulary difficulty and sentence length appear to be the two factors most commonly agreed on as determinants of text readability. The incorporation of polysyllabic, nonfrequent words in complex sentences, with embeddings and transformations, tends to indicate an advanced readability level. Several readability formulas exist; they include Gray and Leary (1935), Lorge (1944), Flesch (1943), Dale and Chall (1948), Spache (1953), Fry (1968), and Aukerman (1972). These authors have attempted to design and measure the factors that cause children to have difficulty with reading materials. The use of these formulas, based on these factors, aids the classroom teacher in *estimating* the appropriateness of certain material for a particular student.

Readability research conducted by Guidry and Knight (1976) indicated that, when the Dale-Chall, Flesch, Fry, and Lorge formulas were used to determine readability levels of the same materials, "the Dale-Chall method seems consistently to be high in its grade-level readability and that a more valid determination can be made by subtracting −0.891 from the final answer, . . . the Fry formula tends to yield a consistently low readability" (p. 556). When using the Fry formula, you will need to add +0.865 as an adjustment grade-level factor. When employing the Flesch and Lorge formulas, the adjustment factors of +0.299 and −0.285 are suggested by Guidry and Knight. With the application of these adjustment factors, it may be possible to use any of these formulas with greater confidence.

One must remember that readability levels are only *approximations* of material difficulty because it is almost impossible to hold constant all the factors (text organization, concept difficulty, semantics, syntax, reader interest) that can affect one's mastery of a given material.

Computation: The Fry Readability Graph

The Fry formula is comparable in accuracy to other

readability formulas. Because it is computed quickly and easily, it is presented here to aid the classroom teacher in determining readability of materials that might be appropriate to students.

Average number of syllables per 100 words

Short words Long words

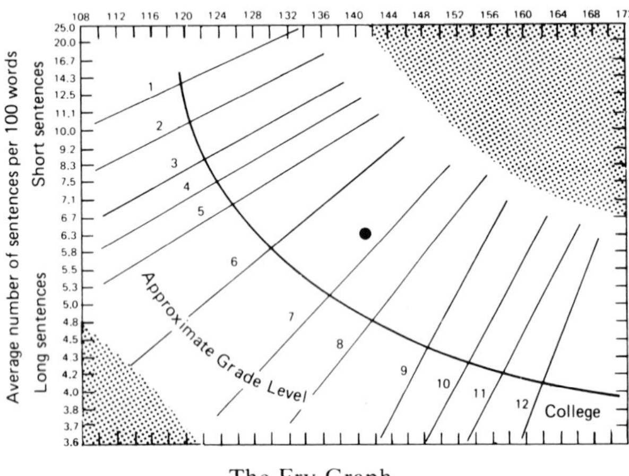

The Fry Graph

Edward Fry, "Readability Formula That Saves Time," *Journal of Reading*, 11:513–16; 575–577 (April 1968). Used with permission of the author and the International Reading Association.

HOW TO USE THE FRY GRAPH

1. Select three 100-word passages from near the beginning, middle, and end of the book. Skip all proper nouns.
2. Count the total number of sentences in each 100-word passage (estimating to the nearest tenth of a sentence). Average these three numbers (add together and divide by 3).
3. Count the total number of syllables in each 100-word sample. There is a syllable for each vowel sound; for example, cat (1), blackbird (2), continental (4). Do not be fooled by word size; for example, ready (2), stopped (1), bottle (2). It may be convenient to count every syllable over one in each word and add 100. Average the total number of syllables for the three samples.
4. Plot on the graph the average number of sentences per 100 words and the average number of syllables per 100 words. Most plot points fall near the heavy curved line. Perpendicular lines mark off approximate grade-level areas.

Example	Sentences per 100 words	Syllables per 100 words
100-word sample, p. 5	9.1	122
100-word sample, p. 89	8.5	140
100-word sample p. 150	7.0	129
Divide total by 3	3) 24.6	3) 391
Average	8.2	130

Plotting these averages on the graph, we find that they fall in the fifth-grade area; hence, the book is about fifth-grade difficulty level. If great variability is encountered either in sentence length or in the syllable count for the three selections, then you should randomly select several more passages and average them in before plotting.

The task of computing readability levels for a complete library of books may be simplified greatly by the use of microcomputers, which are often available in math and science classes or elsewhere in the school. While there are programs available commercially (Goodman and Schwab, 1980; Carlson, 1980), Judd (1981) recommends utilizing the skills of advanced programming students to program in the formula most useful for the situation.

Cautions. While it is easy to use readability formulas, it is equally as easy to misuse them. It is virtually impossible to arrive at an absolute readability level for a text based on the sampling method employed by most formulas due to variables within the textual material. These variables include the fact that introductory chapters of a text are often the most difficult; content area materials often do not evidence a gradation of difficulty; literary devices such as metaphorical and poetic language, tone, mood, and style plus linguistic elements of semantics and syntax are not constant throughout a text. The result of this inconsistency is that there may be varying degrees of reading difficulty within one text, which, in turn, makes a readability score serve only as an *approximation* of difficulty.

Other factors, outside the actual text structure, may also contribute to the "real" readability level as opposed to the level obtained by the formula used. Chief among these factors are the experiential background and interest of the reader. This problem is illustrated in the following exercises. Please read each of the following passages and answer the six questions that follow each passage.

Passage 1

Christmas always meant going to Grandma's house. On Christmas Eve the entire family tramped out to the woods. Dad was in charge of bring back the tree, and the rest of us cut fir branches for house decorations. That evening Grandma would distribute the homemade ornaments. We hung up a cookie universe: suns, stars, moons, and unearthly men with raisin eyes. Mom arranged candles in silvery paper on the branches. With dignity and care, Grandpa chained the tree with yards of cranberries and popcorn. We decorated the tree the way Grandma had when she was young; we were learning tradition.

Questions

1. Who cut the Christmas tree?__________
2. What was Grandpa's job?__________
3. Who was in charge of decorating the tree?__________
4. Why did the author of this paragraph go to the woods?__________
5. What does the phrase "cookie universe" mean?__________
6. How did the author of this paragraph learn tradition?__________

Passage 2

One of the oldest drinks known to man is milk. Man requires liquids as well as solids to remain healthy because he is a mammal, a warm-blooded being. Prehistoric man did not consume as much liquid as modern man. He devoured fruit from the trees he inhabited. However, man had to change his habits to exist on the arid plains. No longer a fruit-eater, he soon began to hunt plains animals. This new activity required much energy; man perspired and needed to drink liquids directly. To this day man needs liquids such as milk to be able to exist.

Questions

1. What does man need to remain healthy?__________
2. Where did prehistoric man live?__________
3. What is a mammal?__________
4. Why did ancient man not have to drink liquids directly?__________
5. What made man change his eating habits?__________
6. What happened to man's body as he hunted animals?__________

Did you find one passage more difficult than the other? Did you score equally on each passage? If you found one passage more difficult, ask yourself, "What factors within the passage created the difficulty?" Both passages, according to readability formulas, are identical. Here are the statistics on each of the passages:

	Christmas	Milk
Number of words	100	100
Number of sentences	8	8
Average sentence length	12.5	12.5
Number of syllables	146	146

This chart demonstrates some of the pitfalls of relying exclusively on readability formulas to determine passage difficulty. If your score was significantly higher on one of the passages, it may have been because you found that passage more interesting than the other passage. You may have performed better on one passage than the other because of your experience; you may have celebrated Christmas in the same way as the people in the passage. On the other hand, you may have performed less well because of a lack of experience; you may not have celebrated Christmas at all, and therefore, you would not have been able to read the passage from an experiential point of view.

From a psycholinguistic point of view, you may have found more difficulty reading the "Milk" passage than the "Christmas" passage. On the surface, the two passages are similar (number of words, syllables, etc.), but if you analyze the two passages carefully, using some of the recent findings from linguistic and information processing research, you will discover the following facts about the "Milk" passage.

It contains several instances where the reader has to *double* process; that is, the reader has to unravel the sequential encoding of contrastive semantic features to extract the appropriate feature of the second semantic element. To process information about the habitat of later-day man, the reader has to distinguish between prehistoric and later-day man and the habitat of each (prehistoric man, trees; later-day man, dry plains). However, the complexity of double processing is compounded in this passage because the contrastive semantic features are interrupted by the addition of an unrelated element. "However, man had to change his *habits*."

A second example of the necessity for double processing that occurs in this passage is entwined with a cognitive overloading phenomenon. The reader is forced to store that information while processing a positive proposition, "he soon began to hunt plains animals." While not dependent on the negative transformation, the positive elements of the proposition may be affected by cognitive overloading and/or by the inclusion of contrastive semantic features within the same proposition.

An additional consideration in the analysis of the differences between the "Milk" passage and the other passage is a question of complexity of cognitive functioning. The reader is required to sort "prehistoric man" from "man" and the habitats of each by processing inferred relationships between the concepts; that is, the reader has to extrapolate unwritten relationships. For example, the following facts are not stated explicitly: (1) man moved from the trees, (2) the dry plains did not have fruit, (3) man needed to gain food and liquid supply from a source other than fruit, (4) fruit was the source of liquid, (5) gathering fruit did not force man to exert himself.

As these examples illustrate, there is more to determining the readability level of textual material than counting syllables or sentences and performing mathematical computations on their numbers. Use these formulas with caution and as tools to establish probable rather than absolute grade-level equivalents for reading material.

DIAGNOSING INDIVIDUAL NEEDS

While it is important to be prepared to help your students by understanding the range of reading levels they may exhibit and to have determined readability scores for the materials you have to offer them, it is more important, indeed vital, to your role in teaching reading to diagnose the reading needs of each individual. To accomplish this complex task, your first step is to evaluate your students to determine their strengths and needs. Through diagnosis, you will be better able to plan prescriptive programs to develop their individual skills. Do not be alarmed; although we are suggesting that you will need to develop the skills of individual students, we are not suggesting that you must work with each child in isolation. Chapter 15 is designed to aid you in understanding and implementing flexible grouping techniques that are necessary for prescriptive teaching.

To begin a diagnostic process, you need to consider the following points:

1. The strengths and needs of the children.
2. The role of diagnostic evaluation in the classroom. Remember, evaluation is a process of decision making that can be used to diagnose and plan a curriculum.
3. The knowledge brought by the children to a specific topic.
4. The skills needed to pursue the study of this topic.

In thinking about these areas, you are already evaluating the competencies of your students.

While a re-emphasis on the processes of diagnostic evaluation may seem to be a contemporary focus, the topic is ageless. Early norms of school evaluation consisted of oral recitation because the major goal of most colonial educators was to train students to recite from memory. As written materials became more readily available, measures of evaluation began to include essay or problem-solving tests. Standardized testing became part of educational evaluation at the turn of the century when Alfred Binet and Therese Simon (1905) developed standardized intelligence tests in an attempt to differentiate normal from retarded children. They eventually broadened their studies to include the measurement of intelligence of all children.

IQ Versus IF

Intelligence tests, as they are currently designed, do

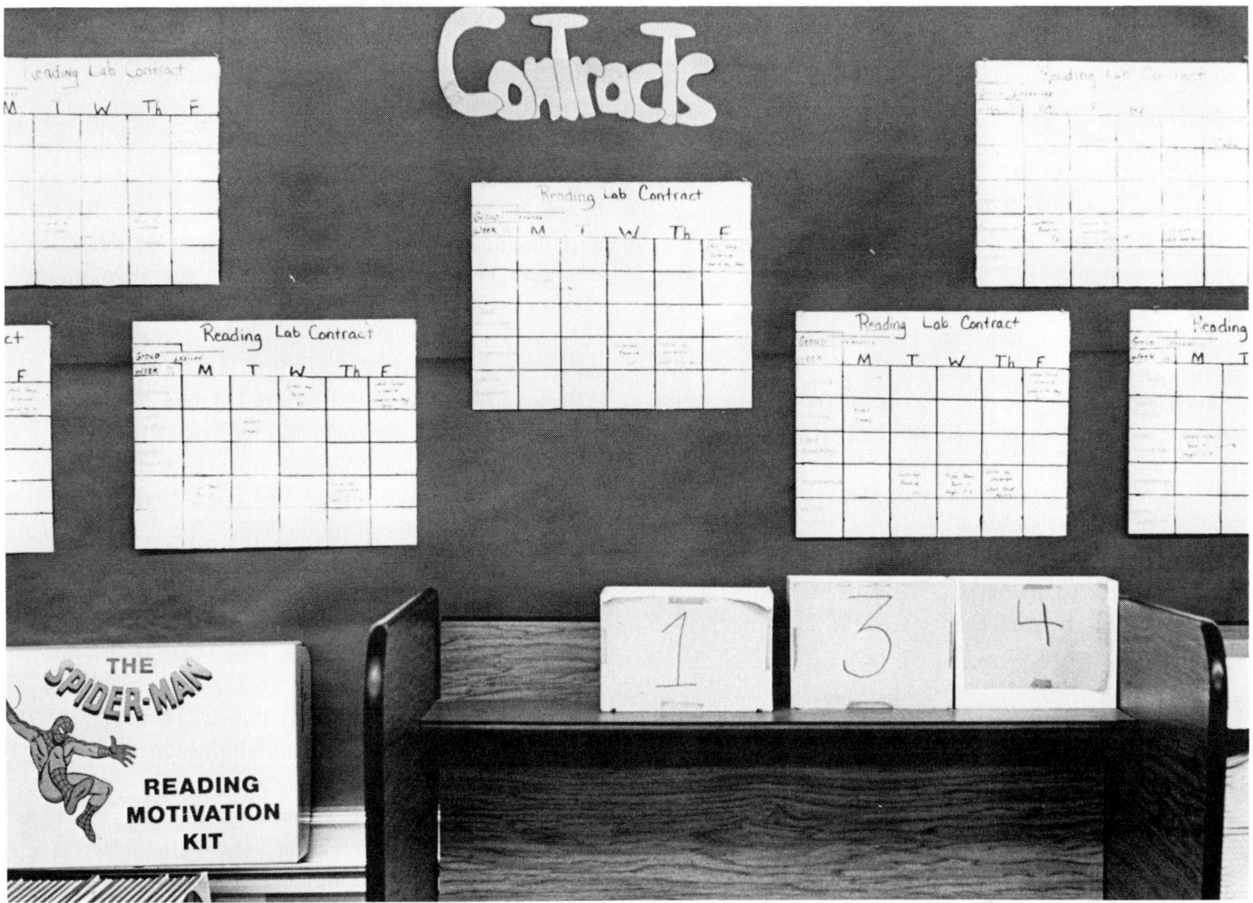

In order to diagnose the reading needs, your first step is to evaluate your students to determine their strenghts and needs. You can then formulate student contracts based on your assessment. (Photo by Linda Lungren.)

not measure intellectual potential (IQ). Instead, they measure one's present level of *intellectual functioning* (IF). Intellectual functioning is a measure of one's cultural experiences and information that are acquired through daily interactions with a variety of stimuli in an environment ranging from significant others to tangibles. If a child has been exposed to cultural experiences that are measured on a given intelligence task, that child often performs well on such a measure. If the tasks are outside a child's range of experience, that child is often considered intellectually inferior when he or she may only be missing daily exposures to such tasks or interactions.

Cultural exposures, coupled with biological factors, determine the potential of one's mental development (intelligence). One's inherent biological characteristics determine potential, while environment encourages the full or partial development of this potential. It is becoming more clear, as research continues into intelligence testing, that no one test can possibly claim to measure a person's intelligence quotient, which must include both potential and realized intellectual ability. Combinations of tests, using traditional instruments that in reality measure cultural exposure (IF) and electronic devices such as the ERTL Index,* may eventually provide us with an accurate means of measuring an individual's total intelligence potential (Fischer, Hunt, and Randhawa, 1978).

*The ERTL Index is an electronic device that attempts to analyze neural efficiency. Neural efficiency is processed in a period of fewer than three minutes. A helmet equipped with electrodes that are supposed to collect brain waves is placed on the person being tested. A flashing light stimulates the brain,

When a child is born, intellectual potential is determined by biological structures. In certain cases brain damage, chromosome abnormality, or other physical factors may affect potential academic or scholastic achievement. The degree of fulfillment of normal potential is realized through environmental exposures and daily experiences. Thus, IQ should be defined as normal intellectual and biological potential plus present intellectual functioning. Biological functioning is innate (it occurs through the development of the human organism), whereas present intellectual functioning is developed through daily experiences.

Available intelligence tests are unable to measure innate intellectual potential (IQ); however, they do report data regarding one's present intellectual functioning (IF) as a result of environmental exposures. This position was forwarded by Wechsler (1958) when he noted that general intelligence could not be equated with intellectual ability (i.e., that which can be measured on most tests) because it takes into account the individual's entire personality.

Currently existing IQ tests are used to

1. Measure and compare mental endowment.
2. Measure one's capacity for learning.
3. Measure lack of mental capacity.
4. Measure the presence of special abilities.
5. Measure the presence of mental disabilities.
6. Determine school placements.
7. Determine a need for vocational guidance.
8. Determine those in need of counseling.
9. Predict life adjustment abilities.
10. Predict tendencies for juvenile delinquency.
11. Predict college success.

Assuming that intelligence tests are useful in all the situations listed, one begins to question exactly how the term "intelligence" is being defined. Thorndike (1973) helped us to develop such a definition when he stated, "There is not just one unique, but several different kinds of intelligence, namely abstract, social, and practical. The first is manifested by the individual's ability to work with symbols, the second by his ability to deal with people, and third by his ability to manipulate objects" (p. 5). Many existing measures seem to assess one's present functional level in the first area, that of abstraction. While other measures of intelligence may also include verbal, spatial, and numerical factors, all existing IQ tests measure one's present cognitive functioning on a specified set of items. What has been measured is intellectal functioning (IF) rather than intellectual capacity (IQ).

There are certain social, emotional, and cultural influences (affective dimensions) that may affect one's IF. However, you, as a classroom teacher, must also be aware that the IF is influenced by one's drive, persistence, will, and sense of preservation. These psychological factors may be studied within the context of the conative domain. To understand better the IF of the student, you will need to study the *affective* and *conative* or "will" dimensions of learning as well as the child's *cognitive* skills.

In utilizing the results of intelligence tests to analyze the strengths and needs of children, the educator must exercise caution before labeling a child as intellectually inferior in some way. As discussed in this chapter, these tests do not accurately measure the real, biological intellectual capacity of an individual. To base an educational program solely on these test results is a regrettably frequent error. Once labeled as dull or retarded, the child is generally treated that way, and expectations for his or her educational career diminish. When the test scores are viewed as measuring the present level of intellectual functioning, and a program is developed to challenge a child from that point, the intellectual capacity is then tapped and the child can be encouraged to go on to higher educational achievement.

Because existing tests do not measure intelligence (intellectual potential + cultural experiences) but instead measure one's present level of intellectual functioning (IF), we believe that the term *IQ testing* should be replaced by *IF testing*. Perhaps the realization and understanding of the need for this substitution will enable us to avoid erroneous, inappropriate labels. We cannot measure intellectual potential, but we do have some measures that begin to assess one's *present* level of *intellectual functioning* on a given task. Examples of tests

while a computer analyzes the efficiency with which the brain processes the light flashes. An oscilloscope, on which the waves can be monitored visually, and a device to amplify the waves are also parts of the machine. For more detailed information see William Tracy, "Goodbye IQ, Hello EI (ERTL Index), *"Phi Delta Kappan*" (October 1972), 89–94, and J. Trout, G. Packwood, and Barry Wilson, "Ertl's Neural Efficiency Analyzer: Still Promising–But What?" *Phi Delta Kappan* (March 1976), 448–51.

that measure IF and not IQ are the Stanford-Binet Scale and the Wechsler Scale for Children. In the next few pages, we will use the term IF to refer to what has previously been called IQ.

MA + IF. In addition to being interested in a child's IF score and his or her reading level score, teachers are often anxious to determine a student's *mental age.* Why? Because many tests are scored according to the age at which a majority of the population succeeds at a given task. For example, a student who succeeds on the items at the eleven-year level and fails at the twelve-year level has a mental age of eleven. If his chronological age is less than eleven, the child may be considered to be very competent in behaviors being measured by the test. If his chronological age is greater than eleven, he may need instruction or exposure to the behaviors measured by the test.

Mental age (MA) refers to one's level of mental development as compared with others on a given set of standardized tasks. MA is one's IF (present intellectual functioning level) expressed in units of age.

One's MA is easily determined through use of the following formula.

$$\text{MA} = \frac{\text{IF}}{100} \times \text{CA}$$

Thus, if a child's IF is 80 and his CA (chronological age) is 8, his MA is 6.4.

$$\frac{80}{100} \times 8 = \frac{640}{100} = 100\overline{)640} \quad 6.4$$

$$\begin{array}{r} 600 \\ \hline 400 \end{array}$$

Or a child whose CA is 10 who has an IF of 140 has an MA of 14.0:

$$\frac{140}{100} \times 10 = 14.0$$

If we accept that an IF of 120 means that a child has intellectually grown at the rate of 1.2 years for each chronological year until age fifteen, while an IF of 80 means that the student has advanced intellectually at the rate of 0.8 for each chronological year, the commonly used formulas (MA = IF X CA and IF = MA/CA X 100) become easier to interpret.

Determining Reading Expectancy

American educators for decades have utilized this homogeneous system of grouping according to age levels, assuming that the teacher's sophisticated knowledge about personalized curricula emphasizing individualized student progress would result in in-class grouping by actual ability level. As you attempt to implement such personalized groupings within a given grade level, remember that the actual achievement level of each student should be compared with his or her learning capacity, not his or her grade placement.

The following formulas have been designed to aid you in determining your students' reading expectancy level.

BOND AND TINKER (1979)

$$\text{Reading Expectancy Level (REL)} = \frac{\text{IF}}{100} \times \text{Years of Reading Instruction} + 1$$

This formula is interpreted as follows: David, who is an eight-year-old in the second grade, has had two years of reading instruction and has an IF of 120. David's REL is 3.4:

$$\left(\frac{120}{100} \times 2\right) + 1 = \frac{240}{100} = 2.4 + 1 = 3.4$$

(measured in grade levels).

HARRIS AND SIPAY (1978)

$$\text{REL} = \frac{2\text{MA} + \text{CA}}{3}$$

Can you refer to the statistics on David and determine his REL using Harris's formula? First we must determine his MA. Remember,

$$\text{MA} = \frac{\text{IF}}{100} \times \text{CA}$$

Thus,

$$\text{MA} = \frac{120}{100} \times 8 = 9.6$$

Now that we have David's MA we can proceed:

$$\text{REL} = \frac{2\text{MA} + \text{CA}}{3} = \frac{2(9.6) + 8}{3}$$
$$= \frac{19.2 + 8}{3} = \frac{27.2}{3} = 9.1 \quad \text{(reading expectancy measured in years)}$$

The REL, as well as the MA, CA, and IF, is a rough estimate of a child's ability employed with great discretion in your classroom. One must note that the formula of Bond and Tinker (1979) reports the reading expectancy level in *grade-level units*, whereas the Harris formula (1970) reports the REL in *chronological age units*. The importance of these two formulas is the following:

1. It is useful for you to know the approximate level of a child's current capacity for reading so that your expectations are realities for *every* child.
2. It is useful to know both the Bond and Tinker formula and the Harris formula because children are often in grades that do not reflect their current ages; for example, some ten-year-olds are in the third grade and some ten-year-olds are in the fifth or sixth grade.
3. It is useful to know both formulas because some schools have an ungraded system.

UNDERSTANDING AND USING CRITERION- AND NORM-REFERENCED TESTS

Both norm-referenced and criterion-referenced tests can be useful instruments to measure a student's learning ability. The basic difference between the two methods lies actually, as their names suggest, in what the test results are *referenced* to or compared with. *Norm*-referenced tests assess performance of a task in relation to the achievement levels of other people who have taken the same test; *criterion*-referenced assess student performance of a task but do not compare the results with a previously established population. Norm-referenced test results are interpreted in statistical terms including percentile rankings, stanine scores, grade levels, and IFs. Criterion-referenced tests provide information regarding placement on a performance continuum relative to a given behavior, the extreme ends being mastery and nonmastery of the task.

Norm-referenced testing became prominent in the 1930s as only one dimension of the process of evaluation. It is useful to think of norm-referenced tests as survey instruments, designed to measure competency in a broad manner rather than as diagnostic tools (Stanley and Hopkins, 1972). They are useful for measuring student progress when administered infrequently (i.e., each year) and nationally normed tests provide an "external basis of comparison " (Shepard, 1979, p. 29) that highlights a student's or program's relative strengths and weaknesses in the national context. State and local norms are often available, and these may provide a more useful and accurate picture of individual and program accomplishments.

Norm- and criterion-referenced measures differ in the ways in which they are designed, as well as in the type of information conveyed through student responses (see the accompanying table). Criterion-referenced tests can function well as diagnostic instruments due to the precise nature of the test items. Items on a criterion-referenced achievement test must reflect competencies within a specified behavioral domain. For a criterion-referenced instrument to be effective, this domain of behavior must be "well-defined." According to Nitko (1980), " a domain is well-defined when it is clear to both the text developer and the test user which categories of performance (or which kinds of tests) should and should not be considered as potential test items. Well-defined domains are a necessary condition for criterion referencing since the basic idea is to generalize how well an examinee can perform in a broader class of behaviors, only a few of which happen to appear on a particular test form" (p. 465).

The scoring of the criterion-referenced instrument should be designed to provide information about the developed skills and existing needs of a student. If behavioral objectives have been written to define the competencies to be tested within the specified domain, and the test items accurately reflect these objectives, the problem of assessing the examinee's degree of demonstration is minimized. For example, the end product of a criterion-referenced measure should provide descriptive information regarding an individual's degree of competence on a specified task. A criterion might be "Can Linda recite her ABCs?" The criterion is clear, and the assessment is relatively simple. Here Linda is compared with an established criterion; that is, she can or cannot recite her ABCs. The test is criterion-referenced.

The criterion-referenced instrument may be designed to aid the classroom teacher in assessing individual competencies and designing alternate programs based on individual needs. The norm-referenced tests can also look at the individual's competency, as he or she is related to others in the group. The question that is being asked is, "How do the various students rank on the ABC test?" Each of these measures assesses the same behaviors, but each has a different purpose. Therefore, when you are selecting or developing an instrument for use in your classroom, you need to specify your reasons for testing, and you need to specify the criterion being tested. Whether you use criterion- or norm-referenced evaluation, you will need to select your instrument very carefully.

A COMPARISON OF NORM-REFERENCED AND CRITERION-REFERENCED TESTS

Test Feature	Norm-Referenced	Criterion-Referenced
Test design	Design is related to subject matter information and process skills.	Design is related to specific instructional behavioral objectives.
Item preparation	Designed to determine variances among students.	Designed to measure individual competency on a given task.
Item types	Many types are used (multiple choice, true-false, completion).	Many types are used (multiple choice, true-false, completion).
Item difficulty	Moderate; designed to determine a middle range.	Wide variance, but with adequate instructional preparation, responses are generally correct.
Interpreting results	A student is compared with the accomplishments of a norm group by computing his subscore or total test score.	A student's performance on a specified behavioral item is determined by comparing his response to the correct question.
Test availability	Consult Oscar Buros' *Mental Measurement Yearbook* to ascertain information about norm-referenced tests.	The tests, which are often designed by teachers for use in their classrooms, may now also be maintained as part of the *management systems* of many basal reading programs.
Test use	Used to determine a comparative score between one pupil and a normative group and to determine global student achievement.	Used to diagnose student strengths and needs and to evaluate an instructional program.

Until recently, the practice has been to evaluate students against some norm group, whether their own or an arbitrarily chosen group. This has at least two disadvantages: (1) it makes the same children fall at the bottom in every situation, and (2) it encourages the development of curriculum unrelated to the needs of the children. Because of these and other disadvantages, the use of properly designed criterion-referenced tests is encouraged by educators. Two advantages of criterion-referenced tests are (1) comparison problems are minimized because a child is being evaluated *only* against *himself* or *herself* and (2) criterion-referenced tests may be designed informally by the classroom teacher to measure a specific behavior.

A test devised by a classroom teacher is often called an *informal test*. It can be either norm- or criterion-referenced. A standardized test can also be either norm- or criterion-referenced. The distinction between informal and standardized testing is that the latter has been administered to many students and "standardized" before being used in an actual situation. Whether you are using an informal or standardized test, it is essential that the test have the following characteristics.

Validity. The basic question to be answered is "Does the test measure what you think it is measuring?" For example, if a college instructor announces a test and says it will measure understanding and application and then asks five questions related to details on a footnote on page 47, is it measuring what she thinks (or says) it is? Obviously not. We say the test has no content validity. If, as a teacher, you want to measure problem-solving ability through story problems and you proceed to give a page of fifty long-division examples, your test will have no content validity.

Content validity must be established for achievement tests. This may be accomplished by first deciding what it is you intend to measure and then deciding if your test (or the standardized test) gives a representative sample of the entire field you are interested in testing. If it does, your test has content validity.

Researchers often discuss three other kinds of validity: *predictive validity*, *construct validity*, and *concurrent validity*. Predictive validity determines how successful the test is at predicting success or achievement at a future time. Most informal measures in the elementary or secondary level are not concerned with this aspect of validity.

Construct validity refers to the relationship between test scores and other criteria of behavior that relate logically to the test. It examines an ability, aptitude, trait, or characteristic that is hypothesized to explain some aspect of human behavior.

Concurrent validity compares the outcome of a test at approximately the same time as the predictor test is taken. For instance, a vocational interest test may be compared with interests exhibited by members of the vocation already. Designers of elementary school measures that are formal or informal are more concerned with content validity than they are with the other types of validity.

Reliability. Another factor that must be determined is the stability of your test (informal or standardized). If you give a reading comprehension test on Monday and again on Friday, and if the scores are not similar for each student, then the test may not be reliable. Ambiguous test items are not reliable because students are guessing at answers, for the most part, and students seldom guess twice in the same way. Long tests and very difficult tests are often unreliable because students tend to guess from fatigue; very short tests are seldom reliable because the sample of work is so limited that you may or may not have selected the items that the student knows.

A *correlation coefficient* indicates the reliability of a test. The coefficient of correlation represents the relationship between two specific behaviors of a group of students. The tendency of the students to have systematic similar or dissimilar relative positions in the two distributions is reflected through computing a correlation coefficient. A positive correlation exists between the two measures if students who are high or low in one distribution are also high or low in a second distribution. For example, if Catherine receives a high score on each of two measures and Todd receives a low score on each of the same two measures, the correlation coefficient is positive. If $r/tt = .00$ (read: The correlation equals zero), the test is completely unreliable. If $r/tt = 1.00$ (read: the correlation equals 1), the test is completely reliable. Unfortunately, tests are never completely reliable, but a correlation of .75 or .99 is usually acceptable as a measure of reliability.

If a test is both reliable and valid and you want to use it as a criterion-referenced test, you have no further concerns. However, if you want to use it as a norm-referenced test, you must investigate appropriate norming procedures.

Norms. Norms are as important to the teacher as they are to the doctor. If you took a child to be weighed and measured, and the doctor told you that the child was greatly overweight, you would ask, "Overweight compared with whom?" If you felt the comparison to be inappropriate, you would reject the doctor's statement.

The same is true for achievement tests. The score that the child receives may be accurate, depending on the validity and the reliability of the test, but the comparisons you make may be totally inappropriate. A child can *only* be compared with his or her own group—that is, a ten-year-old urban child should be compared with other ten-year-old children in similar urban environments. To make the wrong comparisons is totally misleading and provides no helpful information. In fact, the information may be considered destructive if the child is labeled intellectually inferior because of his score on measures with which he has had no preparation.

A test can also be used if the appropriate norms are not supplied. For example, you may wish to use the score in the context of the child's own classroom group, use the test for a diagnostic purpose, or establish a set of norms for your own school. It really is not a difficult process. Farr (unpublished), a leading reading evaluator, suggested the following procedures for norming your informal reading test:

1. Administer a standardized silent reading test to a group of students (a sample size of one hundred is usually best). Several teachers may cooperate on the project.
2. Develop an informal reading test based on the instructional reading materials used in the classes. Use ap-

propriate questions (as described) and decide on criteria for establishing instructional reading levels.

3. Use the results of the standardized test (1 above) to rank the students from highest to lowest. Use a composite reading score (not subscores) for this ranking.
4. Randomly select three students from each decile of the ranking. That is, select three students from the top ten, select three students from the second ten, and so on, until you have selected thirty of the total one hundred students.
5. Administer the informal reading test to these students.
6. From this procedure you can develop equivalency (IRI reading levels) for students scoring at various points on the standardized reading test.

Let us assume that the students who are being tested are fourth-graders. After you have completed the administration of the standardized test and selected your deciles, you should study the test manual and recode the scores into reading grade levels. The next step is to assume that the scores are accurate for each decile, that is, that students who score at seventh-grade level are capable of performing on other tests at a seventh-grade level. Now you are ready to administer the informal reading test with test questions you have developed. The scores of each of your groups will establish norms for your informal reading test. The following chart illustrates this procedure.

Group	Standardized Test		Mean Informal Reading Test Scores (highest = 10 pts)	Estimated Grade Level
	Mean Raw Score	Mean Reading Grade Level		
Group A	85	7.0	9	7.0
Group B	50	4.0	6	4.0
Group C	30	1.0	3	1.0

From this chart you can see that the scores for your informal reading test are easily correlated with estimated reading levels. However, these scores should probably be used only to determine grade-level criteria. In this case, a score of 6 out of 10 will approximate a reading level score of 1.0. There are several cautions to note if you intend to use this procedure:

1. This procedure only *approximates* a reading level.
2. It is assumed that the objective of your informal reading test conforms to the objectives of the standardized reading test. Your informal reading test may have an entirely different purpose than the standardized reading test, and, therefore, the score may not accurately reflect reading-level ability for this particular task.
3. There is a statistical concern with this procedure. If one student in group A scores 2 out of 10 and most of the other students score 9 or 10 and if the mean is equated at 8, then a score of 8 may not accurately reflect the group's scores. Therefore, you may want to use the median score as the norm instead of the mean score.

In addition to examining reliability, validity, and norming samples when you are choosing a test, you should also consider the following:

1. *Original publication date and/or most recent test revision.* Remember that words and concepts change with each generation. Many children today have never heard of an "outhouse" or an "icebox."
2. *Type of test.* Individual or group scoring; done by hand or machine.
3. *Scoring.* If the test is scored by the testing company, remember to request that the student answer sheets be returned. You can plan instruction if you know the consistency of errors made by the students. An IQ score of 103 or a reading score of 6.2 tells you nothing that will aid your planning.
4. *Availability of test forms.* If you plan to retest after instruction, you will need twice as many forms.

5. *Administration time.* Be careful to measure desired behavior rather than rate.
6. *Cost.*
7. *Availability of subtests.* It is often unnecessary to administer the entire test to measure the desired behavior.* Sometimes one subtest is so highly correlated with all the other subtests in a specific test that you need only to give one subtest to ascertain reading achievement information for a child. To determine if you can use one subtest as a valid predictor of overall achievement, you should consult the statistics provided in the manual for each standardized test.
8. *Legibility.* Of tables, maps, and graphs.
9. *Clarity of directions.* Lack of clarity in giving directions often measures one's ability to interpret directions, as well as, or instead of, the previously desired behavior. The directions should be written in vocabulary appropriate to your grade level. Would it invalidate the test if you explained the directions to your children?

*The term behavior is used in the sense of desired cognitive or affective outcome or performance. Behavioral objectives are explained in detail in Chapter 15.

Some of this information will be found in the manual. However, keep in mind that the manual is written by an author or a publisher, whose major intent is to sell the tests. A less biased review of most tests can be found in the *Mental Measurement Yearbook*, edited by Buros (1968–1975). This reference should be consulted before investing time and money in a testing program.

As a teacher, you will already know a great deal about the abilities of your students. Use testing to fill in the gaps and tell you what you *don't* know. There is little point in overtesting your students. It is important that you know your reason for testing: "What do I want to know about this child?" "How will this knowledge help me in planning better activities for him or her?" After answering these questions, select your instrument, using the previously stated criteria. After scoring, diagnose and plan your curriculum accordingly. No one has to pass or fail as each student is competing only with himself or herself.

Go one step farther and explain to your principal that the standardized tests being given to your class at the beginning of the year are really of little instructional value if you only have a list that supplies you with a single grade-level score for each child. Ask for a breakdown of the test by category and components, for example, vocabulary score and syllabication score.

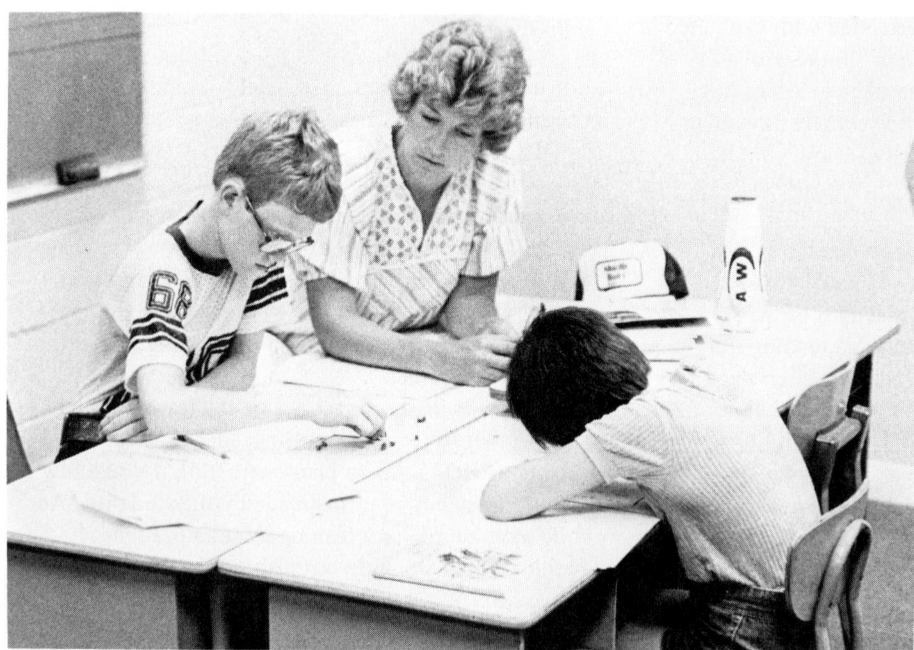

It is important that you know your reason for testing. Ask yourself: What do I want to know about this child? How will this knowledge help me in planning better activities for him or her? (Photo by Linda Lungren.)

As you attempt to analyze student assessment further, you may want to use a *diagnostic test*; an instrument of this type is designed to provide you with a more thorough analysis of individual skill competency. For example, a standard reading survey test will provide you with general information regarding student skill in *vocabulary*, *comprehension*, and *rate*, whereas a diagnostic instrument provides scores in *knowledge of consonant sounds*, *blending*, *syllabication*, *morphemes*, *comprehension*, *study skills*, and *reading rate*. A more thorough analysis of information is provided through the diagnostic test.

Diagnostic tests are often individually administered and require administrative and scoring skills because interpretation may be a complex task. Whichever type of test you use, if it is computer scored, remember to remind the publishing company to return the individual answer sheets so that *continuing diagnosis* can take place.

Standardized achievement test results, which can be used to diagnose and plan instructional needs, can be correlated with informal test results to acquire a more valid understanding of individual student skills. Correlation of standardized and informal tests, if used correctly, will provide a reliable and accurate assessment of student growth.

Informal measures, teacher checklists, textbook tests, and interest and attitude inventories are easily constructed if the teacher is aware of the behavior he or she wants to measure. Do you want to know if the child has map-reading skills or dictionary skills? Do you want to gain some knowledge about Tom's reading vocabulary? The behavior to be measured must be stated clearly so that appropriate materials can be prepared to measure this behavior. Too often, teacher tests are not correlated with material that has been taught. The need for accurate measurement cannot be overemphasized, because student growth is the single most frequently used basis for evaluating teaching methods, teacher effectiveness, curriculum, instructional procedures, and grouping practices.

Assessing the growth of the student is essential for making decisions related to the individualization of his or her program. Student evaluation must be continuous so that program changes can be made in accordance with the progress of the student. Correct use of test results helps the teacher in planning for both group and individual instruction. The process of *diagnosing* the strengths and needs of your students forms your instructional base. Whether your measure has been standardized or designed informally, your instruction should center on the elimination of error, which alters the comprehension of what is read. (Learning to use relevant test instruments effectively requires practice and critical evaluation as to the best application purposes.) It is imperative in the area of testing to never rely on a single measurement instrument to provide the necessary diagnostic information about a student. Test results should serve as a reference point from which to begin diagnostic-prescriptive instruction, never as an end in itself.

The Appendix is designed to acquaint you with standardized reading tests, publishers, and reading skills being measured. It is included to provide you with the comparative information you need to adequately select a test.

Informal Measures

In a diagnostic-prescriptive curriculum, you need as much information as possible about the child to best serve his or her needs. In addition to the standardized tests, you will find that informal assessments also provide you with valuable information regarding the reading competencies of your students. Informal instruments differ from standardized measures because they do not involve the formalized procedures for constructing, administering, and scoring. The quality of the informal measures used in your classroom will depend on *your competency* to design, implement, and evaluate them.

Informal measures that will be useful to you as a reading teacher are *informal reading inventories*, *teacher-made tests*, and the *cloze readability technique.*

IRI: Informal Reading Inventory. An effective and easily constructed diagnostic instrument, the informal reading inventory (IRI) is generally a teacher-made tool designed to assess a student's reading level. Quite often IRIs are made by selecting passages from material at the required grade level and administering them as a silent and/or oral reading exercise. Questions on context and vocabulary help assess the comprehension level of the student. IRIs are useful in determining a student's *independent reading level, instructional reading level,* and *frustration level.* The independent level is believed to be the one at which the student can read successfully with little or no aid because fluency and comprehension are developed well enough to master materials at this level. The student's instructional level is the level at which teacher assistance is required. At this level, the student's fluency and comprehension skills are not as well developed as when he or she reads at the independent level. The frustration reading level signals an area of difficulty to be avoided by the student. The level of the book at the student's frustrational level is too difficult.

For detailed information regarding the development of IRIs, we refer you to

Johnson, M. S., and R. A. Kress. *Informal Reading Inventories.* Newark, Del.: International Reading Association, 1965.

Silvaroli, N. J. *Classroom Reading Inventory.* Dubuque, Iowa: William C. Brown Company, Publishers, 1973.

Interpreting Oral Reading Tests. The number and type of errors made in oral reading provide clues as to a student's reading level and may help in diagnosing any special reading needs. Johnson and Kress (1965) maintain that the child is reading at his independent reading level if he scores 99 to 100 percent (one error) in his oral reading word analysis skills in a 100-word passage. If the child averages two to five errors, or 95 to 98 percent, he is considered to be reading at his instructional reading level. The child has reached his frustrational reading level when he cannot master at least 94 percent of the text.

ADMINISTERING AN ORAL READING TEST

1. Select a 100-word passage from the material you wish the child to read.
2. Ask the child to read the passage orally.
3. Record the following types of errors. The test administrator may record the reading and score the child afterward.

Types of Errors	Correction Procedures
Mispronunciation	Record the incorrect response above the word missed.
Substitution	Record the substituted word above the one missed.
Omission	Circle the omitted word or words.
Insertion	Caret ∧ in the extra word.
Hesitations	Supply the needed word and write Ⓗ if the child pauses for longer than five seconds.
Repetitions	Draw a wavy line under repeated words.

RECORDING ERRORS

"Ho, Ingrid! Ho, Berger!" shouted Mr. Hanson. "Wake up. (THE) The cod fishing starts today!"

"We're ready, Father. (COMING) We just have to put our boots on," answered Berger.

After breakfast they left for the harbor. Their boat was ready. They had cleaned it. The nets were fixed and piled on the side (BESIDE) of the boat.

The children saw the red flag. It started the race for the cod. Mr. Hanson told them, "That gives everyone a fair chance. All the boats can (CAN'T) go when the red flag is dropped."

Soon they were out of the (WE) harbor. Berger and Ingrid helped their father. They threw a net over the side. It went deep into the ocean.

D. H. Madison and R. E. Sterling, *Communities.* (New York: American Book Company, 1979), pp. 91–92.

ADMINISTERING A SILENT READING TEST

1. Prepare questions that determine the student's ability to use various parts of the text (index, glossary, etc.):
   a. On what pages will you find information about prehistoric man?
   b. How does the author define prehistoric?
2. Prepare questions that measure both the *vocabulary* and *comprehension* of what has been read:
   a. Where did prehistoric man originate?
   b. Define the word *skeletal* used by the author in the following sentence.
3. When preparing these questions, you must be careful

to provide items that assess the many operations of comprehension skills. Please refer to Chapter 7 for practice in developing a complex range of questions necessary to assess the comprehension competencies of your students.
4. Direct the students to read the selection.
5. Students can be timed if you are interested in measuring reading rate.

Record Keeping. You may want to devise a chart that will help you to determine student need at a quick glance.

Name	Parts of books	Vocabulary	Recall	Main ideas	Recognition	Translation	Inference	Evaluation	Details
Burnce, Bess									
Chu, Gin									
Cunningham, Denny									
Deering, Michael									
Deleo, Sadie									
Hess, Pearl									
Hill, Gertrude									
Houlden, Marilyn									
Jones, Harold									
Kavanaugh, Denise									
Ramirez, Jim									
Rivera, Juan									

Interpreting Silent Reading Tests. On the silent reading test, the child is believed to be reading at his independent reading level if he is able to answer 90 to 100 percent of the questions correctly. If 70 to 90 percent of the questions are answered correctly, the child is believed to be reading at his instructional level. His instructional plan is now developed.

Careful planning of instructional procedures will eliminate any areas of weakness which were evidenced at this level. The frustrational reading level has been reached if the child cannot answer at least 70 percent of the posed questions.

Informal Reading Inventory Standards

Level	Oral Reading	Comprehension
Independent	90–100%	90–100%
Instructional	95–98%	70–90%
Frustrational	Below 94%	Below 70%

These criteria are presented to guide you in determining student reading levels. Be flexible in using them, because a student may differ only slightly from one of the stated standards and still be reading at one of the levels. Remember, all instruments are designed to facilitate *your* decision making about students' needs and competencies. The final decision is yours; therefore, we encourage you to judge wisely and flexibly, remembering that *you*, not an *instrument*, are the trained teacher.

Consider precautions when employing IRIs:

1. The type of error may be more important than the number of errors.
2. Inventory accuracy may be hampered by teacher inexperience in construction, administration, and scoring.

Teacher-Made Tests. Teacher-made tests are useful for understanding your children's progress. The examples that follow may help you to design some of your own tests.

A simple exercise to test letter discrimination skills is shown here. The target letter is the first letter in each row. Students should draw a circle around the letter that matches it.

Upper Case

M	M	W	N	E
B	P	B	D	R
E	E	F	P	L
T	F	L	I	T
F	F	Y	E	P
O	C	O	Q	G
N	V	M	N	W
V	U	V	W	Y
P	P	R	B	F
I	I	L	T	Y

Lower Case

k	f	k	y	w
g	j	a	g	p
b	b	p	d	q
i	i	l	f	j
v	u	y	n	v
a	e	a	g	o
d	p	d	b	g
o	o	g	p	c
t	f	t	l	y
m	n	u	m	w

A similar exercise can be used to test a student's ability to discriminate the initial or final phoneme in a word. Give them a chart as shown in the following example, omitting the target words. The teacher reads each word, and the student must draw a circle around the letter of the initial or final sound.

Initial Phoneme

television	t	l	p	v
baseball	l	d	b	s
lost	t	s	l	f
water	v	w	m	r
run	n	g	r	t
car	c	r	q	b
fat	t	p	l	f
heart	r	h	b	j
moon	n	m	b	t
girl	j	l	g	t

Final Phoneme

cat	t	k	l	r
hard	p	d	b	r
fun	m	f	n	s
top	b	t	d	p
yes	s	l	t	y
far	g	r	f	p
scream	n	c	m	s
fall	l	f	t	i
log	n	l	p	g
luck	k	l	r	p

The Cloze Technique

The cloze readability technique is an informal measure that is based on the student's ability to comprehend a given text. Assessment is made by judging the acceptability of student responses when supplying missing words deleted from the reading passage. If a student comprehends the passage, he or she should have little difficulty in filling in the blanks. The following example is based on Bormuth's (1968) cloze instrument.

ADMINISTRATION

1. Select a student text, a passage of approximately 250 words.
2. Even if a 250-word passage ends in the middle of a sentence, just use the 250 words.

Manuel Amado, his parents, and his sister, Rachel, were flying from Rio to Brasilia. They had arrived at the airport late. The four of them were the last people to get on the airplane.

Now Manuel sat with his nose pressed against the airplane window. There were tears in his eyes. "Why do we have to leave Rio?" he asked. "I don't want to move away."

Mr. Amado sighed. "I told you, Manuel, I am going to work for our country. To do that I have to live in our capital. My office will be there."

"You children will like Brasilia," Mrs. Amado said. "It is beautiful too, in a different way from Rio. Things there are all new and shiny. Our apartment is completely modern and so is your school."

"But I liked our old apartment in Rio," said Rachel. "It was close to the beach and we could go swimming with our friends. We don't know anyone in Brasilia."

"You will make many friends at your new school," said Mr. Amado. Mrs. Amado added, "And there is a playground and swimming pool near our apartment. Won't that be nice?"

Mr. and Mrs. Amado had been saving the big surprise for last. "Children, guess what will be waiting for us at the airport! A new car!"

"Will we drive around the country on our holiday?" Manuel asked excitedly. "Yes, we will and on weekends too, sometimes," answered his father. "There will be many wonderful things to see."

Suddenly someone called, "Manuel, Rachel, what are you doing here?" There in the aisle stood Pedro Vargas, grinning from ear to ear. "Are you moving to Brasilia too?" he asked. "We didn't see you at the airport."

"That is because we were late," said Manuel. He was so happy to see his friend. "Maybe we will go to the same school. That would be wonderful."

D. H. Madison and R. E. Sterling, *Communities* (New York: American Book Company, 1979), pp. 231–33.

3. Delete every fifth word and substitute a straight line in place of each missing word.
4. A passage should contain approximately fifty straight lines after deletions have been made.

Manuel Amado, his parents, _______ his sister, Rachel, were _______ from Rio to Brasilia. _______ had arrived at the _______ late. The four of _______ were the last people _______ get on the airplane.

_______ Manual sat with his _______ pressed against the airplane _______. There were tears in _______ eyes. "Why do we _______ to leave Rio?" he _______. "I don't want to _______ away."

Mr. Amado sighed. "_______ told you, Manuel, I _______ going to work for _______ country. To do that _______ have to live in _______ capital. My office will _______ there."

"You children will _______ Brasilia," Mrs. Amado said. "_______ is beautiful too, in _______ different way from Rio. _______ there are all new _______ shiny. Our apartment is _______ modern and so is _______ school."

"But I liked _______ old apartment in Rio," Rachel. "It was close _______ the beach and we _______ go swimming with our _______. We don't know anyone _______ in Brasilia."

"You will make _______ friends at your new _______," said Mr. Amado. Mrs. _______ added, "And there is _______ playground and swimming pool _______ our apartment. Won't that _______ nice?"

Mr. and Mrs. _______ had been saving the _______ surprise for last. "Children, _______ what will be waiting _______ us at the airport! _______ new car!"

"Will we _______ around the country on _______ holiday?" Manuel asked excitedly. "_______, we will and on _______ too, sometimes," answered his _______. "There will be many _______ new things to see."

_______ someone called, "Manuel, Rachel, _______ are you doing here?" _______ in the aisle stood Pedro Vargas, _______ from ear to ear. "_______ you moving to Brasilia _______?" he asked. "We didn't _______ you at the airport."

"_______ is because we were _______," said Manuel. He was _______ happy to see his _______. "Maybe we will go to the same school. That _______ be wonderful."

D. H. Madison and R. E. Sterling, *Communities* (New York: American Book Company, 1979), pp. 231–33.

5. If you are unsure of standardization of text difficulty, select twelve 250-word passages that are approximately eight pages apart. This wide range of passages will ensure a representative sample of text difficulty. If you have previously selected a passage that represents difficulty, administer it.
6. Give every student all of the passages.
7. Students are asked to insert the missing words. No time limits are set.
8. Responses are correct even if misspelled.
9. Each correct closure is worth two points.

INTERPRETATION OF CLOZE TEST

1. If a student scores 58 to 100 points, the material being read is at the child's independent level. When a score of 44 to 57 occurs, the material being read is at the child's instructional level. A score below 43 indicates that the material is at the child's frustrational level.
2. Determine mean scores for each passage. When you retest, you will then be able to use only the passage that most closely approximates the mean difficulty of the text.

QUESTIONS AND RELATED READINGS

Now that you have some understanding of the criterion-and norm-referenced measures and processes available to aid you in assessing student competency, we refer you to Chapter 15, "Developing and Managing Your Reading Program," which is designed to aid you in planning and managing the instruction that will facilitate growth in prescribed order.

If you feel that you have not attained adequate knowledge to answer the following questions successfully, we suggest additional related readings.

1. Why is it useful to determine the range of reading levels in your classroom and how is it done?
2. Explain the function of readability formulas, including the pros and cons of relying on their results.
3. Discuss the IF versus IQ controversy.
4. What purpose is served by REL computation and on what is the computation based?
5. What end does diagnosis serve in the reading evaluation process?

5a. Explain the differences between norm- and criterion-referenced tests and their respective uses.

5b. What is the structure and function of the IRI and the cloze readability procedure?

Goal 1: To help the reader to understand the possible spectrum of reading levels in the classroom.

Question 1: Why is it useful to determine the range of reading levels in your classroom and how is it done?

Emans, R. "Teacher Evaluations of Reading Skills and Individualized Reading." *Elementary English* 42 (March 1965), 258–60.

Farr, R., and N. Roser. *Teaching a Child to Read.* New York: Harcourt Brace Jovanovich, 1979.

Mason, G. E., and N. Prater. "Early Reading and Reading Instruction." *Elementary English* 43 (March 1965), 258–60.

Goal 2: To help the reader to assess readability.

Question 2: Explain the function of readability formulas, including the pros and cons of relying on their results.

Irwin, J. W., and C. A. Davis. "Assessing Readability: The Checklist Approach." *Journal of Reading* 24:2 (November 1980), 124–30.

Standal, T. C. "How to Use Readability Formulas More Effectively." *Social Education* 14:3 (March 1981), 183–6.

Tibbetts, S. L. "How Much Should We Expect Readability Formulas to Do?" *Elementary English* 50 (January 1973), 75–76.

Goal 3: To help the reader to understand factors contributing to reading expectancy levels including the concept of Intellectual Functioning (IF) scores.

Question 3: Discuss the IF versus IQ controversy.

Fass, P. S. "The IQ: A Cultural and Historical Framework." *American Journal of Education* 4 (August 1980), 265–92.

Heap, J. L. "What Counts as Reading: Limits to Certainty in Assessment." *Curriculum Inquiry* 3 (Fall 1980), 205–12.

White, M. B., and A. E. Hall. "An Overview of Intelligence Testing." *Educational Horizons* 4 (Summer 1980), 210–16.

Goal 4: To help the reader to recognize the importance of student diagnosis in the evaluation process.

Question 4: What purpose is served by REL computation and on what is the computation based?

Bond, G. L., M. A. Tinker, and B. B. Wasson. *Reading Difficulties: Their Diagnosis and Correction,* 4th ed. Englewood Cliffs, N.J.: Prentice-Hall, Inc., 1979.

Harris, A. J., and E. R. Sipay. *How to Increase Reading Ability,* 6th ed. New York: Longman, Inc., 1978.

Spache, G. D. "Estimating Reading Capacity." In *The Evaluation of Reading*, ed. by H. M. Robinson. Supplementary Educational Monographs, No. 88. Chicago: University of Chicago Press, 1958, pp. 15–20.

Goal 5: To help the reader learn formal and informal student assessment measures.

Question 5: What end does diagnosis serve in the reading evaluation process?

Chall, J. "How They Learn and Why They Fail." *Improvement of Reading Through Classroom Practice.* Conference Proceedings. Newark, Del.: International Reading Association, 1964, pp. 147–8.

Stieflitz, E. L. "Initial Assessment for Individualization." In *Making Reading Possible Through Effective Classroom Management*, ed. by D. Lapp. Newark, Del.: International Reading Association, 1980.

Zintz, M. *Corrective Reading*, 3rd ed. Dubuque, Iowa: William C. Brown, Publishers, 1977.

Question 5a: Explain the differences between norm- and criterion-referenced tests and their respective uses.

Cox, R. C. "Confusion Between Norm-Referenced and Criterion-Referenced Measurement." *Phi Delta Kappan* 56 (January 1974), 319.

Curlette, W. L., and W. M. Stallings. "Ten Issues in Criterion-Referenced Testing: A Response to Commonly Heard Criticisms." *Clearinghouse* 3 (November 1979), 145–9.

Popham, W. J. *Educational Evaluation.* Englewood Cliffs, N.J.: Prentice-Hall, Inc., 1975.

Question 5b: What are the structure and function of the IRI, teacher-made tests, and the cloze readability technique?

Crane, E. H. "Informal Reading Inventories Go Commercial." *Curriculum Review* 5 (November 1980), 424–9.

Dwyer, E. V. "Keeping a Clozed Mind on Reading." *Reading Improvement* 3 (Fall 1980), 170–4.

Jongsma, K. S., and E. A. Jongsma. "Test Review: Commercial Informal Reading Inventories." *Reading Teacher* 6 (March 1981), 686–91.

BIBLIOGRAPHY

Aukerman, R. C. *Reading in the Secondary School Classroom.* New York: McGraw-Hill Book Company, 1972, pp. 19–45.

Binet, A., and T. Simon. *The Development of Intelligence in Children.* Baltimore: The Williams and Wilkins Co., 1905.

Bond, G. L., and M. A. Tinker. *Reading Difficulties: Their Diagnosis and Correction*, 4th ed. Englewood Cliffs, N.J.: Prentice-Hall, Inc., 1979.

Bormuth, J. "The Cloze Readability Procedure." *Elementary English* 45 (April 1968), 426–36.

Bormuth, J. R., ed. *Readability in 1968.* Champaign, Ill.: National Council of Teachers of English, 1968.

Buros, O. K. *Mental Measurement Yearbooks.* Highland Park, N.J.: Gryphon Press, 1968–1975.

Carlson, R. "Reading Level Difficulty." *Creative Computing* 4 (April 1980), 60–61.

Dale, E., and J. Chall. "A Formula for Predicting Readability." *Educational Research Bulletin* 27 (1948), 11–20.

Demaine, J. "IQism as Ideology and the Political Economy of Education." *Educational Studies* 3 (October 1979), 199–215.

Durkun, D. *Teaching Young Children to Read*, 2nd ed. Boston: Allyn & Bacon, Inc., 1976. Chapter opening quotation appears on page 379.

Farr, R. *Reading: What Can Be Measured?* Newark: Del.: International Reading Association, 1969.

_____, ed. *Measurement and Evaluation of Reading.* New York: Harcourt Brace Jovanovich, 1970.

Fischer, D. G., D. Hunt, and B. Randhawa. "Empirical Validity of Ertle's Brain-Wave Analyzer (BWAO2)." *Educational & Psychological Measurement* 4 (Winter 1978), 1017–30.

Flesch, R. F. *Marks of Readable Style: A Study of Adult Education.* New York: Bureau of Publications, Teachers College Press, Columbia University, 1943.

Fry, E. "Readability Formula That Saves Time." *Journal of Reading* 11 (April 1968), pp. 513–6; 575–8.

Goodlad, J. I. *School, Curriculum, and the Individual.* Waltham, Mass.: Blaisdell Publishing Co., 1966.

Goodman, D., and S. Schwab. "Computerized Testing for Readability." *Creative Computing* 4 (April 1980), 46–51.

Goodman, K. S. "Miscue Analysis; Theory and Reality in Reading." In *New Horizons in Reading*, ed. by J. E. Merritt. Newark, Del.: International Reading Association, 1976, pp. 15–26.

Goodman, Y. M. "Reading Diagnosis—Qualitative or Quantitative?" *The Reading Teacher* 26 (October 1972), 32–37.

Goodman, Y., and C. L. Burke. *Reading Miscue Inven-*

tory: Procedure for Diagnosis and Evaluation. New York: Macmillan Publishing Co., Inc., 1972.

Gray, W. S., and B. E. Leary. *What Makes a Book Readable?* Chicago: University of Chicago Press, 1935.

Guidry, L. J., and F. D. Knight. "Comparative Readability: Four Formulas and Newberry Books." *Journal of Reading* 19 (April 1976), 552–6.

Harris, A. J., and E. R. Sipay. *How to Increase Reading Ability*, 6th ed. New York: Longman, Inc., 1978.

Jarolimek, J., and B. Davis. *Lands of Promise.* New York: Macmillan Publishing Co., Inc., 1974.

Johnson, M. S., and R. A. Kress. *Informal Reading Inventories.* Newark, Del.: International Reading Association, 1965.

Judd, D. H. "Avoid Readability Formula Drudgery: Use Your School's Microcomputer." *The Reading Teacher* 1 (October 1981), 7–8.

Legneza, A., and D. Elijah. "The Cloze Procedure: Some New Applications." *Journal of Educational Research* 6 (July–August 1979), 351–5.

Lorge, I. "Predicting Readability." *Teachers College Record* 45 (March 1944), 404–19.

Macedo, D. "Portuguese," personal communication, November 1977.

Madison, D. H., and R. E. Sterling. *Communities.* New York: American Book Company, 1979.

Nitko, A. J. "Distinguishing the Many Varieties of Criterion-Referenced Tests." *Review of Educational Research* 3 (Fall 1980), 461–85.

Potter, T. C., and G. Rae. *Informal Reading Diagnosis.* Englewood Cliffs, N.J.: Prentice-Hall, Inc., 1973.

Rivera, C. "Massachusetts Bilingual Legislation: Impact on the Boston Educational System." Unpublished Paper, Boston University, School of Education, 1976.

Shepard, L. "Norm-Referenced vs Criterion-Referenced Tests." *Educational Horizons* 1 (Fall 1979), 26–32.

Silvaroli, N. J. *Classroom Reading Inventory.* Dubuque, Iowa: William C. Brown Company, Publishers, 1973.

Spache, G. "A New Readability Formula for Primary Grade Reading Materials." *Elementary School Journal* 53 (March 1953), 410–3.

Stanley, J. C., and K. D. Hopkins. *Educational and Psychological Measurement and Evaluation.* Englewood Cliffs, N.J.: Prentice-Hall, Inc., 1972.

Thorndike, R. L. *Reading Comprehension Education in Fifteen Countries: An Empirical Study.* New York: John Wiley & Sons, Inc., 1973.

Vernon, P. E. "Intelligence Testing and the Nature/Nurture Debate, 1928–1978: What Next?" *British Journal of Educational Psychology* 49 (February 1979), 1–14.

Wechsler, D. *The Measurement and Appraisal of Adult Intelligence.* Baltimore: The Williams and Wilkins, Co., 1958.

CHAPTER 13

Reading Instruction as Special Education

The image of myself which I try to create in my own mind in order that I may love myself is very different from the image which I try to create in the minds of others in order that they may love me.

W. H. Auden, 1964

With the implementation of P.L. 94–142, the Education for All Handicapped Children Act, classroom teachers must now strive to educate children with a wider variety of special needs than ever before. (Photo by Linda Lungren.)

GOALS: To help the reader to

1. Appreciate the background and significance of Public Law (P.L.) 94-142 and mainstreaming.
2. Learn the various types of handicapped students who may be present in the classroom.
3. Understand the classroom considerations and teaching techniques for each handicap.
4. Appreciate the nature of learning disabilities.
5. Recognize the particular importance of the classroom teacher in meeting the needs of the learning disabled student.

Just as the educational cry of the 1970s was for every teacher to be a teacher of reading, so the cry for the 1980s may be for every teacher to be a teacher of special education. With the implementation of P.L. 94-142, the Education for All Handicapped Children Act, in 1975, classroom teachers must now strive to educate children with a wider variety of special needs than ever before. In addition to the ever-present disparity of reading levels within one classroom, teachers are now required to integrate or *mainstream* into their instructional framework children with severe visual and/or auditory difficulties, mentally retarded or emotionally disturbed students, and children with learning disabilities. The task certainly appears awesome and daunting at first glance, but with the proper use of personnel, facilities, and funds, plus and understanding of the handicaps afflicting these special students, teaching strategies can be devised to meet this challenge. This chapter provides a brief overview of how and why America is mainstreaming, what the law itself provides, and information about the handicaps delineated in P.L. 94-142 as well as specific techniques and educational considerations that apply to each group. Particular attention is paid to the learning disabled child as this handicap provides specific challenges to the teacher of reading.

MAINSTREAMING AND P.L. 94-142

Historical Background

The handicapped have had an especially long history of social ostracism beginning in ancient times when they were rejected and abused by society. Certainly no thought to providing education for someone with a physical handicap was entertained, let alone providing instruction for the mentally retarded.

The handicapped remained social pariahs until the midnineteenth century when certain changes began. Residential schools to house the blind, deaf, and mentally retarded were established largely through the efforts of such educators and social activists as Horace Mann, Samuel Gridley Howe, Dorthea Dix, and the Reverend Thomas Gallaudet (Cruickshank and Johnson, 1975). Although housing, care, and education for the handicapped was at last being provided, these residential institutions still kept the handicapped out of the mainstream of society, placating humanitarian instincts yet adhering to an "out of sight, out of mind" philosophy. This attitude began to change during and after World Wars I and II when so many men who had been "normal" when they went off to the fighting returned with physical or mental disabilities. At about the same time, the prime moving force in changing public opinion that finally resulted in P.L. 94-142 went into action. This force was the parents of handicapped children.

Litigation

From 1940 when a group of concerned parents timidly began to organize what became the New York State Cerebral Palsy Association, to 1975 when Congress passed P.L. 94-142, the American public has done an "about face" in its attitudes for treatment of handicapped individuals. Civil rights, human rights, and the quality of life have all been major social and political issues in the last four decades, and court cases have often reflected this public concern over the plight of the handicapped. The first major ruling that had an effect on education for handicapped students was in 1954, *Brown* v. *Board of Education*. This was essentially a racial integration decision that found that separate facilities are inherently unequal. Equal education for all was the theme when the Supreme Court stated

> Today, education is perhaps the most important function of state and local governments . . . . It is required in the performance of our most basic public responsibilities . . . . It is the very foundation of good citizenship. Today it is the principal instrument in

awakening the child to cultural values, in preparing him for later professional training, and in helping him to adjust normally to his environment. In these days, it is doubtful that any child may reasonably be expected to succeed in life if he is denied the opportunity of an education. Such an opportunity, where the state has undertaken to provide it, is a right which must be made available to all on equal terms.
(*Brown* v. *Board of Education* (1954) 347 U.S. 483, 493

Two other landmark decisions were the class action suit, *Pennsylvania Association for Retarded Children* v. *Commonwealth of Pennsylvania*, in 1971, and *Mills* v. *Board of Education of the District of Columbia* in 1972. In the former case, the court decided in favor of the plantiffs who represented the mentally retarded population of Pennsylvania who had been excluded from the public education system. In the latter case, the plantiffs included children who had been excluded from public school because they were mentally, physically, emotionally, or otherwise handicapped. Again, the court found in favor of the plantiffs and disallowed the defendant's contention that it was lack of funds that resulted in the exclusion. The court ruled that exceptional children should not be made to bear more of the financial consequences than the normal children. Both cases, but especially the Mills case, are considered to be major precedent-setters in the cause for equal education for all.

Guidelines

Bringing together all the state and federal decisions for the education of the handicapped is Public Law 94–142, the Education for All Handicapped Children Act, passed by Congress in 1975 as an amendment of P.L. 93-380, the Education of the Handicapped Amendments of 1974. P.L. 94–142 became enforceable in 1977. This law has had an enormous impact on the classroom teacher who is essentially responsible for the success of this valiant effort to provide "free appropriate public education" for all children in the United States. The actual law covers every aspect of the issue, from searching out those individuals who are not receiving any education at the moment to funding requirements and the role of the U.S. Commissioner of Education, and has been written about and explained in detail by many authors (Corrigan, 1978; Council for Exceptional Children, 1977; Turnbull and Schulz, 1979). As the focus of this chapter is on the classroom consequences of P.L. 94–142, only the main points that affect you as a teacher are outlined here.

The law's intention is to provide a "free appropriate public school education" to all handicapped individuals between the ages of three and twenty-one years. The key word here with regard to teachers is "appropriate," because it is in seeking to provide the most suitable instruction that P.L. 94–142 delineates four essential guidelines for what occurs in the classroom as well as outside it:

1. Handicapped students will be protected against discrimination in the evaluation process by assuring that the testing materials utilized for placement will be free from racial and cultural bias and when possible will be administered in the child's native language. Tests will have established validity, be administered by trained personnel, and test specific areas of educational need rather than IQ alone. Students with sensory or physical handicaps will be tested in a manner consistent with their handicap. Further protection comes from the guarantee that no single test will be used as the sole evaluation instrument but, rather, other factors, including socialization and physical and emotional development, will be considered by a team of specialists before placement is made. Placement will always be made in a regular classroom unless the total evaluation process contraindicates such a step (Sec. 6.2.5).
2. Handicapped students will be placed in "the least restrictive environment commensurate with their needs." In most cases this indicates placement in the regular classroom, but for many exceptional students combinations of special classes and instructors coupled with instruction in the classroom will best meet their needs. In severe cases, special schools or institutions will be necessary.
3. An individualized education program (IEP) for each child is required. It includes a written statement of the child's present educational level, annual goals, instructional objectives, and any special education or related services provided for the child. The plan must be developed jointly by parents, educators, and, when appropriate, the child in question, and it will be reviewed at least annually.

4. Procedural safeguards have been written into this law to protect the rights of all concerned. Parents have access to all the student's records and have the right to obtain an outside evaluation if desired. They are to be given prior notice for approval of any change in the placement of their child, and they have the right to challenge anything done by the teacher or the school, including the right to court action. The parents and the schools have the right to appeal any decision made regarding the placement of a handicapped student. During any hearing, the child in question will be allowed to remain in school or be admitted to school until the final decision has been reached.

It is obvious from just these few main points why P.L. 94-142 has been called "the most important piece of educational legislation in this country's history" (Corrigan, 1978). The job of the classroom teacher has become more demanding and, at the same time, potentially more rewarding as the challenges of teaching exceptional children pay off for both student and teacher with educational and personal success.

DEFINITION OF HANDICAPPED CHILDREN

The definition of handicapped children as supplied by the original Education of the Handicapped Act, Section 602(1), and amended by P.L. 94-142 includes the mentally retarded, hard-of-hearing, deaf, speech-impaired, visually handicapped, seriously emotionally disturbed, orthopedically impaired or other health impaired, and those children with specific learning disabilities.

Each handicap delineated by this definition is discussed in a separate section of this chapter with the exception of the seriously emotionally disturbed. Children with severe emotional problems would not be placed in a regular classroom and consequently need not be considered here. Children with mild emotional problems may well be in the regular classroom, but for the most part, managing these students is quite similar to managing any other student, as their problems are simply exaggerations of emotions that everyone has. Guidelines must be established as to what constitutes unacceptable behavior, and consistency in enforcing these rules is critical. It has been said that children with emotional difficulties, mental retardation, and learning disabilities have many of the same behavioral and cognitive problems (Hallahan and Kauffman, 1977) as each other, and for this reason teaching suggestions listed for the mentally retarded and learning disabled may be useful for instructing an emotionally handicapped child. (For further reading and references on emotionally handicapped children, see Hallahan and Kauffman, 1978, Chap. 4; Berkowitz and Rothman, 1960; Hewett, 1968.)

The Mentally Retarded

Definition. The definition adopted by the American Association on Mental Deficiency (AAMD) is the one most accepted in the field. It reads: "Mental retardation refers to significantly subaverage general intellectual functioning existing concurrently with deficits in adaptive behavior, and manifested during the developmental period" (Grossman, 1973). The emphasis on a relationship between intelligence, as measured by a standardized intelligence test (e.g., the Stanford-Binet or the WISC-R), and socially adaptive behavior pinpoints the modern concepts of what mental retardation is. In the past, too much importance has been given to a score achieved on a test, so much so that many children who function quite normally, efficiently, and happily in society outside of school become labeled as retarded to their teachers and school adminstrators. As will be stressed throughout this chapter and as seen elsewhere in this text (see Chapter 12), relying solely on an IQ score (or on any other single test score) is misleading as to the student's overall ability and potential and can be harmful to this child in terms of actually limiting his or her academic career.

The categories of mental retardation that are used most commonly are those provided by the AAMD. While based on intelligence scores, these terms are descriptive of functional traits as well. The general breakdown is IQ score 70-55, *mild*; 55-40, *moderate*; 40-25, *severe*; and 25-0 *profound*. The terms EMR (educable mentally retarded) and TMR (trainable mentally retarded) are educational labels that attempt to define the instructional needs of retarded children whose IQ falls within the range of 75-50 and 50-25, respectively. Again, let it be emphasized that to use these scores as hard and fast break-off points for inclusion or exclusion in educational programs is not justified, as the whole individual must be evaluated. Ongoing assessment must be made for mentally retarded students as with every other student because, contrary to many popular ideas about mental retardation, gains in IQ scores are possible, especially for the mildly retarded, with the proper education (Kirk, 1958; Klaus and Gray, 1968).

Classroom Considerations. It is highly unlikely that severely or profoundly retarded individuals would be placed in a regular school environment as their specialized needs generally are met best in residential institutions or in the home. Even a moderately retarded person generally requires a special education situation for academic subjects and may be integrated into the regular school program only for such activities as physical education, music, and art. Chances are that all but the most mildly retarded student would spend part of a day with a specialist and part of the day in the regular classroom, so it is important to coordinate any teaching efforts with those of the specialist.

The mentally retarded child exhibits many of the same behavioral and learning difficulties as does a child with learning disabilities, described in detail later in this chapter. Some of the common problem areas include attention span (Zeaman and House, 1963; Mercer and Snell, 1977), short-term memory (Ellis, 1963, 1970; Borkowski and Wanschura, 1974), and the lack of organizational skills for learning new concepts (Brown, 1974). Language and speech problems may also be present, especially articulation difficulties, and stuttering may be expected (see suggestions in the section on "The Speech Impaired"). Peer relationships may be difficult due to aggressive behavior and negativism, again as may be true for the learning disabled child.

It should be remembered that mildly retarded children may be functioning at a mental age from two to four years below their chronological age and should not be expected to perform the same academic exercises as the other children in the class. In the early grades, they may require readiness training long after the other children have moved on to reading. The emphasis in the secondary grades should be on adult survival skills, vocational training, and successful social interactions that will prepare them to take part in the community once their school days are over. Generally, the more severe the retardation disability is, the more the concentration should be on social functioning skills as opposed to academics. Although much of the academic instruction will be individualized, group activities in which the handicapped child is actively included are important. Being a member of a team and being a partner are essential to developing peer relationships.

Instructional Methods. The most successful technique employed with retarded persons, especially in the severe and profound categories, has been behavior modification or operant conditioning based on B. F. Skinner's research (Robinson and Robinson, 1976). While the mildly retarded may not need a strictly classic approach to behavior modification, it seems that a well-structured program that is very task oriented is applicable. Lessons should be broken down into small tasks that can be completed successfully in a short period of time. As with the learning disabled, the emphasis here is on structure and success. Acceptable behavior should be reinforced immediately, and new information should build directly on what has just been learned. The suggestions for teaching the learning disabled child are equally appropriate for the mildly retarded child in the regular classroom, and the reader is referred to that section of this chapter for further instructional methods.

Teaching Techniques. In addition to those suggestions given in the section of this chapter that addresses the learning disabled school population, the following ideas may be useful for teaching the mentally retarded student.

1. Use the game of "Concentration" (pairs of cards placed face down in random order) to improve visual memory skills. Begin very simply with four to six cards and progress as skill improves.
2. To aid in comprehension skills, highlight main ideas of a story in one color and supporting details in another. Have the student read the color-coded copy first; then present a plain copy and ask him or her to use the colored pencils to mark main idea and details. Student can compare the two copies for immediate feedback.
3. Using a tape recorder, have the child read out material to be learned (vocabulary, spelling words, sequence of a story, facts of a history lesson), listen to the tape, repeat it into the tape using no notes, and then check the answer. Verbal repetition has been found to be effective in teaching the mentally retarded.

4. Old-fashioned drill and repetition may be useful in learning new concepts. Use similar exercises from different series of skills books to re-emphasize an idea (such as parts of speech, sentence construction, vocabulary). Have the student "wallpaper" a cubicle with notebook paper filled with repeated spelling words written in colorful ink. Change the "wallpaper" when the words are learned.
5. Charts showing student successes (such as books read, words spelled correctly, acceptable behavior, participation in class) are a positive reinforcement to behavioral and academic goals. Notes in the form of "awards" or "medals" allow the child to take home commendations from the teacher.

The Hearing Impaired

Definition. Individuals suffering from a hearing impairment are generally classified as either deaf or hard-of-hearing. Definition of this classification has engendered considerable debate, but there are two basic systems for classifying the hearing impaired. The first is a strictly physiological system that is based on auditory performance that can be measured through tests administered by an audiologist. One accepted definition of hearing-impaired is the one offered by Davis (1970), which uses decibels (dB), a measurement for the intensity or loudness of sounds, as a criterion for placement. A hearing loss up to 25 dB is considered normal, from 25 dB to 93 dB is classified as hard-of-hearing, and any further loss beyond 93 dB is categorized as deaf.

The second method of classification is one that is used in educational settings; it is based on the individual's *functional* ability to hear and speak. The preferred definition in this instance was formulated by the Conference of Executives of American Schools for the Deaf:

> A *deaf* person is one whose hearing disability precludes successful processing of linguistic information through audition, with or without a hearing aid.
>
> A *hard-of-hearing* person is one who, generally with the use of a hearing aid, has residual hearing sufficient to enable successful processing of linguistic information through audition.
>
> (Report of the Ad Hoc Committee to Define Deaf and Hard of Hearing, 1975, p. 509)

As with any other attempt to label human beings, these definitions of deaf and hard-of-hearing must be taken for what they are—an attempt to establish a basis for treatment or instruction. The degree to which a hearing loss, however profound, creates a handicap lies within the individual's ability to adjust to the situation and use to best advantage whatever residual hearing exists.

Classroom Considerations. The most noticeable and most devasting aspect of a hearing impairment is the difficulty experienced with acquiring and using communication abilities. This refers equally to language acquisition, speech production, and reading skills. The lack of adequate auditory feedback both from oneself and others, coupled with the inability to hear an adult model speak the language, contributes considerably to the hearing-impaired child's difficulty with language development. Since reading is essentially the translation of a printed code into the sounds that make up language, a hearing impairment that has resulted in reduced language skills usually interferes with learning to read.

Five basic factors influence language acquisition and, consequently, reading skills that should be considered when working with hearing-impaired children (Birch, 1975):

1. The *nature of the hearing loss* relates to the frequencies (tones) and level of intensity that are affected.
2. The *degree* of the impairment refers to the degree of residual hearing that is present.
3. The *age of onset*, or the time when the hearing loss occurred, is extremely important. The later the age of onset, the greater the chance that the person will acquire language in a normal way, thus having a language system upon which to build.
4. *Intelligence level* may be a significant educational factor because children with higher IQs may be better equipped to compensate for their handicap.
5. The *quality of stimulation*, namely, the amount and kind of daily exposure to language, received by a hearing-impaired individual may determine how thoroughly language is acquired.

As with hearing children, perhaps the most important consideration with hearing-impaired children is that they are all individuals and cannot be expected to perform in the same way just because they share a common difficulty. With this in mind, here are some general suggestions for making mainstreaming easier for the hearing impaired:

Seating arrangement. A seat near the front of the room that offers a good view of the teacher as well as the other students is essential for hearing-impaired children, whether they rely on their residual hearing or on speechreading. However, depending on the degree of their hearing loss or their ability to compensate for it, some children may prefer to sit in other parts of the room. Allow the child to experiment with his or her seating arrangement, within reason, always providing the seat near the front if appropriate.

Talking to the child or addressing the class. Try to refrain from moving about and keep your hands, pencil, paper, and so on away from your mouth to provide as clear a sound and image as possible. Remember to write on the board first and then talk to the class rather than speaking with your back to the class. Enunciate clearly and speak at a moderate pace; do not exaggerate speech. When repeating instructions or ideas attempt to rephrase what has been said rather than repeating it verbatim. If the child failed to understand it the first time, the use of new words may help give context clues to the idea. Shouting does not help with the hearing-impaired, and if they are using a hearing aid, the amplification distorts the voice. Be sure to stand where the light is good and not in a shadow or where the child will be facing a glare while trying to see your face.

Attending and Comprehending Skills. Be sure that hearing-impaired children are not just looking attentive but are actually understanding what is going on in class. It is important to check that they understand instructions and assignments and that they are following class discussions. Encourage them to ask questions if they do not understand what was said and to give you feedback on how they are adjusting to the class.

Integration into the Classroom. By using natural opportunities (e.g., a unit on the senses, science lesson, discussion pertaining to broadcasting, sound waves), foster an understanding of the nature of a hearing impairment so that other students will be more at ease with a handicapped classmate's disability. An understanding of why a deaf or hard-of-hearing child may sound unusual or be hard to comprehend when he or she speaks may help the other students to try harder to listen and understand.

Because many hearing-impaired children use some form of amplification (e.g., hearing aid), it is important for the classroom teacher to understand how they work and be able to make minor essential adjustments such as changing a battery or cord. Consult the school specialist for instruction in this area and keep a supply of the necessary items in the classroom.

Instructional Methods. If adminstrators are truly placing handicapped students in the "least restrictive environment," it is highly unlikely that any classroom teacher will be faced with the very specialized task of teaching reading to a hearing-impaired child with no communication skills at all. Before being placed in a regular classroom, whether on a full- or part-time basis, the child will have been taught to communicate by using one or more of the following approaches:

Oral Approach. This method stresses the use of the child's own residual hearing, incorporating amplification, when appropriate, and speechreading, which involves looking at the mouth and face to gain understanding of the words and tone of speech. This method also encourages the hearing-impaired child to learn to verbalize and develop oral language.

Manual Approach. Sign language is essential to this method; this method stresses the point that the deaf and hard-of-hearing should have the means for total expression rather than the often inadequate results achieved when the deaf attempt to produce speech.

Total Communication Approach. This method allows the person to use both methods, oral and manual, to develop communication skills.

There is a tremendous controversy in the profession over which method is best, but unless an interpretor is provided, chances are that only those children functioning with oral skills will be integrated into the regular classroom. Instructional methods that are appropriate for teaching hearing children to read may be useful for the hearing-impaired if they are not based on an auditory system. Visual methods that present new words and concepts in as concrete a manner as possible are most beneficial.

Life experiences are useful instructional vehicles. Just as hearing children need experiences with field trips, neighborhood walks, and guest speakers, so too do hearing-impaired children. Continuing work on syntax and grammar is important for the hearing-impaired child, and the *language-experience* approach is an excellent means for working with the child's own vocabulary while describing new experiences.

Educational media are an excellent resource for providing stimulating material for the deaf. Subtitled films and television programs provide visual stimulation that can be used to the benefit of the entire class, and the use of the computer is a very exciting development for all aspects of education. Hearing-impaired and other special students have used computer systems for learning basic reading skills, generating sentences, writing letters to other handicapped students, and drawing pictures (Geoffrion and Bergeron, 1977; Goldenberg, 1979; Rubenstein and Rollins, 1978).

Teaching Techniques. Here are some suggestions for teaching the hearing-impaired student in the regular classroom.

1. Present new vocabulary words by writing them down, pronouncing them, and using them in several sentences. New words may be written on a list for the child to take home for study with parents or tutors.
2. Provide "previews" of the topics to come by listing the main points and new words so that student may prepare in advance and be more familiar with the material when the class discusses it.
3. Institute a "buddy" or "note taker" system to aid the handicapped student with details missed during class. Note takers are especially useful because it is very difficult for a child to watch the speaker intently and write at the same time. Naturally, note takers also benefit by taking more complete notes.
4. A unit on hearing aids, finger spelling, American sign language, and speechreading with demonstrations presented by the school specialist will be of interest to the whole class and will provide the hearing-impaired child a chance to demonstrate special skills.
5. The use of photographs and illustrations from magazines provides excellent stimuli for vocabulary development. Scrapbooks and photograph albums compiled by the student (using pictures he or she has taken) with captions offering information about concrete items in the pictures or abstract feelings about them is an excellent way in which to improve language skills. Make this an ongoing journal of day-to-day experiences. Some journal entries could be expanded into essays in which the students practice more refined writing skills by making rough, intermediate, and final drafts.

The Speech Impaired

Definition. Speech is the action of reproducing vocally the sounds, in proper sequence, of a language. A speech impairment, then, is a condition that interferes with this sound-producing mechanism and as such is distinct from a language disorder, which is the inability to use or comprehend the actual semantic and grammatical code system by which ideas are communicated. Since language disorders are generally characteristic of other handicaps, (mental retardation, learning disabilities, etc.), they are discussed in the sections relating to the associated condition.

The system for determining if speech is in fact impaired or just deviant is a highly subjective one, depending largely on who is speaking to whom. Strong regional dialects may make speech comprehension impossible to an outsider yet be totally comprehensible and normal to the residents of the area. However, two definitions of speech disorders provide guidelines to determining when and if an impairment exists.

> Speech is defective when it is ungrammatical, unintelligible, culturally or personally unsatisfactory, or abusive of the speech mechanism.
>
> (Perkins, 1971, p. 4)

> Speech is defective when it deviates so far from the speech of other people that it calls attention to itself, interferes with communication, or causes the possessor to be maladjusted.
>
> (Van Riper, 1972, p. 29)

A unit on sign language with demonstrations presented by the school specialist will be of interest to the whole class while providing the hearing-impaired child with a chance to demonstrate special skills. (Photo by Linda Lungren.)

Whether the speech impairment is the result of a cleft palate, cleft lip, or cerebral palsy or stems from some unknown functional factor, it generally falls into (or overlaps) three categories: articulation disorders, voice disorders, or fluency disorders.

Articulation Disorders. These generally consist of errors of sound production involving *omissions* (e.g., ru for run or ift for lift), *substitutions* (e.g., bery for very), *additions* (e.g., puraple for purple), and *distortions* (e.g., consistently mispronouncing /r/ (Perkins, 1971). Misarticulation is common in young children, but by the age of seven or eight, these mistakes should disappear naturally, unless there is in fact a speech problem.

Voice disorders. Although it is very difficult to quantify voice qualities, problems with the voice fall into these areas:

1. Pitch: High or low depending on age and sex of the individual.
2. Intensity: Loudness or volume.
3. Quality: How the voice "sounds": sweet, rough, mellow, for example. Problem qualities are hoarseness, breathiness, and nasality. These may represent vocal abuse or a pathology of the larynx and may need medical treatment.
4. Flexibility: The ability to modulate pitch and intensity to put expression in the voice. Monotone and singsong voices may indicate a problem with flexibility.

Fluency Disorders. When the flow of speech is interrupted to such a degree that it becomes unintelligible to listen to, the speaker may be suffering from a fluency disorder commonly known as *stuttering*. The interruptions consist of repetitions and prolongations of sounds, hesitations, and interjections (uh, uh . . .). While most everyone exhibits occasional fluency dysfunctions, a stutterer has been defined as by Sheehan (1958) as

> a person who shows, to a degree that sets him off from the rest of the population, any one or more of the following groups of symptoms: (1) blockings, stickings, grimaces, forcings, repetitions, prolongations, or other rhythm breaks or interruptions in the forward flow of speech; (2) fear or anticipation of blockings, fear of inability to speak, or related symptoms prior to words or speaking situations; (3) a self-concept which includes a picture of himself as a stutterer, a stammerer, speech

blocker, or a person lacking normal speech fluency. (p. 23)

There is no conclusive evidence as to what causes stuttering, although many theories have been advanced, ranging from underlying emotional conflicts to organic dysfunctions (for discussions of these theories, see Van Riper, 1972; Bloodstein, 1969; Ainsworth, 1970). While the problem of stuttering is a familiar and much imitated disorder, the actual number of stutterers is very small—1 percent of the population (Hull et al., 1969), and the disorder sometimes disappears as mysteriously as it appears (Van Riper, 1973).

Classroom Considerations. Speech impairments can be socially debilitating and emotionally crippling if afflicted persons are not made to feel that they are accepted in spite of their handicap. A speech disorder may create academic problems when the student will not participate in class discussions, ask questions about concepts that are not understood, or becomes so uncommunicative that language ability itself begins to degenerate. The major concern for a classroom teacher of whatever subject, not just reading, is to put the person with a speech impairment at ease in the group and make speaking experiences pleasant and nonthreatening.

It is important that the speech impairment be acknowledged both by student and the teacher so that, together with child's parents, caregivers, and speech clinicians, they can determine how best to help the student fit into the classroom. Acceptance by the other children is important, and here again, as with any other handicap, knowledge of a condition will facilitate understanding. So saying, once the handicap has been acknowledged, it is best to overlook it and concentrate on what the child is saying rather than on how it is being said. Patience and attentiveness are essential to helping a speech-impaired child speak up in class.

Instructional Methods. It is generally believed among speech pathologists that disorders of voice and misarticulation are learned behaviors, not inherent qualities (Schiefelbusch and Lloyd, 1974; Sloane and MacAulay, 1968). Consequently, it becomes the clinician's job to use learning techniques to teach the appropriate new speech skills to the individual. Many of these teaching strategies are highly structured, programmed-learning systems that incorporate behavior modification techniques as well as generally rely on modeling (i.e., imitation) and positive reinforcement.

The clinical process has been described as consisting of three steps that include actually teaching the new skill, transferring the use of the skill to general usage as opposed to only responding to the teaching stimuli, and finally, making a habit of using the skill so that it, in fact, becomes the new way of speaking long after the clinical sessions haved ended. The classroom teacher is an especially important part of this process because the student must be encouraged and reminded to use appropriate speech when participating in classroom discussions.

As imitation is an important aspect of learning to speak clearly, the teacher must be considered as the ultimate model and be conscious of speaking well and clearly. It might also help to seat the child near children who speak especially well or to place the speech-impaired child in a small discussion group with especially articulate peers. Of course, the tape recorder is an excellent tool for use with these children as it can be used for both modeling and monitoring of the child's own speech. As with all handicapped children who require the services of a specialist, there must be an open channel of communication between the classroom teacher and the clinician so that the child has consistency of educational philosophy and reinforcement.

Teaching Techniques. As stated earlier, making speech and language occasions pleasant is perhaps the most important part of the classroom teacher's job when working with mainstreamed speech-impaired children. Fortunately, that objective is equally important for the regular children in the class, so most of the following activities can be used readily for everyone.

1. Stimulate discussion by having students create and present a reader's theater production. Rehearsals should stress articulation and expressive use of voice.
2. Allow older children the use of a camera for taking slides on a subject of their choice and then have the students arrange and present a slide show with either live narration or tape-recorded narrative. Young children may enjoy doing a similar show based on drawings done on rolled paper that can be advanced in a reel-to-reel manner.

3. Make a game out of using descriptive language by blindfolding a student, handing him or her an object, and having him or her describe its qualities. Individual or team points could be scored based on the number of adjectives used or qualities mentioned as well as if the student guesses what the item is. As an individual venture, a "touch" box can be constructed in which various items are placed and the student is asked to describe into the tape recorder how each item feels.
4. A file of pictures and photographs that serve as a stimulus creating stories about events or emotions can be useful not only for written assignments (that could be read orally) but for spontaneous or prepared oral stories that can be taped or read to the class.
5. A group story can be formulated using one of the pictures mentioned earlier by having one student begin a story with a statement and then having each student contribute another statement to the story based on the preceding one. Stories become quite outrageous and language experience can be enhanced further by doing this in small groups so children can have more than one chance to participate in a given story.

The Visually Impaired

Definition. The category of the visually impaired includes individuals who are referred to as ***partially sighted***, which indicates a visual acuity of 20/70 after correction, and *blind*, indicating a visual acuity of 20/200 after correction. As with most definitions regarding individuals, these terms are almost useless as educational criteria for assessing student abilities and needs. The scores that form the basis for this definition are from the Snellen Chart, which only measures distance reading ability. Since reading instruction is done at a close range and since individuals use their residual vision with differing degrees of competency, the numbers 20/70 or 20/200 say very little (Gearheart and Weishahn, 1976). Other classification and measurement scales of visual ability have been proposed that take into account the individual's ability to function in a sighted world and essentially stress that teachers should not base any instruction strictly on test scores but on observation of the student's functional abilities (Genensky, 1970; Barraga, 1970; Harley et el., 1973).

Classroom Considerations. Since reading is largely a visual process, it is obvious that visually impaired students may encounter difficulties with many of its aspects, including concept development, left to right orientation, and clarity of the world image itself (Degler and Risko, 1979). They may be behind their peers in reading level due to a slower reading rate or inappropriate instructional methods (Turnball and Schulz, 1979), but visually handicapped students, whether partially sighted or blind are easily accommodated to the regular classroom when certain considerations and adaptations are instituted coupled with an accurate understanding of individual strengths and limitations.

Putting a child at ease in the school environment is essential to successful instruction. Two key words when working with visually handicapped youngsters are "orientation," which refers to a person's spatial placement in relation to objects in the environment, and "mobility," which refers to the ability to move about in the environment. Mobility and orientation instruction are special skills, and most children will receive this training by a specialist before entering the regular classroom. The classroom teacher must, however, assist in orienting the student to the classroom and school environment. Suggestions for accomplishing this are

1. Spend time with the student in the classroom before the school year begins or, if this is not possible, make time available before or after school. Make sure that the student is comfortable with the surroundings and knows how to find the appropriate desk, books, and materials. Similarly, acquaint the student with the layout of the entire school including the cafeteria, library, and restrooms. When appropriate, ask students who will be in the class with the handicapped child to perform this orientation to assure that the child will be acquainted with some of his or her classmates.
2. Discuss and practice the fire drill procedure and route.
3. If possible, allow extra traveling time for the visually impaired student either before or after the other students.
4. Encourage these students to ask for help when they need it, and instruct sighted students to assist when called upon. Special training provided by a mobility instructor in how to guide a blind or partially sighted person might be both useful and interesting for the other children.

5. Provide ample work space for extra equipment such as braille books, magnifying devices, typewriter, and tape recorder.
6. Be sure to call the child by name, and encourage classmates to identify themselves until the child learns their voices.
7. Include the visually handicapped student in as many of the regular class activities as possible as all the children will profit from this interaction.

Instructional Methods. Any method of teaching reading that agrees with the teacher will no doubt agree with the visually handicapped child as long as the teacher uses a *multisensory* approach and presents concepts in as *concrete* a manner as possible. Blind children and those with extremely low vision rely heavily on auditory and tactile input to process information. Classroom activities and field trips should be explained or narrated to provide a vivid picture of what is going on. New concepts must be explained in nonvisual, concrete terms. Whenever possible, tactile experiences should be provided to illustrate elements or characteristics of the concept being discussed. For example, instead of saying that a mouse is a small, furry animal, say that a mouse can be held in the palm of your hand and provide a piece of fur for the student to stroke. Better still, of course, would be to present a real mouse. Models can be useful for concept development as long as they are not overused to the point of presenting the child with a distorted or limited idea of reality (Ward and McCormick, 1981).

Most of the techniques listed in the paragraphs that follow are useful for children who have low vision or who are blind; however, special consideration must be made for differences in these groups.

Low vision. These children should be seated to avoid glare and may wish to use a portable lamp. Proper illumination, be it bright or dim, and print that is very clear is perhaps more important than the size of the print (Sykes, 1972). Large-type books are available for those children who require them. If a student with low vision has trouble keeping lines of print separate, encourage the use of a marker or the sweep of the hand to keep the eyes on line.

Large type books are available for those students who require them. They are available in many areas including large print piano music. (Photo by Linda Lungren.)

Blind. Braille is of course the main tool for use in teaching reading to the blind. Fortunately, braille instruction is usually done by specialists; however, a sight knowledge of braille is very useful for the classroom teacher. In addition to the readiness required for regular reading (Chapter 4), reading readiness for learning braille requires a refined sense of touch. Sorting tasks, proceeding from large, clearly defined items to small, subtle items are quite useful for developing this skill. Suggestions for items to sort are

1. Blocks and cards of differing shapes and sizes.
2. Every day subjects (cutlery, coins, buttons, and spools).
3. Books of different sizes (paperbacks and hard bound).
4. Natural items (shells, pebbles, and nuts).

Teaching Techniques

1. Prereading activities should include discussion of new vocabulary words and concepts using the concrete multisensory approach outlined earlier in this section. For low-vision students, large clear pictures are useful for explaining ideas as well as for promoting creative language-experience stories. To illustrate such concepts as "rough," "smooth," "soft," "hard," "sticky," "slick," "lumpy," "fluffy," and so on cards can be covered with various types of fabrics, cotton balls, plastic, sandpaper, or any number of substances that will provide the desired tactile response. Sound effects and the actual objects themselves are also useful for presenting new ideas to visually impaired students.
2. In the primary grades, labels for objects around the room should be printed in a size large enough to be read by low-vision students and, where possible, in braille.
3. The development of listening skills for the visually impaired is crucial. Tape recorders are essential here and may be used in the following ways:
    a. Record sentences or passages from stories and have the student repeat them into the tape and play back for correction.
    b. On tape, clap out rhythms or create a series of sounds using bells, drums, and so on, and have the children reproduce them onto the tape. This could be used as a game by several students, awarding points for the longest correct series.
4. A reader's theater can be very beneficial to visually handicapped students because it gives them a chance to participate in oral, expressive reading with their classmates. Although their reading rate may be slower than that of the sighted children, with practice an accomplished production can be performed.
5. Plan activities especially for the visually impaired children and include the regular class in the activity. For example, a nature walk with emphasis on smells, shapes, and textures wherein the children are asked to verbalize how things smell and feel is an excellent way in which to build up oral language fluency as well as develop experiences. It also creates an appreciation for the fact that there is more to objects than what they look like.

The Orthopedically and Other Health Impaired

Definition. While this category covers a wide range of disabilities, from cerebral palsy to diabetes to missing limbs, the common characteristic of a person suffering from an orthopedic or health disability is that his or her primary difficulty is the result of a nonsensory physical handicap. There are few common learning problems associated with this group, as many physical impairments have no real effect on cognitive ability or learning potential, while others such as cerebral palsy and spina bifida may have significant neurological complications that contribute to severe communication problems. Perhaps the most common attribute of this group is the psychological aspect of coping with a very obvious disfiguring or life-threatening disability. In this context, as with all the other handicapping conditions discussed in this chapter, individual ability to adapt to a given condition or disease has dramatic impact on the functional severity of the disability, regardless of the medical prognosis.

There are two basic categories of physical disabilities: *orthopedic and neurological impairment* and *other health impairments.* The former includes such conditions as cerebral palsy, muscular dystrophy, spina bifida, epilepsy, poliomyelitis, multiple sclerosis, congenital malformations, and impairments due to accident; the later include cardiac conditions, diabetes, cancer, tuberculosis, sickle cell anemia, cystic fibrosis, hemophilia, and other chronic or terminal diseases (for a general description of these disorders, see Hallahan and Kauffman, 1978, Chap. 8; Meyer, 1978, Chap. 8).

Classroom Considerations. Because federal law (P.L. 93-112, Sec. 502) now requires architectural access and adequate toilet facilities for wheelchairs, the classroom teacher's only environmental concern should be for proper placement of the physically handicapped student in the classroom. Where the student sits should depend on any accompanying sensory handicaps and accessibility (i.e., maneuvering space) to various parts of the classroom (the student's desk, free reading center, individual study carrels, media center, games) so that the disabled student is as free to participate in the same learning options as are the other students with as little special help as possible.

Once the student is physically at ease in the class environment, the teacher's main concern must be to help the child attain a positive self-concept, which, for the physically impaired, involves, to a large extent, fostering independence and an acceptance of the handicapping condition (Bigge and O'Donnell, 1977). Of course family attitude is highly significant in the psychological health of a handicapped child, but the teacher is influential in helping the other students relate to the disabled child, thus easing the crucial task of establishing peer relationships. The teacher must confer with the family and appropriate professionals involved with the child to understand how the child feels about the condition and how much is understood about it. Encouraging honest answers to questions regarding a physical handicap will help classmates to shift their curiosity from that aspect of the child to the child as a person. Self-confidence and well-being are prerequisite to academic achievement, especially in learning to read.

Some practical concerns regarding work load for a physically handicapped individual are absenteeism, fatigue, and motor problems associated with writing. Here are some suggestions for dealing with these problems:

Absenteeism. When practical and appropriate, send work home with classmates who live nearby, allowing the child contact with his or her peers and providing tutoring that benefits both children. If the absense is prolonged or if hospitalization is required, special tutors may be engaged to help the child to keep up with the class work. Encourage the child to keep a journal of thoughts during the confined time, and periodically have the class write letters, make objects, or visit the child when possible.

Fatigue. Many children with health or mobility problems tire easily and the classroom work should be varied to include rest or quiet periods in which the student can read, draw, or nap as indicated. Do not expect a handicapped student to keep up with the pace of the rest of the class but always include the child, providing the choice to rest if he or she is tired.

Writing Problems. Alternatives to hand-writing assignments may include the use of a typewriter (sometimes it is necessary to use a head wand when hand coordination is not sufficient to type with the fingers) or a tape recorder for oral responses.

Instructional Methods and Teaching Techniques. Because the learning problems of the physically impaired may range from those of the mentally retarded to the gifted, it is impossible to offer specific techniques unique to this class of handicap. Suggestions presented in the other sections of this chapter as well as those in Chapters 5 through 9 will be of aid to you in planning instruction that is appropriate for these students. Emphasis should always be on self-help, survival, and social skills, with more academic pursuits based on these initial skills. As with all other special children, never underestimate them! A challenge should always be presented, keeping a careful eye on frustration levels.

Learning Disabilities

Definition. The term "learning disabilities" was introduced by Samuel Kirk in 1963 and has since become the name for a whole group of problems that affect an individual's ability to learn. The most important aspect of a definition of learning disabilities is that it is not one single condition and consequently cannot be treated in one single way. In 1968 the National Advisory Committee on Handicapped Children presented this definition of learning disabilities to Congress for use in funding programs designed for these children:

> Children with special learning disabilities exhibit a disorder in one or more of the basic psychological processes involved in understanding or in using spoken or written language. These may be manifested in disorders of listening, thinking, talking, reading, writing, spelling, or arithmetic. They include conditions which have been referred to as perceptual handicaps, brain injury, minimal brain dysfunction, dyslexia, developmental aphasia, etc. They do not include learning problems which are due primarily to visual, hearing, or motor handicaps, to mental retardation, emotional disturbance, or to environmental disadvantage.

While this definition provides the traditional and legal delineation of learning disabilities, it does not bring the educator much closer to determining what exactly constitutes a learning disability and what to do about it. Although there is rampant disagreement over just about every aspect of any definition of learning disabilities, there is professional agreement about two of the most common components of these definitions.

1. A learning-disabled child does not achieve up to his or her academic potential. This potential is usually measured by comparing scores on a standardized intelligence test with those on a standardized achievement test; however, other methods using formula for ratio discrepancy (Mykelbust, 1968) may provide a more accurate picture of expected achievement versus actual achievement.
2. A learning-disabled child has a wide range of achievement that traverses the academic spectrum. The child may be strong in reading but weak in spelling or math or have excellent oral communication skills but be unable to write a coherent sentence.

The debate is still on over three of the other most common aspects of learning disabilities definitions: presence of brain injury, lack of environmental disadvantage, and lack of mental retardation or emotional handicaps (Hallahan and Kauffman, 1978).

The field of learning disabilities has some of its antecedents in work done by Werner and Strauss with brain-damaged mentally retarded children in the 1930s.* Because many underachieving students were found to have some of the same behavioral characteristics as the brain-injured mentally retarded children, the assumption was made that the children were not learning because their brains were in some way damaged. Although much of this early work has been refuted due to its nonstatistical and introspective nature, the possibilty that neurological disturbances are the cause of learning disorders has been central to research in the field (Cruickshank, 1975). It is now assumed that learning-disabled youngsters are not necessarily brain injured unless neurological testing so indicates. As more sophisticated neurological examinations are increasingly more possible, perhaps the true nature of the relationship between brain dysfunction or damage and learning disabilities will be revealed.

*For a more complete history of the study of learning disabilities, which actually started in the early 1800s, see Wilderholt, "Historical Perspectives on the Education of the Learning Disabled," in *The Second Review of Special Education*, ed. by L. Mann and D. Sabation (Philadelphia; JSE Press, 1974).

The objections to definitions that state that the environment has nothing to do with learning disabilities arise from an increasing awareness that environment strongly affects the realization of potential in nearly every aspect of development—intelligence, aritistic achievement, emotional maturity, and so on. Gearheart and Weishahn (1976) suggest that the exclusion of culturally disadvantaged or different children from classification as learning disabled was to prevent "wholesale placement of black, Mexican-American, Puerto Rican-American, and the very poor of all races in special, segregated, or semisegragated programs" (p. 8). If culturally disadvantaged children exhibit the characteristic behavior pattern of the learning disabled as they are likely to do (Cravioto and DeLicardil, 1975; Hallahan and Cruickshank, 1973), then they too deserve whatever special help is available.

A similar argument is applicable to the exclusion of the mentally retarded or emotionally disturbed individual. If these children are not achieving up to their expected potential, then they too can be considered as learning disabled. Indeed, many professionals (Cruickshank and Johnson, 1975; Hallahan and Kauffman, 1976) feel that the phenomenon of learning disabilities cuts across every IQ level.

A universally acceptable definition of learning disabilities has yet to materialize from the tomes that have been written on the subject. Somewhere between the Advising Committee's statement quoted earlier in this text and the terse contention that "a learning disabled child is simply not achieving up to his potential" (Hallahan and Kauffman, 1978, p. 125) stands a child who for some reason has trouble learning, and it is your job as a teacher to teach that child.

Causes. There appear to be two main causes of learning disabilities; however, as stated previously, since the term *reading disabilities* encompasses a wide range of disorders, it would be far too simplified to state that the condition has only two causes. More accurately, a learning disability is the result of a complex integration of biophysical, emotional, environmental, intellectual, and perceptual difficulties that creates problems of varying degrees. The two most common areas discussed as causes of learning disabilities are biological and organic disorders and environmental factors.

Biological and Organic Disorders. Neurological impairment, the traditional culprit in learning disability cases, may be the result of an unusual prenatal or birth experience (Pasamanick and Knoblock, 1960). Any maternal illness during pregnancy, medication, and use of alcohol or tobacco are now commonly believed to affect the fetus, often in a negative way. Fetal malnutrition due to lack of a proper diet during pregnancy is perhaps another prenatal cause of neurological distress (Birch, 1971). Prolonged labor, lack of oxygen to the child, breech birth, or forceps delivery are also cited as unusual birth experiences. The theory of mixed dominance (for example, preferred use of the right hand and left foot as opposed to a complete preference for one side of the body) claimed that this condition was a sign of a neurological problem that was responsible for learning disabilities (Orton, 1937). The theory has been disproved many times (Belmont and Birch, 1965), but research into the complexities of the relationships between hemispheric dominance and learning continues.

Other theories that have enjoyed media success but have not been supported by research are those of a biochemical nature. Feingold (1975) believes that artifical food colors and flavorings cause hyperactivity, one of the main characteristics of learning-disabled children, and Cott (1972) has attributed a disorder that prevents the body from synthesizing vitamins to be the cause of learning disabilities.

Environmental Factors. While it is evident that children from a disadvantaged environment tend to have learning problems, it is unclear whether these problems stem from emotional-psychological factors or from biophysical factors. Hunger or conflict in the home may prevent a child from concentrating on schoolwork, which presents a learning problem. However, malnutrition or lack of proper medical care can result in neurological disorders that cause learning problems (Hallahan and Cruickshank, 1973).

Another environmental factor may be lack of proper teaching (Bateman, 1973). In this view the phrase "teaching disability" has been used to state that the problem lies more in inefficient instructional methods in the early years than in the ability or disability of a child to learn.

Characteristics. While the characteristics of learning disabled children are divided into categories, it must be noted that children will not fall nicely into line behind a banner marked "language difficulties" or "perceptual-motor disorders." Not all learning-disabled children will display all these characteristics, and conversely some children with no learning problem may be subject to certain problems listed here. This explanation seeks to provide a guideline for understanding the complexities of a learning disability and also to aid in diagnosing a learning disability when one is suspected.

Lack of Appropriate Impulse Control. From the early work of Werner and Strauss (1941) through the more recent research (Tarver and Hallahan, 1976; Sabatino and Ysseldyke, 1972), it has been recognized that learning-disabled children tend to exhibit disorders of attention, hyperactivity, and impulsivity. Rappaport (1964) used the term "inadequate impulse control or regulation" to describe these activities and Cruickshank (1975) summed up all these behaviors as "the inability of the child to refrain from reaction to extraneous external or internal stimuli" (p. 260). The child has difficulty sorting out which elements in the environment require attention and which do not. The result might be disorders of attention, which include a short attention span, perseveration, which is the repetition of an idea in speech or writing, and distractibility, wherein the child is unable to focus attention on the task at hand due to external or internal distractions. Hyperactivity is perhaps one of the best known characteristics of the learning disabled and shows itself in the child who is constantly in motion, whose motor activity is too high for his or her age group. Impulsivity is the inability to control spontaneous inclinations to act or speak regardless of the circumstances and may cause problems both in social behavior and problem-solving ability (Heins et al., 1976).

Perceptual Disorders. Perception is the process of becoming aware of the nature of something through the senses. For the purposes of learning to read, good visual perception is most important to comprehension of the printed symbols that comprise the written code of language. Similarly, auditory perception influences reading ability because the visual symbol of the word must then be related to the sound it represents. Research indicates that poor visual and auditory perception are a common trait of learning-disabled individuals (Leton, 1962;

Devol and Hastings, 1967; Skubic and Anderson, 1970). Consequently, many authorities have advocated strong programs of visual and auditory perception training to improve reading skills. While this training is certainly indicated for some individuals, it does not offer *the* solution to reading problems and should be coupled with other techniques that deal with other aspects of the reading difficulties.

Perceptual-motor problems, or the inability to move the body in accordance with what the mind directs, are also characteristic of the learning-disabled child. These difficulties can be of a gross (large muscle coordination) or fine (small muscle coordination) nature, which will influence everything from the ability to play in motor games to the ability to write legibly. Again, many professionals (most notably Kephart, 1971) advocate programs of perceptual-motor training to improve this coordination, but again it must be stated that these methods alone will not necessarily improve the learning skills of the individual. They are a part of a total program and will serve the child best in a social way by making him or her more accepted by the peer group.

Language Problems. The language problems experienced by the learning disabled may be described as difficulties with "receptive language" and "expressive language" (Hallahan and Kauffman, 1978) or "input" and "output" (Johnson and Myklebust, 1967). The first of these disabilities—receptive or input problems—results from a lack of comprehension of spoken language, which causes difficulty, for example, in following directions and understanding class discussions. Expressive or output disabilities result in the inability to express thoughts using oral language. Complications of the motion of input may produce students who can understand what is spoken but cannot speak the ideas themselves or perhaps who may be able to say what they mean but not write it down. A student with this aspect of a learning disability may mistakenly be taken for one who does not pay attention or is shy about speaking up in class.

Memory and Cognitive Difficulties. Any learning process requires a certain ability to remember information long enough to access it or relate it to some other piece of information. The time required to perform this operation may be short term (e.g., the time it takes to associate the visual symbol to its corresponding sound) or long term (e.g., storing vocabulary and syntax rules), and dysfunctions of either memory type can create learning problems. While research supports the notion that learning-disabled children experience memory deficiencies (Vande Voort and Senf, 1973; Wiig and Roach, 1975), it offers no conclusions as to why they experience this difficulty. Some theories suggest that they lack efficient skill in organizing the material to be remembered (Parker et al., 1975) and that verbal information causes particular memory problems (Farnham-Diggory and Gregg, 1975; Velluntino et al., 1975).

Cognitive difficulties in learning-disabled children may manifest themselves in impulsive problem-solving strategies (Keogh and Donlon, 1972) and conceptual disorders (Walters and Doan, 1962). In a classic study by Werner and Strauss (1941), replicated in 1951 by Dolphin and Cruickshank, learning-disabled youngsters, given a task of sorting objects into groups based on similar aspects, were consistently distracted by nonessential details of the objects, which resulted in bizarre groupings displaying troubled thought processes (e.g., a wire was grouped with a fire engine because it was long and thin like a hose). Although some of this behavior appears creative and in fact is very imaginative (e.g., a whistle and sunglasses go together because policemen may wear them when directing traffic), the problem is that the student loses sight of the main task.

Emotional Instability. Learning-disabled youngsters tend to have frequent mood changes that may be associated with a defective self-concept. Once again, the failure syndrome found so often in underachieving students operates here with the learning disabled. When children fail in learning tasks, they lose confidence, motivation, and self-esteem, which in turn produces more failure in terms of teacher and parental disapproval. Other elements discussed by Rappaport (1964) that operate on the emotional structure of learning-disabled children include a low frustration tolerance and flight from challenge, which may result in a physical or verbal attack on someone if the individual does not achieve immediate success with the task. Overcompensation for insecurities may result in the child reverting to something he or she is successful at which might be totally irrelevant to the task at hand (e.g., singing Gilbert and Sullivan songs or reciting baseball statistics). Control or manipulation of others, power struggles, and negativism are other defense mechanisms that may show up in the behavior of the learning-disabled child in an attempt to cope with a difficult situation.

Classroom Considerations. Due to the complex nature of the learning disabilities handicap, the classroom teacher must keep in mind a wide variety of teaching strategies while trying to meet the needs of these children in the regular classroom. Ranging from the hyperactive child who creates general chaos to the quiet student who cannot seem to follow directions, learning-disabled students should ideally have individualized programs to meet their specific educational requirements yet be allowed to participate with the rest of the class whenever possible to encourage correct socialization. The approaches described in the following sections may be adapted for use either individually or in a class situation. Some additional suggestions to keep in mind while working with learning disabled children are

1. Never *assume* that they have understood directions even if the instructions are perfectly clear to everyone else. Go to the child and ascertain that the directions were indeed comprehended.
2. When the learning-disabled child is working with the class, try to make the exercises short and success oriented. Team games are especially useful when there is no direct individual pressure on the members (e.g., blackboard Scrabble) and if the child can cope with the excitement.
3. Alternative teaching and response methods may be useful with some learning-disabled children, such as the use of a typewriter or tape recorder for completing assignments.
4. Structure the time into small segments with varying activities–quiet independent work, work with a tutor or aide, classroom work, physical work (filing, board games, etc.).

Of greatest importance, the classroom teacher is a crucial person in the life of a learning-disabled child, and the relationship between teacher and student must be as close and as understanding as possible. Rappaport (1966) calls for a "relationship structure," which he defines as the "ability of the adult (parent or teacher or therapist or otherwise) to understand the child sufficiently well at any given moment, through his verbal and nonverbal communications, to relate in a way which aids the child's development of impulse control and other ego functions" (p. 26). This, of course, is the dream relationship between every pupil and teacher; however, it is even more important to children who have met with so little academic and social success that they are caught up in a failure syndrome. In a class of thirty-six children, this becomes an ideal toward which one must nevertheless strive.

Instructional Methods. As has been stressed repeatedly throughout this discourse, learning disabilities are a composite of many difficulties that are unique to each individual; consequently, no one method of teaching will satisfactorily meet the needs of all learning-disabled children or indeed even the needs of any single child with this complex learning handicap.

Many theories or methods of teaching learning-disabled students exist, and it is necessary to compose a comprehensive instructional framework (CIF) for each child, which consists of selecting those methods (or aspects of them) that best remedy the deficiencies exhibited by a particular individual. Once the theoretical methods of instruction are chosen, an individualized educational program (IEP), pinpointing specific goals, techniques, and exercises, can be developed. By first establishing an educational outline based on the major instructional approaches to learning disabilities, the actual teaching techniques and the rest of the classroom program will easily and naturally build up around this theoretical framework.

Hallahan and Kauffman (1978) present five convenient categories of teaching approaches for the learning disabled child that represent a concensus of professional opinion.

Process Training. This theory claims that it is impossible to know what "underlying processes" are used in learning and that, if there is difficulty in learning, the specific psychological process is the target for rehabilitation or remediation. The malfunctioning process most commonly cited is perceptual-motor integration, which is why many learning disability programs have stressed perceptual-motor training. Frostig and Horne (1964),

Getman et al. (1968), and Kephart (1971) are among the most popular proponents of this method of instruction, and generally they stress the acquisition of motor skills, progressing on to matching visual skills to them. Research evidence indicates that process training achieves very little real academic gain for the disabled learner (Hallahan and Cruickshank, 1973);however, as part of a comprehensive instructional framework, the use of visual-motor training in particular may serve to elevate the child's level of coordination, thus improving self-esteem, which may contribute very positively in attitude toward academic success.

Multisensory Approaches. Fernald's VAKT (visual, auditory, kinesthetic, and tactile) method of instruction serves as the standard upon which most other multisensory methods are based (Fernald, 1943). By using all the sensory mechanisms available rather than focusing on just visual and/or auditory, it is felt that the child has a better chance of learning because individuals differ in how they process sensory information, often favoring one mode over another.

Stimulus Reduction. This approach is designed for use with hyperactive and distractible children, and since those characteristics are among the most common found in learning-disabled children, techniques to reduce environmental phase stimuli may be beneficial to all learning-disabled students. This method basically seeks to reduce any source of distraction for the student, be it in the form of environmental factors (ornate bulletin boards, books on a shelf, other children, noise) or an instructional program in which the student is called upon to make choices. Stimulus reduction is accomplished in the latter instance by providing a totally teacher-structured program that elimates the frustration of choice until the child can be educated sufficiently to handle some decision making. Environmental control consists of providing the child with a quiet, relatively stimulus-free work space wherein all of his or her attention can be focused on the learning task (e.g., undecorated walls in a corner of the room or a cubicle). Cruickshank found that, although academic skills did not improve automatically, attending skills did improve, and since attention and concentration are essential to learning, this approach may contribute significantly to the CIF of certain learning-disabled children.

Cognitive Training. Modeling and self-instructional training are two related methods that attempt to teach learning-disabled children with impulsive problem-solving strategies how to slow down and reflect on the task before responding. Both methods utilize an adult or peer model to demonstrate the appropriate behavior and then provide positive reinforcement, either directly or indirectly, for any successes achieved. Self-instruction further provides a verbal stimulus to modeling by developing in the student the ability to "talk to himself" while performing the task, thus using a verbal control. Meichenbaum (1975), a major advocate of the system, provides the following format for self-instructional training:

1. An adult model performed a task while talking to himself out loud (cognitive modeling);
2. The child performed the same task under the direction of the model's instruction (overt self-guidance);
3. The child whispered the instructions to himself as he went through the task (faded, overt self-guidance);
4. The child performed the task while guiding his performance via private speech (covert self-instruction). (pp. 16–17)

Modeling has been found to be very effective in changing student behavior and can be accomplished easily by sitting the child near peers who normally exhibit the desired behavior. Further work on an individualized level can then be instituted if necessary.

Behavior Modification. This system of reinforcing appropriate behavior and ignoring inappropriate behavior has been used successfully with learning-disabled children suffering from hyperactivity and distractibility (Hallahan and Kauffman, 1975) as well as with those requiring improvement in math and linguistic skills (Smith and Lovitt, 1975; Lovitt and Smith, 1972). An important example of the behavior modification technique is the "engineered classroom" devised by Hewett (1967, 1968), which has led to improvements in attention skills by offering tokens or marks for tasks completed successfully or for behavior that is acceptable. Students can then "buy" prizes with their tokens or checkmarks.

Teaching Techniques. As for other handicaps discussed in this chapter, any method of reading instruction with which the teacher is competent and comfortable is acceptable. Certain modifications of the material are necessary for certain types of problems, and suggested techniques for adapting existing academic materials are presented here.

1. Exaggerate the item being taught thus causing the student to focus all of his or her attention on the task. For example;
   a. When teaching new vocabulary words in context, highlight the work with larger print or color.
   b. When teaching minimal pairs (e.g., focusing on the vowels in *bit* and *bet*), highlight the distinguishing letter as above.

Use of a tape recorder or other audio-visual tool provides a useful diversion between reading tasks which can be related to what was just done or preview what is coming up. (Photo by Linda Lungren.)

2. Break up stories, lessons, worksheets, and other assignments into small parts that culminate in success-oriented tasks. For example,
   a. Determine how much the child can read before frustration sets in, and divide the stories into sections than can be handled successfully. Questions about vocabulary, character, setting, and theme and predicting outcomes would be useful after each section to reinforce the skill being taught, aid in recall, and spark interest in continuing.
   b. Provide creative work such as art of writing as well as tasks using a typewriter, tape recorder, or other audiovisual tools as useful diversions between reading tasks that can be related to what was just done or preview what is coming up.
3. If a restricted environment is indicated for certain activities, create "offices" from carrels, partitions, or appliance crates that are free from distracting stimuli. Children may be assigned "office hours" when the space is for their own private use. Behavior modification principles can be applied to "buy" more or less office time (depending on which is considered more desirable by student and teacher).
4. Remember that IEPs for learning-disabled children require a great deal of monitoring to be certain that the correct instructional level is being used and that the instructions are understood. Utilize peer tutors

when possible to help in the lessons thus making use of the modeling technique at the same time. Sharing "office" space with a responsible, well-organized student may foster better skills than if the students work side by side in isolation.

5. Make full use of the multisensory approach, especially in learning vocabulary and in spelling, by extending the kinesthetic and tactile modalities through sandpaper letters, for use on a flannel board, and a box of sand, for tracing out the letters.

Also, see suggestions listed in the section for the mentally retarded.

QUESTIONS AND RELATED READINGS

If you feel that you have not attained adequate knowledge to answer the following questions successfully, we suggest additional related readings.

1. Describe the societal changes that brought about the passage of P.L. 94–142 and how this affects the classroom teacher.
2. Define the following disabilities:
   a. mental retardation
   b. hearing impairment
   c. speech impairment
   d. visual impairment
   e. orthopedic or other health impairments
   f. learning disabilities
3. What are the special learning problems associated with the handicaps listed in question 2? Name several teaching techniques for each.
4. What are the characteristics of learning disabilities?
5. How may the classroom teacher meet the needs of the learning-disabled student?

Goal 1: To help the reader to appreciate the background and significance of P.L. 94–142 and mainstreaming.

Question 1: Describe the societal changes that brought about the passage of P.L. 94–142 and how this affects the classroom teacher.

Berry, K. E. *Models for Mainstreaming.* San Rafael, Calif.: Dimensions, 1972.

National Association of State Directors of Special Education, Inc. *An Analysis of P.L. 94–142.* Washington, D.C.: NASDSE, 1976.

Weintraub, F. J., A. Abeson, J. Ballard, and M. L. LaVor, eds. *Public Policy and the Education of Exceptional Children.* Reston, Va.: The Council for Exceptional Children, 1976.

Goal 2: To help the reader understand the various types of handicapped students who may be present in the classroom.

Question 2: Define the following disabilities:

a. mental retardation
b. hearing impairment
c. speech impairment
d. visual impairment
e. orthopedic or other health impairments
f. learning disabilities

Dunn, L. M., ed. *Exceptional Children in the Schools.* New York: Holt, Rinehart and Winston, 1973.

Smith, R. M., and J. T. Neisworth. *The Exceptional Child.* New York: McGraw-Hill Book Company, 1975.

Teleford, C. W., and J. M. Sawrey. *The Exceptional Individual,* 3rd ed. Englewood Cliffs, N.J.: Prentice-Hall, Inc., 1977.

Goal 3: To help the reader understand the classroom considerations and teaching techniques for each handicap.

Question 3: What are the special learning problems associated with the handicaps listed in question 2? List several teaching techniques for each.

Bigge, J. L. *Teaching Individuals with Physical and Multiple Disabilities.* Columbus, Ohio: Charles E. Merrill Publishing Company, 1976.

Kirk, S. A., and F. E. Lord, eds. *Exceptional Children: Educational Resources and Perspectives.* Boston: Houghton Mifflin Company, 1974.

L'Abate, L., and L. J. Curtis, *Teaching the Exceptional Child.* Philadelphia: W. B. Saunders Company, 1975.

Goal 4: To help the reader appreciate the nature of learning disabilities.

Question 4: What are the characteristics of learning disabilities?

Kauffman, J. M., and D. P. Hallahan, eds. *Teaching Children with Learning Disabilities: Personal Perspectives.* Columbus, Ohio: Charles E. Merrill Publishing Company, 1976.

Wallace, G., and J. A. McLoughlin. *Learning Disabilities: Concepts and Characteristics.* Columbus, Ohio: Charles E. Merrill Publishing Company, 1975.

Wepman, J. M., W. M. Cruickshank, C. P. Deutsch, A. Morency, and C. R. Strother. "Learning Disabilities." In *Issues in the Classification of Children*, ed. by N. Habbs. Vol. 1 San Francisco: Jossey-Bass Inc., 1975.

Goal 5: To help the reader recognize the particular importance of the classroom teacher in meeting the needs of the learning-disabled student.

Question 5: How may the classroom teacher meet the needs of the learning-disabled student?

Goodman, L., and L. Mann. *Learning Disabilities in the Secondary School.* New York: Grune & Stratton, Inc., 1976.

Haring, N. G., and B. Bateman. *Teaching the Learning Disabled Child.* Englewood Cliffs, N.J.: Prentice-Hall, Inc., 1977.

Kaluger, G., and C. J. Kolson. *Reading and Learning Disabilities.* Columbus, Ohio: Charles E. Merrill Publishing Company, 1969.

BIBLIOGRAPHY

Ainsworth, S. "Report and Commentary." In *Conditioning in Stuttering Therapy: Application and Limitations.* Vol. 7. Memphis, Tenn.: Speech Foundation of America, 1970.

Auden, W. H. "The Will of Narcissus." In *The Dyer's Hand and Other Essays.* New York: Random House, Inc., 1964. Chapter opening quotation appears on page 104.

Barraga, N., ed. *Visual Efficiency Scale.* Louisville, Ky.: American Printing House for the Blind, 1970.

Bateman, B. "Educational Implications–Minimal Brain Dysfunction." In *Annals of the New York Academy of Sciences*, ed. by F. F. De La Cruz, B. H. Fox, and R. H. Roberts. 205, (1973), 245–50.

Belmont, L.,and H. Birch. "Lateral Dominance, Lateral Awareness, and Reading Disability." *Child Development* 34, (1965), 57–71.

Berkowitz, P. H., and E. P. Rothman. *The Disturbed Child.* New York: New York University Press, 1960.

Bigge, J. L., and P. A. O'Donnell. *Teaching Individuals with Physical and Multiple Disabilities.* Columbus, Ohio: Charles E. Merrill Publishing Company, 1977.

Birch, H. G. "Functional Effects of Fetal Malnutrition." *Hospital Practice* 4 (1971), 134–148.

Birch, J. W. *Hearing Impaired Children in the Mainstream.* Minneapolis: Leadership Training Institute/ Special Education, University of Minnesota, 1975.

Bloodstein, O. *A Handbook on Stuttering.* Chicago: National Easter Seal Society for Crippled Children and Adults, 1969.

Borkowski, J. G., and P. B. Wanschura. "Mediational Processes in the Retarded." In *International Review of Research in Mental Retardation*, ed. by N. R. Ellis. Vol. 7. New York: Academic Press, Inc.,1974.

Brown, A. L. "The Role of Strategic Behavior in Retardate Memory." In *International Review of Research in Mental Retardation,* ed. by N. R. Ellis. Vol. 7. New York: Academic Press, Inc., 1974.

Brown v. *Board of Education*, 347 U.S. 483, 493 (1954).

Conference of Executives of American Schools for the Deaf. *Report of the Ad Hoc Committee to Define Deaf and Hard of Hearing*, 1975.

Corrigan, D. C. "Political and Moral Contexts That Produced P.L. 94–142." *Journal of Education* 29:6 (1978) 11.

Cott, A. "Megavitamins: The Orthomolecular Approach to Behavioral Disorders and Learning Disabilities." *Academic Therapy* 7 (1972), 245–58.

Council of Exceptional Children. *The Education for All Handicapped Act–P.L. 94–142.* Washington, D.C.: U.S. Office of Education, 1977.

Cravioto, J., and E. Delicardie. "Environmental and Nutritional Deprivation in Children with Learning Disabilities." In *Perceptual and Learning Disabilities in Children: Research and Theory.*, ed. by W. M. Cruickshank and D. P. Hallahan. Vol. 2: Syracuse, N.Y.: Syracuse University Press, 1975.

Cruickshank, W. M. "The Education of Children with Specific Learning Disabilities." In *Education of Exceptional Children and Youth*, ed. by W. M. Cruickshank and G. O. Johnson. Englewood Cliffs, N.J.: Prentice-Hall, Inc., 1975.

Cruickshank,W. M., and G. O. Johnson, eds. *Education of Exceptional Children and Youth*, 3rd ed. Englewood Cliffs, N.J.: Prentice Hall, Inc., 1975.

Cruickshank, W. M., F. A. Bentzen, F. H. Ratzeburg, and M. T. Tannhauser. *A Teaching Method for Brain Injured and Hyperactive Children.* Syracuse, N.Y.: Syracuse University Press, 1961.

Davis, H. "Abnormal Hearing and Deafness." In *Hearing and Deafness*, ed. by H. Davis and S. R. Silverman, 3rd ed. New York: Holt, Rinehart and Winston, 1970.

Degler, L. S., and V. J. Risko. "Teaching Reading to Mainstreamed Sensory Impaired Children." *The Reading Teacher* 32 (May 1979), 921–25.

Devol, S. H., and M. L. Hastings. "Effects of Sex, Age, Reading Ability, SES, and Display Position on Measures of Spatial Relationships of Children." *Perceptual and Motor Skills* 24 (1967), 375–87.

Dolphin, J. E., and W. M. Cruickshank. "Pathology of Concept Formation in Children with Cerebral Palsy." *American Journal of Mental Deficiency* 56 (1951), 386–92.

Ellis, N. R. "The Stimulus Trace and Behavioral Inadequacy." In *Handbook of Mental Deficiency*, ed. by N. R. Ellis. New York: McGraw-Hill Book Company, 1963, 134–58.

———. "Memory Processes in Retardates and Normals." In *International Review of Research in Mental Retardation*, ed. by N. R. Ellis. Vol.4 New York: Academic Press, Inc., 1970 pp. 1-32.

Farnham-Diggory, S., and L. Gregg. "Short-Term Memory Function in Young Readers." *Journal of Experimental Child Psychology* 19 (1975), 279–98.

Feingold, B. F. *Why Your Child Is Hyperactive.* New York: Random House, Inc., 1975.

Fernald, G. M. *Remedial Techniques in Basic School Subjects.* New York: McGraw Hill Book Company, 1943.

Frostig, M., and D. Horne. *The Frostig Program for the Development of Visual Perception: Teacher's Guide.* Chicago: Follett Publishing Company, 1964.

Furth, H. G. "Influence of Language on the Development of Concept Formation in Deaf Children." *Journal of Abnormal Social Psychology* 63 (1961), 386–89.

———. "Linguistic Deficiency and Thinking: Research with Deaf Subjects 1964–1969." *Psychology Bulletin* 76 (1971), 58–72.

Gearheart, B. R., and M. W. Weishahn. *The Handicapped Child in the Regular Classroom.* St. Louis, Mo.: The C. V. Mosby Company, 1976.

Genensky, S. M. *A Functional Classification System of the Visually Impaired to Replace the Legal Definition of Blindness.* Santa Monica, Calif.: The Rand Corporation, 1970.

Geoffrion, L. D., and R. D. Bergeron. *Initial Reading Through Computer Animation*, ERIC Document No. ED 138 929. Durham: University of New Hampshire, 1977.

Getman, G. N., E. R. Kane, and G. W. McKee. *Developing Learning Readiness Programs.* N.Y., New York: McGraw-Hill Book Company, 1968.

Goldberg, E. P. *Social Technology for Special Children: Computers as Prostheses to Serve Communication and Autonomy in the Education of Handicapped Children.* Baltimore: University Park Press, 1979.

Grossman, H. J., ed. *Manual on Terminology and Classification in Mental Retardation, 1973 Revision.* Washington, D.C.: American Association on Mental Deficiency, 1973.

Hallahan, D. P., and W. M. Cruickshank. *Psychoeducation Foundations of Learning Disabilities.* Englewood Cliffs, N.J.: Prentice-Hall, Inc., 1973.

Hallahan, D. P., and J. M. Kauffman. "Research on the Education of Distractible and Hyperactive Children." In *Perceptual and Learning Disabilities in Children. Vol. 2: Research and Theory*, ed. by W. M. Cruickshank and D. P. Hallahan. Syracuse, N.Y.: Syracuse University Press, 1975.

Hallahan, D. P., and J. M. Kauffman. *Introduction to Learning Disabilities: A Psychobehavioral Approach.* Englewood Cliffs, N.J.: Prentice-Hall, Inc., 1976.

Hallahan, D. P., and J. M. Kauffman. "Categories, Labels, Behavioral Characteristics: ED, LD, and EMR Reconsidered." *Journal of Special Education* 11, (1977), 139–49.

Hallahan, D. P., and J. M. Kauffman. *Exceptional Children: Introduction to Special Education.* Englewood Cliffs, N.J.: Prentice-Hall, Inc., 1978.

Harley, R., J. Spollen, and S. Long. "A Study of Reliability and Validity of the Visual Efficiency Scale with Preschool Children." *Education of the Visually Handicapped* 5 (May 1973), 38–42.

Heins, E. D., D. P. Hallahan, S. G. Traver, and J. M. Kauffman. "Relationship Between Cognitive Tempo and Selective Attention in Learning Disabled Children." *Perceptual and Motor Skills* 42 (1976), 233–4.

Hewett, F. M. "Educational Engineering with Emotionally Disturbed Children." *Exceptional Children* 33 (1967), 459-67.

——— . *The Emotionally Disturbed Child in the Classroom.* Boston: Allyn & Bacon, Inc., 1968.

Hull, F. M., P. W. Miekle, R. J. Timmons, and J. A. Willeford. *National Speech and Hearing Survey Report.* Project no. 50978. Washington, D.C.: U.S. Office of Education, Bureau of Education for the Handicapped, 1969.

Johnson, D. J., and H. R. Myklebust. *Learning Disabilities: Educational Principles and Practices.* New York: Grune & Stratton, Inc., 1967.

Keogh, B. K., and G. M. Donlon. "Field Dependence, Impulsivity and Learning Disabilities." *Journal of Learning Disabilities* 5 (1972), 331–6.

Kephart, N. C. *The Slow Learner in the Classroom*, 2nd ed. Columbus, Ohio: Charles E. Merrill Publishing Company, 1971.

Kirk, S. A. *Early Education of the Mentally Retarded:*

An Experimental Study. Urbana: University of Illinois Press, 1958.

Klaus, R. A., and S. W. Gray. *The Early Training Project for Disadvantaged Children: A Report After Five Years*. Monographs of the Society for Research in Child Development 33, Ser. No. 120. 1968.

Leton, D. A. "Visual-Motor Capacities and Ocular Efficiency in Reading." *Perceptual and Motor Skills* 15 (1962), 406–32.

Lewis, R., and D. H. Doorlag, *Teaching Special Students in the Mainstream*. Columbus, Ohio: Charles E. Merrill Co., 1983.

Lovitt, T. C., and J. O. Smith. "Effects of Instructions on an Individual's Verbal Behavior." *Exceptional Children* 38 (1972), 685–93.

Lowenbraun, S., J. Affleck, and A. Archer, *Teaching the Mildly Handicapped in the Regular Class*, 2nd ed. Columbus, Ohio: Charles E. Merrill Co., 1981.

Meichenbaum, D. H. "Cognitive Factors as Determinants of Learning Disabilities: A Cognitive-Functional Approach." Paper presented at the NATO Conference on *The Neuropsychology of Learning Disorders: Theoretical Approaches*, Korsor, Denmark, June 1975.

Mercer, C. D., and M. E. Snell. *Learning Theory Research in Mental Retardation: Implications for Teaching*. Columbus, Ohio: Charles E. Merrill Publishing Company, 1977.

Meyer, E. L. *Exceptional Children and Youth: An Introduction*. Denver, Colo.: Love Publishing Co., 1978.

Mills v. *Board of Education of District of Columbia*, 348 F. Supp. 866, 880, (D.D.C., 1972).

Myklebust, H. R. "Learning Disabilities: Definition and Overview." In *Progress in Learning Disabilities*, Vol. 1, ed. by H. R. Myklebust. New York: Grune & Stratton, Inc., 1968, 1–15.

National Advisory Committee on Handicapped Children. Conference sponsored by Bureau of Education of the Handicapped. Washington, D.C.: U.S. Office of Education, September 28, 1968.

Orton, S. T. *Reading, Writing and Speech Problems in Children*. New York: W. W. Norton & Company, Inc., 1937.

Parker, T. B., C. W. Freston, and C. J. Drew. "Comparison of Verbal Performance of Normal and Learning Disabled Children as a Function on Input Organization." *Journal of Learning Disabilities* 8 (1975), 386–93.

Pasamanick, B., and P. Knoblock. "Brain Damage and Reproductive Casualty." *American Journal of Orthopsychiartry* 30 (1960), 298–305.

Pennsylvania Association for Retarded Children (PARC) v. *Commonwealth of Pennsylvania*, 343 F. Supp. 279 (E. D. Pa., 1972) Consent Agreement.

Perkins, W. H. *Speech Pathology: An Applied Behavorial Science*. St. Louis, Mo.: The C. V. Mosby Company, 1971.

Rappaport, S. R., ed. *Childhood Aphasia and Brain Damage: A Definition*. Narbeth, Penn.: Livingstone Publishing Company, 1964.

——. *Proceedings of the 1965 Pathway School Institute*. Narbeth, Penn.: Livingstone Publishing Company, 1966.

Report to the Ad Hoc Committee to Define Deaf and Hard of Hearing. *American Annals of the Deaf* 120 (1975), 509–12.

Robinson, N. M., and H. B. Robinson. *The Mentally Retarded Child: A Psychological Approach*, 2nd ed. New York: McGraw-Hill Book Company, 1976.

Rubenstein, R., and A. Rollins. *Demonstration of Use of Computer Assisted Instruction with Handicapped Children*. Cambridge, Mass.: Bolt, Beranek and Newman, Inc., 1978.

Sabatino, D. A., and J. E. Ysseldyke. "Effects of Extraneous Background on Visual-Perceptual Performance of Readers and Non-readers." *Perceptual and Motor Skills* 35 (1972), 323–8.

Schiefelbusch, R. L., and L. L. Lloyd, eds. *Language Perspectives—Acquisition, Retardation and Intervention*. Baltimore: University Park Press, 1974.

Sheehan, J. "Projective Studies of Stuttering." *Journal of Speech and Hearing Disorders* 23 (1958), 18–25.

Skubic, V., and M. Anderson. "The Interrelationship of Perceptual-Motor Achievement, Academic Achievement, and Intelligence of Fourth-Grade Children." *Journal of Learning Disabilities* 3 (1970), 413–20.

Sloane, H. N., and B. D. MacAulay, eds. *Operant Procedures in Remedial Speech and Language Training*. Boston: Houghton Mifflin Company, 1968.

Smith, D. D., and T. C. Lovitt. "The Use of Modeling Techniques to Influence the Acquisition of Computational Arithmetic Skills in Learning Disabled Children." In *Behavior Analysis and Education*, ed. by E. Ramp and G. Semb. Englewood Cliffs, N.J.: Prentice-Hall, Inc., 1975, 86–94.

Sykes, K. C. "Print Reading for Visually Handicapped Children." *Education of the Visually Handicapped* 8:4 (1972), 117–26.

Tarver, S. G., and D. P. Hallahan. "Children with Learning Disabilities: An Overview." In *Teaching Children with Learning Disabilities: Personal Perspectives*, ed. by J. M. Kauffman and D. P. Hallahan. Columbus, Ohio: Charles E. Merrill Publishing Company, 1976.

Turnbull, A. P., and J. B. Schulz. *Mainstreaming Handicapped Students: A Guide for the Classroom Teacher*. Boston: Allyn & Bacon, Inc., 1979.

Vande Voort, L., and G. Senf. "Audiovisual Integration in Retarded Readers." *Journal of Learning Disabilities* 6 (1973), 170–9.

Van Riper, C. *Speech Correction: Principles and Methods,* 5th ed. Englewood Cliffs, N.J.: Prentice-Hall, Inc., 1972.

———. *The Treatment of Stuttering.* Englewood Cliffs, N.J.: Prentice-Hall, Inc., 1973.

Vellutino, F. R., J. A. Steger, L. Desetto, and F. Phillips. "Immediate and Delayed Recognition of Visual Stimuli in Poor and Normal Readers." *Journal of Experimental Child Psychology* 19 (1975), 223-32.

Vygotsky, L. S. *Thought and Language.* New York: John Wiley & Sons, Inc., 1962.

Walters, R. H., and H. Doan. "Perceptual and Cognitive Functioning of Disabled Readers." *Journal of Consulting Psychology* 26 (1962), 355-61.

Ward, M., and S. McCormick. "Reading Instruction for Blind and Low Vision Children in the Regular Classroom." *The Reading Teacher* 34:4 (January 1981), 434-44.

Werner, H., and A. A. Strauss. "Pathology of Figure-Background Relation in the Child." *Journal of Abnormal and Social Psychology* 36 (1941), 236-48.

Wiig, E. H., and M. A. Roach. "Immediate Recall of Semantically Varied 'Sentences' by Learning Disabled Adolescents." *Perceptual and Motor Skills* 40 (1975), 119-25.

Zeaman, D., and B. J. House. "The Role of Attention in Retardate Discrimination Learning." In *Handbook of Mental Deficiency*, ed. by N. R. Ellis. McGraw-Hill Book Company, 1963.

CHAPTER 14

Teaching Reading to Students Who Are Learning English

By the time the native child reaches the age of seven, his cultural and language patterns have been set, and his parents are required by law to send him to school. Until this time he is likely to speak only his own local dialect of Indian, Aleut, or Eskimo or, if his parents have had some formal schooling, he may speak a kind of halting English.

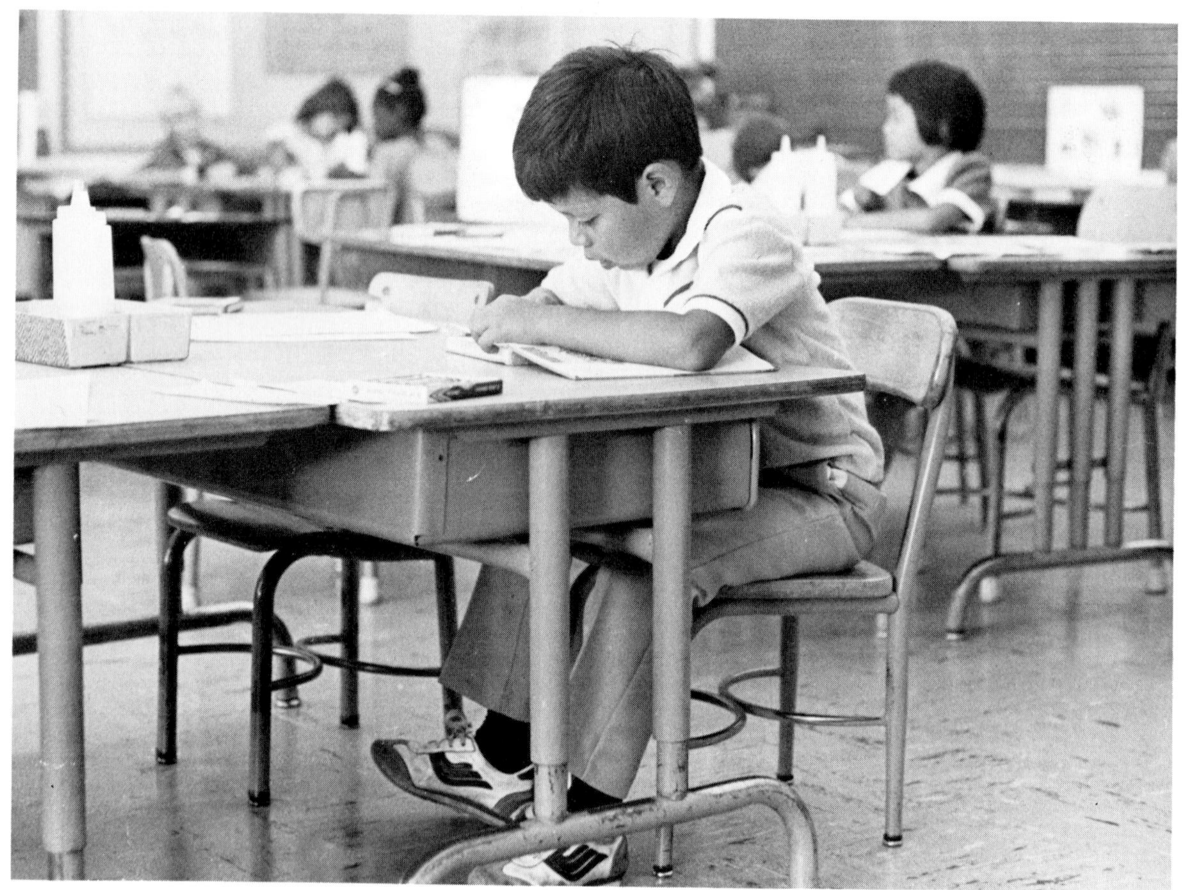

It is important to underscore the fact that bilingual children are *not* disadvantaged. In fact, they have the privilege of two languages. (Photo by Linda Lungen.)

> He now enters a completely foreign setting—a Western classroom. His teacher is likely to be a Caucasian who knows little or nothing about his cultural background. He is taught to read the Dick and Jane series. Many things confuse him: Dick and Jane are two *gussuk* (Eskimo term for "white person," derived from the Russian Cossack) children who play together. Yet, he knows that boys and girls do not play together and do not share toys. They have a dog named Spot who comes indoors and does not work. They have a father who leaves for some mysterious place called "office" each day and never brings any food home with him. He drives a machine called an automobile on a hard-covered road called a street which has a policeman on each corner. These policemen always smile, wear funny clothing, and spend their time helping children to cross the street. Why do these children need this help? Dick and Jane's mother spends a lot of time in the kitchen cooking a strange food called "cookies" on a stove which has no flame in it, but the most bewildering part is yet to come. One day they drive out to the country, which is a place where Dick and Jane's grandparents are kept. They do not live with the family and they are so glad to see Dick and Jane that one is certain that they have been ostracized from the rest of the family for some terrible reason. The old people live on something called a "farm," which is a place where many strange animals are kept: a peculiar beast called a "cow," some odd looking birds called "chickens," and a "horse," which looks like a deformed moose . . . .
>
> So it is not surprising that 60 per cent of the native youngsters never reach the eighth grade.
>
> *Bilingual Schooling in the United States, 1972*

GOALS: To help the reader to

1. Determine the needs of students who are learning English.
2. Understand the linguistic influences in second language teaching and the linguistic differences between several languages and English.
3. Determine the most appropriate methods for diagnosing the reading ability of students who are learning English and students who are bilingual.
4. Appreciate the different methodologies of instruction in teaching reading in the native language as well as reading in English.
5. Learn the appropriate methods of evaluating the effectiveness of materials for students who are learning English.

In most American classrooms there are children learning English as a second language and bilingual children who are not receiving appropriate reading instruction. With this realization, it probably comes as no great surprise to you that a very high percentage of non-English speakers never graduate from high school (Samora, 1968). Although some of the causes for the high dropout rate are not language or culture related, the bulk of them are. Many well-intentioned teachers have taken incorrect steps with bilingual and second language speakers and, inadvertently, have frustrated them to the point of total withdrawal. However, it is not our intention to dwell on the failings of schools. Rather, it is our intention to present a concise body of information about bilingual and English as a second language (ESL) students that will help you to improve your students' language and reading skills. For most of this chapter, we refer to these students as bilingual students.

While it may seem obvious, it is important to underscore the fact that bilingual children are *not* disadvantaged. In fact, they have the privilege of at least two languages. You will have to deal with this language abundance when you are teaching children who are learning English. Sometimes the situation will call for instruction in the native language, sometimes in English, and sometimes in both languages.

LANGUAGE NEEDS OF BILINGUAL STUDENTS

Bilingual children need to speak English before they learn to read English. This may seem obvious, but adult learners, who already read their native language, frequently learn to read English before speaking it. However, a child who does not read at all may need to learn to speak a language before learning to read it.

There are four general categories in which bilingual children require reading instruction:

Experimental/Information/Conceptual Background. Children frequently find it difficult to read about things that are totally outside their experience. The U.S. Office of Education's report cited at the introduction of this chapter has innumerable instances of such lack of background. The Eskimo anecdotes are good examples.

Auditory Discrimination. Because the phonological structures of different languages are never identical, the child from a non-English background may have trouble learning which sounds are relevant in English and which are irrelevent. For example, the initial sound of *key* and *cup* are "identical" in English, but significantly different in Arabic. Similarly, the "k" sounds of *key* and *ski* are identical in English, but different in Hindi.

Vocabulary. In dealing with Hispanic students, for instance, one must beware of "false cognates," that is, words that look or sound similar, but have quite different meanings. For example,

librería	bookstore, *not* library
chanza	joke, *not* chance

Syntax (especially word order). Many languages (e.g., French and Spanish) permit or prefer placement of adjectives after nouns.

La casa blanca	the white house
Les livres jaunes	the yellow books

Other languages (e.g., Russian), do not use the copula verb in the present tense as English does. Speakers of other languages may be confused about the use of "to be" in English, resulting in such forms as

Lamp here
Today he work in store
Freddy in school

Plurals, comparatives, and possessives are other forms that tend to give language learners trouble:

My tooths hurt.
This book is more heavy.
Is black the pen of Rose?

CULTURAL NEEDS OF THE BILINGUAL STUDENT

The need of bilingual children are often special becaues of their ethnic heritage (Ching 1976). Zintz (1975) aptly explains some cultural interference problems that teachers and students may experience.

> Too many teachers are inadequately prepared to understand or accept these dissimilar cultural values. Teachers come from homes where the drive for success and achievement has been internalized early, where "work for work's sake" is rewarded, and where time and energy are spent building for the future. Many children come to the classroom with a set of values and background of experiences radically different from those of the average American child. To teach these children successfully, the teacher must be cognizant of these differences and must above all else seek to understand without disparagement those ideas, values, and practices different from his own.

Perhaps the most important characteristic of any good teacher is his or her ability to accept each child without prejudice or preconception. Children quickly and thoroughly sense rejection by their teachers.. In the case of the bilingual child, the teacher must be quick to accept children's language because it is the language of their homes and their parents. Language and self-concept are so closely intertwined that children can be made to feel foolish and worthless when their "accent" or dialect is ridiculed by their teacher or peers. Trust and confidence between teachers and children must precede linguistic corrections. Through positive interactions with teachers and peers, a child's self-concept will improve tremendously.

DIFFERENCES AMONG BILINGUAL STUDENTS

To suggest that there is one route, one reading methodology for all bilingual and ESL students is utter folly. The complexity of the situation is often overwhelming for the new teacher. However, the following matrix may help you to understand some of the differences among bilingual children with regard to their ability to read and write. There are five different combinations represented in the following matrix:

	Student 1	Student 2	Student 3	Student 4	Student 5
Speaks	Spanish —	Spanish English	Spanish —	Spanish English	Spanish English
Reads	— —	— —	Spanish —	— English	Spanish English

You will note that students, 3, 4, and 5 have no problem per se because each of them speaks and reads at least one language. Teaching student 3 to read in English or student 4 to read in Spanish depends upon several factors: age, the child's progress in English at the present time, and the need for reading in a second language. The following is an example of a prescriptive approach for teaching each of these students.

Student No. 1. Teach oral English before reading instruction in either language. Begin reading instruction in Spanish.*

Student No. 2. Begin reading instruction in one of the two languages, depending on the following factors:

a. Student preference
b. Local expertise
c. Age
d. Cultural factors
e. Family preference

Student No. 3. Begin oral instruction in English. Begin reading instruction in English.

Student No. 4. Begin reading instruction in Spanish (if desired by the student).

Student No. 5. Continue. You are doing an excellent job.

*Depends on student's and parents' concerns.

BILINGUAL EDUCATION TERMINOLOGY

There is terminology used in the field of bilingual and second language education that may not be totally familiar to you. We will define some of these terms, which may help you to understand the role of bilingual education in your school.

TEACHER TRAINING

1. *Bilingual Education:* Teachers are trained to teach in a bilingual setting where the students are often taught in two languages in the course of the day.
2. *TESOL or TESL:* Teaching English to speakers of other languages; teaching English as a second language.
3. *TEFL:* Teaching English as a foreign language.

You will often hear the expression ESL and EFL; these refer to the field of English as a second language and English as a foreign language. ESL is often a component of a bilingual program, whereas EFL would never be used as a component of a bilingual program in the United States.

GENERAL BILINGUAL TERMINOLOGY

1. *Bilingualism* is the ability to function in a second language in addition to one's home language.
2. *Biculturalism* is the ability to behave on occasion according to selected patterns of a culture other than one's own.
3. *Bilingual schooling* is the particular organizational scheme of instruction that is used to mediate curricula in the home language and in a second language.
4. *Bilingual education* is a process by which the learning experiences provided in the home and other educational institutions enable a person to function in a second language in addition to the home language.
5. *Bilingual/bicultural education* is a process in which a person learns and reinforces his or her own language and culture and also acquires the ability to function in a second language.

PROGRAM MODELS

In establishing a bilingual education program, four different types of programs have been used in the United States.

1. Monoliterate program
   Goal: To develop English literacy and literacy in the native language as a link between home and school.
2. Partial bilingual-dual medium differential maintenance program.
   Goal: To develop a language and cultural maintenance. Native language skills are cultivated in all areas except the technical sciences and math.
3. Transitional bilingual program
   Goal: To assist the child in adapting to school and to progress on a par with his or her peers in all subject areas while learning English.
4. Full bilingual program
   Goal: To develop language competency in the native language, as well as in the second language in every subject area.

TEACHING ENGLISH AS A SECOND LANGUAGE

Effective instruction in beginning reading has changed considerably with the current findings of linguistic research. Traditionally, psycholinguists have emphasized that children learn language by imitating what they hear. Incorrect usage and incorrect punctuation were self-corrected when speakers failed to communicate effectively.

Second language teachers who were influenced by this theory began teaching oral language by having children mimic and memorize. Rather than teaching grammatical rules for future independent speaking, they emphasized proper sounds and the acquisition of native-like accents by language learners. The assumption of this approach was that in memorizing enough samples of natural speech, the learner would be able to make proper use of these structures in the appropriate context. Although this approach failed to produce bilinguals, it did demonstrate that learners could perfect their accent in a second language even if they learned it after childhood.

In contrast, transformational/generative grammarians have stressed the ability of all children to generate sentences in their native language that they have neither imitated nor memorized. These linguists have changed many of the objectives of second language teachers. Instead of emphasizing either reading or speaking exclusively, the second language teacher explores the many dimensions of language with the students. The key is to create meaningful contexts that stimulate communication in the new language. Although reading is not to be ignored in this approach, it has been assumed that one cannot, in the early stages, read what one cannot produce orally. As the child moves to a more advanced level in the new language, reading reinforces language and develops it through exposure to new vocabulary, syntactic structures, and cultural contexts.

WHAT THE TEACHER OF READING NEEDS TO KNOW ABOUT OTHER LANGUAGES

Because children from each language group have specific problems with learning to read in English, we will present some possible sources of difficulty for the second language child as well as many insights into the contrasts between the child's language and English.

The languages discussed here have been selected to represent the many languages your children will speak: Spanish, Chinese, Hebrew, and American sign language. You may have the opportunity to work with children whose other language is not one of the languages presented. If this is the case, it is important for you to research the language of your child to understand some basic principles of its sound system and syntactic system. This is crucial to help your child learn to read.

Spanish

Spanish is the second most frequently spoken language in the United States. It is possible that you will eventually work with a Spanish-speaking child. In the next few pages, you will find information useful for teaching a Spanish-speaking child to read English.

The following rules are presented to introduce you to the phonological and grammatical variations between Spanish and English:

1. Spanish-speaking children will have difficulty pronouncing the following vowels:

   /i/ sit /æ/ cat /u/ pull

2. Spanish does not rely on voiced (sit, hit) or voiceless (buzz, bus) sounds for specific contrasting meanings.
3. The speaker of Spanish eliminates or replaces the following sounds in his or her language:

   /v/ voice /θ/ then /z/ zone /j/ juice

4. Words ending in /r/ plus the consonants /d/, /l/, /p/, /s/, and /t/ are pronounced by the Spanish speaker without the final consonant.
5. The Spanish language has no /s/ cluster.
6. The following grammatical differences exist between the two languages:

	English	Spanish
Subject Predicate	The dog sleeps.	The dogs sleeps.
Verb tense	He needed help yesterday.	He need help yesterday.
Negatives	I am not going home.	I no go home.
Omission of noun determiners	He is a dancer.	He is dancer.
Omission of pronouns	She is a doctor.	Is doctor.
Objective ordering	The green dress is beautiful.	The dress green is beautiful.
Comparisons	It is bigger.	Is more big.

The following chart lists some sounds in English that are not present in Spanish:

/p/ point	/z/ pleasure	/h/ hear
/t/ take	/v/ vine, vote	/y/ yet
/k/ car	/r/ rode	/w/ what
/j/ judge	/tt/ cotton	/s/ shoe

This information is useful for you, as a teacher of reading, because you will be able to understand the difficulty which a Spanish-speaking child may encounter when he is trying to read English words which contain these sounds.

Spanish-speaking children may encounter these problems when learning to speak and read English.

PROBLEMS IN THE PRONUNCIATION OF VOWEL SOUNDS

Sound	Example	Possible Error
1. long e	leave, feel	live, fill
2. short i	live, fill	leave, feel

Sound	Example	Possible Error
3. long a	mate, bait	met, bet
4. short e	met, bet	mate, bait
5. short a	hat, cat	hot, cot
6. short o	hot, cot	hat, cat
7. long o	coal, hole	call, hall

PROBLEMS IN THE PRONUNCIATION OF CONSONANTS/ BLENDS IN INITIAL, MIDDLE, AND FINAL POSITION

Sound	Example	Possible Error
1. /θ/ and /ð/	thin, then, path	sin, den, pass
2. /š/	shoe, show, wash	sue, choe, bus or bush
3. /č/	chew, chop, witch	choe or jew, cash, wish
4. /b/	bin, beer, tab, rabbit	pin, pear, tap, rapid
5. /g/	goat, wing	coat, wink
6. /w/	way, wash	gway, gwash (with more proficiency pronounced gwash or watch)
7. /y/	yellow, yale	jello, jail
8. /v/	vest, vail	best, bail

Chinese*

The following is a brief overview of selected variations between English and Chinese. This introduction may be useful if you teach Chinese students.

There are many dialects of Chinese. Mandarin, which is spoken by approximately 70 per cent of the Chinese people, is the national dialect in the People's Republic and Taiwan. Cantonese, another major dialect, is spoken by most of the Chinese families that come to the United States from Hong Kong, Kowloon, or Macao. The Cantonese dialect is the one that is discussed below.

1. The Chinese language does not have as many vowels as English; therefore, a Chinese child learning to speak English may have difficulty with these vowel sounds:

   /ay/ buy   /iy/ meat   /ey/ gait

2. Chinese speakers seldom use consonants in final positions.
3. There is no direct correspondence between English and Chinese sounds:

   rich   shed

4. Many Chinese dialects are devoid of the sounds of consonant clusters:

   calf   swish

5. Some Chinese dialects do not contain consonant clusters for pluralization:

   calves   swishes

6. Chinese speakers may indicate plurals through the use of numerical designations or auxiliary words:

   three dog = three dogs

7. The Chinese speaker expresses grammatical relationships by auxiliary words and word order:

   She gave me two cars. (English)
   Yesterday she give I two cars. (Chinese)

8. Chinese speakers use tone or pitch to distinguish word meanings while speakers of English combine pitch and intonation in sentence meaning.
9. The Chinese speaker may exclude subjects or predicates if the context is understandable:

English	Chinese
It is raining.	It rains.
The car is shiny.	Car shiny.

10. English speakers invert the noun and verb forms when asking questions. The Chinese speaker does not follow this inversion but instead adds empty words *ma* or *la* to the sentence:

English	Chinese
Are you happy?	You are happy ma?

*Information for the section on Chinese was provided by Mae Chu-Chang.

11. Chinese speakers use a time word or phrase to indicate the tense of a verb:

She go "jaw." translates "She went."

In Chinese, there are as many as one hundred spoken dialects, but only one writing system.

Tonal Language. In Mandarin Chinese there are four tones, which can be represented in the following way:

Pluralization. The *plural concept* in English is developed in the following way:

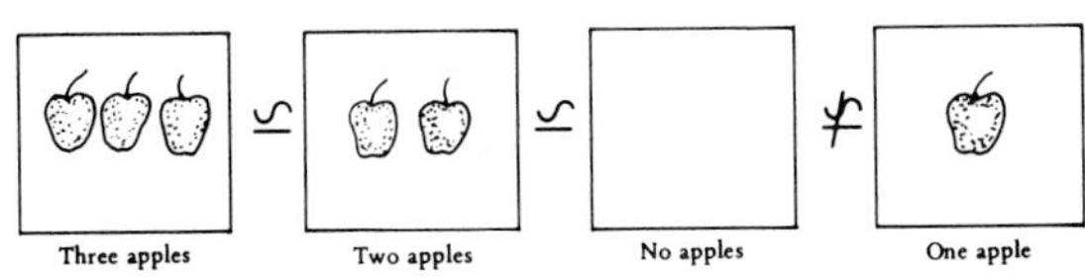

In Chinese, pluralization is similar to the following:

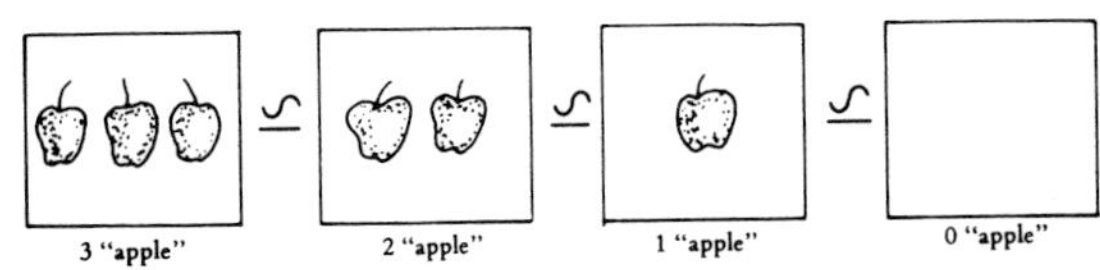

Hebrew*

The phonological and graphemic system of Hebrew is presented in the following chart. This information will help you to prepare an appropriate beginning reading program in English if you are asked to teach Hebrew-speaking children.

*Information for the section on Hebrew was provided by Sharon Frank Hirsch.

	Forms		Name of Grapheme	Graphemic Equivalent in Roman Alphabet	Phonemic Equivalent in English	Cursive Grapheme
	Archaic Grapheme	*Printed Grapheme*				
Consonants	𐤀	א	aleph		glottal	א
	𐤁	בּ ב	bet	b	b, v	בּ, ב
	𐤂	ג	gimel	g	g	ג
	𐤃	ד	dalet	d	d	ד
	𐤄	ה	hey	h	h	ה
	𐤅	ו	vav	v	v	ו
	𐤆	ז	zayin	z	z	ז
	𐤇	ח	het	h	ch (loch)	ח
	𐤈	ט	tet	t	t	ט
	𐤉	י	yed	y	y	י
*used only as final letter of word	𐤊	כּ כ ך*	kaf	k, h	k (hot)	כ
	𐤋	ל	lamed	l	l	ל
	𐤌	*ם מ	mem	m	m	ם*, מ
	𐤍	נ ן*	nun	n	n	ן*, נ
**ayin has two sounds: a weaker general, a Parisian "r"; in modern pronunciation it is not distinguished from alpha.	𐤎	ס	samekh	s	s (hard)	ס
	𐤏	ע	ayin		**	ע
	𐤐	.פּ פ ף*	pey	ph, p	p, f	*ף, פּ
	𐤑	צ ץ*	toade	ts	s (hiss)	*ץ, צ
	𐤒	ק	g ef	K (palatal)		ק
	𐤓	ר	resh	r	r (palatal)	ר
	𐤔	שׁ שׂ	s, in, shin	s, sh	s, sh	שׁ, שׂ
	𐤕	ת	tav	t	t	תּ, ת

Vowel	(hee)	(say)	(eh)	(her)	(aw)	(ch)	(w)
	iy	ey	e	a	o	ow	v
	ִי	ֵי	ֶי			וֹ	וּ

The following is an overview of some syntactic problems that Israelis may encounter when they are learning to read in English:

1. Some verbs that exist in Hebrew as single-word verbs are idiomatic phrases in English:

    to catch a cold, to take a shower, to make friends

2. Hebrew verb forms are inflected for tense, number, and person. In English, one has to examine auxiliaries. Hebrew has no auxiliaries, and a variety of forms do not exist:

    I gave, I was giving, I was given, I give

3. Hebrew has only three basic tenses (past, present, future).
4. Adjectives follow the noun in Hebrew—except for numbers:

    "the beautiful, new, white, home" is expressed as the phrase
    The home, the beautiful, the new, and the white.

5. There is an absence of gender markers in English nouns such as teacher, doctor, lawyer, student, friend. Hebrew nouns are always marked for gender.

Sign Language

The majority of deaf adults in the United States use American sign language as their main channel of communication. The average deaf adult graduates from school with a 4.0 grade-level reading ability. This is an average of their capabilities using the printed English form, not of their capabilities to function within the hearing society. Since their main communicative form is sign language, they can be classified as a linguistic minority.

Users of sign language encounter many of the same problems as bilingual students. To help deaf students learn to read in English, you will have to learn some facts about the structure of sign language. A very brief overview of selected features of sign language is presented now:

FEATURES OF SIGN LANGUAGE

1. Approximately twenty different handshapes are used in sign language.
2. These handshapes when combined with a large variety of movements in space permit very sophisticated communication to take place.
3. Signs are typically produced on the face and head, on the body, and in the space directly in front of the lower head and chest area.
4. Very sophisticated means of indicating subject/agent action and patient/object are used by using arbitrary locations in space to represent objects and persons not present. Sign language makes maximum efficient use of the visual sphere and its perception by the human brain.

This brief presentation of language differences has been intended only as an introduction to the multiple factors that you will need to investigate and understand when you are teaching a bilingual child to read. Although the task seems complex, it is not an impossibility. It is encouraging to note that many Americans are competent readers and speakers of two different languages. With your help, your non-English speakers will soon be reading in English.

ASSESSING BILINGUAL STUDENTS' NEEDS

In this section, you are introduced to tests and instruments that are useful for diagnosing students' difficulties and evaluating student progress. It should be pointed out immediately that most norm-referenced reading tests in English have been standardized on native English-speaking populations. The scores that bilingual students received on these tests must be interpreted with extreme caution and sensitivity.

Where Do I Begin?

The first question you will ask when you are working in English with a second language child is "How much English does the child know?"

In asking this question, you are beginning the process of teaching a bilingual or ESL student to read. The first issue is to assess the child's proficiency in English. It should be emphasized that children have different proficiences within their language ability. In most cases it may be advantageous for you, as the teacher, to conduct a structured, but informal, nonthreatening interview with the child to determine his or her proficiency ease in speaking English.

Most tests that have been designed to assess language dominance have ignored the fact that children have many variations in their language abilities. Sometimes their native language is their dominant, preferred language for a particular task, but sometimes it is not. This seems eminently logical because many adults experience the same phenomenon; that is, a Spanish-speaking adult who studies advanced statistics in England may prefer to use English when he is discussing statistics. Therefore, before assessing a child's language dominance globally, we need to ask, "What is the specific task that the child is being asked to perform?" and "What is the language of the person to whom the child will speak during the instructional period?" The answers to these questions will provide you with a great deal of useful information that will enable you to begin your instructional program.

In determining language proficiency, you will want to extract information about several aspects of language so that you can build a program for each student. An example of such a test that gathers information about the reading, writing, speaking, and listening skills of the bilingual child is the Marysville Test, which is administered in English and Spanish. We have included the reading section of the test. A similar format could be used as the basis for the construction of an instrument for children from language backgrounds other than Spanish.

The Marysville Test

Direction to the Examiner

1. The child should be tested on two separate occasions by separate examiners, unless the teacher is bilingual in English and in the child's native language.
2. The series of questions that follows may be scored as you ask each question.
3. Be certain that you and the pupil are seated in a quiet corner, free from distraction.
4. Make every effort to gain the child's complete attention and tell him that you are going to ask each question only once.
5. Speak in a conversational tone; do not hurry.
6. Do not give emphasis to any of the material that would distort it for the child.
7. Follow the specific instructions for each set of questions.

Administration

Follow the instruction given for each separate page. Use *only* the language of the test. Do not mix Spanish and English.

Scoring

Credit one point for each correct response on each of the four language sections: listening, speaking, reading, and writing.

Test of Reading

Ask the pupil to read the following items. Score correct only an item that is read completely (or letters, characters, symbols of vernacular). Discontinue after three consecutive failures.

1. R. W. X. O. A
2. Me
3. My father
4. Mother and father
5. Upstairs

Write from dictation:

6. You
7. Did
8. Hands
9. Touch
10. Special

In addition to the Marysville Test of Language Dominance, there are several other tests available for assessing the language proficiency of the bilingual child:

Bilingual Syntax Measure, 1973 (grades K–2)
Harcourt Brace Jovanovich, Inc.
Testing Department
757 Third Ave.
New York, N.Y. 10017

Dos Amigos Verbal Language Scales, 1974 (grades 1–4)
Academic Therapy Publications
1539 Fourth St.
San Rafael, Calif. 94901
James Language Dominance Test, 1974 (grades K–1)
Learning Concepts
Speech Division
2501 N. Lamar
Austin, Texas 78705
Spanish-English Language Dominance Assessment, 1972 (grades 1–2)
Professor Bernard Spolsky
The University of New Mexico
1805 Roma N.E.
Albuquerque, New Mex. 87106

PROGRAMS FOR TEACHING ENGLISH AS A SECOND LANGUAGE

One of the best ways in which to teach very young children English, if their first language is not English, is to let them play and learn with children whose first language is English. Young children are less encumbered by introspection and are less self-conscious than older children and adults. They are willing to create new words and to decipher the complex and often unintelligible speech of their peers. However, not all children learn a second language spontaneously. It is foolhardy to think that every second language child will learn English merely because he or she is young. Some children may need rather direct instruction in English as a second language, and older children definitely need formal instruction in English.

Although you may not be teaching any bilingual children at the present time, you may have to do so in the future. If you decide that you need to give direct instruction in English as a second language and you are unsure how to do it, you may want to refer to the following scope and sequence chart:

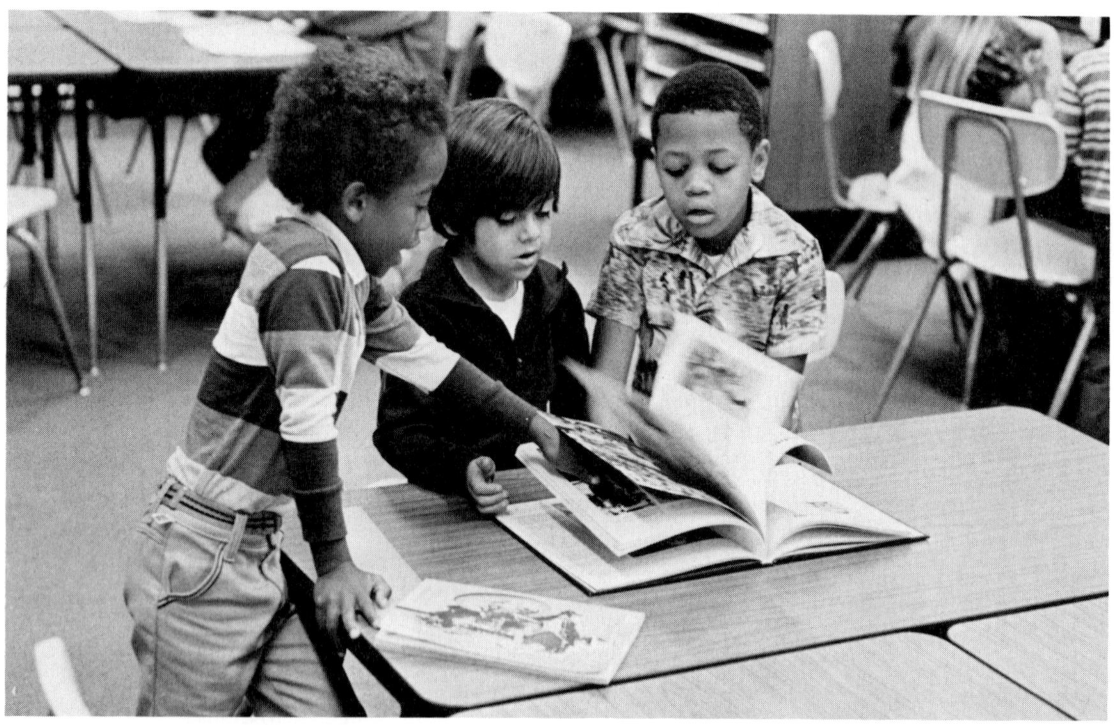

One of the best ways to teach very young children to speak English is to let them play and learn with children whose first language is English. (Photo by Linda Lungren.)

Scope and Sequence Chart

Syntactic Structures	Articulation
Beginning Level	
A. Declarative and question sentence structures 1. Word order of declaratives contrasted with different word order of questions with *be* verbs: *They are* leaving. *Are they* leaving? 2. Use of contracted forms of *be* verbs: *he's, they're, I'm*. Use of pronouns with corresponding form of *be* verb: *she is, they are.* 3. Use of *be* verbs to show action: a. in progress b. of repetitive nature 4. Use of determiners: *the, a, an.* 5. Affirmative and negative short answers to questions with *be* verbs: *I'm* going, *He's not* going.	A. Contrasted intonation contours of declarative sentences, questions, and short answers. B. Stress and accent patterns of requests. C. Articulation of contracted forms of *be* with pronouns *he, she, we, you, it, there.* D. Articulation of the /s/, /z/, and /-ðz/ of third-person singular verbs and plurals as in the words *eats, wins, smashes*, and contractions such as *it's, there's.* E. Unstressed forms of *a, an, the.* F. Articulation of /k/, /g/, /ŋ/: *kick, go, sing.* G. Stress the accent patterns of compound words.
B. Verbs other than *be.* 1. Word order for declaratives compared to order for questions with *do* and *does.* 2. Affirmative and negative short answers to questions with *do* and *does.* 3. *-S* forms of third-person singular used with pronouns (*he, she, it*) and other singular nouns in declaratives, contrasted to plural nouns (*he runs, we run*).	H. Articulation of /t/, /d/, and -ed endings as in *foot, wood, hunted.* I. Articulation of /p/, and /b/ as in *pay, boy.* J. Articulation of /f/ and /v/ as in *calf, move.* K. Articulation of /θ/ and /ð/ as in *thin, those.* a. Contrasting /t/ with /θ/ as in *boat, both.* b. Contrasting /d/ with /ð/ as in *day, they.* L. Articulation of /s/, /z/, /c/ and /j/ as in *mash, pleasure, choose, fudge.*
C. Expression of time (tense). 1. Use of *be* in expressions of past tense in statements and questions (I *was* walking. *Were* they singing?) 2. Irregular verbs which form past tense without *-ed* (use of vowel and consonant contrast) 3. Formation of verbs other than *be* to express past tense using regular rule (*-ed*). a. Past tense forms and placement of verbs other than *be* in declaratives and questions. 4. Forms of short responses to questions asked in past tense (use of *be* or *do* appropriately) 5. Use of *be* verbs + *going to* express future tense (She is going to ride home. They are going to sing.)	M. Articulation of /m/ and /n/ as in *moon, no.* N. Articulation of /l/ and /r/ as in *lose, read.* O. Articulation of /w/ and /y/ as in *wood, yellow.* P. Articulation of front vowels. a. /i/ and /ɪ/: *seat, sit* b. /ey/e/: *say, pet* c. Contrast of /e/ with /ɪ/: *set, sit* d. Contrast of /ɪ/, /e/, and /iy/: *sit, set, seat* e. /æ/: *hat* Q. Articulation of middle vowels. a. /u/ and /a/: *nut, hot* b. Contrast of /a/ with /æ/: *hot, hat* c. /ai/: *tie* d. /u/: *hurt*
D. Formation of questions with interrogative words or word order. E. Negatives. 1. Use and placement of *not* in declaratives (past, present, future) with verb *be.* 2. Use of *not* in questions with *be* 3. Use of *not* in sentences (declarative and question) with *do* and verbs other than *be.* 4. Use of *any, rarely, seldom, few.*	R. Articulation of glides and back vowels. a. /u/ and /ʊ/: *food, foot* b. /aʊ/: *cow* c. /o/ and /ɔ/: *boat, bought* d. /ɪ/: *toy*

Syntactic Structures	Articulation
F. Frequency words. 1. Different positions of frequency words with *be* contrasted to positions with verbs other than *be* (He sometimes walks. He is always late.) 2. Use of *ever* in question patterns; *never* in declarative sentences.	

Intermediate Level

The following skills should be an extension of a solid foundation in beginning level materials.

A. Review of patterns introduced at beginning level.

B. Modification constructions: use of substitute words
   1. How *other* and *another* can be substituted for nouns, contrasted with their use as modifiers of nouns.
   2. Use of objective forms of personal pronouns in object position.

C. Structures in which *me*, *to me*, and *for me* are used with certain verbs.

D. Patterns of word order when expressing manner. John runs quickly.

E. Models: use of *must*, *can*, *will*, *should*, *may*, and *might* in appropriate place in sentence.

F. Techniques for connecting statements.
   1. *and . . . either* contrasted to *and . . . too*
   2. Use of *but*

G. Structures with two-word verbs (verb + particle): *call up*, *put on*.
   1. Structures in which they are unseparated.
   2. Structures in which they are separated.

H. Patterns for answers to why and how questions.

I. Special patterns using *to* and *for*.
   1. *For* and *to* + other words as modifiers following some terms of quality.
   2. Placement of *very*, *too*, *enough*.
   3. Patterns in which nouns or pronouns are used after certain action words.

J. *It* or *there* as subject of the sentence.

K. 'S as a contraction and as a possessive marker.

L. Comparisons.
   1. Structures for comparisons with *different from*, *same as*, *like*, *the same . . . as*, *as . . . as*.
   2. Patterns of comparison using *-er than* and *more than*, *of the . . . -est*, and *the most*.

A. Articulation of consonant cluster. /sp/ as in *special*.

B. Articulation of consonant cluster. /st/, /sk/, /sn/, /sm/, /sl/, and /sw/ as in *step*, *skip*, *snap*, *smell*.

C. Articulation of final consonant clusters. Consonant + /s/, consonant + /t/, consonant + /d/ as in *cats*, *dropped*, *used*.

D. Articulation of final consonant clusters: two consonants + /s/, as in *helps*.

E. Articulation of final consonant clusters: two consonants + /t/, as in *jumped*.

F. Intonation patterns used in comparison.

Syntactic Structures	Articulation
Intermediate-Advanced Level	
A. Review structures introduced at earlier levels.	A. Articulation of final consonant cluster: two consonants + /z/ as in *holds*.
B. Word order pattern and use of relative clauses or embedded sentence to modify nouns. 1. Words used as subject of the embedded sentence: *that, which, who*, etc. 2. *That* and related words in other positions.	B. Articulation of final consonant cluster: two consonants + /d/ as in *solved*.
C. *What, when, who*, in object position.	
D. Embedded sentence of different statement pattern type used in object positions.	
E. Patterns with *have* and *be* in the auxiliary. 1. Present perfect complete *have (has)* + *-ed/-en* form of verb. 2. *Be* + *ing* verb form (used with *yet, any-more, still*). 3. *Have* + *been* + *-ing* verb forms in continuous present perfect structures. 4. Using *be* + *-ed/-en* verb forms. 5. Using *be* with *-ed/-en* and *-ing* in descriptions. 6. Special cases: a. *be* + two-word verbs and *-ing* form b. Use of *had* in those structures	
Special structural patterns	
A. Verb modification 1. *Wish* / *Hope* (that) + declarative sentence. 2. *To* omitted after certain verbs.	
B. Conditionals: 1. Patterns with *should, might, could, must*. 2. Cause and effect sentence structures.	
C. Object structures and modification. 1. Use of *-ing* endings of verbs. 2. Patterns for verbs followed by an object and one or more describing words and/or an *-ing* form. 3. Verbs followed by two nouns with the same reference. 4. *-Ing* endings used in subject position contrasted to their use at the beginning of sentences (referring to the subject)	
D. Logical order of sentences in sequence. 1. Ordering for sentences related by *however, therefore, also, but*. 2. Ordering for sentences related by terms of time or place: *before, after that, then*.	
Advanced Level	
A. Review of all levels.	A. Spelling vowel sounds:

Syntactic Structures	Articulation
B. Review of function words. 1. Auxiliaries: *will, may, can, could, should, might, would, must, have, be, shall, do.* 2. Preposition adverbs: a. Frequently used: *at, by, in, into, for, from, with, to, on, of, off* b. Location c. Direction d. Time e. Comparison	1. /ɪ/ and /i/. 2. Glides /aɪ/ and /r/. 3. Glides /aʊ/ and /oɪ/. Intonation and stress patterns used with comparisons, manner, and time words, and prepositions. Intonation patterns for modals: *could, would, must, should.* Conjunction and intonation pattern with *or* and *but.* Words for degree and for generalizing.
C. Conjunction patterns with *but* and *or.*	Articulation of *to* and *too.*
D. Other complement structures. 1. *Believe / Want / Think / Expect* + declarative sentence. 2. Use of appropriate complementizer words.	

Vocabulary Development

Beginning Level

A. A basic flexible-content vocabulary should include items relevant to the students' everyday experiences, that is,

- Eating and cooking utensils
- Common foods
- Parts of the body
- Articles of clothing
- Furniture
- Telling time
- Numbers: cardinal, ordinal
- Family relationships
- Colors
- Name of occupations
- Days of the week
- Months of the year, seasons
- Common animals
- Various materials: wood, plastic
- Holidays
- Most important geographic names
- Words used to ask directions

B. Pictures and/or objects should be used to explain all of these.

C. Several basic two-word verbs (verbs + particle) for example, *pick up, wait for, hang up, get up.*

D. Concepts of directionality: *in front of, behind, before, after.*

E. Countable and noncountable nouns: *cup* as opposed to *cereal.*

F. Following simple directions:

G. Simple synonyms, antonyms, especially adjectives and prepositions such as *good - bad, on - off.*

Intermediate Level

Extension of vocabulary introduced plus

- Shopping expressions
- Further occupations and responsibilities
- Health and health practices
- Further synonyms and antonyms
- Family names of more distant relatives
- Government agencies
- Clothing materials

Intermediate-advanced Level

- Daily living skills
- Purchasing suggestions
- Directions involving choice
- Derivations

Syntactic Structures	Articulation
Driving	Structural analysis: prefixes, suffixes, hyphenation of words
Traffic regulations	
Postal procedures	Synonyms, antonyms, homonyms (more advanced)
Insurance procedures	
Music, literature, the arts	Educational opportunities
Leisure-time activities	Travel
Government	

Advanced Level

Study skills, information locating and organizing, synthesis of information, and making cross comparisons:

- Propaganda techniques, discerning fact and fiction
- The human body and its actions
    - Evening and morning activities
- Special problems: idiomatic expressions
    - Multiple meanings of words
- Advanced descriptive terminology
    - Attributes of objects (size, shape)
    - Attributes of people (including personality)
- Buying and selling
- Transportation and communication
- Personal and professional contacts (job applications)
- Further government interaction (law, courts, taxes)
- Oral and written reports (books, movies, trips)
- Discussions on American history, geography, climate

Developmentally, all children learn to listen and to speak before they learn to read and to write. Activities in the new oral language should be provided for the bilingual student. These children are speaking and learning English through hand puppets. (Photo by Linda Lungren.)

Language-Experience Method

One of the most effective methods of teaching reading to bilingual speakers is the language-experience method because it elicits language from the child. The teacher or the child, when able, transcribes the oral language, and the child *reads* what he or she has spoken.

All children bring to school many language skills: listening, comprehension, and speaking. The tasks of the reading teacher are to help children develop those skills further and to teach them the graphemes representing the language that they already understand. Developmentally, all children learn to listen and to speak before they learn to read and to write. It is clear that oral language conveys meaning if the speaker and listener share the same set of oral symbols for objects and relationships in their experience. The reading teacher must remember that oral language is the base of the reading process and, until it is developed, reading seems a senseless, futile exercise for the child.

ADAPTING THE LANGUAGE-EXPERIENCE METHOD FOR BILINGUAL STUDENTS

1. Use simple stories and poems for listening exercises and as language models.
2. Provide opportunities for firsthand experiences—outings to the country or city, museums, zoos, and bus or train rides.
3. Have children make phrase books by drawing a picture and writing a short caption beneath it. Young children can dictate their story to you and you can write their words under the picture.
4. Provide model sentences individually or on the board or a large chart.

Today we visited ______________________________.
We saw ______________________________.
My favorite animal was ______________________________.
We traveled by ______________________________.

You may ask, "How do I implement a language experience method for ESL children when they have limited English?" The following lesson presents a language-experience approach with primary-grade children who are not proficient in speaking English.

LESSON PLAN

Topic and Group

The following is a Halloween language experience lesson, designed to introduce new vocabulary words about Halloween to a full-time ESL primary class in which children have different oral and written language skills.

Objectives

A. Classroom objective
The teacher introduces the children to the theme of Halloween, emphasing Halloween vocabulary.
B. Behavioral objective
After being introduced to the vocabulary associated with Halloween, each child will be able to read at least two words related to Halloween that have been added to their word bank, and each child will correctly identify in context the word Halloween and any other word(s) of his or her choice.

Diagnosis

Teacher Observation

The fall season has arrived, and the teacher heard children talking about an American holiday known as "Halloween." He observes the limited descriptive vocabulary being utilized by the children. Halloween books and pictures are then placed around the room to stimulate Halloween vocabulary development.

Strategies

The theme of Halloween is introduced by the teacher as he or she reads a Halloween picture book to the entire class. An experience chart is written by the teacher and dictated by the children. The teacher elicits responses by asking questions such as the following:

What do children do on Halloween? What will you dress up as for Halloween? What will you wear? What do you say when someone answers the door? What are some things we have to be careful of on Halloween?

Each child who is able dictates a word or phrase for the chart. The chart resembles the following:

Things That Remind Us of Halloween

Jaime: scary
Wolfgang: monsters
Cullen: costumes
Denny: candy
Soo-Lin: parties
Pilar: trick-or-treat
Tommy: cold
Nicole: pumpkins
Johanna: excited

Each child is given a word card with Halloween written on it. The children are given a piece of drawing paper to illustrate whatever they like best about Halloween. While the children are drawing, the teacher individually helps each child write another word card of his or her choice for the word bank. The more advanced readers could write several of their own word cards.

When each child finishes his or her drawing, the child will label it or be helped in labeling by dictating to the teacher a descriptive word, phrase, sentence, or several sentences.

Program. In designing and planning your program for young children, it is important to review the designs of other programs. O'Brien recommends the following program.

A SUGGESTED PROGRAM FOR EARLY PRIMARY LEVELS

Structural Activities	Semistructured Activities	Unstructured Activities
Large group Planning time: teacher-directed discussion of 1. Plans for the day 2. Classroom goals 3. Preparation for class projects, field trips, social activities, etc. 4. Classroom rules and regulations 5. Housekeeping task assignments	*Large group* Total class working on such projects as 1. Social living unit activities (charts, displays, talking murals, bulletin boards, indoor/outdoor construction projects, experience charts) 2. Science activities (collections, labeled displays, experience charts, records of experiments, indoor/outdoor gardens, science word dictionaries or files) 3. A classroom newspaper or news sheet 4. Literary experiences, story reading, story telling, poetry, recordings, creative writing 5. Creative dramatics	*Large group* Sharing time period provided for 1. Show and tell experience 2. Reporting on individual or group activities 3. Showing art work, reading creative stories, poems. Library period set aside for independent reading or "picture reading" and listening to "talking books," etc. Demonstration period provided for 1. Creative dramatic presentation 2. Puppet shows 3. Individual talent opportunity 4. Choral reading
Small group Ability group instruction in beginning language and reading: 1. Oral language 2. Vocabulary building 3. Visual and auditory skill-building activities 4. Concept building 5. Language experience activity	*Small group* Groups "cycled" through learning centers for specific learning experiences: 1. Library center 2. Listening-viewing station 3. Reading skills center (games and manipulative devices) 4. Creative writing center 5. Science center	*Small group* Clusters of children involved in cooperative work or play activity
Individual Teacher-directed individual learning experiences such as 1. Programmed instruction in silent reading and perceptual skill development 2. Teacher-constructed tapes and worksheets	*Individual* Individuals assigned to learning centers for specific learning experiences	*Individual* Free-choice activity in learning center Playhouse area, toy or game area, art or crafts area Individual-choice work tasks related to plans of the day

C. O'Brien, *Teaching the Language Different Child to Read* (Columbus, Ohio: Charles E. Merrill Publishing Company, 1973), p. 57. Reprinted by permission.

READING INSTRUCTION IN THE NATIVE LANGUAGE

All children bring to school many language skills. The task of the reading teacher is to help children develop these skills further and to teach them the visual appearance of the language that they already understand. Developmentally, all children learn to listen and to speak before learning to read and write. It is clear that oral language conveys meaning if the speaker and listener share the same set of oral symbols for objects and relationships in their experience. The reading teacher must remember that *oral language is the base of the reading process*, and until it is developed, reading seems a senseless, futile exercise for the child. Many reading programs being developed for bilingual students take this fact into account. Children are first taught to read their native language while doing oral work in the second language. When the oral base in the second language is strong enough, reading is introduced in that language. As early as 1953, many authors concluded that this was the most logical sequence of learning to read and write; they cited studies showing that students who first learned to read in the vernacular made better progress even in the second language reading programs than did students who had spent the same length of time working only on second language reading.

Native Literacy Methodologies in Spanish

Thonis (1976) discusses some traditional methods used to teach reading in Spanish to Spanish-speaking students. These methods mirror many of the approaches used to teach reading in English. The six most frequently used methods are

1. *El método onomatopoético.* This method aims at constant auditory associations of letters and sounds, based on children's experiences. For example, the vowel sound /i/ is the same sound as the squeal of the mouse—"iii."
2. *El método alfabético.* Children are taught the names of letters of the alphabet. Instruction begins with vowel letters. One sound is joined to another: ma - no.
3. *El método fónico o fonética.* This method emphasizes the sounds of the letters of the alphabet with little concern for the names of the letters.
4. *El método de palabras generadoras.* This is a whole-word method.
5. *El método global.* This is a method of teaching both reading and writing using whole words without doing any analysis of component elements, syllables, or letters.
6. *El método ecléctico.* This is a method in which phonics and whole-word strategies are used.

Teaching Individual Words

The question often arises: "If I begin to teach individual words, which words should I teach first?" An obvious answer is to teach the words that appear most frequently in English. The following word list, supplied by the *Heritage Dictionary*, provides us with useful information about word frequency in English. This list may help you in some of the following ways:

1. As a diagnostic instrument for determining an appriate starting point for instruction.
2. As a source for the selection of new words.
3. As a reinforcement strategy, using flashcards.

Heritage List

WORD FREQUENCY

1. English has a distinctive word frequency distribution.
2. Ten per cent of all the words written and printed in books, magazines, and newspapers for children and for adults are *the* and *of*.
3. Ten per cent of all the words written and read are *the*, *of*, *and*, *to*, *a*, and *in*.

BASIS OF THE HERITAGE LIST

1. The *Heritage Dictionary* used a computer to find the separate word forms and their frequencies in over a million words selected from the most technical adult material in all fields.
2. The *Heritage Dictionary* used a computer to find the relative frequency of 86,761 words in 5,088,721 running words, carefully selected from 1,045 textbooks most often used in grades three through nine.

HERITAGE LIST OF SERVICE WORDS

the
of 10%
and
a
to
in
is 20%
you
that
it
he
for
was
on
are
as
with
his
they
at 30%
be
this
from
I
have
or
by
one
had
not
but 35%
what
all
were
when
we
there
can
an
your
which
their
said
if
do
will
each
about 40%
them
then
she
many
some
so
these
would
other
into
has
more
her
two
like
him
see
time
could
no 45%
make
than
first
been
its
who
now
people
my
made
over
did
back
much
before
go
good
new 50%
write
our
used
me
man
too
any
day
same
right
look
think
also
around
another
came
come
work
three
word
must
because
does
part
even
place
small
every
found
still
between
name
should
Mr.
home
big
give
air
line
set 55%
own
under
read
last
never
us
left
end
along
while
might
next
sound
below
saw
something
thought
form
food
keep
children
feet
land
side
without
boy
once
animals
life
enough
took
sometimes
four
head
above
kind
began
almost
live
page
got
earth
need
far
hand
high
year
mother
light
how
up
out
ever
paper
hard
near
sentence
better
best
across
during
today
others
however 60%
sure
means
knew
it's
try
told
young
miles
sun
ways
thing
whole
hear
example
heard
several
change
answer
down
only
way
find
use
may
water
long
little
very
after
words
called
just
where
most
know
get
through
trees
I'm
lady
upon
family
later
turn
move
face
door
cut
done
group
true
half
sentences
red
fish
plants
living
wanted
black
eat
short
United States
run
kinds
book
gave
order
well
such
here
take
why
things
help
put

- years
- different
- away
- again
- off
- went
- old
- number
- great
- tell
- men
- brought
- close
- nothing
- though
- started
- idea
- call
- lived
- makes
- became
- looking
- add
- become
- grow
- draw
- yet
- hands
- less
- John
- wind
- places
- behind
- cannot
- letter
- among
- 4
- A
- letters
- comes
- able
- both
- few
- those
- always
- looked
- show
- large
- often
- together
- asked
- house
- don't
- world
- going

- want
- school
- important
- until
- 1
- hot
- anything
- held
- state
- list
- stood
- hundred
- shows
- tea
- fast
- seemed
- felt
- kept
- America
- notice
- can't
- strong
- voice
- probably
- needed
- birds 65%

- area
- horse
- Indians
- sounds
- matter
- stand
- box
- start
- that's
- parts
- country
- father
- let
- night
- following
- 2
- picture
- being
- study
- second
- eyes
- soon
- times
- story
- boys
- since
- white
- days
- road

- questions
- blue
- meaning
- coming
- instead
- either
- held
- friends
- already
- warm
- taken
- gone
- finally
- summer
- understand
- moon
- animal
- mind
- outside
- power
- says
- problem
- longer
- winter
- Indian
- deep
- mountains
- heavy
- carefully
- room
- sea
- against
- top
- turned
- 3
- learn
- point
- city
- play
- toward
- live
- using
- himself
- usually
- money
- seen
- didn't
- car
- morning
- given
- ship
- themselves
- begin
- fact
- third

- quite
- carry
- goes
- distance
- although
- added
- doing
- sat
- pictures
- possible
- names
- heart
- having
- writing
- real
- simple
- snow
- getting
- rain
- suddenly
- easy
- leaves
- lay
- open
- ground
- lines
- cold
- really
- table
- remember
- tree
- 000
- course
- front
- known
- American
- space
- inside
- ago
- making
- Mrs.
- early
- I'll
- learned
- let's
- least
- problems
- followed
- books
- tiny
- hour
- B
- happened
- foot
- plant

- moving
- care
- low
- else
- gold
- build
- glass
- rock
- tail
- covered
- alone
- reached
- bottom
- walk
- forms
- takes
- check
- dog
- shown
- mean
- English
- rest
- perhaps
- certain
- six
- feel
- fire
- ready
- green
- yes
- built
- special
- ran
- full
- town
- complete
- oh
- person
- Tom
- energy
- week
- explain
- passed
- lost
- spring
- travel
- wrote
- cities
- farm
- circle
- cried
- whose
- bed
- working
- measure

straight
base
mountain
caught
hair
bird
per
wood
running
color
South
class
piece
slowly
surface
river
numbers
common
stop
am
talk
quickly
whether
fine
5
round
dark
glide
past
ball
girl
tried
rather
length
looks
speed
machine
information
except
figure
you're
minutes
free
fell
suppose
natural
ocean
government
lives
trying
horses
the
s
baby
taking
grass
plane
pieces 70%
sides
pulled
follow
beautiful
beginning
moved
everyone
leave
everything
game
system
bring
watch
shall
dry
hours
written
10
stopped
within
floor
Bill
ice
soil
human
trip
woman
eye
milk
choose
north
discovered
houses
seven
easily
famous
pages
late
rocks
flowers
pay
sleep
iron
trouble
store
beside
oil
modern
filled
fun
catch
size
wild
weather
Mother
Miss
carried
pattern
sky
walked
6
main
someone
ones
center
named
field
stay
itself
worked
boat
building
question
wide
village
object
stain
placed
Joe
age
minute
wall
b
meet
record
copy
forest
River
months
especially
dogs
necessary
lower
smaller
he's
unit
flat
7
direction
south
reading
fall
poor
map
scientists
friend
c
language
job
points
music
buy
window
mark
ideas
heat
grow
listen
ask
changes
single
French
clear
material
talking
isn't
thousand
sign
examples
guess
begins
forward
huge
needs
closed
ride
region
largest
answers
nor
period
finished
blood
rich
team
waves
corner
Mary
eat
groups
war
members
fly
yourself
decided
seem
thus
logs
nearly
square
England
moment
North
teacher
happy
changed
products
C
bright
sent
present
plan
played
island
standing
there's
we'll
opposite
barn
sense
cattle
million
anyone
rule
science
helps
farmers
afraid
women
produce
pull
son
meant
broken
interest
ends
woods
Henry
8
inches
street
George
couldn't
reason
difference
tells
maybe
larger
history
mouth
middle
step
thousands
steps
cars
child
opened

thinking
strange
eggs
wish
position
hear
hope
song

missing
France
heard
playing
control
spread
knows
evening
brown
picked
clean
wouldn't
section
spent
Dan
ring
higher
raised
9
weeks
teeth
growing
business
countries
helped
gives
exactly
Jim
King
reach
lot
won't
answered
case
speak
shape
eight
edge
seems
soft
interesting
watched
formed
stories
works
busy

pounds
beyond
seeds
Bob
produced
fingers
send
100
love
materials
cool
laughed
cause
man's
stands
feeling
facts
please
meat
lady
west
glad
British
action
subject
skin
wasn't
I've
Europe
New York
yellow
ships
arms
party
force
test
bad
temperature
pair
ahead
wrong
practice
sand
tail
wait
difficult
general
cover
areas
walls
Africa
showed
safe
grown
cost

wear
act
wings
Paul
bat
arm
believe
major
becomes
gray
died
bones
sitting
wonder
include
interested
describe
electric
sold
visit
15
sheep
I'd
waiting
shoes
30
office
amount
liked
garden
led
note
various
race
developed
bit
clothes
uses
result
greater
fields
New
brother
addition
doesn't
states
dead
weight
thin
stone
hit
wife
contains
row
contain

objects
fit
students
turns
clouds
equal
War
value
yard
Americans
beat
inch
walking
sugar
key
product
desert
bank
farther
won
total
wall
wire
rose
cotton
moves
spoke
rope
rules
four
chance
homes
thick
sight
pretty
12
train
sets
fresh
faster
Washington
drive
lead
break
sit
bought
hundreds
radio
method
gets
king
similar
return
corn
decide

shore
throughout
compare
Sam
dollars
quiet
ancient
Jack
stick
afternoon
silver
nose
century
saying
therefore
flying
level
you'll
death
hole
coast
directions
cross
sharp
fight
capital
Old
fill
deal
patterns
divided
greatest
happens
pass
20
returned
adding
ears
soldiers
type
attention
shouted
gas
World
actually
kitchen
alike
pick
scale
basic
West
President
Uncle
Johnny
happen 75%

EVALUATION

In evaluating a program, it is necessary to examine the difficulty and effectiveness of the materials, as well as the progress of each student.

Difficulty of Materials

In addition to the readability formulas presented in Chapter 12, Spaulding (1956) created a readability instrument to be used for assessing the reading difficulty level of materials written in Spanish. He suggests the following for the selection of a sample of content.

1. In long selections, analyze samples of 100 words every ten pages.
2. In shorter selections, analyze samples of 500 words every 1,000 words.
3. In selections of 500 words or less, analyze the entire passage.

PROCEDURES

1. Count the number of words in the sample.
2. Count the number of sentences.
3. Divide the number of words by the number of sentences. Result is average sentence length.
4. Check the words against the accompanying Buchanan and Rodriguez Bou Word List and count the number of words not on the list.
5. Divide the number of words not on the list by the number of words in the sample. The result is the density or complexity of the vocabulary.
6. Using the table, find the number that corresponds to the density.
7. Find the number that corresponds to the average sentence length.
8. Draw a line to connect the two points of density and average sentence length.
9. The point at which the two lines intersect the central column represents the relative difficulty of the sample.

The Index of Reading Difficulty ranges from 20 to 160 and can be divided as follows:

20–40	Primer level		
40–60	Very easy	40-	Grade 1
		50-	Grade 2
		60-	Grade 3
60–80	Easy	60-	Grade 4
		70-	Grade 5
		80-	Grade 6
80–100	Relatively Easy		Grades 6, 7, 8
100–120	Difficult		Grades 8, 9, 10
120–160	Very difficult		Grades 11, 12, and above

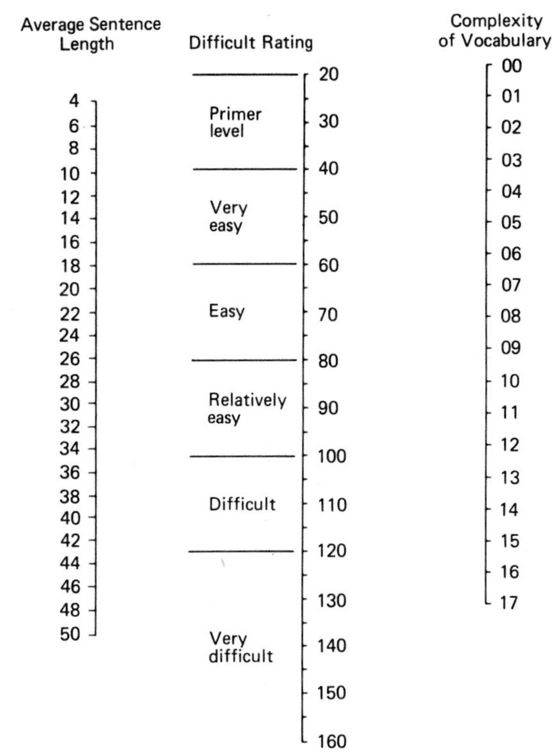

The following word list of Spanish words with their English equivalents has been included for two reasons: it is an essential part of the Spaulding formula, and it will provide teachers who decide to begin instruction in Spanish with the basis of their word program. Before moving on to more difficult words, teachers should be certain that their children can read the words in this list.

BUCHANAN AND RODRIGUEZ BOU WORD LIST (1)

asombrar - to astonish
aspecto - aspect
aspirar - to aspire
asunto - subject
atar - to tie
atención - attention
atender - to attend
atento - attentive
atrás - behind
atrevesar - to go through
atreverse - to dare
aumentar - to increase
aun, aún - even, still
aunque - although
ausencia - absence
autor - author
autoridad - authority
auxilio - help
avanzar - to advance
ave - bird
aventura - adventure
avisar - to notify
ay - alas!
ayer - yesterday
ayudar - to help
azúcar - sugar
azul - blue

bailar - to dance
bajar - to lower
bajo - low
balcón - balcony
bañar - to bathe
barba - beard
base - base
bastante - enough
bastar - to suffice
batalla - battle
batir - to shake
beber - to drink
belleza - beauty
bello - beautiful
bendecir - to bless
bendito - blessed
besar - to kiss
beso - a kiss
bestia - beast
bien (s., adv)* well
blanco - white
blando - soft
boca - mouth
boda - wedding
bondad - goodness
bonito (adj.) - pretty
bosque - forest
bravo - brave
brazo - arm
breve - brief
brillante - brillant
brillar - to shine
buen(-o) - good
burla - mockery
burlar - to ridicule
buscar - to seek

caballero - gentleman
caballo - horse
cabello - hair
caber - to go in or into
cabeza - head
cabo - cape
cada - every, each
cadena - chain
caer - to fall
café - coffee
caida - fall, tumble
caja - box
c(u)alidad - quality
calma - calmness
calor - heat
callar - to keep silent
calle - street
cama - bed
cambiar - to change
cambio - change, barter
caminar - to walk
camino - path, road
campaña - bell
campana - campaign
campo - country, field
cansar - to tire out
cantar - to sing
cantidad - quantity
canto - I sing
capa - cape
capaz - capable
capital - capital
capitán - captain
capítulo - chapter
cara - face
carácter - character
cárcel - jail
cargar - to carry
cargo - burden
caridad - charity
cariño - affection
carne - meat
carrera - career
carro - car
carta - letter
casa - house
casar - to marry
casi - almost
caso - case, event
castellano - Castilian
castigar - to castigate
castigo - punishment
causa - cause
causar - to cause
ceder - cede, to yield
celebrar - to celebrate
celebre - famous
centro - center
ceñir - to surround
cerca - near
cercano - neighboring
cerebro - brain
cerrar - to close
cesar - to cease
ciego - blind
cielo - sky
ciencia - science
cierto (-amente) certain, true
circunstancia - circumstance
citar - to convoke
ciudad - city
civil - civil
claridad - clarity
claro - clear
clase - class
clavar - to nail
cobrar - to collect
cocer - to sew
coche - coach
coger - to catch
cólera - anger
colgar - to have
colocar - to arrange
color - color
columna - column
combatir - to combat
comedia - comedy
comenzar - to begin
comer - to eat
cometer - to commit
comida - food
como, cómo - how, as, like
compañero - companion
compañía - company
comparar - to compare
complacer - to please
completo - complete
componer - to compose
comprar - to buy
comprender - to understand
común - common
comunicar - to communicate
con - with
concebir - to conceive
conceder - to concede
concepto - concept
conciencia - conscience
concluir - to conclude
conde - count
condenar - to condemn
condesa - countess
condición - condition
conducir - to conduce
conducta - conduct
confesar - confess
confianza - confidence
confiar - confide
conforme - in agreement
confundir - confuse
confusión - confusion
confuso - confused
conjunto - joined
conmigo - with me
conmover - affect
conocer - to know
conocimiento - knowledge
conque - condition
conquista - conquest
consagrar - to consecrate
consecuencia - consequence
conseguir - to obtain
consejo - advice
consentir - to allow
conservar - to conserve
considerar - to consider
consigo - with him
consistir - to consist
constante - constantly
constituir - to constitute
construir - to contract
consuelo - consolation
consumir - to consume
contar - to count
contemplar - contemplate
contener - to contain
contento - glad
contestar - to answer
contigo - with you
continuar - to continue
continuo - continuous
contra - against
contrario - contrary
contribuir - to contribute
convencer - to convince
convenir - to convene
conversación - conversation
convertir - to convert
convidar - to invite
copa - cup
corazón - heart
corona - crown
correr - to run
corresponder - to correspond
corriente - current
cortar - to cut
corte - court
corto - short
cosa - thing
costa - coast
costar - to cost
costumbre - custom
crear - to create
crecer - to grow
creer - to believe
criado - bred, raised
criar - to raise
criatura - child
cristal - glass
cristiano - Christian
cruel - cruel
cruz - cross
cruzar - to cross
cuadro - picture
cual, cuál - which, which one
cuando - since
cuándo - when
cuanto, cuánto - how much - as much as
cuarto (s.) - room
cubrir - to cover

cuello - neck
cuenta - account
cuento - story
cuerpo - body
cuestión - dispute
cuidado - care
cuidar - to take care of
culpa - blame
culto - cult
cumbre - top
cumplir - to fulfill
cura - cure
curiosidad - curiosity
curioso - curious
curso - course
chico - boy

dama - lady
daño - harm
dar - to give
de - prep. of, from
debajo - under
deber - to owe
débil - weak
decidir - decide
decir - to say
declarar - to declare
dedicar - dedicate
dedo - finger
defecto - defect
defender - to defend
defensa - defense
dejar - to leave
del - of the
delante - in front of
delicado - delicate
demás - others
demasiado - too much
demonio - demon
demonstrar - to demonstrate
dentro - inside
derecho (-a) - the right to
derramar - to spill
desaparecer - to disappear
descansar - to rest
desconocer - not to know
describir - to describe
descubrir - to discover
desde - since
desear - to desire
deseo - wish
desesperar - to become desperate
desgracia - disgrace
desgraciado - unfortunate
deshacer - to undo
desierto - desert, deserted
despedir - to emit
despertar - to awaken
despreciar - to scorn
después - after
destinar - to destine
destino - destiny
destruir - to destroy
detener - to detain
determinar - to determine
detrás - in back of
día - day
diablo - devil
diario - diary
dicha - luck
dicho (s.) - saying
diente - tooth
diferencia - difference
diferente - different
difícil - difficult
dificultad - difficulty
difunto - dead
digno - worthy
dinero - money
dios - God
dirección-direction
directo - direct
dirigir - to direct
dischoso - lucky
discreto - discrete
discurrir - to contrive
discurso - discourse
disgusto - displeasure
disponer - to dispose
disposición - disposition
distancia - distance
distinguir - to distinguish
distinto - distinct
diverso - diverse
divertir - to divert
dividir - to divide
divino - divine
doblar - to fold
doble - fold
doctor - doctor
dolor - pain
dominar - dominate
don, D. - Mr.
donde, done - wherever, where
doña, Da. - Mrs.
dormir - to sleep
drama - drama
duda - doubt
dudar - to doubt
dueño - owner
dulce - candy, sweet
dulzura - sweetness
durante - during
durar - to last
duro - hard

echar - to throw
edad - age
edificio - building
educación - education
efecto - effect
ejecutar - to execute
ejemplo - example
ejercer - to execute
ejército - army
el, él - he, the
elegir - to elect
elemento - element
elevar - to elevate
ella - she
emoción — emotion
empensar - to pawn
empezar - to begin
emplear - to employ
emprender - to undertake
empresa - enterprise
en - in
enamorar - to make love to
encantador - enchanting
encanto - enchantment
encargar - to order
encender - to light
encerrar - to enclose
encima - on top
encontrar - to find
encuentro - encounter
enemigo - enemy
energia - energy
enfermedad - sickness
enfermo - sick
engañar - to fool
engaño - deception
enojo - anger
enorme - large
enseñanza - teaching
enseñar - to teach
entender - to understand
enterrar - to bury
entero - complete
entonces - then
entrada - entrance
entrar - to enter
entre - between
entregar - to turn in
entusiasmo - enthusiasm
enviar - to send
envolver - to enfold
época - era
error - error, mistake
escapar - to escape
escaso - scarce
escena - scene
escalvo - slave
escoger - to select
esconder - to hide
escribir - to write
escritor - writer
escuchar - to listen
escuela - school
ese, ése - that, that one
esfuerzo - spirit, vigor
eso - that
espacio - space
espada - spear
espalda - back, shoulders
español - Spanish
esparcir - to scatter
especial - special
especie - kind
espejo - mirror
esperanza - hope
esperar - to wait
espeso - thick
espíritu - spirit
esposo - husband
establecer - to establish
estado - state
estar - to be
estatua - statue
este, éste - this, this one
estilo - style
estimar - to estimate
estrecho - narrow
estrella - star
estudiar - to study
estudio - studio
eterno - eternal
evitar - to avoid
exacto - exact
examinar - to examine
excelente - excellent
exclamar - to exclaim
exigir - demand
existencia - existence
existir - to exist
experiencia - experience
experimentar - to experiment
explicar - to explain
exponer - to expose
expresar - to express
expresión - expression
extender - to extend
extensión - extension
extranjero - foreigner
extrañar - to banish
extrano - strange
extraordinario - extraordinary
extremo - extreme

fácil - easy
facultad - faculty
falda - skirt
falso - false
falta - lack
fama - fame
familia - family
famoso - famous
fantasía - fantasy
favor - a favor
favorecer - to favor
fe - faith
felicidad - happiness
feliz - happy
fenómeno - phenomenon
feo - ugly
fiar - to bail
fiel - faithful
fiesta - party
figura - figure
figurar - to figure
fijar - to make firm
fijo - firm
fin - end
final - final
fingir - to fake
fino - fine
firme - firm
físico - physical
flor - flower
fondo - fund
forma - form
formar - to form

formidable - formidable
fortuna - fortune
francés - French
franco - Frank
frase - phrase
frecuente - frequently
frente - front
fresco - fresh
frío - cold
fruto - fruit
fuego - fire
fuente - fountain
fuera - outside
fuerte - strong
fuerza - strength
función - function
fundar - to raise
futuro - future

galán - courtier
gana - desire
ganar - to win
gastar - to spend
gato - cat
general - general
género - class, kind
generoso - generous
genio - genius
gente - people
gesto - gesture
gitano - gypsy
gloria - glory
glorioso - glorious
gobernar - to govern
gobierno - government
golpe - stroke, hit
gota - drop
gozar - to enjoy
gracia - grace
gracioso - funny
grado - grade
gran(-de) — grand, big
grandeza - grandeur
grave - ponderous
griego - Greek
gritar - to scream
grito - shriek
grupo - group
guapo - handsome
guardar - to keep
guerra - war
guiar - to drive
gustar - to like
gusto - taste

haber - to have
habitación - residence
habitar - to dwell
*habiar
hacer - to do
hacia - toward
hacienda - estate
hallar - to find
hambre - hunger
harto - satiated
hasta - until
he aquí - here is
hecho (s.) - made or done
helar - to freeze
herida - wound
herir - to wound
hermano - brother
hermoso - handsome
hermosura - beauty
hervir - to boil
hierro - iron
hijo - son
hilo - thread
historia - history
hogar - home
hoja - leaf
hombre - man
hombro - shoulder
hondo - deep
honor - honor
honra - reverence
honrar - to honor
hora - hour
horrible - horrible
horror - horror
hoy - today
huerta - irrigated land
hueso - bone
huevo - egg
huir - to escape
humanidad - humanity
humano - human
humo - smoke
hundir - to submerge

idea - idea
ideal - ideal
idioma - language
iglesia - church
ignorar - ignore
igual - equal
iluminar - illuminate
ilusión - illusion
ilustre - illustration
imagen - image
imaginación - imagination
imaginar - to imagine
imitar - to imitate
impedir - to hinder
imperio - empire
imponer - to impose
importancia - importance
importante - important
importar - to matter
imposible - impossible
impresión - impression
impreso - printed matter
imprimir - to print
impulse - impulse
inclinar - incline
indicar - indicate
indiferente - indifferent
individuo - individual
industria - industry
infeliz - unhappy
infierno - hell
infinito - infinite
influencia - influence
ingenio - inventive
inglés - English
inmediato - immediate
inmenso - immense
inocente - innocent
inquieto - restless
inspirar - to inspire
instante - instant
instrumento - instrument
inteligencia - intelligence
intención - intention
intentar - to intend
interés - interest
interesante - interesting
interesar - to interest
interior - interior
interrumpir - to interrupt
íntimo - intimate
introducir - to introduce
inútil - useless
invierno - winter
ir (-se) - go, to go
ira - wrath
isla - island
izquierdo - left
jamás - never
jardín - garden
jefe - chief
joven - young
juego - game
juez - judge
jugar - to play
juicio - judgment
juntar - to join, connect
junto - together
jurar - promise
justicia - justice
justo - just
juventud - youth
juzgar - to judge

la - fem. the
labio - lip
labor - work
labrador - farmer
lado - side
ladrón - thief
lágrima - tear
lanza - lance
lanzar - to throw
largo - long
lástima - pity
lavar - to wash
lazo - bow
lector - reader
lecho - bed, couch
leer - to read
legua - league
lejano - distant
lejos - far
lengua - tongue
lento - slow
letra - letter
levantar - to lift
leve - of little weight
ley - law
libertad - liberty
librar - to set free
libre - free
libro - book
ligero - fast
limitar - to limit
límite - limit
limpio - clean
lindo - pretty
línea - line
líquido - liquid
lo - art. neut., the
loco - crazy
locura - insanity
lograr - to gain
lucha - struggle
luchar - to struggle
luego - later on
lugar - place
luna - moon
luz - light
llama - call
llamar - to call
llano - even
llanto - flood of tears
llave - key
llegar - to arrive
llenar - to fill
lleno - full
llevar - to take
llorar - to cry

madre - mother
maestro - teacher
magnifico - magnificent
majestad - majesty
mal (-o)—adj., bad, badness s. o adv.
mandar - to command
manera - manner
manifestar - manifest
mano - hand
mantener - maintain
mañana - tomorrow
máquina - machine
mar - sea
maravilla - wonder
marcar - to mark
marchar - to march
marido - husband
mas, más - more, conj. but
masa - dough
matar - to kill
materia - matter
material - material
matrimonio - matrimony
mayor - greatest
†me
médico - doctor
medida - measure
medio - half
medir - to measure
mejor - better

*Habiar: word misspelled or does not exist.

†me = first person, personal pronoun; dative, accusative, and reflexive of Yo.

mejorar - to improve
memoria - memory
menester - need, want
menos - less
mentir - to lie
mentira - a lie
menudo - small
merced - mercy
merecer - to deserve
mérito - merit
mes - month
mesa - table
meter - to put in
mezcla - mixture
*mi, mí
miedo - fear
mientras - while
militar - military
ministro - minister
minuto - minute
mio - mine
mirada - glance
mirar (v.) to look
misa - mass
miserable - miserable
miseria - misery
mismo - same
misterio - mystery
misterioso - mysterious
mitad - half
moderno - modern
modesto - modest
modo - mode
molestar - molest
momento - moment
montaña - mountain
montar - mount
monte - mountain
moral - moral
morir - to die
mortal - mortal
mostrar - to show
motivo - motive
mover - move
movimiento - movement
mozo - young man
muchacho - boy
mucho - much
mudar - move
muerte - death
mundo - world
murmurar - murmur
música - music

muy - very

nacer - to be born
nación - nation
nacional - national
nada - nothing
nadie - no one
natural - natural
naturaleza - nature
necesario - necessary
necesidad - necessity
necesitar - to need
necio - stupid
negar - to deny
negocio - business
negro - black
ni - neither, nor
ninguno - none
niño - boy
no - no
noble - noble
noche - night
nombrar - to name
nombre - name
norte - north
nota - grade, mark
notable - notable
notar - to note
noticia - news
novio - bridegroom
nube - cloud
nuevo - new
número - number
numeroso - numerous
nunca - never

obedecer - obey
objeto - object
obligación - obligation
obligar - obligate
obra - work
obscuridad - obscurity
obscuro - obscure
observación - observation
observer - observe
obtener - obtain
ocasión - occasion
ocultar - conceal
oculto - hidden
ocupación - occupation
ocupar - occupy
ocurrir - occur
odio - hatred

ofender - to offend
oficial - official
oficio - occupation
ofrecer - offer
oído - ear
oír - to hear
ojo - eye
olor - odor
olvidar - to forget
opinión - opinion
oponer - to oppose
oración - prayer
orden - order
ordenar - to order
ordinario - ordinary
oreja - ear
orgullo - pride
orígen - origin
orilla - shore
oro - gold
otro - other

paciencia - patience
padecer - to suffer
padre - father
pagar - to pay
página - page
país - country
pájaro - bird
palabra - word
palacio - palace
pan - bread
papel - paper
par - pair
para - for
parar - to stop
parecer (v.) - to seem
pared - wall
parte - part
particular - particular
partida - departure
partido - party
partir - to depart
pasado - past
pasar - to pass
pasear - to take a walk
paseo - stroll
pasión - passion
paso - pace, step
patria - native country
paz - peace
pecado - sin
pecho - chest

pedazo - piece
pedir - to ask
pegar - to stick
peligro - danger
peligroso - dangerous
pelo - hair
pena - penalty, pain
penetrar - penetrate
pensamiento - thought
pensar - to think
peor - worse
pequeño - small
perder - to lose
perdón - pardon
perdonar - to forgive
perfecto - perfect
periódico - newspaper
permanecer - to stay
permitir - to permit
pero - but
perro - dog
perseguir - to follow
persona - person
personaje - character
personal - personal
pertenecer - to pertain
pesar (v. o s.) - to weigh, or cause regret
peseta - coin
peso - weight, dollar
picar - to prick, pierce
pico - beak
pie - foot
piedad - piety
peidra - rock
piel - skin
pieza - piece
pintar - to paint
pisar - to step on
placer - pleasure
planta - plant
plata - silver
plato - dish
plaza - market
pluma - pen
población - population
pobre - poor
poco - scanty
poder (v. or s.) to be able, power
poderoso - powerful
poeta - poet

política - politics
político - political
polvo - dust
poner - to put
poquito - a little bit
por - prep. by, for
porque - because
por qué - why
porvenir - time to come
poseer - to possess
posesión - possession
posible - possible
posición - position
precio - price
precioso - precious
preciso - precise
preferir - prefer
pregunta - question
preguntar - to ask
premio - prize
prenda - piece of jewelry
prender - to turn on
preparar - to prepare
presencia - presence
presentar - to present
presente - present
presidente - president
prestar - lend
pretender - to pretend
primero - first
primo - cousin
principal - principal
príncipe - prince
principio - principle, beginning
prisa - in a hurry
privar - to deprive
probar - to try
proceder - proceed
procurar - ask for
producir - produce
profundo - profound
prometer - promise
pronto - soon
pronunciar - pronounce
propiedad - property
propio - own
propener - propose
proporción - proportion
proporcionar - to proportion
propósito - purpose

*mi, mí: mi = singular possessive pronoun, my; mí = personal pronoun, oblique case of pronoun Yo, used after preposition.

proseguir - to pursue
protestar - to protest
provìncia - province
próximo - next
prueba - proof
publicar - to publish
público - public
pueblo - town
puerta - door
puerto - port
pues - conj. because
punta - point
punto - dot, period
puro - pure

que, qué - that - what?
quedar (-se) - to stay
queja - complaint
quejarse - to complain
quemar - to burn
querer - to love
querido - loved one
quien, quién - who who?
quienquiera - whoever
quitar - to take away
quizá, quiza(s) - maybe perhaps

rama - branch
rápido - fast
raro - strange
rato - a while
rayo - ray
raza - race
razón - reason
real - real
realidad - reality
realizar - realize
recibir - receive
recién - recent
reciente - recently
reclamar - reclaim
recoger - pick up
reconocer - to know
recordar - remember
recorrer - to go over
recuerdo - remembrance
reducir - reduce
referir - refer
regalar - give away
región - region
regla - rule
reina - queen
reinar - to rule
reino - kingdom
reir - to laugh
relación - relation
relativo - relative
religión - religion
religioso - religious
remedio - remedy
remoto - remote
rendir - subdue
reñir - quarrel
reparar - to repair
repartir - to divide
repetir - to repeat
replicar - to reply
reposar - to rest
reposo - repose
representar - to represent
república - republic
resistir - to resist
resolución - resolution
resolver - resolve
*respe(c)tar
†respe(c)to
respirar - to breathe
responder - to respond
respuesta - answer
resto - rest
resultado - result
resultar - to result
retirar - to retire
retrato - picture
reunión - meeting
reunir - to meet
revolver - to resolve
rey - king
rico - rich
ridículo - ridiculous
riesgo - risk
rigor - rigor
rincón - corner
río - river
riqueza - richness
risa - laughter
robar - to steal
rodar - to move
rodear - to surround
rodilla - knee
rogar - to plead
rojo - red
romper - to break
ropa - clothes
rosa - rose
rostro - face
rubio - blond
rueda - wheel
ruido - noise
ruina - ruins
rumor - rumor

saber (v.) - to know
sabio - wise
sacar - to take out
sacerdote - priest
sacrificio - sacrifice
sacudir - to shake
sagrado - sacred
sal - salt
sala - living room
salida - exit
salir - to go out
saltar - to leap
salud - health
saludar - to greet
salvar - to save
sangre - blood
sano - healthy
santo - saint
satisfacer - satisfy
satisfecho - satisfied
se - to know
seco - dry
secreto - secret
seguida - continued, successive
seguir - to follow
según - according to
segundo - second
seguridad - security

triunfo - triumph
tropezar - stumble
**tu, tu
turbar - confuse

ultimo - last
††un, uno (-a)
único - only one
unión - union
unir - to unite
usar - to use
uso - use
usted - you
útil - useful

vacío - empty
vago - lazy
valer - to protect
valiente - valiant
valor - value
valle - valley
vanidad - vanity
vano - vain
vapor - vapor
variar - vary
vario - various
varón - boy
vaso - glass
vecino - neighbor
vela - candle
velar - to watch
vencer - to conquer
vender - sell
venganza - revenge
venir - to come
venta - sale
ventana - window
ventura - fortune
ver - see
verano - summer
veras - reality
verbo - verb
verdad - truth
verdadero - truthful
verde - green
vergüenza - sham
verso - verse
vestido - dress
vestir - to dress
vez - turn, time
viaje - trip
vicio - vice
víctima - victim
vida - life
viejo - old
viento - wind
vino - wine
violencia - violence
violento - violent
virgen - virgin
virtud - virtue
visión - vision
visita - visit
visitar - to visit
vista - view
visto - obvious, clear
viudo - widower
vivir - to live
vivo - alive
volar - to fly
voluntad - voluntary
volver - to return
voto - vote
voz - voice
vuelta - turn

y - and
ya - already, right away
yo - I

*Respectar = to concern, regard; respetar = to respect, revere.
†Respecto = relation, proportion; respeto = respect.
**Tu = personal pronoun, second person, m. or f., thou; tu = possessive pronoun, m. or f. (pl. tus), thy.
††Un, una = indefinite article, a, an.

Selection of Materials

In planning a bilingual program you will need to purchase a variety of materials. If you are in a position to purchase materials for use in your own classroom or in your school, you will probably want to establish criteria for their selection.

	Yes	No
1. Teacher Competency		
a. Must you be a content specialist to successfully use the materials?	_____	_____
b. Must you be bilingual to use the materials?	_____	_____
c. Are the materials usable by inexperienced teachers?	_____	_____
d. Does the publishing company or the school system provide consultants to instruct you in the use of the materials?	_____	_____
2. Learners		
a. Do the materials provide for student differences in intelligence, experience, and language fluency?	_____	_____
b. Do the materials contain stories of equal interest to both males and femals?	_____	_____
c. Do the materials contain high-interest, low-vocabulary selections?	_____	_____
3. Program Sequence		
a. Does the developmental sequence of the program closely parallel the natural development of language learning?	_____	_____
b. Does the program build on the natural language strengths of the student?	_____	_____
c. Does the program make provisions for the development of all the language arts?	_____	_____
d. Does the program provide for content area skill development?	_____	_____
e. Do the materials provide for individualizing instruction?	_____	_____
f. Are the materials free from cultural stereotyping?	_____	_____
g. Can the materials be integrated within an existing program?	_____	_____
4. Program Packaging		
a. Do the materials contain charts, filmstrips, flashcards, and other supplementary materials?	_____	_____
b. Are the supplementary aids easily used by children?	_____	_____
c. Are materials provided for reinforcement, review, and evaluation?	_____	_____
d. Are the costs consistent with available program funds?	_____	_____
e. Are program time constraints consistent with time allowances for classroom implementation?	_____	_____

Student Progress

Most educators agree that literacy is measurable, but they do not always agree upon the most appropriate instruments for measuring student progress. We cannot "protect" our students or ourselves from accountability. The argument about standardized tests is not whether to use them, but which ones should be used. "Which instruments adequately assess the abilities of bilingual students at their present stage of development in English?" If a student age five or fifteen is just beginning English instruction, let us be absolutely certain that our tests take into consideration this level of limited exposure to English. By way of example, we present the following fictional test item.

Instructions: Read this brief passage and answer the two questions that follow.

"There he is up around the bend;
come on down over here," Ian said.
"We will box him in and ambush him
like Butch Cassidy used to do with the Sundance
Kid."

Answer the following:

1. To whom is Ian talking?
2. What is Ian's suggested plan of action?

There are very few polysyllabic words in the passage; most of the words are monosyllabic. The only word to be counted as a difficult word, using the Dale-Chall readability formula, would be *ambush*. Almost any young native English speaker would be able to comprehend this passage, but it would be extremely difficult for someone just learning English for the following reasons:

Syntax: The syntax is complex; *used to* is a sophisticated structure.
Idioms: This brief selection uses two idioms that the bilingual student may not be able to understand, "*up around* the bend" and "*Come* on down *over* here."
Cultural/experimental background: The child needs to have some knowledge of Butch Cassidy to appreciate the passage fully.

There are many items in this short passage that would be impossible for a bilingual student to interpret. A second example may illustrate the point further:

Had he gone to the dentist on time, his mother wouldn't have yelled at him.

Again, a young native English speaker probably would be able to interpret this utterance, but a bilingual child, recently exposed to English, would have an extremely difficult time comprehending this complex English syntactic pattern.

We urge extreme caution when using any standardized test to measure the reading growth of bilingual children. Further, we urge you to analyze the test thoroughly and to interpret it in light of the student's present level of functioning in English. If test items are based on complex syntactic structures, English idioms, and English lexical items demanding a specific cultural experience, make a note of the items and interpret your student's scores according to your knowledge of his or her level of English proficiency.

Clinical Reports

After considering the theoretical information presented in the evaluation section of this chapter, it may be useful for you to analyze the case of Gladys, age thirteen. We present the entire case including the diagnosis and planned strategies. After reading it, we would like you to answer these questions:

1. Is this diagnosis adequate?
2. Do the strategies meet the needs that were discovered in the diagnosis?
3. Would you eliminate any of these suggested strategies?
4. Would you include any strategies that have not been mentioned in this report?

Name: Gladys
Age: 13

Overview of Test Scores*

Skill	Test	Score
Listening Comprehension	1. Durrell Listening and Reading	2.8
	2. Durrell Analysis	Grade 3
	3. Marysville Test	Average 3

Oral reading	1. Durrell Analysis	High school grade
	2. Gray Oral Reading Test	3
Silent reading	1. Spire	Low second
	2. Durrell Analysis	High second
	3. Stanford Diagnosis (literal)	2.8
Word-attack skills	1. Durrell Analysis	Grade 6
	2. Spire	Grade 6
	3. San Diego Quick Assessment	Grade 7
	4. Botel Test	7.2
Sight vocabulary	1. Durrell Analysis	Grade 6
	2. San Diego Quick Assessment	Grade 6
	3. Peabody Picture Vocabulary Test, English	100

*Note: The scores of these tests must not be interpreted in the same way as they are interpreted for a native English-speaking child. This student is in the process of learning English. (This report is based on a clinical study report by Sharon Hirsch.)

Strategies and Materials

Objectives	Strategies	Materials
1. To use the simple past tense of regular and irregular verbs orally and in written English.	The student will be helped to discriminate between sounds of present and past—that is, look, looked, bake, baked, by taping several combinations and having her circle the correct response from choices presented in print. Second, she will be asked to write words she has heard. She will be given no visual cues. She will be given much practice repeating sentences with past and present tense verbs. She will also be asked to retell stories in the past that had been presented in the present.	Teacher prepared taped materials, ditto sheets, informal stories to be retold in the past.
2. To use adjectives in the comparative and superlative forms both orally and in writing.	With the student we discussed questions about family and school such as, "Who is the smallest one in your class?" "Who is the youngest one in your family?" Also involve student in completing cloze written work such as "He is the______one in the class," "She is______than he is," etc.	Several ESL texts contain these drills, but informal teacher-prepared materials may also be used.

Objectives	Strategies	Materials
3. To learn to write English sentences with the proper subject-verb-object word order in declarative and interrogative sentences.	Play sentence games and do some structured work with scrambled sentences.	Sentence Cubo, Scrabble, informal worksheets of disarranged sentences.
4. To listen to the structure, "used to" and to use it in structured responses, free speech, and written responses.	Elicit student responses about a story written in the "used to" form and discuss the things she *used to do* before coming to the United States.	Simple teacher-prepared story utilizing this structure.
5. To listen to the conditional structures, "If I were . . . I would . . ." and "If I had seen . . . I would have . . ." and to use these structures in speech and in writing.	Using the same technique as objective 4, discuss questions such as "What would you have done if you had done, seen, traveled," etc.	Informal stories and written exercise sheets.
6. To follow the details and sequence of events in stories more carefully.	Through detailed elicitation (oral) of details in stories provide student with support and contextual clues for remembering sequence.	Informal stories used in above exercises as well as short newspaper articles.
7. To read stories independently for personal enjoyment.	Discuss newspaper articles and books she has read and ask her to report on the books in writing upon completing them	*News for You* Laurback Literacy Association, newspaper in easy English and Scholastic Reading series.
8. To understand and be able to accurately use the conjunctions but, because, although, so, since.	Through oral exercises, consisting of incomplete sentences and through stories using these words, try to distinguish one from another and then ask Gladys to complete structured written drills.	Teacher-prepared materials such as "I was born in Paris although (a) I do not speak English, (b) I do not speak French, (c) I live in Paris, (d) I like life in France."

Suggested Readings for Gladys

Achieving, Venturing, Searching. Encounters Series, Reality in Reading and Language. Cambridge Book Co., 1971.

Fitzhugh, Louise. *Harriet the Spy.* New York: Harper & Row, Publishers, 1964. An award-winning novel of a teenage girl written simply enough for Gladys to enjoy reading it.

Pringle, Laurence. *City and Suburb: Exploring an Ecosystem.* New York: Macmillan Publishing Co., Inc., 1975. A good introduction to reading in the content areas. Some difficult vocabulary but much valuable content material of particular interest to someone who has had both urban and rural experiences.

Stoltz, Mary. *Fredou.* New York: Harper & Row, Publishers, 1962. A human interest story of a teenager, done in large print and well written.

Zevelle, Emily Chevey. *Garden of Broken Glass.* New York: Delacorte Press, 1975. An illustrated novel dealing with the problems of an urban teenager, especially in regard to his family.

Now, let us try to answer the original questions:

1. Is this diagnosis adequate?
2. Do the strategies meet the needs that were discovered in the diagnosis?
3. Would you eliminate any of these suggested strategies?
4. Would you include any strategies that have not been mentioned in this report?

QUESTIONS AND RELATED READINGS

If you feel that you have not attained adequate knowledge to answer the following questions successfully, we suggest additional related readings.

1. Explain how the needs of the bilingual student are being met by bilingual education.
2. Explain the linguistic factors involved in teaching bilingual students.
3. How do you diagnose the reading problems of a bilingual student?
4. Explain several methodologies of teaching reading to bilingual students.
5. Describe the evaluation component of a bilingual program.

Goal 1: To help the reader to determine the needs of students who are learning English.

Question 1: Explain how the needs of the bilingual student are being met by bilingual education.

Alatis, J. "The Compatability of TESOL and Bilingual Education." *English as a Second Language in Bilingual Education*, ed. by J. Alatis and K. Twadell. Washington, D.C.: TESOL, 1976.

Hines, M. "A Critique of the U.S. Commission on Civil Rights Report on Bilingual Bicultural Education." In *English as a Second Language in Bilingual Education*, ed. by J. Alatis and K. Twadell. Washington, D.C.: TESOL, 1976, 218–27.

Thonis, E. *Teaching Reading to Spanish-Speaking Children.* Newark, Del.: International Reading Association, 1976.

Goal 2: To help the reader to understand the linguistic influences in second language teaching and the linguistic differences between several languages and English.

Question 2: Explain the linguistic factors involved in teaching bilingual students.

Smith, F., ed. *Psycholinguistics and Reading.* New York: Holt, Rinehart and Winston, 1973.

Steffensen, M., C. Joag-Dev, and R. Anderson. "A Cross-Cultural Perspective on Reading Comprehension." *Reading Research Quarterly* 15:1 (1979), 10–29.

Wilkinson, A. "Oracy in English Teaching." In *Language and the Language Arts*, ed. by J. S. DeStefano and S. E. Fox. Boston: Little, Brown & Co., 1974, pp. 64–70.

Goal 3: To help the reader to determine the most appropriate methods for diagnosing the reading ability of students who are learning English and students who are bilingual.

Question 3: How do you diagnose the reading problems of a bilingual student?

Ching, D. *Reading and the Bilingual Child.* Newark, Del.: International Reading Association, 1976.

O'Brien, C. *Teaching the Language Different Child to Read.* Columbus, Ohio: Charles E. Merrill Publishing Company, 1973.

Thonis, E. *Teaching Reading to Non-English Speakers.* Newark, Del.: International Reading Association, 1976.

Goal 4: To help the reader to appreciate different methodologies of instruction in teaching reading in the native language as well as reading in English.

Question 4: Explain several methodologies of teaching reading to bilingual students.

Been, S. "Reading in the Foreign Language Teaching Program." *TESOL Quarterly* 9 (September 1975) 313–321.

Past, K., and A. Past. "A Bilingual Kindergarten Immersed in Print." *The Reading Teacher* 50 (May 1980), 907–13.

Thonis, E. *Teaching Reading to Spanish-Speaking Children*, Newark, Del.: International Reading Association, 1976.

Goal 5: To help the reader to learn the appropriate methods of evaluating the effectiveness of materials for students who are learning English.

Question 5: Describe the evaluation component of a bilingual program.

Ching, D. *Reading and the Bilingual Child.* Newark, Del.: International Reading Association, 1976.

O'Brien, C. *Teaching the Language Different Child to Read.* Columbus, Ohio: Charles E. Merrill Publishing Company, 1973.

Thonis, E. *Teaching Reading to Non-English Speakers.* New York: Macmillan Publishing Co., Inc., 1970.

BIBLIOGRAPHY

Bilingual Schooling in the United States. Washington, D.C.: U.S. Office of Education, 1972. Chapter opening quotation appears on page 72.

Ching, D. *Reading and the Bilingual Child.* Newark, Del.: International Reading Association, 1976.

Hirsch, S. "Informal Diagnostic Instruments of English Language Skills." In *Proceedings of the Boston University Bilingual Reading Laboratory*, ed. by J. Flood. Boston: Boston University of Education, 1976, 84–90.

Moores, D. *Educating the Deaf: Psychology, Principles and Practices.* Boston: Houghton Mifflin Company, 1978.

National Education Association. *The Invisible Minority*, Washington, D.C.: NEA, 1966.

O'Brien, C. *Teaching the Language Different Child to Read.* Columbus, Ohio: Charles E. Merrill Publishing Company, 1973.

Past, K., and A. Past. "A Bilingual Kindergarten Immersed in Print." *The Reading Teacher* 50 (May 1980), 907–13.

Ruddell, R. *Reading-Language Instruction.* Englewood Cliffs, N.J.: Prentice-Hall, Inc., 1974.

Samora, J. *The Educational Status of a Minority*. Washington, D.C.: U.S. Office of Education, 1968.

Spaulding, S. "A Spanish Readability Formula." *Modern Language Journal* 40 (December 1956), 435.

Steffensen, M., C. Joag-Dev, and R. Anderson. "A Cross-Cultural Perspective on Reading Comprehension." *Reading Research Quarterly* 15:1 (1979), 10–29.

Thonis, E. W. *Teaching Reading to Non-English Speakers.* New York: Macmillan Publishing Co., Inc., 1970.

———. *Teaching Reading to Spanish-Speaking Children.* Newark, Del.: International Reading Association, 1976.

Unfinished Education: Outcome for Minorities in Five Southwestern States. Washington, D.C.: U.S. Government Printing Office, 1972.

Zintz, M. *The Reading Process.* Dubuque, Iowa: William C. Brown Company, Publishers, 1975.

CHAPTER 15

Developing and Managing Your Reading Program

It is the possibility of improved learning that makes classroom organization such an important topic, and teachers along with parents and all concerned citizens are interested in that. Good organization should mean improved learning because it should lead to more efficient and effective use of a teacher's time, increased attention to the most serious student problems, individual and group sessions for all students, and increased student/teacher interaction time.

R. Farr, 1980

Crucial to the success of a management system is a continuous process of evaluation both by you as a teacher and by your students. Students can also aid you in record keeping and organization once you have prepared a place for their personal folders. (Photo by Linda Lungren.)

GOALS: To help the reader to

1. Recognize the factors contributing to effective classroom management.
2. Learn how to develop and implement thematic teaching.
3. Learn successful grouping techniques.
4. Recognize behavioral objectives as an essential instructional tool.
5. Sample a variety of instructional methods.
6. Recognize the importance of continuous evaluation.

The foundation of a well-functioning reading instruction program is a definition of reading upon which teaching strategies are based. We have encouraged you throughout this text to develop just such a personal, working definition of reading to help you determine the structure of your program. The implementation and management of your well-thought-out program is as great a challenge as the initial development of your teaching strategies. This chapter is designed to help you organize—and operate smoothly—your reading program by incorporating the principles of systems management while taking into account the individual needs of your students. Crucial to the success of such a system is a continuous process of evaluation both by you as a teacher and by your students as the principal users of your system.

It would seem that, when an institutionalized program is not *really* meeting the individual needs of the students or the teachers, a more efficient change in the system would be welcome. However, it appears to be in the nature of things that people are resistant and reluctant to throw out what they know even if familiarity has bred contempt. As O'Donnell and Moore (1980) found, the "stumbling blocks" to organizational change in education can be placed in seven categories:

1. Administration
2. Parents
3. Community
4. Resources
5. Assessment and evaluation
6. Willingness to change
7. The problem of working with large numbers of students

They further suggest that "the most persuasive and obvious stumbling block was the self-fulfilling prophecy: 'But our school just doesn't have the staff or resources to do it; therefore, I can't do it' " (p. 187).

These stumbling blocks can be overcome, and an innovative, efficient management system designed to meet the needs of those involved in a classroom reading program can be implemented. The classroom teacher will, however, need to establish an interactional base for this system, which includes parents, students, teachers, administrators, school boards, and community leaders, all working together with mutual, well-correlated goals. The educational management system scheme (on page 463) may help to clarify the many facets of an educational management system, illustrating factors that contribute to the operational structure of such a system. We present this scheme in the framework of the following simulation.

THE FOUNDATION: A WORKING SYSTEM

"School is fun this year!" seven-year-old Shannon was overheard telling her younger brother Eric. "We get to read fun books and we don't just have to read our readers. This year I like reading as much as science!"

Shannon's parents were surprised by these accolades because Shannon had never expressed praise for the Castle Rock Elementary School Reading Program before. Her parents were anxious to understand their daughter's change of attitude, so they called Ms. Cunningham, Shannon's teacher, and arranged to visit the school.

During their visit with Ms. Cunningham, Shannon's parents realized that the way in which the classroom was managed contributed greatly to the success of the reading program. Ms. Cunningham explained that she believed learning environments should include provisions for

1. Giving *all* children specific information regarding their competencies.
2. Encouraging student participation in the planning of program goals.
3. Having all students participate in evaluating their own progress.

EDUCATIONAL MANAGEMENT SYSTEM

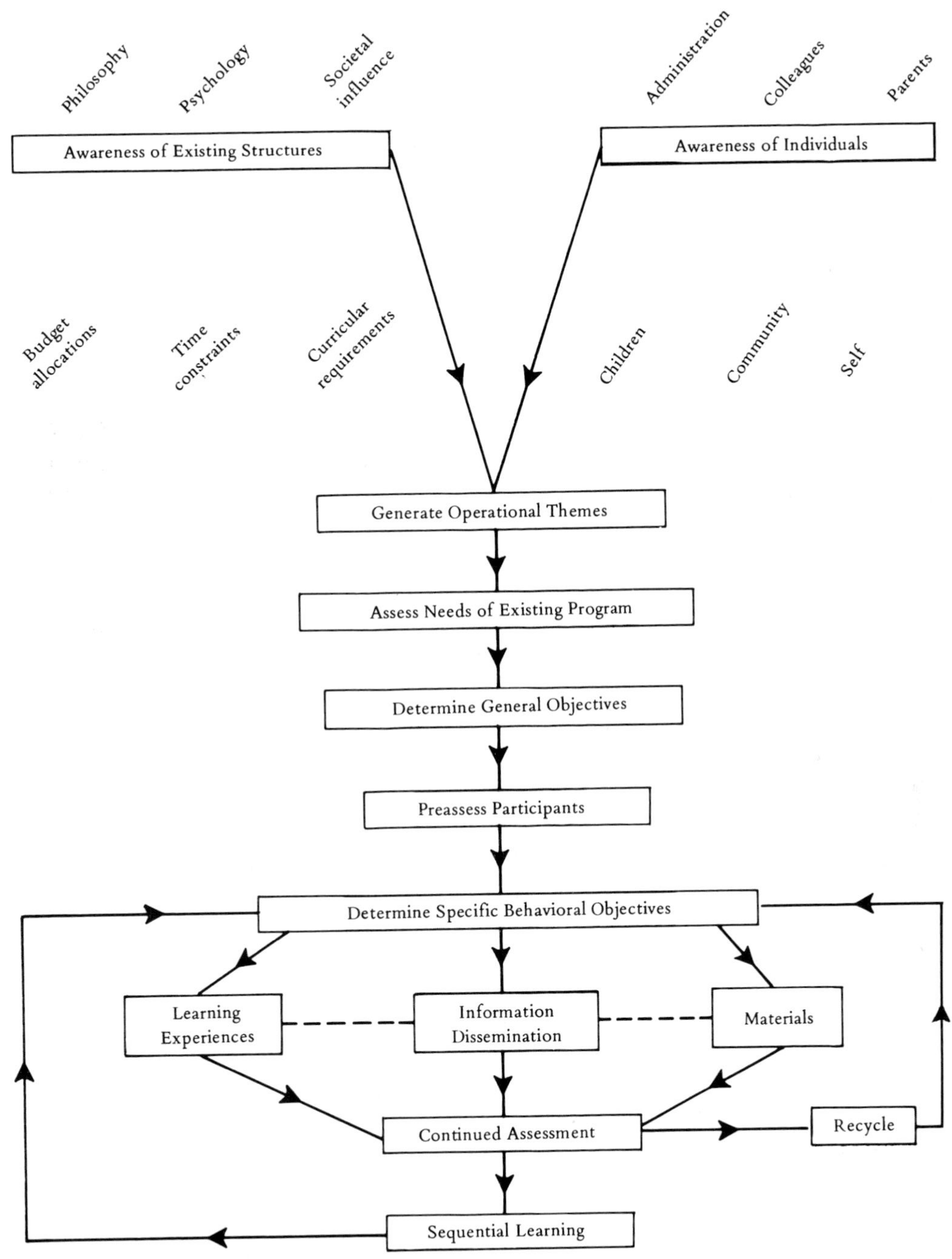

4. Encouraging students to make decisions about participation in alternate learning activities designed to accomplish the specified goals.

Ms. Cunningham explained further that these beliefs were best accomplished if she viewed herself as a classroom manager, because in this role she could work alone or with children to determine

1. Reading program goals
2. Student competencies
3. Procedures for individual or group progress
4. Techniques and materials needed to implement appropriate procedures
5. Achievement of the goals, student competencies, processes, and techniques

Ms. Cunningham realized that, once she had developed a working philosophy of education, she had to determine specific means for helping her students to accomplish their goals. Too often, classroom teachers intend to implement a very personalized model of education, but they are unable to do so because they lack the skills needed to manage one. The use of management systems in educational planning is expanding following the lead of business management, which, since the 1950s and 1960s, has made increasing use of advance technology in this area. Through such a system, the teacher is able to compare student growth with stated objectives and reschedule or recycle student programs according to exhibited competencies. Many textbook companies have been developing basal reading series that provide the teacher with a management system model, for example, *Ginn 720* (1976), *Houghton Mifflin Reading Program* (1981), *Rand McNally Reading Program* (1981), and *Holt Basic Reading* (1980). (For a complete review of these and other basal reading series components, see Aukerman, 1981.)

Let us explore the processes of defining and developing a management system further by focusing our attention on Shannon's classroom. Where is it located? What is the socioeconomic stratification? What is the school building like? How involved are the parents? Who exactly are the individuals in Ms. Cunningham's classroom? and What existing curricular and societal structures predetermine classroom interactions?

EXISTING STRUCTURES AND INDIVIDUALS

Consideration must be given to the existing structures that directly affect the happenings within the classroom. Although some of these structures may be governed by you (philosophy and psychology), others (societal influence, budget allocations) may be outside your range of authority, and still other areas (curricular requirements, time schedules) may have been established before your arrival, but can be changed.

You need to be familiar with all the structures in your environment and the extent of your decision-making power regarding each. You may gain initial insights into this area through social and professional interactions with colleagues and administrators. A review of existing school policies, as well as curriculum guides, will offer you some insights into the parametric structure of the existing curriculum. As you begin to collect information about existing structures, remember to ask the following questions:

1. How is the day divided?
2. Is the time schedule predetermined? By whom?
3. Is your classroom self-contained?
4. What special teachers (music, art) or special services (gym, theater) are provided?
5. Is there an organized curriculum committee? If so, how can you join?
6. What funds are available to you?
7. How are text materials adopted?

Questions such as these may be asked during an early interview. Always attempt to compare the answers you receive with your philosophy of teaching. Is there compatibility? If so, you will avoid conflict later on. If not, can alterations (compromises) be made by you?

One motivation for becoming a teacher is the enjoyment of working with other people to help children learn. Consequently, it is important to consider your own feelings about education and how you relate to others.

Who am I? For whom am I working? Answers to these questions may be found through your interactions with the administration, colleagues, parents, community, children, and yourself.

ADMINISTRATION

1. What appear to be the major objectives of the administration?
2. How are these objectives related to education?
3. How is their apparent philosophy similar to or different from mine?
4. What are the line-staff relationships (line of command) within this administration?
5. *What* decisions are made by *whom*?

COLLEAGUES

1. Who are my colleagues?
2. Do there appear to be any major educational beliefs shared by the majority of this faculty?
3. What are the faculty's initial impressions of me?
4. What will be my role as a member of this educational community?
5. What decision-making responsibilities are mine?

PARENTS

1. Who are the parents of my children?
2. What are their values with regard to the educational training of their children?
3. Are they heavily involved with the decision-making processes of this school?
4. How do they view the existing faculty and administration?

COMMUNITY

1. Is the surrounding community well represented (economically, socially) by the family makeup of the children within my classroom?
2. What segment of the community controls school-board decision making?
3. What are the apparent and less apparent and less apparent feelings of the school board with regard to the administration, faculty, and education?

CHILDREN

1. Who are my children?
2. What have been their life exposures thus far?
3. What may be their projected life goals?
4. Are their life exposures similar or dissimilar to mine?
5. What will be their projected view of me?

SELF

1. What will be my function in this educational community?
2. Do I harbor any prejudices or fears with regard to the people within the community?
3. Are there any barriers that may interfere with my functioning effectively?
4. If so, how is it possible to alter these barriers?

As a veteran or as a beginning teacher, you continually need to pursue answers to these questions. When Ms. Cunningham made these inquiries, she found that the children in Shannon's class were like students in most primary grades: multi-ethnic and culturally diverse, with various dialects, levels of cognitive development, levels of sensory and perceptual readiness, degrees of physical health, degrees of social and emotional development, various interests and attitudes about learning, and a great variety of oral and silent reading skills.

Ms. Cunningham realized that if she were to attempt to meet the learning needs of each of her twenty-six children, she would have to acquaint herself with the existing *program structures* in her school. She began by

1. Reviewing the specific sequence of reading skills covered in the school basal reading program. Because she realized that the levels of student reading ability within a primary grade might range from readiness to intermediate, Ms. Cunningham designed a scope and sequence checklist of reading skills, ranging from preprimer to sixth grade, that included skills in areas such as visual and auditory perception, blending, phonics analysis, and structural and contextual analysis.
2. Reviewing specific terms such as *independent*, *instructional*, and *frustrational reading levels*.
3. Surveying school libraries and closets to determine the range of available reading materials.
4. Reacquainting herself with her principal's and colleagues' philosophies about reading instruction.
5. Surveying community attitudes toward reading instruction.

OPERATIONAL THEMES

After Ms. Cunningham had collected some general understanding of the existing structures and individuals within her educational community, as well as their decision-making effects on the management of her classroom, she began planning her classroom curriculum. She thought about general student interests and needs to determine the *topics* she hoped to share with her children. Although she added to and altered this list to accommodate her students' interests, she never confused her role with her students. She was employed to prepare, manage, manipulate, evaluate, and replan the educational environment.

You may intend to share in the decision-making situations with your children, but never lose sight of the fact that your experiences are broader and more far-reaching than those of your children. These differences are, however, of *degree*, not *exclusion*. Many of these themes will be provided through the management system of the basal program you are using.

At this point, let us brainstorm to determine the general themes you may plan to share with your students.

Life cycles (biological, emotional, social)
Making choices (family, school, friends)
Exploring your environment (geographically, culturally, emotionally)
Life in the American past (family, environment, economic structures)
Building a nation (the U.S. Constitution, interstate and international relations)

As you add to this list of themes, keep in mind the fact that themes may be operating simultaneously because some of your students will not have the same interests or the same levels of readiness. Your intent in any theme will be to convey the basic skills of communication as well as the skills and areas of information that eventually will result in the development of independent learners.

> Students need to learn far more than the basic skills. Children who have just started school may still be in the labor force in the year 2030. For them, nothing could be more wildly impractical than an education designed to prepare them for specific vocations or professions or to facilitate their adjustment to the world as it is. To be practical, an education should prepare a man for work that doesn't yet exist and whose nature cannot even be imagined. This can be done only by teaching people how to learn, by giving them the kind of intellectual discipline that will enable them to apply man's accumulated wisdom to new problems as they arise, the kind of wisdom that will enable them to *recognize* new problems as they arise.
>
> (Silberman, 1970, pp. 83–4)

It may be helpful to select themes that facilitate the incorporation of science, math, and social studies lessons. Think of your themes as topics that may be expanded to become an integrated curriculum unit.

To aid in the development of an independent learner, you must remember that the student will have difficulty venturing beyond the sphere of indoctrination while developing independent learning skills if he or she cannot read, write, or engage in problem-solving activities. Your task is to introduce basic communication and study skills in a practical, useful, synthesized, and interesting manner. That's some task! But whoever told you that the effective teacher's job was easy? Through the selection of topical themes, you have begun the process of *thematic teaching*, which is simply the process of integrating content area learning, language arts, and study skills into a manageable, practical, interesting learning endeavor.

NEEDS OF THE EXISTING PROGRAM

Once Ms. Cunningham had selected some general themes, which she had altered after assessing student interest, she attempted to assess the needs of the existing program. In making this program assessment, she asked questions such as

1. What previous themes have been explored at this grade level?
2. Do these themes apply to the objectives of the system?
3. Am I infringing on material that my colleagues may cover?
4. What resources are available to me?

After thinking about the existing curriculum, Ms. Cunningham attempted to develop general program objectives.

General Objectives

Based on the survey of the existing program, the following general objectives were designed. Objectives were to be mastered through the programmatic themes Ms. Cunningham had selected. For example,

Theme	General Objectives
Life cycles	1. Define a life cycle. 2. Develop an understanding of the life cycle of plants. 3. Develop an understanding of the biological life cycle of animals. 4. Promote an awareness of emotional and psychological cycles in humans. 5. Establish an appreciation for each stage of life from birth to death. 6. Develop a personal awareness of one's own physical and emotional place in the cycle. 7. Evaluate personal and societal feelings about life and death.
Exploring your environment	1. Develop an awareness of self. 2. Identify significant others. 3. Identify geographic boundaries. 4. Identify cultural boundaries. 5. Compare strengths and weaknesses of boundary limitations. 6. Evaluate a social change you can affect.

As Ms. Cunningham planned these general thematic objectives, she became more aware of the interrelatedness of the content areas and of the basic skills that each child would need to study this topic successfully. For example, within the thematic study of "exploring your environment," the child encounters geography, history, sociology, and mathematics, as well as reading, writing, and speaking. Through the integration of these areas, the learner explores standard, basic content skills while exploring areas of practical self-interest.

> The statement that individuals live in a world means, in the concrete, that they live in a series of situations. And when it is said that they live in these situations, the meaning of the word *in* is different from its meaning when it is said that pennies are "in" a can. It means, once more, that interaction is going on between an individual and objects and other persons. The conceptions of situation and of interaction are inseparable from each other. An experience is always what it is because of a transaction taking place between an individual and what, at the time, constitutes his environment, whether the latter consists of persons with whom he is talking about some topic or event, the talked-about being also a part of the situation; or the toys with which he is playing; the book he is reading (in which his environing conditions at the time may be England or ancient Greece or an imaginary region); or the materials of an experiment he is performing. The environment, in other words, is whatever conditions interact with the personal needs, desires, purposes, and capacities to create the experience which is had. Even when a person builds a castle in the air he is interacting with the objects which he constructs in fancy.
>
> (Dewey, 1938, pp. 43–4)

Ms. Cunningham realized that, because children enter a given learning theme with varying amounts of readiness for the experience, it is important to assess entering competencies when one is planning to individualize the instruction.

Student Preassessment

In a study on teacher decisions regarding reading instruction, Borko et al. (1981) asked the question, "Do teachers use all of the available information about students to form reading groups?" (p. 452). The short answer to their question is "no," teachers tend to base these decisions largely on information about reading ability rather than on any other aspect of the child or situation. While grouping strictly by reading ability has been popular in the past, it is now felt that other information such as the child's interests, attitudes, and emotional needs should be considered.

To determine individual needs, Ms. Cunningham began the process of diagnosing student competencies. Through *formal* measures, such as standardized reading tests, and *informal* measures, such as observation scales, teacher-made checklists, interest inventories, and textbook placement exams, Ms. Cunningham assessed each child's

1. Sensory and perceptual developmental needs
2. Emotional and social needs
3. Knowledge of oral reading, noting each child's difficulties with sight words and knowledge of vowel situations, consonant elements, and structural and contextual clues
4. Silent reading comprehension skills, focusing attention on inferential and evaluative comprehension skills.
5. Interests

Based on this initial diagnosis, groups were designed according to student interests and student needs. Correlation of student needs and interests became possible because Ms. Cunningham first determined the reading needs of each child; then she was able to accommodate student interests through alternate activities.

Implementing Groups

Once instructional levels have been determined through informal and standardized testing, it is possible to group students for instruction according to their skill development needs, their achievement, their interests, purposes for reading, and attitudes toward reading. The practice of grouping allows for individualization of instruction and provides for economy of teacher effort and increased student participation. It is more efficient for a teacher to instruct a group of children with similar needs, interests, and purposes than it is to work with a total classroom of separate individuals. Grouping allows materials to be matched to the learner more effectively than would be possible if instruction were geared to a class. Grouping according to individual assessment is beneficial to the learner because the instruction is matched with interests, needs, purposes, and skills. With this in mind, Ms. Cunningham began her program by creating the following grouping patterns.

Reading Level	Number of Students	Needs	Grouping Plans
P	1	Has difficulty understanding concepts of space, time, color, number, and value.	*Group A:* Utilize child's interests to employ language experience activities to further conceptual development as well as to introduce and reinforce basic beginning reading word-recognition and comprehension skills.
1^1	1	Has a limited sight vocabulary, which decreases minimal literal comprehension.	
1^2	1		
2^1	3	Has difficulty with patterns of organization, comparison, contrast, cause and effect.	*Group B:* Develop organizational skills that effect reading comprehension.
2^2	6		
3^1	6	Reads at grade level in basal text.	*Group C:* Reinforce basic oral and silent reading skills while extending fluency and mastery of study skills.
3^2	4		
4^1	2	Reads independently above grade level.	*Group D:* Develop study skills and aid child in transferring and applying them to content area situations.
4^2	1		
5^2	1	Reads independently well above grade level.	

Although there are four groups that have various reading levels within this classroom, it should not be taken to indicate that there may be only four groups within any given class or that there must be at least four groups.

First, there may be individuals who already possess the reading behaviors that have been set as the terminal outcome of instruction prior to the initiation of instruction. The teacher has two options for proceeding with the instructional program for these students: they may be allowed to advance to a new and different program, or they may proceed with the original program independently with minimal teacher guidance.

Second, other individuals may emerge who are unable to handle the materials required in the instructional program because they lack the skills that are necessary for dealing with the content. They would be totally incapable of benefiting from the instructional program as it is now planned. These children would be considered to be functioning on the frustrational level. To make instruction meaningful for them, the program would have to be revised to begin with the skills that the students already possess and build the skills that are needed to master the original program.

Finally, another group of students may emerge, a group that can handle the materials and the instructional program but whose members still require teacher guidance and instruction. These students can be considered to be functioning at the instructional level, and they may proceed with the program as it was originally devised. There can be as many groups as necessary to meet the needs of the learners, but teacher energies must be taken into consideration. It may be that, in a given class, there are no students at the frustrational level when working within a certain theme; however, at the same time, students may be at various points within the instructional level. A teacher may form two, three, four, or five groups within the instructional level, each with different skills, interests, and purposes.

Because grouping is intended to increase participation for students, materials used for instruction are not necessarily uniform for all groups. For instance, the practice of grouping elementary school readers into "red," "blue," and "yellow" birds has often been the extent of grouping. Having each group use the same materials, purposes, and teaching methods, but at differing rates, is highly questionable because purpose, teaching methods, and materials should be modified, changed, and geared to meet the needs of the learners in a specific group in accordance with the various themes being pursued.

It should be remembered that grouping must be based on students' thematic interests whenever possible and that groups will have to change accordingly. Groups are also modified according to specific instructional objectives. As a child progresses through the program and fulfills the objectives, the group for which that program has been formed may become unnecessary for all the learners because each student does not necessarily progress at the same speed. If the objective has been met or if it is determined to be unrealistic, the group may be dissolved. New objectives may then be formed for different purposes and different instructional objectives. The same individuals may or may not be part of both groups. Also, children who progress faster than others may profit from working independently.

For grouping to be effective, not only do specific instructional objectives need to be defined, but constant evaluation of student progress is necessary to maintain the validity of the group. Although grouping allows a teacher to make pedagogical decisions based on the group rather than on each individual in the class (Russo, 1978), never forget that the groups are comprised of individuals who do not remain static.

The fact that children's skills constantly develop as a result of instruction emphasizes the need for continual evaluation, regrouping, and elimination of some groups and formation of new groups. Groups should be viewed as temporary and changing. At the same time, it should be recognized that not all students need to be included in groups all the time. This is especially true of students capable of functioning at the independent levels.

The testing instruments that can be used in grouping are much the same as those that are used in determining reading levels: standardized tests, informal tests, textbook tests, and teacher observations. The standardized reading tests can be used to provide evaluations of reading levels to determine groups if the skills measured by the test are the same as those included in the instructional program and are tested in the same manner as the skills to be taught. Informal tests also provide reliable indications of reading levels for the creation of groups, because they are constructed from the actual materials used in the programs and contain questions related specifically to instructional goals. The validity of the informal test for groups and for determining reading levels if often dependent on the competence of the teacher who devises it. Finally, teacher observations and textbook tests are especially useful in grouping. Such measures can provide a readily available means of assessing student progress toward attaining the objectives of the program.

Successful grouping practices are contingent on the definition of what is to be taught, how it is to be taught, and the anticipated terminal behavior. (Photo by Linda Lungren.)

In summary, successful grouping practices are contingent on the definition of what is to be taught, and the anticipated terminal behavior. It is also dependent on continuous assessment of student behavior, on flexibility of established groups, and on changing the instructional program to meet the needs of the students. In general, the following steps should be followed in using tests for grouping:

1. Define the objectives of the instructional program and the methodology for teaching the objective.
2. Preassess student reading behavior by using a standardized test (if it matches the objectives and definitions established for the instructional program), an informal test, a teacher checklist, and/or any combination of the three.
3. Form groups according to preassessment (e.g., reading levels, thematic interests, purposes for reading, content of instruction, and student attitudes).
4. Evaluate student progress continuously by using informal tests, teacher checklists, or standardized tests (which match the instructional objectives) with the intent of moving students to independent activities if possible or regrouping on the basis of new instructional goals where the original ones have been met. Prepare to eliminate groups when they are no longer necessary.

Once Ms. Cunningham had determined group composition and needs, she had to determine specific behavioral objectives for each learner or for each learning group.

Specific Behavioral Objectives

While some researchers (Hambleton et al., 1978) feel there is a trend toward using "domain specifications" (Popham, 1975) or "amplified objectives" (Millman,

1974), it is still essential for a teacher to understand and accurately use behavioral objectives.* A review of the literature (Lapp, 1972b) suggests that the acceptance or rejection of behavioral objectives as a relevant component to a thematic reading program has been based largely on speculation rather than on research.

Unfortunately, the training of prospective teachers, which includes instruction in writing behavioral objectives, often is not accompanied by training in the utilization of such objectives. The teacher is never sure of the value of behavioral objectives in thematic curricular planning and evaluation. According to Gilpin (1962), an adequately prepared teacher can develop instructional objectives more effectively if the following questions and procedures are followed:

1. What is it that we must teach?
2. How will we know when we have taught it?
3. What materials and procedures will work best to teach what we want to teach? (p. viii)

Guidelines such as these may encourage you, as a teacher, to define objectives before beginning to teach a lesson. Mager (1962), for example, specified five steps to follow in the development and use of behavioral objectives:

1. A statement of instructional objectives is a collection of words or symbols describing one of your educational intents.
2. An objective will communicate your intent to the degree you have described what the learner will be doing when demonstrating his achievement, and how you will know when he is doing it.
3. To describe terminal behavior (what the learner will be doing):
   a. Identify and name the overall behavior act.
   b. Define the important conditions under which the behavior is to occur (given and/or restrictions and limitations).
   c. Define the criterion of acceptable performance.
4. Write a separate statement for each objective: the more you have, the better chance you have of making clear your intent.
5. If you give each learner a copy of your objectives, you may not have to do much else. (p. 52)

There are many instances when a general objective is contrived and then designed into a behavioral objective. For example, a classroom objective may be to introduce children to the theme of community helpers. The following example is a behavioral objective derived from such a broad objective:

Given a lesson that introduces the topic of community helpers, the child will be able to name at least one such community helper and describe his or her role in the community with complete competency.

Why is an objective of this type needed or used by the teacher? When asked to state in specific behavioral terms what he or she wants to accomplish by a specific lesson, the teacher will be able to determine:

1. If the accomplishment of the stated objective is really of any value to the total development of the child.
2. If the child has accomplished the objective:
   a. If there are related objectives within the theme that are to be designed and utilized at this time.
   b. Methods of instruction and performance level needed for implementation of related objectives.
3. If the child has not accomplished the objective:
   a. Whether the objective can be accomplished by this child at this time.
   b. Whether the performance level of the objective was too difficult.
   c. What new methods of instruction are needed to better enable the child to accomplish the objective.

Curricular program evaluation depends on a clear explanation and explication of the behaviors that you are attempting to measure. While the teacher may choose from a variety of evaluative models, she must be careful not to base her total evaluation on a few specified behaviors that have been outlined previously in behavioral terms. We should never be so naïve as to believe that measured behaviors are the only positive occurrences within classroom settings. Teachers must be so aware of their children and their programs that they can intelli-

*A behavioral objective is composed of three criteria: (1) the operational *conditions* existing when the behavior occurs, (2) the terminal *behavior* occurring as a result of planned instruction, and (3) the level of *performance* needed for mastery.

gently estimate growth that has not yet been planned and/or measured objectively.

When the classroom teacher becomes skilled at using behavioral objectives, an abbreviated system may be used, and once the terminal behavior has been clarified, the rest becomes relatively simple. The reluctance to use objectives is quite similar to the reluctance of many educators to use instructional technology, such as teaching machines and audiovisual equipment.

Many educators believe that, if children are in a classroom setting that allows technology to "dehumanize" them, it is the fault of technology rather than the person determining the objectives and the procedures for meeting the objectives. Television sets, radios, phonographs, programmed machines, and other such technological hardware serve only as mechanical teacher aids. The planning does *not* come from the machine. The hardware is value-free. The teacher must distinguish between reality and fraud. If we consider textbooks and chalkboards as teacher aids, perhaps we could say that technology has always been part of the classroom. Materials and objectives *should not dictate* curricula. Teachers should plan thematic curricula using aids that facilitate the learning process.

The following frames are presented in an attempt to help you to develop skill in writing behavioral objectives.

Frame 1

Behavioral objectives

A behavioral objective is a statement that describes the

1. setting under which a specified behavior will occur.
   (external conditions)
2. type of behavior that is to occur.
   (terminal behavior)
3. level of success that must be achieved.
   (acceptable performance)

Frame 2

External conditions

The setting under which a specified behavior will occur. Examples of correct statements of external conditions are

1. Given a list of basic sight words . . .
2. Following a lesson on vowel digraphs . . .
3. After discussing various English words borrowed from German . . .
4. After comparing the basal and linguistic methods . . .
5. Given a simulated phonic rule . . .
6. Following a discussion of the history of standardized readiness tests . . .

An acceptable statement of *external conditon* is one that describes the exact settings or conditions that will exist during or precede the learner's display of the terminal behavior.

Frame 3

Examples of *incorrect* statements of external conditions are

1. To be able to . . .
2. To have knowledge of . . .
3. To enjoy . . .
4. To learn by . . .
5. To discuss . . .

These examples are incorrect because they do not state the exact conditions under which the terminal behavior will occur.

What must precede the occurrence of the desired behavior?

Frame 4

Terminal behavior

The type of behavior that is anticipated. Examples of correct statements of terminal behavior are

1. The student will be able to identify . . .
(verbally, visually)
2. The student will be able to recite . . .
3. The student will be able to list . . .
4. The student will be able to read . . .
(in writing, verbally)

An acceptable statement of *terminal behavior* is one that describes the anticipated behavior with such specificity that it cannot be misinterpreted.

Frame 5

Examples of *incorrect* statements of terminal behavior are

1. The student knows . . .
2. The student will enjoy . . .
3. The student appreciates . . .
4. The student believes . . .

These examples are incorrect because the behaviors are not stated in a manner that can be adequately interpreted and measured.

What type of behavior will be accepted as evidence that the learner has achieved the stated objective?

Frame 6

Acceptable performance

The level of performance that must be evidenced before a specified behavior can be accepted. Examples of correct statements of acceptable performance are

1. . . . at least ten of the following sight words.
2. . . . both initial phonemes.
3. . . . five vocabulary words in three minutes.
4. . . . 40 percent of the basic sight words.
5. . . . all the addition problems on page 126.

An appropriate statement of *acceptable performance* is one that describes how well the learner must perform before his behavior will be accepted.

Please complete the following activities. If you have difficulty, refer to frames 1 through 6.

Activities

Activity 1: Developing a Behavioral Objective—Reading

You are preparing a unit of study that attempts to facilitate understanding of propaganda. Throughout this unit you plan to rely heavily on the language experiences of the children.

Attempt to develop a statement of external conditions (the setting under which a specified behavior will occur) for the preceding brief unit description.

External conditions (refer to frames 2 and 3)

Now can you add a statement of terminal behavior (a type of behavior that is to occur as a result of planned instruction)?

Terminal behavior (refer to frames 4 and 5)

Finally, add a statement of acceptable performance (degree of competency).

Acceptable performance (refer to frame 6)

Now put your sections together and decide what role this behavioral objective has in curriculum planning.

Activity 2: Developing a Behavioral Objective—Drama

You are preparing a unit of study that attempts to facilitate understanding of the dramatic function of setting. Throughout this unit you plan to rely heavily on the language experiences of the children.

Please attempt to develop a statement of external conditions (the setting under which a specified behavior will occur) for the preceding brief unit description.

External conditions (refer to frames 2 and 3)

Now can you add a statement of terminal behavior (a type of behavior that is to occur as a result of planned instruction)?

Terminal behavior (refer to frames 4 and 5)

Finally, add a statement of acceptable performance (degree of competency).

Acceptable performance (refer to frame 6)

Now put your sections together and decide what role this behavioral objective has in curriculum planning.

As suggested in the educational management system (page 463), after determining your behavioral objectives, you can begin the process of designing instruction that will enable the implementation of your objectives.

Learning Experiences, Information Dissemination, and Materials

Once Ms. Cunningham has determined group composition, needs, and objectives, she had to determine *methods of instruction* for each group. Although she reinforced reading and language arts skills whenever she taught content-specific subjects, she had also decided to allot one hour each morning for reinforcing through basal programs the processes and skills of reading. Because Ms. Cunningham realized that she would not be able to meet with each group for the entire period, she decided to develop methods of instruction that could be operationalized without her immediate physical presence. She would *manage* the entire program, but she would not be involved verbally with the direct instructional input of each activity.

Ms. Cunningham realized that this was possible because the development of specific behavioral objectives enabled her to determine the nature of the learning experience as well as the method and materials that would be used to convey the information. To enable you to understand this procedure better, let us look at the following behavioral objective.

Behavioral Objective. After having completed a unit of study dealing with the topic of dinosaurs (external condition), the child will be able to exhibit the following behaviors without error (acceptable performance):

1. List the time periods in which dinosaurs lived (terminal behavior).
2. Discuss the various types of dinosaurs (terminal behavior).
3. Evaluate scientific methods employed to gain information about dinosaurs (terminal behavior).

The nature of the learning experience is the study of dinosaurs:

1. Types
2. Habitat
3. Relationship to man
4. Methods of data collection

The information regarding dinosaurs can be conveyed to the student through a variety of ways, some of which are (1) the teacher, (2) the text, and (3) technology. When we refer to technology, we want to include the following materials:

1. Reference books
2. Trade books
3. Magazines
4. Maps
5. Models
6. Films
7. Records

We have attempted to classify the materials as classroom aids to enable you to understand better their total utilization. A program designed and managed by the classroom teacher, with activities that do not require direct verbal input on the part of the teacher, becomes possible through the use of instructional technology. In this way, instructional technology is logically defined as classroom aids.

CLASSROOM AIDS

Audio Aids. Audio equipment primarily includes record players, radios, language laboratories, telelectures, and tape recorders. The portability and relatively low cost of the record player and radio increase their classroom utility. The tape recorder is another very versatile device because special sounds can be kept and replayed whenever the user wishes. The tape recorder can be used to highlight developmental language creativity by designing a *sound collage* that involves collecting environmental or commonplace sounds on tape, camouflaging these sounds through speed modification and tape loops, and then organizing and combining the sounds to form new combinations of sounds.

The sound collage can be used in a variety of ways: as a composition of its own, in a study of sound classification, or as a stimulus for creative writing. In addition, the composition can be used to introduce twentieth-century art forms or as background sound effects for an original dramatic production.

The *language laboratory* is used primarily to offer students instruction in foreign languages. Students listen to a recording and then verbally model the sounds they have heard. The teacher is able to monitor this experience through a mechanical device that enables him or her to listen to the conversation. The idea of the language laboratory has been incorporated within many technological reading programs for elementary schoolchildren because of its ability to provide specialized individualized attention for children in developing language and listening skills.

The *telelecture* enables groups of students to listen to prearranged conversations with renowned speakers. For example, a class studying the undersea world might greatly desire to speak personally with Jacques Cousteau.

Audio devices can be used in isolation or in conjunction with visual aids to create the setting necessary for one to totally experience pictorial representations. For example, music by Palestrina would enhance one's learning about the Renaissance. A similar experience might involve one's listening to Debussy while studying Impressionism. Audio devices not only offer the means to reach large groups, but they also provide an opportunity for a great variety of individual student tutoring. The role of the teacher becomes less burdensome because the teacher is freed from repeating lessons.

Visual Aids. Visual aids primarily include chalkboards, bulletin boards, opaque projectors, filmstrip and overhead projectors, teaching machines, and textbooks. Of all visual aids, the *textbook* is the one most frequently used. In many classes, the textbook is the major information source, and teachers are viewed as extensions of textbooks. However, in some classrooms, the teacher actually serves as the central factor synthesizing information from many textbook sources. The chalkboard is closely identified with this process because it has been used in learning situations for decades as a tool by which information can be transmitted.

Another long-time classroom material utilized as a means of transmitting information has been the display or *bulletin board*. Two-dimensional demonstrations are often found on felt, bulletin, or display boards. Through these sources, information can quickly be either conveyed or reinforced.

The *filmstrip* projector is certainly the most commonly found projector in American schools. Filmstrips, made from 35mm film, can be used by individuals or groups of students. This instructional device also serves to free the teacher for working with individuals who are having difficulty with particular concepts.

The use of the slide projector utilizing carrousels of slides has many possibilities for imparting visual information as well as sparking creativity. By combining tapes and groups of slides that are prepared commercially, by the teacher or by the students themselves, an audiovisual production can be obtained. With the accessibility of inexpensive cameras and slide development, the slide show can serve as a means of personal expression for student work.

Optical reflection is the principle on which the *opaque projector* operates. A darkened classroom is required for use because light is reflected off the projected material. This projector is widely used by students who wish to view photographs, drawings, documents, or other such materials. The opaque projector, like many other visual and audio aids is a means of transmitting information with the total aid of the classroom teacher.

The *overhead projector* is another device found in many school environments. It is used to transmit information to both large and small groups and presents tables, graphs, and lists with considerable clarity.

Teaching machines that convey information on just about every subject are found in many classrooms. Although automated features may be characteristic of some teaching machines, this is not standard. Teaching machines differ primarily in their presentation of information and questioning.

Many educators look askance at programmed material and teaching machines because of their early use as review, drill, and testing. Although today's programs do still serve these objectives, they are also being designed to *individualize* programs for *independent* study.

Educational programs completing and supplementing visual devices use the student's sense of sight. Visual aids can be employed in tutorial situations because they can be used to recreate the past, provide three-dimensional effects, present abstract information, represent microscopic life, and utilize natural color.

Through audio, as well as visual, aids the following positive educational results are made available: *individualized instruction* becomes a reality because the classroom teacher is aided with instructional implementation, curriculum materials based on *sequential development* are made available, students are matched with materials according to their strongest *learning modality,* and the classroom teacher is provided with *planning time*.

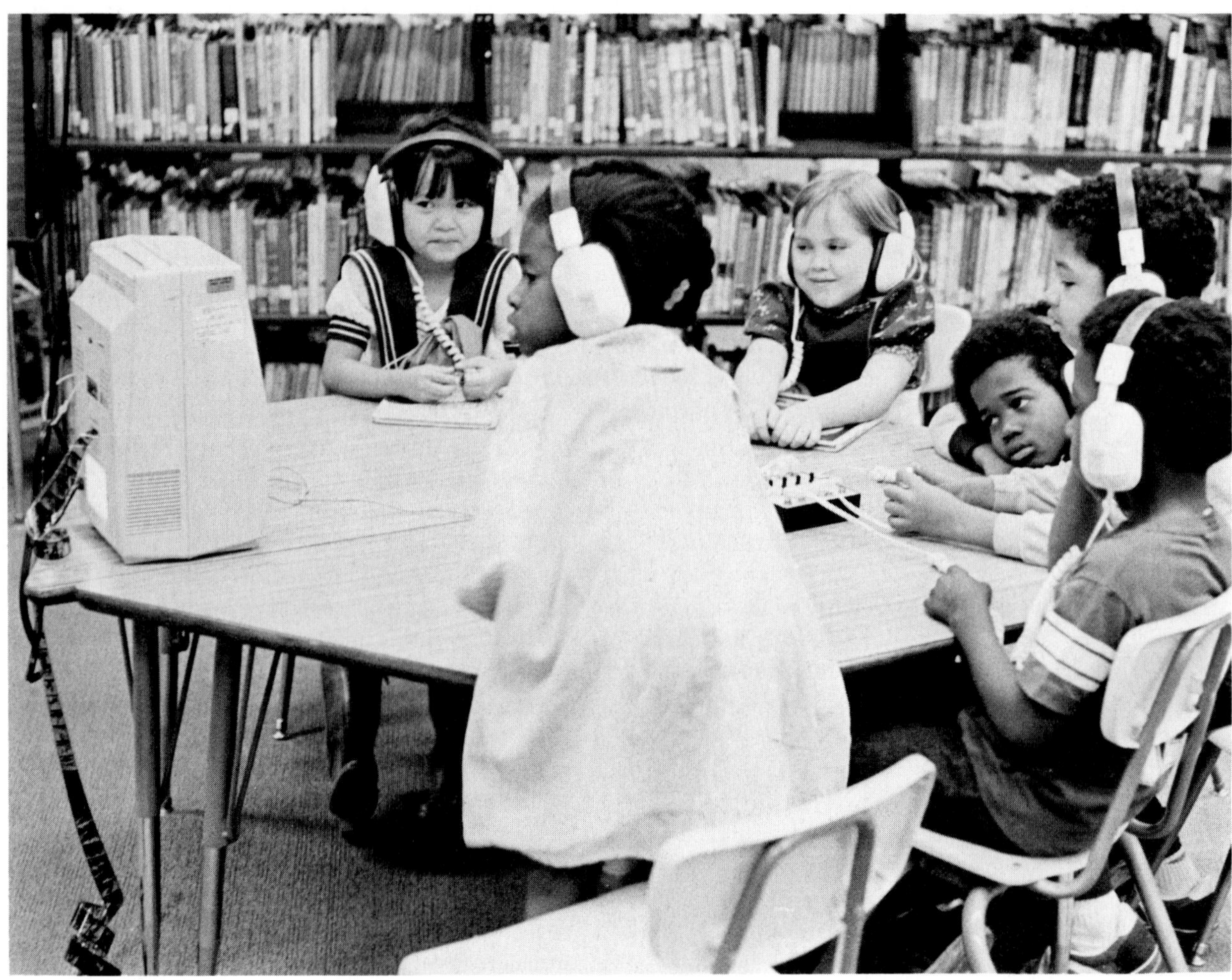

Visual aids can be employed in tutorial situations because they can be used to recreate the past, provide 3-dimensional effects, present abstract information, and utilize color. (Photo by Linda Lungren.)

Multisensory Aids. Technological materials involving more than one sense in the learning experience are commonly referred to as multisensory aids. Motion pictures, television, sandtables, sandpaper cutouts, indented objects, and felt or velvet boards are the most common multisensory aids found in educational settings.

The use of motion pictures involves primarily the senses of hearing and sight as well as the extension of emotional and other human experiences. Simplicity of operation and a vast range of personal involvement have been two prime factors in encouraging motion picture adoption as a teacher aid. Students can explore their own world and those of others through film.

Television is a medium that has advantages similar to those of film. While offering children the possibility of exploring the lives of others, television also capitalizes on the present, providing students with an opportunity for involvement in events as they happen.

Cognitive and psychomotor development are possible through the use of technological materials that involve the tactile and visual senses. Learning involving multisensory aids is strongly encouraged for young children in the process of developing reading readiness skills. Multisensory aids can be inexpensive and adaptable to a variety of learning experiences. Whenever you employ technology, continuously evaluate its effectiveness for a particular subject area or goal accomplishment.

Computer Aids. Computers in their simplest form have been part of the educational scene since the 1950s. The first educational computer, the analog, was limited in implementation accuracy because of its restrictive measurement potential. The analog was followed by the digital computer, which can be used for addition, subtraction, multiplication, and division and for drawing pictures and doing language translations. Through the use of computer-assisted instruction the interests, motivation, and range of information provided to students can be greatly expanded.

Through the use of computer–assisted instruction the interests, motivation, and range of information provided to students can be greatly expanded. (Photo by Linda Lungren.)

The use of technology in an educational setting must be carefully implemented, and educators must be fully aware of the following concerns:

1. Who prepares the materials?
   a. Goals
   b. Programs
   c. In-service training
   d. Research
   e. Evaluation
   f. Funding
2. Who is responsible for program control?
   a. Administration
   b. Faculty
   c. Community
   d. Materials
   e. Funds
   f. Values transmitted
3. What is the role of the teacher?
   a. Developer
   b. Diagnostician
   c. Implementer
   d. Evaluator
   e. In-service model
4. How are students affected?
5. What are the community relations?

When it is used *correctly*, technology can help you personalize your learning environment. Ms. Cunningham found that her students had to take a very *active* part in the learning process. Ms. Cunningham was able to use all these resources by designing prescriptive learning packets for each student.

Learning Prescriptions. Each packet contained the daily learning assignments as well as grouping arrangements for each student. Assignments and grouping arrangements were determined through *formal* and *informal assessment techniques*. Ms. Cunningham had developed this program very deliberately because her purpose was to *meet the various needs* of all her students, while *maintaining a manageable program*. Classroom arrangement facilitated the development of individual needs and accommodated short-term grouping situations. Grouping arrangements were reassigned as student skills developed and changed. Grouping patterns (see the accompanying room arrangement) also varied according to the content area being studied at any given time, as well as the changing interests of the students.

The particular reading class that Shannon's parents saw included:

1. Four students who were members of group D and one child from group C reading directions, discussing plans, and building science incubators. These children were working in the *building production area*.
2. Three youngsters from group C discussing their answers to a set of story questions that involved their ability to *sequence* information as well as *predict* and *hypothesize* future similar events. These children were working in the *committee meeting area*.
3. Five children, also from group C, working independently on their assignments. These children were dispersed throughout the *independent study area*, as well as the *library*, because their learning prescriptions required use of the card catalog and reference books.
4. Two children from group B sitting together in the *independent study area* reading a newspaper story and developing a time line. This activity aided the children in understanding sequential development, which is essential for total comprehension.
5. One child also from Group C and three from group B in the *listening area* listening to a newscast. All these children were interested in media and social-political events. Their assignment was to listen for cause-effect social happenings presented by the newcasters. After the newscast these children were asked to survey the morning newspaper to determine if they had interpreted the newscast accurately.
6. Four other children from group B in the *independent study area* completing worksheets taken directly from their basal program.
7. One student from group A in the *listening area* equipped with a headphone set. He was listening to and reading a primer. This activity reinforced basic sight-word reading skills.
8. Two other children from group A with Ms. Cunningham in the *private conference tutorial area* discussing a basal story they had just finished reading.

"How does everyone know what to do?" Shannon's

parents asked Ms. Cunningham. She told them that she used a system of management through learning prescriptive contracts. She explained that this approach enabled children to take responsibility for their work tasks. The prescriptive contract was simply a note to each child that specified (1) daily goals, (2) assignments and time schedule, and (3) grouping arrangements. Each child's prescriptions were kept in a manila folder for easy reference. The following prescriptive contract appeared in Shannon's file:

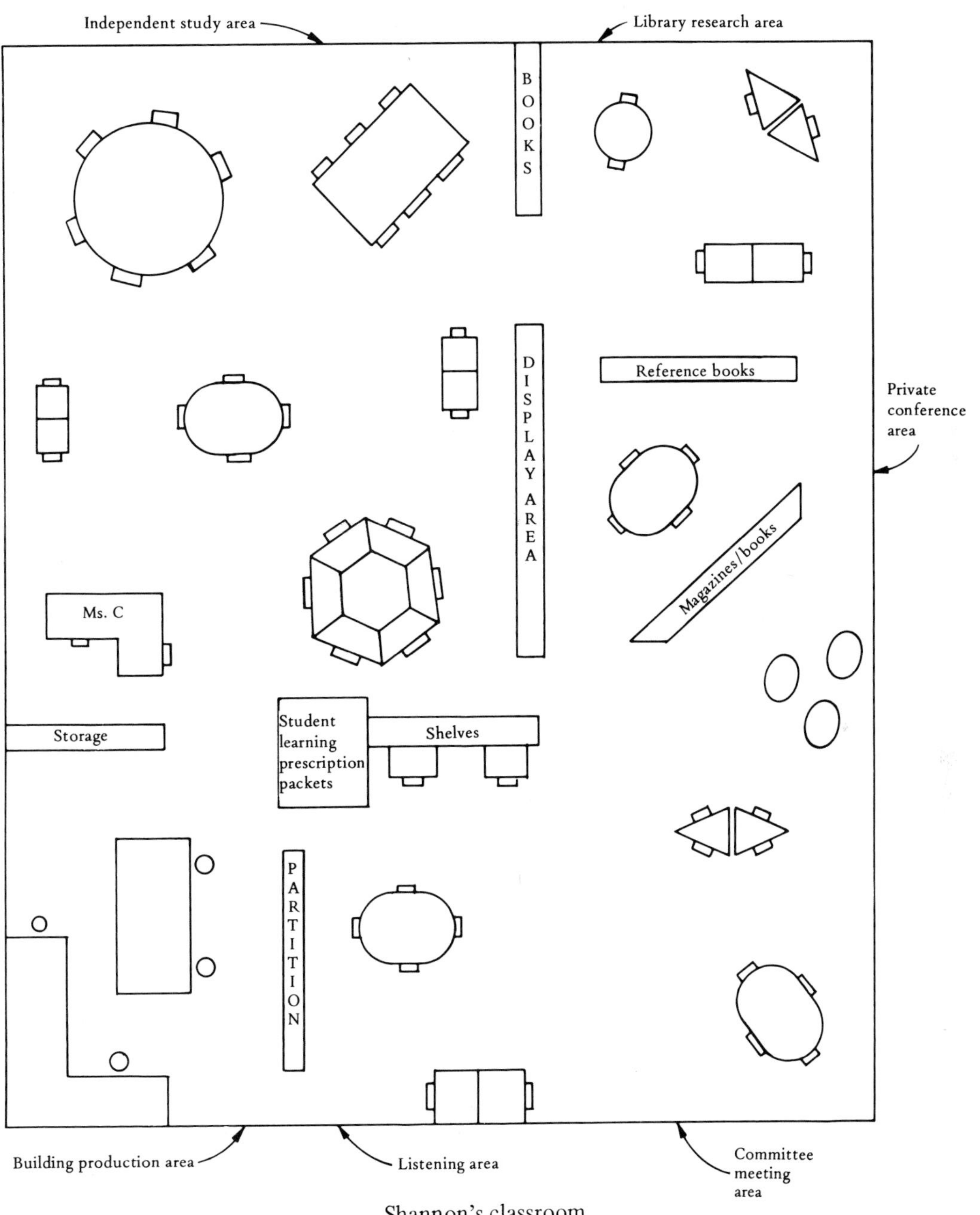

Shannon's classroom.

Good Morning, Shannon!
How is Duchess? You're lucky to have such a nice dog. Did you have fun with her on Saturday? Tell me about it when you and I have some free time.
Please work on the following:
9:00–10:30

1. Reading level 9, p. 32, End-of-Unit Test
2. After the test, you may do any *two* of the following:
   a. Work on a crossword puzzle in the library.
   b. Go to the listening area and select a book about an American inventor. Put on headphones and listen to the tape and read your book. After listening and reading, write three character traits you share in common with the inventor.
   c. Browse through the library and select and read a book you might enjoy.

Shannon, as soon as I have a free moment, I'll help you check your test and give you further reading assignments for Tuesday and Wednesday.

10:30–10:45 Recess—Have a nice break.

10:45–11:30

Math—Complete your math assignment from last Friday. If you have trouble with the multiplication problems, please ask Denise, Mary, or Harold for help. Also, finish lesson 6 in your math text. Continue to work on this task on Tuesday and Wednesday.

11:30–12:15

Science (Monday–Wednesday)—Work with your group on the science experiment we discussed last Thursday. Refer to contract sheet No. 23 for specific instructions.

12:15–1:15 Lunch

1:15–2:00

Social Studies—Meet in the independent study area. Complete your project. I'll assign new groups on Tuesday.

2:00–2:15 Recess

2:15–2:30

On Monday please meet me in the private conference area. We'll talk about your work. On Tuesday and Wednesday you may use this time to finish a task of your choice, or you may choose a new area of interest. You might like to read the new *Ranger Rick Science Magazine*.

2:30–3:00

Complete the unfinished tasks or engage in
1. reading your library book.
2. working crossword puzzles.
3. reading a magazine.
4. selecting and completing an art activity listed in the art activity file.
5. resting and reflecting on your day.

Shannon, if you have anything you want to share with me, please write it on the attached sheet. Have a good day and I'll see you tomorrow.

Although each child's tasks were clearly stated in the prescriptive learning packet, Ms. Cunningham continually mingled with groups of children, as well as individuals, to determine if any immediate issues needed to take precedence over the prescriptive task. Each child had many individual encounters with Ms. Cunningham during any given day.

While observing Shannon's class, her parents realized that individualized prescriptive learning packets did not mean that every child in the class was working on a different task in a different subject area. Students were *grouped* by needs and interests. The program was very *manageable*.

Shannon's parents asked about the time constraints of evaluating the learning prescriptions. Ms. Cunningham explained that she had initially been overwhelmed by the evaluation component of this program, but she had decided to make her program succeed by devising a manageable plan for evaluating everyone's learning prescriptions. She knew that, although she was a dedicated teacher, she also had many personal responsibilities and was, therefore, unable to devote *entire* evenings or weekends to school management.

She explained that continuous evaluation was an essential part of this program because succeeding assignments were based on the competencies and needs of each child as they completed their tasks. From her initial attempts at evaluating the learning prescriptions,

Ms. Cunningham concluded that approximately ten to twelve minutes were required to review a student's completed prescription. Because Ms. Cunningham was responsible for developing and evaluating learning prescriptions for twenty-six students, she decided to develop each prescription for three-day periods. She was only required to review seven to nine folders daily. Ms. Cunningham believed that this one- to two-hour process required no more of her time than had the daily grading of individual workbooks and worksheets that accumulated before she attempted to individualize her instruction.

Ms. Cunningham explained that during the day she made minor evaluations whenever time permitted. Immediately after school, she continued the process of evaluating and grading student's work. Evaluations not completed during the day were finished during the evening or the next morning before school.

When developing, evaluating, and replanning a child's prescriptive program, Ms. Cunningham asked herself the following questions:

1. Is the child completing the learning task successfully?
2. How can I continue to motivate this child?
3. Does the child work better at long or short assignments?
4. How can I best reinforce each student's learning successes?
5. What type of materials are most meaningful and interesting to this child?
6. How can I encourage the child to take more responsibility for his or her learning?
7. What learning techniques encourage the effective development of memory skills?
8. How can I best help this child to transfer what has been learned in one subject area to other areas?
9. How can I best encourage the child to synthesize and generalize the information being learned?
10. How can I best encourage the child to make evaluative decisions about the validity of the information being learned?

By answering these questions, Ms. Cunningham was able to continually evaluate *what* had been mastered and to *plan* the next step for each child. You may also want to pursue these questions if you are interested in implementing Ms. Cunningham's program strategies.

Continued Assessment, Recycling, and Sequential Learning

Once the specific objectives have been designed and information has been conveyed, we must determine varying means of disseminating information for those students who have not reached mastery, as well as develop sequential learning for others who have achieved the prescribed competency level.

A classroom plan would look like this:

Theme		
To introduce a group of second-grade students to Earth as a planet.	To introduce a group of children to the concept of propaganda in written text.	To introduce a group of third-graders to the concept of measured length.
Objectives		
1. Develop knowledge of the conditions that are needed for life on the planet Earth.	1. Develop an understanding of the various types of propaganda.	1. Develop an understanding of the following terms: meter, centimeter, millimeter.
2. Gain an understanding of the movement and size of the planet Earth.	2. Gain an ability to detect written bias and the underlying viewpoint of the bias.	2. Gain an understanding of the use of the meter stick to measure length.

Student Preassessment

Informal or formal measures to determine each student's knowledge of the planet Earth, as well as his or her ability to read the available topical materials.

Informal or formal data collection in an attempt to determine each student's knowledge of propaganda, as well as the ability to read the available topical materials.

Informal or formal data collection in an attempt to determine each student's knowledge of measuring length, as well as the ability to read the available topical materials.

Behavioral Objectives

1. After a discussion of the sizes and movements of the planets, the student will be able to draw and correctly discuss the dimensions of the planet Earth.
2. At the conclusion of a unit of study focusing on living conditions of Earth, the student will discuss, with average competency (allow individual criteria), how air, water, light, warmth, and soil make life possible on Earth.

1. After completing a unit of study dealing with propaganda, the student will be able to circle all the sentences in a paragraph that reveal bias and tell which viewpoint the author holds.
2. Given several sample advertisements or paragraphs, the student will be able to label all those evidencing the following types of propaganda: bad name, bandwagon, testimonial, card stacking.

1. After a discussion of standard and informal measures of length, the student will be able to correctly measure, to the nearest meter or centimeter, all presented objects of various lengths.
2. Having completed a unit of study dealing with the terms *meter*, *centimeter*, *millimeter*, the student will be able to verbally or in writing correctly define each.

Procedure

1. Teacher directed (lecture).
2. Student-teacher directed (plays, games, discussions).
3. Student directed (reports, panels).

After having planned and implemented the theme, you must continue to evaluate.

Evaluation

Through informal and formal measures, one must make the following decisions:

1. Determine if the objective has been met.
   a. Determine if there are related objectives to be designed and utilized at this time.
   b. Determine procedures for implementation of new objectives.
2. Determine if the objective has not been met.
   a. Determine if the objective should be terminated at this time because it is unrealistic.
   b. Determine which criterion of the stated objective has failed (acceptable performance level, external conditions, terminal behavior).
   c. Develop new procedures or external conditions or acceptable performance levels to meet the initial objective if you have determined that the objective is relevant to your situation.

After making decisions related to the mastery of materials, you may regroup and proceed. Thus, through the aid of an educational management system, we have surveyed, planned, implemented, reimplemented, or sequenced an integrated theme. Continuous evaluation is the prime ingredient for success in a program of this type. A system of management enables you, as a teacher, to state clearly the desired terminal behaviors, evaluate instructional effectiveness, and determine sequential learning.

Mastery of instruction may be affected by the amount of instructional time utilized for topical presentation, background readiness of your students, manner or method of presentation, complexity of material, and student interest. As suggested in earlier chapters, instruction needs to be carefully sequenced in order to encourage the children to *formulate* the concept, *interpret* the information, and *apply* the learned principles and facts. Piaget (1959), Gagné (1965), Bloom (1967), and Taba (1967) offer many insights into the educational procedures that should be used when you are sequencing instruction.

As you review the effectiveness of your simulated classroom, we encourage you to consider the following facts:

1. Sequencing instruction through the aid of a management system enables you to avoid a hit-or-miss, ineffectual type of teaching.
2. Sequencing instruction through the use of a management system enables children to proceed according to their developing competencies.
3. Sequencing instruction through the aid of a management system enables you to manage complex skills better by presenting them in smaller, subordinate parts.
4. Sequencing instruction through the aid of a management system enables you to develop a clearer understanding of *how children learn*.

You must remember that a program of this type is certainly not a "new idea." You will be able to succeed in your attempts if you always remain cognizant of the following facts:

1. Students are not "on their own" in learning. The degree of decision-making responsibility shared by the student must be commensurate with his or her experience and ability. It is *the teacher's* responsibility to plan the program and thus guide each student's independence and initiative in learning situations. The learner will, however, have a new role in the individualized program. A child will no longer be found resting contentedly in a program where all the decisions are made for him or her. You will provide each with options, and from these options the child will choose what, where, when, and how to pursue the learning task. Children in your classroom will no longer know the frustrations of being tagged a "slow learner." Through individualized learning prescription, children will no longer pursue learning in a lock-step fashion.
2. The degree of program individualization must depend on the *task* to be accomplished, the readiness exposures of the child for the given task, and your abilities to manage multiple methods for accomplishing a given task. You may be more successful in your attempts to individualize your program if you start with only one content area. Once you are successful with initial attempts, you may want to expand the program. You are the program manager. Be careful not to design a program you are unable to manage.
3. Use the materials you currently have to individualize your program. Do not use a lack of materials as an excuse for not individualizing your curriculum. Your *incentive* is the prime factor in the success of these initial attempts.
4. The major portion of your time will be spent in *planning* instructional procedures that may be executed independently by your students. This will be difficult for you in the beginning because you have previously spent as much time *implementing* as *planning*. Your planning of learning prescriptions will be based on what the child has previously accomplished. You may want to develop anecdotal file cards or checklists to enable you to assess the competencies as they are acquired by each individual student.
5. Students will be involved with both the *implementing* and *correcting* responsibilities of their learning. Because each learning prescription will be designed with the learner as the central focus, students will feel that their efforts have been worthwhile.
6. As a teacher you are responsible for the individual development of *each* child. Your professional exper-

tise must be conveyed in a variety of ways if each child is to intellectually and emotionally grow from the encounter. You cannot teach children only today's body of literal facts and expect them to be critical decision makers tomorrow. Your curriculum must encourage this growth by being custom tailored to each learner.

This program will become a reality only if you believe that there is *no one best way* to learn. If this is your belief, select a small portion of your curriculum and begin the process of designing a manageable individualized program. You may be most comfortable following Ms. Cunningham's model by attempting to personalize your reading program. Whatever your choice, good luck in your endeavors.

QUESTIONS AND RELATED READINGS

If you feel that you have not attained adequate knowledge to answer the following questions successfully, we suggest additional related readings.

1. What considerations must be evaluated when planning a classroom management system?
2. Explain the process and value of interrelating your curriculum through thematic teaching.
3. On what basis should groups be formed and how should they be used?
4. Of what value are behavioral objectives in a reading program?
5. Discuss the range of materials and equipment available for instructional purposes.
6. How is individualized instruction facilitated through continuous evaluation?

Goal 1: To help the reader to recognize the factors contributing to effective classroom management.

Question 1: What considerations must be evaluated when planning a classroom management system?

Emmer, C. T., C. M. Evertson, and L. M. Anderson. "Effective Classroom Management at the Beginning of the School Year." *The Elementary School Journal* 80:5 (1980), 216–24.

Indrisano, R. "Reading–Managing the Classroom Reading Program." *Instructor* 4 (January 1978), 117–20.

Mangieri, J. N. "Characteristics of an Effectively Organized Classroom." In *Making Reading Possible Through Effective Classroom Management*, ed. by D. Lapp. Newark, Del.: International Reading Association, 1980, 10–26.

Goal 2: To help the reader to learn how to develop and implement thematic teaching.

Question 2: Explain the process and value of interrelating your curriculum through thematic teaching.

Chaney, B., and D. Zjaivin. "Our Dinosaur Sits in the Front Row." *Instructor* 8 (March 1981), 44–51.

Fletcher, D. "ERIC/RCS Report: Interdisciplinary Perspectives in Teaching High School English." *English Journal* 69 (February 1980), 81–4.

Kohl, H. "Using Themes Significant to Children." *Teacher* 96:8 (April 1979), 16, 18–20.

Goal 3: To help the reader to learn successful grouping techniques.

Question 3: On what basis should groups be formed and how should they best be used?

Hauze, J. "A Second Look at Small Group Instruction." *Clearing House* 53:8 (April 1980), 376–8.

Lapp, D. "Beyond the Redbirds, Bluebirds, and Yellowbirds." *Reporting on Reading* 5 (March 1979), 1–9.

Williams, M. H. "Does Grouping Affect Motivation?" *Elementary School Journal* 73 (December 1972), 130–7.

Goal 4: To help the reader to recognize behavioral objectives as an essential instructional tool.

Question 4: Of what value are behavioral objectives in a reading program?

Allen, D. I., and R. T. White. "Learning Objectives and Teaching Strategies." *Canadian Journal of Education* 5:2 (1980), 23–42.

Smith, P. G. "On the Logic of Behavioral Objectives." *Phi Delta Kappan* 53 (March 1972), 429–31.

Thiagarajan, S. "Individualizing Instructional Objectives." *Teaching Exceptional Children* 12:3 (Spring 1980), 126–7.

Goal 5: To help the reader to sample a variety of instructional methods.

Question 5: Discuss the range of materials and equipment available for instructional purposes.

Fitzgerald, M. J. "Asking Questions with the Help of Pictures and Slides: Some Language Games." *English Language Teaching Journal* 34:4 (July 1980), 277–81.

McCabe, J. "A School Computer, Yours for the Asking." *Creative Computing* 6:9 (September 1980), 48–53.

Stevenson, V. J. "Switched-on Learning: Education Through Modern Media." *American Annals of the Deaf* 125:6 (September 1980), 714–20.

Goal 6: To help the reader to recognize the importance of continuous evaluation.

Question 6: How is individualized instruction facilitated through continuous evaluation?

Barth, R. S. "Pupil Evaluation and Teacher Growth." *Independent School* 39:2 (December 1979), 21–2, 25–9.

Hillerich, R. L. "Continuous Assessment of Instructional Needs in Reading." In *Making Reading Possible Through Effective Classroom Management*, ed. by D. Lapp. Newark, Del.: International Reading Association, 1980, 116–45.

John, J. L. "Reading Assessment–The Third Dimension." *Reading Horizons* 19:3 (Spring 1979), 235–6.

BIBLIOGRAPHY

Alkin, M. C. *The Use of Behavioral Objectives in Education: Relevant or Irrelevant.* ED035067 Microfiche. Los Angeles: University of California, Los Angeles Center for the Study of Evaluation, May 9, 1968, 27 pp.

Ammons, M. "The Definition, Function, and Use of Educational Objectives." *The Elementary School Journal* 62 (May 1962), 432–6.

Aukerman, R. C. *The Basal Reader Approach to Reading.* New York: John Wiley & Sons, Inc., 1981.

Barrett, T. C. "Taxonomy of Cognitive and Affective Dimensions of Reading Comprehension." Unpublished paper.

Binet, A., and T. Simon. *The Development of Intelligence in Children.* Baltimore: The Williams and Wilkins Company, 1916.

Bloom, B. S., ed. *Taxonomy of Educational Objectives. Handbook I: Cognitive Domain.* New York: David McKay Co., Inc., 1967.

Borko, H., R. J. Shavelson, and P. Stern. "Teachers' Decisions in the Planning of Reading Instruction." *Reading Research Quarterly* 16:3 (1981), 449–66.

Burnett, R. W. "The Classroom Teacher as a Diagnostician." In *Reading Diagnosis and Evaluation*, ed. by D. L. DeBoar. Vol. XIII, Part 4, Proceedings of the Thirteenth Annual Convention. Newark, Del.: International Reading Association, 1970, p. 4.

Burr, C. "Writing Behavioral Objectives: A Self-instruction Module." *Queensland Science Teacher* 6 (February 1980), 24–57.

Combs, A. W. *The Professional Education of Teachers.* Boston: Allyn & Bacon, Inc., 1965.

Dewey, J. *Experience and Education.* New York: Macmillan Publishing Co., Inc., 1938.

Durr, W. K. *The Houghton Mifflin Reading Program.* Boston: Houghton Mifflin Company, 1981.

Farr, R. "Foreword." In *Making Reading Possible Through Effective Classroom Management*, ed. by D. Lapp. Newark, Del.: International Reading Association, 1980. Chapter opening quotation appears on page v.

Fay, L. C. *Rand McNally Reading Program: Young America Basic Series.* Lombard, Ill.: Riverside Publishing Company, 1981.

Gagné, R. M. *The Conditions of Learning.* New York: Holt, Rinehart and Winston, 1965.

Gilpin, J. G. "Foreward." In *Preparing Instructional Objectives*, ed. by R. F. Mager. Palo Alto, Calif.: Fearon Publishers, 1962.

Hambleton, R. K., H. Swaminathan, J. Algino, and D. B. Coulson. "Criterion-Referenced Testing and Measurement: A Review of Technical Issues and Developments." *Review of Educational Research* 48:1 (Winter 1978), 1–47.

Hammond, R. L. *Evaluation at the Local Level.* Miller Committee for the National Study of ESEA Title III. Washington, D.C.: U.S. Office of Education, 1967.

Johnson, R. K. "JH/MS Idea Factory: Designs for Middle School Interdisciplinary Studies." *English Journal* 69:2 (February 1980), 59–62.

Lapp, D. "Behavioral Objectives Writing Skills Test." *Journal of Education* 154 (February 1972), 13–24. This test may be secured from Educational Testing Services, Princeton, New Jersey.

——. *The Use of Behavioral Objectives in Education.* Newark, Del.: International Reading Association, 1972.

——. "Can Elementary Teachers Write Behavioral Objectives?" *Journal of Education* 155:3 (February 1973), 13–9.

——. "Individualized Reading Instruction Made Easy for Teachers." *Early Years* 7:6 (February 1977), 63–67, 73.

Mager, R. F. *Preparing Instructional Objectives.* Palo Alto, Calif.: Fearon Publishers, 1962.

Millman, J. "Criterion-Referenced Measurement." In *Evaluation in Education: Current Applications*, ed. by W. J. Popham. Berkeley, Calif.: McCutchen Publishing Company, 1974.

O'Donnell, M. P., and B. Moore. "Eliminating Common Stumbling Blocks to Organizational Change." In *Making Reading Possible Through Effective Classroom Management*, ed. by D. Lapp. Newark, Del.: International Reading Association, 1980, 186–215.

Piaget, J. *The Language and Thought of the Child*, 3rd ed. New York: The Humanities Press, Inc., 1959.

Popham, W. J. *Educational Evaluation.* Englewood Cliffs, N.J.: Prentice-Hall, Inc., 1975.

Tests

GUIDE TO READING TESTS AND MEASUREMENTS

The following is a list of reading tests currently in print. It is designed to be a quick reference for teachers and other practitioners in deciding which tests are appropriate for their use. This listing is similar in format to an earlier list compiled by Roger Farr in "Reading: What Can Be Measured?"* For example, if a tester wants to identify a student's abilities in comprehension, he or she simply looks at those tests marked "*x*" under the comprehension column.

The tests have been divided into seven categories: (1) readiness, (2) general reading survey tests, (3) diagnostic, (4) oral reading, (5) study skills, (6) special fields, such as content area skills, and (7) miscellaneous. The tests are listed alphabetically by name and include the following information:

1. *Title of test*. This is the title listed on the front cover of the test. The date on which it was first published and the most recent revision are given below the title. If an asterisk (*) precedes the test title, it indicates that the test is known to be an individual test.

2. *Grade*. This is the suggested grade level for use of the test as indicated by the publisher. In some cases, only the age levels are supplied. However, these have been converted to the nearest grade-level equivalents.

3. *Number of forms.* Some tests have alternate forms available for pre- and posttesting of the examinees.

4. *Approximate time (in minutes)*. The approximate time required to administer the test is listed, according to information given by the publisher.

5. *Publisher*. The publisher's name has been abbreviated in the interest of conserving space. An index listing the complete name and address of each publisher follows the test guide. Many times the test publisher is very willing to send sample tests on request, or samples may be available at a college of education library.

6. *Author(s)*. These are names found in the test booklets.

7. *"Designed to assist in the evaluation of . . .".* This information was obtained through the listing of subtests provided by the publisher and also from *Tests in Print* by Oscar Buros. Any skills that do not belong under the given categories are listed under "Other."

8. *Volume and test number in Mental Measurement Yearbooks and page number(s) in Reading Tests and Reviews I (RTR I)* or *Reading Tests and Reviews II (RTR II).* This provides a quick index to the critiques compiled by Buros in *Mental Measurement Yearbooks.*† A double asterisk (**) indicates that the review came from another source, which can be found at the bottom of the page.

These reviews written by professionals throughout the country should be studied before any test is selected. Although the critiques in *Reading Tests and Reviews I* or *II* are identical to those in *Mental Measurement Yearbooks*, they are both listed for those situations in which the tester has access to only one of the references.

The first column gives the volume number of the *Mental Measurement Yearbook* and the number of the test as it appears in that volume. The number of the most recent review of the test is listed. The "Reading Test and Review" column gives the page number on which the description and critique of the test appears. Some tests are not described in either volume.

To give an example, the entries for the California Phonics Survey are 7:714 and RTR I:338. The first set of numbers indicates that a critique of the test can be found in Buros' *Seventh Mental Measurement Yearbook* and is test 714 listed in that volume. The second number stands for page 338 in *Reading Tests and Reviews I*, where a critique of the test can also be found.

*Roger Farr, "Reading: What Can Be Measured?" ERIC/CRIER Reading Review Series, 1969.

†Oscar Buros, *Mental Measurement Yearbooks.* Highland Park, N.J.: Gryphon Press, 1978.

READINESS TESTS

Name of Test	For Grades	No. of Forms	Approx. Time (in min.)	Publisher	Author(s)	Speed	Vocabulary
ABC Inventory to Determine Kindergarten and School Readiness, 1965	K–1	1		**RC	N. Adair G. Blesch		x
Academic Readiness and End of First Grade Progress Scales, 1968	1	1	5–10	AP	H. Burks		x
American School Reading Readiness Test, 1941; rev. 1964	K–1	1	45	BM	W. E. Pratt R. V. Young C. A. Whitmer G. Stouffer		x
Analysis of Readiness Skills: Reading and Mathematics, 1972	K–1	1	30–40	HM	M. Rodrigues W. Vogler J. Wilson		
*Anton Brenner Developmental Gestalt Test of School Readiness, 1945; rev. 1964	K–1	1	3–10	WPS	A. Brenner		
APELL Test: Assessment Program of Early Learning Levels, 1969	Pre K–1	1	40	EC	E. Cochran J. Shannon		
Barclay Early Childhood Skill Assessment Guide, 1973	Pre K–1	1	10	ESD	L. Barclay J. Barclay		
*The Basic Concept Inventory, Field Research Edition, 1967	Pre K–1	1	15–25	FEC	S. Englemann		
Binion-Beck Reading Readiness Test for Kindergarten and First Grade, 1945	K–1	1	40	APC	H. S. Binion R. L. Beck		
A Checklist for the Evaluation of Reading Readiness	Pre K			JS	J. Sanacore		
*Childhood Identification of Learning Disabilities, 1974	Pre K+			WLC			

*Individual test.
**The publisher's full name and address follow this listing: for example, RC is the abbreviation for Research Concepts.

Comprehension	Word Recognition and Attack	Spelling	Auding	Other	Vol. and Test No. in *Mental Measurement Yearbooks*	Pages in *Reading Tests and Reviews, I* or *II* (Buros)
				Readiness skills—draw a man, characteristics of objects, number, and shapes	7:739	RTR II: 129–30
x				Perceptual motor, memory, number recognition, word recognition, emotional aspects	8:795	RTR II: 130–31
				Alphabet, word-matching discrimination, memory of geometric forms, following directions	5:675	RTR I: 219–20
				Visual perception of letters and identification, counting, identification of numbers; English or Spanish	8:796	
				Number recognition, ten-dot gestalt sentence, gestalt draw-a-man	7:742	RTR II: 131–32
				Visual discrimination, letter names, premath skills, language, nouns, verbs	8:794	
				Sensory tasks, motor perceptual skills, environmental exploration, visual and auditory imitation, self-concept, task-order skills, social interaction	8:423	
				Basic concepts, pattern awareness, statement repetition	7:743	RTR II: 132–33
				Picture vocabulary and discrimination, following directions, memory for story, motor control	3:514	RTR I: 128–29
			x	Visual discrimination, left-to-right orientation, oral language development, concept development, social and emotional development, motor coordination		
				Visual motor, speech, visual abilities, hearing, fine and gross motor skills, psychological perceptual abilities		

Name of Test	For Grades	No. of Forms	Approx. Time (in min.)	Publisher	Author(s)	Speed	Vocabulary
CIRCUS: A, 1974; 14 subtests	Pre K–K	1	15 each	ETS			x
Clymer-Barrett Prereading Battery, 1966; rev. 1967	K–1	2	90	PPI	T. Clymer T. Barrett		
Cognitive Skills Assessment Battery, 1974	Pre K	1	20–25	TCP	A. Boehm B. Slatan		x
*The Contemporary School Readiness Test, 1970	K–1	1	105	MRCP	C. Sauer		
Delco Readiness Test, 1970	K–1	1		DRT	W. Rhoades		
Diagnostic Reading Tests—Reading Readiness, 1947; rev. 1972	K–1	1	Untimed	CDRT	F. Triggs		x
Early Detection Inventory	Pre K	1	45	FEC	F. McGahan C. McGahan		
Evanston Early Identification Skill, Field Research Edition, 1967	K–1	1	10–45	FEC	M. Landsman H. Dillard		
*First Grade Screening Test, 1966–69	K	1	30–45	AGS	J. Pate W. Webb		
Gates-MacGinitie Reading Tests—Readiness Skills, 1939; rev. 1969	K–1	1	120	TCP	A. I. Gates W. MacGinitie		
Gesell Developmental Tests, 1964; rev. 1965	K–5	1	20–30	PE	F. Ilg L. Ames		
Harrison-Stroud Reading Readiness Profiles, 1949; rev. 1956	K–1	1	80–90	HM	M. L. Harrison J. B. Stroud		
Initial Survey Test, 1970; rev. 1972	K	2	120–150	SP	M. Monroe J. Manning J. Wepman E. Gibb		

Comprehension	Word Recognition and Attack	Spelling	Auding	Other	Vol. and Test No. in *Mental Measurement Yearbooks*	Pages in *Reading Tests and Reviews, I* or *II* (Buros)
			x	Visual discrimination, perceptual-motor coordination, letter and numeral recognition, comprehension of oral language, problem solving	8:7A	
			x	Visual discrimination, visual-motor performance, auditory discrimination	7:744	RTR I: 15
x				Visual-motor coordination, color and shape identification, auditory and visual memory, symbol discrimination, letter naming, and visual-auditory discrimination	8:797	
			x	Colors, science, health, social studies, numbers, handwriting, listening/comprehension, reading	7:745	RTR II: 137–8
				Visual motor, visual discrimination		
				Relationships, coordination, left-to-right approach, visual discrimination	8:754	
				School readiness tasks, social-emotional behavior responses, motor performance	7:746	RTR II: 138–40
				Identifying children expected to have school difficulties	7:747	RTR II: 140–42
				Intellectual deficiency, central nervous system dysfunction, emotional disturbance	7:748	RTR II: 142–3
x	x		x	Visual discrimination, following directions, letter recognition, visual-motor coordination	7:749	RTR I: 143–5
				Readiness to start school	7:750	RTR II: 145–6
			x	Using symbols, visual discrimination, using context, names of letters	5:677	RTR I: 265–6
			x	Language meanings, visual ability, letter recognition, sound-letter relationships, mathematics	8:799	

Name of Test	For Grades	No. of Forms	Approx. Time (in min.)	Publisher	Author(s)	Speed	Vocabulary
*An Inventory of Primary Skills, 1970	K–1			F	R. Valett		
Keystone Ready to Read Tests, 1954	K	1		KVC			
Kindergarten Evaluation of Learning Potential, 1963; rev. 1969	K–1	1		CTB	J. Wilson M. Robeck		
Lee-Clark Reading Readiness Test, 1931; rev. 1962	K–1	1	20	CTB	J. M. Lee W. W. Clark		
Lippincott Reading Readiness Test (including Readiness Checklist), 1965	K–1	1		JLC	P. H. McLeod		
Macmillan Reading Readiness Test, Revised Edition, 1965–1970	K–1	1	75–90	MC	A. Harris L. Sipay		x
*Maturity Level for School Entrance and Reading Readiness, 1950; rev. 1959	K–1	1	20	AGS	K. Banham		
McHugh-McParland Reading Readiness Test, 1966; rev. 1968	K–1	1		CSB	W. McHugh M. McParland		
Metropolitan Readiness Tests, 1976 Edition, 1933–1976	K–1	2	105–110	PC	M. E. McGauvran J. R. Nurss		
Monroe Reading Aptitude Tests, 1935	K–1	1	40–55	HM	M. Monroe		
Murphy-Durrell Reading Readiness Analysis, 1949; rev. 1965	K–1	1	60	PC	H. A. Murphy D. D. Durrell		
PMA Readiness Level, 1974	K–1	1	10–15	SRA	T. Thurstone		
*Parent Readiness Evaluation of Preschoolers, 1968; rev. 1969	Pre K–3	1	60–90	PII	A. E. Ahr B. Simons		

Comprehension	Word Recognition and Attack	Spelling	Auding	Other	Vol. and Test No. in *Mental Measurement Yearbooks*	Pages in *Reading Tests and Reviews, I* or *II* (Buros)
				Administered by parent: body identification, alphabet, numbers, draw a man, mathematics, class concepts, paragraph reading		
				Visual readiness skills		
				Association learning, conceptualization, self-expression	7:751	RTR II: 146–7
				Letter and word symbols, concepts	7:752	RTR II: 147-9
				Readiness skills	7:753	RTR II: 149–50
	x		x	Visual discrimination, rating scale, letter names, visual motor	8:801	
				Maturity level, behavior	6:847 4:572	RTR I: 374
			x	Visual discrimination, identifying letters, rhyming words, beginning sounds	7:754	RTR II: 150–3
			x	Alphabet, numbers, matching, copying, draw a man, word meaning, rhyming, language skills	8:802	
			x	Visual, motor, articulation	3:519	RTR I: 133
			x	Sound recognition, learning rate, letter names	8:803	RTR II: 159–61
			x	Verbal meaning, perceptual speed, number facility, spatial relations	8:804	
x			x	Administered by parent: verbal associations and descriptions, motor coordination, visual and auditory memory	7:759	RTR II: 161–4

Name of Test	For Grades	No. of Forms	Approx. Time (in min.)	Publisher	Author(s)	Speed	Vocabulary
Pre-Reading Assessment Kit, 1972	K–1			CTB	Ontario Institute for Studies in Education		x
Pre-Reading Screening Procedures, 1968; rev. 1969	1	1	40	EPS	B. Slingerland		
Prereading Expectancy Screening Scales, 1973	K–1	1	25–35	PEI	L. Hartlage D. Lucas		
Preschool and Kindergarten Performance Profile, 1970	Pre K–1			EPA	A. DiNola B. Kaminsky A. Sternfield		
Preschool Screening Instrument, 1973	K–1			FW	V. Kurko L. Crane H. Willemin		
Primary Academic Sentiment Scale, 1968	Pre K–2	1	50	PII	G. Thompson		
Reading Inventory, Probe 1, 1970; rev. 1973	1–2			ATC	Diagnostic Reading Committee S. Warner W. Myers		x
Reading Readiness Form A, 1953; rev. 1960	K–1	1	30–45	STS	O. Anderhalter R. Colestock		
*Riley Preschool Developmental Screening Inventory, 1969	Pre K–K	1	3–10	WPS	C. Riley		
*School Readiness Checklist, 1963; rev. 1968	K–1	1	10–20	RC	J. Austin J. Lafferty F. Leaske F. Cousino		
*School Readiness Survey, Second Edition, 1967–1975	K–1	1	15–30	CPP	F. Jordan J. Massey		x
School Readiness Test, 1974–1977	K–1	1	60	STS	O. Anderhalter		
Screening Test for the Assignment of Remedial Treatments, 1968	Pre K–1	1	60	PII	A. E. Ahr		x

Comprehension	Word Recognition and Attack	Spelling	Auding	Other	Vol. and Test No. in *Mental Measurement Yearbooks*	Pages in *Reading Tests and Reviews, I or II* (Buros)
x			x	Symbol perception		
			x	Visual discrimination, visual perception memory, letter knowledge	7:732	RTR II: 121–3
			x	Predicting reading problems: visual sequencing, letter identification, visual/auditory spatial awareness	8:805	
				Social, intellectual, and physical abilities		
			x	Memory auditory and visual, understanding language, motor skills, closure		
				Motivation for learning, level of maturity, and independence from parent	7:760	RTR II: 164–5
x			x	Visual discrimination		
			x	Uses of things, likenesses in words, listening for "c" and "d" sounds		
				School readiness: design, draw a boy or girl	8:806	
				Checklist to be used by parents	7:762	RTR II: 165–6
				Number concepts, discrimination of form, color naming, symbol matching, general information	8:807 7:763	RTR II: 166–7
x	x		x	Handwriting and number readiness, letters, visual discrimination	8:808–9	
			x	Visual memory, discrimination, copying	8:445	

Name of Test	For Grades	No. of Forms	Approx. Time (in min.)	Publisher	Author(s)	Speed	Vocabulary
Screening Test of Academic Readiness, 1966	K–1	1	60	PII	A. Ahr		x
Steinbach Test of Reading Readiness, 1963	K–1	1	45	STS	M. Steinbach		
Thackray Reading Readiness Profiles, 1974	K–2	1	70	HS	D. Thackray L. Thackray		x
*Valett Developmental Survey of Basic Learning Abilities, 1966	Pre K–1		60–70	CPP	R. Valett		
*Van Wagenen Reading Readiness Scales, 1933; rev. 1958	K–1	2	30	VW	M. J. Van Wagenen M. Klaeger		x
Watson Reading-Readiness Test, 1960	K–1	1	50–60	HC	G. Watson		

READING SURVEY TESTS

Name of Test	For Grades	No. of Forms	Approx. Time (in min.)	Publisher	Author(s)	Speed	Vocabulary
Academic Promise Tests, 1959; rev. 1969	6–9	2	90	PC	G. Bennett M. Bennett D. Clendenen J. Doppelt J. Ricks, Jr. H. Seashore A. Westman		
ACER Primary Reading Survey Tests, 1971–1973	1–6	2	23–40	ACER	M. Clark W. Renehan B. Rechter		x
ACT Proficiency Examination in Corrective and Remedial Instruction in Reading, 1975–1976	13+	1	180–210	ACTP	New York State College Proficiency Examinations Program		
Adult Basic Education Student Survey, 1966–1967	12+	2	300	FEC	E. Rasof M. Neff		

Comprehension	Word Recognition and Attack	Spelling	Auding	Other	Vol. and Test No. in *Mental Measurement Yearbooks*	Pages in *Reading Tests and Reviews, I* or *II* (Buros)
				Letters, picture completion, copying, picture description, human figure drawings, relationships, numbers	7:765	RTR II: 168–9
			x	Identifying letters, memory of word forms, language ability		RTR I: 16
			x	Visual discrimination, draw a man	8:810	
			x	Physical development, tactile discrimination, visual discrimination, language development and fluency, conceptual development	7:767	RTR II: 171–5
				Range and perception of information, opposites, memory open for ideas, word discrimination	3:520	RTR I: 134–5
				Subjective, objective (teacher's ratings), physical, social, emotional, and psychological readiness	6:851	RTR I: 377–8

Comprehension	Word Recognition and Attack	Spelling	Auding	Other	Vol. and Test No. in *Mental Measurement Yearbooks*	Pages in *Reading Tests and Reviews, I* or *II* (Buros)
				Verbal, numerical, and abstract reasoning; language usage	7:672	
x	x				8:714	
				College accreditation of nontraditional study or advanced placement	8:715	
x	x			Arithmetic subtests	7:2	

Name of Test	For Grades	No. of Forms	Approx. Time (in min.)	Publisher	Author(s)	Speed	Vocabulary
American School Achievement Tests: Part 1, Reading, Revised Edition, 1941–1975	2–3	2	25–35	BM	W. E. Pratt G. Stouffer, Jr. J. Yanuzzi		x
Primary Battery; rev. 1975							
Intermediate Battery; rev. 1975	4–6	2	25–35	BM	(See Reading Primary Battery)		x
Advanced Battery; rev. 1975	7–9	2	30–40	BM	(See Reading Primary Battery)		x
American School Reading Tests, 1955	10–13	2	80	BM	W. Pratt S. Lore	x	x
Basic Reading Inventory, 1978	Pre K–8	3		WBC	J. Johns		
Brown-Carlsen Listening Comprehension Test, 1953–1955	9–16+	2	50	HBJ	J. Brown G. Carlsen		
Buffalo Reading Test for Speed and Comprehension, 1933; rev. 1965	9–16+	2	35	MEW	M. Wagner D. Schubert	x	
Burnett Reading Series: Survey Test							
Primary I, 1966; rev. 1969	1.5–2.4	2	50	STS	R. W. Burnett		x
Primary II, 1966; rev. 1969	2.5–3.9	2	50	STS	(See Primary I)		x
Intermediate, 1967	4.0–6.9	2	50	STS	(See Primary I)		x
Advanced, 1967	7.0–9.9	1	50	STS	(See Primary I)	x	x
Senior, 1968; rev. 1970	10.0–12.9	1	50	STS	(See Primary I)	x	x
California Achievement Tests: Reading, 1970 Edition							
Level 1; rev. 1971	1.5–2.0	2	65	CTB	E. W. Tiegs W. W. Clark		x
Level 2; rev. 1971	2–4	2	68	CTB	(See Level 1)		x
Level 3; rev. 1971	4–6	2	70	CTB	(See Level 1)		x
Level 4; rev. 1971	6–9	2	75	CTB	(See Level 1)		x
Level 5; rev. 1971	9–12	2	75	CTB	(See Level 1)		x
California Survey Series: Survey of Reading Achievement, 1959							
Junior High Level	7–9	2	45	CTB	E. W. Tiegs W. W. Clark		
Advanced	9–12	2	45	CTB	(See Junior High Level)		

Comprehension	Word Recognition and Attack	Spelling	Auding	Other	Vol. and Test No. in *Mental Measurement Yearbooks*	Pages in *Reading Tests and Reviews, I* or *II* (Buros)
x					8:717	
x					8:717	
x					8:717	
x					5:621	RTR I: 219–20
x					**	
				Immediate recall, following directions, recognizing transitions, word meanings, lecture comprehension	6:739 5:577	
x					3:477	RTR I: 86–8
x	x				7:682	RTR II: 49–51
x	x				7:682	RTR II: 49–51
x	x				7:682	RTR II: 49–51
x					7:682	RTR II: 49–51
x					7:682	RTR II: 49–51
x	x				8:719	
x	x				8:719	
x	x				8:719	
x	x				8:719	
x	x				8:719	
					6:815	RTR I: 334–7
					6:815	RTR I: 334–7

**K. Jongsma and E. Jongsma "Test Review: Commercial Informal Reading Inventories," *Reading Teacher* 34 (March 1981), 697–705.

Name of Test	For Grades	No. of Forms	Approx. Time (in min.)	Publisher	Author(s)	Speed	Vocabulary
*The Carver-Darby Chunked Reading Test, 1970; rev. 1972	9–16+	2	35	RP	R. Carver C. Darby, Jr.	x	
Classroom Reading Inventory, Third Edition, 1965; rev. 1976	2–10	3	12	WCB	N. Silvaroli		x
Commerce Reading Comprehension Test, 1956; rev. 1958	12–16+	1	65	DPS	I. Halfter R. McCall		
Comprehensive Reading Scales, 1948; rev. 1953	4–12	1	Untimed	VW	M. Van Wagenen		
Comprehensive Tests of Basic Skills: Reading, Expanded Edition; rev. 1976; Six Levels							
Reading							
Level B	K.6–1.9	1	90	CTB			
Level C	1.6–2.9	1	101	CTB			x
Reading and Reference Skills							
Level 1	2.5–4.9	1	105	CTB			x
Level 2	4.5–6.9	1	99	CTB			x
Level 3	6.5–8.9	1	92	CTB			x
Level 4	8.5–12.9	1	91	CTB			x
Contemporary Classroom Reading Inventory, 1980	1–7	3		GS	L. Rinsky E. de Fossard		
Cooperative English Tests, Reading Comprehension, 1940; rev. 1960	9–12 13–14	3	45	AW	C. Derrick D. P. Harris B. Walker	x	x
Cooperative Primary Tests: Reading, 1965; rev. 1967	1.5–2.5 2.5–3.0	2 2	35 35	AW	ETS		
Davis Reading Test, 1956; rev. 1962							
Series I	11–13	4	55	PC	F. B. David C. C. Davis	x	
Series II	8–11	4	55	PC	(See Series I)	x	
Delaware County Silent Reading Test, Second Edition, 1965	1.5–8	1	45–90	DCRA	J. Newburg N. Spennato		x

Comprehension	Word Recognition and Attack	Spelling	Auding	Other	Vol. and Test No. in *Mental Measurement Yearbooks*	Pages in *Reading Tests and Reviews, I* or *II* (Buros)
				Efficiency, accuracy	7:684	RTR II: 52–5
	x	x		Hearing capacity level	8:749	
					5:624	RTR I: 221
x	x			Letter sounds	8:721	
					8:721	
x				Reference skills	8:721	
x				Reference skills	8:721	
x				Reference skills	8:721	
x				Reference skills	8:721	
					**	
x				English, expression	8:49	
	x		x		8:722	
x					6:786	RTR I: 291–3
x					6:786	RTR I: 291–3
			x	Interpretation, organization, structural analysis	7:686	RTR II: 56–7

**K. Jongsma and E. Jongsma, "Test Review: Commercial Informal Reading Inventories," *Reading Teacher* 34 (March 1981), 697–705.

Name of Test	For Grades	No. of Forms	Approx. Time (in min.)	Publisher	Authors(s)	Speed	Vocabulary
Durrell Listening-Reading Series, 1969–1970				HBJ	D. Durrell M. Hayes M. Brassard		
Primary Level	1–2	2	180				x
Intermediate Level	3–6	2	195				x
Advanced Level	7–9	2	190				x
Edwards Reading Test, 1980	1–8	2		HE	P. Edwards		
Ekwall Reading Tests, 1964	Pre K-9	4		AP	E. Ekwall		
Emporia Reading Tests, 1964							
Primary	1	4	40–60	BEM	M. Barnett M. Sanders A. Seybold D. Carline E. Eaton S. Studer		x
Elementary	2–3	4	25	BEM	(See Primary)		
*Intermediate	4–6	4	35	BEM	(See Primary)		
Junior High	7–8	4	35	BEM	(See Primary)		x
Fountain Valley Teacher Support System in Reading, 1971–1975	1–6	1	21	RZA			x
*Functional Readiness Questionnaire for School and College Students, 1957	1–16	1	5	RSSC	E. Taylor H. Solan		
Gates-MacGinitie Reading Tests							
Primary A, 1926; rev. 1972	1	2	50	HM	A. I. Gates W. MacGinitie		x
Primary B, 1926; rev. 1972	2	2	50	HM	(See Primary A)		x
Primary C, 1939; rev. 1972	3	2	60	HM	(See Primary A)		x
Primary Cs, 1926; rev. 1965	2.5–3	3	15	HM	(See Primary A)	x	
Survey D, 1939; rev. 1972	4–6	3	60	HM	(See Primary A)	x	x
Survey E, 1939; rev. 1972	7–9	3	60	HM	(See Primary A)	x	x
Survey F, 1969; rev. 1972	10–12	2	60	HM	(See Primary A)	x	x
Gilliland Learning Potential Examination, 1966; rev. 1971	K+	1		MRCP	H. Gilliland		

Comprehension	Word Recognition and Attack	Spelling	Auding	Other	Vol. and Test No. in *Mental Measurement Yearbooks*	Pages in *Reading Tests and Reviews, I* or *II* (Buros)
			x	Vocabulary listening	7:728	RTR II: 113–7
			x	paragraph listening	7:728	RTR II: 113–7
			x	reading	7:728	RTR II: 113–7
					**	
					**	
			x	Matching objects, like words, phonetic recognition	7:687	RTR II: 57–8
x				Sentence and para. reading	7:687	RTR II: 57–8
x				Paragraph reading	7:687	RTR II: 57–8
x				Paragraph reading	7:687	RTR II: 57–8
x				Phonetic and structural analysis, study skills	8:725	
				Physical and emotional readiness	6:835	RTR I: 360
x					8:726a	
x					8:726a	
x					8:726a	
x				Accuracy	8:726a	
x				Accuracy	8:726a	
x				Accuracy	8:726a	
x					8:727	
x				Visual memory, nonreading and noncultural	7:351	

**K. Jongsma and E. Jongsma, "Test Review: Commercial Informal Reading Inventories," *Reading Teacher* 34 (March 1981), 697–705.

Name of Test	For Grades	No. of Forms	Approx. Time (in min.)	Publisher	Author(s)	Speed	Vocabulary
Gray-Votaw-Rogers General Achievement Test, 1934; rev. 1963							
Level 1	1–3	4	70–80	SV	H. Gray D. Votaw, Sr. J. Rogers		x
Level 2	4–6	4	170	SV	(See Level 1)		x
Level 3	7–9	4	170	SV	(See Level 1)		x
Group Reading Assessment, 1962; rev. 1975	2–3	1	30	HS	F. Spooncer		x
Group Reading Test, 1968–1969	K–5	2	20	HS	D. Young		x
*The Illinois Test of Psycholinguistic Abilities, Revised Edition, 1961; rev. 1968	Pre K–5	1	45–60	UI	S. Kirk J. McCarthy W. Kirk		
Individual Placement Series—Reading Adequacy "READ" Test, 1961, rev. 1966	12+	1	20	PRA	J. Norman	x	
*Individual Pupil Monitoring System—Reading, 1974	1–6	2	60–180	HM			x
Informal Reading Assessment, 1980	Pre K–12	4		RMN	P. Burns B. Roe		
Instructional Objectives Exchange: Objective Collection in Judgment: Analyzing Fallacies and Weaknesses in Arguments, 1974	7–12			IOW	R. Morrow		
Inventory Survey Tests, 1968–1969							
Intermediate	4–6			SF	M. Monroe		x
Upper Grades	7–8			SF	M. Monroe		x
IOWA Silent Reading Tests, 1973 Edition							
Level 1	6–9	2	140	PC	R. Farr		x
Level 2	9–14	2	136	PC	R. Farr		x
Level 3	11–16	2	96	PC	R. Farr		x

Comprehension	Word Recognition and Attack	Spelling	Auding	Other	Vol. and Test No. in *Mental Measurement Yearbooks*	Pages in *Reading Tests and Reviews, I or II* (Buros)
x		x		Arithmetic reasoning and computation	6:10	
x		x		Arithmetic, science, language, literature, social studies, health and safety	6:10	
x		x		Arithmetic, science, language, literature, social studies, health and safety	6:10	
				Aural discrimination and sentence completion	8:728	
	x			Visual stimuli	8:729	
			x	Visual-motor association, auditory and visual decoding, motor encoding	8:431	
x					7:773	RTR II: 177–8
x	x			Discrimination study skills	8:763	
					**	
				Fallacies of relevance, insufficient evidence and ambiguity, arguments that compare context and soundness of arguments		
x	x			Dictionary skills		
x	x			Dictionary skills		
x				Directed reading and efficiency	8:730	
x				Directed reading and efficiency	8:730	
x				Reading efficiency	8:730	

**K. Jongsma and El Jongsma, "Test Review: Commercial Informal Reading Inventories," *Reading Teacher* 34 (March 1981), 697–705.

Name of Test	For Grades	No. of Forms	Approx. Time (in min.)	Publisher	Author(s)	Speed	Vocabulary
Lee-Clark Reading Test, 1931; rev. 1965							
Primer	1	1	30	CTB	J. M. Lee W. Clark		
First Reader	1–2	1	30	CTB	(See Primer)		
*McGrath Test of Reading Skills, Second Edition, 1965; rev. 1967	1–13	1	5–10	MRC	J. McGrath	x	x
McGraw-Hill Basic Skills System: Reading Test, 1970	11–14	2	76	CTB	A. Raygor	x	
McMenemy Measure of Reading Ability, 1964; rev. 1968							
Primary	3	1	70	RM	R. A. McMenemy	x	x
Intermediate	5–6	1	60	RM	(See Primary)	x	x
Advanced	7–8	1	75	RM	(See Primary)	x	x
Maintaining Reading Efficiency Tests, 1966; rev. 1974	7–16	1	40	DRD	L. Miller	x	
Mastery: An Evaluation Tool—Reading, 1974; rev. 1976	K–9	2	10 per subtest	SRA			x
Metropolitan Achievement Tests: Reading Tests, 1932; rev. 1971							
Primary 2	2.5–3.4	3	60	PC	W. Durost H. Bixler G. Prescott I. Balow J. Wrightstone		x
Elementary	3.5–4.9	3	50	PC	(See Primary)		x
Intermediate	5.0–6.9	3	50	PC	(See Primary)		x
Advanced	7.0–9.5	3	50	PC	(See Primary)		x
Metropolitan Achievement Tests: Reading, 1978–1979	K–12	1	40	PC	R. Farr G. Prescott I. Balow T. Hogan		x
Minimal Reading Proficiency Assessment, 1972	12			TM	T. McDonald		

Comprehension	Word Recognition and Attack	Spelling	Auding	Other	Vol. and Test No. in *Mental Yearbooks*	Pages in *Reading Tests and Reviews, I* or *II* (Buros)
			x	Visual stimuli, following directions	6:795	RTR I: 308–11
			x	Visual stimuli, following directions, completion, inference	6:795	RTR I: 308–11
	x				7:692	RTR II: 66–7
x				Skimming, scanning, flexibility, retention	7:704	RTR II: 78
x					7:693	RTR II: 67–9
x					7:693	RTR II: 67–9
x					7:693	RTR II: 67–9
x				Reading efficiency	8:731	
x	x			Study skills and math objectives	8:766	
	x				8:732	
	x				8:732	
x					8:732	
x					8:732	
x	x		x	Visual discrimination, auditory discrimination, phoneme-grapheme consonants, phoneme-grapheme vowels, rate of comprehension, skimming, scanning	**	
				Minimal reading proficiency for graduating seniors		

**E. Fry, "Test Review: Metropolitan Achievement Tests." *Reading Teacher* 34 (November 1980), 196–201.

Name of Test	For Grades	No. of Forms	Approx. Time (in min.)	Publisher	Author(s)	Speed	Vocabulary
Minnesota Reading Examinations for College Students, 1930; rev. 1935	9–16	2	55	UMP	M. Haggerty A. Eurich		x
Monroe's Standardized Silent Reading Test, 1919; rev. 1959	3–5 6–8 9–12	3	4–5	BM	W. S. Monroe	x	
Municipal Tests: National Achievement Tests: Reading (Comprehension and Speed), 1938; rev. 1957	3–6 6–8	2	37–38	APC	R. K. Speer S. Smith	x	
National Achievement Tests: High School Reading Test, 1939; rev. 1952	7–12	2	40	APC	R. K. Speer S. Smith		x
National Achievement Tests: Reading Comprehension Test, 1953; rev. 1957	4–9	1	35	APC	L. D. Crow M. J. Kuhlmann A. Crow		
Nelson-Denny Reading Test, 1924; rev. 1976	9–16+	2	35	HM	M. J. Nelson E. Denny J. Brown	x	x
Nelson Reading Test, Revised Edition, 1931; rev. 1962	3–9	2	35	HM	M. J. Nelson		x
New Developmental Reading Tests—Intermediate Tests, 1959; rev. 1968	4–6	2	75	LC	G. Bond B. Balow C. Hoyt		x
OISE Achievement Tests in Silent Reading: Advanced Primary Battery 1969–1971	2	2	110	GU			x
*Peabody Picture Vocabulary Test, 1959; rev. 1965	Pre K–12	2	10–15	AGS	L. Dunn		
Pressey Diagnostic Reading Tests, 1929	3–9	1		BM	S. L. Pressey L. C. Pressey	x	x
Primary Reading Assessment Units, 1973	1–3	1	10–15	OISE	E. Campbell P. Tracy E. McErlaine		x

Comprehension	Word Recognition and Attack	Spelling	Auding	Other	Vol. and Test No. in *Mental Measurement Yearbooks*	Pages in *Reading Tests and Reviews, I* or *II* (Buros)
x					3:491	RTR I: 104–5
x					6:798	RTR I: 312–5
x				Following directions	8:741	
x	x			Noting details	5:634	RTR I: 225–6
x					5:647	RTR I: 231
x					8:735	
x					6:802	RTR I: 320
x				Reading for information relationships, interpretation, appreciation	7:697	RTR II: 71–4
x	x				8:736	
				Verbal abilities	8:222	
x						
				Recognizing feelings, main ideas and details, sequence, following directions, maps, charts and graphs	8:737	

Name of Test	For Grades	No. of Forms	Approx. Time (in min.)	Publisher	Author(s)	Speed	Vocabulary
Primary Reading Survey Tests, 1973							
Early Primary	2			SF	A. Schiller K. Goodman J. Wepman J. Manning E. Gibb M. Monroe		
Late Primary	3			SF	(See Early Primary)		
Primary Reading Test: Acorn Achievement Tests, 1943; rev. 1957	2–3	2	40	PA	W. Stayton F. Ranson R. Beck		
Progressive Achievement Tests of Reading, 1970	3–9	2	40	NZCER	W. Elley N. Reid		
Public School Achievement Tests: Reading 1928; rev. 1959	3–8	2	45	BM	J. S. Orleans		
RBH Basic Reading and Word Test, 1968; rev. 1969	Disadvantaged adults	1	25–30	RBH			x
RBH Test of Reading Comprehension, 1951; rev. 1963	12+	1	25	RBH			
RBH Scientific Reading Test, 1950; rev. 1969	12+	1	65	RBH			
Reading Comprehension Test, 1963; rev. 1968	College Entrants			WM	W. McCartney		
The Reading Progress Scale, 1970; rev. 1975	3–12 13–14	2 2	15 15	RP RP	R. Carver R. Carver		
Reading for Understanding Test		1		SRA	T. Thurstone		
Junior Edition, 1963	3–8						
Senior Edition, 1963; rev. 1965	8–12						
General Edition, 1959; rev. 1969	5–16						

Comprehension	Word Recognition and Attack	Spelling	Auding	Other	Vol. and Test No. in *Mental Measurement Yearbooks*	Pages in *Reading Tests and Reviews, I* or *II* (Buros)
		x		Mathematics		
x	x			Word opposites	5:642	RTR I: 230
x				Literal and inferential comprehension of narrative, descriptive, and expository passages	8:738	RTR II: 74–5
x	x		x	Oral reading accuracy	6:807	RTR II: 14
					7:700	RTR II: 75–6
				For use in business and industry	7:701	RTR II: 76–8
				For use in technical companies	7:772	RTR II: 176–7
x						
					8:740	
						RTR I: 6

Name of Test	For Grades	No. of Forms	Approx. Time (in min.)	Publisher	Author(s)	Speed	Vocabulary
SRA Achievement Series: Reading							
Level 1, 1954; rev. 1968	1–2	2	185	SRA	L. Thorpe D. Lefever R. Naslund		x
Level 2, 1954; rev. 1968	2–4	2	120	SRA	(See Level 1)		x
Multilevel Edition, 1963; rev. 1969	4–9	2	77	SRA	(See Level 1)		
SRA Reading Record, 1947; rev. 1959	6–12	1	30	SRA	G. T. Buswell	x	x
STS: ASK: Reading, 1974; rev. 1976	1–2	1	185	STS	O. Anderhalter F. Shands		
	3–4	1	145	STS	(See above)		
	5–6	1	165	STS	(See above)		
	7–8	1	165	STS	(See above)		
Schrammel-Gray High School and College Reading Test, 1940; rev. 1942	7–16	2	30	BM	H. Schrammel W. Gray	x	
Sequential Tests of Educational Progress: Reading, Series II, 1956; rev. 1972	4–6 7–9 10–12 13–14	2	55	AW	ETS		x
Stanford Achievement Test: Reading Tests, 1973 Edition							
Primary 1, rev. 1974	1.5–2.4	2	120	PC	R. Madden E. Gardner H. Rudman B. Karlsen J. Merwin		x
Primary 2	2.5–3.4	2	120	PC	(See Primary 1)		x
Primary 3	3.5–4.4	2	110	PC	(See Primary 1)		x
Intermediate 1	4.5–5.4	2	115	PC	(See Primary 1)		x
Intermediate 2	5.5–6.9	2	110	PC	(See Primary 1)		x
Advanced	7–9.5	2	75	PC	(See Primary 1)		x
Stanford Achievement Test: High School Reading Test, 1965–1966	9–12	1	45	HBJ	E. Gardner J. Merwin R. Callis R. Madden		
Sucher-Allred Reading Placement Inventory, 1968; rev. 1973	1–9	1	20	E	F. Sucher R. Allred		

Comprehension	Word Recognition and Attack	Spelling	Auding	Other	Vol. and Test No. in *Mental Measurement Yearbooks*	Pages in *Reading Tests and Reviews, I* or *II* (Buros)
x				Verbal pictorial association, language perception	7:706	RTR II: 79–80
x					7:706	RTR II: 79–80
x					7:706	RTR II: 79–80
x				Everyday reading skills	4:550	RTR I: 177–8
x	x			Study skills	8:748	
x	x			Study skills	8:748	
x	x			Study skills	8:748	
x	x			Study skills	8:748	
x					3:500	RTR I: 112–3
x					8:744	
x	x			Word study skills	8:745	
x	x			Word study skills	8:745	
x				Word study skills	8:745	
x				Word study skills	8:745	
x				Word study skills	8:745	
x				Word study skills	8:745	
x					7:707	RTR II: 80–1
x	x			Oral reading, independent, instructional, and frustrational reading levels	8:746	

Name of Test	For Grades	No. of Forms	Approx. Time (in min.)	Publisher	Author(s)	Speed	Vocabulary
Tests of Reading; Inter-American Series, 1950; rev. 1973							
Level 1 Primary	1	2	28	GTA	H. Manuel		x
Level 2 Primary	2–3	2	35	GTA	(See Level 1)	x	x
Level 3 Elementary	4–6	2	50	GTA	(See Level 1)	x	x
Level 4 Intermediate	7–9	2	50	GTA	(See Level 1)	x	x
Level 5 Advanced	10–13	2	50	GTA	(See Level 1)	x	x
Survey of Primary Reading Development, 1957; rev. 1964	1–2 2–4	2 2	30–60 Not reported	ETS ETS	J. Harsh (See above)		
Survey Tests of Reading, 1931; rev. 1932	3–6 7–13	1			L. O'Rourke	x	
Survey Test of Vocabulary, 1931; rev. 1965	3–12	2	25	OP	L. O'Rourke		x
Tests of Academic Progress: Reading, 1964; rev. 1966	9–12	1	60	HM	H. Smith D. Scannell		
Traxler High School Reading Test; rev. 1967	10–12	2	60	BM	A. Traxler	x	x
Traxler Silent Reading Test, 1934; rev. 1969	7–10	4	46–53	BM	A. Traxler	x	x
Van Wagenen Analytical Reading Scales, 1953; rev. 1954	4–6 7–9 10–12	1	Untimed	VW	M. Van Wagenen		
Wide-Range Achievement Test, Revised Edition, 1976	1–12	1	30	GAD	J. F. Jastak S. R. Jastak S. W. Bijou		
Wide-span Reading Test, 1972	2–9	2	35	TN	A. Brimer H. Gross		
Williams Primary Reading Test, 1926; rev. 1955							
Primary 1	1	2	35	BM	A. Williams		
Primary 2	2–3	2	35	BM	A. Williams		
Williams Reading Test for Grades 4–9, 1929	4–9	1		BM	A. Williams		

Comprehension	Word Recognition and Attack	Spelling	Auding	Other	Vol. and Test No. in *Mental Measurement Yearbooks*	Pages in *Reading Tests and Reviews, I or II* (Buros)
x				English and Spanish language forms	7:711	RTR II: 86–7
x				English and Spanish language forms	7:711	RTR II: 86–7
x				English and Spanish language forms	7:711	RTR II: 86–7
x				English and Spanish language forms	7:711	RTR II: 86–7
x				English and Spanish language forms	7:711	RTR II: 86–7
x	x			Form comparison, pictorial-narrative reading	7:709	RTR II: 84–5
x				Accuracy	7:234	
x				Making inferences and evaluations	7:710	RTR II: 85–6
x					7:712	RTR II: 87–8
x					7:713	RTR II: 88–90
x				Making inferences, interpretation		
x	x	x		Oral reading, arithmetic	8:37	
x	x				8:747	
					5:658	RTR I: 246

DIAGNOSTIC TESTS

Name of Test	For Grades	No. of Forms	Approx. Time (in min.)	Publisher	Author(s)	Speed	Vocabulary
California Phonics Survey, 1956; rev. 1963	7–12+	2	45	CTB	G. M. Brown A. B. Cottrell		
Classroom Reading Inventory, Third Edition, 1976	2–10	3	12	WBC	N. Silvaroli		
Cooper-McGuire Diagnostic Word-Analysis Test, 1970; rev. 1972	1–5+	2	Not reported	CES	J. Cooper M. McGuire		
Cooperative Primary Tests: Word Analysis, 1965; rev. 1967	1.5–3	2	40	AW	ETS		
*The Denver Public Schools Reading Inventory, 1965; rev. 1968	1–8	1	30–40	DEN			
Diagnosis: An Instructional Aid: Reading, 1974	1–4 3–6		Not reported Not reported	SRA			
Diagnostic Examination of Silent Reading Abilities, 1939; rev. 1954	4–6 7–9 10–12	1	Untimed (except Rate Test)	VW	A. Dvorak M. Van Wagenen	x	x
*Diagnostic Reading Examination for Diagnosis of Special Difficulty in Reading, 1929	1–4			ST	M. Monroe		
*Diagnostic Reading Scales, Revised Edition, 1963; rev. 1975	1–6+	1	50	CTB	G. D. Spache	x	
Diagnostic Reading Tests, 1947; rev. 1974	K–4	2	Not reported	CDRT	F. Triggs		x
Lower Level	4–8	4	30	CDRT	F. Triggs	x	
Upper Level	7–13	4	50	CDRT	F. Triggs	x	x
Diagnostic Reading Test: Pupil Progress Series							
Primary Level I, 1956; rev. 1968	1.9–2.1	2	40–50	STS	O. Anderhalter R. Gawkowski R. Colestock	x	x
Primary Level II, 1956; rev. 1968	2.2–3	3	50–60	STS	(See Primary Level I)	x	x
Elementary Level, 1956; rev. 1970	4–6	2	50–60	STS	(See Primary Level I)	x	x
Advanced Level, 1956; rev. 1970	7–8	2	50–60	STS	(See Primary Level I)	x	x

Comprehension	Word Recognition and Attack	Spelling	Auding	Other	Vol. and Test No. in *Mental Measurement Yearbooks*	Pages in *Reading Tests and Reviews, I or II* (Buros)
				Vowel confusion, blends	7:714	RTR II: 90–2
	x	x		Independent, instructional, frustration, reading levels, hearing capacity	8:749	
	x				8:750	
	x	x			8:751	
				Instructional, independent and capacity reading levels	7:716	RTR II: 92
x	x			Study skills	8:752	
x	x			Study skills	8:752	
x				Making inferences, perception of relationships	3:480	RTR I: 89–91
	x			Oral reading, mirror reading		
x	x		x	Phonics	8:753	
x	x				8:754	
x	x				8:754	
x	x				8:754	
x	x			Word content relation, words in use, recalling information, locating information, reading for descriptions	7:718	RTR II: 94–7
x	x			Following directions, words in use, recalling information, reading to locate information, reading for description	7:718	RTR II: 94–7
	x			Study skills; table of contents, selection of best source, reading for directions	7:718	RTR II: 94–7
	x	x	x	Letter recognition, sight words	7:718	RTR II: 94–7

Name of Test	For Grades	No. of Forms	Approx. Time (in min.)	Publisher	Author(s)	Speed	Vocabulary
*Diagnostic Screening Test: Reading, 1976	1–12	1	5–10	FH	T. Gnagey		
Domain Phonic Tests, 1972	K–4	1	Not reported	OB	J. McLeod J. Atkinson		
Doren Diagnostic Reading Test of Word Recognition Skills, 1956; rev. 1973	1–4	1	60–180	AGS	M. Doren		
*Durrell Analysis of Reading Difficulty, New Edition, 1937; rev. 1955	1–6	1	30–90	HBJ	D. D. Durrell		
*Gates-McKillop Reading Diagnostic Tests, 1926; rev. 1962	2–6	2	60	TCP	A. I. Gates A. McKillop		x
Gillingham-Childs Phonics Proficiency Scales, 1966; rev. 1973	2–8	1	10–15	EPS	A. Gillingham S. Childs B. Stillman		
Group Diagnostic Reading Aptitude and Achievement Tests, 1939	3–9	1	60–70	NPC	M. Monroe E. Sherman	x	x
Group Phonics Analysis, 1971	1–3	1	10–15	DES	E. Fry		
*Individual Phonics Criterion Test, 1971; rev. 1976	1–8	1	30–45	DES	E. Fry		
Individual Pupil Monitoring System—Reading	1–6	2	60–180	HM			x
Individualized Criterion Referenced Testing: Reading, 1973; rev. 1976	K–8	2	Not reported	EDC			
LRA Standard Mastery Tasks in Language, 1970							
Primary I	1	1		LEA	D. Smith J. Smith R. Cabot		
Primary II	2	1		LEA	(See Primary I)		
McCullough Word-Analysis Tests, 1960; rev. 1963	4–6	1	70	PPI	C. M. McCullough		
McGuire-Bumpus Diagnostic Comprehension Test, 1971; rev. 1972	2.5–3 4–6			CES	M. McGuire M. Bumpus		
*McGrath Diagnostic Reading Test, 1974; rev. 1976	1–13	1	30	MPC	J. McGrath		

Comprehension	Word Recognition and Attack	Spelling	Auding	Other	Vol. and Test No. in *Mental Measurement Yearbooks*	Pages in *Reading Tests and Reviews, I* or *II* (Buros)
x	x	x		Phonics/sight ratio, frustration level, consolidation index	8:755	
	x				8:756	
	x	x	x	Letter recognition, sight words	8:757	
x	x	x	x	Naming letters, visual memory, learning rate, oral reading	5:660	RTR I: 248–9
	x	x	x	Alphabet, oral reading, syllabication	8:759	
	x	x	x		8:760	
	x	x	x	Visual and motor abilities, arithmetic	6:825	RTR I: 348
			x	Numbers, letters, alphabetizing, syllabication, final *e* rule	8:761	
					8:762	
x	x		x	Study skills	8:763	
					8:764	
			x	Letter matching		
	x		x	Letter naming and writing, word naming and writing		
				Phonetic and structural analysis (seven tests)	7:719	RTR II: 97–9
				Literal, interpretive, analytical, and critical reading		
x	x	x	x	Letter recognition	8:765	

Name of Test	For Grades	No. of Forms	Approx. Time (in min.)	Publisher	Author(s)	Speed	Vocabulary
Mastery: An Evaluation Tool: Reading, 1974; rev. 1976	K–9	2	3 per subtest	SRA	Center for the Study of Evaluation, UCLA		x
Objectives Referenced Bank of Items and Tests: Reading and Communication Skills, 1975	K–12+	2 formats	5 per objective tested	CTB			x
Ohio Diagnostic Reading Test (a special form of Stanford Diagnostic Reading Test)							
Level I, 1966	2.5–4.5	1	133	OTS	B. Karlsen R. Madden E. Gardner		x
Level II, 1966	4.5–8.5	1	100	OTS	(See Level I)	x	x
*Phonics Knowledge Survey, 1964	1–6	1	10–30	TCP	D. Durkin L. Meshover		
Phonovisual Diagnostic Test, 1949; rev. 1958	3–12	1	15	PHI	L. D. Schoolfield J. Timberlake		
Power Reading Survey Test, 1973; rev. 1975	1–3 4–6 7–12	1	Not reported	BFA	W. Blanton J. Laffey E. Robbins C. Smith		
Prescriptive Reading Inventory, 1972; rev. 1977							
Level I	K–1	1	75–85	CTB			
Level II	K.5–2.0	1	75–78	CTB			
Level A	1.5–2.5	1	190–200	CTB			
Level B	2.0–3.5	1	175–185	CTB			
Level C	3.0–4.5	1	175–185	CTB			
Level D	4.0–6.5	1	160–150	CTB			
Interim Tests: Experimental Edition, 1973; rev. 1977	K–6.5	1	5–10 per skills test; 20–25 per comprehension booklet	CTB			
Primary Reading Profiles, 1953; rev. 1968	1–2 2–3	1	95–100	HM	J. B. Stroud A. N. Hieronymous P. McKee		

Comprehension	Word Recognition and Attack	Spelling	Auding	Other	Vol. and Test No. in *Mental Measurement Yearbooks*	Pages in *Tests and Reviews, I or II* (Buros)
x	x	x		Phonics analysis, study skills	8:766	
x	x		x	Literal comprehension, critical comprehension, interpretive comprehension, reference skills	8:767	
x			x	Syllabication, beginning and ending sounds, sound discrimination, blending		
x			x	Syllabication, beginning and ending sounds, sound discrimination, blending		
				Names of letters, consonant and vowel sounds, syllabication	7:720	RTR II: 99–101
		x		Phonetic weaknesses	6:829	RTR I: 350–2
x	x			Study skills	8:768	
x			x	Letter names	8:769	
x			x	Visual reasoning	8:769	
x	x			Sound and symbol recognition, phonic analysis	8:769	
x	x			Sound and symbol recognition, phonic analysis	8:769	
x	x			Phonic analysis and translation	8:769	
x	x			Phonic analysis and translation	8:769	
x				Tests for each of the prescriptive reading inventory objectives	8:769	
x	x		x		5:665	RTR I: 252–4

Name of Test	For Grades	No. of Forms	Approx. Time (in min.)	Publisher	Author(s)	Speed	Vocabulary
Ransom Program Reading Tests, 1974; rev. 1975	K–6	1	Not reported	AW	G. Ransom		
Reading Diagnostic Probes, 1970							
Probe 1	2–5	1		ATC	S. Warner W. Myers		
Probe 2	3–9	1		ATC	S. Warner M. Myers R. Herbert		
Reading: 10X Objectives-Based Tests, 1973; rev. 1976	K–6	2	5–10	IOE	J. McNeil N. Paxton L. Paulson		
*Reading Miscue Inventory, 1972	1–8+	1	45	MC	Y. Goodman C. Burke		
Reading Skills Diagnostic Test, 1967; rev. 1971	1–8	1	Not reported	BP	R. Bloomer		
*Roswell-Chall Diagnostic Test of Word Analysis Skills, 1956; rev. 1959	2–6	2	5–10	EP	F. Roswell J. Chall		
Silent Reading Diagnostic Tests, 1955; rev. 1970	2–6	1	90	LC	G. Bond B. Balow C. Hoyt		
*Sipay Word Analysis Tests, 1974	1+	1	10–20	EPS	E. Sipay		
Skills Monitoring System: Reading, 1974–75	3–5	1	45–60	PC			
*SPIRE Individual Reading Evaluation, 1970: rev. 1973							
Spire 1	Pre K–6	1	20–30	NDE	H. Alpert A. Kravitz		
Spire 2	4–10	1	20–30	NDE	H. Alpert A. Kravitz		
*Standard Reading Inventory, 1966	1–7	2	30–120	KPC	R. McCracken	x	x

Comprehension	Word Recognition and Attack	Spelling	Auding	Other	Vol. and Test No. in *Mental Measurement Yearbooks*	Pages in *Reading Tests and Reviews, I* or *II* (Buros)
x				Location and study skills	8:770	
			x	Consonants, blends, vowels		
x	x				8:771	
				Psycholinguistically analyzes where miscues are made as reader extracts meaning; qualitative as well as quantitative analysis	8:790	
				Letter-sound identification, phonetic words and sounds, inconsistent words and phrases, letters and words in context	8:772	
	x			Syllabication	6:831	RTR I: 354–5
	x		x	Word analysis, synthesis, word parts	7:722	RTR II: 103–6
				Letter names, visual and phonic analysis and visual blending (sixteen tests)	8:775	
x					8:776	
x	x			Oral reading, instructional, frustration, and independent reading levels	8:773	
				Oral reading, instructional, frustration, and independent reading levels	8:773	
x				Oral reading	7:723	RTR II: 106–7

Name of Test	For Grades	No. of Forms	Approx. Time (in min.)	Publisher	Author(s)	Speed	Vocabulary
Stanford Diagnostic Reading Test, 1966; rev. 1976							
Red Level	1.5–3.5	2	150	PC	B. Karlsen R. Madden E. Gardner		
Green Level	2.5–5.5	2	165	PC	(See Red Level)		x
Brown Level	4.5–9.5	2	113	PC	(See Red Level)	x	x
Blue Level	9–13	2	Not reported	PC	(See Red Level)	x	x
Test of Individual Needs in Reading, Seventh Edition, 1961; rev. 1971	1–6	2	25–50	MRCP	H. Gilliland	x	
Test of Phonic Skills, 1971	K–3			HR	K. Smith H. Truby		
Test of Reading Comprehension, 1978	1–8	1	10–25 per subtest	PRE	V. Brown D. Hammill J. Wiederholt		x
Wisconsin Test of Reading Skill Development: Word Attack, 1970; rev. 1972							
Level A	K–2	2	105	NCS	W. Otto D. Stewart E. Askov V. Van Blaricom K. Kamm M. Harris P. Miles		
Transition Level	1–2	2	110	NCS	(See Level A)		
Level B	1–3	2	120	NCS	(See Level A)		
Level C	2–4	2	175	NCS	(See Level A)		
Level D	3–6	2	65	NCS	(See Level A)		
Woodcock Reading Mastery Tests, 1972; rev. 1973	K–12	2	20–30	AGS	R. Woodcock		

Comprehension	Word Recognition and Attack	Spelling	Auding	Other	Vol. and Test No. in *Mental Measurement Yearbooks*	Pages in *Reading Tests and Reviews, I or II* (Buros)
x			x	Phonetic analysis	8:777	
x	x		x	Auditory vocabulary	8:777	
x	x		x	Auditory vocabulary	8:777	
x	x			Scanning and skimming	8:777	
x				Oral reading, word analysis	7:726	RTR II: 110–3
		x	x	Phonics rules—vowels, consonants, blends, digraphs		
				Inferring relationships, syntactic similarities, sequencing, reading directions; math, science, and social studies vocabulary	**	
			x	Readiness skills—rhyming, shapes, letters, and numbers, consonants	8:778	
			x	Rhyming, consonants, blends	8:778	
				Consonants, vowels, rhyming, digraphs, contractions, possessives, compound coordination, plurals	8:778	
				Consonant blends and variants, vowels, diphthongs, plurals, homonyms, antonyms, synonyms	8:778	
				Three-letter blends, silent letters, syllabication, accent, possessives	8:778	
x	x				8:779	

**E. Jongsma, "Test Review: Test of Reading Comprehension," *Reading Teacher* 33 (March 1980), 703–8.

ORAL READING TESTS

Name of Test	For Grades	No. of Forms	Approx. Time (in min.)	Publisher	Author(s)	Speed	Vocabulary
*The Burt Word Reading Test, 1921; rev. 1976	K+	1	5–10	HS	C. Burt P. Vernon		
*Cutrona Reading Inventory, 1975	K–6 7–12+	1	10	CEI	M. Cutrona		
*Flash-X Sight Vocabulary Test, 1961	1–2	1	10	EDL	G. Spache S. Taylor		x
*Gilmore Oral Reading Test, 1951; rev. 1968	1–8	2	15–20	PC	J. Gilmore E. Gilmore	x	
*Gray Oral Reading Test, 1963; rev. 1967	1–16+	4	Not reported	BM	W. S. Gray	x	
*McGrath's Preliminary Screening Test in Reading, 1973; rev. 1976	1–13	1	1–3	MPC	J. McGrath		
*Neale Analysis of Reading Ability, Second Edition, 1957; rev. 1966	1–7	3	10–15	SMP	M. Neale	x	
*Oral Reading Criterion Test, 1971	1–7	1	10–15	DFS	E. Fry		
*Oral Word-Recognition Test, 1973	1–13	3	1–2	MPC	J. McGrath		
*Reading Classification Test, 1972; rev. 1976	2–6	1	5–25	ER	H. Williamson I. Ball		
*Reading Miscue Inventory, 1972	1–8	1	45	MC	Y. Goodman C. Burke		
*Salford Sentence Reading Test, 1976	1–5	3	2–3	HS	G. E. Bookbinder		
*Slosson Oral Reading (SORT) Test, 1963	1–12	1	3	SEP	R. Slosson		
*Standardized Oral Reading Check Tests, 1923; rev. 1955	1–8	5	1–3	BM	W. Gray	x	
*Standardized Oral Reading Paragraphs, 1915; rev. 1955	1–8	1	3–8	BM	W. Gray	x	

Comprehension	Word Recognition and Attack	Spelling	Auding	Other	Vol. and Test No. in *Mental Measurement Yearbooks*	Pages in *Reading Tests and Reviews, I* or *II* (Buros)
				Pronunciation	8:783	
				Word pronunciation, independent reading, instructional reading, frustration reading	8:784	
				Sight and experience vocabulary	6:841	RTR I: 367
x				Accuracy	8:785	
					6:842	RTR I: 367–70
				Word pronunciation	8:786	
x		x	x	Blending and recognition of syllables, accuracy, names and sounds of letters	6:843	RTR I: 370–3
				Independent, frustration, and instructional reading levels	8:787	
					8:788	
				Word pronunciation	8:789	
x				Using grammatical and meaning cueing systems	8:790	
					8:791	
				Oral reading	6:844	RTR I: 373
				Accuracy	8:792	
				Accuracy	8:793	

TESTS OF STUDY SKILLS

Name of Test	For Grades	No. of Forms	Approx. Time (in min.)	Publisher	Author(s)	Speed	Vocabulary
College Adjustment and Study Skills Inventory, 1968	13–16	1	15–20	PGP	F. Christensen		
Comprehensive Tests of Basic Skills: Reading, Expanded Edition, 1968; rev. 1976							
Level 1	2.5–4.9	1	105	CTB			x
Level 2	4.5–6.9	1	99	CTB			x
Level 3	6.5–8.9	1	92	CTB			x
Level 4	8.5–12.9	1	91	CTB			x
The Cornell Class-Reasoning Test, 1964	4–12			UI	R. Ennis W. Gardiner R. Morrow D. Paulus L. Ringel		
The Cornell Conditional-Reasoning Test, 1964	4–12			UI	R. Ennis W. Gardiner J. Guzzetta R. Morrow D. Paulus L. Ringel		
The Cornell Critical Thinking Test, 1961; rev. 1971	7–12 13–16	1	50	UI	R. Ennis J. Millman		
The Cornell Learning and Study Skills Inventory, 1970	7–13 13–16	1	30–50	PEI	W. Pauk R. Cassel		
Effective Study Test, 1964–1972	8–12 11–13	1	35–45	ESM	W. Brown		
Evaluation Aptitude Test, 1951; rev. 1952	12+ 16+	1	55	PA	D. Sell		
IOWA Every Pupil Test of Basic Skills, Test B, New Edition Elementary Battery, 1940; rev. 1947	3–5	3	55	HM	E. Lindquist H. Spitzer E. Horn M. McBroom H. Greene		
IOWA Tests of Educational Development, Test 9, Use of Sources of Information, 1942; rev. 1967	9–12	2	35	SRA	E. F. Linquist L. Feldt		

Comprehension	Word Recognition and Attack	Spelling	Auding	Other	Vol. and Test No. in *Mental Measurement Yearbooks*	Pages in *Reading Tests and Reviews, I or II* (Buros)
				Taking notes, exams, class participation, personal adjustment, time distribution	7:777	RTR II: 183-5
x				Reference skill, science, math, social studies, language expression, and mechanics	8:721	
x				(See Level 1)	8:721	
x				(See Level 1)	8:721	
x				(See Level 1)	8:721	
				Deductive logic		
				Deductive logic		
				Critical thinking	7:779	RTR II: 187
				Goal orientation, lectures, textbook, examination mastery	8:815	
				Reality orientation, study organization, writing behavior (note taking), reading behavior examination behavior	8:816	
				Neutral syllogisms, emotionally toned syllogisms, emotional bias, indecision	5:691	RTR I: 275-7
				Study skills: map reading, use of references, use of index and dictionary, graphs	4:588	RTR I: 210
				Use of sources of information	6:858	RTR I: 381-2

Name of Test	For Grades	No. of Forms	Approx. Time (in min.)	Publisher	Author(s)	Speed	Vocabulary
A Library Orientation Test for College Freshmen, 1950; rev. 1961	13	1	50–60	TCP	E. Feagley D. Curtiss M. Gaver E. Greene		
Library Tests, 1967; rev. 1972							
Test 1: Library Survey Test	7–8	1		PFC			
Test 2: Library Sources and Skills Test	9–10	1		PFC			
Test 3: Library Sources and Uses of Information	11–12	1		PFC			
Logical Reasoning Test, 1955	9–16+	1	25	SSC	A. Hertzka J. Guilford		
National Test of Library Skills, 1967; rev. 1971	2–4 4–12			ATC	F. Hatfield I. Gullette W. Myers		
Nationwide Library Skills Examination, 1962; rev. 1963	4–12	1	40–45	ES	D. Honz		
OC Diagnostic Dictionary Test, 1960	5–8	1	20	OPC	K. O'Connor		
Peabody Library Information Test					J. Moore		
Elementary Level, 1940	4–8	1	35	ETB	L. Shores		
High School Level, 1940	9–12	1	35	ETB	(See Elementary Level)		
College Level, 1938; rev. 1940	13–16	1	37	ETB	(See Elementary Level)		
SRA Achievement Series: Work-Study Skills, 1955; rev. 1969	4.5–6.5 6.5–8.5 8.5–9.0	2	80	SRA	L. Thorpe D. W. Lefever R. Naslund		
Study Attitudes and Methods Survey, 1972; rev. 1976	9–16	1	35	EITS	J. Michael W. Michael W. Zimmerman		

Comprehension	Word Recognition and Attack	Spelling	Auding	Other	Vol. and Test No. in *Mental Measurement Yearbooks*	Pages in *Reading Tests and Reviews, I* or *II* (Buros)
				Library skills	6:859	RTR I: 382
				General information, periodicals, oral and written reports, Dewey decimal system, dictionary, reference books		
				Reader's Guide, scholarly terms, Dewey decimal system, research organization, encyclopedia, card catalog		
				Alphabetizing, Dewey decimal system, card catalog, reference books, using sources of information		
					5:694	RTR I: 279–80
				Arrangement and parts of a book, card catalog, reference books, indexing		
				Library skills	6:860	RTR I: 382
				Dictionary skills	6:861	RTR I: 382–3
				Library study skills	3:538	RTR I: 148–9
				Library study skills	3:538	RTR I: 148–9
				Arrangement of books, dictionary, encyclopedia, periodicals, reference books, bibliography	3:538	RTR I: 148–9
				References, charts	7:780	RTR II: 187
				Academic interest, academic drive, study methods, study anxiety, manipulation, alienation toward authority	8:818	

Name of Test	For Grades	No. of Forms	Approx. Time (in min.)	Publisher	Author(s)	Speed	Vocabulary
Study Habits Checklist, 1957; rev. 1967	9–14	1		SRA	R. Preston M. Botel		
Study Habits Inventory, Revised Edition, 1934; rev. 1941	12–16	1	10–20	CPP	C. Wrenn		
Study Performance Test, 1934; rev. 1943	9–16	1		WL	H. Toops G. Shover		
Study Skills Counseling Evaluation, 1962	9–16	1	10–20	WPS	G. Demos		
Study Skills Surveys, 1965; rev. 1970	9–16	1	15–20	ESM	W. Brown		
Study Skills Test: McGraw-Hill Basic Skills System, 1970	11–14	2	56	CTB	A. Raygor		
Survey of Study Habits and Attitudes (SSHA), 1953; rev. 1965, 1967	7–12 12–14	1	20–25	PC	W. Brown W. Holtzman		
Test of Library/Study Skills, 1975		1	50	LA	I. Gullette F. Hatfield		
Level 1	2–5						
Level 2	4–9						
Level 3	8–12						
Test on Use of the Dictionary, 1955; rev. 1963	9–16	1	30–40	RLC	G. Spache		
The Uncritical Inference Test, 1955; rev. 1967	12+			ISGS	W. Haney		
Watson-Glaser Critical Thinking Appraisal, 1942; rev. 1964	9–16+	2	50–60	PC	G. Watson E. Glaser		

Comprehension	Word Recognition and Attack	Spelling	Auding	Other	Vol. and Test No. in *Mental Measurement Yearbooks*	Pages in *Reading Tests and Reviews, I* or *II* (Buros)
				Study skills		
					3:540	RTR I: 150–2
				Study time distribution, study conditions, taking notes, taking exams, habits and attitudes	6:865	RTR I: 384–6
				Study organization, study techniques, study motivation; Spanish edition available	8:819	
				Problem solving, library information, study skills and habits	7:781	
				Study habits and attitudes (efficiency, attitude toward teachers, educational objectives)	8:820	
					8:821	
		x		Pronunciation, meaning, usage derivation	6:886	RTR I: 386
				Inference, recognition of assumptions, deductions, interpretation, evaluation of arguments	8:822	

Name of Test	For Grades	No. of Forms	Approx. Time (in min.)	Publisher	Author(s)	Speed	Vocabulary
Wisconsin Tests of Reading Skill Development: Study Skills, 1970; rev. 1973							
Level A	K–1	1	25	NCS	K. Kamm D. Stewart V. Van Blaricom		
Level B	1–2	1	65	NCS	K. Kamm D. Stewart V. Van Blaricom		
Level C	2–3	2	130	NCS	K. Kamm D. Stewart V. Van Blaricom J. Allen M. Ramberg		
Level D	3–4	2	160	NCS	K. Kamm D. Stewart V. Van Blaricom J. Allen M. Ramberg E. Weible J. L. Marshall D. Sals		
Level E	4–5	2	190	NCS	(See Level D)		
Level F	5–6	2	195	NCS	(See Level D)		
Level G	6–7	2	180	NCS	(See Level D)		
Work-Study Skills: IOWA Every-Pupil Tests of Basic Skills, Test B, New Edition, 1940; rev. 1947							
Elementary	3–5	2	55	HM	H. F. Spitzer E. Horn M. McBroom H. A. Greene E. F. Lindquist		
Advanced	5–9	2	90	HM	(See Elementary)		

Comprehension	Word Recognition and Attack	Spelling	Auding	Other	Vol. and Test No. in *Mental Measurement Yearbooks*	Pages in *Reading Tests and Reviews, I or II* (Buros)
				Position of objects, measurement	8:823	
				Picture symbols, measurement, graphs	8:823	
				Measurement, graphs, tables, alphabetizing, color keys	8:823	
				Scales, graphs, tables, index, table of contents, dictionary, fact and opinion	8:823	
				Directions, scales, graphs, dictionary, references	8:823	
				Maps, scales, graphs, schedules, dictionary, library skills	8:823	
				Maps, graphs, schedules, outlining, references	8:823	
				Map reading, use of references, index, dictionary, alphabetizing	4:588	RTR I: 210
				Map reading, use of references, index, dictionary, graphing	4:588	RTR I: 210

SPECIAL AND CONTENT AREA TESTS

Name of Test	For Grades	No. of Forms	Approx. Time (in min.)	Publisher	Author(s)	Speed	Vocabulary
Adult Basic Reading Inventory, 1966	Functionally illiterate adolescents or adults	1	60	STS	R. Burnett		x
ANPA Foundation Newspaper Test, 1969; rev. 1972	7–9 10–12	2 2	40–50 40–50	ETS ETS	American Newspaper Publishers Association Foundation		
IOWA Tests of Educational Development							
Test 5: Ability to Interpret Reading Materials in the Social Studies, 1942; rev. 1967	9–12	2	70	SRA	D. F. Lindquist L. Feldt		
Test 6: Ability to Interpret Reading Materials in the Natural Sciences, 1942; rev. 1967	9–12	2	70	SRA	D. F. Lindquist L. Feldt		
*Reading/Everyday Activities in Life, 1972	5+	1	50–90	CP	M. Lichtman		
Robinson-Hall Reading Tests, 1940; rev. 1949	13–16	5	15	OSU	F. Robinson P. Hall		x
SRA Reading Index, 1968; rev. 1974	Age 14+	1	25–30	SRA	B. Campbell L. Macaitis		x
Tests of General Education Development							
Test 2: Interpretation of Reading Materials in Social Studies; 1944; rev. 1970	9–16	7	120	VTS	Examination Staff of the U.S. Armed Forces Institute		
Test 3: Interpretation of Reading Materials in the Natural Sciences, 1944; rev. 1970	9–16	7	120	VTS	Examination Staff of the U.S. Armed Forces Institute		

Comprehension	Word Recognition and Attack	Spelling	Auding	Other	Vol. and Test No. in *Mental Measurement Yearbooks*	Pages in *Reading Tests and Reviews, I* or *II* (Buros)
			x	Context reading, sight words	8:811	
				Newspaper reading ability	7:768	RTR II: 175
				Reading materials in social studies	6:853	RTR I: 378
				Reading materials in natural sciences	6:853	RTR I: 378
				Functional literacy	8:812	
x				Reading ability for art, geology, history, and fiction	4:575	RTR I: 197–8
x	x			For job applicants with poor educational backgrounds	8:813	
					7:771	RTR II: 176
					7:770	RTR II: 176

MISCELLANEOUS READING TESTS

Name of Test	For Grades	No. of Forms	Approx. Time (in min.)	Publisher	Author(s)	Speed	Vocabulary
*Auditory Discrimination Test, 1958; rev. 1973	K–3	2	5–10	LRA	J. M. Wepman		
Basic Reading Rate Scale, 1971	3–16	2	15	RP	R. Carver M. Tinker	x	
*Botel Reading Inventory, 1961; rev. 1970	1–12	2	4–25	FEC	M. Botel C. L. Holsclaw G. C. Cammarata		
Composite Auditory Perception Test, 1973	1–3			AC	B. Witkin K. Butler D. Hedrick C. Manning		
*Concepts About Print Test, 1979	Pre K–Primary	1		HE	M. Clay		
Cumulative Reading Record, 1956 Edition, 1933; rev. 1956	9–12	1		NCTE	M. M. Skinner		
Dolch Basic Sight Word Test, 1942	1–2	1	35	GP	E. W. Dolch		
Durrell Listening-Reading Series							
Primary Level, 1969; rev. 1976	1–2	2	180	HBJ	D. Durrell M. Hayes		
Intermediate Level, 1969	3–6	2	195	HBJ	D. Durrell M. Brassard		x
Advanced Level, 1969	7–9	2	190	HBJ	D. Durrell		x
Durrell-Sullivan Reading Capacity and Achievement Tests, 1937; rev. 1945	2.5–4.5	1	30–50	HBJ	D. Durrell H. Sullivan		x
	3–6	2	30–50	HBJ	D. Durrell H. Sullivan		
*Dyslexia Schedule, 1968; rev. 1969	1		20–25	EPS	J. McLeod		
†Frostig Developmental Test of Visual Perception, Third Edition, 1961; rev. 1966	Pre K–3	1	30–45 40–60	CPP	M. Frostig D. Lefever J. Whittlesey F. Maslow		
*Harris Tests of Lateral Dominance, 1947; rev. 1958	1–adult	1	10–15	PC	A. Harris		

†Both group and individual administration.

Comprehension	Word Recognition and Attack	Spelling	Auding	Other	Vol. and Test No. in *Mental Measurement Yearbooks*	Pages in *Reading Tests and Reviews, I* or *II* (Buros)
			x		8:932	
					8:814	
	x			Phonics skills, opposites	7:727	RTR II: 113
			x	Attention span, short-term memory, following directions, integrating information, recognizing language units and structure		
				Book orientation, lines of print, page sequence, directionality of words, relationship between written and oral language, words, letters, spacing, and punctuation	**	
	x			Basic sight words		
			x	Sentence reading	7:728	RTR II: 113–7
			x	Paragraph listening and reading	7:728	RTR II: 113–7
			x	Paragraph listening and reading	7:728	RTR II: 113–7
				Verbal and nonverbal subtests	5:661	RTR I: 249–50
				Questionnaire to be completed by parents	7:729	RTR II: 117–8
				Eye-motor coordination, spatial relations, perceptual abilities	7:871	
				Hand, eye, and foot dominance	5:761	

**Y. Goodman, "Test Review: Concepts About Print Test," *The Reading Teacher* 34 (January 1981), 445–8.

Name of Test	For Grades	No. of Forms	Approx. Time (in min.)	Publisher	Author(s)	Speed	Vocabulary
*Individual Reading Placement Inventory, Field Research Edition, 1969	Youths and adults with K–7 reading levels	2	10–35	FEC	E. Smith W. Bradtmueller		
The Instant Word Recognition Test, 1971	1–4	2	15–25	DES	E. Fry		
Jordan Left-Right Reversal Test, 1973; rev. 1974	1–6		20–25	ATP	B. Jordan		
*Keystone Visual Screening Tests, 1933; rev. 1971	Pre K–adult	1		KVC			
Learning Methods Test, 1954; rev. 1955	K–3	1	85–100	MCI	R. E. Mills		
Mertens Visual Perception Test, 1969–74	K–1	1	20–30	WPS	M. Mertens		
Michigan Speed of Reading Test, 1932; rev. 1937	6–16	2	15	PC	E. Greene	x	
Minnesota Speed of Reading Test for College Students, 1936	12–16	2	15	UMP	A. Eurich	x	
National Test of Basic Words, 1970	1–5			ATC	S. Halpern		
OC Diagnostic Syllabizing Test, 1960; rev. 1962	4–6	1	15–20	OPC	K. O'Connor		
*Ortho-Rater, 1942; rev. 1958	16+	1		BLI			
Perceptual Forms Test, 1955; rev. 1969	K 1	1	10	WHLR	C. McQuarrie F. Sutphin G. Curry		
Pictographic Self-rating Scale, 1955; rev. 1957	9–16	1	35	PA	E. Ryden		
Reader's Inventory, 1963	9–16+	1	10–20	EDL	G. D. Spache S. Taylor		
*Reader Rater with Self-scoring Profile, 1959; rev. 1965	10–12+	1	60–120	BRP		x	x
*Reading Eye II, 1959; rev. 1969	1–16+	8	4	EDL	S. Taylor H. Frackenpohl J. Pettee	x	

Comprehension	Word Recognition and Attack	Spelling	Auding	Other	Vol. and Test No. in *Mental Measurement Yearbooks*	Pages in *Reading Tests and Reviews, I or II* (Buros)
				Present language potential, independent, instructional, and frustrational levels	7:730	RTR II: 118–21
	x				8:780	
				Relative frequency of letter and number reversals	8:434	
				Visual functions, necessary for individual reading	5:780	
	x			Learning methods, training and testing	6:836	RTR I: 360–3
				Spatial recognition, visual memory, visual perceptions related to reading—design production and completion	8:437	
					3:523	RTR I: 136–7
					2:155	RTR I: 61–2
	x			Service words		
				Syllabication skills	6:827	RTR I: 350
				Visual discrimination, perception of depth, color discrimination	5:783	
				Visual-motor coordination	7:872	
				Attitude toward classroom and study activities	6:701	
				Attitude	7:733	RTR II: 123–4
x				Reading habits, summarizing, skimming	6:837	RTR I: 363
				Fixations, regressions, span recognition, grade level of reading skills, efficiency, visual adjustment, directional attack	7:734	RTR II: 124–6

Name of Test	For Grades	No. of Forms	Approx. Time (in min.)	Publisher	Author(s)	Speed	Vocabulary
Reading Versatility Test, 1961; rev. 1968							
*Basic Level	5–8	2	40–50	EDL	A. McDonald M. Alodia H. Nason G. Zimny J. Byrne	x	
Intermediate Level	8–12	2	40–50	EDL	(See Basic Level)	x	
Advanced Level	12–16	2	40–50	EDL	(See Basic Level)	x	
*Roswell-Chall Auditory Blending Test, 1963	1–4	1	Not reported	EP	F. Roswell J. Chall		
SRA Tests of Educational Ability, 1962 Edition							
Level 1, 1958; rev. 1963	4–6	1	52	SRA	L. Thurstone T. Thurstone		
Level 2, 1958; rev. 1963	6–9	1	67	SRA	(See Level 1)		
Level 3, 1957; rev. 1963	9–12	1	45	SRA	(See Level 1)		
SRA Tests of General Abilities, 1957; rev. 1960	K–2 2–4 4–6 6–9 9–12	1	35–45	SRA	J. Flanagan		
Screening Test for the Assignment of Remedial Treatments, 1968	Pre K–1	1	60	PII	A. Ahr		

Comprehension	Word Recognition and Attack	Spelling	Auding	Other	Vol. and Test No. in *Mental Measurement Yearbooks*	Pages in *Reading Tests and Reviews, I* or *II* (Buros)
x				Span of recognition, fixation, apparent number of lines, regressions and fixations per 100 words	7:735	RTR II: 126–7
x				Skimming and scanning rate and comprehension	7:735	RTR II: 126–7
x				Skimming and sçanning rate and comprehension	7:735	RTR II: 126–7
					6:830	RTR I: 352–4
				Language, reasoning, quantitative	6:495	
				Language, reasoning, qualitative	6:495	
				Language, reasoning, qualitative	6:495	
				Information, noncultural reading	6:496	
			x	Visual memory, visual copying and discrimination	8:445	

Name of Test	For Grades	No. of Forms	Approx. Time (in min.)	Publisher	Author(s)	Speed	Vocabulary
Screening Tests for Identifying Children with	1–2.5	1	66	EPS	B. Slingerland A. Ansara		x
Specific Language Disability, 1962; rev. 1974	2.5–3.5		66		(See Level 1)		
	3.5–4		66		(See Level 1)		
	5–6		110-125		B. Slingerland		
Sequential Tests of Educational Progress: Reading Series II, 1956; rev. 1972	4–6 7–9 10–12 13–14	2	55	AW	ETS		
*Spache Binocular-Reading Test, 1943; rev. 1955	1-adult	1	2–4	KVC	G. D. Spache		
Understanding Communication (Verbal Comprehension), 1956; rev. 1959	9–16	1	20	EITS	T. Thurstone		
Wide Range Vocabulary Test, 1937; rev. 1945	3–16	2	10	PC	C. R. Atwell F. L. Wells		
Word Discrimination Test, 1958	1–8	2	15–20	MUAA	C. Huelsman, Jr.		

Comprehension	Word Recognition and Attack	Spelling	Auding	Other	Vol. and Test No. in *Mental Measurement Yearbooks*	Pages in *Reading Tests and Reviews, I* or *II* (Buros)
			x	Visual perception and memory, kinesthetic memory	8:446	
				Ability to recall ideas, translate ideas, and make inferences; ability to analyze motivation and presentation; ability to criticize	8:744	
				Eye preference in reading	6:959	
x					6:840	RTR I: 365-6
					3:169	
	x				7:736	RTR II: 127

LIST OF PUBLISHERS

AB	Allyn & Bacon, Inc. 470 Atlantic Avenue Boston, Mass. 02210
AC	Alameda County School Department 224 W. Winston Avenue Hayward, Calif. 94544
ACER	Australian Council for Educational Research P.O. Box 210 Hawthorne, Victoria 3122 Australia
ACTP	American College Testing Program P.O. Box 168 Iowa City, Iowa 52240
AEC	Allied Education Council P.O. Box 78 Galien, Mich. 49113
AGS	American Guidance Service, Inc. Publishers' Building Circle Pines, Minn. 55014
AP	American Press, Inc. 111 Fifth Avenue New York, NY 10003
APC	Acorn Publishing Company Psychometric Affiliates Box 3167 Munster, Ind. 46321
AR	Arden Press P.O. Box 844 Huntington Beach, Calif 92648
ATC	American Testing Company 6301 S.W. Fifth Street Fort Lauderdale, Fla. 33317
ATP	Academic Therapy Publications 20 Commercial Blvd. Novato, Calif. 94947
AW	Addison-Wesley Publishing Company, Inc. 2725 Sand Hill Road Menlo Park, Calif. 94025
BEM	Bureau of Educational Measurements Emporia Kansas State College Emporia, Kans. 66801
BFA	BFA Educational Media 2211 Michigan Avenue Santa Monica, Calif. 90406
BLI	Bausch and Lomb, Inc. Rochester, N.Y. 14602
BM	The Bobbs-Merrill Company, Inc. 4300 West 62nd Street Indianapolis, Ind. 46468
BP	Brador Publications, Inc. Livonia, N.Y. 14487
BRP	Better Reading Program, Inc. 230 East Ohio St. Chicago, Ill. 60611
BYUP	Brigham Young University Press 205 University Press Building Provo. Utah 84602
CA	Curriculum Associates, Inc. 94 Bridge Street Newton, Mass. 02158
CDRT	Committee on Diagnostic Reading Tests, Inc. Mountain Home, N.C. 28758
CEI	Cutronics Educational Insttute West 56th Street Bayonne, N.J. 07002
CES	Croft Educational Services, Inc. P.O. Box 15 Old Greenwich, Conn. 06870
CP	CAL Press, Inc. 76 Madison Avenue New York, N.Y. 10016
CPP	Consulting Psychologists Press, Inc. 577 College Avenue Palo Alto, Calif. 94306
CSB	Cal-State Bookstore 25776 Hillary Street Hayward, Calif. 92542

CTB	California Test Bureau/McGraw-Hill Book Co., Inc. 1221 Avenue of the Americas New York, N.Y. 10020
CTD–ETS	Cooperative Test Division Educational Testing Service Publication Order Services Princeton, N.J. 08541
DCRA	Delaware County Reading Consultants Association c/o Nicholas A. Spennato Delaware County Public Schools Court House Annex Media, Penn. 19063
DEN	Denver Public Schools Department of Purchasing 900 Grant Street Denver, Colo. 80203
DES	Dreier Educational Systems, Inc. 320 Raritan Avenue Highland Park, N.J. 08904
DPS	Department of Psychological Testing DePaul University 25 E. Jackson Blvd. Chicago, Ill. 60604
DRD	Developmental Reading Distributors 1944 Sheridan Avenue Laramie, Wyo. 82070
DRT	Delco Readiness Test 111 Linda Lane Media, Penn. 19063
E	Economy Company P.O. Box 23508 1901 North Walnut Oklahoma City, Okla. 73125
EC	Edcodyne Corporation 1 City Blvd. West Suite 935 Orange, Calif. 92668
EDC	Educational Development Corporation P.O. Box 45663 Tulsa, Okla. 74145
EDL	Educational Developmental Laboratories, Inc. McGraw-Hill Book Company 6253 Hollywood Blvd., Suite 1103 Hollywood, Calif. 90028
EITS	Educational and Industrial Test Service P.O. Box 7234 San Diego, Calif. 92107
EMH	E. M. Hale & Co. 1201 S. Hastings Way Eau Claire, Wisc. 54701
EP	Essay Press P.O. Box 5 Planetarium Station New York, N.Y. 10024
EPA	Educational Performance Associates, Inc. 563 Westview Avenue Ridgefield, N.J. 07657
EPS	Educators Publishing Service, Inc. 75 Moulton Street Cambridge, Mass. 02138
ER	Educational Resources 19 Peacedale Grove Nunawading 3131 Australia 789
ERB	Educational Records Bureau Cooperative Tests and Services 21 Audubon Avenue New York, N.Y. 10032
ES	Educational Stimuli Telegram Building Superior, Wisc. 54880
ESD	Educational Skills Development, Inc. 179 East Makwell Street Lexington, Ky. 40508
ESM	Effective Study Materials P.O. Box 603 San Marcos, Tex. 78666
ETB	Educational Test Bureau Publishers' Building Circle Pines, Minn. 55014
ETS	Educational Testing Service Publication Order Services Princeton, N.J. 08541
F	Fearon Publishers Pitman Learning, Inc. Educational Division 6 Davis Drive Belmont, Calif. 94002

FPC	Follett Publishing Company 1010 W. Washington Blvd. Chicago, Ill. 60607
FH	Facilitation House Box 611 Ottawa, Ill. 61350
FSC	Foster & Stewart Publishing Corporation 500 Kelin Rd. Buffalo, N.Y. 14221
FW	Fort Worth Independent School District 3210 W. Lancaster Fort Worth, Tex. 76107
GAD	Guidance Associates of Delaware, Inc. 15216 Gilpin Avenue Wilmington, Dela. 19806
GC	Ginn and Company P.O. Box 2649 1250 Fairwood Avenue Columbus, Ohio 43216
GP	Garrard Publishing Company 1607 N. Market Street Champaign, Ill. 61820
GS	Gordon Scarsbrick Dubuque, Iowa 52001
GTA	Guidance Testing Associates 6516 Shirley Avenue Austin, Tex. 78756
GU	Guidance Centre University of Toronto 1000 Yonge St. Toronto, Ont. M4W SK8 Canada
HBJ	Harcourt Brace Jovanovich, Inc. 757 Third Avenue New York, N.Y. 10017
HC	Hammond, Inc. 515 Valley Street Maplewood, N.J. 07040
HE	Heinman Educational Books 4 Front Street Exeter, N.H. 03833
HM	Houghton Mifflin Company Wayside Road Burlington, Mass. 01803
HR	Harper & Row Publishers, Inc. Keystone Industrial Park Scranton, Penn. 18512
HS	Hodder-Stoughton Educational P.O. Box 702 Dunton Green Sevenoaks, Kent England TN13 2YD
IOE	The Instructional Objectives Exchange 11411 W. Jefferson Blvd. Culver City, Calif. 90230
IPAT	Institute for Personality and Ability Testing 1602 Coronado Drive Champaign, Ill. 61820
ISGS	Internation Society for General Semantics P.O. Box 2469 San Francisco, Calif. 94126
JHP	Johns Hopkins Press Baltimore, Md. 21218
JLC	J. B. Lippincott Company E. Washington Square Philadelphia, Penn. 19105
JS	Joseph Sanacore Reading Coordinator Hauppauge School District 600 Town Line Rd. Hauppauge, Long Island, N.Y. 11787
KPC	Klamath Printing Company 320 Lowell Klamath Falls, Ore. 97601
KVC	Keystone View Company Division of Mast Development Company 2212 E. 12th Street Davenport, Iowa 52803
LA	Larlin Corporation P.O. Box 1523 Marietta, Ga. 30061
LC	Lyons and Carnahan, Inc. Rand McNally College Publishing Co. P.O. Box 7600 Chicago, Ill. 60680

LEA Learning Research Associates, Inc.
1501 Broadway
New York, N.Y. 10036

LRA Language Research Associates, Inc.
Box 2085
Palm Springs, Calif. 92263

MC Macmillan Publishing Co., Inc.
866 Third Avenue
New York, N.Y. 10022

MCI Mills Center, Inc.
The Mills School
1512 E. Broward Blvd.
Fort Lauderdale, Fla. 33301

MEW Mazie E. Wagner
500 Klein Rd.
Buffalo, N.Y. 14221

MPC McGrath Publishing Company
P.O. Box 535
Whitmore Lake, Mich. 48189

MRC McGrath Reading Clinic
15944 W. McNichols Rd.
Detroit, Minn. 48235

MRCP Montana Reading Clinic Publications
419 Stapleton Bldg.
Billings, Mont. 59101

MUAA Miami University Alumni Association
Muskin Alumni Center
Miami University
Oxford, Ohio 45056

NCS NCS Interpretive Scoring Systems
4401 W. 76th Street
Minneapolis, Minn. 55435

NCTE National Council of Teachers of English
1111 Kenyon Rd.
Urbana, Ill. 61801

NDE New Dimensions in Education, Inc.
160 Dupont St.
Plainview, N.Y. 11803

NPC C. H. Nevins Printing Company
311 Bryn Mawr Island
Bradenton, Fla. 33505

NZCER New Zealand Council for Educational Research
Education House
178 Willis Street
Wellington 1
New Zealand

OB Oliver and Boyd
Croyton House
23 Ravelston Terrace
Edinburgh, Scotland EH4 3TJ

OISE Ontario Institute for Studies in Education
252 Bloor St. West
Toronto. Ont. M5S IV6
Canada

OP O'Rourke Publications
P.O. Box 1118
Lake Alfred, Fla. 33850

OPC O'Connor Reading Clinic Publishing Company
Box 447
Roscommon, Mich. 48653

OSU University Publications Scales
Ohio State University
20 Lord Hall
124 W. 17th Street
Columbus, Ohio 43210

OSUP Ohio State University Press
Hitchcock Hall, Rm. 346
2070 Neil Avenue
Columbus, Ohio 43210

OTS Ohio Testing Service
Division of Guidance and Testing
State Department of Education
751 Northwest Blvd.
Columbus, Ohio 43212

PA Psychometric Affiliates
Box 3167
Munster, Ind. 46321

PC The Psychological Corporation
757 Third Avenue
New York, N.Y. 10017

PE Programs for Education
Box 85
Lumberville, Penn. 18933

PEI Psychologists and Educators, Inc.
Sales Division
211 W. State Street
Jacksonville, Ill. 62650

PFC Perfection Form Company
1000 North Second Avenue
Logan, Iowa 51546

PGP Personal Growth Press, Inc.
Box M
Berea, Ohio 44017

PHI Phonovisual Products, Inc.
12216 Parklawn Dr.
P.O. Box 2007
Rockville, Md. 20852

PI Psychological Institute
P.O. Box 1118
Lake Alfred, Fla. 33850

PII Priority Innovations, Inc.
P.O. Box 792
Skokie, Ill. 60076

PPI Personal Press, Inc.
20 Nassau St.
Princeton, N.J. 08540

PRA Personnel Research Associates, Inc.
1435 South LaCienega Blvd.
Los Angeles, Calif. 90035

PRE Pro Ed
Austin, Tex. 78768

PRF Purdue Research Foundation
Personnel Evaluation Research Service
Division of Educational Reference
Purdue University
West Lafayette, Ind. 47907

PSP Public School Publishing Company
Division of the Bobbs-Merrill Company
4300 W. 62nd St.
Indianapolis, Ind. 46468

RBH Richardson, Bellows, Henry and Company
355 Lexington Avenue
New York, N.Y. 10017

RC Research Concepts
1368 East Airport Rd.
Muskegon, Mich. 49444

RLC Reading Laboratory and Clinic
University of Florida
Gainesville, Fla. 32601

RM R.A. McMenemy
3028 N.E. Brazee Street
Portland, Ore. 97212

RMN Rand McNally College Publishing Company
P.O. Box 7600
Chicago, Ill. 60680

RP Revrac Publications
10 West Bridlespur Drive
Kansas City, Mo. 64114

RSSC Reading and Study Skills Center, Inc.
c/o Taylor Center for Controlled Reading and Research
75 Prospect Street
Huntington, N.Y. 11744

RZA Richard L. Zweig Associates, Inc.
20800 Beach Blvd.
Huntington Beach, Calif. 92648

SEP Slosson Educational Publications, Inc.
140 Pine Street
East Aurora, N.Y. 14052

SF Scott, Foresman & Company
1900 E. Lake Avenue
Glenview, Ill. 60025

SHTS State High School Testing Service for Indiana
Purdue University
West Lafayette, Ind. 47907

SMP St. Martins Press, Inc.
175 Fifth Avenue
New York, N.Y. 10010

SPS Seattle Public Schools
Seattle, Wash. 98104

SRA Science Research Associates, Inc.
259 E. Erie St.
Chicago, Ill. 60611

SSC Sheridan Supply Company
c/o Sheridan Psychological Services, Inc.
P.O. Box 6101
Orange, Calif. 92667

ST Stoelting Company
1350 S. Kostner Avenue
Chicago, Ill. 60623

STS Scholastic Testing Service, Inc.
480 Meyer Rd.
Bensenville, Ill. 60106

SUP Stanford University Press
Stanford, Calif. 94305

SV Steck-Vaughn Company
P.O. Box 2028
Austin, Tex. 78768

TCP Teachers College Press, Columbia University
1234 Amsterdam Avenue
New York, N.Y. 10027

TM Thomas F. McDonald, Director, Reading Program
Phoenix Union High School Program
2526 W. Osborn Rd.
Phoenix, Ariz. 85017

TN Thomas Nelson and Sons
81 Curlew Drive
Don Mills, Ont. M3A 2R1
Canada

UI University of Illinois Press
54 E. Gregory Drive
P.O. Box 5081, Sta. A
Champaign, Ill. 61820

UMP University of Minnesota Press
2037 University Ave., S.E.
Minneapolis, Minn. 55414

VTS Veterans' Testing Service
c/o General Educational Development Testing
Service of the American Council on Education
One Dupont Circle, Suite 30
Washington, D.C. 20036

VW Van Wagenen Psycho-Educational Research Laboratories
1729 Irving Ave. South
Minneapolis, Minn. 55411

WBC William C. Brown Company, Publishers
2460 Kerper Blvd.
Dubuque, Iowa 52001

WHLR Winter Haven Lions Research Foundation, Inc.
P.O. Box 1045
Winter Haven, Fla. 33881

WL Wilbur L. Layton
3604 Ross Rd.
Ames, Iowa 50010

WLC Westinghouse Learning Corporation
5005 W. 110th Street
Oak Lawn, Ill. 60453

WM McCartney, William A.
P.O. Box 507
Kaneohe, Hi. 96744

WPC Webster Publishing Company
Division of McGraw-Hill Book Co., 28th floor
1221 Ave. of the Americas
New York, N.Y. 10020

WPS Western Psychological Services
12031 Wilshire Blvd.
Los Angeles, Calif. 90025

Name Index

Subject Index